Rufus J. Haight

The Modern Cemetery

Rufus J. Haight

The Modern Cemetery

ISBN/EAN: 9783337083908

Printed in Europe, USA, Canada, Australia, Japan

Cover: Foto ©ninafisch / pixelio.de

More available books at **www.hansebooks.com**

Modern Cemetery

Volume III

March, 1893--February, 1894

R. J. Haight, Publisher

Chicago

INDEX.

A.

*An Italian Campo Santo.... 6
Ancient Cemetery at the World's Fair, An.... 61
Abandonment of Cemeteries.... 62
Allowances for Tombstones.... 67
Architectural Foliage.... 81
At the Sign of the Skull.... 90
Approaching Millenium, The.... 101
Annual Report—Greenwood Cemetery, Brooklyn, N. Y.... 22
—Forest Hills, Boston, Mass.... 22
—Spring Grove, Cincinnati.... 70
—Mount Auburn, Boston.... 140
—Swan Point, Providence, R. I.... 140

B.

Burial Reform.... 4, 20
Burial Expenses.... 37
*Belmont Memorial, The, Newport, R. I.... 40
Burial by Contract.... 130
Bellefontaine Cemetery, St. Louis, Mo.... 136

C.

Cemetery Stocks.... 1
Cemetery Notes.... 10, 21, 34, 46, 54, 68, 83, 93, 104, 116, 128, 143
Congressional Cemetery at Washington, D. C.... 18
Cemetery Reports.... 22
Cemetery Gardening.... 25
Conveying Lots.... 32
Condemnation of Lands for Cemetery Purpose.... 37
*Chapel in Grove Hill Cemetery, Shelbyville, Ky.... 43
Correspondence.... 47, 58, 95, 107, 118, 130, 143
Cemeteries of Paris, The.... 53
Cemetery Lots on Easy Payments.... 55
Cemetery Superintendents' Ass'n.... 58
*Crown Hill Cemetery, Indianapolis.... 64
Care in Selecting Memorials.... 65
Coming Cemetery, The.... 67
Chapel and Conservatory, Oakland Cemetery, St. Paul, Minn.... 79
Convention Echo.... 79
Classic Epitaph, A.... 81
Cemeteries of Chicago.... 82
Cemetery Rates in City of Mexico.... 89
Cremation.... 23, 71, 93, 118, 135
Chinese Monument, A.... 93
Cemetery of the Huns, A.... 101
Constitutionality of Condemnation for Cemetery Purposes.... 124
Cemetery Planting.... 133
Cemetery Walks.... 138

D.

Destroying Moles.... 20
Disposal of Cholera Dead, The.... 21
Dedication of Street by Cemetery Association.... 49
Derivation of "Hearses".... 55
Death Rates of Great Cities.... 122

E.

Extracts from Rules and Regulations of Edgewood Cem't'y, Nashua, N. H.... 29
Extract from Annual Report, Lowell Cemetery, Lowell, Mass.... 45
*Ex-President Harrison's Monument, Indianapolis.... 65
Epitaphs.... 69, 142
*Entrance to Lakewood Cemetery, Minneapolis, Minn.... 75
*Entrance to Oakland Cemetery, St. Paul, Minn.... 77
*Edgewood Cemetery, Nashua, N. H.... 80
*Evergreen Cemetery.... 115
English Funeral Flowers.... 117

F.

Funeral Reform.... 50
*Fall Effects at Graceland.... 100
Foreign Funeral Customs.... 143

G.

Greenhouse in the Cemetery, The.... 15
Greenwood Cem'tery, Brooklyn, N. Y.... 16
God's Acre.... 33
Grave Digger, The.... 113
Gardener's Burial, The.... 114

H.

*Hardy Herbaceous Plants.... 3
How a Superintendent can Advance the Welfare of his Cemetery.... 9
*Hints on Rock Gardens.... 35
Hardy Shrubs and their Protection against Drought.... 98
*Harleigh Cemetery, Camden, N J.... 122

I.

Is Flower Planting Desirable in the Modern Cemetery?.... 88
In a Cemetery.... 93

K.

*Kensico Cemetery, The.... 90

L.

Landscape Gardening.... 11, 44
Location of Monuments Authorized by Statute.... 55
Leaning Tower of Pisa.... 70
Leaves, What to do with them.... 108
Lincoln's Address at Gettysburg.... 135

M.

MODERN CEMETERY, THE.... 1
Mexican Funerals.... 7
Mt. Hope Cemetery of Boston not Subject to Legislative Control.... 14
Macadam Roads.... 23
*Monument in Fairmount Cemetery, Newark, N. J.... 42
*Monuments of India.... 60
*Monumental Notes.... 70
Mound Builders.... 71
Ministerial Aid in Cemetery Improvement.... 109
Metric System, The.... 111
Mary Magdalene's Grave.... 118
Mt. Royal, Montreal, Canada.... 123
Marion Harland's Notes on Cemeteries at Port Said, Egypt.... 125
*Mortuary Chapel and Conservatory at Mt. Pleasant Cem'y, Toronto, Ont.... 127

N.

*New Office and Residence, Fairmount Cemetery, Newark, N. J.... 10
Notings at Wneback Cemetery.... 57
*Notes from Graceland.... 87

O.

Ornamental Grasses.... 91
Offices and Waiting Room, Evergreen Cemetery, Portland, Me.... 115
Ornamental Fruiting Shrubs.... 138

P.

Power of Trustees to Sell Land Purchased for a Cemetery.... 13
*Pere la Chaise, Paris.... 36
Plea for Slate Headstones, A.... 39
Plea for Cremation.... 42
Plant Early.... 91
Powers over Burial Places.... 136

Q.

Questionable Burials.... 124
Question Box.... 108, 120, 131, 144

R.

Rules and Regulations, Forest Lawn Cemetery, Omaha, Neb.... 5
*Riverside Cemetery, Defiance, Ohio.... 8
Reconveying Lots in Trust.... 13
Rules Regarding Stone Work at Spring Grove, Cincinnati.... 17
*Rhodes' Memorial Chapel, The, Pine Grove Cemetery, Lynn, Mass.... 22
Right of Widow to Control Burial of Deceased Husband.... 28
Rules and Regulations.... 47, 56, 106, 140
Rules for the Employes of the Cemetery of Spring Grove, Cincinnati.... 94
*Riverside Cemetery, The, Rochester, N. Y.... 102
Runic Monuments.... 126
Rights of Owners of Cemetery Lots.... 134

S.

*Single Grave Sections, The.... 2
Suggestions Regarding Stone Work.... 5
Spiritualistic View of Cremation, A.... 20
Springbank Cemet'y, Aberdeen, The.... 32
Suggestions to Lot Holders.... 33, 56, 114
Seventh Annual Convention of the Association of American Cemetery Superintendents.... 45, 59, 73
Superintendents' Convention, The.... 63
Schneider System of Cremation, The.... 71
Should all Lots Front on Paths or Avenues?.... 98
Superintendent, The.... 106
*Shrubbery.... 110
South American Cemetery, A.... 112

T.

To Cemetery Officials.... 12
Tuberous Rooted Begonias.... 18
Trimming Graves.... 32
*Talk on Road Making, A.... 50
Title to Cemetery Lot Acquired by Adverse Possession.... 63
Trees as Memorials.... 99
Telford Highways.... 113
Trees as Tributes to the Dead.... 121
Tax on Graves.... 135

U.

Unconstitutional Local Legislation.... 134

V.

*View in Marion Cemetery, Marion, Ohio.... 19
Vases and Urns.... 30
Vigorous Appeal for Reform, A.... 62
Validity of Mortgages of Public Cemeteries by Corporations.... 85
Validity of Statutory Authorized Bequest to Cemetery Association.... 86
Visit to the Graveyards of Hamburg.... 92
Vacation Reminiscences.... 95, 107, 118

W.

Why a Cemetery is so Called.... 7
What a Superintendent Should Be.... 23
Woking Crematorium.... 31
Wooded Island at World's Fair, The.... 44
Why the Funeral?.... 46
Water Works at Oakwood Cemetery, Red Wing, Minn.... 47
Woodlawn Cemetery, N. J.... 123
Winter Care of Trees and Shrubs.... 124

Y.

Younglove Monument, Lakeview, Cleveland.... 103

THE MODERN CEMETERY.

THE MODERN CEMETERY.

AN ILLUSTRATED MONTHLY JOURNAL DEVOTED TO THE INTEREST OF CEMETERIES

R. J. HAIGHT, Publisher.
246 State Street, CHICAGO.

Subscription $1.00 a Year In Advance.   Foreign Subscription $1.25.
Special Rates on Six or More Copies.

VOL. III.   CHICAGO, MARCH, 1893.   No. 1

CONTENTS.

	PAGE
THE SINGLE GRAVE SECTION	2
*HARDY HERBACIOUS PLANTS FOR THE CEMETERY	3-4
BURIAL REFORM	4
RULES AND REGULATIONS	5
SOME SUGGESTIONS REGARDING STONE WORK	5
*AN ITALIAN CAMPO SANTO	6-7
*RIVERSIDE CEMETERY, DEFIANCE, O.	8
HOW A SUPERINTENDENT CAN ADVANCE THE WELFARE OF HIS CEMETERY	9
*NEW OFFICE AND RESIDENCE BUILDING, FAIRMOUNT CEMETERY, NEWARK, N. J.	10
CEMETERY NOTES	10-11
LANDSCAPE GARDENING	11
PUBLISHER'S DEPARTMENT	12
*ILLUSTRATED.	

THE MODERN CEMETERY enters its third volume with this issue, and we may be pardoned for a few personal remarks. When starting the MODERN CEMETERY two years ago the publisher fully realized what had been the fate of many publications in the doubtful sea of journalism and also recognized the field in which he was to labor as a comparatively limited and exceedingly difficult one in which to make a very pronounced success. He had however, been identified with the Association of American Cemetery Superintendents, since its inception, and having been for many years engaged in a business that brought him into contact with cemetery interests, was impressed with the fact that there was need of more general knowledge on matters pertaining to cemetery management. Especially was this need apparent in the rural districts, where owing to the want of cemetery literature the burial places were being sadly neglected, and it was in the hopes of being instrumental in shedding at least a faint light in these gloomy places that the MODERN CEMETERY was established. While the publication has fallen short of what it is our desire to make it, yet it is gratifying at this time to say that it has been well received, and in the words of many of its subscribers is "doing a good work." For the many valuable contributions which have assisted so largely in making the MODERN CEMETERY what it is the publisher is grateful, and to all who have assisted in the work he returns his sincere thanks.

This issue of the MODERN CEMETERY is mailed to a large number of non-subscribers and from such of our readers we solicit one or more subscriptions. The index for volume two that accompanies this issue will acquaint you with what has already appeared in these columns, and is indicative of what may be expected in the future. The object of the MODERN CEMETERY is to disseminate among those identified with cemetery work information of an instructive nature. It aims to interest lot owners by familiarizing them with the most approved plans for lot embellishment, and by acquainting them with all that is most desirable in the maintenance of a cemetery, be it large or small. To this end the practice, which already obtains in many cemeteries, of subscribing to extra copies of the MODERN CEMETERY for distribution among trustees, and lot owners will be found desirable. On another page will be found subscription rates for one or more copies. A number of testimonials could be shown as to the efficacy of this plan.

* * *

It is peculiarly within the province of such a publication as the MODERN CEMETERY to yield what influence it can in the consummation of such reforms as give promise of correcting what may be designated as existing evils in prevailing mortuary customs. That there are many such goes without saying, therefore burial reform in its various phases will as heretofore be advocated. Cremation, which very naturally comes under this head has our unqualified endorsement for reasons æsthetical as well as sanitary. With the progress this custom is now making, and the appropriateness of locating crematoriums within cemetery grounds the time cannot be very far distant when they will have become a necessary adjunct to every modern cemetery.

A New York stock broker who is making a specialty of cemetery stocks, has the following advertisement in one of the leading magazines:

"Very few people are aware of the fact that the shares of cemeteries in large cities are not only absolutely safe, but pay enormous returns on the investment. They are so profitable that they are rarely offered for sale. Send for my circular, 'Cemetery Stocks as an Investment,' and you will understand why they yield such incredible profits to stockholders."

The statutes of several States prohibit conducting cemeteries for private gain and it will not be surprising if the publishing of such an advertisement does not lead to a desire on the part of the public for a more general adoption of such laws.

The Single Grave Section.

In the November issue of the MODERN CEMETERY the single grave section of Graceland cemetery, Chicago, Ills., is illustrated in such a way that the reader can obtain a very good idea of what that section is, although little is said about it in the text. In the December number our good friend, Mr. Salway, treats on the same subject intelligently and interestingly. Coming from such a source it is authority based on long practical experience, he being not only superintendent of the leading cemetery in the United States but president of the A. A. C. S. We were glad to hear from him for the further reason that he has spoken thoughtfully. It is not my purpose to enter into any argument as to the best plan for and management of a single grave section, but to give a simple statement of the plan we have at Forest Hills, for I imagine that we cannot all do alike and if we could, I do not believe it would be wise. Were we starting a new cemetery we might be glad perhaps to adopt the plan of one of the places alluded to and consider ourselves among the fortunates if we succeeded as they have. The single graves in Forest Hills are not what is frequently known as paupers' graves; they are sold at a fixed price, the parties purchasing them taking a receipt in regular form, and so long as the graves are occupied by the departed friends of the purchaser or his legal heirs, that gives them the right to their use, but should the dead be removed to any other cemetery, the graves then revert back to the corporation. Should the owner buy a lot in the cemetery he is allowed the full price paid for the grave or graves, paying for the reinterment from the grave to the lot. The advantages of such a plan are commendable, as there are a great many people who do not want a lot, no matter how small, and there are others who want only three or four graves, whose limited means will not allow them to purchase even a small lot, with perpetual care. These graves are all well kept. Wishing to make myself clearly understood, the accompanying diagram will illustrate the way in which our single graves are arranged. The sections are all in grass, each one is 17 feet 6 inches wide, exclusive of the intervening walk and any given length according to the space set apart. Each grave is 7'x2'-8" at the head of the grave, if for one stone only, the lower base cannot exceed 2'-4"x1'-5", and in very few cases is that much called for. For two or three graves a stone or one base can be of proportionate length, but no wider. Looking at the diagram, No. 1 is occupied by a child under ten years of age; No. 2, a full-sized body; 5 and 6 is owned by one person and is designed for husband and wife, with one stone for both graves, and so on the same way until you get to Nos. 25 and 26 and, on the other side of the same section, 29 and 30, the same party having bought these four graves, two on each side entitle them to the whole space between the heads of the graves in the center of the section. As shown in diagram, instead of separate

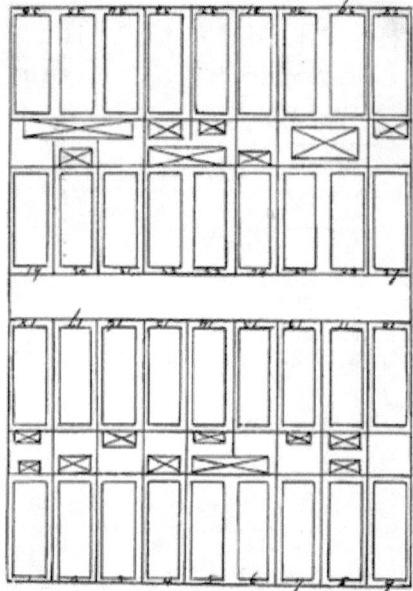

PLAN OF A SINGLE GRAVE SECTION, "FOREST HILLS," BOSTON.

stones for each grave a small granite monument occupies this central space on a base 2-0 square and 5 feet high. This is virtually a small lot, owned by a worthy man who lost his wife. He wanted to do the best he could in the shape of a burial place; this much he could do, and provide a place for the remaining members of the family should they require it. Had we not such a place I do not know where he could have provided one within his means and have been satisfied. Pass along to 34, 35 and 36, these are owned by one person, he placed one stone at the head which answers for three or even more if needed, as they are allowed to bury two deep. The reader will see that some graves have no stones, others smaller ones as their owners' tastes dictate. The height is governed by the thickness of the stone, which must be set to the satisfaction of the superintendent on a solid foundation of stone and cement laid as deep as the bottoms of the graves, some few stones are marble, but the large majority are granite, all of neat designs. This variety, we think, adds to the appearance of the section much more than it would if each one were obliged to conform to a set pattern or style. Where there is no stone and an interment has been made a small mound, not over three or four inches high, is formed, which shows that the grave is occupied by a small or full grown person, according to the length. The space between the front lines of the headstones, including the walk, is 17 feet, and in the summer time, when the flowers and the myrtle are at their best, it is a pleasing spot; nothing unsightly is allowed. A large number of graves are planted and cared for by an annual payment in advance, and the revenue derived from the care of the myrtle graves and those planted with flowers is sufficient to pay for the labor of caring for each section during the season, which are kept in good order. During the year 1892 the sales of single graves was nearly one a day. A large class of our most respectable and worthy citizens are accommodated with this system, and the interest they manifest in their care is commendable and far greater than that of many of the lot holders. A good, well located, carefully managed single grave section should be in every cemetery, and is an addition to it, for there is no class of people that appreciate what is done for them more than the proprietors of the single grave sections.

The following rules govern our sections:

No more than two adults, or one adult and two children under ten years of age, will be allowed to be interred in one grave.

Whenever a grave shall become vacant by the removal of the body or bodies therein, the land shall revert back to the corporation. But in case the owner thereof become a purchaser of a lot in the cemetery, the original price for the grave shall be allowed in part payment for the lot. The graves are not transferable.

No enclosures nor posts will be permitted in any of the single grave sections.

JOHN G. BARKER.

Forest Hills Cemetery, Jamaica Plain, Mass.

Hardy Herbacious Plants for the Cemetery.

THE PLANTAIN LILIES.

FUNKIA SUBCORDATA OR PLANTAIN LILY.

These are handsome hardy border plants, well worthy of more consideration than they usually receive. They have ornamental foliage, some finely variegated, when not in flower, exceedingly showy when in flower, showing to best advantage in considerable groups and forming a fine feature along with other suitable plants in rockeries or sloping banks, or even in a mass of some extent on the open lawn with the grass growing right up to their leaves. It is hardly a single grave plant, but rather to be used in general ornamentation.

The genius is known botanically as Funkia, named after a German botanist, all so far as known are natives of China and Japan, embracing eight species and some garden varieties. One under the name of F. grandiflora has been for a long time under cultivation in this country, the flowers are very fragrant, and are pure white, four inches long, bearing some twelve or fourteen on a scape or stalk. Time of flowering from July to September. Leaves ovate eight to nine inches in length by four to five inches broad, sometimes known as F. japonica. Others with white flowers are, lancefolia or lanceleaved, flowers one to one and one-half inches long on stalks scarcely a foot high flowering in August. Leaves four to five inches long, lance shaped. A variety, albo-marginata, both leaves and flowers August larger and each leaf variegated finely with white that renders it additionally attractive as a border plant. Sieboldtiana has white flowers with a pale lilac tinge two inches long coming in June, ten to fifteen on a flower spike. Leaves ten to twelve inches broad and quite glaucus. Sub-cordata, flowers white, four inches long, often fifteen flowers on a stalk in August. Leaves pale green, six to nine inches long by three to five inches broad. The other species have flowers not so conspicuous, the best being fortunei pale lilac, and ovata bluish lilac, longest known in gardens along with grandiflora. The character of the roots are tuberous, leaves dying down in the fall, easily divided by a division of the roots in the spring, do best left a considerable time without removing.

There is another closely allied group, indeed sometimes classed with these, under the name of Hemerocallis or Day Lily, with orange or yellow flowers, mostly natives of Europe, that except in the wildwood part of a cemetery can scarcely be called good cemetery plants.

EARLY FLOWERING HARDY PLANTS.

The modern cemetery is something in the way of a people's park as an attraction after the winter is over. Almost before the trees begin to leave out there are many hardy herbacious plants, flowering at the time of the spring bulbs, that may be made a great attraction. They are mostly humble growing plants and harmonize well with crocus, snowdrops, tulips and other similar bulbs, and like them look well either growing thickly out of the grass or in patches, under or bordering trees and shrubbery. The following are examples and even though some are but wild flowers, they should be planted in large irregular groups thick enough to be effective, never as isolated single plants.

Phlox subulata, ground or moss pink, flowers pink, purple or rose color, sometimes white, does best in a dry sandy or rocky soil, often in flower in April. Two other species divaricata and bifida come a trifle later with bluish or purple flowers. Of the Erythroniums or Dogtooth violets, the Americanum has leaves beautifully dotted and marbled with violet and white. The true Dogtooth violet of Europe, dens-canis, has purplish, rose or whiteish flowers, leaves blotched with purplish brown. The grandiflorum, also a North

American species, has larger flowers with plain leaves. For a blue flower, very early in flower and a mass of color, the common dwarf border iris or flower de luce, could be made good use of. It does not last long in flower but it comes at a time when flowers are flowers, at least in the north. Then there are the true violets, of course where they will stand nothing can equal in early spring the sweet scented English violets. In their absence however, or even with them, the wild violets of our woods and by ways planted thickly are a revelation in their peculiar color. There are very few places in this country where they may not be had for the digging up, and grown so as not to be smothered by other plants, as they often are in a wild state, they are a bouquet of color. As there are almost two dozen species enumerated as natives of North America, it shows how plentiful the true violets are with us. The common blue violet cuculata, to be met with everywhere, has no less than half a dozen distinct types or natural varieties and includes among them the palmate or hand leaf, the cordate or arrow-leaved, larkspur-leaved, the pedatea or birds-foot, and bicolor, a very handsome flower with the two upper petals deep violet and almost velvety like a pansy. This variety is not common like some of the others, Gray giving it as occurring sparingly from Massachusetts to Maryland, etc. With such a stock of native violets to choose from it is strange something has not been done with them as with the English violet and the pansy, to improve them by raising garden hybrids. Some of the wild kind flower all summer long as it is. The English primroses, cowslips and polyanthus where they will stand, would be charming plants, as would the English daisy, pansy and other similar plants but that could not be in the West or prairie country, as it would require too much protection, which is not a point we are now considering, as it is not such plants as are to be kept in cold frames and the like, and afterwards planted, but a class that will stand out altogether, and come up in the spring as though to the manner born. There are many parts of this country and protected nooks where the latter plants would do like natives, and surely nothing could be more inviting in early spring than to have our phloxes, violets, bluets, spring beauties, dodecathias, Greek valerian, and other native spring flowers come into blossom along with primroses, daisies, sweet violets, Johny-jump-ups and a whole host of old time favorites. This class of plants want no formal planting to be effective. The more natural they spring out of the ground the better. Irregular flower masses, one color and kind merging into one another in patches of different sizes here and there, would be preferable to having them scattered all over the ground with scarcely enough in any one place to be noticeable, and thereby aid nature by art and good taste. EDGAR SANDERS.

ERYTHRONIUM AMERICANUM OR DOG TOOTH VIOLET.

BURIAL REFORM.

In a paper read before a recent meeting of the Church of England Sanitary Association at Westminster, on the subject of "Earth to Earth Burial," the author advocated earth burial, but contended that such burial should be upon scientific and sanitary principles, which consisted in the placing of the body in actual contact with the earth, and not more than three feet below the surface, in not allowing one body to be superimposed upon another, and the planting the ground in order that it may be purified and made fit for the reception, if necessary, of a second body after the lapse of a generation. If burials were conducted in this way in any decently porous soil (any soil, in fact, except a stiff clay), there was no doubt that with proper intervals the soil could be used over and over again without danger of offense, and that the work would probably be done with increasing efficiency as the earth grew more fertile. There should be no tombstones, but a cloister should be set apart for the reception of memorial stones, etc. The pomps and vanities which had grown up round the simple act of interment had become intolerable, and there could be no doubt that the limited popularity which cremation enjoyed was largely due to the fact that it afforded a ready means of escape from the oppressive products of superstition and vulgarity.

Dr. Richardson, who presided over the meeting, in remarking on the great change now taking place in the churches, in relation to the physical advancement in sanitation, said: It was a most hopeful sign of the times to see the learned body of the clergy, who had themselves acquired the art of standing first in the class of long and healthy lives, putting forth their strength to lead the whole community into the best physical methods by which the same wealth of life might be attained. It accorded well, too, with the work of the clergy for them to teach the laws of health as a part of their own mission. The clergyman had unrivalled advantages as a teacher of the principles of health. He commanded an attention and authority essentially his own. Moreover, there were some questions of a sanitary kind which the clergy were bound now to study and impart, because the subject formed part of their vocation. The disposal of the dead, less the expensive system of burial that has so long prevailed, and less the unwholesome system of packing the dead in the earth that had so long prevailed, was one of those questions. The clergy were bound to unite with sanitarians in discussing whether ashes to ashes, or dust to dust, or one or the other, according to circumstances, should from henceforth be the solemn and accepted function for the disposal of the human dead.

The meeting of the Burial and Mourning Reform Association was held subsequently, when the following resolutions were adopted:—"That this meeting deprecates undue exposure to mourners at the graveside." "That this meeting urges upon cemetery authorities the desirability of heating the cemetery chapel, and providing a tent for the shelter of mourners at the graveside"; and, "That this meeting invites the rich to set an example of economy and simplicity at funerals with a view to proving that economy in the burial of the dead is no mark of want of respect."

RULES AND REGULATIONS.

Every cemetery should be governed by certain rules and regulations, which should be printed in pamphlet form for distribution among lot owners. While this has been done in most of the large cemeteries, where the rules are very much alike, we will, for the benefit of the smaller cemeteries, publish in this department such rules as commend themselves for general adoption. Contributions are solicited.

Extracts from the Rules and Regulations of Forest Lawn Cemetery, Omaha, Neb.

The sub-division of lots by the lot owner is not allowed.

The joint purchase of a lot is not recommended, but when it occurs, the board of trustees, on application in writing if deemed expedient may allow a transfer duly executed by either owner to the others, but to no other persons. No transfer is valid until entered on the cemetery records, and no transfer of a lot by sale or otherwise by a lot holder, without the consent of the board of trustees, will be recognized by the association.

To prevent the excessive and unsightly crowding of tombstones, not more than one monument, grave stone or mark exceeding two feet in height above the surface of the ground, shall be permitted in any entire lot.

Grave stones or marks must be placed at the head or foot of the grave, and must be placed upon foundations not less than four feet deep, and not less than twelve inches square, unless the stone be a single piece, in which case a depth of three feet below the ground will be sufficient. No grave stone or mark can be set in a socket.

No fence, coping, or enclosure of any kind will be permitted on burial lots. Boxes, shells, toys and similar articles scattered upon the graves and lawn, are inconsistent with proper keeping of the ground and will not be permitted.

Every lot holder should have a diagram on the back of his or her deed, or other convenient place for reference and mark every interment thereon. This method will enable them to point the precise location for each grave, without going to the grounds, and thus prevent misunderstanding and mistakes, which occur from an imperfect description of location. One interment only should be made in the same grave, unless at a great depth or when necessity seems to require it.

The land marks or corner stones indicating the boundaries of the lots will be set even with the surface of the ground, by the superintendent at the expense of the lot owners.

No elevated mounds over graves will be permitted, as it is impossible to mow the grass or keep it alive and green on mounds. No lot shall be filled above the established grade. All family burial lots and all single graves will be sodded and kept in good order by the association, and without charge.

The superintendent will plant trees and shrubs in accordance with the general plan for the ornamentation and embellishment of the grounds. No additional planting by the proprietors of lots will be permitted, except by consent of the superintendent.

All preparation of flower beds, planting and trimming, must be submitted to the superintendent, and all work done by the gardeners of the cemetery, the charges for which will be as follows, payable in advance:

For digging up and planting flower beds, gardeners per hour..30

Teams, when hauling is necessary, per hour........50
Care of flower beds after planting; for the season..
Beds filled with geraniums, verbenas, etc., per square foot.................................10
Mixed beds of geraniums and foliage plants, per square foot.................................15
Fine foliage beds, per square foot.................20

No flower beds to be dug up in the cemetery larger than the plants furnished will plant properly.

No horse must be left on the grounds unfastened. Drivers must remain on their seats or by their horses during funeral services. Carriages will not be allowed to turn upon any avenue.

Except in cases of emergency when lots are required for immediate use, the superintendent will not attend to the selection or sale of lots on Sunday.

Some Suggestions Regarding Stone Work.

Every monument or marker should have a foundation extending below the frost line, and the foundation should be put in by the cemetery at the expense of the lot owner. A substantial foundation ensures the permanency of the superstructure. Foundations should be the same size as the base that is to rest upon it, and should be laid nearly flush with the surface. Bottom bases should be level enough to set true on the foundation without requiring to be brought up to a level by the use of chips. Such work is not substantial and should not be allowed in any cemetery.

If headstones are used, footstones are superfluous, one mark at a grave is sufficient. Tall marble slabs should be prohibited. Doweling marble slabs to sandstone bases, or setting the markers in socket bases is unstable and is prohibited in some cemeteries. If a family monument is to be erected, a low granite marker in one piece is the best possible means of marking the grave.

Coping and railing around lots should not be allowed. Aside from the fact that in time it will become unsightly, it, even when new, detracts from the surroundings, and is entirely out of place. Modern cemeteries prohibit such enclosures, and many of the older cemeteries are gradually taking them out and adopting the continuous lawn plan.

There should be but one monument to each lot and the graves around it should be marked in a manner that will harmonize with the monument. Lot-owners should be encouraged to keep in mind the surroundings of their lot, and not their lot only, when selecting a design for a monument. Too much care cannot be exercised in making such a selection, and duplicating designs on adjacent lots should be avoided.

Quality, rather than quantity, is most desirable in monuments as in everything else; therefore sandstone bases (so often used to secure greater height) should give place to a material that will be more in harmony with the monument. Variety in color may be desirable on a section, but it is in poor taste in a single monument.

An Italian Campo Santo.

A MARBLE STATUE IN THE CAMPO SANTO, GENOA.

WHILE Rome is the city of tombs, and Florence the home and workshop and temple of art, and Pisa has the sacred soil, and Bologna has a throng of sepulchres that have the gift of beauty, it is in Genoa that the most remarkable evidence is found of development in the artistic decoration of graves. The city is in many ways entitled to the name she bears the Superb. The climate is singularly alluring, soft and brilliant. The mountains that enclose her form a barrier that guards Genoa from the chill of the Alps, and the Mediterranean tempers the airs of distant Spain and Africa. The orange trees glow with green and gold in the winter, and the palms and ferns receive the sunshine and repel the frost. It is to Italy and southern France that the invalids are sent from the harsh climates of northern Europe, and they often go too late. Here, on one of the old streets nigh the harbor, is the house where Daniel O'Connell died, and a tablet with medallion in the wall by the window where he breathed his last, revives recollection of his strenuous life and strong career, so peacefully closing at last on this sunny shore.

On an eminence that commands a charming view is the tomb of Smithson, the founder of the Smithsonian Institution, a noble monument of one who was himself a mystery, and giving his fortune with a genial trust to do good in a distant land, made his name one of happy relations for all time—a household word in the mouths of countless millions of a great nation.

The long line of low arches and weather-beaten walls of an aqueduct, bearing the tribute of mountain springs to Genoa, is on one side of a white road leading into the foothills where the Apennines stand back for a little space from the sea, and on the other side a shallow stream sparkles over wide beds of gravel and polished stones, where the washerwomen toil. After driving for half an hour into the country there is an enclosure of many acres, heavy walls, plain and grim, on the exterior, and within marble halls and colonnades, inclosing a field of graves under a multitude of crosses and decorated with offerings, some of which are quaint in their crude simplicity.

Quickly the unique reputation of the Campo Santo of Genoa is explained, for many of the tombs are marvels of art, and are surprises in beauty and taste. Beside this, dingy and crowded Westminster abbey becomes a second-hand store of funeral bric-a-brac; and the things that are curious in startling originality of design are more notable than those that are attractive through delicacy of workmanship. First, one sees that art still lives in Italy; that whatever she has lost, her sculptors are not unworthy their surpassing inheritance of glory. Indeed, art is like the sunshine in the air, and an inspiration for the people from the cradle to the grave.

Here in the palace of the dead the human figures, as always, are of the highest interest, and they alone would declare to the competent observer that in the race whose fathers conquered the old and discovered the new world the vital forces are found still with the "fatal gift of beauty." The marble that is so dexterously and divinely cut is as of the perfect purity of snow new fallen and drifted, and whether it is the cunning of the hand that carves or the daintiness of the material, there is in the work an airy grace, and only the clear lines tell that the forms are not conjured out of crystal but chiselled in stone. On one side the corridor is open to the golden air, on the other walls as of pearl rise to the stainless roof.

There is the sepulchre of a father, and at the door his son is in his arms and weeping, receiving his blessing. They are parting at the gate of the grave. There are children mourning by the tombs of their parents, perfect likenesses, charming attitudes, sorrowful expressions. There are widows and widowers mourning for lost companions, and it is not unknown that men who have found second mates walk where the dead repose, and see themselves in melancholy attitudinizing.

The story is told of a Frenchman—France is far away and affords the needed perspective—that a friend said to him: "I saw you at the funeral of your wife, and sympathized with your grief." "Ah," exclaimed the mourner, "you should have seen me at the tomb; there I was terrible!" It must be an odd sense of posing in a dramatic situation that a lady, who has buried a husband and figures a pensive statue at his grave, takes a second man who has had the happiness to win her, and presents herself to him, a statuesque affliction over the dust of the dear departed. More sculptured widows than widowers are found in the Genoese Campo Santo, and the guides who know the ways of the world and the fashion of the times point out those who are distinguished for harvesting a crop of second affection, and wind up the stories of the survivals of love and repetitions of matrimonial experiment by telling of the streets upon which the originals of the marble mourners reside, with the occupation in which they are engaged, adding anecdotes that are apt, and aid the formation of character that is picturesque. The portraitures of men and women in business clothes the sculptors achieve are only too accurate, having not unfrequently the authentic severity of photography; the hardness discoverable in what may be termed, with conventional inaccuracy, the living statuary, disappears in the draperies that seem exquisitely soft, and to sway with the gentle undulations of graceful movement. The flowers are as lilies and pale roses, the laces all of fairy texture. There is a young girl who seems to float over the flowers upon

Why a Cemetery is So Called.

Webster says a cemetery is "a place where the dead bodies of human beings are buried." But that is all he says, and there is not a 5-year-old child in the land that could not tell us as much without referring to his "Unabridged." In tracing the derivation of the word I find that the root is in an old Jewish word "caemeteria," meaning dormitories or sleeping places. Later on the form of expression was changed to "requietorium." In that section of "Camden's Remains" which has the heading of "Concerning British Epitaphs," I find the following (page 583, edition of 1630). "The place of burial was called by St. Paul 'sematoria,' in the respect of a sure hope of a resurrection." The Greeks call it "caemeterion," which means "a sleeping place until the resurrection." The old Hebrew word for cemetery means "the house of the living," the idea being that death is only a protracted sleep that will terminate on the day when Gabriel blows his trumpet.— *Chicago Tribune.*

GALLERY IN THE CAMPO SANTO.

which she walks, angels robed in mist, women's forms almost undraped, but clothed in a radiance of purity that shields the loveliness that is sacred, from the gaze of the uncouth. There are majestic figures full of nobility, speaking of high courage and generous daring and devotion, and of mournful fate and grievous destiny. One turns away from the Campo Santo of Genoa with a sense of deep experience, touched with sadness, conscious that, though art may be longer than time, and adorns with shapes of humanity and suggestions of divinity the gates of death, it is not art that can ask in triumph, "Where is the sting of death and the victory of the grave?"

Italy, Europe, Asia, America, the continents and islands of the sea are graveyards; the earth with all its oceans is a tomb, and there is nothing imperishable except the invisible.—*Cosmopolitan for March.*

Mexican Funerals.

A funeral is treated with much respect in Mexico. None so proud who will not lift his hat to do it reverence. The burial is on the day of death if possible, and the priest repairs to the house and celebrates divine service for the repose of the departed soul upon an improvised altar of flowers and candles. This is in full view of passers by on the street, who respectfully kneel on the pavement. Others in the distance see them and also kneel, so that for two or three blocks up and down may be seen men, women and children on the open street in the attitudes of prayer. This, however, more correctly describes the practice of the poorer people. The upper strata of society is more reserved in its devotions.

One street in Mexico, near the National Palace, called the Calle Tabaqueros, is filled from end to end with coffinmakers, whose wares, in different stages of completion, are piled on the curb in gruesome confusion. The wayfarer who pauses a moment to look at the unusual scene is immediately surrounded by the tradesmen, who inquire, in voluble Spanish, if he wants a coffin. —*N. Y. Times.*

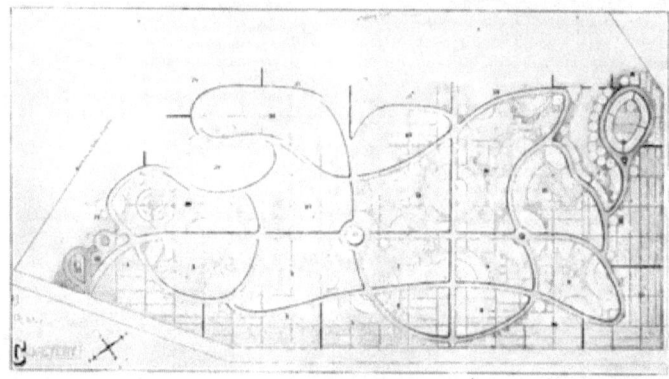

PLAN OF RIVERSIDE CEMETERY, DEFIANCE, O.

Riverside Cemetery, Defiance, O.

As early as 1846 a number of citizens organized the Defiance Rural cemetery, then containing only ten acres of available ground, and used until 1883, when the same went into the hands of the city. Realizing that the area was too limited for a growing town, the trustees petitioned the council to condemn 50 acres of adjoining grounds, which was accomplished with an outlay of about $100 per acre. Bordering on the Auglaize River with several natural ravines cutting into the plateau and a liberal growth of native trees, the tract presents many features well adapted for cemetery purposes, and the trustees will spare no means in making it one of the most charming burial places in northwestern Ohio.

The accompanying sketch of the lot plan shows the distribution of the sections by winding drives, which are ample, well constructed and well drained. At present sufficient ground is graded to place on sale some 1500 lots, portions of which are reserved by sections for members of the Catholic church.

The chapel and vault stands in an elevated position near the entrance convenient to reach for the purpose for which it is designed. The walls are built of Bedford lime stone with handsome trimmings of Portage red-stone and altogether the work is a handsome piece of masonry. The chapel room is 22x34 feet with an additional bay for the lowering apparatus. The gothic windows are filled in with opalescent and jewelled glass of appropriate designs, admitting a soft and sacred light. The ceiling is open work and finished in natural pine, while the massive doors, window frames and handsome wainscoting are of white and red oak, the floor of Georgia marble and the walls of stucco delicately tinted from a terra cotta to a light blue. There is also a handsome mantel and open grate that the room may be pleasantly warmed in inclement weather. The vault below is one large room well ventilated and well secured, with ample accommodations for about 60 bodies. The entire cost of vault and chapel is said to be about $8,500.

Great credit is due Mr. George W. Bechel, the superintendent and treasurer, who has given a great deal of his time to the development of the plans of grounds and buildings from the beginning, and who, together with the president, F. W. LeSueur, and the secretary, J. R. Wilhelm, are aiming to give Defiance a modern cemetery.

The plans for Riverside cemetery, as well as for the chapel and vault, were made by Frank Eurich, superintendent of Woodlawn cemetery, Toledo, O., and give promise of presenting a harmonious whole when reproduced upon the grounds.

CHAPEL AND RECEIVING VAULT, RIVERSIDE CEMETERY, DEFIANCE, O.

How a Superintendent Can Advance the Welfare of His Cemetery.

Editor Modern Cemetery:

You have asked me to give thought to what I consider two very intricate questions, viz.: "how can a superintendent advance the interests of a cemetery?" and "Does the welfare of a cemetery depend upon the superintendent?"

There is such a dissimilarity between cemeteries that to answer these questions intelligently and have them satisfactory to the person who suggested them is somewhat difficult.

It is regrettable that many superintendents do not take that hearty interest in the advancement of their cemeteries that the position demands. Of course there are numerous worthy examples, superintendents whose loyalty and devotion to the best interests of their charge are given without stint, their best time and thought being always at the disposal of the trustees, for the best good of their places.

To advance the interests of a cemetery the superintendent must have the most cordial support of his trustees, they must harmonize; and this leads me to say that while I know some trustees are totally unfit for the position they hold as such, the superintendent must respect their opinions and give them due thought and consideration; if they are wrong they will not get right by the superintendent hitting them all the time, and who knows but the superintendent may be off a little himself. I know of a superintendent whose experience will be of interest in this connection. He has been the subject of the most radical changes that could be brought about. The trustees did not set themselves up as knowing more than he did about the working of the grounds or the arrangement of the labor, but they did not approve of the unbusinesslike manner in which the office work and some of the departments were managed, and which had been in operation many years; they were determined that a better system should be adopted. Well, that superintendent needed pity at that time, and did he not swallow some bitter pills! but, my brother, listen again, who were these trustees that were doing all this? Were they men who held only ordinary positions in life, and never handled anything more than a small weekly stipend? No, they were gentlemen that were all managing large and successful business interests themselves; and why should not the same methods that made them successful be applied to the business interests of the cemetery, and work equally as well? The new methods were applied, faithfully, and with a firm determination that success must follow. The superintendent was given to understand that he, and he alone, must manage and be held solely responsible for everything that took place, select his own men without any interference from any one. All instructions came from the superintendent, the foremen in all departments looked to him for their orders, and he (the superintendent) receiving his instructions from the trustees, to whom he was expected at all times, especially at the stated meetings, to give an intelligent account of all his doings. I hear some saying that is bringing things down pretty fine; so it is, but it is the better plan. Why? Because your willingness to cooperate with those whom the proprietors have placed in charge of your cemetery to see that they are faithfully dealt with, is proof that you are on the alert to fill your position to their best interests. The confidence of that board of trustees in their superintendent has no limit, and the respect he has for them is unbounded, while they give ample proof of their confidence in him by the magnanimity of their interest in his comfort and welfare. Now, my brother, have I succeeded in showing you the starting point in which a superintendent can advance the interests of a cemetery. The trustees and the superintendent must have unbounded confidence in each other. Am I right?

My next point is that the superintendent must make the wants of the proprietors and those who are constantly becoming such, the chief object of his thought; he must remember that death brings everyone in contact with him; he must be a sympathetic man, and for the time being enter as fully into their sorrows as possible. My brother, don't be impatient if a bleeding heart keeps you a little while when you are in a hurry, telling you what is to them the greatest loss that ever was, never fail to say a kind word, remembering that we, too, if not already, cannot tell how soon we may need sympathy in the same way, but, never forgetting that kind words never die. Would you advance the interests of your cemetery, then get the sympathy and good will of the proprietors; you can have it, and give them yours in return. Again, the superintendent should be a man that in studying the interests of his place, should go to other places, confer with other superintendents, exchange ideas, and modes of work, and go at his own work with the expectation that he has a lifelong situation. He may not be able to adopt what others do as a whole, but their ideas should set him to thinking, which will greatly aid him in working out plans that he can adapt to his place vastly better than he could if he did not do anything but stop at home. I am inclined to say (parenthetically perhaps) that he should join the A. A. C. Supts.; yes, and subscribe for the MODERN CEMETERY, which will aid any progressive superintendent. What else? Read all books that will help, landscape especially, make himself acquainted with the trees shrubs and flowers of his locality, find out what will be best suited to his place, and in so doing he will not only be interested, but find it of great profit to be familiar with these things. In such a way a superintendent can advance the interests of his cemetery. Try it.

In replying to the second question, Does the welfare of a cemetery depend upon the Superintendent? the answer depends upon the intent of the question,—if it means upon a financial return, I say, No, for the reason that the superintendent is not the financial head, do not adopt the prices. I know more than one cemetery where, for instance, the price paid for lots is ridiculously low; I also know we all can't be a Greenwood, a Spring Grove, or a Mt. Auburn, but as a matter of business, why should not the work done in the cemetery command a sufficient revenue to pay for itself, the same as any other business? There are a few cemeteries belonging to cities in various localities that sustain themselves, there are others that receive some revenue from the city treasuries to help pay expenses (which in some cases include useless officials who must have a place), others are run as stock companies and made to pay good dividends, and are usually on a liberal basis, others on the mutual plan, where there are no dividends and where the trustees receive no compensation. I do not see how a superintendent can be held responsible for the financial welfare of a cemetery under any of these conditions, unless it be the mutual plan, and then he cannot control the appropriations of the trustees, but where good prices are obtained and no one is looking for dividends or where the citizens expect lots at the lowest possible prices and relies upon the city to make an annual appropriation equal to the deficiency. I can see where the superintendent has a measure of responsibility. The financial management might be discussed at great length, though any further allusion here seems uncalled for, but I must say in this connection, where a reasonable amount of labor is allowed, the superintendent is of course responsible for a fair return.

The other view is this, I fear too many (not all) are in the habit of doing to a great extent as others do. This will not answer; you cannot run in each other's rut successfully. True, there are some few things which we can all adopt in common, which I am sure will readily suggest themselves. I could mention other points and make my ideas clear from observation and past experience, but personality not being allowed and very wisely, too, I know of no pen, except that of the rambler, perhaps, that would dare to expose a feature which some superintendents are obliged to endure, which they know is not practical, but being subordinates must comply with higher authority, while their own interests demand silence.

Again, if you, Mr. Superintendent, are in a progressive place—and why should you not be—no matter how small, you must advance with the people you serve, especially in the laying out of lots and care of the grounds, you must be prepared to advise the proprietors in such advanced ideas, that you will be able to mould their ideas and plans to the best advantage. If you do not keep well posted yourself, how can you lead others to be fully up to all advanced ideas of improvements in the care of their lots and you yourself in the welfare of the place?

So I conclude that, in a measure at least, the welfare of the cemetery does depend upon the superintendent, and if you have the interest of the place at heart you would not want it any other way. To be successful you must give it your first and best consideration, and be assured it will be appreciated, for there is great reward in conscientious faithful service.

New Office and Residence Building, Fairmount Cemetery, Newark, N. J.

We are indebted to Mr. Charles Nichols, superintendent of Fairmount cemetery, Newark, N. J., for the following description of the new building recently completed on those grounds:

The building is fifty feet square, constructed of brown stone and is modern in all its appointments. On the first floor are the offices for the superintendent and assistant superintendent, a map room, a large fire-proof vault and a commodious waiting room provided with toilet rooms. The second and third floors are for residence purposes; there are six rooms on the second and three on the third floors, with all of the modern conveniences. It is lighted by gas and heated by the hot water system, which has given perfect satisfaction the past winter. The building cost $17,000. Another improvement at Fairmount is a new entrance and gateway. Four massive brown stone posts support heavy iron gates, those on the driveway being 12 feet 6 inches in width and the side gates 4 feet 6 inches. The cost of this improvement was $2,145. The new avenue in the grounds, which approaches this entrance, is twenty-five feet wide laid with Telford, with a low granite coping on either side.

Father Henrici, leader of the Economist Society, of Economy, Pa., who died recently, had a remarkable funeral. The body was simply wrapped in a sheet, and laid in a coffin of rough pine boards painted black, and without handles or name plate. It was taken to the cemetery in a wagon. The Economites are buried side by side in one long row, with no headstone or anything to tell where they lie. No distinction was made in the case of Father Henrici. The society is worth $52,000,000 and its members are sworn to celibacy.—*Progression*.

CEMETERY NOTES.

The annual report of Harmony Grove cemetery, Salem, Mass., states that seventeen iron fences were removed during the past year.

The affairs of Woodland cemetery, DesMoines, Ia., which have always been controlled by the city government, are said to be in such a condition as to require investigating. An expert accountant has been appointed to examine the books.

Fairs, suppers, raffles, lectures and other forms of entertainment have been given for the purpose of raising funds for cemetery purposes, but it has remained for a congregation of Polish Jews to give a dance for this object, and it was a Sunday dance at that.

It is unnecessary to mention the desirability of removing the fences and hedges as the argument is eloquently made by a comparison with other parts of the cemetery where the lawn system has been adopted.—Directors' report, Evergreen cemetery, New Haven, Ct.

Very successful fairs have been held by the Sandy Hill Cemetery Association, Paterson, N. J., and the Ladies' Cemetery Association, East Weymouth, Mass. In each place a varied programme was given and the entertainment continued several evenings. The results were very satisfactory and a handsome fund realized to commence needed improvements.

A bill has been introduced in the Ohio legislature amending section 6185 of the revised statutes so as to read as follows:

The court may also, in settlement, allow, as a credit to the executor or administrator, any just and reasonable amount expended by him for a tombstone or monument for the deceased, *and for any just and reasonable amount he may have paid to any cemetery association or corporation as a perpetual fund for caring for and preserving the lot on which said deceased is buried;* but it shall not become incumbent on any executor or administrator to procure a tombstone or monument or to pay any sum into such perpetual fund.

In the 51st report of the Lowell cemetery, Lowell, Mass., President Charles L. Knapp recommends revising the present by-laws, under which the cemetery has been operated since 1841, and makes several suggestions that apply with equal force to many other cemeteries situated similarly to that at Lowell. He suggests having the governing board or trustees consist of six members instead of twice that number as at present, on the well-grounded theory that as the number in such bodies increases the efficiency decreases. But if this pruning be too radical, he adds, the present twelve might continue and the direct management might devolve upon an executive committee of three trustees who should fulfill prescribed duties for a term of three months, when they should be succeeded by three more, so continuing by quarterly periods through the year. In this way the labor would be more equally distributed than is the case to-day, and all trustees would have an opportunity of learning where the cemetery is located. On the subject of lots and their care the report suggests that in case a lot-owner fails to pay for work ordered by him and properly performed for him within three months from time of presentment of bill, the superintendent be ordered to refuse to do further work upon the lot in question. That in case of a lot purchased, no deed shall be delivered until full payment is made, and that failing to pay in one year's time, the purchaser shall forfeit all claim to the lot and be dealt with as shall be decided by the board of trustees. That no money should be received for perpetual care of a lot until the lot in question is put in proper condition for its proper maintenance. Furthermore, that in all cases the superintendent should fix the amount of money to be deposited and necessary to secure the care expected by the lot owner. The president also calls attention to the necessity of a state law that shall prevent the selling of a cemetery lot by heirs at law when such lot is in use for the original purpose for which it was purchased. As the laws are to-day, no man's lot is secured against the greed of those who follow him, save by extraordinary legal precautions, which expensive legal process it should not be necessary to take. The report shows the cemetery to be in a prosperous condition.

The annual report of the directors of Evergreen cemetery, New Haven, Conn., suggests several reforms and invites the co-operation of the lot owners in bringing them about. "One of these," the report says, "is the abolition of the unnatural efforts sometimes resorted to to preserve the bodies of the dead. This is a delicate question, for almost every one whose loss of a friend is recent, possesses to a greater or less degree, a desire that the body of that friend should be preserved as long as possible, and yet to the sober second thought of that individual no good reason therefor can suggest itself; on the contrary the idea is rather repulsive than otherwise. In these days when cremation is being so vigorously agitated in some quarters, and the argument is so much used in favor of that process and against inhumation on sanitary grounds if for no other reason, all attempts to preserve the bodies of the buried beyond the time limited by nature herself, ought to be discouraged. That the body should return to and mingle with the earth in a natural way admits of little doubt.

Towards the abolishing of Sunday funerals we respectfully ask the use of your influence. Of course it is not in all cases possible to avoid them, but in a great majority of cases it is possible, and there is no good reason why we should not join in the growing tide rising against them. There is a rapidly increasing tendency in this direction. Sunday funerals are objectionable because of the throngs of mere idle curiosity seekers which they oftentimes attract, and for the opportunities of parade and display which they afford. Both of these things are contrary to the quiet and solemnity which should characterize a funeral. They are objectionable because the clergy, whose attendance at such a time, if never before, is demanded, have already quite as much to do on that day as they have time for; and they are further objectionable for the reason that they unnecessarily employ the services of men who are entitled to one day in seven, as much as other men, and because they can usually take place upon the second or last day of the week, as well as upon the first."

Landscape Gardening.

"A peculiar quality of nature's arboreal and floral material, as found in wild habitats, is that it rarely fails to satisfy our sense of the beautiful and interesting. This is true in a degree that cannot be claimed for stiffly arranged geometrical effects in landscape adornment.

"Observe a pleasing natural landscape or wild plantation, and you will feel at once that it has an irresistable charm, arising not so much from the kind of growths that may happen to be present as from the way in which the various features within range of the eye-meadow, trees, shrubs, vines, plants, etc., are distributed. Such things as straight lines or angles are almost unknown in natural landscapes. Variety as found in the position of trees and other growths in their forms and colors, both as to foliage and flowers, in the distribution of open areas, thickets, water and hills over the surface, is the rule of nature's gardens. How pleasing and restful is such scenery to the eye!

"The very term landscape, or landview, indicates the basis of the chief charm found in all beautiful natural landscape scenery. Open areas of meadow or lawn, skirted by masses of shrubs and adorned here and there with isolated clumps of trees or single specimens, forming vistas in a number of directions please us most. To have the center of a lawn-area occupied by trees tends to produce a restful effect on the mind of the beholder, and at the same time serves to set forth in perfection the beautiful trees and shrubs of the place.

"If open area is the key-note of the vista feature of beautiful natural landscapes, then it may be said that groups and masses afford the key-note of effective natural planting. An exception may seem to be found in the case of isolated specimens of trees, etc., but even these, pleasing as they are in a fine landscape, seem all the finer if so located as to appear related to some marginal group or projection. Usually a clump of two or three trees will look better than single specimens."—*Elias A. Long in American Gardening.*

The London *Undertakers' Journal* heads an article descriptive of Jay Gould's mausoleum in Woodlawn cemetery, thus: "How $80,000 were wasted." Whether or not it was wasted is debatable, but that the money could have been expended in a manner that would have conferred more good on a greater number of people is beyond a doubt.

Publisher's Department.

Our readers are invited to call the attention of those in authority at their respective cemeteries to the subscription rates printed on another page. Every cemetery trustee as well as those more actively identified in the work should read the MODERN CEMETERY.

Mr. John Amschler, superintendent Woodlawn cemetery, Edwardsville, Ill., has sent the MODERN CEMETERY a sketch of a device used by him for protecting flowers, etc., on graves when it becomes necessary to excavate between two graves. The "protector" is nine feet long with sides three feet high. In position it has this appearance: ∧ The frame may be made of battens joined by strap hinges and covered with light boards. A small chain at either end will prevent the frame from spreading. The ridge may be covered with sheet metal or oil cloth.

Trade catalogues received: Ellwanger & Barry's supplementary catalogue of rare and choice trees, shrubs and roses. B. M. Watson, Old Colony Nurseries, Plymouth, Mass., wholesale price list trees, shrubs, etc. Rules and Regulations Mount Greenwood Cemetery, Chicago. Dell Park Cemetery, Natick, Mass.

Mr. Alexander Henry, superintendent of Uniondale cemetery, Allegheny, Pa., departed this life on February 11th. Mr. Henry was an exemplary man and in a long career earned the respect of a large proportion of Allegheny's citizens. He had been a member of the Association of American Cemetery Superintendents since 1888.

The manufacture of metallic flower wreaths, crosses and similar ornaments for memorial purposes, has assumed very large proportions in England and on the continent. One London concern which is said to carry a stock of about ten thousand designs, do a yearly business aggregating several hundred thousand dollars. Metal and porcelain is used in the manufacture, and they are used alike by all classes.

A great deal has been said at conventions, and from time to time has appeared in these columns, on the subject of making the MODERN CEMETERY a medium for the discussion of topics of general interest to those engaged in cemetery affairs. The year that has just closed marks a decided improvement in point of contributions over those made to the first volume and we are desirous of making still greater improvements in our third volume. It is a fact almost too well known to require reiteration that there are very few persons having a knowledge of the practical workings of a cemetery, who are not employed at some cemetery and have their time fully occupied with their regular duties, this necessarily makes it difficult to secure a corps of regular contributors to the MODERN CEMETERY. Such is not the case with most other journals. The field for literary workers having enlarged from time to time until it embraces nearly all the arts and sciences, but as there is nothing peculiarly attractive about the practical side of cemetery affairs, the literary workers have not taken it up, so that it devolves entirely upon those engaged in the work, who shed all the light possible on the many subjects connected with the care and management of cemeteries. The conditions of all cemeteries are by no means alike, each may be said to possess features peculiar to itself, but there is still so much in common between all cemeteries that the experiences of one will be helpful to another. Especially is this true of the smaller country cemeteries, where there is such need of improvement. We therefore urge upon our readers the good they can do by a free discussion through the columns of the MODERN CEMETERY of subjects pertaining to this most important work.

Wanted.

The head gardener of the U. S. national cemetery at Vicksburg, Miss., wants situation in cemetery to take charge of greenhouses, flowers and shrubs. Or if preferred would take entire charge of grounds. Leaving on account of climate. Best of references. Please address George Farrant, National Cemetery, Vicksburg, Miss.

To Cemetery Officials.

Although the time for the seventh annual convention of the Association of American Cemetery Superintendents is still some months hence, many members are already planning to be present, and many more would gladly do the same if their private means would justify the expense of the trip. This association was not organized for mutual protection or financial interests, nor is its object to act as an "intelligence office," but its constitution clearly states that its object is " the advancement of the interests and the elevation of the character of cemeteries in America." Surely, therefore, every cemetery represented at our annual meetings by the superintendent or some other one of the officials, will reap as much benefit as the representative himself, and for this one reason alone our association ought to be liberally encouraged by all officials having charge of burial places. Not only the larger cemeteries are appealed to but the small as well, for it is even more essential that the smaller places should co-operate with us in sending a representative to the annual conventions and cheerfully bear the expense of the trip. As our profession requires the closest and most faithful attention throughout the year, and very few are allowed to enjoy an annual vacation, could a cemetery management show its appreciation of the services of an efficient and conscientious superintendent better than by granting him an annual vacation with full pay, sending him to the conventions of this association and allowing and paying the legitimate expenses?

Can you appreciate our efforts in your interest and the advantages that have been and will be derived from these annual meetings? They have been of great importance and the benefit derived from them by all who have attended former meetings and who will attend those in the future cannot be estimated; they will continue to grow largely in usefulness to those who will participate, and such cemetery officials who will withhold and begrudge the small appropriation it requires to send their representative to our conventions will make a great mistake and will be deprived of many beneficial results.

Gentlemen of Boards of Trustees and officials of cemeteries in general, you are cordially invited to make preparations and allowances to send your superintendent or come yourselves to our seventh annual convention, which will be held in that beautiful city, Minneapolis, Minn., commencing Tuesday, Aug. 22, 1893, and continuing four days. FRANK EURICH, Sec'y and Treas.

Notice to Cemetery Boards.

The undersigned, who for over ten years was superintendent of Cedar Hill cemetery, Newburgh, N. Y., would be pleased to correspond with cemetery boards who are starting new grounds, or re-arranging of old cemeteries as to the grading of lawns, arrangement of lots, plans and location of vaults, mapping of grounds and the keeping of records; as well as the most modern ideas of conducting funerals. Would advise by mail or would make a short engagement in starting grounds. Address, Wm. B. Westervelt, 7 Dubois street, Newburgh, N. Y.

THE MODERN CEMETERY.

THE MODERN CEMETERY.

AN ILLUSTRATED MONTHLY JOURNAL DEVOTED TO THE INTEREST OF CEMETERIES

R. J. HAIGHT, Publisher.
243 State Street, CHICAGO.

Subscription $1.00 a Year in Advance.   Foreign Subscription $1.25.
Special Rates on Six or More Copies.

VOL. III.   CHICAGO, APRIL, 1893.   No. 2

CONTENTS.

	PAGE
POWER OF TRUSTEES TO SELL LAND PURCHASED FOR A CEMETERY	13
RECONVEYING LOTS IN TRUST	13
MOUNT HOPE CEMETERY OF BOSTON NOT SUBJECT TO LEGISLATIVE CONTROL	14
THE GREENHOUSE IN THE CEMETERY	15
GREENWOOD CEMETERY	16
EXTRACTS FROM THE RULES REGARDING STONE WORK AT SPRING GROVE CEMETERY, CINCINNATI	17
THE CONGRESSIONAL CEMETERY AT WASHINGTON	18
TUBEROUS-ROOTED BEGONIAS	18
*A VIEW IN MARION CEMETERY, MARION, O.	19
BURIAL REFORM	20
A SPIRITUALISTIC VIEW OF CREMATION	20
DESTROYING MOLES	20
THE DISPOSAL OF CHOLERA DEAD	21
CEMETERY NOTES	21
MEMORIAL CHAPEL, PINE GROVE CEMETERY, LYNN, MASS.	22
CEMETERY REPORTS	22
MACADAM ROADS	23
CORRESPONDENCE	23
PUBLISHER'S DEPARTMENT	24

*ILLUSTRATED.

Power of Trustees to Sell Land Purchased for A Cemetery.

Prior to the year 1883, the inhabitants of Orcas Island, Washington, or that portion of the inhabitants near Arbutus Point, on East Sound, had used a certain portion of government land as a public burying ground. In the early part of that year is was thought desirable by some of the inhabitants of that portion of the island to obtain the title to said tract, which resulted in the purchase of twenty-six acres from the government, the patent to which was issued to three persons who were to act as trustees for the others, the island having been canvassed, and the people generally having contributed a dollar each towards paying for the land, though some gave more. On account of a large portion of the land being uneven, rocky and unsuitable for burial purposes, and a village having grown up and adjoining the two or three acres used as a cemetery, the trustees deemed it advisable to dispose of the balance of the property held by them and to remove the old cemetery to another and more eligible site. This was done with the concurrence of a majority of the contributors, who attended a meeting called by one of the trustees by postal card. When the new ground was procured, the privilege was given every one of the original contributors who desired, to select a lot in the new cemetery "without money and without price." An action was, however, brought by some of the contributors for the purpose of having cancelled and annulled the conveyance made by the trustees of the old cemetery, it being claimed that they had violated their trust. The Superior Court of San Juan county agreed with this, but the Supreme Court of the State (case entitled Guthrie v. Tullock) reversed its decision, holding that the purpose for which the land was sold and the use to which the proceeds were devoted, was but to carry out the purpose of their trust, and that there was nothing in their action suggestive of bad faith or unfairness on the part of those who acted as trustees, and that the trust had been executed in accordance with the expressed will of those for whom it was held. Furthermore, said the court, it did not appear that any of the original contributors were to have any fixed, certain, or aliquot part of the whole tract, but it was the general understanding that each one should have a burial lot in the cemetery, the dimensions of which were never fixed, and a right to vote at meetings. In all other respects the contributors were to have no rights other than those enjoyed in common by all the other residents of the island. By reason of their contributions merely, the contributors in this case were not entitled to any rights in the property purchased, for it is well settled that a mere general contribution to a fund for the purchase of land, the title of which is taken in another, will not create a trust in favor of the donor, unless, at the time of the purchase, it is understood that the person contributing to the fund is to have a certain proportion, such as a half, quarter, or other aliquot part, of the whole tract purchased. It is quite common for societies having in charge the building of churches or public hospitals to solicit subscriptions for the purpose, but no one ever supposed that by such general donation he became an equitable owner of a proportionate share of such church or hospital.

Reconveying Lots in Trust.

Some months ago mention was made in these columns of an incident that transpired in Boston wherein was recited the fact that a young man had secured a loan from a money lender and gave as collateral security the deed to the burial lot in the Mt. Hope cemetery where his father and mother were buried. At the expiration of sixty days the note remained unpaid and the broker demanded that the bodies be removed and the lot duly transferred to him. The trustees declined to recognize the legality of the transaction, and refused to make the transfer. Whether or not the broker has brought suit against the cemetery we are not informed, but the chances are that he will lose the money he has advanced.

The idea of securing positive assurance of the undisturbed interment of their friends seldom occurs to lot owners and but comparatively few cemeteries offer their lot owners suggestions on the subject.

* * *

Mr. Timothy McCarthy, superintendent of Swan Point cemetery, Providence, R. I., writes that a case quite similar to that of Mt. Hope happened at Swan Point recently, but no special notice was taken of it as the cemetery has no law preventing a lot owner from disposing of his lot to a friend or any one else. He cites an instance that has come under his observation where a man removed the body of his wife to a single grave section in another cemetery and disposed of the valuable lot in which she was first interred. Mr. McCarthy suggests the discussion of laws bearing on the important subject, and we would be pleased to hear from cemetery officials who have such laws in force.

* * *

To render a burial lot safe from the cupidity of heirs the safest plan is to reconvey the lot to the cemetery corporation in trust and to designate who shall be entitled to interment therein, or, as is suggested by the cemetery of Spring Grove at Cincinnati, O., purchasers may secure the same object under a declaration of trust, which is issued to those desiring it instead of the certificate of ownership. The form of reconveyance in use at Spring Grove reads as follows: I give and devise to the proprietors of the cemetery of Spring Grove my lot in the cemetery of Spring Grove, located in Hamilton county, Ohio, designated as lot No.   , in Section .... to be held by them and their successors forever in trust for the permanent interment thereon of myself and (here insert names of persons whose interment thereon are to be permanent) wholly free from all control of my heirs at law or any other person whatsoever; but to permit the interment thereon of (here insert names and description of those who are to have the right of interment thereon subject to ordinary rules and regulations as to removals) as "any member of my family," or "my children and their families," or "my heirs," etc.

Mount Hope Cemetery of Boston Not Subject to Legislative Control.

It has just been decided by the Supreme Judicial Court of Massachusetts, in the famous Mount Hope cemetery case, that the state legislature does not have the power to transfer this cemetery to any one, so that the new corporation formed for taking it cannot do so without paying the city of Boston for it. Of course, the underlying principle of this decision will be as applicable to any other similar cases. After reviewing the statutes of 1849 and 1855 authorizing the purchase of Mount Hope cemetery by the city, the court says:

"There can be no doubt that the city held the cemetery not only for the burial of poor persons, but with the right to make sales of burial lots rights to any person who might wish to purchase them, whether residents or non-residents. With these duties, and also with these rights and privileges, the city has acquired and improved their property. It is not as if the land had been procured and used exclusively as a place for the free burial of the poor or of inhabitants of Boston. In addition to these purposes, the city has been enabled to provide a well-ordered cemetery, with lots open to purchase, under carefully prepared rules and regulations, and thus to afford to its inhabitants the opportunity to buy burial places, without being compelled to resort to private cemetery companies, where the expense would probably be greater; and it has done this upon such terms that the burial of its paupers has been practically without expense in the past, and it has about forty acres remaining, the proceeds of which when sold, would go into the city treasury, but for the requirements of statute 1889, chapter 265, which requires the city to transfer to the newly-formed corporation called "The Proprietors of Mount Hope Cemetery" without compensation this cemetery, with the personal property pertaining thereto and with the right to any unpaid balances remaining due for lots already sold, and the annual income of certain funds held for the perpetual care of lots. If such transfer is made, all the city would retain would be the right to bury such persons as it is or may be by law obliged to bury in a certain prescribed portion of the cemetery. Its previous conveyances of lots and rights of burial are expressly confirmed.

"But it is apparent from the considerations heretofore expressed that this is not property which is held exclusively for purposes strictly public. The city of Boston is possessed of much other property which in a certain sense and to a certain extent is held for the benefit of the public, but in other respects it is held more like the property of a private corporation. In view of all these considerations, the conclusion to which we have come is that the cemetery falls within the class of property which the city owns in its private or proprietary character, as a private corporation might own it, and that its ownership is protected under the constitution of Massachusetts and of the United States, so that the Legislature has no power to require its transfer without compensation * * Moreover the legislative power over municipal property, when it exists, does not extend so far as to enable the legislature to require a transfer without compensation to a private person or private corporations.

"There are other reasons leading to the same result. The first is that the duties of the city in respect to providing a burial-place for the poor and for persons dying within its limits are not taken away. The city is still bound to provide one or more suitable places for the burial of persons dying within its limits and it is still bound to bury its paupers and indigent strangers. If this cemetery should be conveyed away, under the provisions of the statute of 1889, the city would be bound to provide another. Certainly the mere continuance of the city's right to bury in a limited portion of the cemetery such persons as the law requires it to bury is not a provision adequate to meet the requirement, and by the report of the facts the portion referred to is not likely to suffice even for the burial of paupers for any great length of time. The city is bound to provide a suitable place for the interment of persons dying within its limits; not poor persons only, but all persons; and the burial of the dead in ground not sanctioned by the city authorities, is strictly forbidden. But the duty of burying paupers, and of providing a place for the interment of all persons dying in Boston, is not imposed upon the new corporation."

Five grave robbers are on trial at DesMoines, Ia., for despoiling graves in Woodland cemetery for local medical colleges. Despite the most convincing evidence the jury in the first trial disagreed, making another trial necessary. In the meantime the party who is known to have concocted the ghoulish plot, has jumped his bond and left for parts unknown.

The Greenhouse in the Cemetery.

There is scarcely a rural cemetery now worthy of the name in the West at least, that has not its greenhouse department for the growing of cut flowers, and more particularly for the preparation of all kinds of summer blooming plants to be used for the decoration of the grounds and lots in summer. Even the village cemeteries in which the superintendent is gardener, sexton, etc., combined in one, make some effort in this line, either as part of the cemetery proper or in some cases perhaps, part the perquisite of the important position of sexton, all looking towards the decoration of the grounds in summer with flowers. Old fashioned hardy herbaceous plants are all right, no lover of gardening will decry against them. They have an individuality all their own and when rightly used have a charm not less so. But that other large class of plants ordinarily known as bedding plants, that either from their nature or changed into the condition by the skill of the gardener to be all summer bloomers, or rich with colored foliage, often of the most intense colors, if as the saying goes, has previously been run into the ground, are not going to disappear to suit the dictates of a fashion, and cemetery managers will do well to bear the thought in mind.

It so happens (the writer thinks often advantageously) that in many of our older and best cemeteries, there is necessarily at least two distinct features. One, the older part, that will with difficulty be brought to conform to the more modern idea of lawns, trees, shrubbery and few flowers, and the newer addition that is started and managed with this idea exclusively, to say nothing of those started of late and entirely on the new lawn idea, so that as in many minds there are many opinions, each can select those that suits them best, although we suppose ultimately, on the principle of the survival of the fittest, and increased taste in the people the lawn idea will generally prevail. At any rate it will be a long time before the masses will take kindly to a mere bit of lawn with a stone marker to show their lot, with no flowers, or grassy grave to mark the spot where the loved ones are buried. It is wholly different with that smaller number who can command a large lot, mayhap with a single memorial tablet or monument, notable for its very impressiveness or cost, its fine keeping and part of a system extensive enough to form a pleasing whole.

OAK WOODS CEMETERY, CHICAGO, AS AN EXAMPLE.

As the writer has for many years known Mr. Alex. Reid, the gardener, and knew that a great breadth of glass is part of the establishment, we ran down the other day to see how things looked, and on this occasion made the acquaintance of Mr. Bellet Lawson, the able superintendent who has recently taken charge.

In all there are some fourteen greenhouses, but as that gives but a vague idea, suffice it to say they cover an area of about 35,000 feet, outside of the cold frames in which are now coming into flower some 40,000 pansies. Two of the houses have roses, others carnations, callas and a large quantity of Dutch bulbs with other seasonable plants all for cut flower purposes, and we are assured now that none are sent into the city markets, nor will they be hereafter. The demand for flowers and plants for their patrons alone and for cemetery purposes rendering it unnecessary, besides the objectionable features of turning the consecrated grounds devoted to the dead to a money-making speculation in competition with legitimate florists.

PRINCIPAL STOCK GROWN.

Being a little curious to find out how many plants of the principal kinds are grown we find they will foot up a good way on towards half a million. For example of these few kinds there are used:

Alternantheras of sorts	100,000
Echiveras, " "	50,000
Geraniums, " "	50,000
Coleus, " "	25,000
Pansies, " "	40,000
Asters, stocks, phlox and other similar plants,	50,000
Total	315,000

This list indicates pretty clearly the vast quantity of achiranthus, echiveras or, hen and chickens grown, which is also supplemented with lots of cineraria, maritima, centauria, Madame Saleroi geraniums, and similar plants, neither of which are of much use in gardening except as used in ribbon bedding style, that appears as one may easily infer by a view of the grounds in summer an important feature, encouraged by the management and wanted by lot owners.

It seems that the silver foliage plants are used greatly here alternately with the red achiranthus and thus relieves and brightens up the thousands of yards of line color work done, even if more advanced superintendents of the modern cemetery deprecate it. Just as soon as the pansies and other spring flowers begin to open up, the lot owner's especially those having single graves begin to purchase, and we are assured here as elsewhere that planting is asked for in the case of new made graves almost up to frost time in the fall, although perhaps they are told it may not last a week if early frost comes. We suppose it safe to say the management at least among many cemeteries are not unmindful of the money in this plant-growing, but surely if a thing is done at all it should be done well, and such appears to be the condition of the greenhouse department as managed here. There is no manner of doubt but it more than pays its way, abundant material being at hand and in the cemetery, for such as are bound to decorate lots and graves with foliage or flowering plants, and hence easier controlled than when purchased outside and strangers allowed to do the planting.

CHRYSANTHEMUMS IN THE FALL.

As these houses are most of them empty towards the end of summer, a great sight of 6,000 or 8,000 of chrysanthemums are grown. The stock is now being propagated and as the houses become empty along in midsummer the young plants are set out on the benches. Heretofore no effort has been made here to grow the monster single stem flowers, but a good medium sized flower, and when several houses are a sheet of bloom they are exceedingly attractive.

A fine stock of Harrisi lily, azaleas, hyacinths, tulips, crocus, and other seasonable flowers were in bloom to suit Easter-tide, which is always taken advantage of by lot owners to decorate graves, etc. At Oak Woods no effort is made in the way of big ornamental conservatories. The houses are well although plainly built just such style as florists might use who understood their business.
EDGAR SANDERS.

Greenwood Cemetery.

[Mr. Halford L. Mills, of London, Eng., the author of the following article on Greenwood cemetery, Brooklyn, N. Y., recently visited this country and has written his "impressions" for the London *Funeral Directors' Journal*. Mr. Mills is known throughout England as one of the foremost movers in funeral reform; he is at the head of the Reformed Funerals Co., is an advocate of cremation and has probably done more than any other person to do away with the gloomy funeral practices that were so long observed in that country. Mr. Mills expresses surprise at the comparatively few crosses to be seen in our cemeteries and has promised THE MODERN CEMETERY an article on the subject.]

I think it was Ward Beecher who said that the New Yorkers go to Brooklyn to sleep, to die, and to be buried, and among the many places that are provided for the final reception of their bodies, "Greenwood Cemetery" is by far the most noted.

The chief object of the ambition of a thriving New York merchant is, before his death, to obtain a brown stone mansion on Fifth avenue, and when this is achieved his next business is to build an enormous structure as his mausoleum in Greenwood Cemetery. By-the-bye, whence came we with that word "mausoleum?" which every cemetery official that I ever heard attempt to use it distorts by accenting the "o" in the middle of the word instead of the "e" in the final syllable. The good Queen Artemisa II. little knew that she was enriching the human language for all time, when in the 4th century before the Christian era, she erected a splendid structure to the memory of her husband, Mausolus, King of Caria, a Phoenician colony, which became a kingdom in Asia Minor. Whether that is surpassed by the magnificence of the present structures in Greenwood Cemetery, I must leave to the Americans to decide; probably they would claim in this matter, as in many others, that they have "licked Creation."

At Greenwood Cemetery, I found myself to be one of the very few travelled Englishmen who have taken pains to inform themselves in reference to the peculiarities and customs of American interment and cemetery management generally. Occasionally a cemetery superintendent from England, or one who had some proprietary interest in an English Cemetery company, has looked in for a short period; but I found myself so cordially welcomed by Mr. L. J. Wells, the superintendent, who is a civil engineer by profession, and has had charge of that cemetery for 45 years, that I spent half a day there with very great pleasure. In extent it is about one square mile, actually 474 acres; and as I drove about in it for hours, partly in an independent way and partly with the superintendent in his brougham, I am able to say that there is nothing like a waste space in it, but that the whole of its surface is most carefully as well as beautifully and artistically arranged, laid out and filled up, so that there is no point at which the perspective is not an entertainment.

Unlike the cemeteries that we are accustomed to, it is bounded by main roads on all sides; these make eight entrances a possibility, a great consideration for funeral traffic, both in regard to the size of the place, and the fact that no central spot has to be reached by all funeral traffic, as is the case with us where the service is to be held in the cemetery church—the universal custom in America being to hold the religious service in the house of the deceased and to then go straight to the grave side; having entered the cemetery gate the funeral proceeds to the grave by vale and crescent, dell and dale, arbour and lake— for there are no fewer than eight lakes, some natural and some artificial within the walls of Greenwood Cemetery—the cemetery roads in labyrinthian confusion are beyond the complexity of a maze. It is naturally an undulating spot, and in every respect the natural advantages have been heightened by art. Each eminence in it is named, there is "Glade Hill" and "Ocean Hill," which is the highest, and commands a view of the entrance from the Atlantic Ocean to New York Harbor.

One peculiarity of Greenwood Cemetery—a point in strong contrast to what we are accustomed to here, though I believe only in accord with the universal custom of the American continent—is that it is not a dividend earning, nor a rate-paying concern, but is a "corporation" formed exclusively for the purpose of providing burial accommodation, and all of its revenue is spent upon itself. There is in the first place a handsome remuneration made to all who take part in its administration. The equipment of the whole place is perfect and admirable to an extent far beyond our ideas. It possesses a fund of $1,370,586 for the permanent care and improvement of the cemetery in addition to a special trust fund, for the permanent care of lots which have been sold, of $322,278.

The staff of the cemetery comprises, carpenters, painters, blacksmiths, engineers, 200 men, 20 horses, and steam roller; an engine pumping-house with power to lift water 150 feet, which is extracted from five wells and by which the lakes and reservoir are kept full; a mechanical stone crusher, and suitable premises for carrying on the work in every department. The stone for their roads is raised in their own grounds, and they have a mechanism, of the superintendent's invention, for breaking the stone to a suitable size for road-making, so arranged that the stone unloads and deposits itself, after leaving the crusher, by gravity. There is also a special police corps authorized to watch the stonemasons and to inspect their work in laying foundations, etc., who are responsible both to the superintendent of the cemetery and to the city police commissioner for their duties and character.

Within the cemetery, there is a building capable of containing a crematory when it is considered the demand will justify it. There are also sheltered pagodas in various suitable parts of the cemetery, to which are attached toilet rooms for men and women; and there are the same conveniences to be found at the chief entrances.

The busy season is the summer; during the hot weather children die off very rapidly from many diseases. The interments in the summer sometimes number eighty a day. There are no common interments in Greenwood Cemetery, on the contrary, some of the grave spots are of ample dimensions, and the cost of many of them would be alarming to an English undertaker's customer. A Mr. Thomas Berry has just purchased one lot for $3,750.00. I saw the Niblo family mausoleum that stands on a plot for which they paid $100,000.00, and spend $500.00 a year in keeping it up. The Steinway mausoleum contains 128 catacomb compartments and cost $100,000.00. There are many such mausoleums adorning the prominent parts of the cemetery, and often a number of them together.

A carriage drive in the cemetery for the sake of viewing it was a new experience; it is a fact that wagonettes (called in America "carry-alls") ply at the entrance of the cemetery and earn a living by driving parties about in the cemetery at one dollar an hour; the drivers of these wagonettes are showmen, and point out to one the different points of interest.

One of the earliest immigrant families was the Whitneys. Their chapel tomb is large enough for a service, and a service is actually held within it annually on the 28th day of May.

The tombs are of a different order to what we are accustomed to here, particularly having no crosses—a cross is quite a rarity. It is difficult to believe that you are in the cemetery of a Christian people when every memorial of any pretension is an illustration of classic heathen art. These are peculiarities about some of them; in one case five marble posts stand like guardians in front of the tomb, on each post a lamp was kept burning from the time of the decease of the first to that of the last member of the family. Horace Greely's tomb is made of type metal, and bronzed. John Matthews' sculptured sarcophagus bears a full length recumbent statue of him; on each corner of the four pillars there are correct portrait statues of different members of the family in marble: above this a canopy of richly carved stone rises to height of 36 feet, and upon it a representation of Mr. Matthews leaving England for America at the age of 21 years, so poor that when he landed in New York he shouldered his own box from the quay to the city.

Beautiful tombs raised by public subscription cover all the unknown dead, such as the 105 who were unrecognized victims of the Brooklyn theatre fire.

The "receiving vault" is peculiar: a sort of catacomb with arched passages, the arches enclosed in solid iron doors; each arch providing for twenty-four bodies. This "receiving vault" is for temporary interment, and contains at the present time about 1,500 bodies, placed there whilst a permanent provision is made for their interment in other parts of the cemetery. The rent upon each is $6.00 per quarter. There is no stipulation as to what coffins are to be used, but contagious cases are not admitted. Access to the higher shelves in the vault is obtained by a very ingenious trolly which works along the corridors and has an adjustable platform.

RULES AND REGULATIONS.

Every cemetery should be governed by certain rules and regulations, which should be printed in pamphlet form for distribution among lot owners. While this has been done in most of the large cemeteries, where the rules are very much alike, we will, for the benefit of the smaller cemeteries, publish in this department such rules as commend themselves for general adoption. Contributions are solicited.

Extracts From the Rules Regarding Stone Work at Spring Grove, Cincinnati.

Double head or foot-stones embracing two or more graves are prohibited.

But one mark will be allowed at any grave.

No gravestone or mark can be set in a socket or with a dowell. Granite is recommended for monuments or markers. Limestone, sandstone and soapstone for monumental purposes is not permitted.

On lots where graves are arranged with a view of placing a family monument, all gravemarks must be placed at the end of grave farthest from the monument. Such marks must be not less than six inches thick and four inches high with the inscriptions cut on top.

At single graves in sections set apart for children and in fractions of lots, gravestones shall not exceed four inches in height. No stone will be permitted at any single grave over two feet in height.

Where fences or other structures on any lot have by reason of neglect become objectionable in the judgment of the Board of Directors, they are authorized to have same removed, in which case the outline of the lot shall be preserved by corner stones or proper land marks having the owner's initials, number of section and lot cut thereon, at the expense of the cemetery.

The Congressional Cemetery at Washington.

The Congressional cemetery lies about a mile southeast of the capitol at Washington, on the bank of the Potomac river. Its surroundings are peaceful, for the city has grown in just the opposite direction and left it standing, as it did a hundred years ago, amid the peaceful tranquility of rural surroundings. Here lies all that is mortal of two vice presidents of the United States, a British envoy, a Prussian minister, senators and representatives in Congress, admirals and major generals, associate justices of the supreme court of the United States, an Indian chief of renown, and scattered among and about them, the remains of hundreds of men and women whose names have never graced the printed page. It is an odd place. Not quaint—the "modern improvements," which permeate it so thoroughly, have taken from it the quality of quaintness. But new and old, fresh and quaint, famous and commonplace make a strange combination on each side of its narrow paths and little-frequented drives. Its very name is an oddity, for, from its inception, it has never been strictly a congressional cemetery. It was originally a private enterprise and when Congress determined to favor it with its patronage when distinguished men were to be buried at the public's expense, the owners named it the Congressional cemetery on much the same principle on which the London haberdasher writes "Purveyor to the Prince of Wales" at the head of his business announcement. The circumstances which moved Congress to select an official burial place was the necessity due to the excessive cost of transportation at that time, of burying at the capital members of Congress who died there in the discharge of their public duties. According to the original plan, monuments of a modest character were erected over the remains of all the senators and representatives who were buried there; but this was soon modified by the addition of a provision under which cenotaphs of a similar design and character were to be erected in memory of members of Congress who might be buried elsewhere. As the government reservation in the original cemetery was not well defined, the graves of the distinguished dead were very irregularly arranged, and, but for the peculiar style of the monument which marks each one of them, it would be difficult to distinguish them at a distance from the last resting places, ancient and modern, which lie between and about them. The Congressional mile-stone on the road to eternity rested on a brick foundation. Its base was a square block of sandstone on which rested another square block of the same stone somewhat smaller in size. On these rested a cube or "die" on whose paneled side was inscribed the name of the deceased together with his official title, his age and the date of his death. They stand side by side in long rows in the Congressional cemetery as bare and as meaningless as the little foot-stones that mark the graves of the soldier dead at Arlington; more meaningless, in fact, for the foot-stones mark a grave while most of the blocks of stone in the Congressional cemetery mark nothing but a memory. The custom of erecting cenotaphs was abandoned in 1876 when the house of representatives during the discussion of an appropriation for seventeen cenotaphs, determined that it was time to discontinue the erection of useless monuments. An act was passed at that time providing that where an actual interment of a member of the house of representatives or of the senate took place in the Congressional cemetery, the sergeant-at-arms of the legislative body of which he was a member should cause a monument of granite with suitable inscriptions, to be erected over the grave. The main drive of the cemetery is called Congress avenue and along one side of it are long rows of congressional monuments.

Tuberous-Rooted Begonias.

Mr. John G. Barker, superintendent of Forest Hills cemetery, Boston, read an interesting paper on the subject of Tuberous-Rooted Begonias before the Massachusetts Horticultural Society last month. After tracing the history of the plant from its earliest introduction in England from Bolivia and Peru and quoting the opinions of many eminent floriculturists on its adaptability to open air culture, Mr. Barker said:

I believe there is the greatest future before it of any plant of recent introduction. We have been too apt to think it would not flourish except under glass, and therefore it has not been given a fair trial as a bedder. We have grown it moderately at Forest Hills until last year; then quite extensively, having planted out some thousands of them in different parts of the grounds, in large and small beds and on graves, in all cases they were the best beds of flowering plants in the cemetery, affording a remarkable variety of color—white, yellow, orange, rose, scarlet and crimson, in numerous shades. Then their comparison with other flowers shows greatly in their favor. The geraniums thus far have taken the lead as the best bedders; but how a rainstorm destroys geranium flowers, especially of the single varieties! but with the begonias it is not so; they are bright again in twenty-four hours, flowers and foliage standing up in bright array.

At Forest Hills we must have large quantities of bedding plants and of the best. The introduction of the Crozy cannas and the tuberous begonia forms a great advance. It is to be hoped they will soon take the place of the faded coleus, and perhaps others may as well be spared, as they reflect no credit upon a well-managed place. I think there is very little character to the so-called "foliage bed." One can get material at a dry goods store, with which to produce as good an effect. I do not include in this remark the sub-tropical beds, but those filled with so-called foliage plants. Flowering plants are decidedly better. What "foliage"

VIEW IN MARION CEMETERY, MARION, O.

bed can compare with a solid mass of tuberous begonias, or a large bed with Crozy cannas in the centre, surrounded by a broad belt of heliotrope and tuberous begonias as a border? Such a bed is not only an object of beauty, and a delight to all observers, but if some cut flowers are desired, here they can be had. If one wishes a good bed of flowers, a bright vase, a cheerful window, or some choice cut flowers for decoration, the tuberous begonias will not disappoint either desire. We have need of only single varieties for our bedding purposes, and depend upon seedlings alone. Our method of culture has been as follows: The seed was sown Jan. 4, in shallow boxes, in light soil, sifted fine, covered very slightly and pressed down firm with a smooth board, then watered gently but thoroughly with Scollay's rubber sprinkler, and placed in a temperature of 60 degrees and shaded from the sun. They germinated Jan. 24, and by Feb. 24 were ready, and were pricked out one inch apart, in other shallow boxes filled with the same kind of soil as before. They were kept shaded until established, then they were grown in full sunlight, until the sun got very warm, when a little shade in the middle of the day was very beneficial. From these boxes they were shifted to deeper boxes—say three inches—and set four inches apart, and as soon as established, were exposed to all the light and air possible, in order to harden them off for planting out, which was done from June 1 to 15. They like a deep, rich soil and plenty of water, being gross feeders. After the frost has destroyed the foliage, the tubers can be lifted and gradually dried off in boxes, in plenty of air and light. When dry they should be packed in shallow boxes and stored in a dry, cool place. In the spring, when they show signs of growth, they should be potted in as small pots as will hold them, and shifted into larger pots as they require, until planted out. These directions will serve for the window gardener as well as the greenhouse culturist.

A View in Marion Cemetery, Marion, O.

The above illustration affords an excellent idea of the beauties of the lawn plan. The monument is simple yet imposing in its solidity, no inclosures or high grave markers mar the landscape nor is it broken by useless paths, not even the tops of corner posts or lot marks are visible and every sign of exclusiveness is banished. Each lot owner shares in the beauty of the adjacent lots and the result is a pleasing whole. In what marked contrast is this plan with that where the stone laden lots join each other in unbroken lines, crowding out nature with art of a questionable order and robbing the place of its chiefest charm.

BURIAL REFORM.

The Kansas City Ministerial Alliance, composed of the leading ministers of that city, have spoken in no uncertain language on the subject of burial reform. They urge greater simplicity in floral offerings and recommend a discontinuance of Sunday funerals.

Dr. L. Morgan Wood, of Detroit, Mich., addressed the Michigan Funeral Directors' Association last month on the subject of "Funeral Reform." He referred to the exorbitant use of floral displays as an "immoral tendency." The poor man who has no such offerings is laid away, he said, as we ought all to be, in a neat well-trimmed box. In referring to long funeral sermons he said: "The custom is the old-fashioned idea come down to us on one leg. The old-fashioned preacher used to go to a funeral with a red bandanna handkerchief filled with cayenne pepper so that he could shed tears at the proper moment. He thought he had to. No matter if the deceased was shot while robbing a bank, the preacher thought he had to call him a gloriously good man for the sake of the feelings of the mourners." The speaker took advanced ground on the subject of Sunday funerals and advocated a combination on the part of those interested in the abolishing of them.

The Rev. Dr. J. M. Weaver, of Louisville, Ky., in discussing funeral reform before the Ministerial Association in that city, has suggested having funeral services held in the evening, with a private burial the following morning. There are many reasons why such an arrangement would be desirable, especially in the larger cities, and in fact evening services are already quite common in Brooklyn. They certainly insure a more private funeral which is greatly to be desired.

Some day says a writer in the Pittsburg *Dispatch*, we will learn so much of the meaning of death, and will think so much of the bright and victorious and spiritual side of it, that we will dispense with all symbols which accept its lower and transient and physical significance. In that day we will have no more pagan tombstones. We will come to realize that the best memorial of a good man is not a stone in a graveyard, but a good deed, bearing perpetual interest of loving kindness, testifying not to death, but to life. The great cemeteries are gardens of despair—not despair of immortality, but of brotherly love. They are full of monuments built with misspent money. One who drives through their avenues, looking thoughtfully from side to side, remembers the request for bread which was answered with a stone. So much might have been done to add to the light of life, to uplift and save men, to keep the memory of the dead blessed—and here are these useless piles of carved rock, which are not even beautiful! A scholarship in a school, a lectureship in a college, books for a library, a picture for a public gallery, an endowment for a charity, a window in a church—any one of these is immeasurably better than a cold stone.

A Spiritualistic View of Cremation.

Many religious bodies are looking into the subject of cremation at the present time, among others the Spiritualists, who predict that before many years this will be the universally accepted mode of burial. They, and indeed many Christian communities, believe so fully in the resurrection of the spiritual body that there seems much inconsistency in the efforts made to preserve the earthly body as long as possible after death, and appreciating this they are beginning to deprecate the process of embalming, the use of brick graves, etc., and to advocate cremation.

This subject is causing much agitation and being very ably discussed in England just now, but from a purely sanitary standpoint, and from this point of view and leaving all sentiment out of the question, it would seem to commend itself very highly. One is startled to learn that in the last 30 years, in spite of many administrative reforms, no less than 70,000 preventable deaths from disease have occurred in England. The clergy of the Established church are interesting themselves deeply in the need of sanitary reform in regard to old church-yards and other burial grounds, and at a meeting of the Church of England Sanitary Association held last month a paper was contributed by Mr. F. Scott, in which he dwelt on the tardiness of the English people to adopt any new sanitary system. He seemed to favor earth burial, but that the soil should be porous, and the body placed in actual contact with the earth; while Dr. W. B. Richardson, at the same meeting, suggested that there be a crematorium as well as a burial ground in connection with every large church, so there might be a choice in the method of burial. Something of the kind may come to be necessary before very long, for a little further on in the journal containing this account, we see that in digging a grave in a churchyard twelve skulls were exposed! The good people of the district have decided that they really need a cemetery or at least more burial room.

Destroying Moles.

A writer in the *American Florist* says: My plan to get rid of these pests is to mix a small quantity of arsenic in a little corn meal and after making holes at intervals in the runs drop in small pellets of the meal. This method was completely successful.

A time-saving clergyman at Leamsley having to attend two funerals on the same day, a fortnight since, kept one waiting twenty minutes for the other, says the London *Funeral Director*. The graves were thirty yards apart, and this obliging priest performed the ceremony at a point half-way between. The result was that few, if any, of the mourners in either party could hear what was being read, and the sublime burial service of the Church of England was turned into a farce.

CEMETERY NOTES.

Chicago capitalists are said to have purchased a 300-acre tract of land lying near Wheaton, west of the city, which they will convert into a cemetery.

In a contested will case at Lowell, Mass., wherein the deceased bequeathed to the Lowell cemetery the sum of $2,000 for the care of her lot, the courts have decided that the legacy must stand. By its charter the cemetery corporation is authorized to receive bequests for the care of lots in accordance with the terms of the will and on this provision the court based its decision. The sum paid to the treasurer was $2,120, which included interest while the matter was in litigation.

In the annual report of the Pittsfield, Mass., cemetery Secretary Stevenson, in referring to a new section, says:

A good opportunity is here furnished to show the advantage of proper regulation, such as requiring a deposit for perpetual care, limiting the size of head-stones and number of monuments, so that the lot owner can judge if he does not get a better return for the money expended under such regulations than without them. It is not always the amount of money expended which insures the best results in an attractive and well cared for lot. In these new sections we hope to show to the purchaser the way in which experience teaches that his money can be expended to give the most satisfaction to himself and those who follow him.

According to the Denver *Republican* the city officials are involved in a scandalous scheme to defraud the city out of money under a contract for the removal of bodies from the old city cemetery to Riverside cemetery. Graves in which interments were supposed to have been made were found to contain no trace of a human body, and other evidences of fraud were discovered. Desecrating the graves of the dead and robbing the living in such a manner as this cannot receive too severe retribution. Verily the greed of the average city politician knows no bounds, and the less he has to do with the cemeteries the better it will be for all concerned.

The Riverside Cemetery Co. at Rochester, N. Y., contemplate introducing an electric funeral car for use on the street railways of that city. One end of the car will be fitted up to receive the casket and the balance of the car will afford accommodation for thirty mourners. A hearse will meet the car at the cemetery gate. The economy of such a system, aside from its other obvious advantages, must in time cause it to supersede, to a great extent, the present method of conducting funerals.

The pastor of a Methodist church at North Adams, Mass., took occasion during his Easter sermon to refer to the utter neglect of the cities of the dead in that community. He said that "in that city of culture, with its beautiful scenery, fine residences and superior educational privileges, it seemed very strange that so little care or thought should be given to this matter and mentioned certain facts in connection with these places of burial which left a deep impression." There are many communities in which the neglected burying grounds would afford a fruitful subject for ministers to dwell upon. It is to be regretted that they do not preach upon them oftener.

A very beautiful and impressive adjunct to an aristocratic official Parisian funeral is the presence in the procession of the carriage of the deceased, the horse or horses, led by grooms in mourning liveries, and the lanterns lighted and veiled in long streamers of semi-transparent crape. The effect is at once sombre and picturesque, and is especially striking at the obsequies of some great personage, such as M. Thiers, Gambetta, or Victor Hugo. Nobody, not even the nearest relative of the defunct, is permitted to occupy the vehicle. —*Ex.*

The Disposal of Cholera Dead.

In a paper on this subject read by W. F. McLean, of Elyria, O., before the Ohio State Board of Health at Columbus last month, the speaker said that while he considered cremation the ideal method of disposing of the dead especially in cases where death was the result of contagion or infection, he was of the opinion that the expense of building and maintaining crematoriums would be extremely burdensome to the smaller cities, and in view of the method not having yet attained universal recognition, he felt that other methods were more likely to be pursued. He recommended the use of a hearse or dead-wagon constructed especially for the purpose. This should be in the form of an oblong box of sufficient size to hold a casket, and made of 2-inch plank as nearly air tight as possible. The box should be open only at one end and be provided with rollers to facilitate handling the casket. The box should be covered with black cloth and mounted on the running gears of an ordinary wagon. Bodies immediately after death should be wrapped in a winding sheet saturated with a strong solution of bi-chloride of mercury (1 oz. to 1 gallon). Burial without a casket would be preferable in which case the body could be laid on a board and covered with a pall. After being placed in the grave the body should be entirely covered with quick-lime and then with earth.

The effect of applying quick-lime in a sufficient quantity to a dead body, would be to burn or dry out all the moisture from the tissues. The gases would unite to form nitrates, phosphates, sulphates, etc., and the body would crumble into dust without giving off poisonous gases. Should there be much moisture present in the body, or soil in which it is buried, the quick-lime would unite with the water and form calcium hydrate which unite fats to form lime soap, which is insoluble in water, and would not be carried in the water currents but filtered out in the earth through which it passed. An excess of quick-lime would give nearly the same results as cremation. The main difference being the time consumed in producing these results.

The Rhodes Memorial Chapel, Pine Grove Cemetery, Lynn, Mass.

This chapel, recently erected in Pine Grove cemetery, was bequeathed by will by Mrs. Lydia Newhall Rhodes as a memorial to her husband, the late Amos Rhodes. It will be known as the Rhodes memorial chapel. The building is of granite with free stone trimming and tile roof. Its dimensions are 60x30 feet and it has a seating capacity of 125. Each end is ornamented with a large rose window. The various colored glass heightened by the sun's rays, presents a most beautiful sight. The interior is finished in hard pine and is carpeted and upholstered in a most thorough manner. Every detail has received the best attention. Work was commenced in the spring of 1891 and completed the past summer. The cost was about $25,000. Shipley, Rutan & Coolidge, of Boston, were the architects, and Norcross Bros., of Boston, were the contractors and builders. It was consecrated Jan. 10th of the present year, that day being the anniversary of the birth of the donor. No fee will be charged for its use. As one enters the cemetery gate a fine view of the chapel is obtained, it being situated on rising ground at the head of Main avenue a short distance from the entrance. It is not only an ornament to the grounds, but fills a long felt want. The donor sleeps on the hillside but a few feet distant, and to stand by her grave a fine view can be had of her generous gift. Could she but hear the words spoken in her praise that have met the ears of the writer, she would indeed feel that her generosity was more than appreciated. There stands the building nestling among those noble pines that have braved the storms of years, reaching out their protecting arms, and there it will stand after they have succumbed to the hand of time. As generation after generation reads the tablets on either side of the vestibule they will learn to honor the name of Lydia Newhall Rhodes.

S.

Subscribe for THE MODERN CEMETERY, $1.00 a year.

≫|Cemetery Reports.|≪

The annual report of the Greenwood Cemetery, Brooklyn, N. Y., presents some interesting figures. The receipts from the sale of lots amounted to $175,552; for use of receiving tomb, $12,763; for opening graves and vaults, $31,897. The labor account including cost of opening graves and care of same was $116,587. Improvements, maintenance and contingent expenses exclusive of labor on trust lots increased the sum to $167,542. The fund for the improvement and permanent care of the cemetery amounts to $1,501,969, and the fund for the special and permanent care of lots to $356,593. The latter fund was increased during the year $34,315. This deposit exceeds that of any previous year and evidences the appreciation of lot owners of the utility of such a fund. The largest individual deposit made during the year was $2,000. An average of 214 men were employed in various capacities; the lowest number being 116 in January, and the highest 302 in June. Thirteen hundred hedges were removed from around lots. It cost $21,259 to mow and remove the grass. The cemetery owns twenty horses and during the summer months hire half as many more.

From the twenty-fifth annual report of the Forest Hills cemetery, Boston, we make the following extracts: Receipts from the sale of lots and graves $60,802, the Perpetual Care Fund was increased $26,682 and the Permanent Fund $5,019. The former fund now amounts to $324,330. 905 interments were made during the year, making the total number to January 31st, 26,193. There were fifty-three iron fences, two hedges and three curbings removed. 316 markers and 42 monuments were erected. 34 lots that had been originally sold without perpetual care were placed under such care. The lots now under care number 2,577 and 558 are under annual care. 12 lots were deeded to the cemetery in trust.

The annual report of Fairmount cemetery, Newark, N. J., shows the expenditure of about $18,000 for permanent improvements during the past year. The receipts from the sale of 125 lots and 671 single graves, $30,178; expenditures for salaries and labor, $19,349. 4,095 lots have been sold, of this number 1,735 are under perpetual care. In addition to this 610 lots and graves received special care. 46 monuments and 99 markers were erected. Interments for the year, 1,381, making a total of 26,643 to Jan. 1, '93. 23 men are employed in summer, 12 in winter.

The annual report of Pine Grove cemetery, Lynn, Mass., says: On all new lots sold a portion of the purchase money is deposited, the interest of which is for the perpetual care of the lots. This amount deposited largely reduces the income from the sale of lots, but is a benefit to the community and the commissioners believe that it is the best plan that could be adopted. Any lot owner can place his lot under perpetual care by depositing the sum of $33.33⅓ per hundred feet contained in the lot. This fund has increased the past year, by the sale of new lots, $6,425; by deposit on old lots, $1,449, and now amounts to $68,845. Interments during the year of 1892 were 655, of which 370 were in private lots and 258 in public ones. 181 monuments and tablets were erected. The total expenditures for the year were $32,311.49; receipts, $28,689.21.

Macadam Roads.

For all the talk about macadam roads one may travel a long distance before seeing one that is constructed on the principles that Macadam himself laid down. The underlying principle of his system was that the stone should pack together so closely that, no matter what kind of a vehicle drove over the road, not one of the stones would be disturbed; but, in our so-called macadam roads, vehicles crush and grind the stones in every direction. Macadam's plan was to have all the stones that formed the upper stratum of the road so small that all could go through a two-inch ring. This small size of stone when thoroughly rolled, pack together so tightly that it would take a very small wheel indeed to drive the stone apart. In this case, there is no grinding or crushing of the stones, and the road bed has to do nothing more than bear the dead weight of the vehicles. When these roads needed repairing, which under his system was very seldom indeed, the surface would be torn up by a pair, or even four horses with a heavy drag harrow, and the new resurface applied. When rolled down this was almost as good as a new road. It would be amusing if it were not so costly to the tax-payers, to see the manner in which the so-called macadam roads of our country are repaired, especially in the vicinity of large cities, certainly, in the vicinity of Philadelphia. After some three or four inches are worn away, the custom is to put three or four inches of broken stone, some of the stones nearly as large as goose eggs over the road surface. The wheels then grind up these stones or push them away in every direction, so that in the course of a few months like coffee in a mill, these are ground completely to powder. Within the knowledge of the writer, a resurfacing of this character, costing $3,000, placed on a road 80 feet wide and 600 feet long, was ground to mud within twelve months. Such macadam roads as these, and such repairing of the so-called macadam roads, are the best illustration of municipal ignorance; possibly, that could be adduced. In the management of public affairs we expect more loss than in private ones, but the ignorance displayed in the making and care of macadam roads beats all.—*Meehans' Monthly for April.*

⇒Correspondence.⇐

Editor Modern Cemetery:
I heartily endorse your sentiments on cremation. Too much cannot be said in favor of it. My long experience in cemetery work has taught me that cremation is the only safe and proper mode of disposing of the dead. A. J. GOSHORN,
Hamilton, O.   Supt. Greenwood Cemetery.

PROVIDENCE, R. I., April 11th, 1893.
Editor Modern Cemetery:
DEAR SIR.—In your interesting number of the MODERN CEMETERY for March it is stated that "cremation as a burial reform has the unqualified endorsement of the official organ of the Association of Cemetery Superintendents" and that "the time is not far distant when crematoriums will be a necessary adjunct of every modern cemetery." I was not aware that our association were advocating this reform, and therefore think that the above quotations are as unjust to our organization as they are erroneous and misleading to the public. The much abused "landscape lawn plan" and kind old "Mother Earth" are still good enough for me.
Yours sincerely,   TIMOTHY MCCARTHY,
Swan Point.

While the MODERN CEMETERY is the official organ of the Association of American Cemetery Superintendents, no allusion whatever is made to that fact in the editorial referred to. In giving his endorsement to cremation the editor did not wish to imply that he was voicing the sentiment of the Association of Cemetery Superintendents and had no intention whatever of placing the Association in a false light before the public.

* * *

TOLEDO, O., April 17, 1893.
Editor Modern Cemetery:
The sentiment favoring cremation is fast growing instead of diminishing, as many seem to believe, and when you say in your editorial of March number that the time is not far distant when a crematory will be a necessary adjunct to a modern cemetery it has my approval. After all, the severest protest comes from the religious side, but why it is hard to comprehend. Cremation does not interfere with any creed or belief, and there can be no difference regarding eternal life; for the soul, if it is immortal, cannot be destroyed by heat because of its immortality, even if it remains in the body after death, and the cremated body will be just as surely resurrected on the day of judgment as the one that has been burnt at the stake, or that had slowly decomposed in the earth, or that had been swallowed by the monsters of the sea.

That the incineration of the dead is fast gaining favor with the enlightened public as a sanitary and esthetic method to dispose of the same is shown by the following taken from the report of the president of Forest Hills cemetery, Boston, Mass., viz.: "We also ask permission to apply to the Legislature for authority to build and maintain a crematory for the incineration of the dead, or for the sale of land to be built upon for that purpose.

"The subject of cremation is now *prominent in our community and has many adherents*. Should the demand justify it your trustees would like to be in position to act in the matter."

Much more could be said in favor of incineration, but the object of this communication is only to show that modern cemeteries are already beginning to make preparations for crematories.
Respectfully,   FRANK EURICH,
Supt. Woodlawn Cemetery.

What a Superintendent Should Be.

In the March number on page 9 is an article worth reading by all superintendents. After serving some twelve years in cemetery management I find there is still much to learn. I think on a superintendent taking charge of a cemetery, be it large or small he should not be content to follow in the footsteps of his predecessor, but should say to himself. If I have my health I am going to make this cemetery second to none on the continent, in the way of ornamental and landscape art. Were this the rule many of our large grounds would present a far neater appearance than they do to-day. I believe he should have full charge of men, and, in fact, with everything on him should be the responsibility. He should, as required, present his views in writing to the trustees, who, if they have confidence in him would aid him in carrying out his views, but to be able to do this he must be a good landscape gardener, give his whole time to his duties, not leaving too much for his assistant or foreman to look after. He must be strictly honest and straightforward, courteous at all times to those employed by him, he must be civil and obliging to the lot owners, particularly the ladies, and having by these means gained the good-will of trustees, lot-owners and working men he cannot fail to promote his own interests, and the welfare of the cemetery.

Deer Park, Ont.   HENRY THOMPSON, Supt.

Association of American Cemetery Superintendents.

WM. SALWAY, "Spring Grove" Cincinnati, O. President.
T. M. McCARTHY, "Swan Point" Providence, R. I., Vice President.
F. EURICH, Woodlawn, Toledo, O., Secretary and Treasurer.

The Seventh Annual Convention of the Association will be held at Minneapolis on Tuesday, August 22, 1893, and will in all probability continue four days.

Publisher's Department.

The receipt of Cemetery Literature and Trade Catalogues will be acknowledged in this column.

TO ADVERTISERS. THE MODERN CEMETERY is the only publication of its class and will be found a valuable medium for reaching cemetery officials in all parts of the United States.

TO SUBSCRIBERS. Cemetery officials desiring to subscribe for a number of copies regularly to circulate among their lot owners, should send for our special terms. Several well-known cemeteries have already adopted this plan with good results.

Contributions on matters pertaining to cemeteries are solicited. Address all communications to R. J. HAIGHT, 243 State Street, Chicago.

Cemetery literature received: Charter, By-Laws, etc., of the Cemetery of Spring Grove, Cincinnati, O., accompanied by a lithograph map of the grounds, prepared by Earnshaw & Punshon, engineers. Twenty-fifth annual report of Forest Hills cemetery, Boston. Plan of addition to Springdale cemetery, Clinton, Iowa, Chas. P. Chase, C. E. Annual Report, Elmwood Cemetery, Rockville, Conn.

A Rochester, N. Y., paper states that Mr. J. H. Shepard is to superintend the planting of three thousand trees and shrubs at the new Riverside cemetery this spring. The stock is from Ellwanger & Barry's nurseries and will comprise a choice collection of great variety. The company has expended nearly $50,000 in improvements and will continue beautifying the grounds after the most approved plans.

Mr. Fred. von Holst, supt. Greenwood cemetery, Argo, Colo., is desirous of receiving rules and regulations of some of the principal cemeteries, his cemetery is just being established and he will return the compliment in the near future.

After a service of forty-five years as superintendent of Greenwood cemetery, Brooklyn, N. Y., Mr. L. J. Wells has been relieved by the trustees of the arduous duties connected with that position and will henceforth fill the office of consulting engineer. Mr. Wells has been in very poor health for a number of years and it is hoped that with lessened duties he may soon recover his impaired strength. His successor as superintendent is Mr. Eugene Cushman.

> "Light be the turf of thy tomb!
> May its verdure like emeralds be!
> There should not be the shadow of gloom
> In aught that reminds us of thee.
> Young flowers and an evergreen tree
> May spring from the spot of thy rest
> But not cypress nor yew let us see;
> For why should we mourn for the blest."
> —*Byron.*

Wanted.

Situation as superintendent of cemetery. Good references furnished, correspondence desired. Address, S. L. BROWN, 88 Wenham street, Forest Hills, Boston, Mass.

Wanted.

Situation as superintendent of cemetery, by a person of experience. Was associated with the late Adolph Strauch for some years. Best of references. Address, "R. G.," care MODERN CEMETERY.

Notice to Cemetery Boards.

The undersigned who for over ten years was superintendent of Cedar Hill Cemetery, Newburgh, N. Y., would be pleased to correspond with cemetery boards who are starting new grounds, or re-arranging of old cemeteries as to the grading of lawns, arrangement of lots, plans and location of vaults, mapping of grounds and the keeping of records; as well as the most modern ideas of conducting funerals. Would advise by mail or would make a short engagement in starting grounds. Address, Wm. B. Westervelt, 7 Dubois street, Newburgh, N. Y.

I desire to call the attention of cemetery officials and all others requiring the services of a landscape architect to the following unsolicited letter of commendation. W. W. PARCE, Rochester, N. Y.

OFFICE OF RIVERSIDE CEMETERY ASSOCIATION,
ROCHESTER, N. Y., March 31, 1893.

MR. W. W. PARCE, City:

Dear Sir,—Before you leave the city I want to say to you, on behalf of the trustees of the Riverside cemetery, that we are more than pleased with your work as a landscape architect in connection with our cemetery grounds.

The design which you furnished in advance, and which you have developed during the past year and which will be carried out by your successor, we are sure will compare favorably with any other cemetery grounds in this country.

We are frank to say, as you leave us, that the only errors, and they are exceedingly few, which have been made are the result of insistance on the part of the trustees that certain lines should be followed out, and that were we to do the work over again, we should give you the fullest scope and would allow you to carry out your design without a word of dictation or even a suggestion.

You can rest assured that should any of the trustees require the services of a landscape architect you will be the man above all others whom they would employ.

With best wishes for your continued prosperity along your professional line, we are,

Very truly yours,
RIVERSIDE CEMETERY ASS'N.
By DEAN ALVORD,
Treasurer and Manager.

THE MODERN CEMETERY.

THE MODERN CEMETERY.
AN ILLUSTRATED MONTHLY JOURNAL DEVOTED TO THE INTEREST OF CEMETERIES

R. J. HAIGHT, Publisher.
334 Dearborn Street, CHICAGO

Subscription $1.00 a Year in Advance.   Foreign Subscription $1.25.
Special Rates on Six or More Copies.

Vol. III.   CHICAGO, MAY, 1893.   No. 3.

CONTENTS.

CEMETERY GARDENING—*O. C. Simonds*	25
RIGHT OF WIDOW TO CONTROL BURIAL OF DECEASED HUSBAND	28
RULES AND REGULATIONS	29
VASES AND URNS—*Edgar Sanders*	30
WOKING CREMATORIUM	31
THE SPRINGBANK CEMETERY, ABERDEEN	32
TRIMMING GRAVES—*C. McArthur*	32
CONVEYING LOTS	32
SUGGESTIONS TO LOT OWNERS	33
GOD'S ACRE—*H. W. Longfellow*	33
CEMETERY NOTES	34
ROCK GARDENS—*T. McCarthy*	35
PUBLISHER'S DEPARTMENT	36
THE METRIC SYSTEM	III

Cemetery Gardening.

Probably all will agree that the characteristic features of a cemetery should be seclusion, quietness and beauty, and in designing cemeteries the landscape gardener seeks to secure these effects. It is desirable in the first place to separate the place where we lay our dead from the buildings and busy thoroughfares of the living. A suitable location helps to do this, but after a site is chosen nothing will add to the seclusion so much as an irregular belt of planting along the boundaries. A stone wall or a fence gives a stiff, formal line, and conveys the information that this line is the boundary of the cemetery. A hedge does the same thing, and, moreover, a hedge must be trimmed. With one of these boundaries we feel our limitations. We know that beyond these there is a different world, and the unity of effect is broken; but with an irregular belt of trees and shrubs along the boundary, running up and forming the sky line at one place, dropping to show a distant city or village, a valley, a mountain or a water view at another, and at all points shutting out incongruous objects near at hand, we feel that there is no boundary. The distant view, the sky, and all that is seen from the grounds we wish to make beautiful, belong to these grounds. There may be a fence as a partial protection from intruders, but this should be enclosed and hidden by the boundary of planting. In addition to separation from the outside world, it is desirable in large cemeteries to hide one part from another. Those who are suffering from a great grief like to be alone. The contour of the land sometimes gives this seclusion. Shrubbery is very useful for this purpose, and so are evergreens, where there is room for them.

Seclusion helps to give quietness, but there is a difference between the two effects. The pretentious stone archways so often seen at the entrance gates of cemeteries help to give seclusion, but they disturb the effect of quietness and repose which we seek, and so it seems to me they are in poor taste, no matter how good their proportions or how carefully they are designed. The roads, the walks and the fences, which used to be so common in cemeteries, tend to destroy the restfulness that should prevail. So, also, do extensive flower-beds and even the monuments and headstones. Mr. Strauch reduced the number of driveways to those actually required; he replaced the gravel walks with grass walks, that formed part of a continuous lawn. He abolished the use of fences, railings, chains and coping about individual lots. He was the first to make a cemetery even more beautiful than a park.

Modesty and simplicity are never more appropriate than when they help to give character to our final resting places, which should be restful not only to the dead but to the eyes of the living. Glaring white stones, challenging the attention of all passersby, are therefore especially bad. The stone structures so often erected in cemeteries by lot-owners or their families as monuments to themselves not only destroy the quiet, simple effect which should prevail, but they seem inappropriate in every way. They call attention to the names they bear, and the men those names represent, in a bold, conceited manner. In a large majority of cases they are ugly in design. They do not extend one's fame or reputation. They are intended to last for all time, but who will care for them at the end of a hundred years? Of what advantage will they be to this or any other generation?

The great difficulty in making burial grounds beautiful has been their division into small lots, and the individual ownership of these lots, with the privilege of erecting or placing on them any structure which fancy may dictate. The most beautiful and peaceful spot in the world might be selected for what is frequently called a city of the dead; the most skillful landscape-gardener might make a design that would bring in all the pleasing vistas—that would so locate the drives and select and place the planting as to allow nature to show all her beauty of form and color, all her gracefulness and dignity—and yet, without strict rules and limitations the effect might be entirely spoiled in a few years. Where there should be a broad, undulating lawn, we might see nothing but a mass of stonework. The owner of a small area of land might plant a tree on it and cut off an important view, or he might wish to cut down a tree that has been developing its beauty for a century, and which, on account of its dignity and grandeur, controlled a portion of the plan. The great diversity of tastes, opinions, superstitions and prejudices that must be consulted or controlled make cemetery landscape-gardening the most difficult branch of the art. The progress that has been made in recent years has come about through rules that at first met with much opposition, but which have been generally approved by the public after the results of their enforcement have been seen.

There are a few recognized principles which may help solve special problems. The drives should be as few as possible, and enable carriages to come within a reasonable distance, say 150 or 200 feet, of every point in the cemetery. The grades should be easy, not exceeding a rise of six feet in one hundred. The direction followed should generally be curved, the curve being more pleasing in itself than a straight line, and having the additional advantage of continually bringing new objects into sight, and shortening the average distance traveled to reach given points of the cemetery. The curves selected for the drives may usually be so placed as to save expense in grading, and also make the land on either side higher than the roadway. This arrangement again is justified not only by the pleasing effect produced, but by a practical advantage as well, the sloping ground bringing the surface water to the catch-basins and sewers that must be made to drain the roads. It is necessary at times to make a carriage-way along a side hill, so that the land on one side must be lower than the roadbed; but what-ever relations the lawn surface bears to the road surface, they should be nearly tangent to each other at the dividing line. The most economical and satisfactory method of constructing a road will usually be that followed by Macadam. In small burial places that are very seldom used, sod drives sometimes serve good purpose. A curved driveway will often enable us to utilize a bit of nature to advantage which would be lost or destroyed if straight lines were followed; but double curves should be avoided as far as possible.

Broad, open spaces, giving cheerful effects, may be secured by placing large lots along the margins of sections, or grouping such lots by themselves. A vista may be preserved by placing a grass walk in the center of the open space, having the lots front this walk, and the monuments, if any are erected, located on the rear part of the lots. A quiet, uninterrupted stretch of lawn, so essential to an effect of repose and beauty, is unattainable where all the ground is utilized for graves, and each grave is allowed to have a conspicuous marker. The rules of cemeteries have gradually been restricting the height of these markers. There is hope for the future in the prospect that the time will come when all headstones or foot-stones will be limited to the level of the turf, and made of material of subdued color. The ideal cemetery would be one in which every effort is made to develop the beauty of the grounds as a whole, the results being a memorial park. This would imply a certain affection or regard for the burial place as a whole on the part of those interested in it—a broadening of their ideas, perhaps—but would not preclude the idea of having a special attachment for a given spot, and distinguishing that spot in some appropriate way. What better way is there than to have a bed of violets or ferns, a cluster of golden rods, an iris, a lily or a rose springing from the earth, and year after year filling the space with beauty and perfume? A vine may creep lovingly over the grave that is to be honored, or a lilac, honeysuckle or spirea may be planted on the spot, spreading its graceful sheltering branches all about, and perhaps making a home for a thrush that will send forth the sweetest music day after day. Or, again, what more fitting memorial for a dignified, venerable old man than a tree, which may live for centuries, and which, by its sturdiness, its growth, its life, its spreading branches, its struggles against storms, its beauty and majesty, symbolizes in so many ways the life that is remembered! There are hundreds of beautiful plants that will lend themselves themselves to comforting sentiments, and mean much to hearts that are stricken, while to the casual observer they simply form part of the beautiful, harmonious work of art—"the one art," as Mr. Robinson says, "in which we have the happiness of possessing the living things themselves, and not mere representations of them."

A sheet of water may add greatly to the beauty of a cemetery and help to give the peaceful quiet effect already mentioned. The outline should be varied so as to bring only a portion of the surface of the water in sight from any one point. The margins should be graded in a natural manner, and not in imitation of railway embankments. The projecting points of land may be accented by covering them with trees and shrubs, which will send their branches over the water and give deep shadows and reflections.

In making selections for planting, we should seek those things which give cheerfulness. Deciduous trees and blossoming shrubs are really more appropriate than Norway spruces. Evergreens ought, however, to be plentifully used, because they give us color during the six months of the year when other trees are leafless. Their somberness can be relieved by having a variety of them. Just after a fall of snow there is nothing somber about the young Austrian pines, as they hold a white ball at the end of each branch, and nothing more graceful than the young hemlocks with their fleecy burdens. How pleasing, too, in the winter and early spring, are the red and purple of the dogwoods, the soft grays and browns of the honeysuckles, willows and syringas, the green of the corchorus and sassafras, and the white bark of the birches! The strawberry and barberry bushes, which Mr. Powell commends so highly on account of their ornamental fruit, are just as appropriate for a cemetery as for home grounds, and to them should be added the snowberry, Indian currant, high-bush cranberry, wild roses and bittersweet. We usually think of our colder months as dreary and monotonous, but occasionally when a winter's rain is frozen as it falls, and all the delicate spray-like branches of our shrubs become encased in ice, the most costly jewelry is not to be compared with the magnificence of the following morning, when each branch glistens in the sunlight with every conceivable color.

Nearly every one will remember the delight with which we as children greeted the first wild flowers of spring. Some are fortunate enough to enjoy these spring effects all through life, and the flowers which produce them should be planted wherever they will find a congenial home. The groups of shrubs, whose branches touch the ground destroy some grass, but they compensate for this by making capital places for bloodroots, trilliums, hepaticas, violets, tulips, snowdrops, crocuses, hyacinths and all the early spring flowers which ripen by the time the shrubs are in full leaf.

I have often been told by residents of small towns and country places that the beautiful effects produced by landscape gardening can be easily obtained in the cemeteries near large cities, "where they have plenty of money, but must not be expected with us, where we have to get along on so little." This is a great mistake. Natural beauty is not expensive. Usually in country places, all the trees, shrubs and herbaceous plants really necessary to produce the effects desired can be had for the labor of digging them. The best things supplied by nurseries—that is, the things that are hardy and will usually take care of themselves—can be had for very little money. What is really needed more than money is an appreciation of the simple, commonplace beauty that nature is creating all the time, a little taste, and a love for our plant neighbors that will make us move them in a tender manner, without mutilation, to where they are needed, and supply them with the nourishment they require in the shape of good soil.

Any one writing an article on this subject should at the outset acknowledge the services of the late Adolph Strauch, who did more than any other man to develop the art of landscape gardening in cemeteries. Dozens of burial places near our leading cities are indebted to his suggestions for their most attractive features. So far as I have observed, the beauty of the landscape effects produced by him at Spring Grove, Cincinnati, is not surpassed or equaled by that of any other cemetery, unless it be at Oakwoods, near Troy, N. Y., where an associate and intimate friend of Mr. Strauch has developed views that are remarkably attractive.

Objections are frequently made to setting aside so much land for burials. "That any portions of the earth," says Mr. Norton, "should be given absolutely in fee and forever to a dead body, set off and preserved eternally simply to mark the spot where a dead body was taken back into the elements of earth, seems to me in itself a strange idea." But when cemeteries are established and developed in accordance with the true principles of landscape gardening, all cause for criticism vanishes, because they may be made as useful to the living, as refining and instructive as any public park. Think for a moment of what might be the history of a park-like cemetery! At first, by its beauty, its quietness, its harboring of native songsters, it helps to assuage the grief of the living at the loss of their friends. After serving this useful purpose for a few generations, its actual use as a place of interment should cease, but if it is unspoiled by intruding and offensive monuments, imprudently proclaiming our childish self-conceit, it continues to grow in dignity and grandeur with the added years. Its trees become patriarchs. The people who walk admiringly through its groves and open glades say to themselves: "For this beauty which we enjoy we are indebted to the kindly, unselfish feelings, the wisdom and foresight of our forefathers, from whom we are proud to have descended." At all times such a cemetery stimulates in the community so fortunate as to possess it an appreciation and love for the beautiful things of this world, and encourages the development of such things about the homes of the living. What can be more useful than that which soothes the sorrows and adds to the pleasures of life! — O. C. SIMONDS, *In American Gardening*.

Right of Widow to Control Burial of Deceased Husband.

The right of the widow to control the burial of a deceased husband, as against the next of kin, has been passed upon by the Supreme Court of Rhode Island in the case of Hackett v. Hackett, 26 Atlantic Reporter, 42. The question was raised on a bill in equity being filed by Thomas Hackett to compel Arreletta Hackett to return the body of her late husband, Thomas F. Hackett, to its place of original sepulchre, from which she had removed it without the consent of the said Thomas Hackett, the father and next of kin of said Thomas F. Hackett.

The deceased was the owner of a burial lot, one of a family group, in St. Mary's Roman Catholic Cemetery in the village of Crompton, where he was buried, with the acquiescence of his widow. About six months afterwards she caused the body to be exhumed, and buried in the Riverside Cemetery in the city of Pawtucket. She claimed that she was justified in doing this, because: First, her husband had requested her not to permit his body to be buried in a Roman Catholic cemetery, but in a Protestant cemetery; second, she did not consent to his burial in St. Mary's Cemetery, but, being overcome with grief, and with physical prostration, from nursing her husband in his last sickness, she yielded, under protest, to the demand of his relatives, for the burial aforesaid, so far as to offer no resistance thereto, on account of their threats to take forcible possession of the body, and of her aversion to the disgrace of any strife over his remains; third, as the widow of said Thomas F. Hackett, she claimed the right to control the place of burial, and had not surrendered this right.

Upon the first and second grounds set up in the answer the court did not hear testimony, preferring first to consider the third ground, in which the widow claimed the right to control the place of burial, as against the next of kin, which might be decisive of the case.

In a former case (Pierce v. Proprietors) it was held that, while no one can be considered as the owner of a dead body, in any sense whatever, yet there is a quasi property in the custodian, in the nature of a trust for the benefit of all who have an interest in it, which the court will regulate. In that case a widow removed the remains of her husband, which with her consent, had been buried in his own lot, and there had rested about 13 years. The court held that, as the complainant, a daughter, was then the owner of the burial lot which had been invaded, and so was the custodian of the remains, they should be restored to the place from which they were taken. There are other cases of this sort, where the question has arisen as to the right of the next of kin, after burial; notably the cases of Wynkoop v. Wynkoop, 42 Pa. St. 293, 82 Amer. Dec. 506, with notes. Report of Hon. S. B. Ruggles, (The Law of Burial,) 4 Bradf Sur. 503; Renihan v. Wright. (Ind. Sup.) 25 N. E. Rep. 822. In Bogert v. City of Indianapolis, 13 Ind. 134, where the question was whether the city or the next of kin should have control of an interment, the court decided in favor of the next kin. In all these cases general expressions were used by the courts to the effect that the next of kin had rights exclusive of all others. Such expressions were appropriate to the case under consideration, but are not to be taken as authority upon the question which is now before us. In Pierce v. Proprietors, and Wynkoop v. Wynkoop, the right of a widow to remove the remains of her husband, against the will of the next of kin, was denied upon the ground of her consent and long acquiescence in the burial; but those cases do not decide that the next of kin had a superior right to that of the widow at the time of the burial. The third conclusion of Mr. Ruggles, in his report, cited above, is "that such right, in the absence of any testamentary disposition, belongs exclusively to the next of kin." But in a note to Weld v. Walker, in 14 Amer. Law Review (volume 1, N. S.,) 62, it is said that Mr. Ruggles added a note to the original report, in explanation of the term "next of kin," stating that it was not employed for the purpose of denying or questioning the legal right of a surviving husband to bury his wife's remains, or to reinter them if disturbed. In Snyder v. Snyder, 60 How. Pr. 368, the right to select a place of burial was awarded to a son, instead of the widow. The son was born of a former marriage, and the widow was a second wife, who had been married to the deceased but four years, with no children; and the last two years of his life had been spent in a lunatic asylum. The widow desired the remains to be buried in a lot owned by her father, and the son desired to bury them in a lot owned by the deceased at his former home, in Connecticut, by the side of his first wife and deceased children. Under these circumstances the court decided in favor of the son. The judge giving the opinion concluded with these words: "I mean to recognize the fact that circumstances may exist which should give the widow the preference over the son, but in this case I think the claim of the son is to be preferred." We know of no case, says the court, that denies to a husband, who was not separated from his wife, the right to select the place of burial. Even in case of a separation the husband has been held liable for the expense of interment, which had been incurred by a relative of the wife without his knowledge or consent. Ambrose v. Kerrison, 10 C. B. 776. In Durell v. Hayward, 9 Gray, 248, the court assumes "the indisputable and paramount right, as well as duty, of a husband to dispose of the body of his deceased wife by a decent sepulture in a suitable place." See also, Cooney v. Lawrence, 11 Pa. Co. Ct. R. 79. But if as a rule, where there have been no discordant relations, a husband has the right to bury his wife, why should not the widow have the same right with reference to his remains? A woman is naturally quite as sensitive in such a matter as a man. It would be quite as great a shock to her to have the body buried against her wishes as it would be to a man. Hers is a relationship closer than that of kindred, for it is the teaching of Holy Scripture: "A man shall leave father and mother, and shall cleave to his wife, and the twain shall be one flesh." The chances of complications by remarriage are no greater in her case than in that of a man, and the reasons which give the right to the husband are equally applicable to her. It would be a shock to the sensibilities of humanity to say that the reasonable wishes of a wife in regard to the burial of her husband should not be entitled to paramount respect, when such a right would be accorded to him. It is useless to say that a married woman cannot make a contract, for as a widow she is under no disability and the funeral expenses are a preferred charge on the husband's estate. This is not a question of contract, nor of liability, but of sentiment and propriety. In no case is it an absolute right, but, as this court has already said "a sacred trust for the benefit of all who may from family or friendship, have an interest in it," which should be properly administered; and, as we now say, primarily administered by the wife, due regard being had to the circumstances of the case. As remarked by the court in Scott v. Riley, 16 Phila. 106: "A legal right of this character should be based upon natural affection or moral obligation. It should accomplish the object in a becoming manner." It is also added that to give this right to the next of kin takes from the widow the right to bury her dead, and gives it to kindred, who, perhaps, had no affection for her husband, and very little of his blood in their veins. It also gives the right to classes, which might lead to unseemly contentions. In 10 Alb. Law J. 71, reference is made to the Secor Case, heard in the supreme court of Kings county, which was a suit by a widow to enjoin a son from removing the remains of his father, which had been buried by the widow without dissent, to a lot purchased by the son for a family burial place, pursuant to instructions from his father, and partly with his own money. The court granted the injunction against the son. Mr. Justice Pratt remarked: "Those bound by the closest ties of love to the deceased while he was alive should render these sacred rights and they ought not to be left to others."

For these reasons the court concluded that, as a general rule, the primary right to control the burial of a husband should be with the widow, in preference to the next of kin, dependent, however, upon the peculiar circumstances of the case, or the waiver of such right by consent or otherwise. In all the cases the matter of consent is a controlling element, where the body has been buried. In the present case it is claimed that there was simply non-resistance, coupled with a protest, on account of threats and fear of a disgraceful scene, but no consent by the widow. If consent obtained by coercion, or by an undue advantage taken of one's physical and mental prostration, be sufficient to vitiate a mere contract, for a stronger reason should it be so in a case which touches far more keenly the feelings, privileges, and comfort of one bereaved by death. So, in Weld v. Walker, 130 Mass. 422, under precisely similar allegations, a husband was allowed to remove the body of his wife, after burial, from a lot owned by members of her family to a lot owned by himself.

Extract from Rules and Regulations of Edgewood Cemetery, Nashua, N. H.

Owners of lots or graves will be required to keep the same in good condition, and can have them properly attended to upon application to the secretary or superintendent and payment of the fee therefore. No outside parties will be permitted to contract for the care of lots: this, however, shall not prevent any lot owner cultivating or caring for, in person, his own lot. No work will be performed upon any lot upon which there remains on the first of April an unpaid bill of any preceding year. The superintendent may, under the direction of the trustees, notify owners of neglected lots of their condition, and in case of continual neglect, so as, in the opinion of the Committee on Grounds, to impair the general appearance of the cemetery, such lots may be put in order by the trustees at the expense of the owners thereof.

The owner of the right of burial in any lots may, by the deposit of 50 cents for each square foot in said lot, create a permanent fund, the income to be used forever to top-dress, cut, and take care of the grass on the lot, and water the same when provided for, any remaining income from the fund to be used by the Board as it shall deem to be for the best interest of the lot.

The owner of the right of burial in any lot may, by the annual payment of one cent for each square foot in said lot, provide for the top-dressing, cutting and care of the grass, and watering same when provided for.

Vases and Urns.

While a very general use of vases, urns, etc., is not recommended in modern cemeteries, and in fact are entirely prohibited in some, yet they are to be found in most cemeteries, and it must be admitted that when judiciously used and properly planted form attractive features. Indeed there are cemeteries in which vases of standard bronze or artistically carved granite answer the purpose of memorials to the departed without detracting in the least from the surrounding landscape, and by their artistic outlines, lend a charm to many a spot.

A vase, or urn of a truly artistic design is rarely aided by what may be called ordinary bedding and trailing plants, nor do the plants seem happy in the combination. But there is a class of plants that does seem appropriate, and they are to be found among palms, aloes, and such plants, that have a sort of classical make up, and that do not hide or interfere in the chasest design of the vessels in which they may be planted. Except where vases of very artistic design are used trailing plants should be the main feature, hence the more nearly the vase or basket is completely covered the more pleasing the effect.

In Lincoln Park in this city there is a broad walk called the Mall, lined by low trees, it is perhaps a quarter-mile long, with a magnificent prospect at either end. Plain flower beds and large vases of plants alternate the entire distance. These vases are of the simplest possible description, they are manufactured in the parks, and act as mere receptacles for the plants. From the first they are so covered in the planting that they are in effect a pyramid so to speak, of foliage and flowers. The accompanying engraving which first appeared in the *American Florist*, will show plainly the manner of construction.

The boxes are made of common boards, securely fastened to an upright, solidly set in the ground. The soil used has much to do with a full summers growth, and in those at Lincoln park, the gardener uses that of a medium texture, if too heavy it turns to mud when watered and then bakes like a brick.

It requires to be sufficiently porous to admit of water passing through it. To this soil one-third well rotted cow manure at least a year old is added.

When filling the vases, about a peck of horn shavings is added, being far preferable to bone meal by actual trial.

Tall geraniums are grown each year from the old plants for this vase filling, those on the outside being from the largest of the yearlings grown for the purpose. In the upper box, which is 2 feet in diameter at the top, 15 inches at the bottom and 12 inches deep, are some of the large geraniums in the center, around these a mixture of silver leaved geraniums, cineraria, maritima, centaureas, interspersed with smaller geraniums. Then a few calceolaria annua for its yellow, sweet alyssum, verbena hybrida for its color, ivy leaved geraniums, nasturtiums, a few lobelias and an occasional marguerite.

In the bottom box, which is 3 feet across the top, and 2½ feet deep, the first row around the center is of tall geraniums, but not large enough to show over the center. Then follows much the same as in the upper box with the exception of the trailing plants. For this purpose those growing freely and with good long vines are selected and include vincas, single petunias, maurandia barclayana, german ivy, lophospermum scandens and nasturtiums, always effective for this purpose.

Vases planted so thickly as these are and such a mass of green to be supported from such a small share of earth, need attention and lots of water, more particularly after midsummer. Some of the plants are also put in at first for immediate effect, and cannot stand the crowding. The vases require going over just as do bedding plants, some trimmed out, others pinched etc., so that reasonable uniformity in growth is obtained.

In other words the more nearly the vase part is entirely hidden the greater the effect in this style of plant growing. It is always well to bear in mind when filling vases of iron and stone, except the very largest, the sun striking so fully on them, usually heats the soil to such a degree that the roots of ordinary plants cannot stand it. Not every one is acquainted with this fact, hence when requested to fill such vases it is well to remind customers that the chances of ordinary basket or vase plants doing well in them is not nearly so likely as if in wood, or if the plants are so thickly planted as to obstruct the direct rays of the sun.

Many iron vases are made too shallow or with such small space for soil, it is useless to fill them with any thing else than plants like live-for-ever, aloes, ice plants and such like plants that withholding of water may dry up some but cannot kill altogether.

In case from any cause these commonly constructed vases cannot be covered entirely at the stalk, as with the park examples, with growing plants, then some aid may be rendered by covering the boards with rough bark of trees.

The common ivy may be successfully used in part to relieve this bark space, as there is appropriateness of design always in causing the ivy to clamber on anything made all or in part of the natural bark of the tree.

EDGAR SANDERS.

Woking Crematorium.

The Crematorium at Woking has no part or parcel with the great Walhalla to which it is such a near neighbor. It is especially for the supercession and abolition of earth sepulture that the modern funeral pyre has been established. Anything less suggestive of death and corruption than the Crematorium at Woking it would be impossible to imagine. Entering the ample gate which abuts upon the road, there is a broad gravel drive leading down a gentle slope and lined on each side with shrubs and banks of luxuriant bloom. It resembles the entrance to a beautiful garden and on the left is a cheerful little red brick cottage which might be the gardener's home. Swinging baskets laden with flowers hang round the porch, and the house itself seems set in a cushion of flaming scarlet blossoms. There is nothing gruesome in the cheery occupant of this cheery cottage, and yet for many years he has had charge of all the operations which have gone on at the Crematorium. He talks in a certain grave way about his business, but otherwise is a short, genial little person, with twinkling black eyes, and answers all questions with the air of a man who has nothing to conceal. Going down the sloping road under his guidance, the visitor finds himself in a gravelled yard in front of a chapel. Here, again, the place is enclosed with thick-growing trees and shrubs, and is made bright and sunny with flowers. The chapel is not large. It contains about fifty chairs, a gallery, a small desk for the clergyman or minister, and a rest for the coffin. But what at once attracts attention are the rows of stone niches in the wall behind the desk. The remains of cremated persons are first placed in urns of stone about eighteen inches long, ten inches high, and a foot in breadth, and many of these urns are again enclosed in costly wooden boxes, highly polished, and sometimes strongly bound in metal. They usually bear small plates giving the name, age, and date of death, and about fifty of them stand in the niches at the rear of the chapel. It was curious to see the little urn containing the handful that the fire had left of Nasmyth, the inventor of the steam hammer; and in two adjoining niches lay the ashes of the late Lord Bramwell and Lady Bramwell, the urn in each case being tied with ribbon and sealed with wax. They lie there waiting for the completion of a receptacle which will contain the remains of both husband and wife. I found on enquiry that in most cases the relatives preferred to take the ashes and bury them in some cemetery near their homes; but there were many elected to have the remains interred in the pleasant little grass plat behind the Crematorium. The "graves" there are only a foot deep, and just large enough to take the boxes I have described. It is not often that there is a great number of people present at these cremation services, but the little caretaker told me it was rare to see any outbursts of grief, such as are witnessed at ordinary funerals. With regard to the religious part of the proceedings it, of course, varies according to the body to which deceased may have belonged; but in the case of members of the Church of England, the "graveside" passages are either omitted or the clergyman substitutes "We therefore commit his body to the flames" for "We therefore commit his body to the ground." After the service the coffin is taken through double doors at the side of the chapel into the furnace chamber, but a thick wall screens the apparatus from the sight of relatives and friends. This room is of bare brick, with tiled floor, lighted from the roof, and in the center stands the furnace. This also is of brick, and is rectangular in construction, about 10 feet high and 8 feet across, and about 12 feet long. The coffin is placed on a long narrow "trolly," running on rails on a level with the floor of the cremating chamber, which is already at white heat. The massive iron door is quickly opened, the trolley is pushed by a long handle down a little incline, and when it has fully entered the chamber it has left its burden lying upon a series of iron rings, where every part is exposed to the flames. The trolley is withdrawn, the massive iron door shut, and the valves are opened through which pure flames pour with a rush from a large furnace, at the end of the space where the coffin lies. The operator has means of watching the process through small holes in the side of the cremating chamber, and at one time the friends of the cremated person were permitted to do so, but this is now forbidden. If the friends are willing to have the body consumed without the coffin the operation is completed in about forty-five minutes, but if the coffin is also burnt it occupies about an hour and a quarter. The fumes from the chamber pass through another furnace before being discharged into the atmosphere, so that nothing escapes from the tall red chimney, which one sees from the railway, but hot air and the products of coal combustion. There is no difficulty in separating the ashes of the coffin from the ashes of the body, one being black and the other white. That the practice of cremation is growing is evident. Last year there were ninety-nine bodies disposed of in this way, and this year there have already been over sixty.—*London Funeral Director.*

The Springbank Cemetery, Aberdeen.

The "Granite City" is proud of its new 16 acre cemetery at Springbank. A local journal, after expatiating on the beauty and convenience of the cemetery and the admirable manner in which it is laid out, says:—The ground was sown with long grass seed last autumn, and upwards of 4,000 shrubs have been planted. These are thriving extremely well, and include cypresses of various kinds, yews, black American spruces, bay laurels, laburnums, wild cherries, Irish yews, limes, willows and horse chestnuts for shade, and a great number of different kinds of flowering shrubs. Prominent among the features of the cemetery are the gateways and railings. The latter extend to nearly 400 feet, and rise to a height of 4 feet; of this length 110 feet belongs to the approaches to the gateways. From the inclined nature of the ground in various parts, it has been contrived that the railing should run on throughout on a level. All the castings, especially in the ornamentation of the gates, are of a classic nature, and are confined to the introduction of a run of foliage carried along under the top rail, and lines and curves relieved with enriched pateras in the centre and lower parts. The whole, when seen in its full expanse, presents a delicate lace-like appearance. There are two sets of entrance gates, one on each side of the grounds. Each set consists of a double gate opening to a width of 14 feet for carriages; the height in the centre is about 10 feet, and at the sides are two wicket gates 4 feet in width. The civic coat of arms appears on the centre panels of each of the two principal gates, while the corresponding panels of the wickets show the entwined monogram of the company. Access to the lodge and offices is obtained through an extra wicket gate of simpler design than the others. The whole of the gates harmonise with the railings, but the details are much more elaborate in execution, and in addition a number of sand hour-glasses, urns, and other quaint old devices emblematic of time and eternity are interspersed with designs of wreaths and inverted torches. None of these obtrude themselves harshly, but are so skilfully disposed as to be in perfect consonance with the general design. The gates, which are hung on handsome and substantial granite piers, were made by Messrs. McDonald, Stephen & Co., of Glasgow. The size of the cemetery is considerable, there being room for upwards of 4,000 lairs. The whole cost of the land and laying out of the ground was over £8,000, and of this sum one-half goes to Mr. Geo. Duguid, builder, Aberdeen, who was contractor for the buildings and earthwork. The cemetery is under the superintendence of Mr. James Mackie, Springbank Cemetery, Aberdeen, Scotland, who has had an extensive experience in practical and landscape gardening. The plan of the grounds and buildings was executed by Mr. Alexander Brown, of Messrs. Brown & Watt, architects, Aberdeen, and carried out under his careful supervision. Before settling on his design Mr. Brown visited a number of cemeteries in the south, and several of their most striking features are advantageously introduced into the new Springbank Cemetery.

Trimming Graves.

Editor Modern Cemetery.

As the trimming of graves with evergreens is often requested in Pittsfield cemetery, I adopted a plan in 1889, which is simple and inexpensive. I take four 2x12 spruce planks, eleven feet long, planed and painted green, and lay two on each side of the grave. On the two nearest the grave I lay sprigs of hemlock on the under side of the planks, the tops of the sprigs extending a little more than half-way across the grave, and nail a strip of board over the butts, holding them firmly on the plank. The casket is lowered and the sprigs come back again to their place. The material to fill the grave is covered with spruce boughs, so the open grave and the filling is not seen. For this we charge one dollar. About half of our interments are done in this way.

C. McArthur, Supt.

Pittsfield, Mass.

Conveying Lots.

Apropos of the suggestion by Mr. McCarthy that the laws on the subject of conveying cemetery lots be discussed in these columns, Mr. P. O. Sharpless a trustee of the Marion, O., cemetery calls attention to the laws of that cemetery. The law of the State of Ohio provides that "Burial lots shall be for the sole purpose of interments, subject to the rules prescribed by the association and shall be exempt from taxation, execution, attachment or any other claim lien or process whatever, if used for burial purposes and in no wise with a view to profit."

According to the rules of the cemetery no transfer of any lot will be permitted without the consent of the trustees. When such permission is granted the lot is first reconveyed to the trustees and a new deed issued. The form of deed in use conveys the right of possession forever and provides "that the lot shall not be transferable and shall be subject to the rules of the Association in force at time of purchase or that may be adopted hereafter." The trustees are empowered to repurchase lots from non-residents.

Suggestions to Lot Owners.

If you are not already the owner of a cemetery lot do not put off selecting one until the grim messenger makes it a painful duty. If done when the mind is free from a burden of grief the selection is apt to be far more satisfactory.

Do not purchase too small a lot, as is frequently done only to be regretted later on. Where it is agreeable, have a group of family lots adjoining each other and act together in the selection of such monuments or other objects placed upon the lots. If good taste prevails such an arrangement will result in a harmonious and pleasing effect.

Do not neglect to provide means for the permanent care of your lot. In many cemeteries a permanent fund is secured by appropriating a certain proportion of the receipts from the sale of lots. Lot holders are not prohibited however from making additional provision for the care of the lot and the memorials thereon.

Familiarize yourself with the rules governing your cemetery and do what you can to assist in their enforcement. In the larger cemeteries, people are sometimes disposed to object to what seems arbitrary measures for the protection of the grounds but if they were not necessary they would not have been adopted.

It is not every visitor to "God's Acre" who has the proper regard for its sanctity.

Remember that your lot is but one of many and do not seek to improve it without some regard for the surrounding lots. Above all things do not strive to excel your neighbors in the size of your monument. Ostentation should find no abiding place in a cemetery.

The character of a cemetery need not be governed by its size. All of the beautiful features of the lawn plan may be enjoyed in the small country burying grounds as well as in the large park-like city cemeteries, if the lot owners will but study how best to accomplish the desired result.

Mr. Charles L. Knapp, president of Lowell cemetery, Lowell, Mass., is making a brave effort to rid his cemetery of the unsightly enclosures that still mar the beauty of many of the lots. He has addressed an appeal to all lot owners whose lots are enclosed in any way, from which we take the following extract:

Is not the present enclosing structure about your lot in the Lowell cemetery a positive detraction from the general surroundings, if not a disfigurement to the lot itself? The president's boldness in addressing you upon this matter—a matter, 'tis true, peculiarly your own affair—is only equalled by his deep interest in the general improvement of the cemetery as a whole. He detests the iron fence or the shrubbery hedge. He has, by the co-operation of others concerned with him in the direction of cemetery affairs, induced the demolition of scores of the unsightly objects, and he hopes to bring about their final and complete extermination.

"If you will authorize the superintendent of the cemetery to remove the same, it will be done at once, carefully, and without leaving trace or scar, all, too, without expense to you. If the material is of iron, it will be sold and the proceeds enclosed to you by the treasurer of the association."

In the last annual report of the Town Officers and committees of the Town of Vernon, Ct., the cemetery report is supplemented by an appeal to lot owners to give more attention to the care of their lots. The appeal is prefaced by an extract from a similar appeal issued by the directors of Oak Hill Cemetery, Evansville, Ind., and published in these columns sometime ago, and concludes as follows:

We cannot bear to think that our memories will wither in the hearts of our friends, much less our kindred, when the first grass that grows above us shall fall beneath the frost. And it is a sad commentary that this urgent call has to be made. We ask you, shall the last resting places of our dead become a scene of dilapidation, or shall the work of beautifying go on with renewed vigor? Shall the hearts of the thousands who visit our cemeteries be pained by the shadow of desolation, the sure marks of parsimony and unquestionable evidence of thoughtlessness and neglect, or shall they be delighted by proof written in tree, shrub and flower, and well kept walks and cleanly lots of refined, tender, lasting love of a people who cherish their own as they do themselves? Let us awake to our duty, and by caring for their silent homes, pay the tenderest of all tributes to the memory of departed worth. Then, when we go to muse upon their virtues, to draw inspiration for good from mute mounds, to recall our hearts from earth to Heaven, whose love and hope directs our vision to them, the surroundings will be in unison with our feelings, and every external evidence will soothe and calm the hearts of those who sorrow or meditate on the vanity of all earthly greatness, the reward of purity and personal worth. We will not then make our dead a charge upon a *portion* of our lot owners, who do their duty, but upon all alike who are interested.

God's Acre.

I like that ancient Saxon phrase which calls
The burial ground, God's Acre. It is just;
It consecrates each grave within its walls,
And breathes a benison o'er the sleeping dust.

God's Acre! Yes, that blessed name imparts
Comfort to those, who in the grave have sown
The seed that they had garner'ed in their hearts,
Their bead of life, alas! no more their own.

Into its furrows shall we all be cast
In the sure faith that we shall rise again
At the great harvest, when the Arch-Angel's blast
Shall winnow, like a fan, the chaff and grain.

Then shall the good stand in immortal bloom,
In the fair gardens of that second birth;
And each bright blossom mingle its perfume
With that of flowers, which never bloomed on earth.

With thy rude plowshare, Death, turn up the sod,
And spread the furrow for the seed we sow;
This is the field and Acre of our God,
This is the place where human harvests grow.

H. W. LONGFELLOW.

CEMETERY NOTES.

By an act of the legislature the trustees of Oak Hill cemetery at Herkimer, N. Y., have been authorized to assess lot owners a sum not to exceed one dollar a year for the care of the grounds.

Lot owners at Dover, N. H., are contributing one dollar each to a fund to be expended for flower-beds at the principal cemetery.

A custom that has been observed at Framingham, Mass., for the past forty years, is the holding of an annual May festival in the town hall for the benefit of the cemetery fund. The festival, which is in the nature of a fair or bazaar, is in charge of the ladies of the town, and a handsome sum is usually realized with which to beautify the cemetery.

The family of the late Thomas Clark, of Amesbury, Mass., have contracted for a granite gateway, to be erected as a memorial to him at the entrance to Mt. Prospect cemetery.

A citizen of Ft. Wayne, Ind., has presented the Lindenwood Cemetery Association with a pair of imported white swans.

The annual report of Health Commissioner Ware declares that the general health of the city of Chicago has never been as good as at present. Since January, 1890, there has been a steady decrease in the annual death rate, which is now lower than in any city in the United States or Europe of over 500,000 inhabitants. In 1891 the death rate per 1,000 was 22.20; for the municipal year just closed the rate from all causes has been 18.23, and from natural causes 17.04 per 1,000.

After expending $1,000 in improving an addition to Rose Hill cemetery at Macon, Ga., and disposing of a number of burial lots, the city officials were enjoined by property holders from making further use of the grounds for burial purposes. The enjoiners claim that the land is part of a reservation that cannot be disposed of for such purposes.

Cave Hill cemetery, Louisville, Ky., has been particularly unfortunate with its water fowl. Sometime ago a pair of black swans were killed by a guard, and recently a beautiful pair of white swans have fallen prey to dogs.

Joseph A. James, sexton of Walnut Hill cemetery, Belleville, Ill., has filled that position since 1854, in which time he has dug 16,000 graves.

The remains of Jefferson Davis are to be placed in Hollywood cemetery, Richmond, Va., on the 31st of this month. Hollywood contains many distinguished dead, of state and national repute. Two of the presidents, Monroe and John Tyler, General Pickett, of Gettysburg fame, and many others are interred there.

Arbor Day was fittingly observed at many country cemeteries as an occasion for cleaning up preparatory for spring.

Marysville, Cal., proposes holding a floral carnival as a means of raising funds for cemetery improvement.

At the request of a large number of lot owners the Flemingsburg, Ky., cemetery authorities have drawn the color line, and will henceforth sell no more lots to negroes. This action, it is stated, was made necessary because of the manner in which the colored people violated the sabbath.

A real estate syndicate of New York and Brooklyn has bought the Union cemetery in the latter city and will transform it into building lots. The cemetery covers ten acres and during the forty years of its existence 40,000 interments have been made; $200,000 was realized from the sale.

A change in the political complexion of municipal affairs at Cleveland, Ohio, has cost that city the services of an efficient official, Capt. L. W. Bailey, who for thirteen years has been identified with the city cemeteries, having been obliged to retire to make room for a new appointee.

The government has been making some handsome improvements recently to the national cemetery near Alexandria. The road leading to the cemetery has been macadamized, and at the main entrance iron gates have been placed, elaborately ornamented with two large United States coats-of-arms, cast in bronze. A handsome octagon-shaped rostrum, for use on Decoration Days, constructed of ornamental iron work, with tile floor, and a broad stairway, is another improvement. The wooden flagstaff has been replaced by one of fluted iron, seventy-five feet high. A fountain has been placed a short distance from the main entrance and lodge, the waste water of which is conveyed in a pipe to a miniature lake, filled with various species of fish. About one-fourth of the enclosure is devoted to flowers and shrubbery.

The War Department is preparing to erect similar iron rostrums within the national cemeteries at Annapolis, Md., Yorktown, Va., Fort Donaldson, Tenn., and Fayettesville, Ark.

The desire for poetic obituaries in Paris has led to a new profession, whose followers style themselves "professional panegyrists." They are to be found near the large cemeteries, where sorrowing relatives give them a brief sketch of the deceased and the professional pens an ode for the soul of the departed; a few sous pays the bill.

Lightning struck the tower at the entrance to Cave Hill cemetery, Louisville, Ky., recently, and did several hundred dollars worth of damage. A marble statue, representing the "Guardian Angel," which surmounted the tower at a height of 118 feet, was uninjured, but its pedestal was so badly shattered that a new one will have to be put in.

Magnolia cemetery, Charleston, S. C., was established in 1850. Since that time two thousand lots have been sold and eight thousand interments made. The cemetery has a permanent fund of $35,364, which is accumulated by a deposit of 20 per cent. of all lot sales. The perpetual care fund amounts to $15,265.

Floral Park cemetery, Binghampton, N. Y., is located on a plateau just beyond the city limits. It is fifty feet above the surrounding lands and eighty feet above the Susquehanna river, and affords a fine view of the city and surrounding hilly country. The cemetery is under the management of a board of nine trustees, who have adopted a set of modern rules and regulations for the maintenance of the grounds. One-half of the amount received from the sale of lots is placed to the credit of the permanent fund. In stormy weather a large tent is erected over graves during funerals, for which service no charge is made. A handsome memorial chapel has been erected near the entrance to the grounds and lot owners have the privilege of using it for funeral services without charge.

The annual report of Woodlawn cemetery, New York, for 1892, states that 514 hedges have been removed from around lots, leaving but thirty-seven lots in the entire cemetery of 400 acres, thus enclosed. One hundred and seventy-seven monuments, estimated at $97,450, and four mausoleums at $52,500, were erected. Receipts for lots and single interments, $124,350. There were 2,179 interments, making the total number 42,225. The cemetery was opened in 1865.

At a recent meeting of the trustees of Marion cemetery, Marion, Ohio, the resolved to sell no lots hereafter without an endowment for perpetual care. A uniform price of twenty-five cents a foot is now charged throughout the grounds, and of this sum 10 cents a foot goes to the perpetual care fund.

Hints on Rock Gardens.

Editor Modern Cemetery.

Your desire to give to the readers of THE MODERN CEMETERY some suggestions on Rock Gardens, or Rockeries, should certainly meet with my sympathy, because I could "speak of danger's rugged path where I, too, oft have been." And because of my love for these things, I have endured more odium than for all my other dissipations combined.

While building an immense and outlandish boulder wall last winter, a lady and gentleman riding by stopped, and the gentleman, after asking a great many questions, remarked: "I suppose you intend to cover those rocks with vines, etc., sometime?" "Yes, sir," I replied, "that is the intention." He says, "Won't that look elegant?" "Elegant?" his wife says, "do you

A ROCK GARDEN.

call that elegant?" Such is fame, and such is the penalty of making rock work.

An incline, or elevated position, will show off rock to the best advantage. And if these do not exist naturally, they must be created, by depressing the ground in one place, and using the material to raise or elevate it in another, finishing off with good loam, leaf mould, etc., according to the variety or class of plants to be grown. After you have treated all the land intended for this use, and all the little hills and valleys look easy and natural to the eye, *you can then plant your rocks*. The amount shown out of ground will depend on the size of the material that can be obtained. Be careful not to use too many stones—this is the hardest part to learn. The idea is to create pockets, or spaces, and small rocks are placed to create these, and to keep the soil from washing away. Do not fill these pockets too full as to shed all the rain. In arrangements of this kind a greater variety of plants can be grown than would always survive in a mixed border, as the pockets, or spaces, prevent the strong growing plants from

A BED OF ALPINE FLOWERS.

robbing their weaker neighbors. When rocks are natural to the ground, and stick out occasionally, help nature to show those rocks off by removing some of the earth from around them, trenching and enriching thoroughly; add a few smaller stones as above. This is the happiest arrangement, because man had the least to do with it. It is doubtful if any of these things—artificially created—look well, conspicuously placed, or in the glaring sunlight. Trees, and especially evergreens, as a background, help such things amazingly. For more particular information (in the language of cemeteries), apply to the superintendent on the grounds.   TIMOTHY McCARTHY.

Swan Point, Providence, R. I.

THE MODERN CEMETERY.

CEMETERY ADORNMENTS

Makers of

Artistic Iron Vases

With Reservoir Attach'nt, especially adapted for cemeteries.

Bronzed Iron Bouquet Holders
For Cemeteries.
20, 25, 30 and 40c. ea.

Iron Settees and Chairs
Ornamental and restful.

Wood and Iron Settees
For the avenues in cemeteries, Parks, Etc.

CEMETERY SIGN POSTS—"Perpetual" and "Annual Care," "Keep Off Grass" Sign Plates, Metal Wreaths, Crosses, etc.

We have just issued a NEW ILLUSTRATED CATALOGUE of above goods which we will send to any address on application.

M. D. JONES & CO.
76 Washington St., BOSTON, MASS.

MONUMENTAL ILLUSTRATIONS

Cemetery Officials desirous of making a collection of choice Monumental Illustrations should subscribe for

The Monumental News....
INTERNATIONAL EDITION
An Illustrated Monthly Journal.

61 HANDSOME PLATE ILLUSTRATIONS of public and private monuments, mausoleums, etc., are furnished with a year's subscription in addition to a large number of illustrations and a fund of interesting matter in text.

Subscription, $2.50.

R. J. HAIGHT, Publisher,
334 Dearborn St., Chicago.

The civilization of a people is indicated by the manner in which they bury their dead as much as in any other way. At any rate, we have learned more about the nations of antiquity from their graveyards than from any other source. Our religion does not attach importance to the perpetuation of the terrestrial body, and the theory of the modern cemetery is that the last resting place of the dead should be one in which the living may find pleasure and delight.—*The Artist, Rochester, N. Y.*

TERRA COTTA
Grave and Lot Marks

A new invention for marking and numbering graves and lots, on lawn plan. Cheap, sensible and durable. No cemetery can be up to the times without them.

MISHLER BROS.,
RAVENNA, O.

RAILROAD, Farm, Garden, CEMETERY, LAWN, POULTRY and RABBIT FENCING. Thousands of miles in use. Catalogue FREE. Vouched for. McMULLEN WOVEN WIRE FENCE CO., CHICAGO, ILL.

Preserve your copies of The Modern Cemetery by using a Handy Binder. Price 50 cents.

LAWN GRASS SEED

Vaughan's SEED STORES.

CHICAGO, 88 State St.
NEW YORK, 26 Barclay St.
Best Grade, Any Mixture at Trade Prices.
CANNAS, CALADIUMS and all BULBS.

Studebaker "LITTLE GEM"
SPRINKLER
CAPACITY 150 GALLONS.
FOR CEMETERIES AND PARKS.

The "Little Gem" is made with 4 inch tires and may be used in watering lawns and gardens without doing them any injury. It is well made throughout and is the most complete two-wheel sprinkler on the market. Descriptive circular, prices, etc., upon application. If desired, send for catalogue of larger sprinklers. Mention the Modern Cemetery and address.
STUDEBAKER BROS. MFG. CO.,
SOUTH BEND, IND.

TO TAKE PLACE OF WIND MILLS

HOT AIR PUMPING ENGINES

A Windmill
is unreliable because it depends upon the elements for its power; hydraulic rams also depend upon favorable conditions and waste as much water as they secure. Steam pumps require skill and hand pumps demand labor and time.

DE LAMATER-RIDER OR DE LAMATER-ERICSSON
Hot-Air Pumping Engines
are especially designed for pumping water, and from shallow streams or any kind of well. They are simple, safe and reliable, require no steam and have no valves. They require very little heat to operate them, and can be arranged for any kind of fuel.

Send for illustrated catalogue to
THE DE LAMATER IRON WORKS,
87 South Fifth Avenue,
NEW YORK.

FENCES (Wire, Iron & Steel) CRESTINGS VASES (Reservoir & Centre Drainage)
Do You Want

**LAWN ORNAMENTS — CHAIRS, SETTEES &c. &c.
STABLE FIXTURES, WIRE WORK NETTINGS &c.**
Send For No. 31 Address BARBEE WIRE & IRON WORKS,
Catalogue 44 & 46 Dearborn St. CHICAGO, or LaFayette Ind.

THE MODERN CEMETERY.

THE MODERN CEMETERY.
AN ILLUSTRATED MONTHLY JOURNAL DEVOTED TO THE INTEREST OF CEMETERIES

R. J. HAIGHT, Publisher.
334 Dearborn Street, CHICAGO.

Subscription $1.00 a Year in Advance.   Foreign Subscription $1.25.
Special Rates on Six or More Copies.

VOL. III.   CHICAGO, JUNE, 1893.   No. 4.

CONTENTS.

CONDEMNATION OF LANDS FOR CEMETERY PURPOSES. 37
BURIAL EXPENSES... 37
PERE LA CHAISE, PARIS... 38
SLATE HEADSTONES... 39
THE BELMONT MEMORIAL, NEWPORT, R. I... 40
WOODED ISLAND AT WORLD'S FAIR... 41
A PLEA FOR CREMATION... 42
CHAPEL, GROVE HILL CEMETERY, SHELBYVILLE, KY... 43
LANDSCAPE GARDENING... 44
EXTRACT FROM LAWS OF LOWELL CEMETERY, LOWELL, MASS... 45
PROGRAM SEVENTH ANNUAL CONVENTION A. A. C. S... 45
CEMETERY NOTES... 46
WHY THE FUNERAL?... 46
WATER WORKS, OAKWOOD CEMETERY, RED WING, MINN... 47
EXTRACTS FROM RULES OF FLORAL PARK CEMETERY, BINGHAMPTON, N. Y... 47
PUBLISHER'S DEPARTMENT... 48

Condemnation of Lands for Cemetery Purposes.

The right to condemn land for what is deemed to be a public use is given by statute to counties, towns, school districts, railroad companies, parties who desire to flow land, and to others. In all these cases the right may be exercised on the failure of the parties to agree. No good reason can be given why an exception to this should be made in the case of cemetery associations. Thus declares the Supreme Court of Errors of Connecticut in the case of the Westfield Cemetery Ass'n. v. Danielson.

Section 1871 of the General Statutes of that state provides, among other things, that the owner of any cemetery, who wishes to enlarge its limits by adding land, the title to which he cannot otherwise acquire, may prefer a complaint for liberty to take the same. The words, "the title to which he cannot otherwise acquire," it was contended, limits the right to take land under the statute to cases where it is, strictly speaking, impossible to acquire title in any other way. The claim was that, if the owner of the land refuses to sell at any price, the land may be taken under the statute, but if is he willing to sell at some price, however unreasonable, that price must be paid, and the land cannot be taken under the statute. If, for instance, the owner of land reasonably worth $100 is willing to sell it for $500, and refuses to sell for less, then the price demanded must be paid, or the cemetery association cannot obtain the land at all. To this the court would not assent and said that the language of the statute, in itself considered, is not fairly susceptible of such a construction. In the great majority of cases where land is sought to be taken to enlarge a cemetery, the parties will be unable to agree about the matter. The owner will demand a price either in fact exorbitant, or which the other party deems to be so. The owner will refuse to convey unless his price is paid, and the other party will refuse to pay it. Under such circumstances, it may be fairly said that the title cannot be acquired at all, otherwise than by condemnation proceedings. In using the language in question the legislature did not have reference to an absolute impossibility to acquire title, but to a relative and practical impossibility, arising out of circumstances which would naturally, and did ordinarily, prevent the voluntary conveyance of the title by the owner. In short, it had reference to the ordinary case of a failure of the parties to agree, after a fair attempt to do so.

The safety of the living requires the burial of the dead in proper time and place; and as this court said once before, inasmuch as it may so happen that no individual may be willing to sell land for such use, of necessity, there must remain in the public the right to acquire and use it under such regulations as a proper respect for the memory of the dead, and the feelings of the survivors, demands. And as it is of the utmost importance that such a right should be preserved unimpaired, a construction of a statute, relating thereto which essentially destroys it ought not to be adopted, unless the language employed will fairly admit of no other.

Burial Expenses.

The law seems well settled that an executor or administrator of a deceased person is liable for the suitable and reasonable burial expenses of his testator or intestate, if he have assets sufficient for that purpose; and if such personal representative, by reason of absence or neglect, fail to furnish such burial, in the first instance, he is liable to the one who incurs such expenses, so far as he has assets of the deceased in his hands. This is the decision of the Supreme Court of New York in the case of Kittle v. Huntley. It also holds that an expenditure of $127, for burial purposes is not unreasonable where the deceased left an estate of $800. In this case it was also insisted that it was competent to inquire into the price of caskets as between the manufacturer or wholesale dealer and the undertaker or retail dealer, and that the witnesses should have been compelled to answer that inquiry, or their testimony given stricken out. That doctrine the court said it was not prepared to subscribe to where the article of merchandise, as here, has a market value, as fixed by the trade as between the undertaker and his customers. The cost price between the manufacturer and the undertaker would not in such a case furnish a correct criterion as to the price between the undertaker and his customers, and an inquiry into it would lead to unsafe and unprofitable speculation on the part of the court or jury as to the rate of profit which should be charged by the undertaker, and would not be evidence of the market value between the last-named parties; that value must be measured by the market price between the undertaker and his customers as regulated by competition and the law of demand and supply.

Pere La Chaise, Paris.

WITHIN the limits of the city of Paris, that gay, bright, beautiful capital of France, where one sees more of life, fashion and gaiety, than in any other city in the world; where to be vivacious, charming and happy at all times, seems to be the principal object and duty of life, is situated the grandest, most impressive and gloomy cemetery in the world! Strange incongruity, as though under the sunny skies of this lovely land, this laughter-loving people needed something solemn and awful to remind them of the change and passing away of all things.

It is a positively gruesome place to visit, and one hurries through, as though performing a self-imposed duty or penance. And yet the ashes of more illustrious dead are gathered together here than in any other spot in the world.

This famous cemetery was presented to the Jesuits late in 1700, by Pere La Chaise, the confessor and advisor of Louis XIV, hence its name. When the Jesuits were expelled from France this property changed hands many times, until finally bought by the municipal authorities early in 1800. Originally about fifty acres, it now exceeds two hundred, and about fifty burials a day take place here. There are twenty-two cemeteries near Paris, and unlike our American institutions of the kind, are all owned by the city. The poor dead are buried in what are called "Fosses Communes," long trenches, containing thirty or forty coffins, placed several deep. This mode of burial costs about four dollars, and at the end of five years the ground is cleared and used all over again. Graves can also be leased for ten years for ten dollars. The wealthy, of course, buy separate lots outright, as we do here, and erect magnificent monuments; one hundred dollars being the cost of a piece of ground six feet square, a family lot is usually about the length and breadth of a casket, the caskets being placed on top of each other, in graves not infrequently thirty feet in depth.

This is truly a "city of the dead," with its short streets and long, broad avenues, all paved with cobble stones, and tombs and monuments of all sizes and designs crowded together like rows of city houses. Near the chapel, which is fifty-six feet long by twenty-eight wide, quite a plain-looking building, though commanding a magnificent view of the city, we find the graves of Bellini, Cherubini, Talma, and Chopin, the latter whose melancholy and dreamy nature is represented by a drooping figure in white marble, leaning on a cross. The pathetic life-story of Abelard and Heloise is memorialized by a handsome sarcophagus, over which is an imposing Greek canopy, built partly of the remains of the convent Abelard founded; the remains of the lovers, who died in the twelfth century, were never found. Here, too, is the tomb of the blind poet and faithful translator, DeLille, and is fast falling to decay; the great master of romantic fiction, Honore de Balzac, is suitably remembered by a fine monument, bearing a head and bust of himself in marble; this stone throws a protecting shadow over the grave of his most ardent admirer, Emil Souvestre. A mammoth slab of white marble marks the grave of the historian and poet, so well known to America, Jules Michelet. On an eminence we find the monuments of Beranger, the poet; Foy, the orator and general; and a handsome marble to the Countess Demidoff. Near here are the graves of Napoleon's marshals, conspicuous among them that of Souchet, who rose from the ranks of a private soldier.

The remains of the great Fontaine were interred in this cemetery as early as 1804, having been removed from the Holy Innocents. Near this grave is the tomb of Moliere, and both are enclosed by a rather high iron railing. We noticed many of these railings, sometimes enclosing a single grave, and again used as a sort of decoration on top of a tomb or monument, while the general tributes of love and remembrance are tawdry bead wreaths, sometimes a number on one grave; as compared with the profusion of natural flowers scattered over the graves of our own dead, these seemed fantastic and unsightly in the extreme.

In the Jewish quarter of the cemetery we found the famous chapel of the Rothschilds, overshadowed by some handsome trees, and near it a tomb of Egyptian design, to the memory of Rachel, the renowned actress, also the grave of Fould, the French statesman. In a beautiful spot, fragrant with natural flowers and surrounded by a hedge of ivy, though with no monument of any sort, lie the remains of Marshal Ney, who, with his troops, turned against his king and espoused the cause of Napoleon, and was afterwards arrested, condemned and shot. Near one of the entrances are the graves of the tender poet, De Musset, under a drooping willow, and the composer, Rossini.

One peculiar monument, we noticed, had six hands carved in marble, which in the deaf and dumb alphabet spell the name of Sicard, the good abbe, who did so much for these afflicted people.

It is quite a relief to follow up a visit to Pere La Chaise, as soon as may be, by a ramble through one of own our modern American cemeteries; to stroll over velvety lawns, around dainty knolls, in and out of winding avenues, alive with the warbling of happy birds, and beautiful natural flowers, the many fine trees and shrubs, the clear lakes, the fine monuments, with an utter absence of railings or fences, and the amount of space, convey a feeling of rest and freedom; and a dreamy peace steals over one, a serene calm and restful happiness, and death, the "grim destroyer," is robbed of its ghastliness, and here presented in an almost tender aspect.
P. H. KERBY.

A Plea for Slate Headstones.

Whoever visits the cemeteries of the land—and there are few of us who are not brought thither from time to time upon the saddest of errands—cannot but be struck by the unfortunate results which have attended the efforts of sorrowing friends to do honor to the dead. Most cemeteries are to the eye mere collections of unhappy specimens of the stone-cutter's art, or rather of his want of art. They are uncouth where they should be graceful, oppressive where they should be soothing, aggressive and conspicuous where they should be simple and inconspicuous; they in one way or another violate all the principles of symmetry and artistic propriety, and only too often they are vulgar monstrosities of stone, which serve to advertise the stone-cutter and to disfigure the graves of the dead.

When one considers that all these stones are put here to mark an affection which death could not conquer; that they stand for so much love and sorrow, it makes the heart ache to feel the incongruity between the hard, vulgar monument and the thing they are meant to signify. Says a writer in the *Boston Courier*, marble is cold in color and texture. It is quickly discolored, so that it is unsightly and offensive to the eye, the effect of time being less pleasing than in the case of almost any other stone that could be chosen. Granite is coarse and of unpleasant texture if unpolished, while the high looking-glass surface that results from polishing it is the most vulgar in effect that the ingenuity of the stonecutter has thus far been able to compass. Sandstone is pleasant to the eye, but it so quickly loses the words which affection has committed to its keeping that it is hardly to be counted among the materials available for this purpose.

In view of these facts there seems nothing better to do than to return to the custom of our fathers and return to the use of slate. There is nothing which more satisfactorily stands our climate, both in respect to durability and to appearance. To the eye the soft, low tone of the stone is always pleasant, and the material is one which has the great merit of not seeming to lend itself readily to those ornate and obtrusive structures of which so many specimens unfortunately disfigure the cities of the dead throughout the country. The finer varieties, fine and velvety of texture, are capable of receiving carvings of delicacy and intricacy, and of preserving them through the trying weather of our destructive winters. On the whole, there is no other stone so satisfactory for this use, and it is a pity that it should not be more generally adopted. There is at some cemeteries, a foolish regulation forbidding the erection of slate tablets, but the rule is fortunately not a general one, and so thoroughly is the public tired of the use of marble and granite that there is every reason to believe that it will soon return to the good old custom of the early days of New England, when necessity and common sense combined to hold people to a fashion which was the best that has ever obtained in the matter of gravestones in this country.

By the adoption of urn burial, all that relates to the artistic embellishment of a cemetery would be at once placed on a very different footing.— *God's Acre Beautiful.*

THE AUGUST BELMONT MEMORIAL, NEWPORT, R. I.

The Belmont Memorial.

The August Belmont memorial in the Island cemetery Newport, R. I., is one of the most beautiful examples of monumental art in this country. It is Grecian in design and was made from plans furnished by R. M. Hunt, the New York architect. The proportions of the structure are so nicely drawn that it is less imposing than a statement of the dimensions would lead one to presume, writes a Newport correspondent. From the center of a semi-elliptical platform, with a frontage of thirty-two feet, rises a Grecian temple twenty-two feet in height and ten feet in depth. At the corners of the temple are square marble pillars, with Ionic capitals, which support a massive entablature, with cornice and frieze, enriched with carved mouldings. Two beautifully modelled caryatides flank either side of the entrance to the temple, and while acting as mute sentinels to the tomb, support the ends of an arch that joins the two front pillars. The spandrels are adorned with carved palm branches. The walls on three sides of the structure are of single blocks of marble and rise to the height of the caryatides. Above this are open semicircular spaces, in the center of each stands a Grecian urn. Inside of the temple is a massive sarcophagus of polished red Scotch granite, and carved upon it are branches of laurel, oak and palm. Wing walls, ten feet in height, on either side of the temple, curve from it to handsomely designed pillars at either end of the structure. Marble benches follow the inside of the wall, the upper portion of which is formed of panels of lattice work in marble. The rail surmounting the wall is finely polished and carved, and, in fact, every part of this chaste memorial has been executed with the utmost care. The marble is from the quarries at Lee, Mass., over one hundred tons of it being used in the work, which cost about $30,000.

From a Paris Tombstone.

"Here lies Anathese Bardoux, who died at the age of 72, leaving his fortune to his youthful and amiable widow. On account of the great difference of their age, the deceased was to her a second father."

REAR VIEW, BELMONT MEMORIAL.

The Wooded Island at the World's Fair.

We fancy if there is any thing specially interesting that can be applied to cemetery decorations at the World's Fair, it will be the treatment of what is rightly called the Wooded Island, the lagoons that surround it, and the canals, ponds and lakes in other parts of the ground.

It may however be a fact that even these may hardly fit, the ususal environments of a cemetery, any more than the white palaces in such grand style may be ordinary building. But the nove'ty of treatment and ends to means and transcendent beauty as a whole is well worth a moments study.

The more one takes into account what this piece of land was, say two years ago, and sees it as it is to-day the more impressed one must become with the general treatment as a whole. But the island is the principal part of what we have now in mind and that is most likely to be a good object lesson for cemetery work. There the occupation of the island with my exhibits, was an afterthought principally through the instrumentality of Chief Thorpe, for some good place to show off ornamentals in the way of shrubs and hardy garden plants generally.

The idea of Landscape Architect Olmsted was massing this whole area of some 18 acres almost as a natural jungle, with little to attract ordinary sight seers or for close inspection if at all to botanical students or lovers of wild wood scenery.

It was a happy thought to combine the two, leaving to the land-scape department of the grounds, an outer edge of thickly planted shrubberry and water loving plants, and the center to exhibits of ornamental plants arranged as far as may be in a half natural manner into groups with lawns and abundance of walks interspersing them. One of the most noticable methods of treatment, unique in itself, requiring some courage to carry out, is that the outer edge forming the lagoon from landward is treated absolutely artificially, representing stone abutments, heavy balustrade and parapets, with massive vases, equidistant, with large statuary of animals guarding the bridges, and broad stone steps leading down to water landings, while the opposite shore of the island itself, has every thing of an artificial appearance carefully excluded.

The very shrubbery one could aver was not put there by the hand of man but placed there by nature herself. The banks absolutely destitute of any set design, here cropping out in small patches, half water, half soil, vegetation springing up half in the water half out, indentations of water here, the reverse there, sometimes forming miniature islands, again in others large enough for the abode of water fowl, and even a hunter's cabin, all totally unkempt so far as the gardeners art is concerned, the one side absolutely nature, the other as marked art, and yet no incongruity as a whole.

We say advisedly it took courage to combine these two diametrically opposite methods on the same piece of water, and a water that was to have floating on its bosom the gay gondolas of Venice, with the picturesque dress of the gayer gondol'er.

Willow and other water loving p'ants spring directly out of the water, meeting those on partially dry land and still others on the higher main land, these banks of greenery form the principal part, the willows, alders, dogwoods, sedges and other water loving plants of our native flora.

Rhododendrons, azaleas and kindred plants, a veritable old fashioned rose garden, with edges of clematis, and boundaries of sweet peas are there, and when the roses are past their best, masses of gladioli, dahlias and other plants will take their place.

There also may be seen paeony beds, and pansies, canterbury bells and auriculas, Californian golden poppies, fox-gloves and the stately hollyhock. The useful phlox and masses of evening primroses, the wee crimson tippet flower of Bobby Burns.

These are the smaller, then there are groups of shrubs of all kinds, including a picturesque Japanese garden and buildings on the north and opposite their tea gardens across the lagoon. Waterfowl and electric launches skim the surface of the water along side the gay gondola. All is animated with life, and yet does the main island give in sailing around the most restful appearance of quiet nature, on the one side buildings in marble whiteness of colossal size—the other natures lovely green. The combination is fine in the extreme and certainly affords no end of fine points for everybody to look into who has any thing to do with laying out of grounds and surely to tho e who are in charge of public parks, cemeteries and large private grounds.

On the main Columbian and other canals, the treatment on the contrary is wholly artificial. In front of the vast art palace sloping grassy banks and closely shaven lawns prevail. In others excellent examples of terrace gardens, with monster vases of the simplest design, although made of staff are colored to exactly imitate terra-cotta, the green of the palms and yuccas that the vases are filled with contrast well with the white stone work beneath. The reddish color of the vases is every way preferable to any other that could be chosen.

In this part of the horticultural display as in that in the horticultural building itself, there is plenty to admire.

But the Nursery exhibit on Midway Plaisance confined to fruit trees and evergreens is a disgrace to the nurserymen of the country. Not a half dozen exhibits all told are here worthy of more than a passing mention.

A foreigner seeing this for the first time would certainly have but a poor opinion of the Nursery business of the United States to have done no better than this.

EDGAR SANDERS.

Written for The Modern Cemetery.

A Plea for Cremation.

In nearly all the countries of Europe it has been found necessary to regulate, by legislative enactment, the distance of graveyards from human habitations, and at which wells could be sunk.

In Italy, for example, the prohibited distance is about 360 feet. In France and Austria the distance is about double that of Italy, but that is found to be entirely inadequate, and at a council convened at Brussels in 1852, it was held that 1,200 feet was the least distance regarded as protective. And after further consideration of the subject, many physicians regard this as insufficient, and Prussia passed an act prohibiting the laying out of a cemetery within 3,500 feet of any dwelling.

To bring the matter nearer home, the report of the Board of Health at New York City in 1806, recommended the removal of all graveyards from the City. After sixteen years this law was put into force. Among the condemned spots was the Potter's Field, which was believed to be the cause, in 1814, of an outbreak of diarrhea and typhoid fever in its vicinity. This is now known as Washington Square, and even now, says a good authority, the atmosphere is affected by the gases which arise from the ground and that on this account it is almost impossible to preserve the health of children who are brought up in the lower stories of houses which surround the Square.

According to the *British Medical Journal*, when the plague visited Barbary in 1873, the people of Marah who obtained their supply of water from wells in proximity to a burial ground, were attacked, while the residents of another portion of the town, where water from another source was used, escaped entirely from the disease.

Many other instances could be adduced showing the injurious effects produced by drinking water procured from the neighborhood of graveyards. In France and England it has been found necessary to discontinue the use of wells near the repositories of the dead.

* * * * * *

Why should Chicago be so far behind other cities in this country and in foreign countries regarding cremation? There are quite a number of crematories in the United States, and the custom is becoming so common it is ceasing to cause comment.

There are those who object to incineration of the human body on account of religious scruples, and there are those who are sure the custom prevailed among the Jews, but there is nothing in the New Testament to prohibit it. When the objection was made that it was opposed to the Resurrection, an eminent Christian remarked, How will it be with the blessed Martyrs?

One has only to look at most country churchyards and burying-grounds, with the sunken mounds, broken, moss-covered stones, and over-grown, neglected and forgotten graves, to have all sentiment of repugnance toward incineration removed.

It is only a question of time, and perhaps, at the farthest, two or three generations, when we shall all be forgotten and there will be none to care for, or shed a tear over the spot where our poor old bodies have turned to dust. And how much better that the handful of pure, clean ashes should be scattered over a bed of pinks, to enrich the soil in which they grow, that they might give pleasure to those we loved and left behind, than that the slowly decaying matter should pollute the air and water and plant the seeds of death among the living.

Yes, let us bestir ourselves, and quickly provide the means to return these poor deceased bodies to their primary elements, freed from the seeds of disease, as soon after the release of the emancipated soul, as it is proper to do so. And set the example to the world that the protection and defence of the living casket in which the precious gem of life is incased, is of far more consequence than the way the dead body is disposed of after the loved spirit has taken its flight.

LOUISE ROCKWOOD WARDNER.

Robbing graves of flowers is a practice that many cemetery officials have to contend with. Numerous reports of such thefts have been received of late. In one instance the depredator was a woman, who visited the cemetery in the early morning hours, and after securing all the flowers she could well make way with she exposed them for sale on one of the principal thoroughfares of the city. Here she did a flourishing business until detected in her nefarious traffic. In the larger city cemeteries thieving is by no means confined to flowers, but includes almost everything of a portable nature that can be taken away without arousing suspicion. Ribbon thieves are said to be common in New York cemeteries. A woman was arrested in that city sometime ago who had made a practice of stealing the ribbon from bouquets and floral ornaments in one of the principal cemeteries.

THE MODERN CEMETERY.

CHAPEL.—GROVE HILL CEMETERY, SHELBYVILLE, KY.

Chapel in Grove Hill Cemetery, Shelbyville, Ky.

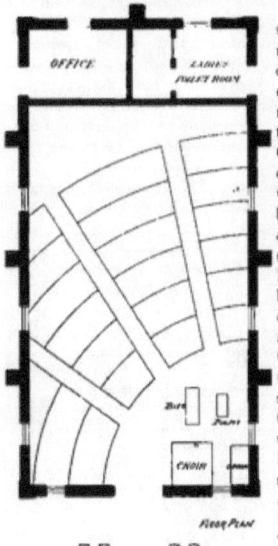

FLOOR PLAN OF CHAPEL.

Beautifully situated in the midst of a grove of grand old forest trees is the recently completed chapel in Grove Hill Cemetery, Shelbyville, Ky. The building is 24 x 48 feet, and is constructed of Bedford, Ind., limestone. The exterior walls are rock-faced, with cut stone trimmings of the same material. On the inside the walls are finished in sawn stone smooth rubbed, and pointed with black mortar. The floors are tiled, and all of the wood work is in yellow pine and antique oak, the design of the Gothic ceiling being particularly effective.

Stained glass windows admit a subdued light into this well appointed sanctuary, which, as will be seen by the accompanying sketch, is provided with all the requirements of the modern chapel. The building cost over $5,000 and is to be used by lot-owners free of charge. Mr. Lynn T. Gruber of L. H. Gruber & Sons, Shelbyville, Ky., was the architect. We are indebted to Mr. George W. Reily, Secretary and Superintendent, for photographs of the chapel and other views in the cemetery.

At New London, Conn., a woman was recently convicted of stealing flowers from Cedar Grove cemetery and sent to jail for three months. If more of the thieves were dealt with in this manner the practice would be less common.

Newtown, Long Island, that cemetery-ridden suburb of New York, is thankful to Governor Flower for his recent veto of a bill that promised to increase the number of cemeteries in the vicinity. If there is any community in this country likely to suffer from the proximity of cities of the dead that place was Newtown, where, for years, thousands of New York's dead have been buried annually.

Landscape Gardening.

Of all the conquests which the modern landscape gardening art has made, that of the cemetery is the most happy and complete. Here the greatest obstacles of conventionalism and prejudice had to be overcome. The cemetery is bound up in the emotions, and it has become in no small measure one of the forms of expression of religious feeling. Consider the form which the burial-ground takes in different religious denominations. Contrast the low tombstones and "verdant sculpture" of the Friends with the profusion of architectural effects of other denominations. The ordinary cemetery is of all places the most hideous. The glistening tombstones, with their teeth cut deep in inscriptions, are so many skulls and cross-bones, forcing upon the unhappy visitor the harshest and coldest aspects of life and death. The rusting iron-work, vases of withered flowers, tawdry doves and angels, are suggestive only of the death and decay of all things. The graveyards still reflect the loveless dogmas of preceding generations. The modern garden cemetery, like the modern religious impulse, seeks to assuage the cheerlessness and sternness of life and to substitute that free and gracious charity which was the mission of One who came to rob death of its hideousness.

* * *

America must have the credit for the landscape cemetery. So long ago as 1825, Jacob Bigelow began his efforts which led to the organization of Mt. Auburn cemetery by the Massachusetts Horticultural Society; for while this cemetery comprises none of the modern landscape features, it was the first American suburban cemetery, and perhaps the first effort at cemetery ornamentation by a horticultural organization. The modern art owes its definite origination to Adolph Strauch, who died in 1883. It is therefore only a generation old. No other country has such admirable examples of cemetery landscape gardening as this, and most of them have none. Over one hundred cemeteries in various parts of the land have been directly influenced by the artist, and some of them are among the best models of landscape gardening in existence. As if to show that the deepest prejudice can be the most thoroughly overcome, many of these cemeteries are less trammeled by traditions and conventions than any other style of landscape improvement. They are the exact antipodes of the cemeteries of a generation back—every feature which men once thought indispensable to a burial place has been swept away. The first and most important of the innovations is the absence of the old-fashioned high, glaring tombstones. It is evident that no landscape effect can be secured so long as these objects obstruct the view and obtrude themselves upon the attention of the observer. And for all purposes of identification—and what other purpose can any tombstone serve?—the modest, low headstone answers every requirement. If a monument exists at all, let it be a common one for all the occupants of the lot. The second great innovation is the presence of the cheery and restful greensward, which is unbroken by copings and steps and grimy walks. The gist of it all is the fact that the cemetery plot is one homogeneous area in which all owners are participants, rather than a patchwork of incongruous and unseemly individual lots. It is one abiding monument to the sanctity of life and death, which inspires the sweetest and most hallowed emotions and abandons forever the lugubrious and forbidding aspects of the graveyard.

* * *

In all this transformation, every thoughtful citizen must have a part. If every community is bound to do its best as its part in the evolution of the race, then the old-time graveyard is doomed! Not that we should tear up the tombstones and grade the soil that is sacred to every heart in the community, not that—but that every simple art should be exercised to make the place more attractive, and that every extension of the present area should be made upon the approved maxims of rural ornamentation. Who shall do this work? The local horticultural societies! Here is a mission in every community which will carry the love of nature and the amenities of life to every home. The present graveyards are essentially bad. Their influence is unwholesome. And in an artistic sense, they are little better than the wash-tub gardens of the topiarists. Nothing is simpler of treatment than the rural cemetery if once the prejudice against improvement is overcome. The natural surroundings and the wild plants lend themselves gracefully to the task. It must all be a labor of ardor and love and a feeling towards rural scenes which is akin to poetry. The first persons to quicken the artistic impulse towards nature were poets and polite authors. Pope and Addison urged the reformation before Switzer demolished the walls, or Kent "leapt the fence and saw that all nature was a garden." If the soft garden-effect serves a purpose anywhere, it must be invaluable in the cemetery, for

"The landscape, forever consoling and kind,
Pours her wine and her oil on the smarts of the mind."
American Gardening.

In the graveyard of the Augustinian Abbey of St. John's, near Enniscorthy, in the south of Ireland, the following custom of burial was observed until about the year 1818, by certain families, says the London *Funeral Director's Journal.* The body being brought to the graveyard in a well-made coffin, the friends assembled around, and the face was uncovered, in order that they might take a farewell look at the loved departed. The body was then taken from the coffin, and laid in the grave, previously prepared with great care, being made 6 ft. or more deep, and at each end was raised a course of stone-work, without mortar, 18 in. or 30 in. high, according to circumstances. Much attention was paid to providing tough green sods, cut from the adjoining alluvial bank of the Slany river; and several of them about 7 ft. long and two ft. wide, each, being well rolled up, were conveyed to the graveyard, and with them the grave was carefully and neatly lined from top to bottom; one the breadth of the grave being laid lengthwise over the ends of the others. In this green chamber was strewed moss (in the season), dry grass and flowers; and a pillow of the same supported the head of the corpse, when laid in this its last earthly bed. One or more stout planks were then placed longitudinally, and the green sods of the side turned over and downwards, completed all but the filling up in the usual way with the clay. The mound being covered with the original green sods of the grave, prayers were then said without any keening or any wailing but the feelings which natural grief gave utterance to, and a particular solemnity is said to have marked every occasion of the kind.

Extract from Annual Report, Lowell Cemetery, Lowell, Mass.

PRICES FOR LOTS, CARE OF SAME, GRAVES AND OTHER WORK.

Single Lots.—15x20 feet, or 300 square feet, $250. Additional space at proportional rates.

Yearly Care.—Single Lots—Grass cut weekly or oftener, as needed, watered, and top-dressed, $4; grass cut, $2.50. Open-top Lots—Grass cut and top raked, $2. Turfing single lots (300 square feet), $10; single graves, $1; prices for double lots, double single rates.

Interment.—For opening grave, $3; child, $2; in case of digging through frost, $1 extra

Use of Receiving Tomb.—For four months, $10; $2 per month after the expiration of four months. The same rates for a child.

Single Graves, including interment, $13.

Brick Graves, $21 to $30.

Reinterment.—(Removal of bodies), $6.

Flowers.—Beds, $2 to $10; filling urns with plants, $1.25 $1.50; planting myrtle on graves, $3; bouquets (at greenhouse), 25 cents each, or for the season, 20 cents each.

Foundations.—Monument foundations, three feet square, $6; 6x3 feet, $12; tablets, $1.50 to $5.*

Use of Chapel Heated, $2.

Charges to Undertakers.—For digging adult's grave (plain), $3 in summer, $4 in winter; child's grave, $2 in summer, $3 in winter; removing dirt and lining, $3 extra; use of boarding and canvases $2; flowers for use in lining, $1 and upwards.

*Foundations for monuments, headstones, or curbing must be built of solid masonry, with good cement or mortar, and be not less than four feet deep for headstones, and six feet deep for monuments, and shall be built under the direction of the Superintendent."—*Rules and Regulations of Trustees.*

Seventh Annual Convention of the Association of American Cemetery Superintendents.

The following is the program of the seventh annual convention of the Association of American Cemetery Superintendents, to be held at Minneapolis, Minn., August 22, 23, 24 and 25:

9 A. M. TUESDAY, AUG. 22, 1893.

Meeting called to order, roll call, receiving new members.
Announcements in regard to meeting.
Announcements of Executive Committee.
President's Address.
Minutes of previous meetings and Secretary's report.
Discussion of the following subjects:

1st. Is the lawn plan to be recommended under any and all circumstances?

2d. Is it essential with the lawn plan that every lot should border on a drive, path or alley? If so, what width?

3d. What gutters are best suited for cemetery drives, and what are the best methods to keep drives and gutters free from weeds?

4th. Paper by B. Chaffee, on "What Constitutes Judicious Planting?"

AFTERNOON.

Visits to Loring Park, lake drives and Lakewood Cemetery.

9 A. M. WEDNESDAY, AUG. 23, 1893.

Roll call.
First paper, "Perpetual Care of Lots," T. McCarthy.
Second paper, "Drainage of Swampy and Wet Lands for Burial Purposes," H. J. Dierning.
Third paper "Sunday Funerals," John J. Stephens.
Discussion of papers and following questions:
"Where Can the Line be Drawn between a Marker and Monument?"
"How best to prevent Graves from Caving."
"How best to Open Graves through Deep Frost."

AFTERNOON.

Visit Parks and Minnehaha Falls.

EVENING.

1st. Report on visit to Lakewood, John G. Barker.
2d. "The Object of our Association," O. C. Simonds.
3d. "Is Flower Planting Desirable in the Modern Cemetery?" Bellett Lawson.

9 A. M. THURSDAY, AUG. 24, 1893.

Take cars for St. Paul to spend the day.

EVENING.

Discussion of papers and questions from question box.
Paper, "Vaults," George W. Creesy.
Paper, "Removal of Bodies," Fred Von Holdt.

9 A. M. FRIDAY, AUG. 25, 1893.

1st. Report on visit to Oakland. T. McCarthy.
2d. "Forestry in Cemeteries," Prof. Green.
Discussions.
Election of officers.
Unfinished business.
New business.
Adjournment.

AFTERNOON.

In hands of Executive Committee.

Mr. A. W. Hobert, chairman of the Executive Committee, has secured the following rates: West Hotel, $3 per day, or $3.50 for room with bath; the Nicollet, $2.50 and $3 per day. Those who prefer the European plan can make reasonable terms at the Holmes Hotel. Mr. Hobert may be addressed care Lakewood Cemetery, Minneapolis.

CEMETERY NOTES.

It is expected that the 1000th cremation at the Fresh Pond crematorium on Long Island will be made this month.

One of the requests of a Tennessee man was that the stone coffin which he had provided for his own use, be filled with whiskey.

Land near Rochester, N. Y., which is said to have cost the Oak Hill Cemetery Ass'n., $300,000 several years ago, was sold at auction recently for $45,000. The cemetery project has been abandoned.

In an article on reminiscences of the old Presbyterian cemetery at Lynchburg, Va., the *News* publishes some quaint extracts from a record of interments kept by the undertaker more than fifty years ago. It was customary to bury the slaves of lot owners in the public ground and some of the following entries refer to them. After giving the name of the party buried, we have "young married lady," "middle aged man," "old man," "young man," "small boy," "married," "poor," "elder in church," "aged man," "stranger," "black girl," "Miss B..s Phil, buried by Cato," "Blank's black girl," etc.

Among other improvements referred to in the sixteenth annual report of the Magnolia cemetery, Charleston, S. C., is a beautiful new lake, covering twenty acres of marsh land. It is the intention to have the lake dotted with islands which will add much to its attractiveness. $150,000 have been expended in making "Magnolia" a model cemetery.

The trustees of New York Bay cemetery, Jersey City, N. J., have resolved to remove all arbor vitae hedges from around lots.

Contracts have been let for a receiving vault of white granite at Forest Hill cemetery, Kansas City, Mo., to cost $13,000.

Why the Funeral?

In a paper entitled, Why the Funeral? read before the Iowa Funeral Directors Association at Webster City recently by the Rev. F. W. Parsons, the writer attributes many of the methods of burial in the past to fear and a consequent desire to be forever rid of the possibility of a returning ghost. It is love, the writer says founded on a belief in immortality that is the cause of the funeral of today. In this he voices a sentiment upon which there is but one opinion. Not so however in his reference to cremation wherein he says:

Cremation or the burning of the body in all probability has its origin in this fear. It is true that this custom is found among highly civilized people as the Greeks and Romans but it did not originate with them. Before ever the Greeks lived or the Roman Empare came into existence, rude and uncivilized tribes, even those of the stone age were accustomed to burn the dead bodies of their friends, and in all probability, fear was the first cause of the custom. Several reasons have been given why the Greeks and Romans practiced cremation. It has been said that they did it for sanitary reasons or lack of space for burial, but whatever may have been the reasons with these people the probabilities are that with the less developed tribes it was a desire to get the dead man entirely out of existence so that his spirit could not come back to haunt or hurt the living.

Cremation will never again be practiced by enlightened people but embalming will become more and more the custom. We will not burn the body because we are afraid of it, neither will we burn it because we have no room to bury it and if sanitary reasons are urged in favor of the horrid custom, embalming will meet all those reasons, and our love for the departed will keep us from destroying their bodies by fire, and cause us to use every possible means to preserve and keep those bodies. I am not speaking as an interested party but bear my prediction upon the fact that love is the prevailing sentiment in the funeral of this age.

It is evident that the writer is not informed as to the progress that cremation is now making and that too among the most enlightened. Advocates of cremation give place to no sect in the firmness of their belief in the immortality of the spirit and it is the very essence of love that prompts them to prefer the purifying influences of the flame to the loathsome certainties of inhumation.

It begins to appear that one of the most pressing needs of Washington is a crematory, writes our correspondent at the National Capitol. There is a growing objection from the property owners in all sections of the city, to the establishment or maintenance of orthodox burying grounds, through the proximity of which drinking water may be contaminated. One of the latest suburban cemeteries here to come under the ban of the suburban resident and real estate man is Graceland. This cemetery was established in 1871, and consists of about thirty acres of high, rolling, gravelly land, which has been planted partly in trees, and promises in time to become a picturesque spot. Unfortunately, however, there is one portion of the cemetery, a strip of about 100 feet wide, running along the Benning's road, which is low and marshy, and in this, as the cheapest part of the cemetery, nearly all the 6,000 interments have been made. The result has been that the burial sites have become much overcrowded and there is said to have been a great deal of sickness in the neighborhood.

A bill was recently introduced in the Senate making it unlawful to inter bodies in this cemetery, the measure providing a penalty of not less than $100 nor more than $500, for any one violating the provisions of the act. It is claimed that the cemetery has practically reached the limit of its capacity, and that the interment there of any more bodies would be dangerous. The Commissioners of the District approved the bill but before it becomes a law, a legal fight is expected as the cemetery officials claim that the charges are unfounded.

Correspondence.

Water Works at "Oakwood," Red Wing, Minn.

Editor Modern Cemetery.

In compliance with your request, and for the reason that I have several times been on the point of making a suggestion that simple descriptions of any cemetery object, fixture, system, method of working, tools used, would be interesting and helpful to many of your readers, I will try for a description of our water system now in process of construction.

First get an idea of our location. We are about one mile back from the Mississippi river, upon the brow of the table lands, and at an altitude above the river of nearly 450 feet. The views from there are, you can imagine, most grand, but as a compensation, the highest stage of water in the river is still "quite a few" trifles too low to irrigate us. Dehydrated feebly expresses the dryness of a dry summer up there.

When the present board took charge of the cemetery we found that two adjacent lots, exactly upon the crest of the highest ground in the cemetery, had not been deeded. These were at once reserved as a site for a drilled well and windmill. Drilling through limestone and sandstone, a good supply of water was reached at 330 feet, filling the six-inch bore 40 feet. A 12 foot steel high-speed mill does the pumping. It stands 60 feet from the ground on a four-post wooden tower, having a base of 17 feet. The foot of each post stands upon a large rock well bedded into the soil, and is held fast by a strap-bolt leaded into the rock.

The tank, which we are just now putting into place, will stand inside the tower upon a framework 11 feet high. It is 11½ feet in diameter at the bottom, 9½ feet at top, and 16 feet in length of stave, thus giving a possible head in the vicinity of the well of 27 feet, and at other points in the cemetery of 40 to 70 feet.

The pipe through which the water is pumped will pass up through a four-inch pipe standing in the center of the tank, and the blocks and tackle for taking up the pump pipe from the well will be hung from the top of the tower.

Our object in placing the tank thus in the tower is, that the whole may be ornamentally enclosed. We can see possible objections to the plan, but have concluded to take the risks.

Galvanized piping will be used for the mains, beginning with two-inch and reducing toward the ends of the lines. The mains will be placed one foot below the surface, and be so provided with drip valves or plugs at the lowest places in the lines, that the entire system can be thoroughly drained at the end of the season; and with street valves to cut out portions of the lines, if necessary.

At proper intervals along the avenues arrangements will be made for connecting hose for sprinkling, and as we have not yet attained to the utterly too, too, half barrels will at present be placed at convenient points, where lot owner can procure water for sprinkling, if desired. Set down to nearly level with the surface, and, provided with hinged covers, they will not be intolerable.

Of course, as a part of our plan, there come in some small lakes (the bed of one of which is already completed), and, possibly, fountains—not large, but large enough for the quiet of a cemetery,—and other alluring thoughts that while away the time during the slow growth of the improvement fund.

D. DENSMORE.

Oakwood, Red Wing, Minn.

LIMA, OHIO, MAY, 29, 1893.

Mr. Editor:—

Your article in the May number of THE MODERN CEMETERY headed—"Right of Widow to control Burial of Deceased Husband" recalls to me a similar case recently tried in our courts here, and in which our company was made party defendants. I refer to the case of Milo Hadsell *et al, v.* Theresa Hadsell and the Vermont Granite Co.

Theresa Hadsell, being the widow and second wife of Almond Hadsell contracted with our company for a family monument, and selected a suitable and roomy site in the country-home cemetery as a burial lot and upon which to build the monument.

Mr. Hadsell was buried by the side of his first wife, in what was termed the Hadsell burial row, located in an unkept part of the cemetery and it was necessary to remove the remains from their location to the new lot on which stands the family monument.

At the time of building the monument, Milo Hadsell a son of the deceased and of his first wife, who was acting as Administrator, obtained an injunction restraining the removal of the remains.

The case was tried in the Court of Common Pleas and the injunction was dissolved; it was carried to the Circuit Court, which body, held that Theresa Hadsell not only had the proper and legal right to remove the remains of her husband to the place selected by her, but also the right to remove the remains of *his first wife* to that place.

Had your May article been published earlier, it would have aided us materially in our case. Such citations are certainly very valuable to many readers of your Journal. I, for one, appreciate them.

WILSON W. BUTLER,

Manager, The Vermont Gran. Co.

RULES AND REGULATIONS.

Every cemetery should be governed by certain rules and regulations, which should be printed in pamphlet form for distribution among lot owners. While this has been done in most of the large cemeteries, where the rules are very much alike, we will, for the benefit of the smaller cemeteries, publish in this department such rules as commend themselves for general adoption. Contributions are solicited.

Extract from Rules of Floral Park Cemetery of Binghampton, N. Y.

No vault or mausoleum will be permitted to be built unless the designs are exceptionally good and the construction is solid and thorough. The designs must be submitted to the Trustees and will not be approved unless the structure would in their judgment be an architectural ornament to the cemetery.

Mounds over graves must be kept low, not extending four inches in height, stone or other inclosures around graves will not be allowed.

No desinterment will be allowed without the permission of the Trustees, the lot owner and the next of kin of the deceased.

* * * * *

The use of metal (except real bronze) in construction of monuments, effigies or other ornamentation is prohibited.

FOREST LAWN, Detroit, Mich.

Association of American Cemetery Superintendents.

WM. SALWAY, "Spring Grove" Cincinnati, O., President.
T. M. McCARTHY, "Swan Point " Providence, R. I., Vice-President.
F. EURICH, Woodlawn, Toledo, O., Secretary and Treasurer

The Seventh Annual Convention of the Association will be held at Minneapolis on Tuesday, August 22, 23, 24 and 25, 1893. See program on another page.

Publisher's Department.

The receipt of Cemetery Literature and Trade Catalogues will be acknowledged in this column.

TO ADVERTISERS. THE MODERN CEMETERY is the only publication of its class and will be found a valuable medium for reaching cemetery officials in all parts of the United States.

TO SUBSCRIBERS. Cemetery officials desiring to subscribe for a number of copies regularly to circulate among their lot owners, should send for our special terms. Several well known cemeteries have already adopted this plan with good results.

Contributions on matters pertaining to cemeteries are solicited. Address all communications to
R. J. HAIGHT, 334 Dearborn St., Chicago.

Cemetery Literature Received: Fourth Annual Report of the cemeteries of Red Wing, Minn. Fifty first annual report Lowell Cemetery, Lowell, Mass., sketch of Harleigh cemetery, Camden, N. J. The Baltimore *Methodist* containing a reprint of the article on "Good Taste on Cemeteries" from *Garden and Forest*.

The fifty-first annual report of the Lowell Cemetery, Lowell, Mass., a copy of which has been received, contains a list of the trust fund lots, giving name of lot owner, amount and date of deposit, outlay for 1893 and condition of account on March 1, 1893. The fund amounts to $50,274, with about 400 lots under care. The publishing of such information commends itself to cemetery officials as a means of stimulating interest in the trust fund.

The Hartman Manufacturing Co., inform us that a large number of their hitching posts have been introduced into cemeteries. The post is made of tubular steel with an ornamental cap and is provided with an anchor that insures permanency if properly set. A wrought steel chain with spring snap is attached to each post. The manufacturers claim that this is the cheapest, neatest and best hitching post made and invite correspondence with cemetery officials in reference to them and their other cemetery specialties.

In his contribution on the Water Works at Oakwood Cemetery, Red Wing, Minn., published on another page, Mr. Densmore makes a suggestion in the opening paragraph, the value of which we have tried time and again to impress upon our readers. These columns are open to all cemetery officials for a discussion of methods, description of buildings or improvements of any nature. Brief articles on any subject of general interest are cordially solicited.

The Lord & Burnham Co., builders of conservatories, green houses, etc., at Irvington-on-Hudson, N. Y., have an exhibit at the World's Fair, which they would be pleased to have cemetery officials visit while taking in the Fair. It is situated on the west side of the Horticultural Building a short distance from the 60th St. entrance.

Visitors to the World's Fair who may be interested in the subject of monuments are invited to visit the office of the Smith Granite Co., at 104 Pullman Building, on Adams St. Owing to the great strike that prevailed throughout New England last year in the granite industry this company was obliged to forego making an exhibit at the Fair, but Manager Young has plenty of fine work in the cemeteries around Chicago and a great collection of artistic designs that he will be pleased to show intending purchasers who may favor him with a call.

Conservatory in Newton Cemetery, Newtonville, Mass., designed and erected by Lord & Burnham Co.

CONSERVATORIES, GREENHOUSES, VINERIES,

SHIPPED TO ANY PART OF THE COUNTRY AND ERECTED COMPLETE, READY FOR USE.

❋ ❋ ❋

Plans Embrace the Latest Improvements.
Unequaled Facilities for Manufacturing.
Thirty-five Years Experience.

ADDRESS, STATING REQUIREMENTS.

Lord & Burnham Co...

IRVINGTON-ON-HUDSON, N. Y.

Catalogue sent on application.

THE MODERN CEMETERY.

THE MODERN CEMETERY.
AN ILLUSTRATED MONTHLY JOURNAL DEVOTED TO THE INTEREST OF CEMETERIES

R. J. HAIGHT, Publisher,
334 Dearborn Street, CHICAGO.

Subscription $1.00 a Year in Advance.   Foreign Subscription $1.25.
Special Rates on Six or More Copies.

VOL. III.   CHICAGO, JULY, 1893.   NO. 5.

CONTENTS.

DEDICATION OF STREET BY CEMETERY ASSOCIATION.	49
A TALK ON ROAD MAKING	50
FUNERAL REFORM	52
THE CEMETERIES OF PARIS	53
CEMETERY NOTES	54
CEMETERY LOTS ON EASY PAYMENTS. LOCATION OF MONUMENTS AUTHORIZED BY STATUTE. DERIVATION OF HEARSES	55
RULES AND REGULATIONS—SUGGESTIONS TO LOT OWNERS	56
NOTINGS AT WABBACK CEMETERY	57
THE MODERN CEMETERY. THE CEMETERY SUPERINTENDENTS ASSCN	58
SEVENTH ANNUAL CONVENTION OF THE A. A. C. S.	59
PUBLISHERS DEPARTMENT	60
EXPRESSIONS FROM SUBSCRIBERS	111

Dedication of Street by Cemetery Association.

An incorporated cemetery association has the power to dedicate to the public for street purposes a strip of land owned by it adjacent to its cemetery. So holds the Supreme Court of California in the case of the Los Angeles Cemetery Association v. City of Los Angeles. (32 Pacific Reporter 240.) And the following facts of the case were considered to show such a dedication. On October 26, 1877, the Los Angeles Cemetery Association, a corporation, was the owner of a tract of land in the City of Los Angeles, which included the strip in controversy, and on that day it filed for record a map of the tract, on which were delineated the usual plats and avenues of cemetery grounds, and along the southerly and westerly sides of which were left blank colored strips, 40 feet in width, the one on the southerly side being now a portion of First street, and the one on the westerly side being the land in controversy. The map also showed that the only entrance to the cemetery was from the strip in controversy, and that the strip opened out at one end into First street, and at the other end into Broderick avenue, public streets of the city. About the time of the filing of this map the association planted along the easterly and inner line of the street in controversy a hedge fence, leaving an opening therein where the entrance to the cemetery was located, and also planted pepper trees for a short distance on each side of such entrance, which hedge fence is still intact, and is now, and has been since the year 1885, a good and substantial fence. In 1885 it moved a fence that had been erected upon the outer or westerly line of the strip into the inner line thereof, and adjoining the hedge fence on the easterly side thereof. Some time about the year 1885, the lands adjoining the strip in controversy on the west side were laid out in lots, and spaces between them for streets, and among other spaces was one 20 feet in width, the full length of and adjoining the said strip, and making therewith a 60-foot strip, known as "Evergreen Avenue." Previous to and since 1885, the association has sold to divers persons a great number of lots in its cemetery, and the only carriage entrance thereto fronts on the strip of land in dispute, about midway between the north and south ends thereof. Since the year 1885, the said strip of land has been continuously used and traveled by the public as a public street, which use has been with the knowledge and consent of the association. On December 15, 1890, the city council of the city of Los Angeles duly passed an ordinance accepting all streets theretofore dedicated, or offered to be dedicated, by property owners for public use. Wherefore the court found that the said strip of land was a part and portion of a public street in the city of Los Angeles, known as "Evergreen Avenue;" that the association had no right to its possession, and that the city was entitled to its possession as a public street. It was claimed, among other things, that the association having been organized as a corporation for cemetery purposes, "had no power, directly or indirectly, to dedicate its land to the public for street purposes." But this claim, it was said, was sufficiently met and answered by the decision of the Supreme Court, reported in 95 Cal. 420, 30 Pac. Rep. 523. That case was between the same parties as this, and the question involved related to the dedication of the 40-foot strip along the south side of the association's tract. It was held that the dedication was made and accepted, and that the strip formed a part of First street. And the use, that commenced as early at least as 1887, and was continued up to the time of the trial, was sufficient to show an acceptance by the public without the formal ordinance passed by the city council in 1890.

A Talk on Road-Making.

Many of our American parks and garden cemeteries contain excellent examples of what a good stone-road suited to our climate should be like. Having observed the fine condition of the drives in Forest Lawn Cemetery, of Buffalo—a magnificent garden burial-ground embracing near 600 acres of land—the editor of *American Gardening*, which was given as follows in a recent issue of that magazine, and to whose publishers the MODERN CEMETERY is indebted for the use of the accompanying illustrations asked Mr. George Troop, superintendent of the

FIG. 1.—CONSTRUCTION OF GUTTER, COPING AND PAVEMENT

grounds, for information about the construction of the roads.

The first question to be determined in road-construction is the proper kind of roadway and the depth of the material. Roads made only of small stone, however carefully laid and compacted together, are found not to be so durable in this country as they are in Europe, where so many good roads of this class were made by Mr. Macadam, who first built them, and built them so systematically and extensively, that this kind of pavement is still called by his name even when, as is now generally the case, only the surface coat is built with Macadam stone. In this country the power of the frost is so destructive every winter, and the road-bed becomes so spongy each spring as the frost thaws out, that a pavement of small stones only has little bond. The small stones sink too readily into the soft subsoil under heavy loads, and a corresponding rut is at once made on the surface. The cohesive power of the pavement being once broken it yields under further travel on the same principle that an arch settles when the keystone is removed.

For these reasons all good roads of the kind usually known as "Macadam roads" have a carefully laid rubble-stone foundation. This method was at first practiced extensively in England by an eminent engineer named Telford. All our so-called "Macadam" roads of any value are of this class, and are sometimes named "Telford Macadam." Figure 1 shows a cross-sectional view, including the gutter and copings, of a portion of Telford road-bed 18 inches thick. Its construction consists in first laying a foundation of any rough rubble-stones of convenient size for handling, and placing them carefully by hand in parallel courses across the road-bed as for a rough street pavement. The nearer such stones can be brought to the general form of paving-stones by judicious breaking, the better the work. Blocks averaging 6 inches in thickness by 12 inches in depth will make strong work, however rough their general shape. They should be placed on edge, with the largest edges down, and be set as closely and firmly together as their rough shape will permit. Where the jagged upper edges project too high for the established thickness of the layer, they should be broken off, and all low places should be filled with suitable chips well packed into place. The whole course should be gone over, and all open spaces be filled by running stones of suitable sizes into all interstices with pounders or heavy hammers. When the surface is level enough for rolling the heaviest roller obtainable should be used, and the rolling be continued until the whole foundation course is perfectly solid and of the right shape and height to receive the Macadam course; that is, the course of small stone.

The depth of this course of small stone will vary with the same circumstances which determine the whole depth of the pavement. Usually it is about one-third of the whole. Thus it will be 4 inches thick if the Telford course be 8 inches, and 6 inches if the foundation be 12 inches deep. The stones may be laid in two courses if the depth be 6 inches, and each course be rolled separately. For the lower course the stones should all be small enough to pass through a 3-inch ring, and through a 1½-inch ring for the upper coat. To make at once a smooth and firm surface it should be dressed with an inch of fine stone screenings or selected gravel of similar quality. This should contain some fine sand or earth loam, just sufficient to sift into the finer chinks and to bind the Macadam stones into one firm crust when well watered and rolled.

For the best work a steam-roller is necessary at every stage, and each course should be rolled until no further impression can be made, or, in other words, until the roller leaves no track behind it. Horse-rollers, however heavy, are very inferior, because the stones shift so easily under the horses' feet. The heavier the draft the greater the disturbance will be. Another defect is the frequent turning necessary, and the impossibility of packing firmly the parts of the road where the horses turn. For ordinary cemetery use a steam-roller of from 5 to 10 tons will suffice. In compacting the surface coat, frequent sprinkling is also necessary. Both sprinkling and rolling should be continued together or alternately until the surface becomes perfectly solid. If, finally, the water from the sprinkler be all shed into the gutter by a water-tight surface, so much the better.

A common error in road-making is to have the pavement too shallow. It must be strong enough to withstand the heaviest traffic to which it may be subject, without yielding when the frost thaws out in the spring. Where the subsoil is exceptionally sandy or gravelly a depth of 6 to 9 inches might answer fairly well, but under ordinary conditions a 12 to 18-inch depth is necessary for a cemetery road subject to much travel, while public highways should ordinarily be still thicker. Few are aware of the great difference in power to support a load between a firm layer 6 inches in depth and a compact mass 18 inches deep. The surface pressure of the passing vehicle will spread through either layer, as shown in fig. 2, in the form of a cone with its apex at the wheel and its base on the road-bed. The area of this base will increase (to use an engineering term) "as the square of the depth." Thus, if the depth of the stone be 6 inches, the weight of the road-bed under the stone will be over 36 inches. If the depth be 12 inches the base will measure 144 inches if 18 inches deep the weight will spread over an area of 324 square inches.

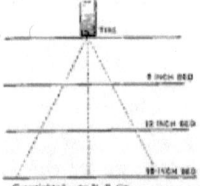

FIG. 2.—SHOWING HOW THE STRENGTH OF A ROAD IS PROPORTIONAL TO ITS THICKNESS.

Thus a pavement of 18 inches is nearly ten times as strong as one of 6 inches, instead of being only three times as strong, as most people would naturally suppose. In a like ratio is the power to resist the upheaving of frosts, especially if the road and road-bed be well drained.

The question of depth being decided for any given case, the excavation at the sub-grade level should conform as nearly as possible to the established grade of the finished road, both in profile and in cross-section, as shown by fig. 3.

The proper form of the finished surface will vary considerably as the grade varies. On a nearly level grade the height of the center above the edges of the gutter should be on a ratio of 1 to 25. This will give a crown of 6 inches for a 25-foot road, or 12 inches if the width be 50 feet. If the grade be steep the crown should be proportionately higher, so that in all cases the water will find its line of quickest descent toward the gutters, and never parallel with them. When newly finished, the crown is better too high than too low, as it will constantly be wearing down under the travel upon it.

Paved gutters to carry off the surface-wash are of the utmost importance wherever the grade is steep or the flow likely to be large under a heavy rainfall. If the grade be less than one foot

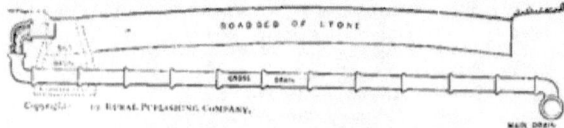

FIG. 3.—CROSS-SECTION OF ROAD-BED.

per hundred, gutters may not be necessary. Well-laid Macadam stone will stand a heavy flow on an easy grade. The width and depth of the paved gutters will vary in proportion to the amount of water to be carried off. If they are not large enough the water will quickly gouge out another gutter in the Macadam along the inner margins. The best work is done with regular blocks, laid lengthwise, as in the best street pavements, but where good cobble-stone is cheaper it may be used. All gutters should have a bed of sand at least 12 inches deep.

The proper laying of underdrains in connection with fine roadways is a matter of great importance, for it largely effects questions of construction and maintenance. If provision be not made for carrying the heaviest rainfalls from the roads, frequent damage of a very aggravating character will be done by severe thunder-storms. It will be cheaper in the long run to provide ample drainage at first. This is a problem that may require elaborate engineering calculations, and some competent expert should be engaged for the purpose.

Catch-basins, such as are shown in fig. 4, to carry off the wash of the road-gutters into sub-drains, should be placed along-

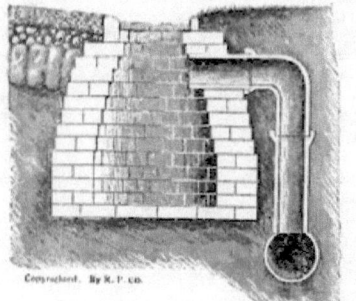

FIG. 4.—CATCH-BASIN AND ITS CONNECTION WITH DRAIN UNDER ROAD-GUTTER.

side the road at frequent intervals. The overflow drain should be near the top of the basin, the bowl of which should be deep enough to hold all the heavier silt of each storm-flow. The inlet gratings should be fine enough to keep out coarse drift, liable to choke up the drain, and yet open enough not to close up readily with fine grass, dead leaves and other light refuse always abundant in a cemetery. The road-drain should be placed where it will not only carry off the surface-water, but also be most effective in draining the subsoil. Where the subsoil is liable to become water-soaked at certain seasons of the year, the road-drain may be placed along one margin of the drive and a small pipe, for sub-drainage only, be laid along the opposite side.

The proper care of the road under ordinary wear and tear is as important as its thorough construction. The old adage of the thrifty housewife, that "a stitch in time saves nine," may be applied to a Macadam road without any great wrench of metaphor. We have only to think of a rut as a rent, and then we can say fitly that as soon as one is seen it should be stitched immediately, or the whole fabric will soon be ripped up. Wherever a rut deep enough to guide a wheel is seen, all horses and drivers will instinctively fall into line and follow its lead. All wheeling on the road will thus be confined to the few inches in width covered by the two tires. The grooves will deepen with wonderful rapidity. Every shower will wash them out, and heavy rains will gouge them into watercourses of whatever size the flow may require. After rents are patched up the seams will long remain, as travel will shun them because they are rough and softer than the body of the road.

To maintain a smooth surface, regular sprinkling is necessary in dry weather. It is needed not only to lay the dust, but also to prevent the surface from breaking up. In a long drought the grit and gravel will be loosened by the horses' feet for several inches in depth, and the particles will be rapidly ground into powder. The surface may be kept comparatively whole by simply keeping it uniformly moist.

On the other hand, in wet weather, it is equally important to scrape off the mud. A muddy road is not merely a dirty one. Wherever there is mud enough to be sticky it will be lifted with the tires, and much grit will be picked up along with it. The mud also prevents water from running off freely, and it is soon worked into slush. In such condition all travel on the road is abominable. The adhesion of the Macadam stones is also soon destroyed by the constant churning of the surface and the softening of the matrix in which they were bedded.

The foregoing details given by Mr. Troop are drawn from many years of successful practice. His conclusion of the whole matter is, that to secure a really permanent road-way, wholly satisfactory at all times, the utmost care must be taken to make the work as substantial as possible at every stage in the first construction. In the subsequent wear and tear of travel, equal care should be given to prevent incidental damage of any character, under all circumstances, and if damage be done in spite of all precautions, it must be promptly and thoroughly repaired. The lesson is one that everywhere deserves wide consideration.

In days when careful attention is bestowed upon the designs of trifling details of our houses, it is to be hoped that we shall soon be ashamed of the present state of what should be the beautiful and unpolluted rest-garden of all that remains of those whom we have known, or loved, or honored in life, or having heard of in death as having lived not unworthy of their kind.

W. ROBINSON.

Funeral Reform.

Extracts from a paper read by Rev. G. P. Fulton before the Indiana Funeral Directors' Association.

In the last two decades there have been some important reforms in the appointments and the conduct of funerals. The old-time shroud has given place to the more appropriate burial suit; and the sensible casket has generally been substituted for the hideous coffin. The hour-and-a-half funeral sermon is a thing of the past; and the people are now dismissed from the open grave, so the sexton may do his work without the nervous anxiety occasioned by a hundred critical eyes watching every shovelful of earth which he handles. There ought to be entire absence of everything like stiffness in the undertaker and all who assist him. Everything should be done in a natural way. Men can conduct themselves with that serious dignity befitting the solemn occasion without those mysterious looks and actions which seem to be expecting the corpse to rise up and speak, and which cause timid, nervous souls to lie awake for hours during the following night, dreaming of the funeral with its solemnities increased a hundred fold, and think more of the lifeless body in the grave than of the deathless spirit which has gone into the presence of its Maker.

Why should every funeral service be conducted with a public parade around the casket? Can any one give a reason, founded either in respect for the dead or in common sense, for the custom of exposing the dead body for fifteen or twenty minutes to the critical gaze of the populace that is prompted by morbid curiosity? And the tired, sorrowing family must submit to the cruel ordeal, because from time immemorial it has been the custom.

But, you say, the friends want to see? Then let them do so, but in a way to spare the family. Let it be understood that the face of the dead will be exposed for an hour, or longer if need be, and if possible in a room where the relatives will not be annoyed by those who come and go; there let kind friends come and say their silent farewell to the dead. Then when all the members of the family have taken their last leave of the loved body, close the casket, and let the religious services follow. After a short service, the character of which must be determined by the convictions of the minister officiating, the wishes of the family, and the circumstances of the occasion, quietly bury the dead and leave the re-opening of the casket to the agent of Him who has said, "I am the resurrection and the life."

A Sunday funeral may be a necessity; but there are sufficient reasons why funerals should occur on Saturday, or be postponed until Monday if it can reasonably be done.

The Sunday funeral that monopolizes the regular monthly, or semi-monthly, hour of worship in the rural district, is a great inconvenience to the pastor and a disappointment to the congregation. In the city the Sunday funerals have become a great burden upon the ministers. This is his hardest day. Body, brain and spirit are taxed to the utmost. A funeral on that day means, for him, an extra service in addition to the four or five which he dare not neglect.

Recently I conducted a funeral service on a Sunday when I was already booked for five services. After leaving the house, I said to a member of the family: "A large company this." "Yes," he answered, "that's why we waited till Sunday. We wanted everybody to come."

Now, gentlemen, I am free to say to you that such a funeral is not only an unjust burden upon the minister, but a flagrant violation of the fourth commandment.

A funeral service, from its beginning to its close, should never occupy more time than twenty to thirty minutes; and oftener, I think, ten to fifteen minutes would be better. Reading some portions of the scriptures, with some well chosen words of comment, or a very brief talk upon some appropriate text, and prayer, should be a sufficient funeral service.

Sorrow, deep and pungent, often finds its best expression in verse; but the soul of poetry is one thing, and the music to which the words are set is quite another thing. Song is not the natural voice of grief, but of joy. Often the hymn selected is so untimely, or the music so inappropriate or badly rendered, that the singing misleads or jars upon the finer sensibilities of the sorrowing ones and results in more harm than good. An appropriate and favorite hymn would be more powerful to comfort if well read by the minister than it could be when indifferently sung by a hastily summoned choir. Would it not be well to discourage the custom of singing at funerals by encouraging the omission of it.

The enormous cost of funerals, especially in the cities, may be greatly reduced by a reform that is within easy reach. The hire of carriages, while the men who furnish them may be reasonable in their charges, is often oppressive. Why should a poor man pay ten or twenty dollars, perhaps more, to convey a large number of people to the cemetery? Would it not be better to conclude the services with the benediction before the corpse is carried from the house, and only the family, accompanied by such friends as they have chosen for that purpose, follow it to the cemetery? If others wish to go along let them do so, but at their own expense.

The custom of uncovering heads in the open air had its origin in superstitious notions concerning the dead. It has ever been regarded simply as a reverential act, that could do nobody any particular good; but it must be evident to the thoughtful that it has been fruitful of much harm. The time has certainly come when this custom should go the way of many other things which have been discontinued when scientific examination has shown them to be both dangerous and useless.

Common courtesy requires you to remain uncovered within doors, but a proper regard for your health demand that you wear your hat when without. For myself, the new rule is established. I will not so expose myself when there is no good reason to be given for so doing.

The Cemeteries of Paris.

Few Englishmen are aware of the large number of public cemeteries in and around Paris, says a French writer in *Leisure Hour*. Many know no other than the Pere la Chaise, or Cimetiere d'Est, chiefly because it is a show-place, on account of many monuments of notable persons, described in all guide-books. There are no fewer than nineteen cemeteries under the charge of the municipality of Paris. One of these, at Pantin, near the Fort of Aubervilliers, is upwards of 99 hectares; or about 250 acres, of superficial measure; another, at Bagneux, is about 220 acres. Pere la Chaise is little more than 100 acres, and the great majority of the intra-mural cemeteries are of far smaller dimensions. Montmartre, Bagtignolles, Belleville, Passy, Grenelle, Vaugirard, La Villette, are altogether not equal to the size of Pere la Chaise.

The surroundings of all the cemeteries and the approaches to them are in strange contrast with the solemnity of the scenes inside the enclosures. Rows of marble-cutters' sheds, of makers of wreaths, crowns, and artificial flowers or *immortelles*, with various objects with which to tempt purchasers, mark the nearness of the cemetery. Taverns and drinking shops abound, as with us in London. At certain seasons, especially on "All Soul's Day," each cemetery of any size shows an activity as great as a fair, the sounds of competing vendors and the drink-shop touter destroying any general feeling of religious sorrow. In fact, the crowds of visitors on such occasions are the slaves of custom, and go for excitement more than from genuine feeling. Those who seek to inspect graves or to renew memorials will shun such noisy festivals, and take quieter times for their *in memoriam* visits.

Associated with these busy scenes there are tales told of regularly organized "cemetery robberies," which occupy not an inconsiderable portion of the Parisian criminal class. Each cemetery ha numerous guardians, that of Pere la Chaise having thirty at least. The robberies are, however, most frequent at this place, the numerous chapels and monuments aiding concealment on dark nights, and the objects worth stealing being of more value and more numerous. An everyday theft in all the cemeteries is that of an apparent mourner who obtains entrance by carrying a wreath, which is exchanged for some object more valuable, and the thief leaves the cemetery by a different gate. Many anecdotes about this are recorded in the official reports.

Of late years new regulations have been introduced to meet the new fashion of cremation, directions being given for the various proceedings, and also the tariffs for different classes. But we must omit further reference to this, as well as the curious details given as to the contrivances of the clergy and chief officers to extract as much as possible from the distressed mourners.

It is true that the expenses of the religious service may be entirely dispensed with, and the only charge may be for civil interment. But even in Paris, where it is thought that infidelity and materialism so much prevail, the force of custom and regard for appearances prevent the neglect of the Church, save in comparatively few cases. Of the "enterrements civiles," there were in all 10,581, of which 7,892 were of the pauper and gratuitous class. In the first class there was only one without religious services, second class ten, and in other cases comparatively few, till we reach the *ouvrier* class, the seventh, which numbered 1,448.

The vast proportion of the religious services were in the Roman Catholic Churches, which numbered 39,570; of Protestants, including the Eglise Reformee and the Lutherans of the Confession of Augsburg, there were 1,068; of Israelites, 690; and "divers," including the Greek Church, Mahometans, Buddhists, etc., 67. The religious services of the Israelites are not performed in their place of worship, which would be defiled by the presence of the dead bodies. The civil interments without any religious service in these statistics include those carried beyond the city of Paris, and also the large number of still-born children.

If brevity be the soul of wit, then the following comes dangerously near being witty. It is to be found in one of the Parisian cemeteries, and forms an epitaph on husband and wife, the husband having died first:

   I am anxiously expecting you. A. D. 1827.
     Here I am. A. D. 1867.

Evidently the good lady was determined to have the last word, says the *Funeral Director's Journal*.

CEMETERY NOTES.

The Birmingham, Ct. Cemetery Association has received a bequest of $20,000, for the improvement of the grounds, from the late Mrs. M. M. Huyler.

Geo. Van Atta, superintendent of Cedar Hill cemetery, Newark, O., writes that no vehicles were allowed in that cemetery on Decoration Day. As a precautionary measure, such a rule is commendable where it can be enforced.

Ex-President Harrison has been elected a member of the board of directors of Crown Hill cemetery, Indianapolis, Ind. There are 330,700 soldiers buried in the 83 national cemeteries in this country.

One who signs himself "A Lover of Flowers" has written the Cincinnati *Commercial*, a brief description of "a new plantation," at Spring Grove cemetery, in which superintendent Salway's work is spoken of very highly. The planting covers more than a thousand feet in length and varies from twenty to one hundred feet in width, consisting of choice hardy flowering shrubs, herbaceous plants and bulbs tastefully arranged, and bordered by a grass walk of graceful contour.

After a service of twenty-five years as superintendent of Rural Cemetery, at Albany, N. Y., Mr. J. P. Thomas has resigned. Before taking final leave he was made the recipient of a gold-headed ebony cane from the employes of the cemetery. Marion Randolph, a civil engineer of Albany has succeeded Mr. Thomas.

What is said to be the oldest pear tree in this country stands in Cambridge Cemetery, Cambridge, Mass. It was planted by the original owner of the land in 1635, and is still bearing fruit. The old tree has been patched up considerably, according to a local paper, but gives promise of living for many years to come.

The annual report of Oakland Cemetery, St. Paul, Minn., gives the total receipts for the last fiscal year, ending May 31st, $28,685.55; expenditures in same period, $23,361; $16,700 was received from the sale of lots and single graves. The expenditures for permanent improvements aggregated $8,144, and included new greenhouse costing $2,610, a steel and iron fence one-half mile in length, $5,476, and an extension of the water service. The Perpetual care fund, principal and working combined, is $80,653. President Blakely expresses gratification at the growing interest manifested in the cemetery by lot-owners. Some very fine monumental work has been erected, notably a mausoleum, at a cost of $40,000, by one of the trustees, and a massive family monument, surmounted by statues of Faith, Hope and Charity.

Just how many monuments Mr. George W. Childs, the Philadelphia philanthropist, has erected may never be known. A printers' cemetery at Philadelphia was started by him years ago. A number of soldiers' graves at West Point were marked at his expense, and he has contributed to many other funds of this nature. His latest gift of this nature is to no less a personage than the late astronomer, Prof. Richard A. Proctor, who died in a New York hospital in 1888. Mr. Childs has purchased a lot in Greenwood Cemetery, Brooklyn, where the remains will be interred in October. He has also ordered a granite sarcophagus to be placed at the grave. It will bear the following inscription:

RICHARD A. PROCTOR.
Born Chelsea, England, 1837; Died in New York,
Sept. 12, 1888.
How good! How kind! And he is gone.
Erected by George W. Childs.

Impressive services were held in Oakwood Cemetery, Chicago, at the burial of the unknown dead who lost their lives in the fire on the Worlds' Fair grounds early in the month. The eight bodies were brought to the cemetery on a large catafalque constructed expressly for the purpose and accompanied by the largest funeral cortege ever witnessed in this city. The lot in which the unfortunate firemen were buried was donated by the Oakwood Cemetery Association.

At the annual meeting of the corporators of Allegheny Cemetery, Pittsburgh, Pa., recently held, President Clark, in his report, stated that by actual measurement there were 9,020 lineal feet of iron fencing, and 9,599 feet of granite or stone coping in the grounds out of repair. On an average $3,000 a year has been expended in such repairs, and at his earnest suggestion a resolution was adopted prohibiting any further erection of curbing, coping, fencing or inclosures of any kind. Post stones were also prohibited. A resolution was also adopted empowering the managers to request lot-owners to remove the unsightly inclosures from their lots. The receipts from all sources were $63,054.37; operating expenses, $32,566.45. About $100,000 was expended by lot-owners for thirteen monuments, 406 head and foot markers, thirty-five tombs and two vaults. Interments for the year, 1,146; total number to date, 35,722.

A tombstone in the churchyard of Upton-on-Severn in England is a curious mixture of religious sentiment and worldly wisdom, in about equal proportions:

Beneath this stone, in hopes of Zion,
Doth lie the landlord of the Lion;
His wife keeps on the business still,
Resign'd unto the heavenly will.

SECTION OF AN ANCIENT COLUMBARIUM.

"Cemetery Lots on Easy Payments."

This is the inviting announcement on circulars issued by a Chicago real estate dealer who has embarked in the cemetery business. Some cemeteries may be obliged to resort occasionally to the instalment plan, but here is one that judging from the circular, has been projected with this plan as its main feature. We have not discovered the whereabouts of the cemetery, but the novel enterprise is thus described by the enterprising proprietor.

"If you die we will do the rest. In other words, we will furnish you a lot in a cemetery in which you and your family can be placed to sleep the sleep which knows no waking. Have you ever provided a burial place for yourself and family, or have you been too busy to think of it? We have established a cemetery second to none in beauty and adaptability for the resting-place of the dead. We have located beyond the point where the cause for the removal of the cemetery will ever occur. A point where nature has done so much to beautify the place. The roads will be graveled, shade trees and shrubbery will be planted and many things will be done to aid what nature has so well begun. A six-acre lake with an average depth of ten feet is already on the property. Terms, $3 down and $1 a week until paid for, at which time a deed will be given. In case of death of the buyer, a deed will be given to whom the party may have directed and payments canceled. In case of death of any member of the family after first payment, privilege granted to bury in the lot. In case of sickness of a lot buyer you do not lose your lot, as we extend the payments. The intention is to give you a chance by making a small saving to enable you to buy a cemetery lot while you are able, so that in your old age you will know you have a final resting-place. Think of this subject thoughtfully and do not delay this important matter longer, but buy a lot now in a first-class cemetery at a nominal cost."

A plan that has given the greatest satisfaction to the public, and led to the creation of the nobler cemeteries is that where every lot-owner is a member of the corporation of the cemetery, and where the entire income is devoted to the improvement and perpetual care of the cemetery. Some of these bodies, in addition to forming garden and park-like cemeteries, to which the best in Paris and London are mere stone yards, have already accumulated a considerable surplus, and there is not the least doubt that in a few years they will have a fund the interest of which will be more than sufficient to keep the grounds perpetually in complete order. *God's Acre Beautiful.*

Location of Monuments Authorized by Statute.

Such a statute as that of Massachusetts, authorizing an allowance for the erection of a monument is not to be construed as confining the court to the case of a monument on a lot bought with the intestate's money. Consequently the Supreme Judicial Court of Massachusetts says in the case of Dudley v. Sanborn (34 Northeastern Reporter 181) that where an administratrix has obtained leave to spend a certain sum for the erection of a monument, etc., "in the burial lot of said intestate," but afterwards, preferring that he should be buried elsewhere, buys another lot, with her own money, moves her husband's body and puts up the monument there, the fact that the expenditure is not within the terms of the decree is not conclusive against it, but simply leaves on the administratrix the burden of justifying it when she renders her account.

Derivation of "Hearses."

The word "hearse," or *herse*, is of French origin, and means a harrow or frame for setting candles in, which was formerly used in church ceremonies and at funeral services. In the fifteenth and sixteenth centuries *herses* of great splendor came into use and were erected in the churches over the bodies of distinguished persons. The framework was of iron or brass, sometimes of beautiful workmanship, square, eight-sided, etc., with pillars at the angles and arched framework above, forming a canopy. The whole was hung over with rich clothes and embroidery and lighted up with hundreds of wax candles and decorated with wax images. From this the transition to the modern hearse can easily be traced. In Roman Catholic churches of the present day the *herse* still exists as a triangle with spikes, on which candles are placed.—*St. Louis Republican.*

RULES AND REGULATIONS.

Every cemetery should be governed by certain rules and regulations, which should be printed in pamphlet form for distribution among lot owners. While this has been done in most of the large cemeteries, where the rules are very much alike, we will, for the benefit of the smaller cemeteries, publish in this department such rules as commend themselves for general adoption. Contributions are solicited.

Extracts from Rules and Regulations of Mount Greenwood Cemetery, Mount Greenwood, Ill.

No mounds shall be allowed upon single graves, and mounds upon lot-graves shall not exceed four inches in height.

One monument of proper design, material and workmanship may be erected upon a lot and shall be placed in the center of the lot. Monuments shall not be erected at single graves, nor upon fractional lots of a less area than 120 square feet.

Only one stone, which may be placed either at the head or at the foot of the grave, shall be allowed at a grave. Such markers shall not be less than six inches nor more than twelve inches in thickness, and shall not exceed twenty-four inches in width for adult graves, nor eighteen inches in width for childrens' graves. No marker for a single grave shall exceed eight inches in total height, nor for a lot-grave twelve inches in total height.

All markers shall consist of one piece only, of stone, marble or granite.

Wooden, iron or other crosses, tablets, boxes or miscellaneous objects shall not be placed upon graves or lots. Wire designs containing flowers shall be removed as soon as the flowers fade.

All foundations shall be built by workmen in the employ of the association. A reasonable charge shall be made and an order required from the lot-owner at least fifteen days in advance of the date at which the setting is to be done. No masonry work requiring the use of cement or mortar shall be done or allowed to be done when the weather is such that injury from frost cannot be prevented.

All foundations shall be finished true and level, and two inches below the surface of the ground where lowest. All stone work shall have the surface next to the foundation bedded off sufficiently true and level to allow every part to be in contact with the foundation. The use of spawls between base-stone and foundation or the removal of any part of the foundation to accommodate irregularities or other defective workmanship in the base-stone shall not be allowed. Dealers or manufacturers' cards or advertisements shall not be cut nor marked on any stone, nor placed anywhere within the cemetery inclosure.

* * *

It does not seem to admit of argument that one's duty to those dependent upon him is to own a burial place somewhere. It is inevitable that death's shadow will cross his threshold soon or late. Will he not make his own and the burden upon his family lighter if he anticipates the dark hour from which he has thus far, by God's goodness, been spared.—*Chas. L. Knapp.*

Suggestions to Lot Owners.

The practice of having a diagram of cemetery lots on the back of lot-deeds and keeping thereon an exact record of the interments as they are made, will obviate future disappointments, especially where graves are not marked or proper lot interments are not kept by the cemetery. In some cemeteries diagrams of lots are furnished with the location of each grave numbered thereon. When it becomes necessary to open a grave the lot-owner sends an order designating the grave by its number. The value of such a system is obvious.

In referring to proposed improvements in the local cemetery, the Ottawa, Ill., *Free Trade* wisely suggests that they be made by someone who has made landscape gardening a study, and offers the following as some of the rules that should govern the cemetery:

"No fence, coping or other enclosure of any kind should be permitted about burial lots. Boxes, shells, toys and similar articles are wholly out of place upon graves."

"No elevated mounds over graves should be permitted, as it is impossible to mow the grass or keep it alive or green on mounds."

"Carriages should not be allowed to turn upon any avenue. Drivers must remain on their seats or by their horses during funeral services."

"Foot stones and lot markers should be level with the ground. Head stones should merely give the name and be not more than two feet high. The place for inscriptions is the monument."

It is not strange that there are numerous violations of good taste in the adornments of our burial grounds. In a great majority of cases attention is first called to this subject when a lot is purchased, or when the death of some friend calls for a memorial. Upon a point which has received no previous consideration the idea first presented, however crude, will probably be accepted. While there are some whose own good sense and taste are a sufficient guide in matters of this sort, it is certain that far the greater number rely mainly on opinions not always judicious, derived from others. Many are content with blindly copying some fanciful or quaint conceit which has caught their eye; tolerable, perhaps, while it stood alone, but odious when oft repeated. Others visit the stone cutter's yard, look at his ready-made specimens, and listen to advice, which not even charity herself can suppose to be always disinterested. Or anxious, perhaps, to have something very expressive and original, they concoct with his aid some outre design, and then perpetuate in marble the long enduring folly.—*Cleveland.*

Notings at Waeback Cemetery.

Editor Modern Cemetery.

The people at Waeback are become quite proud of their cemetery. Through the earnest endeavors of a few of their citizens the brush has been cut off the grounds and they have fallen into a warm admiration of the place. It was truly a great improvement—having the brush cut off—and one for which the Waebackians had waited patiently for twenty long years and more. I attended a funeral there the other day and picked up some points that had escaped the brush cutters.

It would seem better that the man in charge of a cemetery should wear a tile hat, so that he might be of equal authority value with the one who does wear one and can't be waived down. A bell-crown is quite nowhere in the emergency of the tile having the floor—or head of the procession. I mention this simply as a possible fact in nature.

The procession was therefore in charge of the tile. Out-flanks are there employed to accompany the procession. Their antics relieve the tedium of the occasion and are, as well, the chief pride of many of the attending citizens. Thus, on our left were five tails, on the right three tails and four dogs—you see, in its infancy, Banker Brown's pup, Tige, had suffered dehorning of the tail. The canines were not required as guards at all, but were simply along to take an outing, for there is nothing that does a Waeback gentleman's heart so much good as to give his beloved dog a chance for diversion in such a famous range as their cemetery is since the brush was cut off.

But these four-footed gods were quiet as usual in their general demeanor, simply visiting rose-tree, headstone and geranium, seriatim, with a wonderful exactitude. On the left there did fall an innocent set-to which only upset the begonia pot that Widow Blake had placed on the grave of her daughter, and on the right Tige bethought himself of a dirt geiser which with zeal and a glad boisterousness he promptly instituted in the soft earth up on the knoll where Jake Smith buried his baby last week. As the projected volleys of dirt were outlined against the sunny sky beyond "the place seemed like very wonderland," and I knew by the look on his face that Banker B. fairly ached to yell out "Bully for Tige!"—Jake Smith wasn't along.

Arrived at the place of burial, the hearse, by a unique system of cramping, see-sawing and exhibition of horse training, was backed toward the side of the avenue. This closely imitates the familiar dumping of goods upon a side-walk from a dray, and evidently is intended to avoid that appearance of oppressive solemnity which in some places is permitted to exist on such occasions. The avoidance is perfect. The pall bearers then take their burden from the hearse, and waiting for no one, following only and implicitly the lead of the tile, step briskly away to the grave. The clergyman was in advance in the procession, and they therefore find him already at the grave awaiting them. By the time the first trembling mourners have arrived upon the scene the casket is well on its journey toward the bottom of the grave. The clergyman proceeds at once with the few closing words of ceremony, probably having in mind how injurious it is for people to be out in the open air for any length of time. Just as he hastily utters his final "Amen!" and turns away the occupants of the second carriage reach the grave—those of the third being at a hurried halfway point. The remaining mourning friends, seeing "it's too late and no use," make no attempt to get near and alight, though feeling not a little chagrin at being so nonchalantly left out. They entertain a strong suspicion that Bro. Cravat, or somebody, has "hurried the mourners."

But it is all over, and at this juncture, by an ancient custom here, the hackmen now take charge. In some cemeteries I have seen the empty carriages driven around a section in an orderly way and stand ready, in a quiet line, to take up their passengers again. But these hackmen executed the more expeditious and exhilarating maneuver of geeing and backing and backing and geeing, hooking their carriage poles into evergreens in front and halting with a whip slash when they bumped up against some inconveniently placed grave stone or urn behind, until they had all "changed ends." Their prompt finesse may scare a few nervous females out of their carriages, but is much more expeditious, and comports more perfectly with the mode of turning the service at the grave, constituting in oratorical phrase, a seemingly harmonious whole. The unloaded carriages are now driven rapidly up into (not by the side of) the groups to be taken up, who, when they have recovered from their fright at the sudden prospect of being run down, scramble into their seats, anxiously expressing the hope that they may yet reach their homes without serious accident. No longer a procession, the carriages now scurry back to town.

I would not say of a certainty that any of the long-home residents out there were actuated by the deeds in their midst to turn themselves in their homes, yet it would strike me as quite safe to assert it were possible.

Other matters noted out there I may refer to later on.

SEM. TERRY.

Your subscription to this JOURNAL is solicited.

Correspondence.

The Modern Cemetery.

The MODERN CEMETERY having recently come to hand, I am naturally brought to the contemplation of the various topics therein treated. The term Modern Cemetery justly implies an institution much improved within the present generation or some assumed limit of time.

If this Modern Cemetery thoroughly satisfies the need required we would prefer to call it also a *Model* Cemetery.

The Cremationist implies by his action that thus far the work fails to meet his peculiar demands, or wishes. The writer having always felt an aversion to that method of hasty extinguishment, naturally hopes to avert it. He does not believe that the animal or physical sensibilities of men can be reconciled to such a system. Age and cold heartless logic sometimes will quench the finer sensibilities and partially prepare us to accept the inevitable, but nature forbids a full reconciliation.

The young, the affectionate, the sensitive, will always revolt at any needlessly hasty destruction of that personal representative form they have sacredly loved to cherish and to remember. Never the less there can be no alternative but the living and dead must separate, and the ordeal should be made as kindly in form and character as possible.

The time honored, quiet religious funeral is compatible with either method, but the interment in Sweet Mother Earth amid cleanly and tasteful surroundings seemed to meet the tender sensitive and humane sentiment better than hasty destruction, as by fire.

The model cemetery will thoroughly respect all requisite sanitary rules, whatever citation of facts brought forward by advocate of cremation the model cemetery must prepare for and fairly meet.

In the model cemetery a system will be devised that effectually prevents the toleration of needless troublesome encumbrances that hinder or prevent the workmen from keeping *every portion of improved ground* clean and tidy.

The system of finance must not depend upon the optional liberality of dead peoples friends; nor can neglect be tolerated because some people die poor; all must have proper interments whether rich or poor and the same principle will apply to the regular necessary care of the graves. The single grave section should be provided with all the care needed to make the external appearance respectable, or their remains a blemish upon the plan which thus fails to meet the *idea* contemplated. All drives, walks and lawns should have ample care and attention. Vaults, tombs, monuments and graves will need attention and occasionally repairs will be needed when they were not anticipated but such a condition must have some proper remedy.

With these general outlines and possibly many more the model cemetery has to cope until the true end or purpose shall be attained, and yet I believe the solution will come. The plan and the effort needed to attain it, are before the people and the people are strong, I am sure they are willing.

The organization known as The Association of American Cemetery Superintendents will prove to be a factor of much force towards the accomplishment of the true ideal, and the testimony they furnish will be weighed with increasing consideration as time advances.

The perpetual care fund is another very important factor, every association that assumes to provide interment should arrange for their work with this in view, and charges for lots must be borne—by those able to meet them, and thus enable the trustees to provide a prudent and regular care.

B. F. HATHEWAY.

Contributed.

The Cemetery Superintendents' Association.

In the course of his daily routine, the average cemetery superintendent has to attempt, with the best means at his disposal, the solution of many problems which may prove more or less difficult according to circumstances, but which are quite sure to cover a tolerable wide range of subjects. About some of these the information he needs can be readily obtained, but there are others which can better be studied with the help of those whose longer or wider experience enables to advise.

To meet this among other wants, there was formed in 1887, the Association of American Cemetery Superintendents who have held annual meetings in some of the larger cities, and who expect to hold their seventh meeting in Minneapolis in August, thereby affording to those who desire to improve, and what superintendent does not, an opportunity not to be neglected, of compaired notes with others engaged in similar lines of work, of listening to papers on topics of special interest and of visiting together such cemeteries as are in the neighborhood, not to mention those which may be visited in smaller parties on the way to or from the meeting.

By comparing his own work and method with those of others, the superintendent is far more likely to become aware of his own short comings, and at the same time is encouraged to improve his standard and to make the most of the opportunities at his disposal. He is also led, almost unconsciously, to take a broader view of things, and is less likely to be satisfied to remain in a rut.

In these days when many of the lot owners travel widely and form their own standards and tastes by what they see, how can the superintendent be expected to satisfy these more critical tastes, unless he also has the opportunity to see some of the work accomplished by others.

The managers and trustees' control of cemeteries are likely to be well repaid for the expense of sending to these meetings their superintendent or some other delegate, many of whom can ill afford the necessary expenditure themselves. A considerable number of the cemetery corporations have already done so with, it is believed, results generally admitted to be satisfactory, and those who have not are urged to make the experiment.

To the members of the A. A. C. S.

As the time for our seventh annual convention is fast drawing near, I take this method to urge upon you, one and all, the necessity of making every effort possible to be on hand and also to try and bring some new member with you. Seldom are such opportunities offered. Minneapolis is a beautiful city noted for her fine park system and cemeteries; St. Paul, her sister city, is nearby and will also be visited, and from the program issued, you can see that we may anticipate a very profitable and enjoyable meeting. Undoubtedly many of you have planned to visit the World's Exposition en route to Minneapolis or on your return trip from there, and for this reason it would be desirable for every member to wear the badge of our association while traveling so that one can recognize another if not personally acquainted. There are on hand both kinds of badges, the button at $1.25, and the pin at $1.00, either of which will be mailed upon receipt of price, and members desiring either will please send in their orders at once.

The executive committee have secured reduced rates at various hotels on the American and European plan, also announce the place where the meetings will be held, and all that is necessary now to make our meetings a success will be for each and every member to be present and to take an *active* part in the proceedings.

All members who intend to be present, and I hope you all will be, are requested to notify the chairman of the executive committee, A. W. Hobert, Supt. Lakewood Cemetery, Minneapolis, Minn., as soon as possible, also those who will have their ladies with them.   FRANK EURICH,
                    Sec. and Treas.

Seventh Annual Convention of the Association of American Cemetery Superintendents.

The following is the program of the seventh annual convention of the Association of American Cemetery Superintendents, to be held at Minneapolis, Minn., August 22, 23, 24 and 25:

9 A. M. TUESDAY, AUG. 22, 1893.
Meeting called to order, roll call, receiving new members
Announcements in regard to meeting.
Announcements of Executive Committee.
President's Address.
Minutes of previous meetings and Secretary's report.
Discussion of the following subjects:
1st. Is the lawn plan to be recommended under any and all circumstances?
2d. Is it essential with the lawn plan that every lot should border on a drive, path or alley? If so, what width?
3d. What gutters are best suited for cemetery drives, and what are the best methods to keep drives and gutters free from weeds?
4th. Paper by B. Chaffee, on "What Constitutes Judicious Planting?"

AFTERNOON.
Visits to Loring Park, lake drives and Lakewood Cemetery.
9 A. M. WEDNESDAY, AUG. 23, 1893.
Roll call.
First paper, "Perpetual Care of Lots," T. McCarthy.
Second paper, "Drainage of Swampy and Wet Lands for Burial Purposes," H. J. Diering.
Third paper, "Sunday Funerals," John J. Stephens.
Discussion of papers and following questions:
"Where Can the Line be Drawn between a Marker and Monument?"
"How best to prevent Graves from Caving."
"How best to Open Graves through Deep Frost."

AFTERNOON.
Visit Parks and Minnehaha Falls.

EVENING.
1st. Report on visit to Lakewood, John G. Barker.
2d. "The Object of our Association," O. C. Simonds.
3d. "Is Flower Planting Desirable in the Modern Cemetery?" Bellett Lawson.

9 A. M. THURSDAY, AUG. 24, 1893.
Take cars for St. Paul to spend the day.

EVENING.
Discussion of papers and questions from question box.
Paper, "Vaults," George W. Creesy.
Paper, "Removal of Bodies," Fred Von Holdt.

9 A. M. FRIDAY, AUG. 25, 1893.
1st. Report on visit to Oakland, T. McCarthy.
2d. "Forestry in Cemeteries," Prof. Green.
Discussions.
Election of officers.
Unfinished business.
New business.
Adjournment.

AFTERNOON.
In hands of Executive Committee.

Mr. A. W. Hobert, chairman of the Executive Committee, has secured the following rates: West Hotel, $3 per day, or $3.50 for room with bath; the Nicollet, $2.50 and $3 per day. Those who prefer the European plan can make reasonable terms at the Holmes Hotel. Mr. Hobert may be addressed care Lakewood Cemetery, Minneapolis.

A World's Congress of Horticulturists will be held in Chicago, commencing August 16th and continuing four days. The official program has not yet appeared, but the array of prominent horticulturists named on the advisory council gives promise of a great gathering, at which many topics of interest will be discussed by practical men.

Association of American Cemetery Superintendents.

WM. SALWAY, "Spring Grove" Cincinnati, O., President.
T. M. McCARTHY, "Swan Point" Providence, R. I., Vice-President.
F. EURICH, Woodlawn, Toledo, O., Secretary and Treasurer.

The Seventh Annual Convention of the Association will be held at Minneapolis on Tuesday, August 22, 23, 24 and 25, 1893. See program on another page.

Publisher's Department.

The receipt of Cemetery Literature and Trade Catalogues will be acknowledged in this column.

TO ADVERTISERS. THE MODERN CEMETERY is the only publication of its class and will be found a valuable medium for reaching cemetery officials in all parts of the United States.

TO SUBSCRIBERS. Cemetery officials desiring to subscribe for a number of copies regularly to circulate among their lot owners, should send for our special terms. Several well known cemeteries have already adopted this plan with good results.

Contributions on matters pertaining to cemeteries are solicited. Address all communications to

H. J. HAIGHT, 334 Dearborn St., CHICAGO.

Under date of July 3rd, Mr. Jesse B. Kimes, of Philadelphia, writes: "Vault orders are increasing right along. Slate is being appreciated wherever seen. Thanks to MODERN CEMETERY."

An announcement that will interest magazine readers appears in our advertising columns. *The Cosmopolitan*, long since recognized as deserving to rank with the leading magazines of the day, has made a radical move in the direction of a reduction of price and is now offered at one-half its former cost. The high standard will be maintained, and in fact the July issue excels any previous number in point of distinguished contributors and matter of general interest.

Street and Shade Trees, and Country Roads are the respective subjects treated in the March and May series of the *Rural Library*, published by the Rural Publishing Co., New York. The topics are ably and interestingly treated by experts whose opinions are worthy of consideration.

Cemetery officials who contemplate attending the World's Fair while on their way to or from the Minneapolis convention can make arrangements for accommodations near the Fair grounds through the publisher of this paper.

There are comparatively few advertisements in the MODERN CEMETERY, and the number can never be very large as the lines of trade that would be benefited by using these columns are limited. It is our wish however to have every class of business that contributes to the materials used in cemeteries represented, and we would esteem it a favor if readers would furnish us with the names and addresses of manufacturers and others from whom they purchase supplies, who are not advertising in the MODERN CEMETERY. We would also ask our readers to read our advertising columns and patronize those who are represented therein, always remembering to name this paper when writing.

Interment Records.

Having had several applications from officials of small cemeteries for an interment record, we have concluded to publish such a book that will be especially adapted to country cemeteries. Ordinarily burial records in the small country towns are kept either by the undertaker or the town clerk, and we are not aware that any uniform system has been adopted. We are desirous of adopting the best and simplest form, and to that end invite suggestions from our readers. There are divers forms of recording interments in use in the large cemeteries, many of which possess features that might be simplified and made practical in a record book suitable for a small cemetery. Readers of the MODERN CEMETERY who can spare the time to submit a form of what they consider the best method for keeping such a record are requested to do so at their earliest convenience. The author of the form or system that is adopted will be compensated for his suggestions.

Situation Wanted.

Wanted position as superintendent of cemetery or park, landscape gardener or foreman in public park. Have had 15 years experience in general horticulture. Best of references. Address, Sexton, care of MODERN CEMETERY.

THE COSMOPOLITAN MAGAZINE AND THE MODERN CEMETERY BOTH FOR $2.00 A YEAR.

THE GREAT ILLUSTRATED MONTHLIES have in the past sold for $4.00 a year. It is a wonder to printers how The Cosmopolitan, with its yearly 1,536 pages of reading matter by the greatest writers of the world, and its 1,200 illustrations by clever artists, could be furnished for $3.00 a year. In January last it put in the most perfect magazine printing plant in the world, and now comes what is really a wonder:

WE WILL CUT THE PRICE OF THE MAGAZINE IN HALF FOR YOU.

Think of it, 128 pages of reading matter with over 120 illustrations—a volume that would sell in cloth binding at $1.00 for only 12½ cents. We will send you The Cosmopolitan Magazine, which has the strongest staff of regular contributors of any existing periodical, and the MODERN CEMETERY, both for only $2.00 a year.

THE NEW HANDY BINDER

Will be found a most valuable invention for keeping the numbers of the MONUMENTAL NEWS in good condition. The method of binding allows the pages to lie perfectly flat, whether one or a dozen numbers are in the binder. Any number can be taken out and replaced without disturbing the other numbers. The binders are strong and durable and have the title of MODERN CEMETERY on the side in gilt, an ornament to any desk or reading table. We will supply them to subscribers in embossed cloth covers, 50 cents. Heavy flexible paper covers for 35 cents. By mail post-paid.

MODERN CEMETERY,
334 Dearborn St., Chicago.

THE MODERN CEMETERY.

THE MODERN CEMETERY.
AN ILLUSTRATED MONTHLY JOURNAL DEVOTED TO THE INTEREST OF CEMETERIES

R. J. HAIGHT, Publisher.
334 Dearborn Street, CHICAGO.

Subscription $1.00 a Year in Advance.   Foreign Subscription $1.25.
Special Rates on Six or More Copies.

VOL. III.   CHICAGO, AUGUST, 1893.   No. 6.

CONTENTS.

AN ANCIENT CEMETERY AT THE WORLD'S FAIR	61
ABANDONMENT OF CEMETERIES	62
A VIGOROUS APPEAL FOR REFORM	62
TITLE TO CEMETERY LOT ACQUIRED BY ADVERSE POSSESSION	63
THE SUPERINTENDENTS' CONVENTION	63
*CROWN HILL CEMETERY, INDIANAPOLIS, IND.	64
*MONUMENTS OF INDIA	66
THE COMING CEMETERY.—ALLOWANCES FOR TOMBSTONES	67
CEMETERY NOTES	68—69
EPITAPHS	69
MONUMENTAL NOTES	70
MOUND BUILDERS—THE SCHNEIDER SYSTEM OF CREMATION.—MARBLE CREMATORIUM	71
PUBLISHERS DEPARTMENT	72
*Illustrated.	

An Ancient Cemetery at the World's Fair.

The burial customs of the ancient Peruvians are curiously illustrated in a section of an old graveyard which is to be seen in the Anthropological building at the World's Fair. Hundreds, perhaps thousands, of years have intervened since these strange people lived and died, yet their bodies have been so perfectly preserved that they are now on exhibition in Chicago in this wonderful World's Fair year. Not even the approximate date of their existence on the earth is known, but it must have been long centuries ago, for the graveyard of Ancon from which the relics and bodies were taken, was in existence before the Spaniards conquered Peru.

Ancon is twenty-three miles from Lima. It is a desert plain on which the rain never falls. Three square miles of these sandy wastes are occupied by the ancient graveyard. The soil is the usual desert sand, beneath which is a deep layer of gravel. What a site for a cemetery! No verdure, no diversity of hill and vale, only the bare, treeless, cheerless desert plain, on which the sun forever beats mercilessly. There is one advantage, however. The graves in this gravelly soil are forever free from moisture, and the desert is so far removed from the usual haunts of men as to be undisturbed. So thought the centuries—old Peruvians when they planned their cemetery at Ancon.

The burial customs of these ancient people were but rude ceremonies, no coffins being used nor lofty monuments reared to mark their resting place. The sand was first scooped away from the surface, and then holes six to twenty feet deep were dug in the hard gravel. In these natural sepulchers were placed the remains of the dead. The arms were first folded across the breast, the legs bent until the knees nearly touched the chin, and then the body was carefully swathed in cloth and leaves and bound fast with ropes of llama wool or human hair. In this way entire families were sometimes buried together. Husband and wife were placed side by side in a sitting posture. Before them were placed pots of oil, bags of corn and bowls of peanuts. On their sides were hung bags of medicine, with tablets bearing inscriptions which have never been deciphered. Beside the wife a work-box, made of plaited reeds and filled with food and utensils of their primitive home, was usually placed. There was also a simple loom made of six sticks, with combs of cactus needles, and spindles of wood often handsomely inlaid with turquoise or shells. In many of these graves beautiful specimens of pottery are found. Thus in this dry, salt gravel these bodies have reposed undisturbed for many centuries and are now taken out in a state of remarkable preservation.

For the last fifteen years or more the burial ground at Ancon has been sadly desecrated. During the war between Chile and Peru, in 1879, 2,000 Chilean soldiers camped near Ancon, and each day hundreds of graves were opened by them in the search for hidden treasure. All over the three square miles of desert which are occupied by the necropolis are strewn skulls, long bones and cloth which have been taken from the graves by the despoilers. Some of the fabrics made by the ancient Peruvians from the wool of the llama on their primitive looms are almost as fine as cashmere. Fanciful designs were stamped on cloth with wooden dies. Entire garments made of human hair have been found, and one piece of cloth is of brightly colored feathers.

The collection of Ancon relics at the World's Fair was made by Mr. George A. Dorsey, of the Archæological department. It is the largest collection of the kind in existence and includes the contents of 127 graves. Of this number but two bodies were found buried at full length. These were wrapped in cloth and covered with leaves. The exhibit at the Exposition faithfully reproduces the cemetery just as it appears at Ancon. The mummies appear at the World's Fair city just as they were placed centuries ago in their stony graves, with their pottery, tools, weapons and food about them. In a long row of cases around the reproduced graves are relics taken from the excavations. Here are pieces of dried fish, sea-crabs and various fruits.

Relics from other Peruvian and Chilean graveyards are also shown in the Anthropological building, and it is gratifying to know that this exhibit will remain as a permanent feature of the museum to be established in Chicago after the Fair. The most curious feature of the entire exhibit is that the ancient Peruvians almost invariably chose a desert spot for their graveyards, as in the little island of LaPlata, about thirty miles off the coast of Ecuador, which is now barren and uninhabited. In the graves on this island were found images of gold and silver and pottery of remarkably fine workmanship. The bodies had crumbled to ashes.

Abandonment of Cemeteries.

The Supreme Court of California has decided the case of the city of Stockton v. Weber against the city. The court found that for about 10 years prior to 1860, Charles Weber was the owner of a tract of land adjacent to the city of Stockton. That he surveyed and platted the same into lots and blocks and public streets, a part of which was a block in question; and said Weber until his death, and since that time his heirs owned said tract so laid out continuously from the year 1860, to the time of the trial. That prior to 1860, said C. M. Weber permitted a number of dead bodies to be buried in said block under a verbal license. That no time was fixed or agreed upon during which they should remain, nor when they should be removed. That said C. M. Weber, deceased, and his heirs, always reserved his and their rights as the absolute owners of said block in fee simple. That no burials were ever permitted by C. M. Weber without a reservation of all his rights in and to said block, and the whole thereof, and he never consented to its use by the public as a burial ground. That no part of it was ever used by the public for a burial ground for five years, nor was there ever an uninterrupted use thereof by the public for any purpose; and that it never was dedicated to nor accepted by the public as a cemetery. The testimony showed that the first interment in that block was in or about 1852, and the last in the spring of 1862, that about 1861, the Rural Cemetery was established; and that prior to the execution of the deed hereinafter mentioned, nearly all the bodies had been removed from that block. The number remaining was not definitely shown, but said to be "six or more." Under the circumstances the court held that notwithstanding one section of the Political Code of that state vests title in the inhabitants of a city or town to lands "used" as a "public" cemetery, another declares a place where six or more bodies are buried "a cemetery," and a third declares no part of the Code retroactive, unless so expressed, the title to the land which has ceased to be used as a public cemetery before enactment of said sections is not affected thereby, but remains in the original owner; and that upon abandonment for cemetery purposes, and removal of bodies, the title would be discharged from such use. The title to the block in controversy therefore remained in Weber notwithstanding the use of the ground for burial purposes, subject to such use, and the abandonment of the ground for such use, and the removal of all the bodies, would leave the absolute title discharged from such use in his heirs. And, when, on the 12th day of May, 1880, said Charles M. Weber, by a deed signed, sealed, and acknowledged by him, and by him delivered to the city of Stockton, sold, granted, bargained, and conveyed to it, for a nominal consideration, said block, to be preserved and kept as an ornamental square, and for the erection of public buildings thereon; provided the city should obtain authority from the legislature, and remove the dead therefrom within certain time, with reverter to the grantor in case of sale or otherwise to private uses, abandonment of the land for cemetery purposes and removal of the bodies was a condition precedent to the vesting of title. Nor is such a condition void as in contravention of a provision of the state constitution forbidding special legislation, since, if other and general legislation could be obtained, it made the condition simply impossible, not unlawful.

A Vigorous Appeal for Reform.

The Rev. Dr. Harcourt, a Methodist minister of San Francisco, delivered a sermon some time ago on the subject of "Undertakers and Funerals." In referring to funerals he said: "The world is growing better, and in the conduct of the funerals of the past as compared with the present, this fact becomes very evident. Some of you who hear me to-night can remember well the time when the death of some neighbor or friend was looked upon as a great occasion for eating, drinking and smoking. A few years ago it was not thought decent to have a funeral without treating the relations and friends to liquors of all kinds—now such a thing is seldom, if ever, heard of. In place of liquors we have flowers—a wonderful transformation.

"Flowers have a very appropriate place at funerals. Yet, it is possible to go to extremes, even in these beautiful expressions of love and sympathy. A single handful of flowers on a plain coffin is often more expressive of love and worth than wagon loads of floral display. The former may speak of undying love and remembrance, while the latter may be but the grand display of a well-filled pocketbook. Now, while I am a believer in, and favor the custom of carrying flowers to the funeral service of the friend, I would not have you wait until your friend is dead before you present the floral expression of your love and esteem. Send some to the sick room, with your card attached, if you cannot go in person. One rose bud for the living will exceed in value one thousand rose buds for the dead! I am an advocate of more expressions of love and esteem for the living and not any less for the dead.

"There is one and one-fourth more money expended annually for funerals in the United States than the government expends for public schools. We are slaves to the tyrant of custom. There is much need of reform and of the establishment of a proper public sentiment in the matter of reducing the expenses of burial. Cremation presents the most feasible measure for remedying the evils of costly funerals.

"I consider it an evil to expose our dead in the churches for public gaze. Some are found in all the throngs that gaze upon the dead in public assemblies who would not have dared to look the person, while living, in the face. Another evil is that of burying our dead on the Sabbath. This is an open violation of the fourth commandment, and also a violation of one of the rules of discipline of the Methodist Episcopal church.

"I utter my protest against burying the dead on the Sabbath in behalf of the carriage-horses that need rest; in behalf of the drivers who should have one day in the week to themselves; in behalf of the grave-diggers; in behalf of the undertaker; in behalf of the ministers."

Title to Cemetery Lot Acquired by Adverse Possession.

The title to a cemetery lot or other land which can be acquired by merely using same for burial purposes is termed an easement, or right of use. Like the fee-simple title to land, an easement, or simple right of use, whether acquired by deed or by possession, may be lost by entry and continuous adverse possession for the statutory period by even a wrong-doer, and his title so acquired cannot be defeated by the owner of the soil, but will by descent pass to heirs at law. The question arises what is the nature and extent of the adverse possession required in order to ultimately ripen into a title to an easement of a burial lot? It seems to us, say the Court of Appeals of Kentucky, in Hook v. Joyce (22 Southwestern Reporter 651), burial of the dead body is the only possession, where claimed and known, necessary to ultimately create complete ownership of the easement, so as to render it inheritable. And as long as it is inclosed as a burial place, or even without inclosure, as long as gravestones stand marking the place as burial ground, the possession is, from the nature of the case, necessarily, and therefore in legal contemplation actual, adverse and notorious. Moreover, there cannot be an actual ouster of possession by an intruder, or running of the statute of limitations in his favor while such gravestones stand there, indicating by inscription the previous burial of another. And non-residence does not divest an heir at law of such easement; the gravestones of his parents being, as long as they stand, conclusive of his claim of ownership as well as right of entry. The case decided was in the nature of an action of ejectment brought by an heir to recover of a purchaser from the city of Paducah of a cemetery lot in which his parents and brother were buried. Nothwithstanding that the city of Paducah purchased a tract of land, including the lot in question, and laid it out for burial purposes in 1847, and sold the lot in 1881 to the person against whom the action was brought, from the fact that it had been held adversely to all the world against all persons for fifteen years, the statutory time in that state to acquire title by prescription. For the reasons above given he was held to have acquired the easement claimed, and was given damages for the removal of tombstones and desecration of the graves of his ancestors which, however, did not exceed $100.

The Superintendents' Convention.

There is every prospect for a large and interesting gathering of cemetery officials at Minneapolis on the occasion of the seventh annual convention of the Association of American Cemetery Superintendents. An excellent program has been prepared and has already appeared in these columns, aside from the profitable discussion of the many papers that it contains and questions that have been sent in, much interest will center in the visits to Lakewood, Oakland and the parks of Minneapolis and St. Paul and their subsequent discussion by John G. Barker and Timothy McCarthy. These gentlemen are superintendents of two of the finest cemeteries in New England, being in charge, respectively, of Forest Hills at Boston, and Swan Point at Providence, and eminently qualified to discuss from an artistic point of view the creations of their brethren in the Northwest. A pleasant and profitable time may be anticipated and it is hoped that the membership of the association will be materially increased from the cemeteries of Minnesota, Wisconsin and Iowa.

Crown Hill Cemetery, Indianapolis, Ind.

Three miles and a half northeast of the center of the city of Indianapolis, adjoining its northern suburbs, and on the highest ground in the vicinity, lies Crown Hill Cemetery. The ground chosen for the site is nearly two hundred feet above the streets of the city; so diversified with hill and plain, gentle modulations and lowly dells, heavy forest and open lawn, that there is not a foot of the ground that can not be conveniently used, nor a foot that can not be made beautiful and grateful to the weary or perhaps grief-stricken visitor.

On the 12th of September, 1863, three pioneer citizens of Indianapolis, who had been chiefly concerned in the planning and extension of the old graveyard, called a meeting for the consideration of the far more important work of establishing a new cemetery. These citizens were James Blake, Calvin Fletcher, Sr., and James M. Ray, all of whom now rest in the home of the dead so largely created by their public spirit. To their initial meeting they invited Mr. John Chislett, then superintendent of the Allegheny Cemetery, at Pittsburg. Mr. Chislett strongly advised the purchase of the Crown Hill site, and the committee, relying very largely on his counsel, purchased the property, which now contains, with recent additions, 348 acres, making it one of the largest cemeteries in the world, and fully entitled, both in extent and beauty, to rank with our leading American cemeteries.

Crown Hill was formally dedicated with appropriate ceremonies on the 1st of June, 1864. The fundamental principle of the organization then promulgated was that all receipts from the sale of lots shall be restricted to the maintenance and improvement of the cemetery; except that, after twenty-five years, any twenty-five corporators of the cemetery may direct the managers, if a fund sufficient for all cemetery uses has been accumulated, to appropriate a portion to the benefit of the poor of Indianapolis. This unalterable provision is a perpetual assurance that the property can never be devoted to speculative purposes. The board of managers is elected annually by the board of incorporators, and vacancies in the latter body are filled by vote of the remaining members. The board of incorporators is therefore self-perpetuating.

It is given to but few men to foresee the changes that time will bring. Thirty years have elapsed since the projectors of Crown Hill Cemetery laid deep and broad the foundations of their philanthropic enterprise, and great are the changes wrought by those thirty years. At the time of the purchase of the site it was thought that it was too far from the city. Now it is evident that it could not advantageously be nearer. Then there was some objection on the score of the distance to be traversed. Now the cemetery is the terminus of three electric street-railway lines and is easily reached from every part of the city. The commanding view afforded from Crown Hill, the beauty and restfulness of its primeval foliage, which under the careful guardianship of the incorporators is destined never to be disturbed amid all the changes of an encroaching civilization, the great extent of the acreage of the cemetery, and the very general favor with which it is regarded by the citizens of Indianapolis—all these and other considerations combine to testify to the wisdom of the original incorporators and the care of their successors.

Crown Hill Cemetery was organized on the principle that every lot-owner has an interest equal to that of the incorporators. On this basis the management has been conducted for thirty years, and to this principle is largely due the remarkable success attained. From a primeval forest, or swampy glade, the greater part of the large tract belonging to the corporation has been converted into a vast and exquisite lawn, studded with native trees and groups of shrubbery, swelling into graceful undulations or sinking into shaded and solitary dells, and everywhere revealing the sedulous care and earnest labors of the superintendent. The simple uniformity and harmony of the grounds is the result of the policy of banishing conspicuous marks of individual interest, except monuments, and, fortunately, this policy has been generally concurred in by the lot-owners. Crown Hill may be said to have gone to the extreme of the tendency to reduce the prominence of individual display, simplifying as far as possible the entire scheme of landscape decoration.

The adoption of this policy is due largely to the influence of the late Mr. Adolph Strauch, formerly superintendent of Spring Grove Cemetery, Cincinnati; also to Mr. John Chislett and, since his decease, to his son, the present superintendent of Crown Hill, Mr. Frederick W. Chislett. The policy of these gentlemen has been, in accordance with modern ideas of cemetery gardening, to make their burial ground as attractive as a park. The glare of monuments and copings has been avoided as far as possible, and the attractiveness of graceful foliage and handsome lawns has been substituted for the bare hideousness of the old-fashioned graveyard. The approaches to the cemetery are along foliage-embowered roads. Within the entrance and close to the ground set apart for a national cemetery, are the chapel and vaults. The vault and chapel combined is a handsome Gothic structure built entirely of Indiana stone. The chapel is in the center of the building, a large room with stained glass windows, tiled floor and walls and groined arched

EX-PRESIDENT HARRISON'S FAMILY MONUMENT, CROWN HILL CEMETERY.

ceiling of carved stone. The vaults are wings on each side of the chapel and connected with it by heavy double sliding doors. The crypts are of heavy stone, each crypt holding one casket and are so arranged and ventilated as to be cool and dry at all seasons. The chapel has a seating capacity of over two hundred. The building cost about $40,000. The monumental attractions are many and varied and include memorials to several distinguished persons. A gray granite shaft twenty feet in height marks the last resting place of ex-President Thomas A. Hendricks, and not far from it is the family monument to Oliver P. Morton. This consists of an ornate marble pedestal surmounted by a life-size bust of the deceased statesman. The family lot of ex-President Harrison is in Crown Hill and will soon be marked by the monument illustrated on this page. Mr. Harrison was recently elected a director of the cemetery. There are over four thousand lot-owners and the total number of interments exceeds fourteen thousand.

A stone coffin weighing 1,500 pounds has been completed in Lexington, Ky., for Stephen Langford, an eighty-year-old land-owner, of Madison County. He is in the best of health, but says he wishes to preserve his body from polecats, minks, and other like animals.—*Casket.*

In endeavoring to perpetuate the memory of the departed by the use of monuments, mausoleums or cemetery work of such character, care should always be exercised in regard to design, material and execution. A monument is not a thing for a day, but is expected to endure for years and that too in a spot fraught with fondest memories. Too many lots, even in our best cemeteries, are marked by inartistic specimens of the stonecutters' art, simply because sufficient care has not been exercised in the selection of design or material, or too much confidence has been placed in the final outcome of a highly colored drawing. It has been the constant effort of many cemetery officials to improve the condition of their grounds by doing away with the hedges, fences and inclosures of whatever kind. Now cannot they take another step and advise with their lot-owners in the selection of suitable memorials. The interest of the lot-owner and the welfare of the cemetery are so closely allied that what is detrimental to one must prove so to both. In regulating the sizes of head-stones that shall be used, cemetery managers have conferred a favor upon lot-owners that they cannot fail to appreciate, and we believe that lot-owners would value the advice and suggestions of cemetery officials in regard to larger memorials.

BUDDHIST TOPE AT SARNATH, BENARES.

Monuments of India.

The history of architecture in India commences with the reign of Asoka, 270 to 234 B.C. It is quite appropriate that the prince, who established the Buddhist church, first discarded the flimsy and perishable material of wood hitherto used for building, and employed the more solid and lasting stone. The earliest stone monuments still existing date from the third century B. C., and for five or six centuries following all architecture that still remains was enlisted in the service of the church.

Besides cutting inscriptions in rock, in the twelfth and the thirteenth year of his reign, Asoka set up a number of pillars throughout his counrty, which made the doctrines of his faith known to his subjects. Of these pillars, *stambhas* or *lats*, as they are called, only a few are still existing. The most complete is that at Allahabad; it gives us an idea of what the hundreds of pillars that have disappeared must have been. Its shaft, 33 feet long, 3 feet wide at the base, and 2 feet 2 inches wide at the summit, resembles the tapering stem of a pine tree. It bore a crowning ornament—a wheel, or perhaps the figure of an animal—which has disappeared. This pillar—which bears the inscriptions of Asoka (250 B. C.); of Samudra Gupta (380–400 A. D.) detailing the glories of his reign; of Jehangir the Mogul emperor (1605 A. D.) commemorating his accession, and which is now placed on a pedestal in the English fort at Allahabad—illustrates the strange vicissitudes of Indian history. Another class of monuments, which have come down to us from the third century, are the towers, *Stupas* or *Topes*, which commemorate an event or mark a spot, sacred to the followers of Buddha; and the Dagobas which contain relics of their lord or one of his saints.

The best known of the topes which still presents distinct architectural features is at Sarnath, where Buddha first expounded the truth, "turned the wheel of the law" to his former disciples. On a mound of brick and stone ruins, half a mile long and a quarter of a mile broad, there are the remains of brick towers and buildings, prominent amongst which is the great tower, as it is called, of Dhamek. In 1835 it was examined by General Cunningham, who gives its measurement as 109 feet 10 inches in height, 292 feet in circumference, 93 feet in diameter at its base. The lower part of the monument has eight projecting faces, each 21 feet 6 inches in width, with intervals of 15 feet between them. In each face, 24 feet above the ground, there is a niche five and a half feet in width and height. Each niche no doubt contained life-size statues of Buddha; the statues have disappeared, but the ornamentation has remained. It consists of a profusion of flowing foliage on each face, on either side of the niche; and of a triple band, 9 feet in depth, the upper and the lower of which represents lotus blossoms and flowers, while the middle contains geometrical designs, all of exquisite beauty, surrounding the whole tower. The upper part of the building remained unfinished; it was to have been encircled, most probably, with pilasters, and covered with a dome. Excavations brought to light an inscription—to judge from the characters, of the seventh century—containing the Buddhist profession of faith: "Of all things proceeding from cause, their causes hath the Buddha explained; (he) hath likewise explained the cause of the cessation of existence."—*The Religions of India.*

SCULPTURE ON TOPE AT SARNATH.

The Coming Cemetery.

In a recent issue of the Rochester, N. Y. *Union and Signal*, there appeared an interesting description of the new Riverside cemetery near that city, which is being developed on the most approved lines. The article gave the substance of a conversation had with an official of the cemetery, which is so thoroughly in accord with modern ideas on cemetery matters, that we reprint it in full:—

"In this age of culture and refinement, people are demanding many changes in habits and customs. Many grotesque customs are permitted simply on account of their antiquity and because they have worked their way into the lives of men and women through many centuries of habit. The conventional cemetery must change its old-time fashion and appear in line with reason, good taste and that simplicity of form which comports with true art.

"The majority of the people have long since learned the lesson of that simplicity which is the soul of art, but from fear of criticism have recoiled from leadership in reform. But now, thanks to education and its enlightening influences, the trend of social taste is towards that simplicity.

"The conventional cemetery has evolved into nothing more inspiring than a stone mason's and marble cutter's show ground, and the lines of true art have been cruelly ignored. The sentiment back of this vulgar display, though, in the main actuated by deep feeling and real affection for the dead, is built upon a false estimate of duty and a desire for ostentation.

"Pride and vanity has done much to mar and disfigure every cemetery in the world, and nothing is more irksome and distasteful to the cultivated mind than the display of acres of unmeaning, ill-formed, impotic and conventional creations of the marble cutter's hands. The coming cemetery is going to be entirely different in many respects to the old. Mother Nature, with its divine art, its glorious diversity of form and color, its inexhaustible resources and its immortal lessons will, under the guiding hands of skillful artists, usurp the place now occupied by the vulgar hand of ostentation.

"The lesson of future cemetery adornment and conduct is learned in that sublime utterance of the Master, who in speaking of the common lilies, exclaimed: 'And yet I say unto you that even Solomon in all his glory was not arrayed like one of these!' Men and women now realize that the highest and most ornate shaft of marble that was ever fashioned by man does not convey so lofty a sentiment of love and devotion, nor teach so sweet a lesson of faith and hope as a common flower fashioned by the hand of God."

Allowances for Tombstones.

One of the questions raised in the case of Howard's Estate recently decided by the Surrogate's Court of Cattaraugus County, New York (23 N. Y. Supp. 836), related to an indebtedness of $300 incurred by the executor for a tombstone to be placed at the grave of the testator. Shortly after the death of testator the executor caused an inexpensive tombstone to be placed at his grave. The remains of deceased were subsequently removed to another burial place, and thereafter the executor entered into an agreement for the purchase of another tombstone for testator at an expense of $300. The expense of a tombstone, if not excessive, will be allowed to an executor, upon his accounting. Wood v. Vandenburgh, 6 Paige, 277. The term "funeral expenses" includes the cost of a suitable tombstone to be erected at the grave of the deceased. Owens v. Bloomer, 14 Hun, 296. This expenditure being such a one as the executor was authorized to make, the only question was as to whether the amount was reasonable or not. In Re Erlacher, 3 Redf. Sur. 8, where the estate amounted to $2,625, it was held that the administrator should be allowed only $250 of the $700 expended by him for monument and inclosing burial lot. In Re Mount, Id. 9, note, the administrator, out of an estate of $938, paid $425 for funeral expenses; and it was held that only $200 should be allowed for funeral expenses, and $50 for a gravestone. In Valentine v. Valentine, 4 Redf. Sur. 265, an expenditure of $350, where the estate was $13,000, was held not unreasonable. So it is apparent that there is no arbitrary rule for determining the question of reasonable funeral expenses and expenses of tombstone, but each case must be disposed of upon its own particular circumstances. In this case there was originally an estate of over $6,000, with accumulations thereon to much more than that sum. The rights of creditors were in no manner impaired by the expenditure, and, as against the legatees under the will of testator, all of whom were collateral, the court said the expenditure of $300 it must be held that the expense incurred is reasonable and proper.

A funeral custom creeping into New York city is the fashion of leaving cards at the tombs of friends who are buried in city cemeteries. Small baskets are placed in the urns of flowers over the graves for receiving the cards. When the family visit the grave they can see who have called and learn to appreciate the sincere devotion of their friends. One would naturally view such a fad with repugnance, but I favor it says a writer in the *Oakland Tribune*, as it will have a tendency to induce people to care for the resting places of the dead more tenderly than is now the custom.

CEMETERY NOTES.

At the instigation of the board of health of Malden, Mass., Holy Cross Cemetery has been investigated and found to contain many violations of the law requiring three-foot graves. Proper reinterment has been required in each instance.

An old rule at Ferncliff Cemetery, Springfield, O., provides that the cemetery gates shall remain closed in the forenoon on Sundays. For some reason it was overlooked or disregarded for some time, but is now being enforced and lot-owners having tickets of admission are admitted on that day from 1 to 6 p. m.

The trustees of the recently organized Edgewood Cemetery, at Nashua, N. H., have engaged the services of a Boston landscape artist to prepare plans for the improvement of their cemetery. Both the old and new portions of the grounds will be treated in the new plan, which contemplates the addition of a lake, an extensive water system and other permanent improvements that will give Nashua one of the most modern cemeteries in the Granite state.

A long-standing dispute between the city of Newark, N. J. and Mt. Pleasant Cemetery Association about assessments on the latter's property has just been settled. The association's charter provided that it should be exempt from assessments until the Chosen Freeholders decided that it should pay them. In 1891 the Freeholders by resolution declared that the time for exemption had passed. The Common Council has decided to cancel the assessments made prior to that time.

By the will of the late Wm. A. Marriott of Altoona, Pa., $9,000 is bequeathed to the Altoona Fairview Cemetery Association. The money must be expended for a chapel and is subject to the further condition that the cemetery shall never become an institution for the profit of its stockholders. Among many other bequests made by Mr. Marriott was one of $1,000 in trust to the mayor of the city, who is to distribute the interest thereon among the deserving poor of the city every winter.

The Supreme Court of Brooklyn has granted a lot-owner a permanent injunction restraining the sale of the Union Cemetery. The Legislature last year passed an act prohibiting any further burials in the cemetery and permitting the trustees to sell the property. When Mr. West, the lot-owner, brought suit, the trustees, it is understood, were negotiating with a building company for the sale of the property and the removal of the bodies. The court held that the deed of plaintiff's lot conveyed to him the perpetual right of burial there, unless, in the exercise of police power of the State, interments were forbidden on account of the public health.

Parched and burned describes the condition of many village burying grounds at this season of the year. Scarcity of water has browned the luxuriant growth of grass and weeds, and in some places the spark from a passing locomotive has fired the dry grass and left everything desolate. The monuments and markers resemble so many spectres arising from their blackened surroundings, and the place looks even worse than it did when shrouded in weeds and rank grass. A little attention in the spring would obviate, in a measure, such an undesirable condition at a time when every "God's Acre" should blossom as the rose.

The Westminster Cemetery Co. of Philadelphia have been enjoined by the city against establishing a cemetery in Lower Marion on the Schuylkill, on the ground that its drainage would pollute the waters of the river and endanger public health. In their answer to the suit the cemetery company asserts that the use of the land for cemetery purposes would not pollute the water or be in any way prejudicial to health. They also state that the act of the Assembly for 1891, prohibiting the establishing of cemeteries within one mile of cities of the first class is unconstitutional.

Russian Jews have a burial custom peculiar to themselves. In that country the undertakers keep handsome, silver-mounted burial caskets, to which the bottom is attached by springs. After the funeral ceremonies are over, and the coffin has been lowered into the grave, the mourners withdraw and the coffin is lifted out, leaving its bottom and the corpse in the grave. These show caskets are let to the poor at reasonable rates, and they can have a fine funeral at small cost. A Norwich, Conn. undertaker had a request for such a coffin the other day, and being unable to furnish it, the Russian community had one made and will use it hereafter.

A Cincinnati judge refused to enjoin the officers of the German Catholic Cemetery from refusing permission to a lot-owner to remove the remains of his deceased children from the cemetery. The plaintiff had become a Protestant, and desired to bury his children in Protestant ground. The judge's holding is that the next of kin have the right to designate where their dead shall be buried, and, the burial once having taken place, there is no right of property in the dead body upon which a claim can be asserted. In the case at bar the children had been buried about four years. Were the plaintiff about to remove to another city, and wished to remove the bodies to his new home, the Court intimated that there might be reason for giving him a hearing, but under the present circumstances his petition must be denied.—*Cincinnati paper.*

The cemetery at Fort Madison, Ia., shows such evidences of neglect that one of the lot-owners asked the editor of the local paper to insert an item to the effect that the treasurer was still living and would be glad to receipt for dues.

Some years ago the city of Dover, N. H., was bequeathed the sum of $5,000 in trust, the interest to be used in caring for the city cemetery. Since that time the annual appropriations have been gradually diminishing until now only the interest from this bequest is used and the people are untaxed for cemetery maintenance. Inasmuch as the grounds are not cared for in the manner they should be, this is no less than a violation of the trust and another argument against having cemeteries under municipal control.

Some months ago a committee of lot-owners was appointed by the trustees of Lowell Cemetery, Lowell, Mass., to procure and recommend a plan for a new gateway. Three prizes aggregating $300, was offered as an inducement for architects to compete, and at the time the competition closed last month fourteen designs had been received. The winner of the first prize was Mr. John Spencer of Chicago, whose design is thus described by the *Lowell Times*:

It is in the style known as Roman Doric, and consists of four columns, two on either side of the gateway, each pair supporting an entablature suitably ornamented, with a wide cornice. The gates themselves are of iron, with bronze panels at the bottom, and are surmounted by an iron cornice of conventional design connecting the capitals of the columns on either side. These stone columns are 16 feet to the top of the capitals, and the height of the entire structure is 21 feet 10 inches. The adaptation of columns and entablature for the purpose of an entrance gateway is original, and the design will give a pleasing and monumental effect. On either side of the driveway is to be a footpath provided with an iron gate of similar pattern, outside of which is a stone pier with suitable cap. The gateway is recessed into the cemetery about ten feet. The whole design is very imposing and would be very effective when viewed from a distance, as well as a nearer view.

[Mr. Spencer holds the responsible position of superintendent of construction with one of our leading firms of architects, and his extended experience has been such as to qualify him for the successful execution of his prize design.—*Ed.*]

"We are revising our recently adopted rules, absolutely prohibiting mounds over graves and limiting the pieces of stone work to one upon each entire lot, that is, but one monument, headstone, grave-mark, or stone structure of any description, *rising above the level of the lawn*, will be permitted; all other marks will be set with their tops level with the lawn, and containing their lettering or inscription upon their upper surface."—*Dean Alvord, Mgr. Riverside Cemetery Assn., Rochester, N. Y.*

Epitaphs.

This collection of English and Scottish cemetery gleanings is furnished by the London *Funeral Directors' Journal*.

The following in Penrith Churchyard is refreshing in these days of deceit, on account of its candor:—

> Here lies the man Richard and Mary his wife;
> Their surname was Pritchard, and they lived without strife.
> The reason was plain—they abounded in riches;
> They had no care nor pain, and the wife wore the breeches.

The owner of this inscription, now resting in Hebburn Churchyard, was probably a Democrat and had some little opinion of himself:—

> This humble monument will show,
> Here lies an honest man;
> You Kings, whose heads are now as low,
> Rise higher if you can!

John Dale was a courageous man. This is the epitaph over his remains in Bakewell Churchyard, Derbyshire:—

> Know posterity that on the 8th of April, in the year of grace 1757, the rambling remains of John Dale were, in the 86th year of his pilgrimage, laid upon his two wives:—
> This thing in life might raise some jealousy;
> Here all three lie together lovingly.

One epitaph in Ilfracombe Churchyard shows faith:—

> Weep not for me, my friends so dear,
> I am not dead, but sleeping here;
> My debt is paid, my grave is free,
> And in due course you'll come to me.

Not far from this we have an example of quiet self-glorification:—

> Here lies a kind and loving wife
> A tender nursing mother—
> A neighbor free from brawl and strife,
> A pattern for all others.

Evidently marriage was not a failure in this case.

What follows was formerly on a tombstone in St. Thomas' Churchyard, Salisbury:—

> Here lies three babes dead as nits,
> God took them off in agie fits;
> They was too good to live wi' we,
> So he took 'em off to live wi' 'ee.

Who dares utter the foul slander that it requires a surgical operation to get a joke into the head of a Scotchman? Let he or she cast their eye over the following, and then sit silent forever. It is on a gravestone in Stonehaven Churchyard:—

> "The place whaur Betty Cooper lies
> Is here or here about;
> The place whaur Betty Cooper lies
> There's neen can fin' it oot;
> The place where Betty Cooper lies
> There's neen on earth can tell,
> Till at the resurrection day,
> When Betty tells hersel'."

THE MODERN CEMETERY.

A MONUMENT IN FAIRMOUNT CEMETERY, NEWARK, N. J.

Monumental Notes.

In one of the new sections of Fairmount Cemetery, Newark, N. J., may be seen the novel monument shown in the above illustration. The pedestal and ball are of Quincy granite and the figure of the child is in bronze, cast from a model by Mr. John Rogers, the New York sculptor. The monument is octagonal in form with a diameter of eight feet at the base and rising to a height of 17 feet 6 inches. Circular inscription tablets ornamented with wreaths of ivy are on each of the eight sides of the die. The sphere above is nearly 5 feet in diameter and so highly polished as to reflect surrounding objects as clearly as a mirror. Resting lightly on this massive pedestal is the life-like figure of a babe modeled a little larger than life. The design, which has been copyrighted, is original with Mr. H. T. Clawson of Newark, the father of the babe, to whom we are indebted for the photograph from which the engraving was made.

* * *

In the interior of the costly mausoleum in which the remains of the late Leland Stanford were recently laid to rest, there are no crypts or vaults commonly found in such structures. In the spacious room, 15 ft. x 22 ft. 3 in., with its floor, walls and ceiling of white marble, are three sarcophagi measuring 8 ft. 6 in. x 5 ft. 6 in. x 4 ft., cut from single blocks of Italian marble and designed expressly for the bodies of father, mother and son. Each sarcophagus is lined with heavy steel plates, is provided with a carved marble cover and bears an appropriate inscription. The mausoleum covers a ground space of 50 x 30 feet and is constructed of Vermont granite. The cost exceeded $100,000.

* * *

"Eminent as a poet, rarely accomplished as a linguist, learned and acute in science—a man without guile," is a portion of the epitaph on the monument recently placed at the grave of the poet James Gates Percival, at Hazel Green, Wis.

* * *

An imposing monument of Georgia granite has just been completed in Oakwoods Cemetery, Chicago, commemorative of the seven thousand Confederate soldiers buried there. A statue in bronze of a Confederate infantryman eight feet in height surmounts the shaft, and bronze relief plates in the die represent "The Call to Arms," "The Lost Cause," "The Eternal Sleep" and the seal of the Confederacy. The memorial was erected by ex-Confederates at a cost of about $7,000.

* * *

The famous leaning tower of Pisa is a campanile or bell tower. It was begun in 1174 by the two famous architects—Bonano of Pisa and William Innspruck. The tower, which is cylindrical in form, is 179 feet high and 50 feet in diameter, made entirely of white marble. It has eight stories, each with an outside gallery projecting several feet from the building, and each decorated with columns and arcades. In the center of the tower a flight of 320 steps passes up to the summit. It is called the leaning tower from the fact that it inclines some thirty feet from the perpendicular, and it is not generally known that this inclination, which gives the tower such a remarkable appearance, was not intentional. At the time it was about half done the error in measurement was perceived, and it was guarded against by the use of extra braces in the further construction of the building and an adaptation of the stone in the highest portion. There are seven bells on the top of the tower, the largest of which weighs 12,000 pounds, and these are so placed as to counteract, as far as possible, the leaning of the tower itself.—*Ex*.

* * *

A receiving vault of brick and stone is in course of erection at Woodmere cemetery, Detroit, Mich. The building will cost $15,000.

Mound Builders.

It is generally believed that the Mississippi Valley and the Atlantic coast were once populated by an agricultural and partially civilized race quite different from the nomadic Indians, though possibly the progenitors of some of the Indian tribes, and that, after centuries of occupation, they disappeared, at least a thousand, and perhaps many thousand years before the advent of Europeans. The theory has been advanced that these people migrated from Asia, and that they passed over Asia to Siberia, across Behring Straits, down the Pacific Coast of America from Alaska and to the Mississippi Valley, and down to Mexico, Central America and Peru. The remains of the Mound-Builders, as this vanished people are called, are scattered over most of the states of the central and lower Mississippi Valley, along the banks of the Missouri and on the sources of the Allegheny. They are most numerous in Ohio, Indiana, Illinois, Wisconsin, Missouri, Arkansas, Kentucky, Tennessee, Mississippi, Alabama, Georgia, Florida, Texas, and are found in the western part of New York and in Michigan and Iowa. These mounds vary greatly in size; in some instances are very extensive and exceedingly intricate, notably those of the Licking Valley near Newark, Ohio, which cover an area of two square miles. In other localities there are some which reach a height of ninety feet. It is not believed that these people had any written language, as no inscriptions or tablets yet discovered indicate this. Many of these mounds have been found to contain skeletons, numerous implements and ornaments, usually composed of stone, sometimes of copper; also rude and coarse pottery of curious design. In substantiation of the belief that these people came from Asia is the fact that in Siberia mounds have been found similar to those in the Mississippi Valley.

The Schneider System of Cremation.

The system of cremation used in the new cremation urn at Cypress Lawn Cemetery, San Francisco, is that invented by Richard Schneider, an engineer who lives in Dresden, Saxony, says the San Francisco *Examiner*. It is the same introduced within the last year at Hamburg, and is probably the best process yet known. Under the Schneider system fuel is put into a gas regenerator and lighted, and when the gas is formed it is mixed with air. During the process of combustion the flame heats the fire-bricks which wall the incineration chamber, and the products of combustion after passing through the chamber and a fire-clay grating are carried off through a flue. After the fire has been burning for some hours the regenerator becomes bright red and the incineration chamber shows a white heat. Then the operation of reducing the human body to ashes may be commenced. The body is placed in a marble sarcophagus, which stands in a niche at the right of the main auditorium of the crematory. A button being pressed, the body is lowered by machinery into the preparation room, where it is stripped and wrapped in a sheet soaked in alum water. It is placed in an iron receptacle whose bottom is covered with a solution of alum and water. The door of the incineration chamber is then swung open and the body is given to the consuming heat. Through an opening in a door of the chamber the official in charge of the operation closely observes the progress of the incineration, and when it is concluded he reverses the gas and air valves and the ashes fall into the ashpit of the crematorium. No fire is visible. A rosy light, the product of more than 2,000 degrees of heat, plays around the shrouded form. No sight could be more impressive, few more beautiful.

The new marble columbarium of the United States Cremation Company at Fresh Pond, Long Island, was dedicated last month with appropriate ceremonies. The building contains niches for 600 urns. In his address, President Lange traced the progress of cremation and among other evidences of its growth in this country said that with the single exception of Japan, more bodies are incinerated yearly in the United States than in any other country, and the custom is constantly increasing. Some of the statistics are of interest. Of the one thousand and ten bodies cremated at Fresh Pond to date, six hundred and fifty were men, two hundred and seventy were women and eighty-eight children. Six hundred and seventy-five of the incinerants were foreign born, and of this number five hundred and ten were Germans. In Paris the number of incinerations ordered by families last year aggregated 139, while in New York they amounted to 200.

The current number of *The Urn* contains a most forcible argument in favor of cremation. It is in the form of an illustrated report of the commission on Sanitation of Cemeteries at Paris, and presents views of seven coffins and their contents in various stages of decomposition as exhumed from the cemetery of Saint Nazaire, Paris. The bodies were exhumed from five months to five years and present an appearance most repulsive, while the condition in which they are reported to have been found is painful to contemplate.

The practice of cremation in Japan appears to have been in vogue from the most ancient times, the investigations of archæologists having established the fact that it was practiced by prehistoric races.

Association of American Cemetery Superintendents.

WM. SALWAY, "Spring Grove" Cincinnati, O., President.
T. M. McCARTHY, "Swan Point" Providence, R. I., Vice-President.
F. EURICH, Woodlawn, Toledo, O., Secretary and Treasurer.

The Seventh Annual Convention of the Association will be held at Minneapolis on Tuesday, August 22, 23, 24 and 25, 1893.

Publisher's Department.

The receipt of Cemetery Literature and Trade Catalogues will be acknowledged in this column.

TO ADVERTISERS. THE MODERN CEMETERY is the only publication of its class and will be found a valuable medium for reaching cemetery officials in all parts of the United States.

TO SUBSCRIBERS. Cemetery officials desiring to subscribe for a number of copies regularly to circulate among their lot owners, should send for our special terms, several well known cemeteries have already adopted this plan with good results.

Contributions on matters pertaining to cemeteries are solicited. Address all communications to
R. J. HAIGHT, 334 Dearborn St., CHICAGO.

We are indebted to Mr. Geo. M. Brunner, Paterson, N. J., for photographs of the lodge and lake in Laurel Grove Cemetery.

A photograph of the vault and conservatory at Mount Pleasant Cemetery, Toronto, Ont., has been received from Mr. Henry Thompson, Superintendent, accompanied by a brief description. The structure is 50 x 100 feet, built of brown pressed brick with brown stone trimmings. The facade is of the gothic order of architecture with triple arches and double doors to the vault, which is kept well ventilated by means of an electric fan. The walls of the vault are 24 feet in height and support steel girders on which is constructed the conservatory and chapel 50 x 50 feet, the latter having a seating capacity of 100 persons. In the vault is located the machinery for lowering bodies from the chapel. The chapel conservatory and three forcing houses are heated by the hot water system.

Our request for suggestions as to the best method of keeping a record of interments has been productive of most gratifying results. Replies, accompanied in several instances by plats, diagrams, portions of record books, etc., have been received from the following named gentlemen, to whom we are indebted for many valuable suggestions, Frank D. Willis, St. Paul, Minn.; J. Mishler, Mogadore, O.; J. B. Russell, Macomb, Ill.; F. Jameson, Allegheny, Pa.; Henry Thompson, Toronto, Ont.; L. Andrews, Southington, Conn.; Geo. L. Transue Easton, Pa.; Wm. S. Moses, San Francisco, Cal.; J. G. Boyd, Louisville, Ky. We shall endeavor to incorporate the most valuable features of each method into our proposed record, and in due course of time produce a system that will be suitable for cemeteries large and small.

Situation Wanted.

Superintendent and landscape gardener with an extended experience desires situation; was nine years in one of principal Massachusetts cemeteries; references. Address S. H. G., care Modern Cemetery, Chicago.

BOOKS

LANDSCAPE GARDENING...
By SAMUEL PARSONS, Jr., Supt. of Parks, New York City. Notes and suggestions on Lawns and Lawn Planting, Laying out and arrangement of Parks, etc. Deciduous and Evergreen trees, shrubs, flowers and foliage—Ornamentation of Ponds and Lakes. 300 pages, nea ly 200 illustrations. Beautifully printed and bound. A charming book for landscape gardeners. Price $3.50. With the Modern Cemetery one year, $4.25.

ORNAMENTAL GARDENING FOR AMERICANS.
By ELIAS A. LONG.—This book has had a large sale among cemetery officials. Cloth binding, illustrated. Price $2.00, with the MODERN CEMETERY one year, $2.75.

THE NURSERY BOOK...
By L. H. BAILEY. A complete hand book of propagation. Paper covers 50 cents, cloth, $1.00.

Any of the above books or any other book or magazine will be sent prepaid at publishers prices.

R. J. HAIGHT, The Caxton Bldg., CHICAGO.

VIEW IN CEDAR HILL CEMETERY, NEWARK, O.

Half-Tone Engravings for Cemeteries

MADE DIRECT FROM PHOTOGRAPHS.

When writing for prices please state size of cut wanted.

R. J. HAIGHT, 334 Dearborn St., Chicago.

THE NEW HANDY BINDER

Will be found a most valuable invention for keeping the numbers of the MONUMENTAL NEWS in good condition. The method of binding allows the pages to lie perfectly flat, whether one or a dozen numbers are in the binder. Any number can be taken out and replaced without disturbing the other numbers. The binders are strong and durable and have the title of MODERN CEMETERY on the side in gilt, an ornament to any desk or reading table. We will supply them to subscribers in embossed cloth covers, 50 cents. Heavy flexible paper covers for 35 cents. By mail post-paid.

MODERN CEMETERY,
334 Dearborn St., Chicago.

THE MODERN CEMETERY.

THE MODERN CEMETERY.
AN ILLUSTRATED MONTHLY JOURNAL DEVOTED TO THE INTEREST OF CEMETERIES

R. J. HAIGHT, Publisher,
334 Dearborn Street, CHICAGO.

Subscription $1.00 a Year in Advance.   Foreign Subscription $1.25.
Special Rates on Six or More Copies.

VOL. III.   CHICAGO, SEPT. 1893.   NO. 7.

CONTENTS.

ANNUAL CONVENTION OF THE ASSOCIATION OF AMERI-
  CAN CEMETERY SUPERINTENDENTS 73
PERPETUAL CARE OF LOTS, *T. McCarthy* 74
*ENTRANCE TO LAKEWOOD CEMETERY, MINNEAPOLIS,
  MINN 76
THE OBJECT OF OUR ASSOCIATION, *O. C. Simmons* 76
*ENTRANCE TO OAKLAND CEMETERY, ST. PAUL MINN. 77
IS FLOWER PLANTING DESIRABLE IN THE MODERN
  CEMETERY? *Bellett Lawson* 77
*CHAPEL AND CONSERVATORY, OAKLAND CEMETERY,
  ST. PAUL 79
CONVENTION ECHOS 79
*EDGEWOOD CEMETERY NASHUA, N. H. 80
ARCHITECTURAL FOLIAGE—A CLASSIC EPITAPH 81
CHICAGO CEMETERIES 82
CEMETERY NOTES 83
PUBLISHERS DEPARTMENT 84
  *Illustrated.

Annual Convention of the Association of American Cemetery Superintendents.

For the first time in its history the Association of American Cemetery Superintendents held its annual gathering west of the Mississippi River, and with such gratifying results in point of attendance and excellence of program that there was but one opinion in regard to the success of the occasion. In accordance with the program the sessions of the seventh annual convention were held at the West Hotel, Minneapolis, commencing August 22d and continuing four days. After the usual preliminary business President Salway read his annual address in the course of which he said:

The individual experience of each member present is different from that of all others, consequently with a liberal exchange of the varied experiences this meeting becomes a vast field from which we may glean the kernels of knowledge unobtainable in any other way. We can, I think look back to the first meeting and see that each one has been of more interest than the one previous, and when contemplating the influence they exert we should be stimulated in our efforts to continue the good work. There is much to be done to remove, or improve old customs and forms now so prevalent in cemeteries which all practical cemetery men know to be superfluous. I refer to lot inclosures, high corner marks, gravel walks between lots, elaborate grave marks, grave decoration in its various forms, fanciful and gorgeous floral decorations for a few summer months and Sunday funerals. This does not comprise the list, but will be sufficient to show that we must, in order to progress, be constantly at work to supplant them with that which is of a more permanent nature, and in harmony with the general landscape. There are existing customs which every one knows to be wrong in general, but more objectionable in some places than in others; take for example the Sunday funeral. Considering the death rate of London, New York and Brooklyn and many other cities whose population numbers into the millions, the stopping of funerals for one day each week is a very serious matter and should be well considered before any legislative action is taken; but in the cities whose population will not exceed 300,000 I believe we might set aside the Sunday funeral with good results. The question of cremation is still an open one and will, I think, adjust itself. The incineration of the human body is not growing in favor as fast as might be expected. Yet it is quite probable that cemeteries of large cities will find it necessary to be provided with crematories on their own grounds.

The making and enforcement of all rules for the good government of cemeteries should be very carefully done and with due consideration for the feelings of those whose property and dead are under our care and keeping.

The superintendent should be the possessor of a tender and kindly nature, having at the same time the ability of deciding what to do and say at the proper time, so that he may preserve the rules without injury or offense to the grief-stricken lot-owner."

In his annual report Secretary Eurich stated that a number of new members had been enrolled since the Baltimore meeting, the total membership now being 138. Financially the condition was all that could be desired.

The subjects suggested for general discussion at this session were: 1st, Is the lawn plan to be recommended under any and all circumstances? 2nd, Is it essential with the lawn plan that every lot should border on a drive, path or alley? If so, what width? 3rd, What gutters are best suited for cemetery drains, and what are the best methods for keeping drives and gutters free from weeds? The first was answered in the affirmative; the second provoked considerable discussion and showed that there was a remarkable diversity of opinion on the subject of alleys and paths. It was voted that it is essential to the lawn plan that every lot should border on a drive, path or alley, and that it is not essential to have spaces between adjoining lots. President Salway recommended the use of benzine as the most effective and least expensive method of keeping cobble stone gutters free from weeds. It should be applied with a sprinkling can. Mr. McCarthy said he had gutters that looked almost too nice. On a well tamped foundation of sand he laid paving stone of different sizes and instead of putting sand in the spaces between the stones, as is commonly done, he used a thin solution of Portland cement. Care was taken to keep the cement away from the surface. Weeds in such gutters are unknown.

Through the courtesy of the officials of Lakewood Cemetery, conveyances were furnished in the afternoon and the superintendents and their ladies were driven through the principal streets of the city to Loring Park and Lakewood Cemetery where, owing to rain, a portion of the program had to be postponed. Arrangements had been made for a banquet on the lawn at Superintendent Hobert's residence, and this, too, was interfered with, but the hospitable superintendent and his wife threw open their doors and entertained their guests in a most enjoyable manner. After partaking of a delicious repast the evening was pleasantly spent, interspersed with singing and music.

SECOND DAY.

There was a largely increased attendance on the second day and several new members were added to the association.

The program for the morning session included the reading and discussion of three papers and as many more subjects from the Question Box. The papers were as follows: "Perpetual Care of Lots," by T. McCarthy, Providence, R. I.; "Drainage of Swampy and Wet Lands for Burial Purposes," by H. J. Diering, New York, and "Sunday Funerals," by John J. Stephens, Columbus, O.

A resolution was adopted to the effect that Sunday Funerals should be discouraged.

Secretary Eurich read a paper sent by Burritt Chaffee of Syracuse, N. Y., on "What Constitutes Judicious Planting." Mr. Chaffee having been detained at home by sickness.

The following is an extract from Mr. McCarthy's paper:

PERPETUAL CARE OF LOTS.

The necessity and importance of making some provision for the perpetual care of cemeteries is now so fully recognized and appreciated throughout the country that it is gratifying to know that the increasing interest and admirable results already obtained owe very much to the influence and intelligent efforts of this association. Such progress is surely sufficient excuse for our existence and some compensation for the labor and expense in attending these annual conventions.

A burial ground (says the writer) unprotected and neglected, presents a cheerless and sad spectacle. It would seem that the dead who lie in such a place had been strangely forgotten by the living, and that philosophy is cold and repulsive which teaches us that the body being an insensible mass of matter may be buried from our sight and never thought of any more, and so inseparably do we connect the feelings and character of the living with the appearance and condition of the place of their dead that Franklin's saying is applicable, "I only need to visit the burial ground of a community to know the character of the people." Hence no cemetery or burial ground to-day is complete or satisfactory which does not show, not only evidences of care and respect paid by individuals and families to the memory of their own dead, but evidences also of that respect which the community of the living should ever bear toward the community of the dead.

Now, while I cannot hope to enhance the importance of this subject, it may be well to call attention to the diversity of opinions and of practice that prevails as to the best method of securing perpetual care, and as the charges and application of this vary in the different cemeteries, I have no desire to recommend a fixed scale of prices for all cemeteries, or any "best plan." In my opinion each cemetery must be governed by the local conditions and advantages of its section of the country, such as the rate of interest, the cost of labor and materials, condition of the soil, severity of the climate, etc., or the exacting taste of your respective communities. All these and many other considerations will govern somewhat the cost of perpetual care. I might say here that the words "perpetual care" (although as smooth and consoling as a life-insurance policy) are too broad and often misleading, and seemingly promise more care than the interest of the fund or money left will admit.

The original intention and meaning of perpetual care in my vicinity included the care of the grass only, and I hear of many disappointments because myrtle graves, watering vases, cleaning head-stones, etc., are not included. Of course all these can be provided for by increasing the fund, and it would be well to have all such things definitely stated in the bond or contract made between the proprietor and the corporation, and thus avoid many misunderstandings in the future.

In my opinion, there are only two or three things connected with a burial lot, the care of which should be included and provided for, viz. the good appearance of the grass and all hardy shrubs and trees, and the cleaning and permanent position of head-stones and monuments. Many other items, some of a perishable existence and doubtful taste, could be readily dispensed with, and we continually discourage perpetuating flower beds (excepting hardy subjects), myrtle graves, vases and the care of hedges, fences, etc.

New cemeteries have no great difficulty in adopting perpetual care, at least for the grass and good appearance of the grounds, but these remarks are intended more for the older cemeteries which it is desirable to rescue from dilapidation and neglect, many lots and ground sold years ago, or before perpetual care was thought of.

To accomplish this, and before appealing to proprietors to leave money for the care of their respective grounds, the cemetery or corporation should do its part and give some assurance of greater neatness and higher keeping of the grounds, and thus secure the confidence and respect of the public.

When perpetual care was adopted in the cemetery under my charge, and when it was understood that dilapidation and neglect would no longer be tolerated, our sales perceptibly increased, and that too to citizens already owning lots in the numerous cemeteries in our vicinity, so that it is very evident that the greater the assurance a cemetery offers against such neglect, not only for our day, but for the future as far as human foresight can suggest, the more surely will it provide what the public demand, the greater will be its success and the higher will what it has to offer for sale be valued.

Swan Point was consecrated in 1847, and perpetual care was not adopted till 1877. During those 30 years many proprietors left money by will or otherwise, and many more who were able and could have done so, but by their delay and the reverses of fortune they have been prevented from making this provision for themselves and their families. Suffice it to say that since the adoption of perpetual care the amount received in any one year exceeded the voluntary contributions of the first 30 years.

ENTRANCE TO LAKEWOOD CEMETERY, MINNEAPOLIS.

About this time a scale of prices was adopted having reference to the care of the grass only. This was headed "Perpetual Care of Lots," and was mailed to the older proprietors as a guide and reminder to place their lots under care, and thus look like the newer sections.

The printing and distribution of this scale of prices was, I think, a mistake, as it deceived many who intended to provide for everything, when by will or otherwise they left only sufficient to care for the grass. The better way would be for the lot-owner or his representative making this provision to visit the cemetery, see the condition of his lot, state what he desires to provide for and obtain the proper information from the superintendent, and with all due respect for cemetery officials, he is the proper one to consult.

Scale of prices for perpetual care of grass only:

100 square feet		$ 50
200	" "	90
300	" "	130
400	" "	144
500	" "	165
600	" "	186
700	" "	206
800	" "	226
900	" "	245
1,000	" "	264
1,100	" "	282
1,200	" "	300

For lots containing over 1,200 feet, 25 cents per square foot.

When the above scale was adopted, some 16 years ago, the basis of our reckoning was 6%. Last year these funds earned only 5% and they are likely to realize still less in the future. So with the rates of interest decreasing and wages, etc. increasing, it may be a question if our scale of prices is not too low, but I will leave this to the convention, and as I said before, each cemetery will be governed by the conditions and advantages of its own section and people.

While the moneys or funds of cemeteries may be under various headings, and not always intelligible, I would suggest at least two funds: A perpetual care fund, which has reference to private lots only, and a permanent fund, the interest of which would be sufficient to care for all the property of the cemetery and meet expenses when there is no further income from the sale of land. This fund should be absolutely fixed, and as carefully guarded as the perpetual care fund. The method of its accumulation may vary, but the principal with the yearly additions and interest, should be allowed to accumulate for a long number of years, or till the land which created them is all sold. I think this fund is of vital importance, but I am anxious to make improvements in my day and so would like to leave its creation to my successor.

This was followed by a discussion of the following subjects: "Where can the line be drawn between a marker and a monument?" "How best to prevent graves from crumbling?" and "How best to open graves through deep frost?"

The discussion of the first subject brought out the fact that cemeteries conducted on the lawn plan restrict the height of stones placed to mark graves and permit but one monument or central structure to a lot. It was

Resolved: That it is the sense of this meeting that all headstones or markers should be limited to the height of the sod or the level or surface of the ground.

The weather in the afternoon being more propitious for sight seeing than on the previous day, the Lakewood Cemetery Co., kindly provided conveyances and gave the party a delightful drive to the parks and pleasure resorts around Minneapolis, terminating in a visit to Lakewood. Under the guidance of Superintendent Hobert and Mr. C. M. Loring a tour of the grounds was made. Lakewood contains about 165 acres of land, charmingly diversified and commanding at its highest points magnificent views of the surrounding country. The imposing granite entrance with its handsome offices, the commodious receiving tomb and chapel and the excellent condition of the grounds, which are conducted entirely on the lawn plan, elicited many words of commendation.

At the evening session John G. Barker of Forest Hills, Boston, made a "Report on the Visit to Lakewood," in which he referred to it in the most complimentary manner. This was followed by an able paper by O. C. Simonds of Graceland Cemetery, Chicago on:

The Object of Our Association.

Our constitution says "The object of this association shall be the advancement of the interests and the elevation of the character of cemeteries in America."

The interests of a cemetery are advanced by anything that aids to its material welfare, such as the introduction of simpler methods, the keeping of better accounts and records, greater economy in the expense for labor and material, dispensing with unnecessary drives and walks, and by preserving the natural beauty of the grounds and doing whatever will add to their attractiveness. We come together once a year to get new ideas from each other in regard to various methods of doing work, to impart our best thoughts and to listen to such criticisms as may be made. We come to test our own work by what we hear and see. A number of cemetery associations have sent their superintendents to visit the leading cemeteries of this country. These associations are satisfied that the information thus gained is worth more than the time and money expended to obtain it. These meetings serve a similar purpose. We do not, perhaps, visit as many cemeteries as we would during a trip made for that purpose, but we can in a few minutes get the opinion of more than fifty members in regard to any subject of general interest. We secure a more extended criticism than we could in any other way.

The interests of cemeteries are also advanced by everything that tends to give them stability, freedom from encroachments and by provisions for their perpetual care and maintenance. The experience of one cemetery may be of great assistance to another in regard to any of these matters.

But our highest mission will not be fulfilled unless we do something to elevate the character of cemeteries. A cemetery serves its purpose when it does two things: First, when it takes care of the dead organic material of human bodies; second, when it serves by its neatness, its beauty, its quietness, its seclusion and its assurance of a permanent resting place to assuage the sorrow of those who have lost their friends. It fills its highest purpose when it accomplishes these two results in a rational manner. What constitutes such a manner is, therefore, a fit subject for our discussion. It is generally acknowledged that the final destiny of a body is to be resolved into the elements of which it was composed. Shall we seek to postpone this process as did the ancient Egyptians? Shall we stow away the bodies of our friends in mausoleums to remain ghastly objects for untold years and perhaps finally be disposed of as mummies are now? Or shall they be placed in the sweet fresh earth to be absorbed and transformed into trees and grass and flowers? Or, again, shall they be dissipated in an hour to the clouds in a colorless vapor? These are questions that concern everybody. Perhaps they should be answered first by physicians and then should be answered in our meetings. Our answer may not have much influence but it will undoubtedly have some—directly through the people we meet, and indirectly through the paper which we were influential in starting. We should discuss these matters so that our personal influence and the influence of our published report will be in the right direction.

If inhumation is recommended, what can be done to bring the body in closer contact with the earth? This is a question that ought to be solved by undertakers, but they are interested in selling as many boxes as possible. We can advocate the use of paper coffins and the omission of the outside box with the calmness of philosophers. But cremation may be endorsed. What effect would the adoption of this method have on the sale of lots in cemeteries? What should be done with the ashes that are left?

With any disposition that may be made of the dead, what should be done with regard to funerals? If, as some aver, they are relics of barbarism, how can they be abolished? The funeral procession comes to the cemetery and friends, neighbors and perhaps strangers and idle curiosity seekers gather around to see how bad the mourners feel, to gaze on some celebrated character that has attended the funeral, or to ask questions about the private affairs of the deceased. If this had not been the custom for ages, could we imagine a more trying ordeal for grief-stricken people to pass through? With all our advancement in material things and even in religion, why have we not adopted some simpler manner of burying our dead, some custom that would accord with our instinctive desire for seclusion and quietness? Perhaps it is because people shrink from thinking of such matters, and they would no doubt like suggestions from those who have to give attention to these things.

In seeking to elevate the character of cemeteries, a very pleasant field of study presents itself which helps to counterbalance the disagreeable part of our work. It is always a pleasure to try to make things beautiful and this pleasure increases with increased efforts so that we learn to appreciate more and more the wonderful beauty of leaf and stem and flower with their infinite variety of texture, shape and color with their waving vistas and changing outlines giving a most interesting boundary to clouds and sky. I cannot help thinking that our cemeteries should be made for the living rather than the dead, that they should be viewed with joy and gladness for their artistic perfection rather than sadness for the dead they hold; that with their beauty of foliage and songs of birds they should exert as refining an influence as good painting or fine music. Such a character, certainly, would not detract from their memorial value. The work of our association may be called complete when not only the cemeteries about all our cities shall become equal to our ideals, but when every little country burying ground instead of being an eyesore, as at present, shall be as beautiful as a charming bit of nature.

In conclusion let me say that the object of our association should be work, not play. We must not regard our meetings as a time for our own pleasure and gratification. Incidentally, we come in contact with some kindred spirits at our meetings, and we have an agreeable change from the ordinary routine of our duties, but I like to think of this as a pleasant change in work rather than a vacation. A vacation suggests a change of thoughts and a throwing off of responsibility. By looking out of the car windows, by going to the cemeteries and parks of the towns we visit, and by listening to what is said at our meetings, we can get ideas from the time we leave home till we return, and nothing will be of more value to the institutions we work for than ideas coupled with good judgment. Our report should embody these ideas in as brief and interesting a manner as possible. Of course there are many things said at our meetings that are not of general or lasting interest. These should be eliminated from our report, not simply to save the expense but to save as well the

THE MODERN CEMETERY.

ENTRANCE TO OAKLAND CEMETERY, ST. PAUL, MINN.

time of whoever may read it. So long as we live up to our constitution and make these annual meetings add to our knowledge and efficiency and so indirectly improve our cemeteries and the tastes of those who use them, our society will prosper and its influence will continue to grow. But when the idea of our individual enjoyment takes precedence, the best days of the society will have passed.

The closing paper of the evening was read by Bellett Lawson of Oakwoods Cemetery, Chicago, on the subject:

IS FLOWER PLANTING DESIRABLE IN THE MODERN CEMETERY.

The desirability of planting flowers in cemeteries is a very debatable question and full of interest to superintendents. So much depends upon the surroundings. By flowers is meant annuals, perennials and other flowers used in florists' work.

Let us take a burial ground conducted strictly upon the lawn system, say for instance, Spring Grove Cemetery, Cincinnati, where every surrounding indicates quietness and repose. The beautifully kept lawns or open spaces surrounded by or dotted with trees and shrubs bearing foliage of different hues and shades of green. Each of those lawns or spaces are beautiful pictures in themselves. The trees being planted to throw light and shade on the sward, heightens the beauty of the picture and the effect upon the spectator is soothing and commands silent admiration. The very sombreness of the surroundings indicates repose, and the mind immediately associates itself with the idea of the suitability of the cemetery as a final resting place.

Beds planted with brightly colored flowers upon such lawns would be extremely out of harmony with the surroundings and would not be desirable.

Flower planting, no matter how artistically the work is done, is palpably artificial and in the majority of cemeteries out of place. A modern cemetery should appear as natural as possible.

Imagine a nicely graded section adorned with trees and shrubs; the landscape artist has expended his energies in making it appear as perfectly natural as possible. A lot-owner whose portion is probably in the most prominent part, conceives the idea of having a bed upon, or a border around his lot. The graves are also adorned with foliage plants until the lot has the appearance of what a brother superintendent justly describes a crazy patch-work quilt. No doubt the work is artistic but it does not harmonize with the surroundings and to the trained eye of a landscape gardener the effect is harsh in the extreme. Lot-owners, as a rule, care nothing for the harmonious appearance of the whole. To the individual lot is what they desire to draw attention.

One great aim of a cemetery superintendent should be to educate the people to the fact that "in simplicity there is beauty." That a cemetery should look natural and park-like, and that the general appearance of the whole should be studied rather than any particular spot. A stupendous task, more especially in localities where the resident migrates from parts where the modern cemetery system is unknown. To their minds the old country church yard with its heterogeneous mass of flowers and vegetation is beautiful and exactly what a burial ground should be. A few days ago the writer counted no less than 34 plants of different varieties (including mint) upon a four-foot grave. Nothing can persuade the owner that it is not the most beautiful grave in the cemetery.

To prevent this class of ornamentation (?) will require stringent rules, the enforcement of which means unpopularity and few officials care to have their cemeteries unpopular. Several who have tried arbitrary rules in this direction have had to modify them in obedience to public feeling.

There are many first-class cemeteries where flower planting is extensively practiced. These are now being styled flower garden cemeteries. The question of the desirability of flower planting is settled as far as they are concerned.

There are also burial grounds where flower planting would prove an improvement, but these places can scarcely be classed among the lawn cemeteries. They are simply grave yards. No great amount of landscape work having been lavished in their construction and the management is a sort of "go as you please."

Then again there is the dollars and cents side of the question. In the majority of cemeteries, both large and small, the desire to make money is paramount, and what should he has to give way to the mighty dollar. So few can afford to sacrifice caste to sentiment, and as most cemeteries are conducted for the money there is in them, flower planting will be encouraged. It is business, simply business.

Where flower planting is considered desirable study should be given to the use, as much as possible, of dwarf growing plants, and such as bear flowers quiet in color, for in few instances do the brighter colors harmonize with the surroundings of a burial ground. For cemetery work nothing looks worse than a bed containing a mixture of tall-growing plants, such as dahlias, lillies, salvia, chrysanthemums, hollyhocks and others too numerous to enumerate. Pretty effects can be obtained with dwarf-growing plants, especially when massed, and they are not visible from a distance, therefore their appearance is not so striking, nor is the appearance of the lawn so broken as by their taller brethren.

In cemeteries where flower growing is encouraged a spirit of emulation soon creeps in, and lot-owners try to outvie each other in their efforts to have their lots look nice, to the great joy of the florist, who acquiesces in the good work (?) and soon the lawns are covered with all manner of designs, regardless of the surroundings, till ofttimes the whole resembles a wild garden in its profusion of bright colored blooms. These beds soon become dried and withered blotches in the landscape, especially during the heat of summer, unless kept well watered each day, meaning more joy for the florist, who, of course, has to be paid additional for watering.

THIRD DAY.

Inclement weather again interfered with the program, necessitating a postponement of the proposed trip to St. Paul.

A paper on Vaults by George W. Creesy of Salem, Mass., was read by Mr. Stone. The paper dealt with the subject from a sanitary point of view. After discussing the subject it was

Resolved: That it is the sense of this meeting that vaults and catacombs be discouraged and if possible prohibited in cemeteries.

A paper on the "Removal of Bodies," by F. Von Holdt of Colorado was read by the secretary.

Mr. Walbridge, who is interested in Woodlawn Cemetery, Toledo, addressed the convention from a layman's point of view. He regarded the work of the cemeteries of this country in the light of a public trust, in the fulfilling of which the greatest care and caution should be taken. Mr. Walbridge illustrated the different attitudes of lot-owners and cemetery officials by relating an anecdote that was received with applause. Two brothers, children of Israel, were negotiating a loan. When the papers were drawn up, the loan was seen to draw interest at 9%. "Oh, Jakey," said the borrower, "what would our parents think if they knew that you charged your brother 9% interest?" "Oh, that's all right," exclaimed the other, "they is up there," pointing heavenward, "and they are looking down and this is 6% for them."

Richmond and Philadelphia were nominated as the place of holding the next annual convention, and although Mr. Hooper of the former city had sent a most cordial invitation to visit the Old Dominion, it was decided to go to Philadelphia.

A motion in favor of establishing local or state associations was lost.

The officers for the past year were unanimously re-elected. They are as follows: President, Wm. Salway, Spring Grove Cemetery, Cincinnati, O.; vice-president, T. McCarthy, Swan Point Cemetery, Providence, R. I.; secretary and treasurer, F. Eurich, Woodlawn Cemetery, Toledo, O. The executive committee for the ensuing year consists of Geo. E. Rhedemeyer, Harleigh Cemetery, Camden, N. J.; Geo. M. Painter, West Laurel Hill, Philadelphia; Wm. B. Walker, Woodlands, Philadelphia, and Geo. W. Creesy, Harmony Grove, Salem, Mass.

An interesting and very comprehensive paper on "Hardy Shrubs and Their Protection against Drouth," was read by Prof. Saml. B. Green of the state experimental farm at St. Anthony.

In the afternoon the party visited Minnehaha Park, where they saw the falls made famous by the immortal Longfellow; the soldiers' home and other points of interest.

FOURTH DAY.

The fourth and last day of the convention was devoted exclusively to St. Paul and was spent in a most enjoyable manner. The interurban electric system conveyed the party from Minneapolis to the city office of the Oakland Cemetery at St. Paul, where they had been invited to assemble as the guests of the trustees of Oakland. Here carriages were in waiting to show the visitors the sights of the city. Oakland was reached after a pleasant drive, where Superintendent Boxell and Secretary Willis escorted the party through the grounds. The cemetery was established in 1853 and comprises about eighty acres of undulating land. Since 1873 it has been conducted on the lawn plan and the improvements since that time have been of a most substantial nature. The receiving tomb and chapel is an imposing structure, standing on one of the highest points. It is built of a grayish stone and is nearly covered with vines. The chapel is a large square room connected with conservatories on three sides filled with flowers. A catafalque in the center of the chapel is used to lower bodies into the tomb, which has a capacity of nearly five hundred caskets. Resuming the carriages the drive was continued to Como Park through the beautiful residence portions of the city and terminating at the Hotel Aberdeen, where dinner was served. After dinner the closing session was held at which an address was made by Mr. Charles Nichols, a trustee of Oakland. Mr. Nichols referred in a humorous vein to the similarity between his name and that of the father of the association and concluded his interesting address as follows:

"It has been my fortune to have held the position of trustee in Oakland Cemetery at St. Paul for very nearly a quarter of a century. It has been a labor of love, and not one of pecuniary compensation. Of all trusts there are none more sacred; and none but those who are impressed with the sacredness and responsibility of this trust are wholly fitted for trusteeship. No greater responsibility rests upon the trustees than the selection and retention of the right man for superintendent. I say retention advisedly; his hands should be strengthened and his pride aroused to do the best work of which he is capable. And whether he be noted for communicativeness or receptivity; whether he exudes information or absorbs it, he should be sent to the annual meetings of your association and his expenses paid. Keep on, gentlemen, with your work. Contact with one another will brighten old and develop new ideas. The superintendent who does not learn enough at each meeting to pay for his time and expenses must either be the veritable 'wise man from the East' or a very dull scholar. The fullness of fruition for each of you should be that at every meeting you grow in grace and in the knowledge of cemetery work."

Mr. McCarthy made an informal report of the visit to Oakland in which he said it was a difficult matter to criticise the cemeteries of St. Paul or Minneapolis.

The convention adjourned to meet at Philadelphia in September, 1894.

Convention Echos.

Philadelphia and Camden next year.

* * *

Seven of the charter members were present.

* * *

As usual the genial Mr. McCarthy was the life of the party.

* * *

Father Nichols arrived late but the hearty greeting he received must have compensated for what he had missed.

* * *

An interesting account of Superintendent Rhedemeyer's trip to Minneapolis appeared in one of the Camden papers soon after his return home.

* * *

The idea of having a brief address from an intelligent layman is a good one and should be encouraged. It is well to hear from the other side occasionally.

* * *

An agreeable feature was the presence of an unusually large number of ladies. They were attentive listeners at the sessions and added to the pleasure of the meeting.

* * *

The local press gave extended notices of the meetings and published portraits of several of the officers and members. The *Times* indulged in a little satire at the expense of what they termed the ultra artistic superintendents.

* * *

An exhibit of the automatic burial apparatus was made by the Scherer Manufacturing Co., of Hartford, Conn. Rain interfered with the practical demonstration of its workings at Lakewood but it was afterwards removed to the hotel, where it was shown in successful operation.

* * *

Mr. Creesy supplemented his paper on Vaults with a number of photographs showing the interior of some of the old tombs in Harmony Grove. The condition of the decaying and moss grown caskets was such as to convince any one that this mode of sepulchre should be discouraged.

* * *

Superintendents Hobert and Boxell of Minneapolis and St. Paul, respectively, were untiring in their efforts to entertain their guests. The creditable program they prepared and the many hospitalities extended by them made the occasion replete with interest and one that marks progress in the history of the Association of American Cemetery Superintendents.

J. J. Stephens of Columbus, O., exhibited the model of a hitching post, a grave protector and a false bottom for use in wet graves. The hitching post is an ingenious device that will do away with unsightly and dangerous posts in cemetery roads if the claims of the inventor hold good. It consists of a tube of sufficient diameter to give easy play to a weight suspended on a chain, all of which is sunk into the ground. The upper end of the tube is protected by an iron cap that lies close to the ground.

Those who enjoyed Mr. Simond's description of the cemetery whose superintendent did not care to join the Superintendents' association because it was a hundred years behind the age will be still further amused at the comment of a prominent citizen recently published in one of the local papers. He says: "It is worse than an old barn yard. There is no way to get up the hill but by a rough ungraded pathway and the whole condition of affairs is such as to reflect severely on someone." This is a lot-owner's opinion of a cemetery whose superintendent said there was nothing for him to learn at the superintendents' convention.

* * *

The following is a list of those in attendance: John G. Baker, Boston, Mass.; *John F. Boerkel, Peoria, Ill.; John M. Boxell, St. Paul, Minn.; M. P. Braill, St. Louis, Mo.; *Chas. M. Chamberlain, Maspeth, L. I.; * J. C. Cline, Dayton, O.; *J. Y. Craig, Omaha, Neb.; Geo. W. Creesy, Salem, Mass.; *John C. Dix, Cleveland, O.; *Frank Eurich, Toledo, O.; Geo. Gilmore, Uhrichville, O.; *Thomas Hand, Minneapolis, Minn.; *A. W. Hobert, Minneapolis, Minn.; L. S. Kilborn, Marshalltown, Ia.; *Bellett Lawson, Chicago; T. McCarthy, Providence, R. I.; *D. Z. Morris, Rochester, N. Y.; W. A. Morrow, Hillsboro, O; Chas. Nichols, Newark, N. J.; *G. M. Painter, Philadelphia; C. D. Phipps, Franklin, Pa.; John Reid, Detroit, Mich.; T. B. Robinson, Des Moines, Ia.; *Wm. Salway, Cincinnati, O.; J. H. Shepard, Rochester, N. Y.; O. C. Simonds, Chicago; E. Smith, Brookline, Mass.; *J. J. Stephens, Columbus, O.; Wm. Stone, Lynn, Mass.; *Geo. L. Transue, Easton, Pa.; Geo. Van Atta, Newark, O.; F. D. Willis, St. Paul, Minn.; †Geo. Ruff, Lincoln, Neb.; †Geo. E. Rhedemeyer, Camden, Pa.; †Geo. W. Beckel, Defiance, O.; H. J. Byers, Lincoln, Neb.; †W. F. Jewson, Mankato, Minn.; †G. L. Kelly, New Albany, Ind.; †G. Scheringer; †Albert Marckhoff, Elgin, Ill.; †William Moorehouse, Hastings, Minn.; †A. Brown, Alaska, Mich.; R. J. Haight, Chicago.
*Accompanied by lady.   †New Members.

CHAPEL AND CONSERVATORY, OAKLAND CEMETERY, ST PAUL.

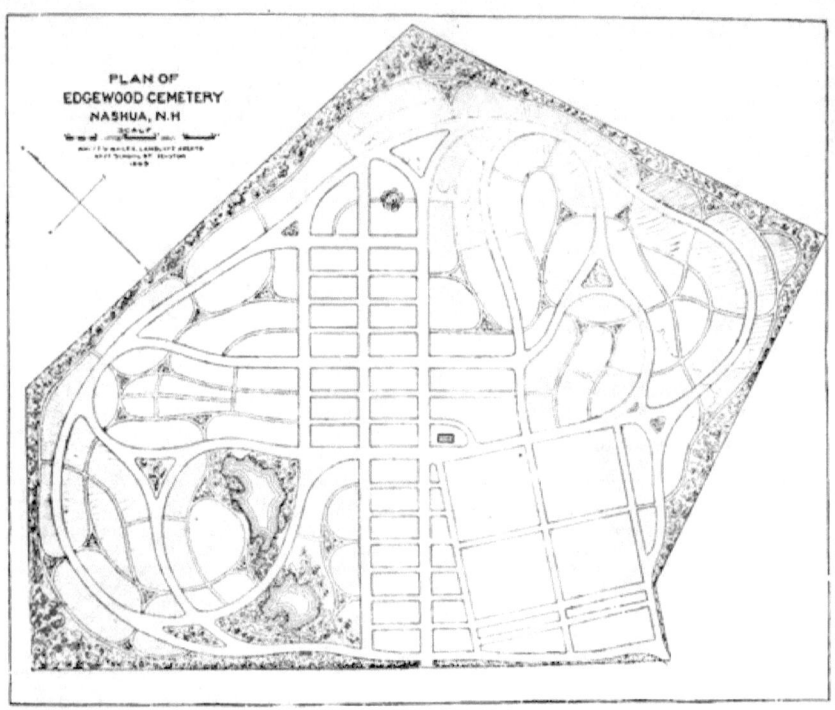

Edgewood Cemetery, Nashua, N. H.

The accompanying plan of Edgewood Cemetery is, as will be seen, the embodiment of two separate plans, one the old rectangular system, another a modern natural system of treatment adapting itself more nearly to the contour of the ground.

As the old portion, that represented by the rectangular system, is nearly if not fully occupied no radical changes could be made and it remained for the landscape architect to combine the two systems so as to make a harmonious whole. New avenues had to be continuations of old ones and no abrupt termination of the first plan could be made at the beginning of the second.

It will be seen by a glance at the plan that one avenue, that which skirts the border of the cemetery, has been made most prominent with all others subordinate to it. It will also be seen that all the new avenues radiate, or have a tendency to radiate, from the center of the cemetery where the present chapel is located. This is designed with a view to the convenience of funerals having services in the chapel. The new avenues are uniformly sixteen feet in width and of easy grade following the natural trend of the ground.

The walks are so designed that every lot can be conveniently approached. They are designed five feet in width and divide the blocks into desirable areas. The blocks, spaces bounded by avenues, are subdivided by walks and these sections into lots. The blocks are lettered alphabetically, A being in the old portion, Z the portion outside the border avenue.

The lots are numbered, one (1) in most cases being the lot in the corner of the block nearest the center of the cemetery. The numbers read around the block from left to right. Hence knowing the number of the lot and letter of the block it is an easy matter to find a particular lot.

The blocks contain from twelve to two hundred odd lots. The lots vary in size from one large enough for six graves to one of twelve graves.

The triangles at the intersection of the walks are to be reserved for planting or other public purposes.

The space shown in the plan as occupied by the pond is a natural hollow, well adapted to the purpose. New portions of the cemetery are to be graded as a whole with a view to giving a park-like appearance and the lots are to conform to the general grade.

The eastern part of the property is heavily wooded and the border and vicinity of the pond are to be planted with ornamental trees and shrubs.

The receiving tomb is located near the entrance and where it will be convenient to approach during the winter months.

The plan has been designed so that any portion can be constructed complete in itself and at the same time working toward the completion of the whole cemetery.

Boston, Mass.   FRANKLIN BRETT.

Architectural Foliage.

To many persons, in their cursory notice of architectural foliage, stray instances of an underlying meaning must occasionally have presented themselves. The Egyptian had used the lotus lily to bear the beams of his temple, binding the stalks together for the model of his pillar, and forming its capital after the flower, says the *Contemporary Review*, probably with definite symbolic intent, for a water lily scarcely suggests itself as suitable for forming a column; we know, however, that that plant was a sacred emblem to him, constantly placed in the hands of his divinities, and interwoven with traditions of Horus and the sun, and knowing this its use becomes reasonable and interesting.

Although the Greek acanthus would seem to have no such fact to support it, yet the legend of its origin bears something of the same spirit. The architect Callimachus is said to have gone to visit the grave of his daughter, upon whose tomb he had previously placed a basket of flowers. The brank-ursine meanwhile had sprung up about the tile upon which the basket stood and encircled its fine lattice with its luxuriant herbage, and this visit the artist immortalized in the Corinthian capital.

To the Roman mind, however, this local circumstance does not appear to have been of sufficient moment for such a position of importance, and in their capitals after this order they employed far more the olive and laurel and parsley, foliage sacred to Minerva, Apollo and Hercules. And in Christian architecture the same intention may have prevailed. Sir Walter Scott's mind seems apprehensive of something of this kind being the case in the stonework of "St. David's ruined pile," when speaking of the monk's garden, he says:

"Spreading herbs and flowerets bright,
Glistened with the dew of night;
Nor herb, nor floweret glistened there,
But was carved in the cloister-arches as fair."

A Classic Epitaph.

Soon after the fall of Gen. Albert Sidney Johnston at the battle of Shiloh and the transfer of his remains to New Orleans, a lady visiting the cemetery found pinned to a rough board that rested on the temporary tomb the following beautiful epitaph, says Memphis *Commercial*. She made a verbatim copy of the weather-beaten manuscript and sent it to one of the New Orleans papers with the request that if possible the name of the author should be published. The exquisite lines went the rounds of the press of this country and England as a model of English composition. Lord Palmerston pronounced it "a modern classic, Ciceronian in its language." The authorship was traced to John Dimitry, a young native of New Orleans. Young Dimitry, though only a boy, served in Johnston's army at Shiloh, and on visiting New Orleans and the grave of his dead chieftain wrote the lines on the inspiration of the moment and modestly pinned them on the headboard as the only tribute he could offer. When the question arose concerning the form of epitaph to be placed on the monument erected to the memory of the dead general the committee in charge with one voice decided upon this, and it is now inscribed upon a marble tablet near the entrance to the tomb:

IN MEMORY.
Beyond this stone is laid,
For a season,
Albert Sidney Johnston,
A General in the Army of the Confederate States,
Who fell at Shiloh, Tennessee,
On the sixth day of April, A. D.,
Eighteen hundred and sixty-two;
A man tried in many high offices
And critical enterprises,
And found faithful in all.
His life was one long sacrifice of interest to conscience;
And even that life, on a woeful Sabbath,
Did he yield as a holocaust at his country's need.
Not wholly understood was he while he lived;
But, in his death, his greatness stands confessed
in a people's tears—
Resolute, moderate, clear of envy, yet not wanting
In that finer ambition which makes men great
and pure.
In his honor—impregnable;
In his simplicity—sublime.
No country e'er had a truer son—no cause a
nobler champion;
No people a bolder defender—no principle a purer
victim
Than the dead soldier
Who sleeps here.
The cause for which he perished is lost—
The people for whom he fought are crushed—
The hopes in which he trusted are shattered—
The flag he loved guides no more the charging lines,
But his fame, consigned to the keeping of that
time, which,
Happily, is not so much the tomb of virtue as its
shrine,
Shall, in the years to come, fire modest worth to
noble ends.
In honor, now, our great captain rests;
A bereaved people mourn him,
Three commonwealths proudly claim him
And history shall cherish him
Among those choicer spirits who, holding their
conscience unmixed with blame,
Have been, in all conjectures, true to themselves
their country and their God.

Cemeteries of Chicago.

The larger and more popular cemeteries of Chicago are too well known to the readers of the MODERN CEMETERY to need any special mention in an article like the following. There are, however, a large number of smaller or more recently established burial places near the Garden city which are well worthy of the attention of every lover of the beautiful in nature and the excellent in landscape art. It is of some of these that we propose to write, as impartially as possible, with a view to describing the chief characteristics of some of the less widely known cities of the dead, wherein sleep so many thousands of the former residents of the great western metropolis.

Calvary is the largest and oldest of the Roman Catholic cemeteries adjacent to Chicago and is by far the most populous city of the dead in the West. It contains 110 acres, and not less than 120,000 bodies have been interred within its limits since its construction in 1859. Previous to 1885 the daily average of interments at Calvary had reached 15. In that year a new cemetery, Mt. Olivet, was opened south of the city, since which time the interments at Calvary have been reduced to an average of 14 a day.

Calvary Cemetery is located south of and adjoining the village of South Evanston, ten miles north from the city hall. It fronts Sheridan Drive and Lake Michigan, and is reached by the Northwestern and the Milwaukee & St. Paul railroads and by the new electric road. The location is an ideal one. The great number of forest trees of every variety, evergreens being mingled with deciduous trees, form a grand contrast to the widespreading marine view afforded by the lake. This combination of wood and water is the chief natural charm of Calvary, in which too often the intruding presence of unsightly railings and cumbrous monuments has detracted from the real beauty of the grounds.

To the west and south of Calvary, and just south of Rosehill, lies another but smaller Catholic cemetery named St. Boniface. This cemetery, which has an area of 36 acres, was consecrated in 1863, and now contains over 26,000 interments. In the new portion of St. Boniface the park system has been adopted, and there is such a marked contrast between the new and old portions of this cemetery that it affords an excellent opportunity to study the advantages of the modern style of cemetery gardening, as compared with the old.

Just south of Graceland is Wunder's Cemetery, a burial ground that was consecrated early in the fifties. Here evidences of neglect are sadly noticeable, and many of the graves are said to have been used repeatedly. Not so in the little Jewish cemetery of five acres adjoining on the south. Here the grounds are in charge of a faithful attendant, strange to say of the Christian faith, who keeps the paths and graves in scrupulous care. Another Jewish cemetery has recently been opened in Jefferson near the village of Dunning.

The west division of the city of Chicago is destined always to contain probably not less than two-thirds of the population of the entire city, and it would be surprising indeed if the western suburbs should not develop some remarkably large and beautiful cities of the dead. Three cemeteries of considerable importance now repose on the banks of the Des Plaines river about nine miles west from the city hall. They are Forest Home, Waldheim and Concordia.

The first of these, Forest Home, comprises nearly 100 acres of land and is, both by nature and art, one of the most beautiful cemeteries in Chicago. Here the lawn system was adopted from the beginning and the uniform park-like appearance of the grounds so much admired by all visitors is a silent but powerful testimony of the excellent results to be obtained by this system. No copings or other means of marking the boundaries of lots are allowed, except corner stones and these are restricted in height, thus making it easy to keep the lawns uniform. The same system has been followed, though not so rigidly, in Waldheim, a German cemetery of 80 acres, just north of Forest Home. This is the favorite burial ground of the German societies, and is carefully kept by them as well as by the individual lot-owners. The burial lot of the anarchists, 1,500 feet square, is a feature of this cemetery.

Concordia Cemetery is the burial ground of the German Lutherans, and comprises 60 acres on the banks of the Des Plaines river at its intersection with Madison street. This cemetery was dedicated in 1872, and the number of interments now reaches 16,000. It was not until 1884, however, that strict rules were adopted against enclosures around lots and other obstructions which were then seen to be disfiguring the grounds. Since that time the beauty of the cemetery has been materially enhanced.

Eight small Jewish cemeteries are located on both sides of the road leading from Forest Home to Riverside. They are the cemeteries of the "Austrian-Hungarian Benevolent Society;" " Aushe Suwalk, Chicago;" "Chewre Aushe Emes;" "Moses Montefiore;" "Ohavo Amuno;" " Bnai Abraham;" "Improved Order of Free Sons," and "Free Sons of Israel." The cemetery of the last-named order, 5 acres in extent, is the largest of these, and is open not only to the members of the order but also to the poor outside of the organization.

The town of Jefferson contains two cemeteries at least which deserve more than a passing notice. One of these is Mount Olive, which is situated near the county institutions at Dunning. Mount Olive is one of the youngest of Chicago's cemeteries. It was opened in August, 1886. In the comparatively short time of seven years that have elapsed since then over 7,000 interments have been made at Mount Olive, and great improvements in the landscape have been effected. The lawn system has been adopted from the beginning over the entire 52½ acres of this cemetery, and the results obtained have been excellent. Mount Olive is a Scandinavian Lutheran cemetery, but the privileges of the cemetery are not confined to any sect or nationality.

In the summer of 1877 a plat of ground in the town of Jefferson, containing 30 acres, but since increased to 50 acres, was purchased by certain Bohemian Catholics, who had become dissatisfied with the burial regulations of their church. This was the beginning of the Bohemian National Cemetery, which is now represented by 36 lodges or societies and contains nearly 10,000 interments. The site of this cemetery presents many natural advantages, but like many another similar enterprise the beginnings were not characterized by wise choice of the park system, and some unsightly structures still remain to detract from the beauty of the view. The newer portions of the cemetery are laid out in accordance with advanced ideas.

South of the city and reposing on the western slopes of the famous Blue Island ridge, are four charmingly located cemeteries, which at once attract the eye and please the sense of the beholder from the exceptional natural beauty of their surroundings. The first or nearest of these gardens of the dead is St. Maria, a German Catholic burying ground, which was consecrated in 1888. This cemetery contains 102 acres of ground, which lies on the western slope of Washington Heights at an elevation of 55 feet above the level of Lake Michigan and from 16 to 20 feet above the level of the surrounding prairie. The grounds are peculiar in that when they were purchased by the cemetery association they were almost treeless. Under the vigorous policy of the management more than 4,000 shade trees have been planted.

Two and a half miles farther south are Mount Greenwood, Mount Olivet and Mount Hope, all occupying an elevation of from 50 to 100 feet above Lake Michigan and nestling among forest trees of ancient growth. Mount Greenwood and Mount Olivet each contain 80 acres. Mount Greenwood was opened to the public in 1879. Here the lawn system is in full operation. The drives and walks are mostly macadamized and are kept in excellent condition. Much attention is paid to beautifying the grounds with flowers and shrubs.

Mount Olivet is a Catholic cemetery and is under the same management as Calvary. It was consecrated in 1885, and has since been much improved.

Mount Hope was designed by its founders to be a model cemetery. It contains 300 acres in the form of a square, and is not only beautifully situated on the slope of the wooded ridge, but has also had all the advantages of the expenditure of a large amount of money and the exercise of the best skill in its landscape gardening. No expense has been spared. Steam pumping works supply water, and a complete system of drainage has been provided. A fine stone chapel, depot, waiting rooms and office were erected at a cost of $20,000 before a body was interred. It is not necessary to state that the park system prevails at Mount Hope. It is there that it is to be seen in the perfection of its loveliness, and nothing could be more helpful to a student of landscape gardening than a day spent in contemplation of Mount Hope Cemetery.

A sign bearing the words "Flirting is Prohibited," has been placed at the entrance to Germantown (Penn.) cemetery.

A firm of Pittsburg undertakers and the St. Mary's Cemetery company were each fined $20 and costs for interring a body for which no burial permit had been issued.

Two cemeteries at Hudson, Wis., were desecrated last month and twenty-two of the most costly monuments damaged. The city offered a reward of $500 for the arrest of the perpetrators.

Laurel Grove Cemetery at Savannah, Ga., was devastated by the destructive cyclone that did such damage in that section last month. Trees, fences and monuments were blown down and ruined.

The mayor of Cherokee, Ia., imposed a fine of $20 and costs upon the wife of a prominent citizen of that place, who had been detected in the act of taking flowers from graves in Oak Hill Cemetery.

An injunction has been granted at Port Huron, Mich., restraining the construction of a drain sewer from the local cemeteries to the lake. The grounds on which the injunction was granted was the alleged pollution of the waters in front of the beaches from where the cottagers secured their water supply.

Lakewood Cemetery, Minneapolis, is beautiful in its neatness and simplicity, a feature that in nearly all cemeteries is too frequently neglected. *John G. Barker.*

Allow me to express my feelings regarding the MODERN CEMETERY. No association can afford to manage a cemetery in our day upon the narrow conception of a single individual be he engineer, landscape gardener and veteran grave digger combined—the MODERN CEMETERY shows him the true work.— *Chas. N. Snyder, Sec'y. West Laurel Hill Cemetery, Philadelphia.*

Association of American Cemetery Superintendents.

W. M. SALWAY, "Spring Grove" Cincinnati, O., President.
T. M. McCARTHY, "Swan Point" Providence, R. I., Vice-President.
F. EURICH, Woodlawn, Toledo, O., Secretary and Treasurer.

The Eighth Annual Convention of the Association will be held at Philadelphia in September, 1894.

Publisher's Department.

The receipt of Cemetery Literature and Trade Catalogues will be acknowledged in this column.

TO ADVERTISERS. THE MODERN CEMETERY is the only publication of its class and will be found a valuable medium for reaching cemetery officials in all parts of the United States.

TO SUBSCRIBERS. Cemetery officials desiring to subscribe for a number of copies regularly to circulate among their lot owners, should send for our special terms. Several well known cemeteries have already adopted this plan with good results.

Contributions on matters pertaining to cemeteries are solicited. Address all communications to
H. J. HAIGHT, 334 Dearborn St., CHICAGO.

Cemetery Literature Received: Rules and Regulations of Cave Hill Cemetery, Louisville, Ky.; Rules and Regulations of the Staten Island Cemetery Association, West New Brighton, Staten Island, N. Y.

Plan of Glenwood Cemetery, Oneida, N. Y., recently re-surveyed, has been received from B. F. Hatheway, landscape surveyor of Stamford, Conn. The margins of the map are illustrated with views of the entrance, receiving vault and other portions of the grounds.

Four boilers made by Hitchings & Co., of New York, will be used for heating the five new greenhouses now under construction at Forest Hills Cemetery, Boston. The Hitchings Co. makes a handsome exhibit of green-houses at the World's Fair and invite the inspection of same by visiting cemetery officials.

W. D. Diuguid of Lynchburg, Va., has just completed a record, comprising five volumes, of the interments in Spring Hill Cemetery. Accompanying the record is a diagram of every lot on which an interment has been made. Only those who have attempted to make up a complete book of this kind for an old cemetery can appreciate the amount of labor connected with it.

In the announcement of the Hartman Manufacturing Co., on another page, may be seen an illustration of one of their Steel Picket Fences which they have recently placed around the cemetery at Plattsburg, N. Y. The company are meeting with marked success in the sale of their steel fencing, which, as may be seen from their printed price list, is supplied at a price within the reach of all cemetery corporations.

Glenwood Cemetery, Mankato, Minn., and Minnecopa Cemetery at South Bend, Minn., were recently visited by vandals and a large number of marble and granite monuments thrown to the ground. Although a large reward has been offered there is no clue to the perpetrators who are thought to have been a party of hoodlums, or as the Mankato *Herald* calls them, human hyenas.

The automatic burial apparatus made by The Scherer Manufacturing Company of Hartford, Ct., consists of a rectangular frame, which is placed on the ground over the grave, leaving the mouth of the grave open. The sides of the frame are hollow and contain the mechanism by which the casket is lowered. From each inner side of the frame strong web bands issue, which, meeting and fastening in the middle, form the support for the casket. A touch of a spring and the casket is lowered noiselessly into the grave. The straps are then disconnected and drawn up into the frame, which completes the operation. The apparatus is made in three sizes: No. 1—7 feet 3 inches by 3 feet; No. 2—7 feet 3 inches by 2 feet 8 inches; No. 3—7 feet by 2 feet 6 inches. To responsible parties the company will send the apparatus on sixty days' trial.

Public monuments should not always be found in the most conspicuous places. In the public square at Gainsville, Fla., stands a monument to yellow fever victims whose bodies were interred in the local cemetery. The monument was erected by subscription and the much frequented square was thought to be the proper place for it. It has just occurred to some of the citizens that a monument telling that the city was once visited by yellow fever is "absolutely frightful to the visiting strangers," and an effort is being made to have it removed to Evergreen Cemetery, where it should have been erected in the first place.

AUBURNDALE, O., Sept. 11, 1893.

To members of A. A. C. S. in particular, and cemetery officials in general:

Before placing my order for the printing of the proceedings of our seventh annual convention, recently held, I would appreciate advice from all who intend ordering extra copies, so as to be governed as to the number likely to be needed.

The proceedings are unusually interesting and instructive and will form quite a valuable pamphlet.

An immediate reply by postal or otherwise is requested as the copy must soon go to press in order to have the report out early. Those who wish to place their definite orders for copies can do so and remit when convenient after receipt of goods.

Respectfully,
FRANK EURICH, Sec. and Treas.

Situation Wanted.

Superintendent and landscape gardener with an extended experience desires situation; was nine years in one of principal Massachusetts cemeteries; references. Address S. H. G., care Modern Cemetery, Chicago.

THE MODERN CEMETERY.

THE MODERN CEMETERY.
AN ILLUSTRATED MONTHLY JOURNAL DEVOTED TO THE INTEREST OF CEMETERIES

R. J. HAIGHT, Publisher.
384 Dearborn Street, CHICAGO.

Subscription $1.00 a Year in Advance.   Foreign Subscription $1.25.
Special Rates on Six or More Copies.

Vol. III.   CHICAGO, OCT. 1893.   No. 8.

CONTENTS.

VALIDITY OF MORTGAGES OF PUBLIC CEMETERIES BY CORPORATIONS..	85
VALIDITY OF STATUTORY AUTHORIZED BEQUEST TO CEMETERY ASSOCIATIONS..	86
*NOTES FROM GRACELAND..	87
IS FLOWER PLANTING DESIRABLE IN THE MODERN CEMETERY?—DISCUSSION..	88
CEMETERY RATES IN THE CITY OF MEXICO.....................	89
*THE KENSICO CEMETERY—AT THE SIGN OF THE SKULL..	90
ORNAMENTAL GRASSES—PLANT EARLY...........................	91
VISIT TO THE GRAVEYARDS OF HAMBURG—CREMATION.	92
CEMETERY NOTES—A CHINESE MONUMENT....................	93
RULES FOR THE EMPLOYEES OF THE CEMETERY OF SPRINGGROVE, CINCINNATI..	94
CORRESPONDENCE...	95
PUBLISHERS DEPARTMENT..	96

*Illustrated.

Validity of Mortgages of Public Cemeteries by Corporations.

Where the purposes for which alone cemetery corporations may be organized are public, rather than private, lands acquired by such a corporation, and platted pursuant to the statute for cemetery purposes, the plat being recorded, and the land to some extent having actually been used for burials, are thereby dedicated to the purpose, exclusively, of the burial of the dead. After such dedication the corporation is without power, for reasons in which the public is concerned, to convey any of such lands, except for the exclusive purpose of burials, or to mortgage the same. Its mortgage is wholly void, and the doctrine of estoppel is not applicable to preclude the corporation from asserting its invalidity. So holds the Supreme Court of Minnesota in the case of Wolford v. Crystal Lake Cemetery Association, 56 Northwestern Reporter 56.

The statement of facts in this case shows that prior to June, 1883, this association was, and ever since has been, an incorporated cemetery association, organized under the Minnesota statute. In that month and year it acquired the title to a tract of land of 40 acres, 10 acres of which became the subject of this action. In the year 1886 the corporation had the entire 40-acre tract platted into lots, avenues, and walks, and the plat thereof, showing that the land was thereby dedicated as a cemetery, to be used exclusively for the burial of the dead, was then recorded. It was designated "Crystal Lake Cemetery." After that, and in October, 1888, the corporation became indebted to Wolford for money loaned to it, and by it used in paying its debts, and in laying out and improving the cemetery grounds. This indebtedness was evidenced and secured by a promissory note of the corporation, and by a mortgage to him of the 10 acres in question, executed pursuant to a resolution of the association's board of trustees. Wolford was induced to accept the note and mortgage securing the same by representations of the association's officers to the effect that this 10-acre tract had not been laid out as a part of the cemetery, or actually devoted to or used for burial purposes. The representations were made in good faith, as the court found, but were untrue and Wolford was deceived thereby. In fact, not only had the platting and dedication, as above stated, been made and recorded, but the whole 40-acre tract had been inclosed by a fence, which on one side, at the entrance, bore the name "Crystal Lake Cemetery." Thirty-four burials had been made on this 10 acres, but close to the south line thereof; and a temporary vault had been erected partly on the same land. That part of the 40 acres lying south of the 10 acres had been laid out and was being used for purposes of burial. The improvements which had been made were almost wholly confined to that part of the grounds. In 1890 Wolford foreclosed his mortgage by the statutory exercise of the power of sale, he being the purchaser at the foreclosure sale. No redemption was ever made. The present action involved the issue of title as affected by the mortgage and its foreclosure. The real questions were whether the cemetery association had power to mortgage the property, and if not, whether it was precluded from asserting its want of power.

The purposes for which cemetery corporations may be organized are public, says the court, rather than private, and the land acquired by such corporations, and devoted to the purposes of burial, are held in trust for public, rather than private, use. Every community needs, and ordinarily has, one or more places set apart and kept for the general burial of the dead. The providing and maintaining of such cemeteries is a matter of public concern, in the same sense as is the establishing and maintaining of roads or parks. The duty or power of doing this may properly be imposed or conferred upon towns, villages, or other political divisions of the state, as is done by the general laws defining the power of such municipal bodies; or, as has been done in Minnesota, the formation of corporations for that purpose may also be authorized. The purpose is equally public whether the one agency or the other is employed for its accomplishment, and in either case lands once legally devoted to and used for burial become appropriated to a public purpose, in such a sense that the power of the body in which the legal title may rest, to use or alienate the same, is restricted. The public character of such corporations, and of the purposes to be subserved by them, as well as the general inalienability of lands legally dedicated to and used for burials, may be asserted, not merely because of the nature of the subject, but also in Minnesota (and in many other states) because the statute justifies it. Here no purpose of private gain or benefit is contemplated by the law, but only the accomplishment, through such corporate agencies, of the same public purposes which, in the absence of such a statute, or in the event of no such corporations being organized, would generally be accomplished by the exercise of powers conferred upon towns, villages and cities.

It is contrary to the policy of the law to allow a corporation to convey or alienate, except for burial purposes, any part of the land thus appropriated, in the manner prescribed by the statute, exclusively for the burial of the dead. Nor can an association, by its own act of alienation, divest itself of the trust which it has assumed under the law over the cemetery once established. Consequently this association was powerless, the court held, when the mortgage referred to was executed, to sell without such restriction, or to mortgage a lot, or any number of lots, even to raise money for the payment of its debts, or to carry on its proper work. As it was wholly beyond the power of the corporation to thus mortgage its cemetery lands, so it could not validate or give legal effect to its void act by ratification, or by acceptance of benefits thereunder. Furthermore, the doctrine of estoppel was not applicable here, as it might have been if the corporation were one created for the accomplishment of private, rather than public purposes, or if the defect consisted only of some irregularity in the exercise of a power. The principle of estoppel could not be applied, so as to subject the public (not merely the corporation) to the very consequences which the restriction of the power of this public agent was intended to prevent.

Validity of Statutory Authorized Bequest to Cemetery Associations.

Such a statute as that of New York state authorizing the incorporation of rural cemetery associations and providing that "Any association incorporated pursuant to this act may take and hold any property, real or personal, bequeathed or given upon trust, to apply the income thereof under the direction of the trustees of such association, for the improvement or embellishment of such cemetery, or the erection or preservation of any buildings, structures, fences or walks, erected or to be erected upon the lands of said cemetery association, or upon the lots or plots of any of the proprietors; or for the repair, preservation, erection, or renewal of any tomb, monument, gravestone, fence, railing or other erection, in or around any cemetery lot or plot; or for planting and cultivating trees, shrubs, flowers, or plants, in or around any such lot or plot; or for improving or embellishing such cemetery, or any of the lots or plots in any other manner or form, consistent with the design and purposes of the association according to the terms of such grant, devise or bequest," creates an exception to the statute against perpetuities, which (in New York) provides that "The absolute ownership of personal property shall not be suspended by any limitation or condition whatever for a longer period than during the continuance and until the termination of not more than two lives in being at the date of the instrument containing such limitation or condition; or, if such instrument be a will, for not more than two lives in being at the death of the testator," and makes such bequests valid. So holds the Surrogate's Court of Rockland County, in re Schuler's Estate (24 N. Y. Supp. 847). It says that this statute against perpetuities is general, and applies to all cases, except where special provision is otherwise made. The same power that created the general prohibition can authorize an exception, and determine that the general provision shall not apply. The legislative power has prohibited generally such perpetuities, and the same power has, as to cemetery corporations, removed such restriction, and bestowed affirmatively the power and right to hold funds for the purposes specified in this will, and it can see no reason why both should not stand with force, the latter as a statutory exception to the general law. This was an application by the Oak Hill Cemetery of Nyack, to compel the payment to its trustees by the executors of the last will and testament of John W. Schuler, deceased, of a bequest of $1,000, and interest thereon, pursuant to a direction of the testator contained in his said will, the same to be invested only on first mortgage bond and mortgage on improved real estate of double the value of such sum, and the interest accruing from the same to be applied by the said trustees in keeping testator's lot in said cemetery grounds in good and proper condition, making such needed repairs as might be required from time to time during the several seasons of the year, to both fences and grounds, as shall be demanded, this trust to be and remain in perpetual continuance. This is different from a bequest of a fund to an executor, to be used to keep the testatrix's burial plot in good condition, which was held to be void in re Fisher's Estate (Surr.) 8 N. Y. Supp. 10, under the above statute against perpetuities. Here the bequest is to the corporation, and according to the foregoing opinion the statute specifically makes such a bequest lawful.

A GROUP OF ALDERS.   A CHARMING VISTA.   CUT LEAF MAPLE.

Notes from Graceland.

A short stop in the sulphurous atmosphere of the train sheds of a great railway terminal, followed by the dreariness and squalor that invariably line a railway route on its way through cities, there a flash of scarlet salvias against the grass, and finally a glad glimpse of green trees. A step through a vine-clad gateway and one feels that turmoil and hard places have drifted out of reach and that ways of pleasantness are at hand.

Graceland is, in the main, like a quiet, well conducted, tasteful home. If ostentation and pretentiousness are there it is under protest, and as far as control goes one finds no lapses from good taste. The landscape effects are so good, the art with which every tree and plantation has been chosen and placed so nearly perfect, that one forgets that brains and brawn have brought it all about.

It seems natural. There is a reason for this feeling in that the planting has been done by rules learned through careful loving study of nature's pictures, and her methods of making them. Trees and shrubbery grow on unmolested, as pruning, in the accepted sense, is not practiced at Graceland. Dead branches are removed, that is all. But to produce the series of landscape pictures to be seen there, art and taste, as well as judgment and knowledge, have been brought to bear in the selection of every tree and shrub, in every combination of them in the various plantations, and in the relation of groups and single specimens to each other. The pictures are careful compositions.

The most has been made of all irregularities of the surface, the treatment being such that a slight elevation becomes in effect a hill; much after the Japanese method of making a landscape of great diversity of level and variety of scope within the space of a few feet, by judicious arrangement of surface, placing of buildings, and planting.

The highest elevation is used as a site for the beautiful chapel of Waupaca granite, a warm reddish stone which is in harmony with the surroundings, and which shows when polished a texture, color and marking almost equal to some precious stones. Near the building are some good elm trees, among the largest ever transplanted, add dignity to the composition and add to the general effect. These together with some still larger ones set out in another part of the grounds are felt as a dominant feature of the landscape from all parts of the enclosure and even outside of it.

The result of allowing trees to grow and develope according to their nature, each being so placed that it can make symmetrical growth unhampered by its neighbors and unmolested by its friends, gives one a new insight into their habits and forms. Some varieties take on aspects so unfamiliar as to make them almost unrecognizable. Most people think of a maple as a tree having a more or less well formed and pleasing top and a bare trunk as high as, or higher, than a man's head.

Those at Graceland are clothed to the ground with graceful branches that narrow the outline of the top as it approaches the surface, and brings the leafage down to the level with a light, lilting swing that is charming. The slender lower branches give the air of children tossing their arms with the freedom of unconscious happy childhood. The trees will be no less delightful in age, when the swaying branches have grown sturdy and form great leafy airy caverns around the trunks. There are other trees than the various varieties of maples left to follow the bent of their inclination, that make pleasant surprises for those who have grown weary of the discouraged lines of trees that are trying to grow in grace in many a Chicago suburb. Among them nothing is prettier than a group of alders with their somewhat oddly combined characteristics of stiff formal boughs and sharply cut dainty foliage disposed on twig and branch in an indescribably graceful and beautiful way.

The elms are in good contrast to the trees having low branches, in their habit of growing a straight clean trunk to a considerable height. The trunk being monumental in form it would be a pity to mask the noble lines of the base of the tree by shrubs as some naturally bare varieties are appropriately treated. Something low and comparatively delicate to nestle in the retreats formed by the subdivision of the base, where the roots spread to brace the tree firmly, would be well; or vines to cling closely and define the form; but anything to break the clean cut columnar lines would be out of place. A stately elm like the one transplanted two years ago to the northern part of the grounds, where it is used as a monument, is seen at its best when it stands, as this one does, sharply outlined against a broad expanse of sward. The inference drawn from Nature's lessons would seem to be that trees with bare trunks are nature's pillars, some of which will fitly be adorned with vines.

There are charming vistas here and there throughout the grounds as the one down Wildwood Drive, (shown in one of our illustrations,) where the planting is particularly happy, the curving road being bordered on one side by trees that in the afternoon make shifting shadow patterns across the roadway, and on the other closely outlined by a thicket of shrubby things that take on new aspects as they are touched by sunlight and shadow through the changing seasons.

FANNY COPLEY SEAVEY,
Chicago.

Is Flower Planting Desirable in the Modern Cemetery?

Mr. Bellett Lawson's paper on this subject appeared in our last issue. The following is an extract from the discussion that followed the reading of the paper at the Minneapolis convention.

MR. MCCARTHY: It is very difficult to advise the best course in this matter, because a great many cemeteries insist they must plant them and cannot do without them. Personally I discourage annual planting, even among the graves, and I invariably discourage it and all phases of flowers, but we have no arbitrary rule against it. They are difficult to care for in the dry season and we know how early the frost nips them, and then the beds are bare. If lot-owners will let me plant the corners of their lots with hardy subjects, I give them the best attention and put in the best material that I can think of. That ornaments their lots, and it also ornaments the grounds. Still if every lot-owner did the same thing it would become monotonous, and would present almost a solid hedge in a few years. I do not want to be understood as not liking or planting flowers. While I may be in favor of discarding the gay colors that Mr. Lawson refers to, I may be buying hundreds of another kind. It is the kind that I choose and there is no question but what a cemetery in the spring with the hardy shrubs, tulips and crocuses and plants of this nature (which might be introduced by the million), would harmonize with the country and the cemetery, and would not be offensive as the gay colors would. The great difficulty of overcoming the planting of flowers is this, that affection will have some outlet and flowers seem to be the most natural one for people to select and it is very difficult to refuse to plant them. If you can suggest any method except an arbitrary rule that no flowers shall be planted, I would like to hear it. There is, of course, such a thing as having this thing too modern, and we must treat this question very carefully. Surely flowers are the most beautiful expressions that people can give or introduce, and although I do not believe in these perishable, gaudy displays or figures that have been so conspicuously introduced, still I am a great lover of flowers.

MR. SIMONDS: We plant a great many flowers, still I don't approve of using the ordinary green house flowers. I do think that we ought to have flowers in the cemetery. They are, of course, beautiful objects, and it is natural to have flowers. We have shrubs, beginning early in the spring, and we have flowers, lilacs and spireas, and later still the elderberries, and later still hydrangias and witchhazel, some have flowers, but we plant trees and shrubs. Then we ought to have herbaceous plants as well; they deserve a place as well as the shrubs, and there are many ways in which flowers can be used that could be effective. If we go out into the woods in the early spring one of the greatest pleasures we have is finding the first spring flowers; the first violets, etc. If we would just bring those plants and similar plants into the cemetery, and put them under the roots of shrubs or under the trees, we would have that same pleasure in the cemetery, and we would have no further expense or trouble, and we would cover the ground that is bare just at the beginning of the year, with something that would be attractive.

Again, for a border of shrubs there is nothing more natural than to have the hardy flowers. Go out into the border of a piece of woods, where you have shrubs coming down and forming the edge of an open space, you will find asters or golden rod and many other of our wild flowers, and I think they should be brought in and used in the cemetery in the same manner.

One of the objections to green house plants is that they are somewhat expensive, and they require a force of men for their work. The fewer men you can have in the cemetery the better, not only on account of the reduction in expenses, but more on account of the quiet effect. If you could have a cemetery without any workmen in it at all you would reach the ideal in that direction. Of course there is another objection to green house plants, coming from the fact that they cannot be planted in this northern climate until nearly June, and then the first frost kills them, so that instead of having a beautiful object we have an ugly spot two-thirds of the year.

PRESIDENT SALWAY: I too, am a dear lover of flowers but our tastes have been cultivated in that direction, perhaps. We will find rich gorgeous colors everywhere. People have their attention attracted by a striking bed of scarlet geraniums, or some other rich gaudy flower, but why not cultivate a taste for the different colored foliage that lasts, say, for instance, the spruce or the cone-bearing family that are permanent in their color. They vary a little, but look at the variety of color and form of habit there is, it is admirable. These are permanent and they are certainly ornamental in every respect. The hardy herbaceous plants mentioned by Mr. Simonds, and the advantage of these I can testify to. They certainly are desirable. They practically take care of themselves as far as the weather is concerned. They need some care of course; everything needs care. We do not have anything that is worth having but what needs some kind of care and protection, but these plants do not need much protection, and there is a great variety that do not need any protection from the weather.

MR. CRAIG: My views coincide with Mr. Lawson's completely, although I am not able to carry them out in my cemetery. I think most decidedly that our modern or lawn cemetery would be better without so many flowers and with a good collection of trees and shrubbery judiciously planted it would be better than we could ever make it with the flower beds. Still I find, like a good many others, that I have to affiliate with lot-owners in some respects.

MR. STONE: I admire grass and I admire flowers, and the latter have always been cultivated quite extensively in the cemetery that I represent. I do not believe in placing them on graves but I do believe in having some for beds on lots when the lots are large enough. I do not believe in planting on graves or small lots. In large spaces growing plants look very beautiful if it is not overdone.

Cemetery Rates in the City of Mexico.

The following is a schedule of prices recently adopted by the council of the City of Mexico for interments at the Dolores Cemetery:

1st. The bodies shall remain undisturbed 7 years and not 10 as hitherto.

2nd. The prices for interments shall be the following: For adults for the term of 7 years: 1st class, $60; 2nd class, $35; 3rd class, $15; 4th class, $8; 5th class, $3; 6th class, free.

For children, or remains, during a similar period: 1st class, $30; 2nd class, $20; 3rd class, $10; 4th class, $4; 5th class, $2; 6th class, gratis.

In perpetuity, for adults: 1st class, $200; 2nd class, $120; 3rd class, $75; 4th class, $45; 5th class, $20.

In perpetuity, for children or remains: 1st class, $120; 2nd class, $70; 3rd class, $50; 4th class, $30; 5th class, $15.

The Philadelphia philanthropist, Geo. W. Childs, has erected a monument in Greenwood Cemetery, New York city, to the memory of Richard A. Proctor, the astronomer, who died in New York of yellow fever, Sept. 12, 1888. Since his death Professor Proctor's body has lain in an unmarked grave in the neglected portion of the cemetery, but the remains are to be removed this month. The monument is of Quincy granite and is surrounded by a brass railing resting on posts of rustic work. At the apex of the stone is a raised star, and on its reverse side is an inscription written by Herbert Spencer.

THE MODERN CEMETERY.

THE RECEIVING TOMB.

The Kensico Cemetery.

This new necropolis of New York, is located on the Harlem division of the N. Y. Central & Hudson River R. R., about fifteen miles from the city limits. It is situated in the midst of an elevated and extensive plateau ranging in height from 300 to 525 feet above the sea with picturesque and historic surroundings, and soil well adapted to the purpose.

A new stone depot of Queen Anne style, perfect in all its appointments and exclusively used for cemetery purposes, forms an entrance to the cemetery.

The receiving tomb which we illustrate is built of stone and granite, contains 178 marble catacombs with a perfect system of interior ventilation, which will make it thoroughly sanitary. The tomb is entered under a stone archway, through a massive iron gate, in front of which are three large Sienna marble tablets; upon the centre one is engraved the names of the trustees; the mosaic floor, stained glass windows, groined arch ceiling, white marble fronts to the catacombs, the large iron gates separating the two rows of catacombs from the main isle where committal services are held, and the general finish of the interior, are all suggestive of a grand crypt to a cathedral. In front of the tomb is a large fountain, and the grounds near by will be purely ornamental.

The artistic treatment of this building and its surroundings has made a most beautiful and attractives pot. All drives, roads and avenues are built on stone foundations. In all landscape work an equal regard has been displayed to convenience, completeness of arrangements and beauty of effect; the winding drives diversifying the scene and breaking the monotony of the old style grave-yard.

Among the attractions soon to be added are a chapel and conservatory; this group of buildings will be conveniently placed near the entrance. Many prominent New Yorkers are interested in Kensico.

The annual report of Spring Grove cemetery, Cincinnati, O., for the year ending September 30th, contains the following statistics, receipts from lot sales etc., $83,042. Expenses for maintenance $75,810. Number of interments, 1,431, total number 55,482. Available resources of the association $256,358. Perpetual care fund $26,000. Sixty-seven men were employed by superintendent Salway.

At the Sign of the Skull.

A strange old tavern have I seen;
The walls are thick, the garden green;
'Tis damp and foul, yet through the door
Do rich men come as well as poor.
They come by night, and they come by day,
And never a guest is turned away.

The landlord, an unwholesome fellow,
Has a complexion white and yellow,
And, though he looks exceeding thin,
Does nothing else but grin and grin
At all his guests, who, after a while,
Begin to imitate his smile.

The guests are a fearful sight to see,
Though some are people of high degree;
For no one asks, when a carriage arrives,
A decent account of the inmates' lives;
But holy virgins and men of sin
Sleep cheek by jowl in this careless inn;

And beautiful youths in their strength and pride
Have taken beds by a leper's side;
But all sleep well, and it never was said
That any kind of complaint was made.
For all people who pass that way
Appear to intend a lengthened stay.

The house has a singular bill of fare,
Nothing dainty, nothing rare;
But only one dish, and that dish meat,
Which never a guest was known to eat,
Night and day the meal goes on,
And the guests themselves are fed upon.

These merry guests are all of them bound
To a land far off, but I never found
That any one knew when he should start,
Or wished from this pleasant house to part.

O, strange old tavern, with garden green!
In every town its walls are seen.
Now the question has often been asked of me
Is it really as bad as it seems to be?

—*Theodore C. Williams in Century.*

Ornamental Grasses.

The more extensive use of the different ornamental grasses should be encouraged by cemetery managers. Pleasant effects can be had by growing them, and their quiet beauty makes them very desirable for cemetery ornamentation. F. N. Gerard, in *Garden and Forest*, says:

For a tall, strong-growing, reliably hard and graceful grass, the variety zebrina of Eulalia Japonica will usually be most satisfactory. Under ordinary culture it makes a large clump some seven or eight feet tall, with strong stems and gracefully reflexing leaves barred with lighter green. In the fall they flower with handsome plumes, very much curled, and are useful for house decoration. The green leaves and stems are also very useful during the season for bold effects in decoration.

A well-grown clump of Pampas grass is very handsome as a detached group, making a fountain of foliage capped with handsome plumes, but it is not always hardy. The Ravenna grass, Erianthus Ravennæ, sometimes does duty with the florists as Pampas grass. It is a green-leaved, tall-growing sort, not so graceful as the Gynerium, but it is more hardy. For a bold effect there is nothing better than Arundo donax, though it is a coarse plant, and needs the gloss of distance. This is easily grown to a height of ten or twelve feet. The leaves are glaucous and clasp thick stems. The casual observer generally asks as to the variety of corn which is being grown. The variegated variety of Arundo donax is a much dwarfer plant, only three or four feet high, and much less coarse in effect. These plants require here a slight protection, a small mound of coal ashes over the roots being satisfactory in preserving them from destructive moisture. I have under trial a large form of Panicum spectabile, sent to me as the variety Gigantea. From seeds sown in the early year there are strong plants flowering in loose panicle, at about seven feet. This is said to be a ten or twelve foot grass, and I should judge that it might reach that height from strong roots. This is said to be hardy and sometimes variegated, though none of my plants have shown more than a white channel on the mid-rib. The leaves midway are about two inches wide, wider than those of the Eulalia, and the plants are distinct from the other large grasses. There is also the typical form of P. spectabile about three feet tall. This is also the height of the beautiful Eulalia gracillima univitatta, which, as many of your correspondents have remarked in your columns, no garden should be without. Eulalia Japonica variegated is of the same height, and the brightest of variegated grasses; it is taller than the Ribbon grass, Phalaris arundinacea, and much less spreading at the roots. Of the still shorter grasses, I fancy most Elymus glaucus, which has a rich glaucous sheen extremely effective. Elymus hystrix was sent me as one of the handsomest grasses in cultivation, but I fail to see any beauty in its foliage or heads of coarse flowers. Pennisetum longistylum is a well-established favorite for its effective heads of bloom. There is a grass in the swamp of the lower part of this state, New Jersey, which has a fur-like ball of bloom, which it has always seemed to me would be effective in cultivation—Pussy grass, in the vernacular—Apera arundinacea. The Pheasant grass is a handsome species, very odd and distinct, the leaves being marked in bright reds and browns. This did not grow very well for me, probably from neglect, for I do not think it a delicate plant, though it had at first glance a look of a plant suffering from some blight or disease.

There are numerous aquatic and sub-aquatic grasses and sedges—of these latter, the exotics Cyperus Papyrus, C. pungens and C. alternifolius being the most satisfactory, though tender. Hydropyrum latifolium (Co-ba of the Chinese) is a perfectly hardy aquatic grass, with a jointed stem from which spring several tall leaves. It is something in the way of "Wild Rice," but a handsomer plant. It has not flowered in the two years it has been cultivated here. In planting edges of ornamental water, it will be found most satisfactory to search neighboring swamps and use the most effective native plant. This course, pursued by Mr. Olmsted, at Chicago, has produced one of the most effective and satisfactory bits of planting in the grounds of the Exposition.

In selecting decorative grasses preference should be given to those which have a long season of growth, as those which flower and mature early are apt to prove unsightly. Scarcely enough use is made of the noble grasses in arrangements of decorative plants. Masses of these, as often seen, have a rather heavy effect, which a well-considered addition of grasses would often relieve.

Plant Early.

Be it in fall or spring, that is our theory and our practice too. In order to have success and pleasure in ornamental trees and shrubs we must be prepared to give them good ground, a good position and good care. If your ground is naturally good dig holes deep and wide, even if you fill them in again before planting to a size just big enough for the roots, this gives the roots good foraging ground for some years. If your soil is poor dig out the holes deep and wide, removing the poor dirt and filling up with good earth; this will give the trees a good start in life. If your garden is bleak and exposed you had better choose trees that will thrive in such a place, as Austrian pines, white spruce, Colorado blue spruce and Douglas fir in the way of evergreen trees; and American elms, rock maples, birches and the like in the way of deciduous trees. But if your grounds are fairly well sheltered by neighboring swells of country or woods, or buildings, then you can gratify your taste as much as you wish in the way of fine varieties. In the way of shrubbery you want something nice, and something in bloom all summer, from the mezereon in early spring till altheas wind up in fall. Fine shrubs want shelter too, but this you can afford anyway; if you have not got it naturally, close board fences, spruce and other hedges and contiguous buildings should be made to supply it. Deeply worked land and good earth make showy, thrifty shrubs. Before planting cut off the tips of the broken roots with a sharp knife or shears, also head in the roots proportionately, and plant firmly. Don't mix fresh manure with your soil in planting, and never put manure about the roots, whenever manure is given it should be applied as a mulching.—*Gardening*.

Evergreens planted in early fall do just as well as when set out in spring. Select a period immediately following heavy rains when the ground is moist and warm. It will induce young roots to push out before severe weather sets in, giving the plants additional strength during the winter.—*Mechan's Nurseries*.

Visit to the Graveyards of Hamburg.

Whoever visits Hamburg this year is likely to go to the cemeteries. A grewsome trip it is to travel over the road where within a few weeks last year trod nearly 10,000 funerals. There are Jewish and Christian cemeteries. The Christian cemetery is well laid out and thickly planted with trees and all kinds of shrubbery. There are driveways, footways and settees. The grounds cover an immense area and scores of laborers are constantly employed, who keep them in superb order. An inspection of the gravestones points plainly enough to the great mortality during those last few days of August and the early weeks of September, last year. Sometimes two or three or four stones within a single family plat bear the same date.

Even many of the graves of the poor are marked, for slabs are cheap, very clever little ones with the inscriptions on them being quoted at the roadside at prices which are equivalent in our money to not more than $4 or $5. The very poor still rest in the trenches where they were buried on those terrible days. At the height of the epidemic almost 700 died per diem, though this rate was maintained for only a short time, and it was out of the question to make the burials in separate graves. These trenches are still unmarked; but it is expected that a monument will be erected, a fit companion-piece to a large sarcophagus in another part of the city which commemorates the fate of many residents of Hamburg, who fell victims to starvation during the severe winter 1813-14, and the cold marble and history books will soon be all that are left to tell of one of the most awful visitations of scourge in modern times.—*Corr. Philadelphia Telegraph.*

The will of the late Jesse H. Griffen of Yorktown N. Y., contained the following clause: "I desire that my corpse may be put in a plain walnut coffin, without any silver plating and carried to Omawalk by some of my friends in an ordinary spring wagon, and that no tombstone should be erected where my mortal remains are reposited in the earth, for I have noticed that people in moderate circumstances are often distressed by trying to follow the example of others who make expensive displays at funerals, and tombstone honors are a truer indication of the vanity of survivors than of the virtues of the deceased. If in passing through this life I can do anything for which posterity will be better and happier it will be sufficient monument to my memory. If I fail in this, let no marble slab bear the witness that one so worthless lived."

* * *

The New England Undertakers' Association are in conference with the faculty of the Harvard University Medical School with reference to establishing an embalming school for the better education of undertakers.

Cremation.

The first crematorium to be built in New England is now in course of construction near the rear entrance to Forest Hills cemetery, Boston. It is a substantial stone structure and with the acre and a half of ground surrounding it will cost $30,000. Oil will be used in the retorts in place of coal or wood ordinarily used.

* * *

Instead of being on the verge of abandoning its property and objects as was published in a Cincinnati paper sometime ago, The Cincinnati Cremation Co., give every evidence of being as determined to succeed as ever. They have recently taken out the old retort in which 215 bodies had been cremated and replaced it with two larger and improved retorts. Secretary Roever writes that there is every evidence of growth of sentiment in favor of cremation.

* * *

In Germany there is to be fresh legislation for the prevention of epidemics; and a proposal is made in the Reichstag for making cremation optional throughout the Empire. In England cremation is, within certain limits, already optional, but there is a strong feeling, partly sentimental and partly religious, against it. The recent debate in the German Reichstag brought out the fact that among all parties, there was a strong inclination to favour this mode of performing the last rites. What the balance of parties is in Germany, in the immediate future, is, of course, at present very uncertain, but there can be little doubt that a new law of a stringent character will be passed for the preventing of epidemics.—*Funeral Directors Journal.*

* * *

In Worcester, England, is a stone erected over the grave of a departed auctioneer of that city, on which "Gone" is inscribed. In a Sussex graveyard, in addition to the initials of the deceased and the date of death, a stone has inscribed in large letters the words "He Was." Two of the strangest as well as the shortest epitaphs are "Asleep (as usual)," on the tombstone of a large individual by one who knew him well, and "Left till called for" is carved on a gravestone in Cane Hill Cemetery, Belfast. A photographer has this inscription over his grave: "Here I lie, taken from life." On the tomb of Charles the Great, first Emperor of Germany, are two words only, "Carolo Magno."—*St. Louis Globe-Democrat.*

* * *

The number of the MODERN CEMETERY which you have sent me is as fine a copy of typographical work, the illustrations as pretty, as I have seen for some time, and would bear a very creditable comparison with any journal with which I am acquainted.—*Franklin Brett, Boston, Mass.*

CEMETERY NOTES.

The city council of San Antonio, Texas, are considering the purchase of 500 acres of land for cemetery purposes.

* * *

I am very much interested in aquatics and think that as a class such plants are worthy of more attention in cemeteries.—*Wm. Stone, Lynn, Mass.*

* * *

Woodlawn cemetery Winona, Minn., Harleigh at Camden, N. J., and Forest Hills at Boston, have materially increased the capacity of their greenhouses this season.

* * *

The Laurel Hill Cemetery Association at San Francisco are erecting a spacious building 35 x 70 feet, to be used as offices, reception rooms and superintendent's residence. The building is of brick with light stone trimmings and elaborate interior finish. It will cost about $15,000.

* * *

Two workmen at Greenwood Cemetery, Brooklyn, quarreled over a trifling remark and fought with sickles. One of the men was nearly decapitated and otherwise horribly mutilated. The other escaped with but few injuries and was imprisoned awaiting the result of his victim's injuries.

* * *

On a plat sixty feet in diameter in the Brockport (N. Y.) Rural Cemetery, a soldiers' memorial of unique design is now in course of construction. It will be in the form of a circular tower ten feet in height, built of rock faced stone. Memorial tablets will be placed on the inner walls and a spiral stairway leads to the top of the tower. The plat is encircled by a twenty-foot drive and the greensward between it and the tower will probably be used for statues, cannon, etc.

* * *

A Boston paper says that the grave of Phillips Brooks at Mt. Auburn is entirely overgrown by the glossy-leaved myrtle, or periwinkle, and upon this dark background fresh flowers are constantly laid. The bishop lies in a simple, old-fashioned grave lot, with an iron fence around it. The gate of this fence is not latched, but swings silently, to admit the countless visitors, who have worn the grass entirely away between the grave and the path below it. Two laurel bushes, which stand on each side of the gate, have been nearly chipped away by those who wish to retain some memorial of the spot.

The MODERN CEMETERY is a splendid periodical.—*J. M. Underwood, Lake City, Minn.*

I consider the MODERN CEMETERY most valuable.—*Geo. E. Smith, Treas. The Rural Cemetery, Worcester, Mass.*

Resolutions Adopted at the Seventh Annual Convention of the Association of American Cemetery Superintendents.

Resolved: That it is the sense of this convention that all Sunday funerals be discouraged as much as possible.

Resolved: That it is the sense of this meeting that all headstones or markers should be limited to the height of the sod or the level of the surface of the ground.

Resolved: That it is the sense of this meeting that vaults and catacombs be discouraged and if possible prevented in cemeteries.

A Chinese Monument.

A piece of unique monumental art in Rosehill is the Chinese monument, which serves also as a sort of altar where the Celestials perform their singular funeral ceremonies. It is near the north gates of the grounds, and is a singular bit of architecture. A central wall or slab eight or ten feet high is surmounted by a graceful bit of scroll work and ornamented with a tablet of gray-veined marble, upon the surface of which are carved in vertical lines the queer Chinese characters, painted black, which probably relate the object of the monument or may contain a prayer to the heathen gods. At either side of the central tablet are two small hollow pillars, square at the base and surmounted by a ball. Holes are cut in the sides of these, and a little door of iron is set near the bottom of each, says a writer in the Chicago *Times*.

The square holes in the side pillars serve as vents for the smoke of the incense, colored paper, rice cakes, sweetmeats and other such things that are supposed to be acceptable offerings to the Chinese gods and which are introduced into the columns through the little iron doors, which are the openings to the fireplaces of the altar.

These pillars and the central tablet rest on a semi-circular hearth or altar with three steps or stages, which are surrounded by a coping. Before the center of the face of the monument, under the inscribed tablet is an iron pan, where the mourners burn joss sticks of perfumed wood, which are equivalent to prayers for the repose of the soul of the dead, each prayer being supposed to ascend as long as the joss stick burns.

It is said that the Chinese invariably bury their dead in the single graves of the cemetery, and never purchase lots, for they do not intend that the bodies of their countrymen shall permanently rest in the unhallowed soil of a Christian land.

In a Cemetery.

Tommy—"All these people haven't gone to heaven, auntie."

Aunt—"Hush, Tommy! Why do you say that?"

Tommy—"Because I read on some of the tombstones, 'Peace to his ashes,' and they don't have ashes only where its very hot.—*Ex.*

Rules for the Employees of the Cemetery of Spring Grove, Cincinnati.

1. All employees must be at the places appointed for roll-call at six-thirty (6:30) A. M.
2. Must be industrious and attentive to their work.
3. Must not hold conversation with the other workmen when at work, only as necessity requires for the proper understanding of their respective duties.
4. Must not smoke, or bring into the grounds anything to eat or drink.
5. Must be courteous, polite and neatly dressed.
6. Must not leave their work without directions to do so, or by the sound of the bell.
7. Must not use profane language under any circumstance.
8. Must not take anything away from the grounds or remove anything from the lots without permission.
9. Must not put tools, or anything else, under or in the branches of trees or shrubbery, but when done using any tool must return it to its respective place.
10. Must take their own tools with them at night, so when coming to work in the morning they may be ready, without having to spend time in looking them up.
11. When passing through the grounds, must pick up all paper or any light rubbish that can be carried in the hand.
12. Must not hunt, trap or shoot without permission.
13. Must not go through or over the fences of the grounds, and must use all dilligence to prevent others from doing so.
14. Must not cross the sections, in going to and from work, except the one on which they are working, and then not to make paths.
15. The men in charge of horses and other animals must treat them kindly and take good care of them.
16. Teamsters, when working with other men, must not leave their work before the bell rings (unless instructed to do so). They must be at the stable at five-thirty (5:30) A. M., that they may have ample time to care for their teams and be ready when the other men arrive.
17. They must not, under any circumstance, receive any compensation for courtesies extended to lot owners or any other persons coming to the cemetery. First violation of this rule will insure instant dismissal.
18. All employees must make themselves acquainted with the rules and regulations of the cemetery, and immediately report any violation of them.
19. The violation of any of the foregoing rules will cause the offender to be suspended for three days, for first offense. Second offense—dismissal from the employment of the cemetery.

WM. SALWAY, Sup't.

An unusual funeral service was recently performed in St. George's Church, New York, by the rector, Rev. Dr. Rainsford. It was over the funeral urn containing the ashes of Mrs. Lillian Poole, the soprano of the Jarbeau Comedy company, who died in Pittsburg and was cremated there. The urn, eleven by eight inches in size, was placed at the head of the middle aisle at the foot of the altar. The metal case containing the ashes was in a handsomely finished cedar box, covered with white satin. On two sides were photographs, one showing her in ordinary dress and the other in the character of *Priscilla*. It was supported by a beautifully carved white pedestal. Dr. Rainsford made no change from the usual Episcopal burial service. When he reached the part, "Dust to dust," he took some ashes from a silver dish and sprinkled them over the flowers on the urn. After the services the urn was removed to the house of her father, where the family will keep it surrounded with lilies of the valley.

* * *

An old-fashioned horizontal marker in one of the cemeteries at Alexandria, Va., supposed to mark the grave of Aaron Burr's only daughter, bears the following inscription:

To the memory of a female stranger whose mortal sufferings terminated on the 14th day of October, 1816, aged 23 years and 8 months.
This stone is placed here by her disconsolate husband, in whose arms she sighed her latest breath and who under God did his utmost to soothe the cold, dread ear of death.
How loved, how valued once avails thee not,
To whom related or by whom begot;
A heap of dust alone remains of thee,
'Tis all thou art and all the proud shall be.
To him gave all the prophets witness, that through his name whosoever believeth in him shall receive remission of sins.—Acts, 10th chapter, 43rd verse.

* * *

The Kansas *Chief* asks what has become of the old-fashioned people who used to rub the backs of their hands over a dead person's face, when the coffin was opened at the grave? We give it up.—*Goshen Democrat*.

They have gone to join those who turn the face of mirrors to the wall, and stop the clock at the hour of a death occuring in the house.—*Western Undertaker*.

And will soon have the company of the few remaining adherents to several equally as superstitious ideas, that obtain in some sections of this country.

Correspondence.

Vacation Reminiscences.

Since the organization of the Association of American Cemetery Superintendents, the annual vacation is looked forward to with much pleasure, not alone from the mere fact that we are to meet at the convention in formal shape, but because of the more acceptable social greeting. Were we to measure the usefulness of the association by the gains made only at the meetings, I think it would take but a short time to wind up. Although I recognize its great value, the social chat and exchange of views in the hotel corridors, the drives to various places of interest, visiting cemeteries and parks, are all means of usefulness, on account of opportunities for practical thought and suggestions which we are enabled to apply in our daily duties.

With these thoughts in our mind, we left our eastern home Aug. 19, with the anticipation of the happiest greetings from our brother co-workers. Our journey was very pleasant, the company of the jovial V. P. adding no little to the occasion. Our ride through the states was one of rare enjoyment. The beautiful scenery, more readily enjoyed than described, added greatly to the pleasure of the first day's trip. Our first stop was at Lowell, which is often called the Spindle City and the Manchester of America, because of the extent of its cotton manufactures. Here we have a member, K. H. Mulno, whom we have met only in correspondence. Onward again and we are soon at Manchester, N. H., a great manufacturing center, and a thriving city of 36,500 inhabitants in 1893. There are two cemeteries here. It has been our pleasure to meet the superintendents of both at our own grounds, but we regret that they are not members with us. A short run and we found ourselves at Concord, N. H., the capital of the state, beautifully situated. Here the great industries of the New England Granite Co. are carried on. Large quantities of dressed and undressed blocks are shipped to all parts of the country. There is a very good cemetery in Concord, I am told, having met the superintendent who is a progressive man, but the writer's persuasive powers did not draw him in as a member of the A. A. C. S. We hope they will all come in, if not to the national body we may have to start a local society for the benefit of those who cannot get so far from home. St. Johnsbury was reached in a rain storm. The great Fairbanks scale industry is carried on here. All through this state and portions of New Hampshire the scenery is very attractive and often grand, the mountains are very high. Our encyclopædia says Mansfield is the highest, 4,430 feet, and there are five others over 4,000 and twelve over 3,500 feet. These ranges, except perhaps on the very summits, are densely covered with spruce (Abies Niger). As we rolled rapidly along, from what little met our eye, we are sure that the flora of this state must be of unusual interest, and with here and there a stop we found ourselves at Montreal after the evening shades appeared, and the beautiful city was to be seen only by the aid of the electric light. A short stroll gave us an idea of the majestic buildings, and the well-arranged beds of flowers in the public squares were greatly enjoyed. The buildings were grand examples of the solid way our cousins across the line have of doing things, and at the same time the attractive and beautiful were well looked after. Thus ended our first day's journey. The next morning when we awoke it was to behold as deserted a looking country as could be imagined, and so we traversed all day with little to interest us, preferring to read and sleep. Occasionally a little fresh verdure was seen in the shape of ferns and flowers in moist places, but the marks of the destructive forest fires was apparent all along, and lamentable to behold. The early evening brought us to the end of our ride on the Canadian Pacific, crossing St. Mary's river and at 7 p. m. we were at Saulte Ste. Marie. A short stop here enabled us to take some fresh air, and view the country; this was quite refreshing. We were soon on our way again. The shades of the second night are upon us and our observations are again ended. As soon as light dawned however, our curtain was lifted and we looked with greater satisfaction than on the previous day upon the evidences of civilization. Large tracts of land had been cleared and cultivated, little settlements here, a saw mill occasionally, and the farmer's house and barn all encouraged us to believe that we were nearing a large city. All this time we were on the lookout for the flora, but saw but little that differed from that of the previous day except in the low places, some splendid patches of that magnificent native plant, Lobelia Cardinalis, of which New England's poet, Holmes, says:

> As if some wounded eagle's breast,
> Slow throbbing o'er the plain,
> Had left his airy path impressed
> In drops of scarlet rain.

And now our observations ceased, as we were told by the courteous porter that we were drawing into Minneapolis. The usual dusting and brushing after a forty eight hours' ride, placed us in fit condition to land. We preferred to walk to our hotel, which gave us needed exercise and a chance to see something of this magnificent western city. Breakfast being over, the next thing in order was an extra good touch by the tonsorial artist on the V. P. and with the usual shine for both, we commenced our vacation in the best of spirits. In our next we will try and gather some thoughts about the convention and Minneapolis.

Editor Modern Cemetery.

A brief resume of my trip to and from the Minneapolis convention may be of some interest to the members of the A. A. C. Superintendents.

Owing to my late arrival at the convention, I was deprived the pleasure of accompanying the association to Lakewood Cemetery, which I regretted exceedingly. This was partially made up for, however, by the pleasant and profitable visit made to Oakland Cemetery, St. Paul, at which all present expressed themselves as being abundantly paid through the courtesy of the members of Oakland Cemetery and the kind attention shown them by Brother Roxell, superintendent. Much favorable comment was made at the fine appearance of Oakland Cemetery, and the well cared for grounds were generally admired.

Having been denied a visit to Lakewood Cemetery, as referred to above, I called on Brother Hobert after the convention adjourned and was cordially received by the capable superintendent, who conveyed me through the beautiful grounds, pointing out recent improvements and prospective ones to be made in the near future. The grounds are conducted strictly on the lawn plan and their beautiful appearance of gentle and varied undulations, ornamented with choice trees, shrubbery, etc., form a grand combination very pleasing to the eye. These in conjunction with the fine lake surroundings seem greatly to enhance the beautiful features of Lakewood Cemetery. This is one of the most beautiful cemeteries that it has ever been our privilege to visit. The courtesy extended me by Brother Hobert was duly appreciated, and will linger in our memory for years to come. The trustees of Lakewood were fortunate in securing the services of such a competent man to supervise their grounds.

After a hurried and entirely unsatisfactory visit to the wonderful Fair, where three months instead of three days would have been requisite for anything like a careful examination, I visited beautiful Spring Grove. I always feel at home under the roof of the hospitable superintendent and his wife and never tire of exploring the charming grounds. The following day found me once more in Newark at the end of a long and enjoyable trip.

CHARLES NICHOLS.

Association of American Cemetery Superintendents.

WM. SALWAY, "Spring Grove" Cincinnati, O., President.
T. McCARTHY, "Swan Point" Providence, R. I., Vice-President.
F. EURICH, Woodlawn, Toledo, O., Secretary and Treasurer.

The Eighth Annual Convention of the Association will be held at Philadelphia in September, 1894.

Publisher's Department.

The receipt of Cemetery Literature and Trade Catalogues will be acknowledged in this column.

TO ADVERTISERS. THE MODERN CEMETERY is the only publication of its class and will be found a valuable medium for reaching cemetery officials in all parts of the United States.

TO SUBSCRIBERS. Cemetery officials desiring to subscribe for a number of copies regularly to circulate among their lot owners, should send for our special terms. Several well-known cemeteries have already adopted this plan with good results.

Contributions on matters pertaining to cemeteries are solicited. Address all communications to
R. J. HAIGHT, 334 Dearborn St., CHICAGO.

Cemetery Literature Received: Thirty-ninth annual report of the Board of Commissioners of Pine Grove Cemetery, Lynn, Mass.; Annual report of Union Dale Cemetery, Allegheny, Pa.

We are indebted to our subscribers who have sent lists of parties from whom cemetery supplies are purchased.

Jesse B. Kimes, Philadelphia, Pa., is furnishing the slate for the new receiving vault at Woodmere Cemetery, Detroit, Mich.

In the recently published annual report of the Union Dale cemetery, Allegheny, Pa., a page is devoted to "Suggestions to Lot Owners" which we are pleased to note were taken from the columns of the MODERN CEMETERY and due credit given.

I will consider it a lasting favor if some of the MODERN CEMETERY readers will suggest a means of exterminating moles. I have tried such remedies as corn soaked in Paris green, raw pork spread with rough-on-rats, the ordinary mole trap, etc., but notwithstanding they continue to increase.—*Alex. Russell, Supt., Camden, N. J.*

Inclosed find names and addresses of eight of our directors, to whom I wish the MODERN CEMETERY sent for one year. Our president is already a subscriber and I am anxious that the other members of the board shall become more interested in cemetery matters and know of no better way to interest them than by their reading the MODERN CEMETERY.—*From a prominent cemetery official.*

The committee appointed at the recent convention to confer with lawn mower manufacturers in regard to certain improvements has heard from one concern who are now experimenting with several appliances designed to meet the requirements of lawn mowers adapted to cemetery work. One of the improvements is a flexible washer to cover the outside hubs of wheels, and another is a flexible rod projecting from front of machine, to prevent the latter coming in contact with monument bases, etc. These experiments are being made by the Caldwell Lawn Mower Co., Newburg, N. Y., whose high-wheel mower has already been introduced in a number of cemeteries.

By a typographical error in last months issue the address of the De Lamater Iron Works was given as 24-26 Cortland St. New York. It should have been 87-89 South Fifth Ave. This company manufacture the De Lamater-Rider and the De Lamater-Ericsson Pumping Engine, a hot air pumping engine well adapted to cemetery uses. An illustrated catalogue will be sent free on application to any one interested.

The McMurray and Fisher patent vault hearse illustrated in our advertising columns this month is a complete and stylish hearse designed expressly for moving bodies from the vault to the grave. It is arranged to be drawn by two or four persons and is what every cemetery association having a receiving vault should have. The trustees of Marion, O., Cemetery Association have used the hearse for sometime and give the following testmonial.
MESSRS. McMURRAY & FISHER, Marion O.

Gentlemen:—We feel that you have perfectly supplied our long felt want of a suitable vehicle for removing the dead from the Receiving Vault to place of Interment. The Vault Hearse is just the thing and we must say for style and finish it is much better than we expected. We consider it indispensible where a vault is in use. Wishing you success in their manufacture we are,

Yours Truly,
P. O. SHARPLESS,
A. H. KLING,   } Trustees Marion Cemetery.
GEO. CRAWFORD.

Cemetery Stock for Sale.

My one-eighth interest in Sylvan Lawn Cemetery, Chicago, is offered for sale. Full particulars on application.
G. L. RAY.
318½ N. Market St., Chicago.

THE NEW HANDY BINDER

Will be found a most valuable invention for keeping the numbers of the MODERN CEMETERY in good condition. The method of binding allows the pages to lie perfectly flat, whether one or a dozen numbers are in the binder. Any number can be taken out and replaced without disturbing the other numbers. The binders are strong and durable and have the title of MODERN CEMETERY on the side in gilt, an ornament to any desk or reading table. We will supply them to subscribers in embossed cloth covers, 50 cents. Heavy flexible paper covers for 35 cents. By mail post-paid.

MODERN CEMETERY, 334 Dearborn St., Chicago.

THE MODERN CEMETERY.

THE MODERN CEMETERY.
AN ILLUSTRATED MONTHLY JOURNAL DEVOTED TO THE INTEREST OF CEMETERIES

R. J. HAIGHT, Publisher.
334 Dearborn Street, CHICAGO.

Subscription $1.00 a Year in Advance.   Foreign Subscription $1.25.
Special Rates on Six or More Copies.

Vol. III.   CHICAGO, NOV. 1893.   No. 9.

CONTENTS.

SHOULD ALL LOTS FRONT ON PATHS OR AVENUES	97
HARDY SHRUBS AND THEIR PROTECTION AGAINST DROUGHT	98
TREES AS MEMORIALS	99
*FALL EFFECTS AT GRACELAND	100
A CEMETERY OF THE HUNS—THE APPROACHING MILLENIUM	101
*RIVERSIDE CEMETERY, ROCHESTER, N. Y	102-103
CEMETERY NOTES	104
*THE YOUNGLOVE MONUMENT, CLEVELAND, O	105
THE SUPERINTENDENT	106
VACATION REMINISCENCES	107
THE QUESTION BOX	108
NOTICE TO CEMETERY OFFICIALS	108
PUBLISHERS DEPARTMENT	108

*Illustrated.

Should all Lots Front on Paths or Avenues?

"Is it essential with the lawn plan that every lot should border on a drive, path or alley? If so, what width?". To this question, after a free discussion the members of the Association of American Cemetery Superintendents in their recent convention at Minneapolis, replied by voting it to be "essential that all lots should front on an avenue or path." The question really at issue was whether every lot should be separated on all sides from the adjoining lot by a path or alley. The resolution which followed the discussion, as given above, deems it necessary that all lots should have an avenue or path frontage, but does not imply that it is desirable that a lot should be entirely surrounded by a path. A subsequent resolution was adopted to the effect that spaces between lots were not essential.

The question was presented by Mr. Cline, of Dayton, Ohio, who at the outset of the discussion, stated that he had propounded the question for the practical purpose of finding out what members who had had more experience than he, would do in laying out his new territory, and in relaying old territory that was not originally provided with alleys.

Would it be essential to have the lots front on alleys or outlets of some kind?

Mr. McCarthy, of Providence, R. I., speaking for his own cemetery, said that they formerly platted their ground with a two-foot space around every lot, but as these spaces became depressed and were a receptacle for all kinds of rubbish they soon became a nuisance. They were then filled up and sodded, but in the newer parts of the cemetery no paths or spaces were left between lots. One lot abuts against an adjoining lot, and the boundaries are marked with granite posts, one post answering for two lots. To furnish access to all the lots they front either on an avenue or a path. The path is continuous and intersected occasionally, but it furnishes a frontage to all the lots that do not front on a drive. If a small piece of ground anywhere is without frontage, it can be reserved for planting with trees or shrubs.

The argument in favor of walks all around lots was supported by Mr. Stephens, of Columbus, O. He thought this the only plan whereby the lawn system could be carried out successfully. He suggested a two-foot grass walk around three sides of every lot. Gravelled paths are out of the question, because they are not in harmony with the lawn plan and people will not keep on the walks, no matter how stiffly defined. The best method is to have all the walks needed but not to define them sharply by shrubbery or any other means. Each tier of lots would border on an avenue or walk, so that monuments could be got in, but the two-foot space all around each lot would appear as part of the lawn. The lots would simply be made two feet wider and longer, only that the space reserved for a path on three sides could never be used for graves or monuments. The cemetery thus gains more lawn, and the lot-owner pays for it, just as he would pay for walks or any other improvement under the old system.

President Salway said that in his cemetery the original plan was to provide walks of from two to four feet around nearly all the lots, but experience had made the directors more economical, and now they allow to each lot an alley on one side only. The future ought to be provided for as well as the present, but with the landscape plan in view at all times, liberal spaces should be reserved for approach to the interior lots from one side. There must be some definite way of getting to the interior lots, because, though the erection of monuments does not always follow soon after the purchase of lots, yet sometime in the future, perhaps fifty, sixty or a hundred years to come, someone will see the necessity of putting up a monument. When all the other lots are occupied, it will be impossible to get a monument to a lot unless there are spaces left for that purpose. The privilege of setting a monument at some future time belongs of right to every lot, and it ought to be preserved. The object is to have enough walks and alleys, but not too many as in the old plan. It is comparatively easy to make no mistake in this regard in laying out new cemeteries on the lawn plan, but it is very difficult to do away with these walks and alleys when once they have been established, as in the old plan. Never should there be a walk on more than two sides of a lot, and all walks should be sodded.

Mr. Rhedemeyer, of Camden, N. J., presented the plan adopted in his cemetery, which proved to be a novel one in some respects. To mark the boundary lines of lots, he uses granite posts, varying in size, 6 x 6, 6 x 12, and 12 x 12 inches. The use of 12 x 12 posts indicates that four lots are adjacent to one another. The posts are creased with a chisel to represent the boundary lines. The cemetery by this plan does not lose an inch of ground. The corner posts are set on a level with the ground, giving a clear sweep of lawn. All walks as far as possible are sodded. A four-foot path leads from one end of the drive to the other, giving access to the lots. The practical advantage of this plan, besides saving ground and preserving the continuity of the lawn, is to save labor and expense.

It was agreed that the policy to be pursued by new cemeteries in conforming to the lawn plan was plain, as compared with the course of the old cemeteries. The difficulty felt by all was to get out of the old plan when once established. The simplest solution of this difficulty is to fill up all paths and alleys and sod them over.

Hardy Shrubs and their Protection Against Drought.

A paper read before the Seventh Annual Convention of the Association of Cemetery Superintendents, by Prof. Green of the Minnesota Experimental Station.

The treatment of the surface soil around trees planted on dry land is a matter that calls for much careful attention. The American public has been educated to thinking that a blue-grass sod in such places should extend close up to the trunks of the trees. In a few years this may become so thick and solid that it will shed water nearly as perfectly as a shingled roof. This is an unnatural condition, and under such circumstances plants cannot reach any great degree of development in dry situations. Where trees naturally make a good growth in dry locations, the surface of the soil is covered with a considerable thickness of leaves and branches that have fallen to the ground. These retard the run of the water and allow it to percolate into the ground and reach the roots of the trees. It also prevents evaporation from the surface soil and keeps the surface soil cooler. For instance, this season the strawberry bed at the experiment station has given far better returns than others in the immediate vicinity, and this success was largely due to the practice of heavily mulching the space between the rows with straw.

At any time during the severe drought, which has prevailed for a considerable period, the soil under the mulch could readily be rolled into pellets, while in adjacent rows, not mulched, the soil was very dry. Analysis of the soil, four inches from the surface, showed that which had been mulched contained 24.3 per cent. of water, while that which was not mulched had 18 per cent. of water. Of the soils three inches from the surface, the mulched contained 20.6 per cent. of water, and that not mulched 15.5 per cent. In either case, the mulch increased the amount of water contained in the soil under it 33⅓ per cent. This is equivalent to an increase of 2.2 quarts of water to each cubic foot of soil, which is equivalent, where a tree is mulched for five feet on all sides, to an increase of 44.3 gallons of water in its upper one foot of soil under the mulch, and there is, probably, nearly as much increase in the second foot of soil. Yet in this case, the soil which was not mulched was undoubtedly near enough to be considerably affected by the water in the mulched rows. The surface soil of some other land on the farm was found to contain only 5 per cent. of moisture at the same time. It is probably fair to assume that the mulched land contained at least 60 per cent. more moisture than that not mulched.

This is a great variation, and often makes the difference between success and failure in growing trees and plants.

People may complain that a mulch is unsightly; but it can often be covered up to great advantage with hardy shrubbery, which also aids the retention of water by shading the ground and protecting it from drying winds. We are apt not to appreciate the value of undergrowth around trees. This is nature's way, and we would do well to follow her in it many times. For covering the mulch symphoricarpos, the hardier spireas, flowering currants, buffalo berry and many other hardy plants are suggested as being desirable; and when properly grouped, make pleasing contrast. The best material for a mulch will vary with that which is easiest to obtain. Hay, straw, bogasse, coal ashes and hard-wood sawdust are good; but any material which is a good non-conductor will answer the purpose.

The importance of shelter, by this I mean wind breaks, can hardly be overestimated. It has been clearly shown that evaporation under the influence of the wind is dependent not only on the temperature and degrees of the same, but also on its velocity, which if impeded, reduces the rate of evaporation. Careful experiments made by the U. S. Signal Service in 1887, showed that with a temperature of the air at 84 degrees, and a relative humidity of 50 per cent., evaporation, with the wind blowing at five miles an hour, was a little more than twice what it was in a calm. At fifteen miles an hour, the wind would evaporate about five times as much water as in a calm atmosphere of the same temperature and humidity. These figures state in exact terms the value of the shelter belts, and many other similar observations could be given to show the value of wind-breaks.

This protection is sometimes best given by a wind-break. It certainly may be given by planting in groves where the trees protect one another from the wind and sun. Newly transplanted trees will often be greatly helped by covering their trunks with hay, straw or other material that will keep off the wind and sun. The hard maple is found in the extreme northern limit of this state in large quantities, forming great forests, yet even at Lake City, 300 miles south of this limit, is liable to serious injury to its trunk, and is not considered a safe street tree unless the trunk is shaded. The same is more or less true of the bass-wood, which is greatly improved by covering its trunk. The mountain ash makes a large tree 200 miles north of this city and yet, here, is liable to sun scald if its trunk is not protected. I have made a considerable study of this subject and have always found the bark much healthier and fresher when protected than when exposed.

To sum up this matter, I would say, in dry locations it is of the utmost importance to have a retentive soil, to mulch, and to protect the whole plant from wind and the trunk from the sun as far as possible.

Trees as Memorials.

To those who have tired of the countless forms of marble and granite for memorial purposes, and yet who feel that some tribute should mark the spot where are laid away the remains of the loved ones gone before, the use of trees will be most gratifying. The idea, though by no means a new one, is not in as general practice as many cemetery officials would like to see it, or as it is likely to be in time. Adolph Strauch, the recognized father of landscape gardening as applied to cemeteries, recommended their use many years ago. He suggested planting trees that were indigenous to the birth places of the deceased, "thus forming an arboretum which in the course of time would afford valuable information to succeeding generations, and be of far more value and use than a great collection of dilapidated stone slabs, monuments, etc." Chateaubriand has expressed himself most beautifully on the subject in these words: "I have seen the memorable monuments to Crœsus and Cæsar, but I prefer the airy tombs of the Indians, whose mausoleums of verdure, refreshed by the morning dew, embalmed and fanned by the breezes and over which waves the same branch where the blackbird builds his nest and utters his plaintive melody." Memorial trees are known to exist in Europe that are now more than 400 years old, and not a few have been planted in this country. In the selection of trees for such purposes, there are many things to be taken into consideration, and the advice of one well versed in such matters should be sought before a selection is made. In this connection it will be interesting to note the remarkable age attained by some trees as given by J. A. Collinson, in a recent issue of *Notes and Queries:*

"Elm, 300 years; ivy, 335 years; maple, 516 years; larch, 576 years; orange, 630 years; cypress, 800 years; olive, 800 years; walnut, 900 years; Oriental plane, 1000 years; lime, 1100 years; spruce 1200 years; oak, 1500 years; cedar, 2000 years; yew, 3200 years. The way in which the ages of these trees have been ascertained leaves no doubt of its correctness. In some few cases the data has been furnished by historical records and by tradition, but the botanical archæologists have a resource independent of either, and when carefully used, infallible. Of all the forms of nature trees alone disclose their ages candidly and freely. In the stems of trees which have branches and leaves with netted veins—in all exogens, as the botanist would say—the increase takes place by means of an annual deposit of wood, spread in an even layer upon the surface of the preceding one."

Paul Scholz superintendent of Metairie Cemetery, at New Orleans, La., committed suicide by shooting himself in the head. Mr. Scholz was a german by birth and won distinction in the Franco-Prussian war. He studied floriculture and engineering in the old country. Fourteen years ago he became sexton of Metairie Cemetery and five years since was made superintendent. Mr. Scholz took much pride in his work and through his efforts many improvements were made in Metairie. It is one of the Crescent City's chief attractions and winter visitors from the frozen north may be seen strolling among its avenues throughout the entire season.

Fall Effects at Graceland.

On the first visit to Graceland to note the fall effects the only hint of the season, in the way of changing foliage was a single spray of flaming orange scarlet leaves held out from a shadowy green recess like a welcoming hand. But there were indications of the close of summer in the odor of ripe vegetation, in the deep blue sky with fleecy clouds piled high and motionless, in the dreamy haze that hung like a veil of thinnest gray blue gauze between one and the middle distance, and in the brooding restfulness that pervaded all nature. No ripple disturbed the smooth surface of the water, and in it lay quiet reflections of the calm beauty of the surrounding view. The tone of the atmosphere was unmistakably that of the "Fall of the Leaf."

Before the second visit, (made perhaps a week later) there had been a frost, and dame nature had been busy with her paints, putting in color sparingly, but with a breadth and freedom, yet at the same time, with an attention to detail that made close attention a delight.

The art of planting at Graceland is well

QUIET REFLECTIONS.

the border of a coppice gleamed masses of color, comparable to nothing but certain sunset clouds. It is neither copper, crimson, scarlet, orange nor gold, but all of them combined. A glorious hue, fit only for nature's use on far off clouds, or in splashes here and there over the gorgeous robe she fashions for her October carnival. With it she decks the pretty little pepperidge trees at Graceland, and right daintily is it worn. Tall oaks are swathed with the beautiful fall colors of Virginia creeper, and its deep crimson adds a touch of color to the gray stone wall that makes its way through the enclosure, forming inviting nooks where one would willingly lie down one day to restful sleep.

After these brilliant bits one notes anew the soft gray green of the Royal willows, and the pleasing contrast between it and the glossy dark green mass of the laurel-leaved willows happily placed close beside them, as well as the still different green of one or two weeping willows standing at the edge of a pond, quiescent when their best friend—the water—is quiet, but waking into life the moment it stirs, and emphasizing the friendly companionship by always floating their slender branches, the same way the ripples run.

AN INVITING NOOK.

shown by the fall color effects. Their beauty is cumulative. Nowhere is there a sudden breaking out of masses of multi-colored foliage. The varieties of trees and shrubs that take on good tints are so placed that at the beginning color is introduced delicately and so working on by subtle graduations there is room for a climax when the right time comes. But that time was not yet. There was just enough brilliancy here and there to arouse the interest and keep one alert as to what beauty spot might be waiting round the next curve. Clumps of crimson sumach glowed among plantings otherwise made up of cool greens, beside a driveway on

Among the most delightful effects are the fascinating tangles of shrubbery where in the Fall, waxen snow berries whiten the drooping twigs; barberries hang in thick fringes of soft rose-red; and gleaming scarlet winter berries make bright tracery among the leaves and branches.

And where the witch hazel lies in ambush to play its merry pranks, tossing its yellow tassels alluringly, then greeting the unwary with a lively fusilade of tiny polished

TRANSPLANTED ELMS.

black missiles from its curious small batteries.
FANNY COPLEY SEAVEY.

A Cemetery of the Huns.

Further investigation has shown that the 500 Huns' graves, discovered by the dean and parish priest of Apar, near Cziko, in the county of Tolna, South Hungary, were evidently not those of men who had fallen on the battle-field, as was at first believed. They formed the regular burying-ground of a colony of Huns, as the skeletons of women and children outnumber those of men. In many cases the remains of man and wife are found in the same grave side by side; but where children are buried with the mother they are placed across her breast. The graves are very narrow and are seven to ten feet deep. They are arranged in regular rows, and the remains, which are without coffins, lie on the back, the feet being turned towards the east and the heads towards the west.

In seven graves, probably those of warrior chiefs, the remains of horses have been found buried with their owners, with their harnesses complete, and adorned with silver or bronze work. On the skeletons of these chiefs a number of very skilfully made ornaments have been discovered, including, for instance, belts of silver and bronze. The weapons are knives, arrow-heads, three-edged javelins, spear-points and axes. Several of these chiefs held in their left hands Roman coins belonging to the end of the fourth century. Among the food found in the graves there were a number of eggs with shells still unbroken. Equally interesting is the fact that in several graves a Roman stylus was found, showing that the Huns of that period were more cultured than had hitherto been believed. One of these styli was artistically made of silver and richly ornamented. It was found in the hand of a woman, with a wax tablet close by ready to be written on. Nearly all the women have massive golden ear-rings, fibulæ and arm-bands, besides knives, hand-glasses and various ornaments of silver, amber, bronze and glass.
—*Vienna Correspondence London Standard.*

The Approaching Millenium.

Take a walk through any of the cemeteries throughout the country and you will believe with us that the fools are slowly but surely passing away. You pass the last resting place of a man who blew into an empty gun. The tombstone of him who lighted the fire with kerosene. The grass-carpeted mound covers the remains of the man who took the mule by the tail. The tall monument of the man who didn't know it was loaded over-shadows the man who jumped from the cars to save a ten rod walk. Side by side lies the ethereal creature who kept her corset laced to the last hole, and the intelligent idiot who rode a bicycle nine miles in ten minutes. Here reposes a doctor who took a dose of his own medicine, and the old man who married a young wife. Right over yonder, in the northwest corner, the breezes sigh through the weeping willows that bend over the lowly bed where lies the fellow who told his mother-in-law she lied. Down there in the potter's field, with his feet sticking out to the cold blast of winter and the blistering rays of the summer sun, is stretched the earthly remains of the misguided regulator, who tried to lick the editor, while the broken bones of the man who would not pay for his paper are piled up in the corner of the fence. Over by the gate reposes the boy who went swimming on Sunday, and the old woman who kept baking powder side by side with strychnine in the cupboard. The old fool-killer gathers them in one by one and by and by we will have a pretty decent world to live in.—*Ex.*

Accompanying an order for a subscription to the MODERN CEMETERY, which by the way was for a lot-owner, Mr. William Stone, superintendent of Pine Grove Cemetery, Lynn, Mass., writes: I think the MODERN CEMETERY is worthy of a much larger circulation. It treats on subjects that can be found in no other paper—subjects that should interest every one who cherishes the grounds wherein rests the remains of some loved one who has only gone a little before.

. . .

The longer the MODERN CEMETERY comes to me the more highly I value it.—*Henry Ross, Supt. Newton Cemetery, Newtonville, Mass.*

OFFICE BUILDING AT ENTRANCE TO RIVERSIDE CEMETERY.

The Riverside Cemetery, Rochester, N. Y.

The directors of the new Riverside Cemetery at Rochester, N. Y., have adopted measures which will insure the very highest degree of perfection in cemetery gardening. Riverside Cemetery occupies a beautiful tract of land, one hundred acres in extent, on the Charlotte Boulevard, four miles from the center of the city of Rochester and easily accessible by electric cars. The location is most advantageous for a combination of natural and artificial beauty, with the boulevard on one side and the Genessee river on the other. The general slope of the land is towards the river, whose high bank—the lowest point of the cemetery being seventy feet above the water—afford natural scenery unsurpassed.

The surface of the ground at Riverside is gently undulating, with just enough diversity to give to the drives and walks that wealth of landscape effects which are unattainable on a flat surface. The ground itself is a clean sand admirably adapted for burial purposes. The natural drainage is excellent and is supplemented by a simple but effective system of artificial drainage. No precipitous banks require protection against the washing of heavy rains. Yet the alternation of knolls and dells makes the spot one of nature's chosen sites for a beautiful garden of the dead.

Natural groves of trees abound in Riverside. Here is to be seen a knoll crowned with a grove of chestnut; there a lake bordered with graceful overhanging elms; or a natural growth of willow and red-stemmed dogwood may be seen by the side of another lake; and approaching the bank of the river, the road leads through a thick grove of maple, oak and other trees, all growing in profusion. Three small lakes nestle under the foot of the hill that leads down from the entrance gateway. What with this rare combination of lake and river scenery and profusion of natural foliage, Riverside possesses all the elements of location and surroundings to make it an ideal modern cemetery.

The actual work of improving the grounds at Riverside did not begin until about a year and a half ago. A large force of men was then put to work grading and filling and preparing a portion of the grounds for burials. The plan adopted does not contemplate any burials near the boulevard. All that portion of the cemetery which is first visible from the boulevard and the entrance is laid out for ornament, the effect being to leave as little indication as possible from the frontage that the park is a cemetery. The ground reserved for burial purposes lies midway between the boulevard and the river, and it was there that the first work of modifying the natural beauties of the site was directed.

In the comparatively short time of a year and a half much has been accomplished. Roads have been laid out in graceful curves along the valleys and around the knolls. Several thousand trees, representing every known variety of foliage, have been planted. The whole cemetery is being sodded with Kentucky blue grass, the intention being to make every part of the grounds a perfect lawn. The natural beauty of the park will thus be ably supplemented by artificial adornment of the highest char-

RECEIVING VAULT, RIVERSIDE CEMETERY.

acter, so that a drive through Riverside, winding in and out among its gently sloping mounds, will be one continual round of pleasant surprises.

The perfection of the park system is the high aim of the Riverside directors. Instead of thousands of grotesque or inartistic marble or stone markers, designed to suit the taste of as many individuals whose knowledge of art is nil, there will be countless varieties of plant, flower, and tree, all cultivated with the highest skill of the landscape artist, and each contributing to the general effect of beauty and harmony. In conformity with this plan the bridge leading across a small stream to the river bank is of the rustic pattern. The view from the high shores of the Genessee is of indescribable beauty and it is most fortunate that this rare natural scene is not to be marred by the too frequent disregard for sysem, harmony or beauty.

To this end the most stringent regulations have been adopted. No copings or fences of any kind will be allowed. But one monument or other ornamental device can be placed upon each lot. All markers must be placed level with the surface of the ground. No device for separating the lots will be visible to the eye, the design being to present to the view a cemetery which shall have all the beauties of a park, which shall be as little as possible suggestive of the gloom of death and as much as possible suggestive of the hope that lies beyond the grave.

The perpetual care of every grave is an essential feature of the lawn system in its perfection, and this feature has been embodied by the Riverside authorities in their deeds. They covenant with every purchaser of a lot that the cemetery shall be perpetually cared for, and to insure this a sum is set apart from the purchase price of every lot to form a maintenance fund for the perpetual care of the cemetery. There can be no " neglected " graves. Every foot of the entire domain will be carefully preserved. There will be no discrimination shown—the poor man's lot being cared for as thoroughly as that of the wealthy. Some method of designating the unmarked graves will be adopted, so that there will be no unknown residents of this city of the dead.

The illustrations presented with this article give a good idea of the improvements that have been made at Riverside during the short time since actual work began. The Riverside Cemetery Association is composed of some of the most substantial business men of Rochester. They have already expended some $200,000 in the development of the cemetery and have interested many prominent citizens in the purchase of lots. It is only a question of a com-

A VIEW IN RIVERSIDE CEMETERY.

paratively short time of such vigorous enterprise as that shown by the officers of the association when Riverside will be one of the most beautiful burial grounds in the state. The officers of the association are: Merton E. Lewis, president; G. W. Sanborn, vice-president; Erastus U. Ely, secretary; Dean Alvord, treasurer and manager; Joseph T. Alling and William C. Walker, directors. The grounds are in charge of J. H. Shepard, an active member of the the Association of American Cemetery Superintendents, whose long experience as superintendent of Oakwoods Cemetery, Chicago, coupled with his natural qualifications eminently fits him for the important position.

CEMETERY NOTES.

The Government of Austria has requested information from our National Government regarding cremation in America.

* * *

Charters recently granted: Mutual Union Cemetery Co., Houston, Texas capital stock $20,000. Riverside Cemetery Co., Roanoke, Va., capital stock $20,000.

* * *

Many village cemeteries were awrecked along the Atlantic coast by the severe October storms. On Solomon's Island gravestones were thrown down, and coffins torn open and the bodies exposed.

* * *

The chime of bells nine in number that pealed forth from the clock tower in the Manufactures Building at the World's Fair will be placed on a costly mausoleum now in course of construction at Glen Cove, Long Island, for the Pratt family, of Brooklyn, N. Y.

* * *

An English law in effect the latter part of the 17th. century required that all bodies should be buried in woolen shrouds. This act was meant as an encouragement to the woolen trade, but was repealed by George III. An affidavit stating that the requirements had been carried out had to be given to the officiating priest, or a penalty paid.

* * *

In the old Cross Street Cemetery, at Canandaigua, N. Y., are three little stones blackened with age standing close together side by side. They bear the dates, January 17, 1813; August 11, 1814; and November 20, 1815 with inscriptions showing them to be in memory of three wives of Moses Goodsell. Just what became of Moses the records fail to show.

The cemeteries of Grand Rapids, Mich., three in number are owned, controlled and regulated by the city through a commission composed of three members who by the provisions of the city charter are vested with "exclusive" power. This under some conditions might be considered a wise policy in as much as it lays the entire responsibility of proper management upon a small committee, but on the other hand it is liable to form an autocratic body who while supposedly carrying out the will of the people in the performance of their duties may assume a "public be—policy" which is anything but desirable in cemetery matters. Judging from the local papers this seems to be the status of affairs at the present time.

* * *

The Younglove monument illustrated in this issue is a unique specimen of monumental art recently erected in Lakeview cemetery, Cleveland, O. It is a massive bowlder of Westerly granite weighing about 35 tons. The weatherworn surface of the stone has been preserved as far as possible. On the face a slight niche has been cut into the bowlder and in it carved in low relief is a female figure typifying Purity. Between the partially clasped hands is the stem of an Easter lily, which lies against her breast in a most natural manner. The relief at no point exceeds one inch in height and is an excellent example of the sculptors art in granite. The family name cut in sunk letters across the face of the stone is the only suggestion of an inscription.

* * *

Queer things happen in cemeteries as well as out of them. An elaborate receiving vault was built in a Massachusetts cemetery last year at a cost of $6,000 and considerable expense incurred in grading, sodding and otherwise beautifying the surroundings, up to the present time however the vault has not been used. The cemetery is under municipal control and the superintendent states that he has never been able to ascertain whether "the committee on city property has turned the vault over to the committee on burial grounds" and in the absence of such knowledge he does not care to take the responsibility of using the vault. Apathy on the part of cemetery committees is not uncommon but it is seldom carried to such an extent as this.

* * *

Two appealed cases of the city of Chicago against Rosehill Cemetery for taxes have recently been decided. The first case for 1890 taxes on eighty acres of land owned by the cemetery company, but which it was claimed, were not used for burial purposes. The lower court held that the land was not exempt, owing to the fact that no burials had been made in

THE YOUNGLOVE MONUMENT, LAKEVIEW CEMETERY, CLEVELAND, OHIO.

the land and no notice given to the assessor that it had been platted for cemetery purposes. Judgment was affirmed and the company will pay the tax assessment of $300. The second case was taxes of 1891, on the same land, amounting to $1,670. The County court gave the city a judgment for that amount. This order was reversed by the Supreme court on the showing of the cemetery company that burials had actually been made on the land during that year.

* * *

A visitor to a prominent Southern cemetery writes to the local paper as follows: "Truly a lovely city of the dead, with very costly monuments, but none of them has any special significance—simply an array of tall slabs that commemorate the wealth of the man." This too common fault in monumental work has done more to bring about the growing antipathy against memorials of this nature than any other. Unfortunately for cemeteries ostentation and art do not go hand in hand. The former aims to show the measure of grief by quantity rather than quality. The beauty of simplicity in memorials has not yet been as fully appreciated by our people as it was by the Greeks but that there is a growing sentiment against the inartistic display of memorials as seen in our modern cemeteries is becoming more and more apparent. With the development of artistic tastes and an appreciation of the beautiful in nature and in art among the masses our silent cities will reflect such characteristics in the same measure that they do the lack of them to-day.

RULES AND REGULATIONS.

Every cemetery should be governed by certain rules and regulations, which should be printed in pamphlet form for distribution among lot owners. While this has been done in most of the large cemeteries, where the rules are very much alike, we will, for the benefit of the smaller cemeteries, publish in this department such rules as commend themselves for general adoption. Contributions are solicited.

THE SUPERINTENDENT.

The by-laws of Cave Hill Cemetery, Louisville, Ky., prescribe the duties of the superintendent as follows:

1. The superintendent shall reside in or near the cemetery.
2. He shall have the general direction and control, under the Board of Managers, of the improvement and grounds of the cemetery.
3. He shall lay out lots in the cemetery, and shall preserve a record thereof, so that the same may be known and easily found should the boundaries become obliterated or changed.
4. He shall see that the regulations of the Board of Managers, with respect to interments, disinterments, the construction of tombs and monuments, and improvement of lots by the holders thereof, be properly observed.
5. He shall have charge and keep an account of the property, tools and implements of the cemetery company which may be on the premises, and shall render to the secretary an inventory and appraised value of the same, to be incorporated in the secretary's annual report.
6. He shall furnish, when required, estimates of the probable expenditures of the coming week or month, or of any proposed work or improvement, and shall, on a fixed day of each week, certify and deliver to the treasurer a pay-roll in which he shall state the number of hands employed, their names, the time they have worked, the rate of wages, and the amount due to each of them. The pay-roll thus certified shall be the guide for the treasurer in paying said wages. The superintendent shall make and preserve a duplicate copy of said pay-roll, which shall always be subject to the inspection of the president and any manager of the company.
7. He shall keep a record, which shall contain an account of all the interments that take place in the cemetery, in the form determined on by the Board.
8. No interment shall take place in the cemetery without a permit from the secretary. This permit shall be handed to the superintendent, who is required to cause the grave to be prepared, but who will not be responsible for its preparation by the time appointed, unless he shall have six hours of day light notice thereof.
9. It shall be the duty of the superintendent to take charge of the keys of the receiving tomb, under such directions as to the use of it as shall be hereafter made.
10. He shall have power to remove from the cemetery any improper and disorderly persons; also to abate nuisances, remove stray animals, rubbish, and unnecessary encumbrances.
11. As agent for the managers, he shall have sole power to employ or discharge workmen for the cemetery, subject to supervision of the president, and to order and arrange their respective duties as the Board may direct, and he shall have the general control and direction of all persons engaged in the grounds, including the sexton and policemen.
12. The Board of Managers have adopted rules for the government and police of the cemetery, and may from time to time adopt more. These it will be the duty of the superintendent to see properly enforced, and to attend generally to the instructions of the Board in reference to the affairs of the cemetery.
13. Inasmuch as it is desired that the lot-holders shall have every facility afforded them in the care of their lots, it is enjoined on the superintendent, in his intercourse with them, to consult their wishes in this respect as far as he can do so, consistently with his other duties.
14. No person in the employment of the company shall be permitted to receive any perquisite for any matter connected with the cemetery, or his duties therein, his salary being considered in full payment therefor.
15. A fire proof safe is provided by the cemetery company for the safe-keeping of the records of the superintendent, and of the keys of the receiving tomb.

THE SECRETARY AND TREASURER, AND SUPERINTENDENT.

Article XII. While the officers filling the above places have each their allotted duties, as herein before set forth, it is very necessary, for the facilitating of the business of the company, that close communication be had between the above-mentioned officers, and it is therefore directed that at least once every working day the superintendent shall call at the company's office to receive any messages or business left there with the secretary, with whom the public have close communication, and which business will come under the control and action of the superintendent. The superintendent will in turn report to the secretary and treasurer any necessary information regarding such business.

THE SEXTON.

Article 3. It shall be the duty of the sexton to superintend the digging of graves and the interments therein. He shall be present and supervise all funerals, and he shall report to the secretary the location on the lot of each grave, and the name of the person whose burial he has superintended, and also aid in locating the graves of persons heretofore buried on lots in the cemetery. He shall be under the general direction of the superintendent, and perform such other duties as may be required of him.

Correspondence.

Vacation Reminisences.

With the closing of our last notes we had just started on our vacation, taking the electrics at the West Hotel for Lakewood Cemetery; after a very pleasant trip of about one half hour we were at the entrance, and as this Cemetery will form the subject of a special article, no allusion is called for at this time. Our impressions of Minneapolis were charming, how could they be otherwise. such hospitality, and such boundless attention, beyond all expectation, made us wish we were twenty years younger, and I am not sure but we should go there and settle. The West Hotel was the headquarters of the association and the superior accommodations cannot be too highly spoken of, it is elegant, in its appointments and at the same time homelike, and unusually comfortable. Of course the flour mills were seen and formed a very interesting feature of our sight seeing, just think of their capacity. The largest flour mills in the world one, the Pillsbury "A" with a capacity of 7,500 barrels per diem, and the Washburn Mills with a combined output of 12,000 barrels. the daily output is 30,000 barrels and they have an annual export of 2,000,000 barrels. Here also to be seen is the Falls of St. Anthony with the enormous capacity of 12,000 horse power, the greatest water power ever utilized in the United States. The parks and boulevards are justly the pride of Minneapolis. The system embracing 1,504 acres has been obtained since 1883. Included within this park system are the beautiful Lake of the Isles, Lake Calhoun, Lake Harriet, Powderhorn Lake, Sandy Lake, and the famous Falls of Minnehaha and Longfellow Glen, Fort Snelling, and its military reservation, the Soldier's home and State park, adjoin the Minnehaha reserve, several of the parks overlook the Mississippi River, and all are connected by boulevards along its picturesque banks, and over the Kenwood hills. The buildings are grand. The new public library erected at a cost of $350,000 is very conspicuous. The City Hall and County Court House with its commanding tower is another elegant structure, the Guaranty Loan Building, with its roof garden and magnificent lookout, here you can see the country for many miles and on a clear day a good idea can be had of the delightful location of this thriving city; the New York Life Insurance towering up eleven stories, the new Lumber Exchange, opposite the West Hotel, and not least by any means that unique and magnificent farmers and mechanics saving bank building which is the most complete and splendidly fitted up and furnished bank we ever saw; and through the courtesy of one of the officers, we enjoyed the privilege of looking all through the different rooms. What shall we say of the private residences, they far exceeded our most sanguine expectations, one of the handsomest is that of Senator W. D. Washburn, also that of A. A. Pilsbury, Mrs. W. W. McNair, Ex. Gov. J. S. Pilsbury, F. G. Winston, J. W. Lawrence, S. C. Gale, S. C. Bell and many others.

The lawns about these and those not mentioned were the best we have ever seen, and showed that much care had been bestowed upon them, we are not envious but we do wish ours were as good, but our guide told us that they had not been good long. the unusual dry summer had caused them to dry very much, but recent rains had brought them up again; if the churches are not attended to, it may be thought we are a godless set, but they were such fine structures and so commanding in appearance that it is next to impossible to pass them by. The most noticable however were the Westminster and First Presbyterian, the Unitarian, the Universalist, and the First Baptist which we are told cost about $200,000. Now for the convention what shall I say that will please all, I shall not try that because failure would be sure; I confess I feel full of criticism, but if I do, some will say, Oh, that's prejudice, he sees nothing good outside of his own limit, and as the proceedings will be read by all, each one had better form his own opinion of what was accomplished. As I read the report in the MODERN CEMETERY, I think the Superintendent who did not gain some information that he could use must be a dull scholar. It seems to me that the thoughts and suggestions were more practical than usual at such gatherings, and that the offhand minute man made the most telling points because he had only his practical experience to fall back upon, but there is a question that was not cleared up, and it seems to me that it might properly form the subject for some of our enlightened brothers to post us up on through the columns of MODERN CEMETERY viz. Where can the line be drawn between a marker and a monument, the man that can settle that is entitled to be an honorary member of the A. A. C. S. Who is he? Where is he? If he exist will he enlighten us. Mr. Simonds paper speaks for itself, and I hope every one will read it again until he is saturated with the excellent thoughts and suggestions it contains. I cannot say that as an individual I endorse Mr. Lawson's suggestions, although I would not be understood as opposing any progressive ideas that may be suggested, anything that will improve our taste should receive its full share of encouragement whether we like it or not. I am glad to say that at a well known cemetery in the East where plants are freely used, especially on the graves, we never possessed anything like the four foot grave alluded to which contained thirty-four plants of different varieties; the owner surely must be alone in thinking that grave beautiful, and a repetition of such planting is undesirable, but where the tendency to such heterogeneous planting exist, I think the power of moral suasion far better than any stringent rule against such work. A few good examples by a good gardener would attract attention, we all know that many cemeteries do and will continue to plant flowers; this is a recognized fact that cannot be set aside with any modern idea, if such planting as is described on p. 78. is tolerated the sooner it is banished the better. but it seems to me the keynote is sounded when he says that one great aim of the Superintendent should be to educate the people to the fact that "in simplicity there is beauty" that is right, let us educate but not drive by any rule. Prof. Green's excellent paper will undoubtedly be read with great interest as it gave just the information in regard to shrubs so adapted to the locality where we met that we are all glad to know about, I find my pen running very easy and I am warned to stop, and without further comment, express the hope that next convention will have the enthusiastic practical turn which characterized this one, only more so.

The fourth and last day at St. Paul was one of much pleasure, that is the capital of Minnesota, and is certainly beautiful for location. *The suburban and river scenery is grand, elegant residences with fine lawns and gardens, parks on a liberal scale, all go to make up the list of attractions to a progressive city, which in 1892 had a population of 160,000. The unbounded hospitality of the Trustees of Oakland Cemetery and the personal attention of Mr. Boxell the Superintendent and Mr. Willis the Secretary was enjoyed very much, the day was beautiful, the drives superb, and the banquet one of the best, and at evening we separated for Chicago or home, with thankful hearts that the A. A. C. S. was organized, and that our seventh annual convention had been held under such pleasant circumstances, and now, Mr. Editor, I fear that these abbreviated notes may be too indefinite to be interesting, especially to those who were with us, certainly they will not need to read them to be reminded of what we enjoyed, but for those who did not go, it may perhaps give them an idea of what they missed, and I feel quite sure, I voice the sentiments of all who were't here, it was an occasion of rare enjoyment, having spoken twice, if the readers of MODERN CEMETERY are not tired of me, you may hear from me once more. B.

*The greater part of the city is built on a plateau or terrace, which is 70 feet higher than the river and is partly surrounded by an amphitheatre of hills.

The Question Box.

An interesting feature of the conventions of the Association of American Cemetery Superintendents is the discussion of queries sent to the "Question Box," and it has been suggested that these discussions may be continued throughout the year, and much valuable information disseminated by an expression of opinions on stated topics through the columns of the MODERN CEMETERY. All questions that may be suggested for discussion will be published and replies cordially invited from any who may choose to say a word on the subject.

As a seasonable question for discussion we have asked a number of subscribers to tell what disposition they usually make of their leaves, and have received the following replies:

I consider the decomposed leaves of deciduous trees and shrubs a very important part of the soil necessary in successful horticulture. Our leaves are put in some out-of-the-way place in the fall and covered with earth. Decomposition is slow, from three to four years being required. Where there is a tendency to clay in the soil this makes an excellent top dressing for lawns. It is also valuable for potting purposes in the green houses.—*J. V. Craig, Omaha, Neb.*

The most of our leaves are spread in layers on a dump-pile composed of leaves, grass, old sod, a little waste earth and occasionally a little manure from the barns. When mixed together this makes, in a few years, good material for use about the cemetery, especially in the greenhouses.—*John M. Boxell, St. Paul, Minn.*

For two reasons I am careful not to mix the pine needles or leaves with those from deciduous trees when raking in the fall. First because they are very injurious to vegetation and second because they make the best covering for myrtle graves and s mi-hardy plants that I wish to leave out through the winter. The rotted deciduous leaves are valuable for mulching Rhododendrons and newly set trees and shrubs.—*Henry Ross, Newtonville, Mass.*

Our experience in rotting leaves has been so unsatisfactory that we burn them and use the ashes for top-dressing.—*W. H. Morrow, Hillsboro, O.*

At Oakwoods, Chicago, the leaves are piled and allowed to rot into leaf mould which Mr. Lawson considers of great value in the greenhouses.

At Mount Hope, Rochester, N. Y., and West Laurel Hill, Phildelphia, the leaves accumulate in such quantiities that the greater part are burned.

There is a good deal of comfort to be gathered from these little old scraps of poetry and somehow they seem to stretch to fit a great grief and shrink to fit a small one. *Hawthorne.*

Association of American Cemetery Superintendents.

WM. SALWAY, "Spring Grove" Cincinnati, O., President.
T. McCARTHY, "Swan Point" Providence, R. I., Vice-President.
F. EURICH, Woodlawn, Toledo, O., Secretary and Treasurer.

The Eighth Annual Convention of the Association will be held at Philadelphia in September, 1894.

Resolutions Adopted at the Seventh Annual Convention of the Association of American Cemetery Superintendents.

Resolved: That it is the sense of this convention that all Sunday funerals be discouraged as much as possible.

Resolved: That it is the sense of this meeting that all headstones or markers should be limited to the height of the sod or the level of the surface of the ground.

Resolved: That it is the sense of this meeting that vaults and catacombs be discouraged and if possible prevented in cemeteries.

Publisher's Department.

Cemetery Literature received: Report of Committee on Gardens, by John G. Barker, chairman. From the transactions of the Mass. Horticultural Society. The Salem *Gazette* from Geo. W. Creesy, with description of an ancient cemetery at Ipswich. The oldest stone bears the date 1647. From Geo. E. Rhedemeyer, Camden N. J., views in Harleigh Cemetery and rules and regulations. From Geo. W. Riely, Shelbyville, Ky., copy of Shelby Sentinel with account of dedicatory services of the new chapel illustrated in the MODERN CEMETERY some months since.

C. C. Abel & Co., of New York, agents for a number of foreign horticulturists and bulb growers have an announcement in this issue that will interest buyers in these lines. The houses represented are reliable and trustworthy. Messrs. Abel & Co., will send price lists etc., on application.

Notice to Cemetery Officials.

The proceedings of the seventh Annual Convention of the Association of American Cemetery Superintendents are being published in pamphlet form and can be procured after December 1st. Members of the Association and all others desiring copies will please send in their orders as soon as possible.

Price 25 cents per copy or at the rate of $2.50 a dozen for (6) copies or more.

FRANK EURICH,
Sec. and Treas. A. A. C. S.
P. O. Address, Auburndale, Ohio.

Cemetery Stock for Sale.

My one-eighth interest in Sylvan Lawn Cemetery, Chicago, is offered for sale. Full particulars on application.
318½ N. Market Street, Chicago. G. L. RAY.

Situation Wanted. A thoroughly competent and experienced business man and landscape gardener, expert in management desires position as superintendent or assistant, speaks German and French. Special attention given to new cemeteries and organizations of companies. Meier, care 47 Moffat Block, Detroit, Mich.

THE MODERN CEMETERY.

THE MODERN CEMETERY.

AN ILLUSTRATED MONTHLY JOURNAL DEVOTED TO THE INTEREST OF CEMETERIES

R. J. HAIGHT, Publisher.
334 Dearborn Street, CHICAGO.

Subscription $1.00 a Year in Advance.   Foreign Subscription $1.25.
Special Rates on Six or More Copies.

VOL. III.   CHICAGO, DEC. 1893.   No. 10.

CONTENTS.

MINISTERIAL AID IN CEMETERY IMPROVEMENT	109
*SHRUBBERY	110
A SOUTH AMERICAN CEMETERY	112
*TELFORD HIGHWAYS	113
THE GRAVE DIGGER	113
SUGGESTIONS TO LOT OWNERS—THE GARDENER'S BURIAL	114
*OFFICES ETC., EVERGREEN CEMETERY, PORTLAND, ME	115
CEMETERY NOTES	116
ENGLISH FUNERAL FLOWERS	117
CREMATORIUM IN CHICAGO—MARY MAGDALENE'S GRAVE—VACATION REMINISCENCES	118-119
THE QUESTION BOX	120
PUBLISHERS' DEPARTMENT	120

*Illustrated.

Ministerial Aid in Cemetery Improvement.

That the dead are all too soon forgotten by this busy bustling world is painfully evidenced by a visit to many a country graveyard or village cemetery, not that our country brethren are less mindful of their dead, but because their cemeteries lack the care that is bestowed on the burial grounds of cities and larger towns.

The famous saying of Benjamin Franklin, "I need only to visit the graveyard of a community to know the character of the people," is true of all ages and all countries. One of the most hopeful signs of our civilization is the modern cemetery, the beautiful garden of the dead, perpetually cared for and ever growing more and more attractive and peaceful as it becomes more populous. But this as yet is the exception rather than the rule. Too many of our cemeteries are still like that visited by a southern clergyman, who describes the fences as falling to decay, the grave stones prostrate and broken, and the graves overgrown with weeds; vaults fallen in and caskets exposed to view; skulls and human bones lying uncovered. The sexton told him that in digging a grave in that part of the cemetery devoted to the burial of the poor, he would be compelled to exhume the remains of as many as three or four bodies, so frequently had this ground been buried over.

Admitted that this state of affairs in a cemetery is an exception rather than the rule, yet it speaks only the more loudly in behalf of the care and preservation of the resting-places of the dead; and the action of this clergyman in denouncing cemetery neglect in his own community is an excellent example for ministers in other localities. Ministers in the best interests of their communities ought to guard well these sacred resting places. They have the power and the opportunity to arouse public interest in the care of cemeteries and no more commendable effort could be made by them. The tendency is too much toward expensive funerals. The elaborate service, the costly funeral trappings, the long procession of mourners, and the epitaph, "Gone but not forgotten," are all a hollow mockery when the narrow house of the departed is allowed to crumble into decay. Our ministerial associations should visit some of these decaying cemeteries and there read "sermons in stones," to supplement their crusade against expensive funerals.

Their influence would be of great weight if directed towards awakening the people from indifference on this subject. Cemetery officials also are often the very individuals who need stirring up. To their apathy and the general lack of public interest is due the shameful neglect to which many cemeteries are subjected. No one whose attention has been called to the fact can fail to appreciate the desirability of making burial places as attractive as possible—to dispel the gloom of the grave and bring in as much of cheer and beauty as is consistent with the surroundings. Thus in the modern cemetery refinement and civilization receive their highest stamp in the beauty, the tender care and the lovely scenery and views amid which lie the dead of our great cities. On the other hand, a neglected cemetery is a public disgrace—a libel on a religious and God-fearing community. Why should remains buried on farms, be brought to the village cemetery for interment if the graves are not to be cared for? Better let each bury in his own door-yard where he can protect the remains of his loved and lost, rather than to deposit them in some mis-called God's acre, where weeds and disorder betray an almost criminal neglect. We are convinced that an important duty devolves on the clergy of this country in the education of public sentiment in this behalf.

A BEAUTIFUL BIT OF PLANTING.

Shrubbery.

Well placed plantings of carefully selected shrubs are coming to be more and more appreciated as decorations for home grounds, parks and cemeteries.

In usefulness and beauty they are unexcelled, but that their use is often abused most suburban enclosures, (one feels that "gardens" would be a misnomer,) bear witness; nearly every one being spotted with a strangely ill-assorted, inappropriate collection of them. Often the assemblage is so motley that one feels no wonder at their failure to harmonize. Even their individual beauty is in some cases lost by their poor position and surroundings.

But a thicket, a coppice or a border of *well chosen* and *well grown* shrubs placed where it belongs, that is to say where it seems naturally to fill a need, complete an arrangement, is another thing and one than which nothing is more pleasing. And if the art of pleasing is the art of living, it is part of out of door art to place beautiful growing things so that they may grow in beauty.

There is much to be learned in making such compositions, but with the excellent horticultural journals now available no one need despair, neither the class that has the artistic taste that is necessary, nor the one that has the practical knowledge of making things grow that is quite as necessary. And good object lessons in planting that combine taste and knowledge are accessible to many.

The landscape gardening of the World's Fair, especially the design and planting of the Wooded Island, must have enlightened a large number of those whom it delighted. But it must be borne in mind that the planting there was to the end of securing good effects in a very short time, and that the choice of plants was not what it would have been had the necessities been less exacting. Such planting lacks the element of permanence that is desirable in nearly all locations but perhaps especially in cemeteries, so that only a part of the shrubs used on the Island would be suitable in such locations. At the same time some of the things used there would serve such a purpose admirably.

And no better object lessons in designing and planting water landscape than those of the Island can be cited, while probably no one will question the desirability of introducing water landscape into every cemetery where it is not a natural feature.

For object lessons that have the double advantage of permanence and more age, those who can visit Graceland Cemetery, (Chicago,) will find all that can be desired, and Mr. Simonds is constantly devising and working out new schemes of beauty.

Among the best of the small trees and larger shrubs used there are pepperidge and thorn trees, lilacs, syringas, bush honeysuckles, elders, common sumach, several viburnums including the bush cranberry, and two or three dogwoods including *cornus paniculata* and the very effective *C. sanguinea*.

As seen on the Wooded Island the cut leaf sumach would be admirable planted with the common variety. It branches and grows lower, and its deeply cut fern like foliage would be in excellent contrast, while bearing a family resemblance, to the plain leaved sort that would make the combination particularly pleasing.

Of the lower growing shrubs used advantageously at Graceland, the most noticable, (at least in the fall,) are barberries both green and purple leaved, snow berries, witch hazel, Indian currant, spirea crenata, the lower cornuses, wild roses and rosa rugosa, the Japanese wild rose which bears such large fruits. But this list would be largely increased, (as would that of taller kinds,) by going through the cemetery with a view to noting all the good things that take turns in calling attention to themselves through the cycle of the seasons. Many of them, indeed, being decorative at more than one stage, notably those varieties that show flowers in spring or summer followed by lovely fruitage and then lengthening their season of attractiveness by an Indian summer of gay foliage, and not even then gloomily settling down to a winter of ugly discontent but brightening things up by their bright colored, highly polished bark.

Some of the lower growing hardy shrubs used on the Island that might well be added to this list are *Cassia Marylandica*, which was beautifully green and thrifty throughout the hot and very dry summer of the Fair, and is pretty when in flower, and the delicately lovely, although hardy, *Tamarax Africans* which is so distinct and desirable in both foliage and flower as to seem an acquisition in cemetery planting, yet I do not ever recall having seen it in one. There could be nothing prettier in their way than the miniature weeping mulberry trees, in the nursery exhibit, each being from four to four and one-half feet high and with gracefully drooping branches that swept out on all sides on the grass for some distance by the time the pretty fruit, with which they were well laden, was ripe. The polished leaves are distinct and the whole effect most pleasing. And the recollection of the beds of lovely *Kadmia Latifolia*, (native mountain laurel,) seen on the Island last June, makes one long to find a similar showing in our parks and home-like modern cemeteries.

Shrubs are largely used in the finishing off method followed at Graceland that leaves no raw edges. Trees and tall shrubs that grow bare stems are in most cases surrounded or bordered, according as they are grown and placed, with those of lower habit, sometimes shrubs of several heights are used to bring the leafage down to the level of roadways or lawns.

There are charming plantings of wedge shaped spaces where roadways diverge; small trees being grouped in the wider part of the narrowing division, the planting carried on with tall shrubs and finished off with the witch hazel and winter or barberries in a way so natural that one involuntarily promises ones self to pass that way for violets in the spring.

A nicely rounded border line of low shrubs that outlines the curve of a road elsewhere is made entirely of the neat growing Indian current, green to the ground.

South of the chapel is an excellent example of shrubbery banked against a building. The foliage of the vine on the wall is carried down to the grass by remarkably well chosen and perfectly placed shrubs, the building seeming to grow out of them. When this bank is white with big snowberries, (species, symphoricarpus racemosus,) it is as satisfactory as a planting can be made.

The small pond is almost hidden by a wealth of shrubbery of well balanced irregularity as to height and density, like a woodland lakelet set in its copses and groves.

The other pond is treated in a more dignified manner as befits its greater size, importance and position.

Here, are well combined bodies of foliage, each passing breeze breaking the mass of the Royal Willows into waves of soft silvery green; there, open glades, but an open vista does not necessitate sudden and unmitigated barrenness, and nearly everywhere the water line is softened by at least a slight fringe of shrubs.

In this respect the borders of the Wooded Island at Jackson Park are artistic in the highest degree.

The combinations were good everywhere, the grouping could scarcely have been improved, the proportion was perfect, and there was so much art in the omissions.

That is, where a view from or towards the water was left it was in just the right place, yet no one felt that it was a made opening. By no means.

The impression was that of nature's planting; the height and density of the bordering plantations gradually diminished, where they ended no one knew, but presently only a tiny islet of tall ornamental grass rose gracefully from the turf, a few semi-aquatic things swayed gently at the water's edge and on its surface some pond lily leaves floating lazily carried the willing eye on to the picturesque or a stately scene beyond.

Any one who has an ornamental pond and the use of shrubs in his intention may well be commended to the graces of the Wooded Island's border, and to the inspiration of the planting at Graceland.
FANNY COPLEY SEAVEY.

The change which has of late taken place in the public sentiment concerning the taste and propriety of inclosures is earnestly commended to the consideration of all lot owners. Only a few years since an iron railing, an inclosure of posts and chains or posts and bars, a hedge or stone coping, was deemed the initial step, and first requisite towards improvement. Even the family monument was deferred as matter for subsequent and secondary consideration. Now, however, in some of the most highly improved cemeteries of the country, inclosures of every kind are prohibited, and it must be admitted that the measure is approved by the best taste and judgment. Some of the most costly and substantial of the earlier styles, such as in their day were regarded as things of beauty and fitness—have given way to different taste, and it only remains a question of a little time, when the cumbrous coping, the latest device in this direction of the useless and in many respects the most objectional of all inclosures, will be looked upon as a striking example of the inappropriate, and as a marvel of misdirected expenditure.—*Calvary, St. Louis, Mo.*

PEPPERIDGE TREES.

A South American Cemetery.

Arrived at the gates of Asuncion's "recoleta" you find women squatting on the ground outside, each with a few dulces, fruits and flowers to sell for the consolation of visitors. But trade can not be brisk, for there are never any visitors, except an occasional foreigner, the followers of funeral processions and on the annual recurrence of All-Soul's day. Entering, you find a bare, unkempt enclosure—which strikes you as being exceedingly small for so old and large a city, until you remember the gruesome custom of piling corpse upon corpse, of borrowed coffins and rented graves for periods of from three months to three years, according to the means or affections of the mourners, and the semi-annual burning of the evicted bones. Although the living are so profuse in their use of flowers, there are few for the dead in this neglected God's Acre—only the faded wreaths of the more recently bereaved. And there are no trees but the useful orange, whose fruit the natives do not hesitate to eat, although its abnormal lusciousness speaks of the decay in which the roots were nourished.

The burial inclosure is crowded with wooden crosses painted black and mural tombs—some of the latter elaborate specimens of the Italian stucco workers' art; others with some architectural merit, but the majority pretty good representations of Dutch bake-ovens. On the tombs of the well-to-do the lack of flowers is compensated by ugly wreaths of black and white beads strung on wires after the French fashion, which gives the mourning relatives little trouble, not being perishable. They have but to place a bead wreath upon the grave of the dear departed and wash their hands of the decorative business for a whole year—until both fashion and religion demand their attention to the spot on All Soul's day. The simple burial places of the poor show the most care—perhaps because in every case the poor cadaver beneath is only a temporary tenant to be presently turned out into the general pile of its former friends and neighbors. Nearly all the black, wooden crosses have placed in front of them two common tin lanterns, each surmounted by a little tin cross, with candles burning inside, and scraps of white linen beautifully embroidered at the ends or finished with a deep fall of nanduti lace are draped around the arms of the cross.

An old church connected with the recoleta is at one side of it, and on the other, strange to say, is an Italian beer garden, where the sorrows of the stricken may be literally "drowned." In it are fruit and flower stands, besides the usual booths devoted to beer, and the contrast between this cheerful and well-patronized garden of Bacchus and the adjoining neglected and forsaken "Field of Saints" (Campo Santo), is something very startling.

The richer classes decorate their family vaults with splendid wreaths and numerous candles, and stand in rows before them, murmuring prayers; but you can not help noticing that most of them are not too much engaged to watch the stranger's every movement with insatiable curiosity. Here and there one sees a poor woman kneeling upon some newly-made grave, her face literally bowed to the dust, which in true Biblical fashion, she has thrown over herself, uttering meanwhile the most heart-rending shrieks and sobs, which seem likely to end in a fit. Naturally your sympathies are aroused and you yearn to go and mingle your tears with hers; when you are amazed to see her suddenly brace up, cease her cries, shake the dirt from her head, leisurely pick out another grave and fall upon it in the same manner, with her face in the dust, beginning anew the sobs and tears more violently than before; and then you understand that she is a professional mourner, hired to weep by the hour at a stated sum, and paid so much per sob. There are real mourners, too, whose grief is undoubtedly genuine, in whose sad eyes one reads that death is always a tragedy, as grim and inscrutable in palace as in hovel.

Let fancy picture to you the extraordinary scene. The crowds of barefooted, black-gowned women, the mumbling priests and hustling sightseers, the wild, pathetic music, mingled with the shrieks of hired mourners, the fragrant heaps of flowers, the odd shapes of the monuments, the quaint old church (in which all this time a corpse was lying), palms and bananas peering over the wall, blue hills in the distance, a wide vista of rolling, wooded, peaceful landscape, dotted with the red-tiled roofs of cottage homes and the yellow glow of fruit-laden orange groves—all bathed in golden sunshine, permeated by human affections, sorrow and helplessness, though rudely expressed, and dominated by the stern, unchangeable fact that the common tragedy is as inscrutable as universal, and that whatever method one may take to assuage his personal sorrow and show his faithful love for the departed the mystery remains as unsolved to-day as when the first man died.—*Fannie B. Ward, in Chicago Tribune.*

An ordinance of the city of Austin, Tex., making it a penal offense to bury the dead within the limits of the city, was declared void recently by a jury in the case of the Austin City Cemetery Association vs. City of Austin. On the strength of this decision the present city cemetery will be extended within the city limits taking in an additional tract of ten acres.

Telford Highways.

The following description of the method of constructing a substantial roadway according to ideas of Telford will impress the reader as thorough, but it suggests an undue and perhaps unnecessary thickness of the separate layers and a consequent waste of material, says *Good Roads*.

A description of the work as done on a road in New York city may be useful. The roadbed is trimmed to the required form, which is a descent of eight inches from the curb along the center strip to the outer curb, and the ground is made firm by the use of a 6½-ton roller.

Upon the prepared roadbed a pavement of quarry stones is set by hand, the stones being from 8 to 10 inches in depth, 3 to 6 inches in width and not exceeding 14 inches in length, and of as nearly a uniform size as possible, with parallel sides.

The stones are laid lengthwise across the road, with the broadest edges down. After being closely set together they are firmly wedged by inserting and driving down with a bar used for that purpose, in all possible places, stones of the same depth until every stone is bound and clamped in the proper position.

CROSS-SECTION OF TELFORD.

The projections of the stones on the top of the pavement are then broken off with a light hammer, and the spalls worked into the interstices not already filled by the process of wedging, by which the pavement is reduced to an even surface of eight inches.

Broken stones of gneiss, of a size to pass through a ring 2 inches in diameter, are then spread evenly over the pavement to such a depth as will make 6 inches when rolled. This layer is then rolled first with a 6½-ton horse roller, so that the steam roller can pass over without difficulty, and when thoroughly compact is in readiness for the top layer.

The top layer is of broken stone of trap rock of a size to pass through a ring 1¼ inches in diameter, spread evenly over to such a depth as will bring the surface to the proper grade. After being made thoroughly compact screened gravel to the depth of about 1½ inches is spread on the top and thoroughly rolled.

Both the stone and gravel are kept well moistened by means of sprinkling carts when the rolling is going on, and the gravel, working down into the interstices under the roller, consolidates the whole material.

When completed, the entire depth of pavement, stone and gravel is 18 inches.

It has been found impracticable to consolidate the stone when placed on the road by the heaviest rolling with a 16-ton steam roller without some binding material. Hard gravel has been used for this purpose as being preferable to loam or other material. When the avenue is first thrown open to travel, the roadway is kept moist by sprinkling, and a man is employed to pick off any stones that may be loosened by the feet of horses, and a 2-horse roller is kept passing over it until it becomes thoroughly compact and smooth.

The Grave-Digger.

There is something terrible about this grim custodian of our frail elements, this inexorable landlord who will sooner or later have the housing of us. We would not willingly make a foe of him, and yet he can never be a friend. He is like a malignant fate, beyond the reach of bribery or propitiation, who obtrudes his hobnail boots and clay-stained overalls into our most solemn visions; he menaces us during our lives, and the lump of earth he flings upon our coffins is the final token of his triumph and our subjection. His rule seems everlasting and his power unshakeable. And yet a little cloud has risen upon the horizon of the grave-digger, the smoke of the crematory. Here is an infringement upon vested right which warms to indignation even that imperturable man. The unseemly innovation makes progress. Verily and indeed its result is to the grave-digger an "unthankful ash."

Yet at last fate must overtake even the grave-digger. Was it accident or retribution that befell him once in a country churchyard when he plied his task recklessly near one of the great altar tombs which our forefathers were wont to rear? He had nearly finished his task when, as he stooped at the bottom of the grave, the heavy tomb fell in, and, like the ungodly recorded by the Psalmist, "he fell in the pit he had digged for others." But the grave-digger is dour and stark to the last; and if the dying tiger can strike hard, what shall we say of the one grave-digger whom the accidents of fortune are recorded to have successfully assailed—the sexton of Yarmouth, who attributed his bankruptcy "to the great falling off in his business consequent upon the scarcity of doctors?"—*The Globe.*

A New York taxidermist has a cemetery on Long Island in which he buries the dead pets of New York society people who do not care to have them stuffed. His little cemetery contains several hundred graves, for which his usual charge is $15.

Suggestions to Lot Owners.

The appearance of the cemetery as a whole, is much more pleasing, where enclosures do not exist. The superiority of a clean shaven expanse of lawn broken only by paths, trees and monuments, over that of grounds covered with railings and other enclosures in various stages of decay, requires no sophistry to make manifest. Experience, too, has demonstrated that even where the greatest vigilance is exercised, lot enclosures speedily become dilapidated. Atmospheric influences invariably produce the result. And as the expense incidental to the maintenance of the enclosures is very considerable, the result being worse than useless, the money thus expended, might better have been thrown away.—*Laurel Grove, Paterson, N. J.*

It should be policy to discourage the erection of vaults. How much better for the health of the living and the honor of the dead, were the money laid out in building vaults, expended on handsome monuments or an increased space of ground, and how much more natural and appropriate to see the grass covered graves of a family, side by side, than to have them remain unmixed with the earth, deposited on cold shelves above ground, and forming separate portions of preserved corruption from which volumes of pernicious gases are continually exhaled.—*Adolph Strauch.*

"The laws of nature," observes Oerstea, "are the thoughts of nature, and these are the thoughts of God." And so the idea followed up in the Lawn system is to confine all improvements to imitations of nature, thus exhibiting in classical chasteness a happy medium between too great simplicity, or nature untutored an unadorned, on the one side and on the other the excessive ornament usually met with where man undertakes to create and not to imitate. Nature's alphabet consists of only four letters, wood, water, rock and ground; and yet with these four letters she forms such varied compositions and such infinite combinations as no language with an alphabet of twenty-six letters can describe. Nature is always great in design. She is also an admirable colorist and harmonizes tints with infinite variety and beauty.—*Laurel Grove Cemetery*, Paterson, N. J.

Many lot owners have by introducing flower borders around their small burial plats, obtained a trifling formality, and disgraced the noble object they wished to adorn. In forming new combinations, rich, perspective, and scenic groupings, we should be very cautious in the selection of suitable places for monumental structures, as well as planting additional trees and shrubs. Fancy shrubberies and flower borders particularly demand limitation. No matter how fashionably patronized, for if immoderately extended, as they very often are, they only mark the triumph of luxury over elegance, and afford a poor compensation for the natural advantages of beautiful green grass plats, that can always be kept in order at little expense.— *Adolph Strauch.*

Sleepy Hollow Cemetery, at Qarrytown, N. Y., has been of late much improved and enlarged. From the character of an old burial ground it has been emerging gradually into an attractive place of sepulture. Within a few years, more than $40,000 has been expended in enlarging its borders and improving the new territory. Forty-seven acres have recently been added and further improvements are contemplated, which will tend to greatly enhance the attractiveness of this beautiful and historic spot, immortalized by Washington Irving and within whose precincts his ashes rest.

The Gardener's Burial.

This is the grave prepared; set down the bier;
Mother, a faithful son we bring thee here
In loving ease to lie beneath thy breast,
Which many a year with loving toil he drest.
His was the eldest craft, the simple skill
That Adam plied, ere good was known by ill;
The throstle's song at dawn his spirit tuned;
He set his seeds in hope, he grafted, pruned,
Weeded and mowed, and with a true son's care
Wrought thee a mantle of embroidery rare.
The snow-drop and the winter aconite
Came at his call ere frost had ceased to bite;
He bade the crocus flame as with a charm;
The nestling violets bloomed, and feared no harm,
Knowing that for their sakes a champion meek
Did bloodless battle with the weather bleak;
But when the wealthier months with largess came
His blazoned beds put heraldry to shame,
And on the summer air such perfume cast,
As Saba or the Spice Isles ne'er surpast.
The birds all loved him, for he would not shoot
Even the winged thieves that stole his fruit;
And he loved them—the little fearless wren,
The red-breast, curious in the ways of men,
The pilgrim swallow, and the dearer guest
That sets beneath our eaves her plastered nest;
The merry white-throat bursting with his song,
Fluttered within his reach and feared no wrong,
And the mute fly-catcher forgot her dread,
And took her prey beside his stooping head.
Receive him, Mother Earth; his work is done;
Blameless he lived, and did offence to none:
Blameless he died, forbidding us to throw
Flowers in his grave, because he loved them so;
He would not have them stifle underground,
But bloom among the grasses on his mound.
 We that have loved, must leave him; Mother, keep
 A faithful watch about him in his sleep.

H. J., in "*Spectator.*"

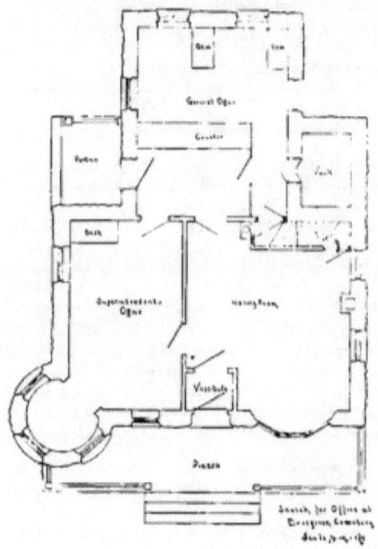

Offices and Waiting Room
EVERGREEN CEMETERY,
PORTLAND, ME.

CEMETERY NOTES.

It is bad enough for men to be selfish during their lives, but to provide for the selfish squandering of money on useless tombstones after they are dead is the sublimation of greed.—Oakland (Cal.) *Enquirer.*

* * *

On the line of the Union Pacific Railway, near the town of Sherman, stands a memorial to Oakes and Oliver Ames, to whose exertions the completion of the road is due. The monument is a pyramidal granite structure 65 feet high and 60 feet square at the base.

* * *

The arched roof of the new receiving vault at the Sacramento, Cal., City Cemetery fell in last month and ten thousand brick covered two workmen who were removing the wood-work from beneath the arch. One of the men was instantly killed but the other escaped with slight injuries.

* * *

A plan to provide work for the unemployed, in laying out the new portion of a cemetery was broached by an alderman of Brockton, Mass., recently. Some $1,212 was reported on hand in the Melrose Cemetery fund. The proposition was to expend this sum in improving the fourteen rough acres of the cemetery by hiring worthy poor men at $1 a day. The board of aldermen concurred in this opinion, and voted that the committee on Burial Grounds carry out some such plan.

* * *

The Odd Fellows' Cemetery, one of the most beautiful burial grounds in San Francisco, is to be turned over to the park commissioners of that city for a public park. The ground for this cemetery was purchased by the Odd Fellows' in 1865, and, as it lies wholly within the city limits, no more territory can be acquired and about all of the lots available have been sold. With the sale of the last lot the career of the cemetery will be practically closed. The trustees will then have $100,000 in the treasury, a sum sufficient to keep the grounds in excellent condition for all time, and it is proposed to donate the grounds and this fund to the city of San Francisco for the maintenance of a perpetual park.

* * *

Chicago police have interfered with a curious Chinese burial custom during the past month. In a little house adjoining Rosehill Cemetery several Chinamen have been at work boiling the bones of their deceased countrymen preparatory to shipping them to China. Some forty-eight celestials repose under the sod of Rosehill. Their remains are all to be exhumed, and, after boiling to remove the flesh, the bones are to be disjointed and sealed up, together with the cue or pig-tail, in tin boxes about thirty inches long and fifteen inches wide and deep, in which they are to be shipped to China and buried in consecrated ground. The Chinese believe that until their bodies repose in consecrated ground their spirits cannot leave the flesh.

* * *

It is gratifying to note that the long-continued stubborn opposition to cremation which has pervaded professional circles of highest influence is rapidly giving way. For years undertaker's as a class have been the strongest foes of incineration, believing it to be inimical to the best interests of their business. Now, however, a change has come. *The Casket*, the well-known undertaker's journal, has taken advanced ground on this subject and demonstrates clearly that it is the best policy for undertakers to follow public sentiment in the matter of cremation rather than to oppose it. Without entering into a recommendation of cremation the *Casket* shows that the practice will not lessen the cost of funerals or in any way interfere with the business of the undertaker. THE MODERN CEMETERY is glad to see this breaking down of prejudice against a practice so little understood and so much undervalued as cremation. In the current number of the *Casket* illustrations of five crematories are given, beginning with the first crematory erected in the United States, the Le Moyne at Washington, Pa., in 1876, and showing the retorts of the Le Moyne and the Lancaster, Pa., crematories.

* * *

C. L. Marston, a trustee of Mount Hope Cemetery, Bangor, Me., has sent the MODERN CEMETERY a photograph of the recently completed entrance to that cemetery. It consists of two granite towers 4ft. 6in. square at the base and 14ft. 6in. in height. The work is ashlar finished and rises in 12 inch courses diminishing from base to cap 1 inch in 1 foot. Each tower is topped by a square urn having polished sides margin lined. Wings 11ft. 6in. in length and 2ft. 6in. in height project from the outsides of the towers and terminate in small posts 2ft. 6in. square. The caps and urns are of white Hallowell granite and the remainder of the superstructure is of dark gray granite from the Lincoln quarries, the contrast in the colors giving a pleasing effect. In the front of each tower there is a polished panel inscribed with name of cemetery and year of incorporation. Mr. Marston writes that the cemetery has been very much improved within the last few years. A chapel has been erected and several lakes, dotted with islands, have been added. The board of trustees take a great interest in making the grounds attractive and are assisted by a well-qualified superintendent.

For funeral flowers there is a decided reaction against stiff designs, though many of them are still made, says the *American Florist*. But flat bunches, or cycas leaves with a knot of flowers, undoubtedly lead. People with a love for the symbolic, however, still crop up, and we heard recently of an order in memory of a departed carpet layer, which consisted of a flight of steps with partially unrolled stair carpet, and on it a broken shears and carpet stretcher! Such monstrosities, however, become rarer every year.

* * *

The old cemetery on High street, in Ipswich, Mass., is one of the oldest places in New England that have been used continuously for a burying-ground for the dead. The oldest stone in this cemetery has this inscription: "E. L., aged 48, 1647." This cemetery contains the remains of many families whose descendants are living in New England, as also some families of whom there are no known descendants in this country. Many of the old tombs in this cemetery have the family coat of arms blazoned on the marble slab, but the relic hunter has made sad work of many of these trophies.

* * *

An English seaman named Frederick Wallace was arraigned before a magistrate recently, charged with damaging a tombstone. It appears that his wife had erected at her own expense a stone to the memory of her son, and had had her own name "Ann" cut therein. The defendant, returning home from a voyage, became incensed at seeing his wife's name on a tombstone, and proceeded to fill up the letters with cement, besides painting and otherwise disfiguring it, to show, as he said, that "Ann was not there, but at home." The court took occasion to denounce this act as of a shameful character, though no damage to the stone was proven.

* * *

Reports of vandalism in cemeteries still continue to come from every part of the country. In previous numbers we have had occasion to mention a number of cases of this kind of an aggravated character that have been reported from Illinois, Wisconsin and other western states. This month news comes from Meriden, Conn., of desecration by vandals at West Cemetery. Many tombstones were overturned and some utterly ruined. Inscriptions on other were defaced. As usual a reward has been offered for the conviction of the perpetrators, but no clue is obtainable. It is really too bad that our cemeteries are so defenseless against the vandalism of tramps or other evil-disposed persons. A sharp watch should be kept and, if caught, the scoundrels should be dealt with so severely as to make them a startling example to other lawless characters.

Chateaubriand, the great French writer, is buried on a lonely rock where he was born. His biographer relates the circumstance as follows:

"The father and mother of the Vicomte Chateaubriand were on board a vessel bound for St. Malo. It was night when they neared the coast and a terrific storm was raging. No boat could venture to the assistance of the crew, and the vessel was wrecked upon a rock not far from the shore. The mother of Chateaubriand passed the night upon the rock and there he was born. When he had reached manhood he desired that, as his life had commenced surrounded by the ocean, so he might sleep in death, guarded by its restless waves. He accordingly purchased the rock and built upon it the tomb in which he now lies. Thus, born amid the tempest of the elements and dying during the lull of a more fearful and scarcely ended storm of human passions, he rests in his lonely tomb mourned over by the waters."

English Funeral Flowers.

The use of colored flowers for wreath and cross making appears to be on the increase, says a correspondent of the *London Garden*. I recently saw a wreath of vallotas, and it is not uncommon to see wreaths in Covent Garden almost entirely composed of colored flowers. I remarked one a few days since made of purple asters. Autumnal-tinted foliage is also used, and has quite a nice effect. There is something appropriate in the employment of foliage in the last stage of its life for funeral decorations. If once the custom of employing white flowers exclusively for this purpose is broken through it may be taken for granted that for some time to come at least comparatively few wreaths will be made of white flowers alone. It has hitherto been a matter of sentiment, for the future it will probably be a question of taste as regards the choice of flowers for wreaths and crosses. It is to be hoped that the change of fashion will be decided and permanent, as we have so many flowers suitable for this purpose that have hitherto been put aside on account of their color. Colored flowers are now much used for the decoration of graves, as many cannot command a supply of white ones.

The great mistake people make in many cases consists in doing too much, whereby they destroy the general good appearance of their otherwise beautiful locations.—*Sleepy Hollow*, Tarrytown, N. Y.

* * *

No advertisements in any form will be allowed on any stone work in the cemetery.—*Laurel Grove*, Paterson, N. J.

CREMATION.

A Crematorium in Chicago.

Recognizing the growing sentiment in favor of cremation in Chicago, and actuated by a desire to supply a public want, the managers of Graceland cemetery have constructed incinerating furnaces in connection with their beautiful chapel. After a careful investigation into the workings of the various systems of generating heat as used in the crematoriums of this country, it was decided to employ oil for the purpose. Experiments have shown the furnaces to work entirely satisfactory, and the public have been duly apprised of the fact that it will no longer be necessary to send bodies to other cities for incineration. The rules that have been adopted provide that in addition to the usual permit admitting the body to the cemetery, when incineration is desired, a certificate to that effect, signed either by the person whose body is to be incinerated or by the one having charge of the body, must be deposited at the cemetery.

It is believed that every incineration should be conducted in as private a manner as possible and not serve to gratify morbid curiosity. For this reason but five persons in addition to the regular attendants will be admitted to the crematory at the time of the incineration. Every incineration shall be attended by some relative of the deceased or representative of the family.

The charge of the use of the crematory is twenty-five dollars. This charge includes a receptacle in which to place the ashes and the use of the chapel, excepting where death occured from a contagious disease. It is suggested that burial in a family lot will be the most satisfactory way to dispose of this receptacle, and in this way the sentiment connected with trees and shrubbery, the songs of birds and quiet landscapes, will be preserved and the cemetery will be a beautiful memorial park.

The late Mrs. Lucy Stone was an advocate of cremation and left instructions that her body be burned in the new crematorium now under construction near Forest Hills Cemetery, Boston. It is stated in the *Urn* that six bodies are in different Boston vaults awaiting the completion of the furnace.

Mary Magdalene's Grave.

Fifteen thousand pilgrims annually visit St. Baume, in Provence, not far from Marseilles, in France, where Mary Magdalene is said to have spent the last thirty years of her life.

The legend, according to the *Nouvelle Revue*, runs that Mary Magdalene came from Judea in a small boat with Lazarus, Martha, the two Marys and Salome, bringing with them the body of St. Anne, the head of St. James the Less, and a few wee bones of the innocents massacred by King Herod. But from early ages this story has been disputed, and the Abbe Duchene, one of the most erudite writers on the early Christian saints and martyrs, considers that the relics of Mary Magdalene were probably sent from Constantinople about the seventeenth century. A Greek breviary, however, speaks of the saint as having died at Ephesus.

The pilgrimages are to a kind of grotto, which is supposed by local tradition to have been the place where Mary Magdalene spent her old age. Be that as it may, it seems that there is no older or more picturesque place of pilgrimage in Europe. In addition there can be seen at St. Baume a forest which has practically been kept intact since the days of old Gaul. The Dominican's convent is practically the only inn in those parts, and every visitor has to put up with the severely plain accommodation provided by a monastic cell, and simple but clean food.

The convent contains about one hundred beds; the lady visitors are served by nuns, the gentlemen by monks. The convent, which is almost as ancient as the grotto, is situated on the edge of a vast rocky chain of hills, and almost opposite the monastery, half up the steep incline, is the famous grotto cut into the solid rock. There a wide platform is hewn out, partly occupied at present by a second convent.

The grotto is about twenty-five yards square, eight yards high, and to all intents and purposes, a chapel. The principal altar is surmounted by a fine statue representing Mary Magdalene praying. It is strange to stand on the spot, apart from the feeling connected with the great saint to whom it is dedicated, and to think of all those who have stood in the grotto.

Correspondence.

Vacation Reminiscences.

In our last notes, we were about leaving St. Paul, our destination being Clinton, Iowa, after a pleasant visit there, and at Elgin, Ill., we went to Chicago, where of course, our interest was centered in the World's Fair. So much has been said about it, that any thoughts we might express would fall into insignificance compared with the able writers who have through the daily press given so many interesting articles of the various departments. We cannot refrain, however, from expressing our great disappointment at the Horticultural department. We went with a good-sized book expecting to fill the pages with useful notes, but, it is as empty now as when we started, not that there was a lack of good things, but that those of real merit, better than we in eastern Massachusetts are accustomed to see, were not to be found, such as the elegant collection of trees, deciduous and evergreen, shrubs and rare plants of H. H. Hunnewell at Wellesley, the fine grounds and splendid collections of trees, shrubs, and plants at the elegant estate of C. S. Sargent and J. S. Gardner, Brookline. The superb collection of trees and shrubs at the Arnold Arboretum, which cannot be equalled in this country, or any other, make us quite content with our home institutions. Yes, and we think justly proud of them, and perhaps having access to these at all times, we were looking for too much at the White City, but we have no doubt that many others enjoyed what we did not appreciate. It would please us to speak definitely of the park system of Chicago, but we can not. A few facts, however, will be of interest. There are nine parks covering nearly 2,600 acres, and boulevards which afford a drive of about 95 miles. It was our pleasure to visit two of these parks. Lincoln so ably managed by Mr. Pettigrew, has improved greatly since our last visit there two years ago. It was especially gratifying to see such a large collection of hardy plants well established, which always add to the permanent beauty of any place, and are now a marked feature of all public grounds of any note. The summer bedding was very fine, and the lily ponds by far the best we have seen, and were very interesting, and evidently much appreciated by the large number of people constantly there giving the greatest evidence of their appreciation. The new greenhouses are a splendid addition, the plants are getting well established, and in a short time will be splendid specimens. A great attraction is the elegant Grant monument, and at night the electric fountain. There are other features no less attractive, with the superb lake front and fine drives, we are inclined to think Lincoln park is at the head of the system. Washington park, located nearer the fair grounds, was visited on a Sunday afternoon, at which time we had a good opportunity to see how the people appreciated the elaborate floral display. There were thousands of people admiring these objects, beautiful or otherwise, as each one determined for themselves, a brief mention of a few of them will perhaps convey a slight idea of what they are. The most attractive or rather striking feature was undoubtedly "Sol's Clock." It is a fine timekeeper, and is at one end of a huge mound that is a perfect panorama of floral wonders. It is said that there is nearly a mile of sweet alyssum in ribbon borders containing over 97,000 heads of bloom. The first words and bars of "Hail Columbia" are written in red and yellow foliage plants, in so large a hand, that truly he who runs may read. There is also a terrestrial globe, on which the continents are quite clearly defined. Then there is a gorgeous butterfly, but to define the species is beyond our capacity. There are other wonders which elicit the warmest and most outspoken admiration of the visitors, but the charm of the place seemed to be centered in the daily calendar, which is complete to the very day. This is a specialty at this park only, and is a wonder to many how it is done. We were informed that the necessary letters and figures were kept growing in boxes, and each day, early in the morning, the needed ones were set in place. There are many attractive raised designs, the shield and flag being quite conspicuous. The aquatics were also a feature of great interest. Very much more might be said of this elaborate display, the vast number of plants, care required, and skill shown in their arrangement, gives to the visitor another evidence that Chicago is not to be beat. A brief visit to Humboldt park, many attractive beds were seen, and a very pretty point is the view of the boulevard which leads to Garfield park. We would have been glad to stop days, where hours had to suffice, and have taken our leisure to see all the attractions, but the next time we go there may not be a World's Fair to prevent us. A hasty glance at Graceland cemetery would have been the subject of a few notes, but it is done better by a writer in the October number of MODERN CEMETERY, we can however, heartily endorse all the writer has said, and will add that to meet Mr. Simonds is always a great pleasure, and we are heartily glad of his success as a leading landscape artist. Long may it continue. And now we bid farewell to Chicago, our vacation is ended, and we shall not be home any too soon. A pleasant trip by the Grand Trunk R. R. to Montreal, where a brief stop was made, from thence through the beautiful Green mountains of Vermont, the scenery of which was so delightful, tended to shorten the otherwise tedious ride. We arrived home amid happy greetings, and soon found ourselves in our accustomed place with our duties cheerfully resumed, refreshed by the change. Glad that we went to Minneapolis, rejoiced that there is one Association of American Cemetery Superintendents, and that we have had the privilege of giving those who could not, and also those who would not go with us, through the columns of MODERN CEMETERY what we have seen and enjoyed, and the only way for such to have a part with us is to become a member of the association, and subscribe for the "MODERN CEMETERY." B.

The Question Box.

Your question column in the November issue of MODERN CEMETERY is a good thing and a step in the right direction. I for one hope it will be kept up, for I venture the opinion that there are as many superintendents that can answer questions, as there are who can ask them. Is not this a good way to be constantly disseminating information?

Some time ago a brother superintendent, asked me to suggest the names of the best works on flowers and their care, and work in a greenhouse and where to obtain them. It seems to me that this question is as applicable now as last spring, indeed more so, for in what way can we spend a portion of the long winter evenings more profitably than in reading and studying up for future work? These were the suggested books: *Gardening*, a semi-monthly publication at $1.00 per annum. *Parson's Landscape Gardening* and *Long's Ornamental Gardening for Americans*, all of which can undoubtedly be procured from the office of the MODERN CEMETERY, 334 Dearborn street, Chicago.

JOHN G. BARKER.

S. H. C., Iowa, asks: Where purchasers of cemetery lots buy or bargain for a lot, bury one body thereon and do not pay for said lot, how is the cemetery to get its pay? Of course deed can be withheld, but what can be done with the body buried thereon? purchaser being execution proof.

[In some cemeteries where lots are sold on time the trustees reserve the right to remove bodies to the single grave section if payment is not made within a specified time, and to sell such lots to other parties. Will cemeteries having had such experience, give MODERN CEMETERY readers the benefit of same.—ED.]

Put me down for twelve copies of the MODERN CEMETERY for 1894, writes Mr. Charles Nichols, of Newark, N. J. * * *

I have just had my MONUMENTAL NEWS for 1891 and '92 bound in one volume, and have 1889 and '90 similarly bound. I treasure them very highly and take much pleasure in perusing their pages.—*Charles Nichols, Newark, N. J.*

Situation Wanted. A thoroughly competent and experienced business man and landscape gardener, expert in management desires position as superintendent or assistant, speaks German and French. Special attention given to new cemeteries and organizations of companies. Meier, care 47 Moffat Block, Detroit, Mich.

Situation Wanted.

Young man, experienced in cemetery management, steady and trustworthy, desires position to take charge, or as assistant superintendent. Apply,
L. B., MODERN CEMETERY.

Association of American Cemetery Superintendents.

WM. SALWAY, "Spring Grove" Cincinnati, O., President.
T. McCARTHY, "Swan Point" Providence, R. I., Vice-President.
F. EURICH, Woodlawn, Toledo, O., Secretary and Treasurer.

The Eighth Annual Convention of the Association will be held at Philadelphia in September, 1894.

Resolutions Adopted at the Seventh Annual Convention of the Association of American Cemetery Superintendents.

Resolved: That it is the sense of this convention that all Sunday funerals be discouraged as much as possible.

Resolved: That it is the sense of this meeting that all headstones or markers should be limited to the height of the sod or the level of the surface of the ground.

Resolved: That it is the sense of this meeting that vaults and catacombs be discouraged and if possible prevented in cemeteries.

Publisher's Department.

Cemetery Literature received: Rules, Regulations and Map of Laurel Grove Cemetery, Paterson, N. J., from M. M. Brunner, supt. Rules and regulations of Calvary cemetery, Cleveland, O., from Rev. G. F. Houck.

Mr. John G. Barker concludes his interesting "Vacation Reminiscences" this month. He has been ever ready to yield his pen at the editor's request, considering it a duty and a pleasure to give what assistance he could towards brightening these pages.

Mr. Frank M. Floyd, superintendent of the Evergreen Cemetery, Portland, Me., has kindly furnished the plans of the new office building at that cemetery which we illustrate in this issue. The building is modern in its appointments, and was erected at a cost of about $4,000.

From a recently published work on the business interests of Salem, Mass., we learn that Mr. George W. Creesy, the Superintendent of Harmony Grove cemetery and a widely known member of the A. A. C. S., has under his management the Harmony Grove conservatories covering an area of 40,000 square feet. Mr. Creesy has served in both branches of the Salem city council, and has been prominently identified with the advancement of the best interests of the city.

Decorating or lining graves for the purpose of robbing the sad rites of burial of one of its harshest features is now practiced quite generally in cemeteries large and small. Evergreen sprays are commonly used for this purpose but where they are scarce various other devices have to be resorted to. To fill this want Mr. A. W. Anderson formerly asst. superintendent of Lakewood cemetery, Minneapolis, Minn., invented a grave lining that has been adopted by a number of cemeteries which is giving entire satisfaction and proving a source of revenue. In Mr. Anderson's announcement which will be found in another column, it will be seen that a material reduction has been made in the price since the lining was first put on sale.

THE MODERN CEMETERY.

THE MODERN CEMETERY.
AN ILLUSTRATED MONTHLY JOURNAL DEVOTED TO THE INTEREST OF CEMETERIES

R. J. HAIGHT, Publisher,
334 Dearborn Street, CHICAGO.

Subscription $1.00 a Year in Advance.   Foreign Subscription $1.25.
Special Rates on Six or More Copies.

VOL. III.   CHICAGO, JAN'Y, 1894.   No. 11.

CONTENTS.

TREES AS TRIBUTES TO THE DEAD	121
*HARLEIGH CEMETERY, CAMDEN, N. J.	122-123
FRANK LESLIE'S EPITAPH	123
CONSTITUTIONALITY OF CONDEMNATION—QUESTIONABLE BURIALS, WINTER CARE OF TREES AND SHRUBS	124
CEMETERIES AT PORT SAID—DEATH RATES OF GREAT CITIES	125
RUNIC MONUMENTS—POWERS OVER BURIAL PLACES	126
*CHAPEL AND CONSERVATORY, MT. PLEASANT CEMETERY, TORONTO, ONT.	127
CEMETERY NOTES	128
*S. S. STONE MONUMENT, CLEVELAND, O.	129
SURVEYOR'S REVIEW OF THE CONVENTION PROCEEDINGS—BURIAL BY CONTRACT	130
AGREEMENTS FOR SELLING LOTS ON TIME	131
THE QUESTION BOX	131
PUBLISHERS' DEPARTMENT	132

*Illustrated.

Trees as Tributes to the Dead.

An extract from a paper on the Planting of Trees read by C. W. Garfield, of Grand Rapids, Mich., before the Illinois State Horticultural Society.

By the way, have you ever thought about the value of trees as monuments? If well chosen, they will stand the changes of years better than marble or even granite. Look to the older grave yards that are within your area of vision, are the slabs of marble standing at various angles in crude shapes and inscribed with cruder characters of any particular credit to those who erected them or do they awaken any particular pleasure in remembrance of the departed? But some of those trees that have grown up there because of sheer neglect of the premises, are really beautiful, and had they been planted there in remembrance of dear ones gone before, would they not be treasures to those who are left, far beyond the cold marble or the lifeless granite?

I remember years ago, a newspaper item that asked the question, "who ate Roger Williams?" and then a description followed of the attempt to disinter the remains of that distinguished pioneer liberal. They found that the root of an apple tree near by had penetrated to the bottom of the grave and following the line of the trunk of the body had bifurcated taking the line of the lower limbs, and in its growth had completely absorbed all there was of the early remains of Roger Williams.

For generations, men, women and children had enjoyed the fruit of that thrifty apple tree. The question of who ate Roger Williams was certainly a pertinent one. And isn't it a delightful thought that when we have left this tenement, all there is that belongs to the earth can be taken up and transformed again into living tissues, the fruits of which can strengthen and delight multitudes of people? In this transformation we know no end. We can trace an immortality that is worthy of a monument, and when the monument itself becomes the means of perpetuating that immortality, is it not glorified? Then why not plant a tree above the grave of the one you loved, it will be a constant reminder of affection, and a delightful tribute to the dead, an attractive symbol to the living.

Don't picture to me a Kingdom of Heaven with streets of gold enameled with rubies or sapphire. Don't try to make yourselves believe that future happiness is dependent upon sitting in a golden rocking chair, even if it is embellished with opals and jasper, but the rather, dream out a scheme of Heaven where beautiful symmetrical trees shall temper the brightness of the sun. Let the immortal praises that perhaps you desire to sing be rendered more sonorous by the delicate sound of the wind pursuing its course through their branches and wafting pleasant harmonies through the fields elysian, and above all things so live up to the ideals of this dream, that you shall be fitted to enjoy such a glorious environment as you have pictured. In order to do this, and that your preparation may be complete, plant lovely trees of the earth about your own premises, bring to yourselves and your loved ones all of the attractions that the wide diversity of tree and shrub growth presents to you on every hand. I am not so certain but with this kind of a preparation one could slide into the next world and scarcely feel the transition. Surely he who loves God with all his soul, his mind and strength, will be in harmony with nature's most attractive features; and the love of trees that typify all that is most noble and beautiful in man, can help to place us in harmony with the great Center and Source of life.

Through the efforts of patriotic women an imposing shaft has been placed at the grave of Mary Washington at Fredericksburg, Va.

THE MODERN CEMETERY.

MAGNOLIA LAKE, HARLEIGH CEMETERY, CAMDEN, N. J.

Harleigh Cemetery, Camden, N. J.

Harleigh Cemetery, located on the Haddon turnpike, about two miles from Camden, N. J., is recognized as one of the leading cemeteries of the state, and its modern improvements are attracting merited attention.

The tract of land now under operation embraces 140 acres, all of which is on the lawn plan. More land is available when required. Though only six years have elapsed since work was begun at Harleigh, there have been to date some 925 interments, and the high aim of its projectors, aided by their able superintendent, Mr. George E. Rhedemeyer, to make Harleigh the first cemetery in the state, if not in the Union, is evident in the substantial and extensive improvements that have already been accomplished.

The topographical characteristics of Harleigh are admirable. The ground is high, with rolling slopes and knolls, and consequently is well drained. Midway along its entire length, the cemetery is divided by a small valley, in the center of which are two pretty lakes. A strip of woodland skirting one side of this valley furnishes a beautiful background of foliage.

Each lawn has its appropriate name, as: Granite, Marble, Haddon, Mt. Hope, Philadelphia, Spring Grove, Ridge, Wood, Terrace, etc. Granite lawn is so named from its numerous shafts and monuments of granite. Marble lawn is similar to Granite both in size and shape. It is a beautiful oval plot occupying the center of the western section of the cemetery, is perfectly level, and its central portion is laid out in lots of the uniform size of 18 feet square. Its velvety green-sward is dotted with monuments and head-stones. Adjoining Marble lawn is Haddon lawn, a circular plot of rare beauty, but recently completed. Terrace, Spring Grove and Ridge lawns are among the most picturesque in Harleigh. They overlook both lakes, Ridge being skirted with trees and separated from the lake by a winding drive. Mount Hope is the lawn intended for single graves exclusively. It is a high, circular knoll commanding an excellent view of the scenery of the park-like grounds. The graves here are arranged in rows, the purchase-price of a single grave being $10, which includes perpetual care. What is to be the largest lawn in the cemetery is now being laid out. It will be known as "Summit" and when fully developed will make an attractive section.

The rules by which Harleigh is governed differ little from those of the leading lawn plan cemeteries of America. Every thoughtful provision is taken by the management to guard against the gloom and exclusiveness of old time burial places, and to secure that which will give beauty and charm to the park-like grounds. Lot enclosures are prohibited, mounds are low and uniform in height and grave markers are restricted to a height of six inches which preserves a more unbroken landscape than is possible where stones of varying sizes is permitted.

Notable among the many tombs is that of the gray poet, Walt Whitman. This is a massive rock-faced structure, in the construction of which eighty one tons of granite were used. It has eight catacombs, and the first body to be placed in it was that of its owner, whose funeral brought to Harleigh the largest number of people ever gathered in

SWAN LAKE, HARLEIGH.

it at one time. The poet's tomb is in a picturesque restful spot, on a side hill amid trees and foliage, and facing one of the beautiful lakes seen in our illustrations. The receiving tomb, a stone structure built into a side hill is appropriately placed amid cheerful surroundings and faces Magnolia lake. There is no charge made for the use of the receiving vault, where the friends purchase a lot in the cemetery.

A feature of Harleigh which is given great importance by the management is that of perpetual care. Every lot and grave sold, carries with it the assurance on the part of the cemetery association that it will be kept in perfect order for all future time. This valuable guarantee is rendered possible by the charge of a slight additional price on all lots sold. A lot 9 x 18 feet can be purchased for $60, which considering the scrupulous care with which the cemetery is kept, is a very moderate expense. Other appointments for the care and comfort of its patrons are also provided. When a new grave is opened the loose dirt is thrown on a canvas and is then covered with green boughs to hide it from sight during the services of interment. After the grave has been filled in it is so carefully sodded that it does not present the unsightly appearance of a new mound. In stormy weather, when the ground is wet and soft, matting is spread on the lawns, and, if rain is falling, a large tent is erected over the grave for protection to mourning relatives and friends at the services.

During the past year, 3,590 square feet of glass

A GLIMPSE OF HARLEIGH.

has been added to the conservatory. This is used principally for cut flowers, as the planting of graves is discouraged. Bouquets or baskets of cut flowers can be obtained by lot-owners at all seasons of the year, and the grounds are kept adorned with suitable displays for a modern cemetery.

Superintendent Rhedemeyer is indefatigable in his efforts to bring Harleigh to a high standard. His training has been in the direction of landscaping, and being in harmony with modern ideas of cemetery management, the improvements he has made have met with approbation from trustees and lot-owners. Mr. Rhedemeyer is a member of the Association of American Cemetery Superintendents and is looking forward with much pleasure to a visit from the members of the Association when they hold their annual meeting in Philadelphia next September.

In Woodlawn Cemetery, New York, a handsome granite monument marks the last resting place of Frank Leslie, the publisher. On the front face of the die is a palette and brushes and a laurel wreath, on the rear is the following inscription:

In memory of Frank Leslie, who was called to rest on the 10th of January, 1880, aged 58 years. His life was ennobled through its whole course by labor and usefulness, and made gracious and beneficent by unfailing sympathy with the needs, the joys and the sorrows of others. The pioneer and founder of illustrated journalism in America, his life work speaks through the artistic and literary monuments he has left behind him. His aim was to popularize art and make it a common helper of men, and so signal was his success that his name has become a household word in the uttermost parts of the earth. An artist born, he went into art and art repaid him in full measure. As a friend he was staunch, as an employer generous and considerate, to the poor a benefactor, as a man true, and to his wife, who raises this stone to his loved and honored memory, he never caused any other grief than his death.

The following inscription is on an engineer's tombstone in a Virginia cemetery:

JAMES E. VALENTINE.
Killed in Collision, Dec. 20, 1874.
Aged, 32 years.

In the crash and fall he stood unmoved and sacrificed his life that he might fulfill his trust.

Until the brakes are turned on time,
Life's throttle valve shut down;
He wakes, to pilot in the crew
That wears the martyr's crown.

On schedule time, on upper grades,
Along the homeward section,
He lands his train at God's round house,
The morn of resurrection.

His time all full, no wages docked;
His name on God's pay roll
And transportation through to heaven;
A free pass for his soul.

Mount Royal, the principal cemetery of Montreal, Canada, has twenty-one trustees representating six religious denominations. The church of England and the Presbyterians have eight each, Methodists, Baptists, Congregationalists and Unitarians supplying the remainder.

Constitutionality of Condemnation for Cemetery Purposes.

It seems to be settled law that lands may be condemned for the purpose of a public cemetery where the public in general have a right to obtain interment, according to a recent decision of the Supreme Court of Indiana in the case of Farneman v. Mt. Pleasant Cemetery Association, and that lands taken for the purpose of enlarging a public cemetery is devoting it to a public use. The court then goes on to hold constitutional such a statute as that of Indiana, which provides that whenever, in the opinion of the trustees of any corporation owning or controlling any public cemetery in any county of the state, it becomes necessary to purchase real estate for cemetery uses, such trustees may file a petition in the Circuit Court of said county, asking for the appointment of appraisers to appraise and assess the value of such real estate. This neither confers judicial power in the officers of the corporation, as the statute does nothing more than confer on the corporation the right to file a petition seeking an appropriation when, in the opinion of its officers, the public necessity may require it, nor does it deprive an owner unjustly of any of his rights, where provision is also made permitting him to except to the report of the appraisers for any cause and to have a trial thereon in the court. That the statute in question did not make provision for damages to land from which the condemned land was to be taken, the Supreme Court refused to consider in this case because there was nothing showing it that the tract ought to be condemned, was not all the land that the person had. This ground of unconstitutionality therefore remains to be raised in some future, proper, case.

Questionable Burials.

A startling condition of affairs has been brought to light in England by the recent trial of a comparatively insignificant case. The evidence given shows that in one cemetery about one hundred still-born children were buried during the year, all received from midwives, whose certificates or declarations were taken, without any inquiry as to their qualifications, with the children, which were buried in common graves. The question of the proper mode of registration of the deaths of still-born children is said to have recently been before Parliamentary committees. This is a matter of great importance, not only across the water, but in our own country and those in charge of cemeteries, whether there is any legislation on the subject or not, cannot be too careful in order not to encourage the commission of crime.

One stone at a grave is sufficient.

Winter Care of Trees and Shrubs.

There is no better time than the present, to examine groves and groups of trees, in order to determine whether they are becoming overcrowded, and to designate those which should be removed to make room for the rest.

The axe is the only remedy for crowding among trees, and when this heroic treatment is necessary, no considerations of sentiment, should be allowed to interfere with its use. At this season, too, it is easier to find where branches are growing too thickly on a tree, and where they are rubbing each other, than it is when they are in full foliage, and in the warm days of midwinter, pruning can be done to an advantage. When it is necessary to remove large branches, they should be sawed close to the trunk, and the edges cut smooth with a sharp knife. Coaltar applied to the wound, will keep out moisture and fungi, and thus prevent decay. Any kind of ochreous paint will answer almost as good a purpose, and it can be easily applied with an ordinary brush. All sprouts should be cut from the trunk and all suckers from its base, but the dead twigs in the heads of the trees can be more easily detected in the summer. Of course all diseased limbs should be amputated, and so should the branches of such trees as Hawthorn or yellow-wood that are badly infested with scale.

A top-dressing of loam, or fine well-rotted stable manure, spread over the roots, will encourage a vigorous growth next year. The dressing should be scattered over a circle as far as the roots extend.

Shrubs, too, must be well fed, if they are expected to make luxuriant growth and show their highest beauty. No cultivator thinks of obtaining a fair crop, in garden or field, without fertilizing his land, and yet too many persons starve their shrubberies, and then wonder why they are thin and unattractive. Of course the shrubs like Coryopsis, Forsythia, VanHauttes, or Thunberg's Spiraea, Cersis, the bush Honeysuckles, and other shrubs which flower early, should not now be cut in severely, since the buds for spring flowers are already formed, and if we cut away the branches we destroy the possibility of flowers next season. If late flowering shrubs have not yet been pruned the work can still be done and this will encourage the growth of wood, which will bears flowers later in the season. In this class are the Althaeas, Hydrangea Paniculata, Indian Tamarisk and others. The pruning of roses which are liable to be killed back to some extent had better be post-poned until spring, so that we can be sure to cut below the dead-wood. *R. A. in Garden and Forest.*

A neglected cemetery is a reflection on the community.

Marion Harland's Notes on Cemeteries at Port Said, Egypt.

After leaving the outskirts of Port Said, there were no signs of human habitation except a few scattered hovels dotting the waste on our left. Right in the desert arose the walls of the cemeteries—the Christian, devoted to the interment of French Roman Catholics and Egyptian Copts, and the Moslem where lie "the faithful" of whatever nationality. We looked in the first, seeing nothing very different from the tall crosses and headstones such as we had beheld in dozens of other foreign burial grounds.— We alighted at the gate of the Moslem cemetery and entered the enclosure. Arid sand for many feet downwards is the substance through which the graves are sunk.

Within a few days after the mound is heaped above the sleeper below, the meeting winds of sea and desert, tear it down and whirl the sand to the four quarters of the enclosure. Hence as soon as may be, a box of the shape and size of the grave is fitted over it. When the relatives can afford it, a structure of similar form in cement takes the place of the wooden case. Upon box and cement are written the names of the deceased, and texts from the Koran.

Above many of the wide tombs arise coop-like constructions, with trellised sides and tops, within which stand pots of dwarf palms, cacti, geraniums, and once in a great while of sickly vines, pathetic to behold in a region where the rain does not fall for months together, and water is sold to the poor by the jar or skinful.

There are no regular walks or avenues, and wherever the graves were not protected by boxes, the sand bore the imprint of many feet. Leading the way to the outermost row of graves, the guide pointed to a line of freshly heaped mounds, to the headboards of which were tied shabby branches of palm leaves, palm branches and artificial flowers, "if you had been here this morning," he explained in execrable French enlivened by insupportable English, "you would have seen two thousand women—perhaps more, maybe less, here crying, and telling how good her husband was, or her child was so sweet; or how she mourned her father, or her sister, or her brother, and did break her heart for her mother, died so long ago. They come so every Friday and cry just the same and ever so hard, pointing to the newer mounds. These are those who were buried of late, and the ladies keep the mounds high until the boards are placed around them—so they be not blown away by the sea wind.

Friday is the Moslem Sabbath, and this pious pilgrimage is a duty to be performed upon the holy day. Hearing the tale we looked with different eyes upon the sandy heaps raised by pitying hands; the already withering memorials lashed to the main headboards, had meaning and poetry, the woman's heart is the same, the world around.

At the end of the row of new mounds was an open grave, "when is this to be filled?" I asked knowing that burying in this tropical country follows with awful rapidity upon death, and supposing that the pit was dug purposely for somebody. The dragoman shrugged his shoulders, Ah! who can know? it may be tomorrow, it may be next week. But there is always one ready. Somebody must come to fill it some day. That also was an old story, known wherever men and women live and die. Heaven forbid that we, or any of our blood should ever die at Port Said.—*Christian Herald*.

Death Rates of Great Cities.

Statistics are given below compiled for the first half of last year by Secretary Carter, of the Maryland Board of Health, showing the mortality in various cities of this country and Europe having a population of more than 100,000.

	Population.	Deaths.	Death rate per 1000.
London	5,849,104	55,895	19.11
Paris	2,424,705	28,673	23.61
New York	1,801,739	23,856	26.47
Berlin	1,665,134	17,181	20.58
Chicago	1,456,000	13,590	18.95
Vienna	1,435,931	18,005	25.07
Philadelphia	1,115,562	12,129	21.95
Brooklyn	978,374	10,682	21.84
St. Louis	520,000	4,802	18.47
Brussels	488,188	4,359	17.86
Boston	487,397	5,816	23.88
Baltimore	455,427	4,806	21.10
Dublin	349,594	4,735	27.05
San Francisco	330,000	3,006	18.21
Cincinnati	305,000	3,000	19.67
Cleveland	290,000	2,538	18.19
Buffalo	290,000	2,361	16.28
Pittsburg	255,000	2,923	22.92
New Orleans	254,000	3,598	28.72
Edinburg	267,000	2,572	19.22
Milwaukee	250,000	2,000	16.00
Louisville	227,000	1,630	14.80
Minneapolis	200,000	1,024	9.60
St. Paul	155,000	745	9.61
Christiana, Nor'y	156,500	1,385	17.75
Denver, Col	150,000	871	11.61
Rochester, N. Y	144,834	1,291	17.87
Reims, France	105,408	1,503	28.62

In cities where the cemeteries do not provide awnings or tents for the protection of mourners at funerals it is becoming the custom for undertakers to provide them says the *Sunnyside*.

* * *

A unique monument has been erected in a cemetery near Boston in memory of the Spaulding family, the famous bell ringers. It consists of a broken bell of polished granite, about three feet in height on a square base. The bell is modelled after the large brass bell formerly used by the elder Spaulding and bears the family name in raised letters.

Runic Monuments.

Runic monuments have been found in Sweden, Norway, Denmark and England and are of very ancient origin. They are called Runic from the fact that they are inscribed with Runes or letters of the Runic alphabet, which was in use by the Angles or inhabitants of the Northern countries—not including Germany—previous to and immediately following the beginning of the Christian era. About 2000 Runic pieces have been found in Sweden alone, and something less than half that number in all the other northern countries. When it is considered that not one of their monuments is less than ten centuries old, the wonder is that any of them are remaining; and it would seem that the practice of erecting Runic stones among the early inhabitants of England and Sweden must have been quite general.

Some of the Runic monuments are in the form of crosses; others represent shields; still others are rude pillars of stone or mere boulders bearing inscriptions; a comparatively few ornamental pieces have been found, in which the stone has been carved into the form of men or of common household utensils. In all of these the symbol of the cross is to be found with such frequency as to argue strongly that the monuments were, with few exceptions, Christian memorials to the dead. They were erected over the graves of the departed, sometimes by a widow to her husband, a son to his father, or an heir of a later generation to a deceased progenitor. In one rich funeral sculpture a lady erected a double canopied slab to her deceased husband, the Dean Nicholas, and to herself. His full-length effigy is carved in the right compartment, but her own, in the left, is wanting, and the Runic inscription is unfinished. Perhaps she thought better of it and—married. Another lady raised her own monument before her death, but afterwards thought it might prevent her marrying again and changing her name, in which case the stone would be useless. She therefore removed it.

In all the instances of good preservation of Runic monuments it is found that an exceedingly hard stone was used, and doubtless this was the custom. Granites are frequent among them and one piece which had withstood the elements exceptionally well was a porphyritic greenstone. It must be borne in mind that where these stones have not been buried in the ground they have frequently been used over and over again for monuments to succeeding generations, so that with this constant re-handling and working over with rough tools the fact of their preservation in anything like recognizable shape for so many centuries is all the more wonderful.

How these monuments were carved is still a mystery. It is supposed by some that the work was done with iron tools; by others the conjecture has been offered that tools of bronze may have been used, but if this be possible the metal must have been hardened by a process of which we know nothing. Against this theory is the fact that the writing on these monuments date from the early iron age. Traces of color have been found on many of these stones, and as some of them are cut in very low relief it is probable that color was applied to heighten the effect. Gilded metal, particularly lead, was used also on these Runic stones.

One of the most celebrated of the Runic crosses was that discovered at Lancashire, England. It was dug up in an old churchyard and was found to be in a remarkably good state of preservation, considering the fact that it must have been at the time of its discovery, 1807, at least ten centuries old. One arm of the cross had been broken off, but the inscription remained. This has been determined to be a Christian burial inscription in the Northumbrian dialect of the Anglo-Saxon. Translated into Latin, the language of the church, it reads:

Orate pro Cynibaldo Cuthberhti.
Pray for Cynibald, the son of Cuthbert.

Powers over Burial Places.

The powers for preventing burial places from becoming dangerous to public health, to be exercised by order in council under the English Burial Act of 1857, are held to be not inconsistent with the exclusive jurisdiction of the Court of Ordinary to authorize the removal and re-interment of remains buried in consecrated burial places or vaults in consecrated ground. The Court of Ordinary will have to in such a case, give authority for removal and re-interment, but may confine the re-interment, to a specified place of burial and provide as to the mode and manner in which the removal and re-interment shall be made, and the interests of relatives guarded.

MORTUARY CHAPEL AND CONSERVATORY, MOUNT PLEASANT CEMETERY, TORONTO, ONT.

Mortuary Chapel and Conservatory at Mt. Pleasant Cemetery, Toronto, Ont.

The accompanying illustration of the new chapel and conservatory at Mt. Pleasant cemetery is from the North Toronto *Recorder*. The new building is constructed immediately over the old receiving vault or mortuary, the iron and terra cotta ceiling of the latter acting as the floor of the superstructure shown in our illustration. The mortuary is built into a side hill, entrance is had to it through a handsome gothic archway, but as is the case with too many side hill vaults the ventilation was bad and the interior damp and forbidding. The happy thought of placing the conservatory and chapel above the mortuary has changed this, for with high ceilings and ample ventilation the air is now kept perfectly pure. The upper portion of the building contains a conservatory 50 ft. square, surrounding on three sides a mortuary chapel, from which it is separated by swing doors and large plate glass windows giving a full view of the flowers, plants, and palms. The bier, situate near the centre of the chapel, is made to descend through a brass-railed richly curtained opening into the chamber beneath, which is hidden from view by upholstered doors that fold over the opening immediately after the descent of the casket. Three large propagating houses occupy the remainder of the space over the Mortuary, while a commodious potting house forms an extension northwards. The conservatory, chapel and forcing houses are heated by hot water obtained from two large boilers situate beneath. Water is pumped from a well in the lower story to a tank in the potting house by means of a force pump driven by an electric motor, which also operates a ventilating fan to be used as occasion may require, the floors are of terra cotta and cement on iron girders, while the floors of the conservatory and chapel are finished with handsome tiling. The work has been executed from the designs of Mr. Edmund Burke, architect.

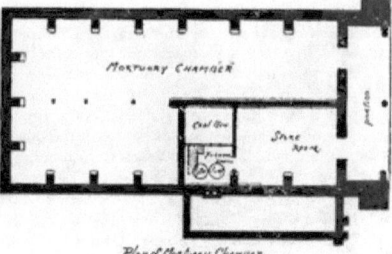

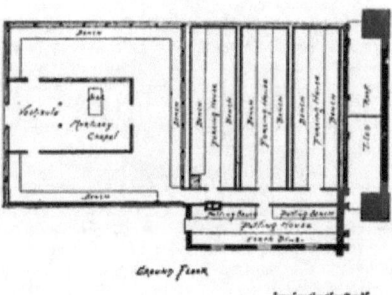

Dr. John W. Shaeffer, convicted of grave robbing at Des Moines, has been sentenced to six months in the penitentiary and his two assistants fined $200. A motion for appeal was denied.

CEMETERY NOTES.

For the purpose of arousing an interest in the religious press to the pressing needs of cemetery reform copies of the MODERN CEMETERY are frequently mailed to such publications throughout the country. Judging from the degree of success that these efforts have apparently met with, it would appear religious editors or more properly speaking editors of religious papers are as apathetic on this subject as the average lot owner. The editor of the *Ave Maria* an influential catholic journal is however an exception. After quoting an extract from our last issue he adds the following, which shows that he is in touch with modern thought on cemetery affairs. Would that others were as much so. "We moderns stare in surprise when we are told that some of the the older nations still hire professional mourners, who are wont to pursue the slow-driven hearse with high-priced lamentations. But what more pitiable example of mourning by proxy than the custom which prompts a lavish expenditure in funeral arrangements, while it allows the grave to lie neglected and overgrown with noxious weeds! Flowers are the language of love; and he must indeed be a Philistine who would not prefer that a few fragrant blossoms, and not mere costly ceremonial, should stand for the outward expression of his grief."

The appearance of most cemeteries is needlessly depressing, if it is not wholly inconsistent with Christian hope. Instead of being a distant, dismal spot, shrouded in the gloom of evergreen trees, the graveyard should stand in view of men, a bright, hopeful, sunshiny place,—a real "God's acre," such as beseems the long, peaceful sleep which precedes the morn of Resurrection."

* * *

Iowa undertakers have caused to be prepared a bill to be introduced in the legislature authorizing the establishing of a state board of embalming. The object being "to regulate the practice of embalming, the care and disposition of the dead, to provide for the better protection of health and prevent the spread of contagious diseases." Persons desiring to enter the undertaking profession are required to qualify before this board, and one member of the board is to be an ex-officio member of the state board of health. Iowa is the first state to take such an important move and the enactment of the bill is confidently looked for.

* * *

Supt. Cushman, of Greenwood Cemetery, Brooklyn, N. Y., Mr. Wells' successor, is reported as saying that it is the intention to fill in all of the lakes, which to his mind "do not add to the beauty of the place because they are continually getting covered with green scum." It is to be hoped that the intentions will not be carried out. While green scum does mar the beauty of any body of water, it can be obviated to a certain extent at some little expense and the authorities of wealthy Greenwood should not let the matter of expense deprive the grounds of what have been in the past one of their most charming features.

* * *

Cleveland, O., has three or four cemeteries under municipal control. A change in the political complexion of the city government brings a corresponding change in the officials and workmen at the cemeteries. Lot owners have long since demurred against these frequent interferences and to prevent their continuance a bill accompanied by a numerously signed petition, has been sent to the legislature, providing for a bi-partisan cemetery board to consist of two republican and two democratic members, in whom shall be vested entire control. We are not aware of the context of the bill, but any movement looking to the divorcement of cemetery control from the political machinery of city affairs should and doubtless will meet with favor.

* * *

The people of Newton, L. I., opposite New York City, are again disturbed over the possible addition of another cemetery. There are at present twenty cemeteries and one crematorium in the town, occupying over 1,800 acres of ground all of which is free from taxation. It is estimated that over 1,500,000 interments have been made and they are increasing at the rate of 40,000 a year. The people will contest any movement contemplating an additional cemetery.

* * *

The annual report of Riverside cemetery, Cleveland, O., states the total receipts of the year were $30,379 and the disbursements $12,257. Of the former amount $25,264 was received from the sale of lots, the sales having been one-third larger than the yearly average for the last ten years. The cemetery has a bonded debt of $41,000 and its assets consisting of cash and personal accounts amounts to $46,209.

* * *

Earnshaw and Punshon, landscape engineers of Cincinnati, have completed plans for Mt. Olivet, the new catholic cemetery in the suburbs of Detroit, Mich. The tract aggregates 200 acres of rolling partially wooded land. A stream flows through the land which will be utilized to form a chain of lakes. Mt. Olivet will be a corporate extension of Mount Elliot, which is now within the city limits and fast filling up.

S. S. STONE MONUMENT, LAKEVIEW CEMETERY, CLEVELAND, O.

The S. S. Stone monument, Lakeview Cemetery, Cleveland, O., is a dignified and imposing piece of memorial work, combining the special features of a family vault, with the artistic effect of the individual monument. It is of the Corinthian order of architecture, enriched with the renaissance, the individual feature being the statue, which is a portrait, heroic size, of the late Silas Stafford Stone, at one time a prominent citizen of Cleveland. The granite used in the construction of this work is the fine Westerly from the quarries of the Smith Granite Co., of Westerly, R. I., who executed the work.

* * *

Vandals at Stroudsburg, Pa., used dynamite to blow open a cemetery vault in an attempt to rob the bodies of jewelry. No valuables were found and the bodies were left undisturbed. The vault, a $30,000 structure, was but slightly damaged.

* * *

The cemetery board of Cadillac, Mich., are endeavoring to raise $1,000 for improvements by giving a series of entertainments during the winter.

Correspondence.

A Surveyor's Review of the "Convention Proceedings."

Editor Modern Cemetery.

Having before me the "Proceedings of the Seventh Annual Convention of Association of American Cemetery Superintendents," I have carefully gone over the several discussions with the purpose of garnering the opinions of leading minds respecting points concerning the planning or lay outs of new grounds. All as with one accord concur in endorsing the "Lawn Plan" and condemning what they term the "Old Plan." I have tried to determine by their debate just what is meant by the new plan or lawn plan and just what belongs to the old plan, as to the latter I am confident they are not referring to church burial grounds or town plats for burial purposes as was every where in use during the last century. I have been laying out cemeteries since 1852; at that date our work was called the park plan, sometimes the new plan and quite frequently the association plan. I would like to say that our methods have been moderately improved but not in any essential sense radically changed, so far as designing or laying out are concerned. We had drives or avenues then, also lawns, and alleys with paths to reach every family lot or single grave, and I may say the same essential features are still recognized among the best maintained and improved grounds. It would be quite just to say that the management has drifted away from the original idea of a park with memorial monuments and low grave marks, large unincumbered vistas with occasional groups of planting, here and there a shady resting place with rustic seats for the invalid or weary pedestrian. They have permitted the useless enclosure to take a multitude of cumbersome forms. The iron railing, posts with chains, curb stones, hedge rows and all such trappings, even the massive corner posts are all encroachments, that should have been kept out of the way.

The park plan, association plan, lawn plan and modern plan are essentially the same but the methods of care should be radically reformed and the American Association of Cemetery Superintendents have taken hold of the work. They are seeming sensible respecting the difficulty they have to treat, but I am sure they will succeed in large measure. The people revolt at arbitrary ruling, but they respect change and indeed covet it. A sacrifice that is voluntary will be counted a virtue and pleasure, but arbitrary destruction will weigh down like vandalism.

I am unwilling to fully concur with the superintendents who would unhesitatingly abandon all graveled walks, because of the expense of keeping in order. Were we to do so the rural cemetery will lose one element which enables the designer to bring out much of the natural beauty that inheres to the ground. Without this means of bringing out the natural undulation, the plan will reduce itself to a mere checker board. Mr. Pres. Salway says, "the walk should follow the contour of the hill," in that he is strictly right, a similar principle will control on the plateaus, slight wrinkles or undulations of surface are sufficient to control or very much modify the range taken for a walk. When this graceful sweep has been fully developed and defined so that the common mind observes the respect paid to it by the artist, he involuntarily exclaims how beautiful!

I am not without an experience in the matter of having roads washed out by storms. I add concurrence in the opinion that walks which cannot be protected against mutilation during storms had better be filled flush with adjacent lawn and sodded over.

All family plats and I will add (single grave interments) should be accessible by carriage drive or public opening, this principle need not and should not unduly increase the amount of graveled walks. Walk spaces may be provided and remain as parts of the lawn, what I claim is that some conspicuous walks so located as to give character and obvious purpose should not be under disguise but brought out in full view so that the way faring man, though a fool, may find and if he wills to do so, can follow it. In some future article I may comment more on other characteristics of the cemetery walk.

B. F. HATHEWAY.

Burial by Contract.

In every great city the poor live by the worldly vanities of the rich. In Paris, they die in the same way. It is the manufacture of innumerable superfluities which makes up the bulk of the industry of the working classes. The French capital has developed an ingenious system by which the poor are furnished with a free burial at the expense of the "pride, pomp, and circumstance" which Dives considers his due on the road to the tomb.

One of the largest best-managed and most profitable industries in Paris is that of the Pompes Funebres, the gigantic monopoly which alone has the privilege of transporting the dead through the streets of Paris in funeral style. It possesses undertaker's material to the value of over 4,000,000 of francs, does some 6,000,000 a year of business, and turns over nearly 2,500,000 of this as clear profit to its accredited owners, the church establishment of the city, after gratuitously and decently burying some three out of every five of the dead as indigent subjects.

Each country and each age have their own fashion of disposing of their dead, from the Patagonian who makes "lion meat," of his spouse, back to the ancient Roman with his ancestral urns. Taken in all, perhaps there is no more reasonable arrangement than that of the thrifty Parisian who manages to have each disposal of the dead carried out decently and in order through the exploitation of a love of lavish display in a minor portion of the community.

One sees nothing of the ghastly side of undertaker's work in visiting the vast premises which have been recently devoted to the use of the Pompes Funebres, away out in the extreme northwest of Paris, in La Villette. There we found "the trappings and the suits of woe," the materials for the funeral decorations and funeral cortege. Take it altogether, a ramble over the establishment is one of the most interesting sights of the city.—*The Forum.*

QUESTION BOX.

Forms of agreement used in selling lots on time have been received from F. W. Chislett, Crown Hill, Indianapolis, Ind., C. M. Chamberlain, Mt. Olivet, Maspeth, Long Island; Geo. E. Rhedemeyer, Harleigh, Camden, N. J.; John Levering, Spring Vale, LaFayette, Ind.; and extract from Charter, of Grove Hill, Shelbyville, Ky., on the same subject from Geo. W. Riely. The two first are reproduced.

THE CROWN HILL CEMETERY.

$............ INDIANAPOLIS, Ind. .... 189..
Received of..
.... /00 Dollars, in cash, and......
promissory notes for...........................Dollars
each, payable in..................................
months from this date, under a conditional contract for the sale of..................................
of Lot No..................in Section No................in The Crown Hill Cemetery.
The rights of the said.............are fully set forth in said conditional contract of sale, a copy of which is found below.

CROWN HILL CEMETERY.

INDIANAPOLIS,.................189..
This certifies, That I have this day paid to The Crown Hill Cemetery, the sum of,......................Dollars, in cash, and have also executed to them my...............
promissory note for.................Dollars each, payable ....months from this date. Such cash has been paid and such note executed by me on the conditional sale to me by said Crown Hill Cemetery of,........................
Lot No............in Section No............in The Crown Hill Cemetery.

But it is expressly understood and agreed that no title to or interest in said lot has become vested in me by reason of such payment or the execution of said note; and that if said note, or any part thereof, or any renewal thereof, in whole or in part, be not promptly paid at maturity then The Crown Hill Cemetery shall have the right, without notice to me, to take possession of said lot, remove any body or bodies buried therein, and all monuments or marking stones to other grounds reserved for single interments, in which event all previous sums of money paid shall be taken as paid for the privilege of the burial of such body or bodies upon said grounds and the occupancy thereof, for the time being, to cover the cost of transferring such bodies, monuments or marking stones, and for the price of such grounds reserved for single interments, to which such body or bodies and such monuments shall have been transferred; and thereafter I shall have no right either at law or in equity to claim any right whatever in and to said lot or any part thereof, or to recover any of the moneys so paid to The Crown Hill Cemetery.

Signed duplicates.

MOUNT OLIVET CEMETERY.

MASPETH, L. I., N. Y. ....18....
Received from..................................
the sum of..........................dollars, in partial payment on account of Lot.......................
........................; the balance of...............
dollars, it is hereby agreed, shall be paid............
on or before the............day of........., 18....
with interest from this date, when the deed will be delivered at the Office of the Cemetery, provided, however, and it is hereby expressly agreed, that in case of any default in the above mentioned payment this receipt shall be null and void, and any payment made on the above mentioned lot shall be forfeited to the Cemetery; and it is further conditioned, that any interment made in the said Lot, in the mean time, shall be considered as temporary, and subject to removal, unless the deed for the said Lot shall be taken within the time above mentioned.

The conditions of sale are quite similar in all of the forms. The Harleigh agreement reads that "the heirs and assigns shall forfeit all right and claim in said lot and the amount paid on account of said consideration money shall be forfeited to said Association as payment to it for the burying of such removed body or bodies." In addition to the right to remove to single grave section for non-payment the Spring Vale agreement contains the following "or at the option and consent of the corporation the re-interment may be made upon any lot bearing price not exceeding, with expense of removal, the amount paid by the delinquent party."

At Spring Vale the receipt embodying conditions of sale, and two notes one at six and one at twelve months are printed on the same page and bound in book form. The two latter remain in the book until they are paid. The stub keeps a record of the transaction. Mr. Chamberlain heartily favors selling lots in this way. At Maspeth, lots are sold on 3, 6, 9, and 12 months time and where reasonable excuse is given the time is extended. Mr. Chamberlain writes that he heartily favors the plan, as in a long experience he has had but two or three occasions for removing bodies.

Association of American Cemetery Superintendents.

WM. SALWAY, "Spring Grove" Cincinnati, O., President.
T. McCARTHY, "Swan Point" Providence, R. I., Vice-President.
F. EURICH, Woodlawn, Toledo, O., Secretary and Treasurer.

The Eighth Annual Convention of the Association will be held at Philadelphia in September, 1894.

Resolutions Adopted at the Seventh Annual Convention of the Association of American Cemetery Superintendents.

Resolved: That it is the sense of this convention that all Sunday funerals be discouraged as much as possible.

Resolved: That it is the sense of this meeting that all headstones or markers should be limited to the height of the sod or the level of the surface of the ground.

Resolved: That it is the sense of this meeting that vaults and catacombs be discouraged and if possible prevented in cemeteries.

Publisher's Department.

It is exceedingly gratifying to note the number of subscribers who have contributed to this issue of the MODERN CEMETERY. Mr. O. C. Simonds furnished the very interesting extract from Mr. Garfield's paper on Trees. Mr. Charles Nichols sent us Marion Harland's account of the cemeteries at Port Said. To Mr. John G. Barker, we are indebted for a description of the new Crematorium near Forrest Hills Boston. Mr. Geo. E. Rhedemeyer furnished data for the article on Harleigh. Mr. Geo. N. Painter favored us with a number of valuable newspaper clippings while several more superintendents names appear in our columns this month. This evinces a spirit of willingness to help make the columns of the MODERN CEMETERY interesting and instructive that is sincerely appreciated by the editor. Contributions, original or otherwise, that are deemed of general interest to cemetery readers are always welcome.

Geo. E. Rhedemeyer, chairman of the Executive Committee, A.A.C.S. has written a stirring letter to the MODERN CEMETERY urging the agitation of the Eighth Annual Convention of the cemetery superintendents to be held in Philadelphia in September. It is certainly none too early to commence discussing through these columns what topics are most desirable for consideration at that time, and cemetery officials are requested to give the subject their attention. Mr. Rhedemeyer says that the committee expect to have an address from the eminent horticulturist, Mr. Thomas Meehan, which of itself will be sufficient to attract a large attendance.

The "Question Box" query last month brought a number of replies, which will be helpful to new cemeteries if not to many others whose rules on the subject referred to need revising. Questions and answers are solicited for this department.

Photographs received, Los Gatos cemetery, Los Gatos, Cala., from Mr. R. F. Robertson, Secretary. Entrance and office of Mount Olivet cemetery Maspeth, Long Island, from Mr. C. M. Chamberlain, Supt.

Cemetery Literature received: Rules and Regulations of Woodlawn Cemetery, Toledo O. Report of interments in Grove Hill cemetery, Shelbyville, Ky. The North Toronto *Recorder* with description of the new conservatory and chapel at Deer Park, Ont., from Mr. Henry Thompson, Supt.

Mr. Frank Eurich, Secretary and Treasurer of the A. A. C. S. and Superintendent of Woodlawn cemetery, Toledo O., has been elected to the office of clerk of that cemetery.

Several new advertisements appear in this issue, will our readers kindly mention the MODERN CEMETERY when corresponding. By patronizing those who advertise in these columns our readers confer a favor upon the publisher.

To the Members of the Association American Cemetery Superintendents:

One copy of the Minneapolis proceedings has been mailed to each and every one, aside from the extra copies to such that had their orders in before December 15, 1893.

Owing to the general depression in business throughout the country I have been unable to secure advertisements as heretofore and this will make it necessary to pay for the reporting, printing and binding our proceedings from membership dues. Those who feel disposed to procure extra copies for distribution among officers and lot holders of their respective cemeteries will please forward their orders and remit at the rate of $2.50 per dozen for six or more copies.

Will also say that, while it may appear premature, it would be desirable for members to bear in mind our next meeting in Philadelphia, and give the matter of topics for papers and discussion some attention and reflection. In the every day routine of cemetery work perplexing questions and problems are constantly presenting themselves, and if such are sent to the Executive Committee or Secretary much material can be procured for interesting papers and discussions.

Members willing to volunteer papers will find more time for preparing same during these winter months than later in the season, when their whole time is taken up with their duties.

Yours sincerely,
FRANK EURICH, Sec'y. and Treas.

ERRATA:—In the list of membership, published in the seventh annual proceedings, the name of Philoh King, Maple Grove, Ravenna, O., was inadvertently omitted, and Geo. W. Creesy, Harmony Grove, Salem, Mass., is incorrectly located at Salem, O.

Situation Wanted. A thoroughly competent and experienced business man and landscape gardener, expert in management desires position as superintendent or assistant, speaks German and French. Special attention given to new cemeteries and organizations of companies. Meier, care 47 Moffat Block, Detroit, Mich.

Situation Wanted.
Young man, experienced in cemetery management, steady and trustworthy, desires position to take charge, or as assistant superintendent. Apply, L. R., MODERN CEMETERY.

Situation Wanted.
By a person qualified to fill position of superintendent and secretary. Several years experience. W. F. L. care MODERN CEMETERY, Chicago.

THE MODERN CEMETERY.

THE MODERN CEMETERY.
AN ILLUSTRATED MONTHLY JOURNAL DEVOTED TO THE INTEREST OF CEMETERIES

R. J. HAIGHT, Publisher.
334 Dearborn Street, CHICAGO.

Subscription $1.00 a Year in Advance.   Foreign Subscription $1.25.
Special Rates on Six or More Copies.

VOL. III.   CHICAGO, FEB'RY, 1894.   NO. 12.

CONTENTS.

CEMETERY PLANTING....................................	133
RIGHTS OF OWNERS OF CEMETERY LOTS............	134
UNCONSTITUTIONAL LOCAL LEGISLATION............	134
LINCOLN'S ADDRESS AT GETTYSBURG.................	135
TAX ON GRAVES, A..	135
CREMATION..	135
*BELLEFONTAINE CEMETERY, ST. LOUIS, MO.........	136
ORNAMENTAL FRUITING SHRUBS......................	138
CEMETERY WALKS..	138-9
ANNUAL REPORTS, SWAN POINT, PROVIDENCE, MT. AUBURN, BOSTON.....................................	140
*RULES AND REGULATIONS, WOODLAWN CEMETERY TOLEDO, O...	140-1
EPITAPHS...	141
FOREIGN FUNERAL CUSTOMS..........................	142
CORRESPONDENCE..	143
THE QUESTION BOX......................................	144
PUBLISHERS' DEPARTMENT.............................	144

*Illustrated.

Cemetery Planting--I.

As in all decorative planting, the landscape plan must first be carefully thought out with a view to pictorial effect. For it is a picture that is to be made, and the prime artistic quality of synthesis must be considered before the analysis which decides details, viz., the position and variety of trees, shrubs, vines and plants best adapted to the production of the desired broad effect. The parts must be subordinated to the whole. Mr. Hamerton's words written of landscape painting, apply so forcibly and admirably to landscape *planting*, that they may well serve as rules for guidance in such work.

He says that in landscape art: "a fine effect is pictorially complete; a common effect usually scattered and comparatively unmeaning; a fine effect has large masses and vigorous appositions; a common effect is apt, (he means *likely*) to be broken and feeble." There, in a nutshell, is a fundamental rule for all decorative planting, be it applied to parks, cemeteries, private grounds or suburban lots.

If one succeeds in applying the spirit of it, the effect can not be less than good. But the rule is not so tangible that it can be handled or measured.

The rules of composition are elusive; vague as the effects of natural landscape on all sensitive minds, but,—just as surely felt. The unfailing guide, however, is to have a reason for every part of the design, and in a cemetery this should not be hard to find. Utility for the purpose in hand is the rock foundation that must underlie all work if it is to stand the test of time.

The best salient feature or features of the natural landscape will be quickly recognized, and readily made the most of by every man of taste who looks and tries for this end, and whatever they may be, will decide the character of the picture he will form in his mind's eye. It may take years to make the picture, but if he sees it clearly at the outset he is sure, in time, to "arrive." It may be that the picture must needs be pastoral, like Graceland, (Chicago), or sylvan like Spring Grove (Cincinnati) or hilly woodland, such as Bellefontaine or Calvary (St Louis) might be if some trees were cleared out of the first, and a judicious cyclone would clear some stones out of them both.

But the desired general effect decided on, there remains the delightful task of working it out in all its charming detail. And while the making of such landscapes in a measure resembles the composition of a landscape painting, it is far more difficult; for the painting represents *one* phase of *one* season and remains unchanged; while the landscape is looked at, enjoyed and criticised in *all* the phases of *all* the seasons. Moreover, the materials of which it is made change in size; and while the painted picture is seen from the point of view chosen by the artist, the made landscape is seen from *all* points of view, and must look right from every one of them.

All of these conditions must be taken into account by the artist who makes these out of door pictures, if that coquettish siren, success, is to attend him on his way. But above all else, perhaps, he must know how and when to hold his hand, or all sense of repose will be lost, and its loss is fatal. Meaningless repetitions of plantings, however good in themselves, will give a spotty, broken effect. Broad stretches of open, unbroken turf bring about repose, rest the eye and set off the scene. In fact they make the view, as without such openings there can be no vistas, and without vistas there can be no landscapes. For trees alone do not make a landscape. An unbroken wall of foliage is not as dreary as one of brick, but it shuts off a view quite as effectually.

A carpet of sward, whether spread on a level,

over gentle slopes, or over hill and dale, may be considered the stage whereon the picture maker is to group and arrange his living figures, place his colors and plan for his masses of light and shade.

It is magnificent work; it is the fundamental art; it was practiced in the garden of Eden, and a garden is still the synonym of Paradise.

FANNY COPLEY SEAVEY.

Rights of Owners of Cemetery Lots.

In the case of Ritchey v. City of Canton, reported in volume 46 of the Illinois Appellate Court Reports, a decision of interest is rendered. A Mrs. Almeda Rush acquired by deed the title to a lot in the Canton Cemetery. Afterwards the Canton cemetery company conveyed all of its cemetery property to the city of Canton in trust for burial purposes. After such conveyance, the city passed an ordinance providing that no grave should be made in the cemetery, except by permission and under the direction of the sexton appointed by the city, under penalty. Subsequently, Mrs. Rush requested a Mr. Ritchey to go upon her lot and dig a grave for the burial of her daughter, which he did without permission of the city sexton, and, in fact, against the will of the sexton, who claimed the right to dig the grave. This action was then brought to recover from him the penalty prescribed for violation of the ordinance referred to. It was not contended that in preparing the grave he violated any other of the provisions or failed to observe any other of the requirements of the ordinances of the city relating to the cemetery, excepting the one prohibiting the digging of a grave in the cemetery without the permission, or under the direction, of the sexton. In the circuit court he was fined $1 and costs. The appellate court reverses that judgment. The court in discussing the rights of the owner of the lot in question, says that though she held by title in fee simple, the lot was subject to the exercise on the part of the city of that inherent and plenary power resting in the state, and by the state delegated to the city, to prohibit all things hurtful to the comfort, safety, and welfare of the inhabitants of the city. But the power of the city to regulate by ordinance the use and the manner of use of the burial lots by persons purchasing from the city after the adoption of such ordinance would not apply to her lot; except to the extent that the provisions of the ordinance were directed to the protection of the health, comfort, safety and welfare of the public. The lot was her property, with all the title and rights of fee simple ownership of cemetery lots located within the limits of a city. One of these rights was the privilege of interring therein the bodies of her dead by her own hand, if she liked, or by the hand of such sympathetic neighbors or friends as might volunteer their service, or by whom she might employ for that purpose. The city might, by ordinance, establish such regulations concerning the manner of digging the grave, its depth, etc., and the interment, as were reasonable in their character and necessary for the protection of the public health and welfare, and she or those who made the grave for her must conform to such regulations. It is to be understood that what is said is different in principle from a case between a city and a person who purchases a burial lot or burial rights in a lot from the city after the passage of such an ordinance.

Unconstitutional Local Legislation.

A decision of unusual significance, setting forth an important principle of wide application, although rendered by a court of inferior jurisdiction is that of the Court of Common Pleas, No. 4, of Philadelphia, in the case of the City of Philadelphia v. The Westminster Cemetery Co., holding unconstitutional a statute providing that it shall be unlawful to ("hereafter") establish any cemetery upon lands located within one mile from any city of the first-class, the drainage from which empties or passes into any stream from which any portion of the water supply for such city is obtained. Such is the Pennsylvania Act of June 8, 1891. The bill filed by the city in this case averred that the Westminster Cemetery Co., had purchased land and established a cemetery within one mile of the city of Philadelphia, and that the surface drainage therefrom emptied into the Schuykill. The objection that this particular Pennsylvania statute is defective on account of its title not being expressive enough, the court over-rules as unavailable. And the further objection that this statute violates the (Pennsylvania) constitutional inhibition against any local law relating to cemeteries, grave-yards, or public grounds, not of the state, is over-ruled on the ground that the statute does not in anywise "regulate" cemetery companies. But the court holds that the statute offends against the constitution in that it is local legislation relating to a belt of land around cities of the first-class. What particular municipal function, attribute, or power, this may be referred to, the court says it does not see. It relates neither to the officers of a city of the first-class, or their duties, or powers, or any municipal purpose. It makes a belt around such cities in adjoining territory by a local, narrow, and arbitrary law. Cemeteries now existing in the city, or within a mile of it, or which may hereafter be located more than a mile off, or even, within the city, are not under the ban of the law. Such legislation cannot be upheld as constitutional. If it is attempted to sustain the Act as a police regulation, it must be remembered that of all laws, those relating to police powers, must be general, and cannot be parceled out in belts of territory.

Lincoln's Address at the Dedication of the National Cemetery at Gettysburg, Pa.

Four score and seven years ago, our fathers brought forth on this continent, a new nation, conceived in liberty, and dedicated to the proposition that all men are created equal.

Now we are engaged in a great civil war, testing whether that nation or any nation so conceived and so dedicated can long endure. We are met on a great battle field of that war. We have come to dedicate a portion of that field, as a final resting place for those, who here gave their lives, that that nation might live. It is altogether fitting and proper that we should do this. But in a larger sense, we can not dedicate—we can not consecrate—we can not hallow this ground.

The brave men living and dead, who struggled here have consecrated it, far above our poor power to add or detract. The world will little note, nor long remember what we say here, but it can never forget, what they did here. It is for us the living rather to be dedicated here to the unfinished work which those who fought here have so nobly advanced. It is rather for us to be here dedicated to the great task remaining, before us, that from these honored dead, we take increased devotion, to that cause for which they gave the last full measure of devotion, that we here highly resolve that these dead shall not have died in vain, that this nation under God, shall have a new birth of freedom, and that government of the people, by the people, for the people shall not perish from the earth. ABRAHAM LINCOLN.
November 19th., 1863.

A Tax on Graves.

The members of the Paris Municipal Council have little difficulty in meeting any deficit in their budget. They are threatened with one now, and consequently have resolved to put a fresh tax on funerals.

Strictly speaking, of course, this will take the form of enhanced fees to be paid by the public, as there are no private undertakers in the French capital. According to the tariff which has been in vogue during the present regime the price of a freehold grave, two square yards in size, is £14, but there is a progressive scale, so that a third yard costs £40 extra, and a fourth the same amount again, while a fifth and a sixth are charged £60 each, and every yard above a sixth costs no less than £80. The municipality proposes to increase the price of the first two yards to £30, and to remodel the scale of charges in other ways, so that it is estimated there will be an increased revenue of £21,520 per annum.
—London Tid Bits.

A Club that Attended Funerals.

The funeral Club of Paris was a ghastly organization. Its object was to attend in a body all public funerals, and private ones where it was allowed. Its meetings were always held in cemeteries, and members invariably dressed in sombre black with crape sashes on their hats. The only music they had was a hand organ, and this played nothing but the dead march in "Saul." All kinds of gayeties, theatres, dances and parties the members were strictly forbidden to participate in at any time; indeed it is difficult to imagine what on earth the men composing the funeral Club had to live for anyhow.
—Boston Home Journal.

÷ CREMATION. ÷

The annual report of the Philadelphia Cremation Society states that 68 bodies were cremated in 1893 and 254 since 1881.

* * *

Oakwoods cemetery, Troy, N. Y., Graceland at Chicago, Forest Lawn at Buffalo, Cypress Lawn at San Francisco, Rosedale at Los Angeles have crematoriums in successful operation. In New York, Boston, Detroit and other cities, the crematoriums are situated within a short distance of prominent cemeteries.

* * *

It has remained for a profound German scientist to suggest that cremation should become popular because it would put an end to the superstitious belief in graveyard ghosts.

* * *

At the recent tuberculosis congress at Paris, it was declared that bacilli existing in the bodies of persons who die of consumption are brought to the surface of the ground by earthworms, and two Lyons physicians demonstrated by the result of actual experiment that the disease may be propagated in this way. Compulsory cremation was therefore urged as one means of guarding against the spread of this dreaded scourge.

General Crook's monument in Arlington cemetery, Washington, is a massive, oblong block of Quincy granite resting upon a low base of the same material. The top of the stone is rock-faced, and three of the sides bear bronze tablets. One gives the names of the Indian campaigns, another the battles of the civil war in which General Crook was engaged, and the third depicts the surrender of Geronimo in the Sierra Madre in 1883. General Crook and his assistants, with the noted Indian chief and several of his tribe, are grouped amid rustic surroundings. The portraiture in the miniature figures is said to be very good.

Bellefontaine Cemetery, St. Louis, Mo.

The history of Bellefontaine is so closely interwoven with that of St. Louis that one would be incomplete without the other. The cemetery, however, is of more recent origin than the city. It was begun in '49 with one hundred and forty acres. These have been gradually added to, by purchase of adjoining farm lands, until it now comprises some three hundred and forty acres lying along the Bellefontaine bluffs that face the Mississippi and extend from St. Louis nearly to the mouth of the Missouri river. The cemetery has a frontage of one mile on Broadway, a thoroughfare about parallel with the Mississippi river, and distant from it at this point some three miles. The bluffs are neither precipitous nor very high, but are in bold contrast to the low lands lying between them and the river by their abrupt elevation, and in that they are heavily wooded. All of the land, however, now included in the cemetery has been owned as farms, and the long sweeping hill-sides that lie back of the first sharp rise, and widen out from the first deep, steep sided ravines, had all been under cultivation for years before being turned to cemetery purposes.

The superintendent of Bellefontaine, Mr. Hotchkiss, an extremely courteous, not to say courtly, gentleman of the old school, has held that position from the organization of the Cemetery Association, which, without being sure of my ground, I fancy is something unique in cemetery history in this country, and am quite sure it is at least very unusual.

Finding the more broken parts of the grounds closely covered with an indigenous forest, made up largely of oaks and elms, his policy from the outset has been to preserve its woodland character. In this he has been most successful. It is strictly a woodland cemetery. The clearings have been closely set with trees in variety, and where the native trees, resenting as is their habit, the intrusion of civilization, have died and been removed, all such openings have been similarly filled.

The first impressions on entering Bellefontaine are seclusion, picturesqueness and trees—evergreens being very prominent. Monuments and stones have not been allowed to obtrude near the several entrances. Barring the lack of waterways, the natural beauty of the cemetery site could not be better; and barring the lack of enough openings for long views through the grounds, the tree planting is good. The trees are fine, but more vistas in the interior parts of the grounds would be an improvement; the effect now seems heavy, and if this is true when all of the deciduous trees are bare, it would seem to indicate a summer suffocation of foliage. The next general impression is that Bellefontaine was intended by nature for a terrestrial

WINTER LANDSCAPE, BELLEFONTAINE CEMETERY.

paradise, but that man has so littered it with stones that it has become typical af an earthly prison.

The lawn plan, in its broad sense, is not accepted here, but that the authorities are leaning that way, although perhaps unknowingly, is evident. Fences and copings around lots are no longer allowed, and trees have always been protected. No evergreens grew wild on these bluffs, but great numbers of them, in well placed groups, have been planted, presumably to give pleasing variety. For the same reason, (it is supposed) artificial waterways have been constructed consisting of a series of ponds and of reservoirs, the latter supplying water for a flowing stream during summer which is rightly regarded as a picturesque feature. It might however, be made more so by a less formal bit of masonry for the larger waterfall—the smaller one seems well designed.

Having done so much for the sake of variety, it would not be going very much farther, and it would be quite in the line of logical sequence, to provide for a still greater diversity by the use of shrubbery, hardy ornamental grasses and aquatic and semi-aquatic plants. More vines would be well too, although in some of the dells wild grapes and Virginia creeper were noted. Then with the opening up of a few interior vistas the thing would be accomplished, with one important exception—stones.

In nomenclature, Bellefontaine is picturesque. The original "beautiful fountain" was a very large spring at the foot of this same range of bluffs, but on the western or Missouri river side, and farther north by some miles. Here on the bluff above the spring the early French settlers established old "Bellefontaine cantonment," and Bellefontaine road, which passes one front of the present cemetery, was in those days the military "trail" connecting this "Post" with St. Louis "Post."

THE MODERN CEMETERY.

Nothing now remains of the old Bellefontaine fortifications, but the old Post graveyard and tombstones are still there. The great spring has been merged in the Missouri river by the erratic changes of current and location of that strangely willful stream, though at low water its location can still be determined. But the old name still clings and makes a most euphonious one for the slightly more modern cemetery of our day. Consecration Dell is appropriate, as here the opening ceremonies occurred; Amaranth and Laburnum hills are arbitrary, but have a pleasant old time flavor that recalls Miss Austen's novels; Mount Repose is a fitting name for one of the heights overlooking the Mississippi where rest a host of the forefathers of St. Louis, their names the warp of city's history; and from Vista Hill one gets broad and splendid views up and down the great river for miles as well as across it and over the fertile levels of Illinois, that are part of the far-famed Valley of the Mississippi. As far as seen there is no plot in Bellefontaine where any attempt at artistic planting has been made. It seems to be an unknown feature of decoration in a cemetery that should lead in this respect, for the natural advantages of the site are far and away beyond anything that can be accomplished on made land, and much of the finest shrubbery thrives well about St. Louis. One has but to visit the interesting and instructive shrubberies connected with the Missouri Botanical Garden to get a long list of varieties that can be seen growing; each with its name attached. And in Calvary Cemetery, right next door, is the Lucas plot than which there could scarcely be anything better in its line, barring the shaft, which is not happy. But Bellefontaine has a bit of stonework that is artistically good in the Wainwright vault or memorial but recently completed. It is unique and deserves a paper to itself. The members of the Association of American Cemetery Superintendents seem to have found out that the world "do move," but there is room for the knowledge to spread.

The Bellefontaine Association is but one of several that should lead in the new movement that is to the end of making the cemeteries of the United States pleasanter places for the living and less gruesome for the dead. The management of Bellefontaine hold that a cemetery without stones would be like the play of Hamlet with the leading character omitted. Would it not rather be more like leaving out the ghost? The ghost of old time notions that obtained in years gone by before even the Centennial, much less the beautiful World's Fair, had awakened us to the fact that there is such a thing as art; that beauty is a part of religion. Yes, whole armies of ghosts stalk abroad there, and in many other cemeteries too, where landscape art and a little good statuary would make tasteful and beautiful resorts instead of the unsightly places they are now. Places where stones of every size and shape, like some unclassified fungi, have sprung up, disagreeably suggestive to the sensitive of poisonous exhalations and of environments to be avoided. Such great crops of stones are neither useful nor beautiful, they are mostly only stupid. Few would think of making the surroundings of their living friends so forlorn, formidable, and devoid of interest. It seems rather unfair to treat them less well when they can no longer speak for themselves. Truly, Hamlet would remain, the tragedy would go on, the cemetery be just as populous. And instead of all interest taking flight with the useless stones that cumber most grave grounds there would, or *should* be the uplifting and never dying interest of beautiful objects. Of well chosen landscape beauty, that is to say, an adaptation of nature's beauties to the conditions of the site, and to cemetery requirements; the beauty of artistic planting; and here and there in this beautiful setting, against this beautiful background there would, or *should*, be sculpture that has received the impress of an artist's mind, instead of senseless blocks of stone that have received no impress save that of a stonemason's chisel.

Rather than be condemned to take ones last rest in such forbidding grounds, where ugly stone ghosts stalk abroad by day as well as by night—

> Commend our bodies to the vasty deep,
> Where clear sea waters flow,
> Where shifting sea weeds sweep,
> Where forms of beauty come and go,
> And gleaming jewels keep
> Watch, through long years and slow
> Of dreamless sleep.

FANNY COPLEY SEAVEY.

The prevalence of pneumonia, lagrippe and similar maladies at this season of the year gives emphasis to the importance of remembering the oft repeated advice about removing hats at funerals. If the attending clergyman or the undertaker fails to intimate to the mourners that they remain with covered heads during the ceremony it is clearly within the province of the superintendent to do so. People should be warned against the dangers consequent upon the observance of this custom. Many fatal results have been traced to it and there can be no disrespect shown either the dead or the living by adhering to a custom that is detrimental to the healthiest of persons. A word of caution to the minister may save many a life.

* * *

I make a three-fold use of the MODERN CEMETERY; first as a text book for myself; second to lend to lot owners to educate them up to modern ideas, and to the editor of our local paper in the hope that he may give, through its means, some instruction to the public.—*H. Hulme, Asst. Supt., Grove Cemetery, New Brighton, Pa.*

A Few Ornamental Fruiting Shrubs.

In planting ground for decorative effect too few of our gardeners take into consideration the value of such work of fruiting shrubs and vines. Landscape gardeners are just beginning to see the possibilities in a judicious selection and arrangement of berry bearing plants, especially those which hold their fruit into late fall and winter, and to realize that these are almost as indispensable as those whose particular beauty lies in their flower or foliage alone.

To the florist and interior decorator these have a value that, with one or two exceptions, is not recognized as it should be. The holly, with its rich glossy foliage and scarlet berries, has come to be an indispensable material for decoration in our Christmas and midwinter festivities, and the beautiful Ilex verticillata, or black Alder, with its heavy laden branches of dazzling scarlet (sometimes yellow) fruit.

Celastrus scandens, or bitter sweet, is a well known American climber abundant in rocky woods, where it climbs to the tree tops and festoons them with its drooping racemes of scarlet fruit. Celastrus articulata is a native of China and Japan. Like C. scandens the orange scarlet fruit is enclosed in a yellow three-lobed capsule or persistent calyx, which opens at maturity and exposes the berry. C. articulata is a much more rapid grower than C. scandens. The racemes are not so large, but are much more abundant, and it is more graceful for decorative purposes. It can be cut in streamers from one to five feet in length. One thing regarding celastruses must not be forgotten. They are all diœcious and in planting care should be taken to secure only seed-bearing plants.

Pyrus prunifolia, Asiatic apples, are extremely beautiful when in blossom in spring, as well as when in fruit. The fruit of the red variety especially hangs well on the trees until after very severe frosts, and the loaded branches are splendid for decorative work. An additional advantage possessed by this fruit is that it makes a jelly of unequaled flavor.

Berberis Thunbergii is a popular Japanese species, and in foliage, flower and fruit is one of the best plants introduced into this country for many years. On moderately poor soil it gives brighter autumn foliage and fruit earlier and heavier than on rich ground. The berries are brilliant from early autumn until the leaves come in the spring. Probably the way to preserve them in best condition, however, would be to cut the branches in early autumn and put them away in moist sand in a light freezing temperature. Not long ago the gentlemen's smoking room in a Newport mansion on a wedding occasion was decorated exclusively with Berberis Thunbergii branches with grand effect.

Ampelopsis heterophylla is a beautiful species from Japan, where it is called the "blind grape." It is a rapid climber, very effective in covering trellisses, etc. The fruit is very striking in color. In the same bunch it will be of all shades from pale green to deep violet, in porcelain, robin's egg and ultramarine and speckled with tiny black spots. The branches grow naturally in fruited festoons from eighteen to twenty-four inches long, but if trained specially for fruiting purposes they could doubtless be produced much longer. There is also a yellow fruited form of this.

Menispermum Canadense, bears its fruit suspended in bunches by slender thread-like stems. The blue-black berries are somewhat lustreless and are in condition only in early fall.—*Jackson Dawson, in American Florist.*

Cemetery Walks.

My former article protested against the indiscriminate filling and abandoning of so-called graveled walks in cemeteries, thereby converting them to lawn and saving expense by mowing instead of keeping gravel clean of weeds and otherwise maintaining a system of repairs.

I promised to add some comments on the characteristics of walks as provided in the cemetery lay out.

The cemetery walk may have two legitimate purposes viz: convenience and appearance, convenient when made useful and pleasurable as a promenade.

Appearance when grandeur or beauty are developed or brought to view. The mind naturally contemplates a feeling of justification when following a path that is unmistakable and deeply provided for use, and the pleasure is also hightened by the fact of a certain indescribable fitness that may be tracable all along the rambling route. On the other hand, a person possessed of common sensibilities will naturally hesitate before venturing upon doubtful territory.

Such as a well kept lawn will always indicate; in fact the sensitive will invariably feel a sense of condemnation and mental pain whenever necessity requires them to tread upon a neatly prepared lawn. I think therefore that walks must be maintained and whatever of expense shall be needed to make them respectable as a sight to behold or comfortable to follow should never for a moment be withheld. Convenience will often require more walks than good appearance demands, and hence there is room to exercise some discretion. When deciding upon the expediency of opening some of the walks to use as such.

THE MODERN CEMETERY.

Some of our cemeteries have been laid out on the contemplated plan that each family lot should have space for a narrow walk on all sides, thus rendering the lot completely isolated from all others. Such a provision serves no essential purpose, adds needless care and labor, generally has proven a nuisance and will be fully condemned I think in future designs.

All family lots and all single graves should be accessible by walks or openings that are free to public use, but some of these alleys or spaces may be tolerated as part of the lawn without real detriment to convenience and often to the advantage of good appearance.

The walks should be all well graded and *adjacent lawns brought into strict harmony with them*, the graveled surface of the walk should not be more than one or two inches below the lawn surface so that no shoulder will appear to annoy the sight or inconvenience the mower in passing from one side to the other.

All material for making the walks should be such as will pack, the surface when finished should please both eye and touch, a walk that comes short of this test will only prove a nuisance. In speaking of materials for filling purposes, coarse materials of any indestructible kind can be used, but the top dressing should be of that quality which *packs firmly*, rolls smoothly and at the same time becomes in every way agreeable to both sight and touch.

Walks thus prepared where not unduly exposed to the wash of storms are not expensive to make or *maintain*. They are never regarded a nuisance, always blend pleasingly with the adjacent lawns and are generally a real help to the landscape as a whole. I suppose their utility will not be questioned, nevertheless I wish to notice a class of walks quite too often found in cemeteries where the projector seems to have entertained only the idea of *contrast to please the eye*, and over looking comfort by selecting and often transporting at unusual cost a kind of coarse pebble to *ornament* a walk which when applied utterly destroys the purpose for which a walk has been supposed to serve.

In view of such conditions many exhibitions of which are duly on file and open to public inspection, I am not surprised to find writers who revolt against the use of all gravel and adopt another extreme to the general discarding of all walks except natures rabbit path through the lawn.

For one I am quite willing to be recorded in favor of good roads, smooth velvety lawns, all these in general as a principle of universal application, but most emphatically do they apply to cemeteries and parks.

The cemetery walk should be regarded a permanent feature well worth a thorough construction and protection. When that has been done the repairing will be light and rarely needed, the monthly care and cleaning will be needed but should be reduced to a minimum cost by permanent work in construction.

B. F. HATHAWAY.

There can be but one purpose served by walks and that is usefulness. I should as soon expect to improve the sky by painting on it the lines described by astronomers or looking at it through a grated window, as to improve the appearance of a lawn by making gravel walks through it, but walks are occasionally useful and so should not be discarded altogether.

I happen to be the superintendent of a cemetery which contains a large number of depressed walks, many of them bounded by stone coping. It also contains a number of sections conducted on the lawn plan in which there are no visible walks, the entire surface being covered with a continuous lawn. The complaints of paths being made by people walking across the grass are much more frequent in that part of the cemetery containing the depressed walks. There is a reason for this. The steps or entrance to a lot from the walk indicate the line of least resistance which one person after another follows. With the continuous lawn there are no restrictions. People walk where they please, and no paths are formed. There are slight exceptions to this rule made mostly by workmen who follow the spaces or paths left between lots in removing surplus material or taking in stone, but this is temporary and at its worse does not hurt the appearance of the lawn nearly as much as it would be injured by a gravel walk.

A lawn is a much more agreeable thing to walk on than a gravel walk, no matter how well the latter may be made. I think the testimony of superintendents of cemeteries in which all or any part is conducted on the lawn plan, would be unanimous in favor of the continuous lawn. It not only looks better than the other but it saves expense and also saves the trouble of putting up signs saying "keep off the grass."

S.

Twenty years ago the McCutchenville, O., Cemetery association purchased additional ground, and the trustees gave their notes for payment of the same. The notes have been renewed but never paid and the owner of the land, brought suit against two Trustees to collect over $1,000 principal and interest. The court decided against him, and he was not only required to pay costs but also to surrender the notes.—*Ex*.

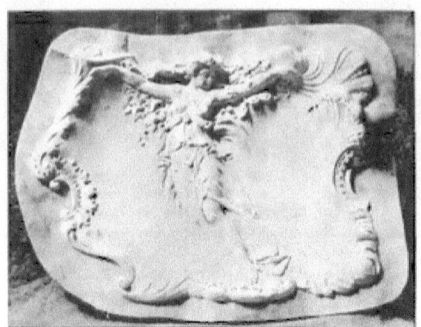

BRONZE MEMORIAL TABLET. H. W. BEATTIE, SC.

CEMETERY NOTES.

The forty-sixth annual report of the directors of Swan Point cemetery, Providence R. I., for the year ending December 1893, contains the following statistics:

Average number of men employed per month during the year, 50; interments during the year, including 67 to the receiving tomb, 319; total number of interments, 12,951; brick and slate vaults built, 94; foundations to monuments and tablets built, 206; hedges removed from lots, 2; curbing removed from lots, 5; land sold during the year, 10,723 square feet; number of lots put under perpetual care, and upon which bequests have been made, 1258; number of lots under annual care, 588; number of lots under partial care, 274; number of lots not under care, 993; whole number of lots sold to date, 3115.

In common with many other corporations, the cemetery felt the continued depression of the times, especially noticeable in the reduced receipts from the sale of burial lots. It has been the desire of the directors to help relieve, as much as possible, the great distress among the laboring people by continuing all work that could be done advantageously through the winter, 75 men were employed for this purpose.

* * *

The sixty-second annual report of Mount Auburn Cemetery, Boston, Mass., shows the past year to have been a moderately prosperous one. The Repair Fund was increased $35,926.70 and now amounts to $771,684.38. The Permanent Fund gained $10,459.96, making that fund $330,880.76. The General Fund increased 8,046.38 and now amounts to $100,382. Receipts for sale of lots and use of receiving tombs $16,461.50. For labor and material on lots $55,148. Expenditures for labor and salaries $45,890.70. Interments 509, removals from cemeteries 43, total to December 31, 29,837. Number of headstones erected 331, monuments 54, no curbing or coping was put in. Iron fences removed 16, granite curbing removed 7, tombs removed 1.

Plastic Marble.

In one account of Rome the author mentions five or six slabs of plastic marble as being in the possession of Prince Borghese. Being set on end, they bend backward and forward; when laid horizontally and raised at one end they form a curve; if placed on a table and a piece of wood or any other substance is laid under them they fall into a kind of curve, each end touching the table. Abbe Fortis was told that they were dug up near the town of Mondragon, in the kingdom of Naples. The grain is like that of fine Carrara marble, or perhaps of the finest Greek. They seem to have suffered some attack of fire. A slab of marble similar in every respect to those described, and highly polished, has been exhibited for more than twenty-five years at the British Museum. M. Fleuvian de Belvac succeeded in making common granular limestone, a granular quartz, completely flexible by exposing to a certain degree of heat. In Lincoln cathedral, England, there is an arch built of white marble which is quite elastic, yielding to a heavy tread, and returning or rebounding to its original position on true elastic principles.—*Ex.*

Extracts from Rules and Regulations, Woodlawn Cemetery, Toledo, Ohio.

Each deed for a family lot will be accompanied with a plat of the same showing the arrangement of the graves thereon, and the location of a monument.

No lots will be regarded as sold until fully paid for. If interments are made before such time, the Association reserves the right after demand and neglect to pay, to remove the bodies to the single grave allotment and place the lot on sale.

No lot or parcel of land shall be defined by any so-called fence, railing, coping, hedge, embankment or ditch.

Boxes, shells, toys, wire-screens and designs of any description and similar articles scattered upon graves or lots are inconsistent with the proper keeping of the grounds, and will not be permitted.

Chairs, settees and benches of any material, rustic work and so-called ornaments and architectural objects are considered injurious to the beauty, dignity and repose of the cemetery, are therefore forbidden, and will be removed from lots without further notice. Persons will be furnished with camp-chairs free of charge for use while in the cemetery.

Planting within the narrow limits of a cemetery lot so as to avoid overcrowding and encroachment on adjoining lots requires the intimate knowledge of the habits of trees and shrubs, and the size which they attain, and it must be done only with the approval and under the directions of the superintendent.

Mounds should be kept flat or nearly so as it is

VIEW IN WOODLAWN CEMETERY, TOLEDO, O.

impossible to make grass live or to mow properly on high mounds, therefore no mounds raised above four inches at the centre will be allowed, and in no case will growing flowers be permitted on them, nor flowers in pots. Such found in violation of this rule will be removed. This does not interfere with placing bouquets or cut flowers on graves, if properly secured. Myrtle on graves is not recommended, but will be permitted provided no mound is raised, and the care of same is placed with the superintendent.

To secure a good effect in the cemetery it is essential that every portion of it should be well cared for as partial neglect would mar the beauty of the entire surroundings. Therefore all the care of the lots is assumed by the Association; the avenues and walks will be kept in good condition, trees and shrubbery will be trimmed and pruned, the turf will be kept mowed without extra charge to lot owners.

Unusual outlays are from time to time necessary on every lot by the impoverishment of the soil, the decay of trees and shrubs, or the effect of time on vaults, monuments, markers, etc. In order to provide for these contingencies for all time to come it is advisable that each lot owner, by will or otherwise, leave or deposit with the cemetery association a sum of money, the principal of which is to remain untouched, and the interest to be used on said lot as occasion may require. The association will therefore receive in trust any such sums.

No grave markers will be permit-

ted to exceed sixteen inches in height above the sod, the width and thickness to be in proportion, but none will be allowed to embrace two or more graves. Those less than six inches shall not be placed higher than eight inches, and none less than four inches thick will be permitted.

Foundations for grave markers, monuments and other superstructures will be built only upon the lot owners written orders, giving size of base, etc. The bottom of the lower base must be squared sufficiently to allow it to rest firmly on the foundation, as no wedging will be permitted.

In no instance will permission be given to erect vaults or tombs as a receptacle for bodies above ground in localities where they will be objectional and injurious to surrounding lots.

No burial shall take place from the Public Vault on Sunday or a Holiday.

WOODLAWN CEMETERY, TOLEDO, O.

EPITAPHS

Hang her an epitaph upon her tomb.
—*Shakespeare.*

I have some books from which might be culled, from time to time, interesting excerpts for your paper. They are, "The Book of Epitaphs," "Gleanings from God's Acre," "A Collection of Quaint and Curious Epitaphs," and "Curious Epitaphs." The latter has a Bibliography of Epitaphs, giving a list of over 100 books confined to this subject, one of which, I note, is as early as 1631.

The one to Admiral Byng begins:

"To the perpetual disgrace of public justice."

The admiral having been a sacrifice to the rage of the public for a naval defeat in 1757.

The inn-keepers have several variants of:

"This world's an inn and I her guest;
I've eat and drunk and took my rest
With her awhile, and now I pay
Her lavish bill and go my way."

At Chatham there is one on a drunkard:

"Weep not for him, the warmest tear that's shed
Falls unavailing o'er the unconscious dead;
Take the advice these friendly lines would give,
Live not to drink, but only drink to live."

Over the remains of Mrs. Freland is inscribed, however:

"She drank good ale, strong punch and wine,
And lived to the age of ninety-nine."

Here's a dexterous weaving of spiritual and temporal:

"Beneath this stone, in hope of Zion,
Doth lie the landlord of the 'Lion';
His son keeps on the business still,
Resigned unto the Heavenly will."

On a baker's monument it says:

"Blessed are they who in the Lord are dead,
Though set like dough, they shall be drawn like bread."

This is a literal copy of a game-keeper's epitaph:

"My gun's discharged, my ball is gone,
My powder's spent, my work is done."

Those to the Typothetæ are numerous and notable for their punning in their trade, among which are Franklin's familiar one and another to:

L. Gedge, printer,
Like a worn out character, he has returned to the Founder,
Hoping he will be recast in a better and more perfect mould.

Of John Hippisley, a comedian, his tombstone says:

"When the stage heard that death had struck her John,
Gay Comedy her sables first put on;
Laughter lamented that her fav'rite died,
And Mirth herself ('tis strange) laid down and cry'd.
Wit drooped his head, e'n Humor seemed to mourn
And solemnly sat pensive on his urn."

The Parish clerks have their innings, thus:

"The vocal powers here let us mark
Of Philip, our late parish clerk.
In church none ever heard a layman
With clearer voice say 'Amen.'"

Hogarth's begins:

"Farewell, great painter of mankind,
Who reached the noblest point of art,
When pictured morals charm the mind,
And thro' the eye correct the heart."

Of course the (apocryphal) epithet that Rochester is said to have written on Charles II.'s by the latter's request is here:

"Here lies the mutton-eating king,
Whose word no man relied on;
Who never said a foolish thing,
Or ever did a wise one."

and also the king's comment:

"If death could speak, the king would say,
In justice to his crown,
His acts they were the ministers's,
His words they were his own."

West Laurel Hill, Philadelphia.   H. J. S.

A Venerable Grave-Digger.

Epitaph upon an ancient Dublin Grave-Digger who, it is computed, during a period of 22 years among the Tombs, prepared the last resting place for some 6,000 of his fellow-citizens.

Here lies Pat Doyle,
His working days are done.
He who made many graves,
Now sleeps in one.
He died lamented,
And a hearse and four
Drove him in splendour
From the "Buggie" * door.
In brass-bound coffin
He went home to earth,
What more was wanted
To attest his worth!
He had a Wake, too—
'Twas a gorgeous feast—
Whisky galore there was
For man and beast.
The "Boys" attended,
There was Mick and Bill,
And all the neighbours
Kindly drank their fill.
"Pat" did his duty,
Both alive and dead,
For any mortal
Could more praise be said?
When I, like him,
Am freed from further toil,
I don't expect the praise
I've given Doyle.

—London *Funeral Directors' Journal.*

*This tabernacle of dirt and poverty is known in the region about Harold's Cross as "The Buggie Barracks." Fifty-four human beings live, and move, and have their being in this single edifice.

Foreign Funeral Customs.

Funerals in Europe differ from those in this country as widely as can be imagined. In France a funeral custom in vogue at present is for the mourners at the obsequies of some person of limited means to follow the hearse in an omnibus. This conveyance, which is black, has the words "Omnibus Funerane," inscribed in silver letters on either side, so that the careless outsider should not bounce into the midst of a mourning multitude. While the Parisians are looked upon as a gay and frivolous people, their respect for the dead is unequaled by any other city in the world. Whenever a hearse appears along the streets, all noise seems to cease, and one would think that animation had suddenly become suspended. Rich or poor, young or old, the lifeless form that two days ago might have passed along unheeded is treated with the utmost respect. The flying vehicles that during his life would have run over him in their rapid course now stopped suddenly; the men take off their hats and bow their heads until the rear of the cortege has passed, and the women stop and express their conventional sorrow by courtesying. A most painful custom at French funerals is the posting at the exit door of the church wherein the ceremonies take place, of the male head of the deceased person's family, whose duty it is to shake hands with every person who has been present at the obsequies. An impressive adjunct to an aristocratic official funeral is the presence in the procession of the coupe of the deceased, the animals led by the grooms in mourning livery. The effect is sombre and picturesque.

In Germany the hearses used in funerals are peculiar, and consist of a sort of combination hearse and hack. In the forward part is a place constructed for the casket, while in the rear are seats for the near relatives. Another style there consists of a low wagon, long and with squatty wheels, something like a flat car.

In England to a remarkable extent the old Lutheran custom prevails. Sometimes a hearse is used to carry the casket, and the mourners walk in the street behind, and sometimes the body is carried on the shoulders of bearers through the streets. Next to the manner of laying out the dead and preparing them for their eternal sleep comes the idea of perpetuating their memory. This is usually done in the way of an elaborate monument, and in this respect considerable advancement has been made during the last 50 years. The demand half a century ago was for simple designs, in tombstones and monuments, and even 25 years ago anything like ostentatious display or adornment was regarded as bad form. The fashion has, however, greatly changed, and it is now considered the correct thing to have a monument very elaborate as a token of respect for the departed relatives.

Correspondence.

Editor Modern Cemetery.

The original of the accompanying communication was written at the request of the editor of the *Casket* who wished my opinion on a newspaper article in which it was stated that bodies invariably turned over in their coffins. The idea is so absurd that to write seriously on it was out of the question. Some of the MODERN CEMETERY readers may wish to express themselves on the subject.

CHARLES NICHOLS.

We have carefully read the article on "Corpses turning over in graves," and conclude that the theory advanced by the *Herald* correspondent, (Bath, England), is a ridiculous misconception.

The writer of the silly article must have been either *non compos mentis*, or was endeavoring to create a sensation—if the former he cannot be blamed, if the latter he has lamentably failed to carry his point, or to convince even the most credulous. He assures us that in Cochin China, Siam, and several of the Oriental countries, they bury with the face downward, so that in thus burying the "corpse will right itself by turning over."—We have had charge of Fairmount Cemetery going on 24 years, and during that period have made about 1800 removals of bodies from one part to another of the cemetery, also of bodies that were removed to, and from the cemetery, and have always found on examination that the faces were upturned, same as when they were buried. When there was nothing left but the bones, they occupied a position showing that they proved our assertion. Let us hope and pray that this man at Bath, England, will previous to his decease either request, or direct his relatives and friends to strap him down securely in his coffin right side up, With Care, so that he will not be able to turn over in his grave.

CHAS. NICHOLS.

* * *

BALTIMORE, FEB. 12TH, 1894.

Editor Modern Cemetery:

If I were to meet some of our brother superintendents in conversation I might interest them, failing to meet them I will try to write something.

My text is "Limit and Eliminate," foot stones, name (or step) stones and boundary posts. Not in an arbitrary or dictatorial manner, but quietly, determinedly, with constant iteration and reiteration.

They are obstructions to the lawn mower. Some of our lot holders have consented to the leveling of graves and the removal of foot stones and others have permitted the head stones, (slabs) that will not stay perpendicular, to be laid horizontal. They become object lessons to point the way for others. Two hundred lot enclosures have been removed, viz. iron railings, bars, chains, hedges and marble curbing.

Some lot holders have removed all the stones from their lot, putting one stone in the center.

For boundary markers I have suggested a three cornered stone with lettering on top. The advantages are, that it gives to every lot holder four stones. The angles show clearly the location of the lot and where two or four stones come together they are not objectionable.

C. W. HAMILL.

Mount Olivet Cemetery.

[Mr. Hamill is to be congratulated on what he has accomplished with his lot owners.—*Ed.*]

QUESTION BOX.

Moneywort.

I would like to ask whether superintendents permit the planting of moneywort on their grounds and what their experience has been with it? Is there a good manual published on the care of greenhouses?—H. H., Grove Cemetery, New Brighton, Pa.

Ants and Moles.

How can I exterminate ants and moles?—T. A. H., Wildwood Cemetery, Salamanca, N. Y.

Trimming Graves.

What is the most economical way in which to trim or decorate a grave and what is the usual charge? *Novice.*

Association of American Cemetery Superintendents.

WM. SALWAY, "Spring Grove" Cincinnati, O., President.
T. McCARTHY, "Swan Point" Providence, R. I., Vice-President.
F. EURICH, Woodlawn, Toledo, O., Secretary and Treasurer.

The Eighth Annual Convention of the Association will be held at Philadelphia in September, 1894.

Resolutions Adopted at the Seventh Annual Convention of the Association of American Cemetery Superintendents.

Resolved: That it is the sense of this convention that all Sunday funerals be discouraged as much as possible.

Resolved: That it is the sense of this meeting that all headstones or markers should be limited to the height of the sod or the level of the surface of the ground.

Resolved: That it is the sense of this meeting that vaults and catacombs be discouraged and if possible prevented in cemeteries.

Publisher's Department.

The receipt of Cemetery Literature and Trade Catalogues will be acknowledged in this column.

TO ADVERTISERS. THE MODERN CEMETERY is the only publication of its class and will be found a valuable medium for reaching cemetery officials in all parts of the United States.

TO SUBSCRIBERS. Cemetery officials desiring to subscribe for a number of copies regularly to circulate among their lot owners, should send for our special terms. Several well known cemeteries have already adopted this plan with good results.

Contributions on matters pertaining to cemeteries are solicited. Address all communications to
R. J. HAIGHT, 351 Dearborn St., CHICAGO.

Cemetery literature received: Map of Metowee Valley Cemetery, Granville, N. Y., from B. F. Hatheway, Stamford, Conn. Lot Plan of Calvary Cemetery, Cleveland, O., from F. Eurich, Toledo, O. By-Laws, Rules and Regulations of South Mound Cemetery, New Castle, Ind., Lakewood Cemetery, Minneapolis, Minn. Hamilton, O. News with annual report of Greenwood Cemetery. History, constitution, etc., Oberlin Cemetery Association, Oberlin, O.

Trade catalogues received: John Saul, Washington, D. C., New and Rare Plants; Nanz & Neuner, Louisville, Ky., Seeds, Plants and Bulbs. Jas. Vick, Rochester, N. Y., Seeds and Plants. Wm. Deering & Co., Chicago, Mowing Machines. W. R. Shelmire, Avondale, Pa., carnations, coleus, etc.

Sydney Heminsley, Sr., for the past fifteen years superintendent of Cedar Lawn cemetery, Paterson, N. J., and a member of the A. A. C. S., died early in the month.

Wm. Deering & Co., of Chicago, invite the attention of cemetery officials to their horse lawn mower advertised in this issue. This mower which was the only horse lawn mower to receive an award at the World's Fair is recommended as being easily operated and very effective. The manufacturers will send a handsomely illustrated catalogue and full particulars on application.

George E. Painter, superintendent of West Laurel Hill cemetery, Philadelphia, and Miss M. Heiner of that city were married February 6th. The MODERN CEMETERY extends congratulations.

Mr. Eugene Cushman, superintendent of Greenwood cemetery writes to the MODERN CEMETERY that the statement credited to him last month in reference to filling in the lakes at Greenwood on account of green scum is not in accordance with the facts. One of the lakes has been filled in and another one probably will be, but not for the reasons stated.

Several new aspirants for cemetery trade in the way of flowers, shrubs, trees etc., will be found in our advertising columns this month. Our readers who may require new stock will find it to their interest to address the advertising patrons of the MODERN CEMETERY and when corresponding they will confer a mutual favor by mentioning the name of the paper.

The executive committee of the Association of American Cemetery Superintendents are especially desirous of receiving suggestions in the way of topics or matters for discussion at the next convention to be held at Philadelphia. Communications addressed to Geo. E. Rhedemeyer, Harleigh cemetery, Camden, N. J., who is chairman of the committee will receive attention. When the subjects for discussion are of sufficient importance to justify the writing of papers upon them it is necessary to make the assignments at the earliest possible time, it will therefore facilitate the work of the committee if members who contemplate offering suggestions will do so at once.

Situation Wanted.
Young man, experienced in cemetery management, steady and trustworthy, desires position to take charge, or as assistant superintendent. Apply, L. R., MODERN CEMETERY.

Situation Wanted.
By a person qualified to fill position of superintendent and secretary. Several years experience. W. F. L., care MODERN CEMETERY, Chicago.

THE MODERN CEMETERY

VOLUME IV.

March, 1894—February, 1895

R. J. HAIGHT, Publisher.
CHICAGO.

INDEX.

A.

A Canine Graveyard.................107
A Plea for Centralizing Country Cemeteries.............................2
*A plea for the Old Style...........107
All Saints Day in New Orleans......101
*Ancient Monuments—Artemisia and the Mausoleum......................51
Annual Convention of American Cemetery Superintendents...45, 74
*Aquatic Garden, Pine Grove Cemetery, Lynn, Mass....................88
Are we going from one Extreme to Another............................79

B.

Burial Reform..................13, 25

C.

*Calvary Cemetery, St. Louis, Mo....27
*Cedar Hill Cemetery, Hartford, Conn.,..............................116
Cemetery Entrances..................61
Cemetery Greenhouses..........126, 136
Cemetery Memorials other than Grave Monuments....................49
Cemetery Notes......4, 20, 33, 46, 57, 69, 82, 94, 104, 118, 130, 140
*Cemetery planting......6, 15, 31, 42
Cemetery Reports...9, 22, 47, 58, 131, 133, 142
Cemeteries from the Sanitary View Point..............................50
Chinese Sanitary Burial............106
Common Law Dedications..............1
Correspondence..10, 35, 72, 94, 107, 119, 141
Cremation.............23, 48, 58, 96, 132

D.

*Death as a Friend..................38
Decoration Day......................45
*Dickson Memorial Chapel, Salem, Mass...............................41
Dry Rubble Foundations.............123

E.

Electric Funeral Cars...............19
Embalming as a Sanitary Measure...122
*Entrance to Montefiore Burial Grounds, Minneapolis, Minn......21
Epitaphs...........................144
Extremes in Cemeteries.............106

F.

*Fall in Graceland, Chicago........123
*Illustrated.

Forethought necessary in acquiring Land for Cemetery Purposes......110
Foundations.........................83
Funeral Customs of Ancient Nations 90
Funeral Reform...............109, 133
Fungicides..........................50

H.

*Hardy Herbaceous Plants for Cemeteries.........................67, 79

I.

Individual Rights and State Removals................................98
Injury to trees.....................17

L.

Lawn Grass..........................72

M.

Memorial Trees......................41
*Metairie Cemetery, New Orleans, La.,64
*Mt. Auburn and some of its Famous Dead...............................89

N.

New Greenhouses, Allegheny Cemetery, Allegheny, Pa..............139

O.

*Oakwood Cemetery, Austin, Minn....127
*Oakwoods Cemetery, Chicago........52
*Obelisks...........................55
Ornamental Cemetery Monuments considered as Trade Fixtures....42

P.

*Pine Grove Cemetery, Whitinsville, Mass..............................114
Planting and Good Planting........143
Police Power of States over Burial Grounds............................70
Power to take Land in Iowa..........70

Q.

Question Box..............11, 36, 48

R.

Removals from unpaid for Lots..70, 101
Rubble and Concrete Foundations...113
Rules and Regulations...8, 22, 35, 47, 84

S.

*Shrubby Herbaceous Perennials......91
*Shrubs for Cemeteries........99, 138
St. Johns Churchyard, New York....119
*St. Roch's Chapel, New Orleans...111

*Sleepy Hollow Cemetery, Concord, Mass..............................134
Some Canons of Criticism......91, 100
Some Parasitic Growths and Recipes for their Removal............80
Some Rights of Officials of Cemetery Associations....................127
Suggestions to Lot Owners...7, 83, 119
Suitable Trees and Shrubs for a Modern Cemetery......................86

T.

*The Archer Mausoleum, Woodlawn Cemetery, Dayton, O...............5
The Cemetery in the Country.........2
The Cemetery Superintendents Convention..................60, 61, 66
The Education of the Lot owner....97
The Friends Burial Ground, Brooklyn, N. Y..........................62
The Garden........................106
*The G. P. Morisini Mausoleum, Woodlawn Cemetery, New York..129
*The Houghton Monument............142
*The Humboldt Monument, Berlin....30
The Law with regard to Removal of Bodies............................44
The Lily Pond......................20
The May Mausoleum.................102
*The Mather Monument, Lakeview Cemetery, Cleveland, O............43
*The McKay Mausoleum, Pittsfield Mass...............................40
The Modern Cemetery, a Social Force..............................63
*The Patterson Monument, St. Louis, Mo................................56
*The Shaw Mausoleum, St. Louis, Mo 18
The Soil of Graveyards.............68
The Use and Abuse of Boulder Monuments............................122
Thoughts on Transplanting...........9
To Shakespeare......................7
Treasured Tears....................46
Trees and Shrubs—The Lawn........131

V.

Validity of Ordinance Relating to Places of Burial..................134

W.

*Westlawn Receiving Vault, Canton, Ohio...............................92
Women in Westminster Abbey.......117
*Woodlawn Cemetery, Toledo, O....102

THE MODERN CEMETERY.

THE MODERN CEMETERY.
AN ILLUSTRATED MONTHLY JOURNAL DEVOTED TO THE INTEREST OF CEMETERIES

R. J. HAIGHT, Publisher,
334 Dearborn Street, CHICAGO.

Subscription $1.00 a Year in Advance.   Foreign Subscription $1.25.
Special Rates on Six or More Copies.

Vol. IV.   CHICAGO, MARCH, 1894.   No. 1.

CONTENTS.

COMMON LAW DEDICATIONS	1
A PLEA FOR CENTRALIZING COUNTRY CEMETERIES	2
THE CEMETERY IN THE COUNTRY	2
CEMETERY NOTES	4
*THE ARCHER MAUSOLEUM, WOODLAND CEMETERY, DAYTON, O.	5
*CEMETERY PLANTING, II	6
SUGGESTIONS TO LOT OWNERS—TO SHAKESPEARE	7
RULES FOR STONE WORK IN GRACELAND CEMETERY, CHICAGO	8
THOUGHTS ON TRANSPLANTING—CEMETERY REPORTS.	9
CORRESPONDENCE	10
THE QUESTION BOX	11
ASSOCIATION OF AMERICAN CEMETERY SUPERINTENDENTS	12
PUBLISHER'S DEPARTMENT	12

*Illustrated.

With this issue THE MODERN CEMETERY enters its fourth year, and we take the opportunity of cordially thanking all who have helped us along to the success attained. The very nature of the office of the MODERN CEMETERY requires the co-operation of all interested in the work and while earnestly hoping for the continued assistance of our many old contributors, we shall be very happy to find the list extended, for the broader the field of information and experience the more valuable the product.

Common Law Dedications.

The United States Circuit Court of Appeals has reversed the decision of the Circuit Court in the case of the Board of Commissioners of Mahoning County v. Young, holding that while lot No. 96 is held by a conditional title, yet the breach of condition relied upon as creating a right of re-entry is excused because the breach was the act of the law. This was an action brought by Charles C. Young to recover the possession of this lot, which had been dedicated in 1802, with lot No. 95, to be used as a "burying ground," by his father, John Young, who originally platted the village of Youngstown, Ohio. The original plat made of the town was defectively acknowledged under the Ohio statute regulating the acknowledgement and registration of town plats. The result was, as the court holds, to constitute a common law dedication of lot No. 96 and other public places shown on the plat. That is to say, the public were thereby given the right to use lot No. 96 as a burying ground, but no more; the absolute title to the estate not being transferred. Down to 1868 this lot was used as a burying ground. In that year the council of Youngstown passed an ordinance by which all interments in the old burying ground were thereafter forbidden, and the remains of those already interred there, which should not be removed by friends and relatives before April 1, 1869, were ordered removed at public expense. This ordinance was executed, and all bodies removed. In 1874 the legislature provided that the county seat of Mahoning County should be removed to Youngstown, and in pursuance of the conditions imposed, lot No. 96, with other property, was conveyed by ordinance to a committee of five citizens charged with the duty of erecting the court-house, to be used as a site for the same and other public buildings. But lot No. 96 was not so used. It was contended, on Young's behalf, that the dedication being conditional, and only giving the right to use the lot for burial purposes, the subsequent action of the city authorities was a breach of the condition which gave him the right of re-entry. While generally the owner of the absolute title may resume possession whenever there has been a full and lawful abandonment of the use for which the dedication to use is made, the court holds that the breach is excused when the act of the law has prevented the further use of the property for the purposes intended by the grantor. The cessation in this case was the direct result of the law, which prohibited a longer use. Therefore, there was no forfeiture. Moreover, in such a case, the village or city council being but trustees, holding the title and protecting the use, the people of the municipality being the beneficiaries under the trust, the council, in their character as trustees, can do no act to defeat the beneficial interest of the public. Consequently, the trustees cannot without the voluntary acquiescence of the people abandon the use or defeat the estate. On these grounds the Court of Appeals decides against Mr. Young, and lays down the general principles stated.

A Plea for Centralizing Country Cemeteries.

With the rapid advancement our nation is making in the appreciation and culture of art, our outlying districts are not enjoying the true and the beautiful in nature and in art, as applied to their cemeteries, as they might if they were more united.

As matters now exist, every village and almost every district of a few miles in extent, that has been settled or is occupied largely by a class of people in any sense united, as by relationship, religion or nationality, have established and make for a time an effort to maintain (all that it claims) "a burying ground." Doubtless there are many good reasons for the establishing of many of these grounds, and there are also many things to make these spots desirable and endearing to a community, but it has been found practically impossible to maintain with any degree of respectability these small burying grounds. The reasons for this are various; the principal one however is that because of their small extent, the few families interested become scattered in a few years so that the grounds are left with no one to properly care for them. But to argue against these small burying grounds will not be so effectual in preventing a new lot being platted each year, as will a well directed effort to substitute something better. The day has arrived when this should be accomplished. Many states by law authorize the establishment and maintenance of cemeteries by the public authorities.

The advent of the MODERN CEMETERY to current literature will yield a profitable influence in the betterment of cemeteries. It will be a great aid in creating a more extended feeling that a cemetery is a place of art, not alone as man makes it but also as God would have it, by the provisions he so richly provides in nature.

Thanks to our landscape engineers for the beautiful examples of their art which they are scattering over the land. These will have a great tendency toward creating a unity of interests such as will enable undertakings to be perfected at proper locations.

The frequency with which, or at what points cemeteries should be established will depend largely on the population of the territory to be accommodated. In rural districts it is seldom necessary to have more than one cemetery for each one hundred square miles of territory, provided such grounds can be somewhat centrally located. They should however be located according to the center of population of the district, which will have a tendency to bring them within a pleasant distance of some town or village such as usually occur at about such intervals as is embraced in the above territory. In many of the older states the counties are divided into civil townships of such extent as would make it well, especially if under public management, to have one cemetery for each township. The location of cemeteries at as frequent intervals as above mentioned will not enable them to be made of such extent or character as would be desirable from an art view, but would about meet the absolute requirements of the people, as matters will exist for some generations to come. But even these should be no barrier in the way of each city or town of any considerable size being provided with a sufficient high class ground. Each county should in addition to what has been suggested, make provisions on a broad and liberal scale for the establishment and maintenance of a country cemetery at the county capitol that would meet local requirements. But to get these matters before the masses of the people properly, there must be an active interest and effort manifested by cemetery authorities, landscape engineers, and local engineers or surveyors as well. In fact if the local engineers and surveyors would cultivate and embody a little more art in some of their work they could be of aid in abolishing the stingy little rectangular real estate speculation "grave yards," dotted over the land.

The establishing of a main county cemetery is a subject of sufficient importance for an article of itself which may be submitted later.   J. C. W.

The Cemetery in the Country.

Rural cemeteries, as a general thing, are greatly neglected. Not because those who have friends buried there are forgetful or unmindful of the dead, or are unwilling to do their share of work in making the place beautiful, but because of a lack of system in the work done. I have often thought that if a few of the leading women of a country community would take the matter in hand, a great deal might be done to improve the appearance of our rural cemeteries. The first step should be the organization of an improvement society, which should enlist the assistance of all the people interested. There need be but little "red tape" about it—the less there is the better is its chance of being successful. Those who are lot owners in any cemetery will almost invariably give countenance and aid to any scheme calculated to make it attractive, and the judicious expenditure of a small amount of money in combination with willing labor by interested parties will produce satisfactory results in one season.

ORGANIZING FOR WORK.

There should be a committee to decide what is to be done, and some one selected to act as superintendent in carrying out the plans of this committee, people who donate labor being required to work under his instruction. Without such a committee and such a superintendent there will be no unity of aim, much less of action. Individual tastes will be brought into action, and because these tastes differ widely there will be an utter lack of that harmony upon which everything depends. The committee should be made up of persons having good taste, and when the work is put into their hands they should not be hindered by suggestions from outsiders. Such a committee would receive suggestions, but it should be made to feel entirely free in accepting or rejecting them. There are always those in every community who cannot give labor but who can and will give money and from small sums obtained in this way shrubs and plants for general use may be purchased. I am convinced that it is only necessary for some one to make a start in this direction in each community, to make it possible to accomplish great things in the way of improving country cemeteries. I would urge that some action should be taken at the proper season, and that an interest be aroused which should manifest itself in action. When a few persons in each community see what may be accomplished by united and systematic work, an enthusiasm will be created which will spread to others, and soon all will take pride in contributing to the undertaking.

AVOIDING ELABORATE EFFECTS.

I would suggest that elaborate effects be avoided. To make them successful requires more knowledge of landscape gardening and other matters of similar nature than can be commanded in a country neighborhood. Aim to bring out the natural beauty of the place. Work over the soil until it is in a condition to be seeded with lawn grass, after removing all weeds and bushes which have taken root there. Wherever there is a living tree or shrub that has in it any beauty, leave it, but go over it and remove all weak or superfluous growth, and prune it into something like symmetrical shape. But in doing this avoid, if possible, the mistake of making it take on a prim, stiff look. Study nature's plans and imitate them as closely as you can. In bare spots set out shrubs and hardy perennials. Plant bulbs here and there to brighten the place in early spring. If there are no trees plant them, but do not place them in regular rows nor after any set rule or pattern. Go into some city park and see how the intelligent superintendent of it has allowed trees of native growth to remain in natural groups, and note the charming effect thus secured, and then go back and try to plant your trees in such a manner that they shall look when they are grown as if they were native there. Aim to make the entire cemetery look like a park if you want to make the most of its beauty. In doing this I am aware that the boundaries of lots must be ignored to some extent, and fences of all kinds must be discouraged. Do away with all that indicates a division of the place, and blend it all into one pleasing whole.

No covering is prettier for a grave than the green sward. The grass always seems to me like a coverlet which nature spreads above those who lie down to rest.

SELECTING PLANTS AND SHRUBS.

In selecting plants and shrubs for cemetery use choose only hardy kinds, for they will not be likely to get that care in autumn which is necessary to the half-hardy sorts. In choosing flowering plants I would not confine the selection to white flowers. Some persons seem to think that no bright color ought to be used about the dead. But God made all the flowers and they are appropriate everywhere. Why should there not be brightness where the dead are at rest? No spot can be made too beautiful for their resting-place, and it cannot be made attractive in the highest degree if we ignore color. There are not many shrubs suitable for cemetery use, because those which grow there must be able, in a large degree, to take care of themselves after being planted. The Deutzias and Spireas are among the best we have. The Lilac is fine for planting in conspicuous places. For groups nothing is finer than Hydrangea *Paniculata grandiflora*. This plant is as hardy as it is possible for any plant to be, and has the peculiar merit of being late in blossoming.

Another most charming late-blooming plant is a new variety of the Japan Anemone, which is put upon the market this spring for the first time. It originated in a garden near Rochester several years ago, and is doubtless a seedling from the old single variety, Honorine Jobert. Unlike that variety, the new one is double. Its flowers are large, exceedingly beautiful and not too perishable. It has been given the singularly inappropriate name of Whirlwind, but the inappropriateness of name does not detract from the beauty of its flowers. This I consider one of the best hardy plants of the herbaceous class for cemetery use. The herbaceous Spireas, both pink and white, are very beautiful. So are the Aquilegias, in white, blue, crimson and yellow. The perennial Coreopsis, *C. lanceolata* of the catalogues, is a charming yellow flower, blooming freely and constantly throughout the season. Achillea, both pink and white, is desirable. So is the Iris. Among the larger shrubs the Weigelias take high rank as desirable cemetery plants. Plant the white and pink varieties together and a fine contrast and perfect harmony are secured. For early spring blooming the Japan Quince, with its intensely bright scarlet flowers, is very effective.

ROSES AND VINES.

Among the Roses suitable for cemetery use Madame Plantier takes first place. It is perfectly hardy in most localities. It makes a very free growth, sending up scores of slender branches, which in June are laden with great clusters of rather small but perfect flowers of a pure white. The old Provence Rose should have a place in all grounds, because of its great beauty and wonderful sweetness. So should the Scotch and Austrian Roses, because of their profusion of bloom. The climbing Roses and the hybrid perpetuals I cannot recommend for general use, because they will seldom do well without good care and protection, which they cannot be sure of receiving.

Vines are not used as much in cemeteries as they ought to be. If there are trees large enough to support them, plant Virginia Creepers or Bittersweets. These can be found growing in most old pastures and along the banks of streams. Another most charming vine to clamber over trees or old stumps or rock work is our native Clematis. Its feathery white flowers are exceedingly beautiful, and I have often wondered why the superintendents of cemeteries do not make more frequent use of this plant.

CHOOSING NATIVE SHRUBS.

We have many native shrubs which are suitable for use in cemetery work. The Sumach makes a most brilliant display of color in fall. Some of the Alders are remarkably appropriate, for their spikes of rich scarlet fruit remain on through the winter, and if we plant them in positions where they can have a background of evergreens against which to display their brilliance nothing can be more effective.

Such native plants as the Goldenrod and Aster should not be overlooked. They seem particularly appropriate in the decoration of a country cemetery, if planted in such a manner that they retain their own wild grace, and given positions similar to those they select when left to choose for themselves. The wild rose is beautiful anywhere, and when we see it growing in the home of the dead it seems to take on a fresh beauty and a charm unnoticed before. And bulbs, such as the Tulip, Hyacinth, Crocus, Lily and Snowdrop, may be made very effective in cemetery work, because they are entirely hardy.— *Eben E. Rexford in Ladies Home Journal.*

An epitaph in Mt. Zion churchyard, near Washington, D. C., reads:

Little Samuel
Died Jan. 21, 1887,
1 year, 2 m. 4 da, 3 hours
and 20 minutes old.

CEMETERY NOTES.

Rocky hill sides and ravines that at one time formed what was considered worthless portions of the Wyltwick Rural cemetery at Kingston, N. Y., have been converted into most desirable sections. This was accomplished by the removal of a large quantity of stone and the use of hundreds of tons of earth for filling in. The cemetery is provided with water from a living spring, and is available at five different points. Mr James Hargreaves, superintendent, informs us that the use of brick graves covered with blue stone flags is becoming quite general.

* * *

The Forest Hill cemetery association of Newark, N. J., has been re-organized into a cremation society. It is their intention to build a crematorium to cost about $12,000.

* * *

The Highland Cemetery Co., of Covington, Ky., recently completed a building equipped with all modern conveniences for the use of their visitors. As a place of shelter in inclement weather, it will be greatly appreciated by lot owners.

* * *

One of the features of a new cemetery company recently started at Norristown, Pa., is a provision whereby every stockholder who purchases a lot or lots can utilize fifty per cent of the amount of his stock in payment therefor, having the amount credited to him as advance dividends on his stock.

* * *

A Philadelphia paper says, "An undertaker who is known as a 'hustler' has devised a scheme for securing patronage which is not looked upon with favor by his colleagues. He was recently presented with a building lot in the suburbs, but instead of using it to erect a house on, he has cut it up into small sections and now anyone who calls upon the undertaker to inter a relative, unless he has a lot of his own, is presented with a piece of ground in which the remains may be laid."

* * *

We are indebted to Mr. J. C. Cline, superintendent of Woodland Cemetery, Dayton, O., for a photograph of the Archer Mausoleum illustrated in this issue and recently completed at Woodland. The mausoleum is 20 x 14 feet, substantially constructed of massive blocks of Barre granite and has a handsomely finished interior with a capacity for sixteen adults. Staniland, Merkle and Staniland of Dayton, O., were the designers and builders.

THE ARCHER MAUSOLEUM, WOODLAND CEMETERY, DAYTON, O.

The authorities of Pere la Chaise, in Paris, are annoyed at the revival of a very grim hoax. A Russian princess is said to have left a million francs to any person who should spend a whole year and a day consecutively in the little chapel raised over her tomb. The body was in a glass coffin in the center and the walls were covered with mirrors, so that the watcher, could he keep awake, would have no possible escape for his thoughts to anything more agreeable than the corpse. No occupation or relaxation was allowed but that of reading by the light at the head of the coffin. No conversation was to be permitted and food was only to be brought to the chapel once a day. One hour for exercise was to be confined to a stroll among the tombs. The offer of $200,000 in this way brought an avalanche of applications from all sorts of persons. Widows were numerous. The obligation of silence for a year and a day had no terror for them. They would be able to wag the tongue all they wanted when they had the million. Men of all degrees of impecuniosity and neediness applied. The cemetery people would like to have the perpetrator of the joke in Pere La Chaise.

The permanence of sepulchral architecture is an object so desirable as to entitle it to special attention. The dilapidation and disfigurement of structures reared for the dead, have been too common to excite surprise but can never be witnessed without pain. Owing to numerous causes of decay and displacement which are ever in action, it should be made a primary consideration to guard against them. Respect for the dead, respect for ourselves, and a just regard for the taste and feelings of all whom either affection or curiosity may attract to the cemetery, demand so much at least, of those who shall make improvements in Oak Ridge. This is a matter in which all are interested for whatever the precaution and care used by some, if others, through inattention suffer their grounds and monuments to become neglected, painful contrasts will soon offend the eye, and the entire grounds will suffer a serious injury.

It is not possible wholly to prevent the effect of atmospheric influence, but proper care in the erection of monuments will greatly counteract and long retard the footsteps of decay.—*Oak Ridge, Springfield, Ill.*

PEPPERIDGE TREE, GRACELAND CEMETERY, CHICAGO.
Photographed when the branches were sparkling with ice.

Cemetery Planting.—II.

As may easily be seen and remembered, plan invariably precedes plant. When the planter has decided to which one of Nature's notes his composition is to be keyed, it goes without saying that the key must not be lost if harmony is to prevail. The artist will find certain harmonious transitions possible without losing the key, and will be able to work out permissible diversity without disturbing the unity of the scheme as a whole.

But this unity must be preserved. Everything must be in character and the spirit of the place should never lose the restfulness that is in keeping with its purpose.

The feeling awakened in cemetery visitors will be more often one of peace, rather than of bitterness and repining, as the subtle influence of scenery harmoniously composed on naturalistic principles is substituted for dreary wastes of stones—an influence that is more or less felt by all, though undefinable, in fact often scarcely understood, but strong and far reaching as silent influence always is.

After deciding where to plant comes the question of what to plant, reversing the hap-hazard way in which so-called decorative planting is usually done. When the plantations and the groups necessary to the plan come to be considered in detail, the end in view, aside from the subordination of its parts to the large general effect, will include planting for a succession of good effects throughout the seasons. Necessarily this means that some parts will be especially attractive at one time and other parts at other times; but it should also mean no barren, ragged or noticeably unattractive spots at any time, not excepting winter. By selection provision can be made for good premeditated winter effects to help out those that Nature, with her large hearted generosity, supplies gratuitously.

She makes everywhere a lovely fret work of interlacing twigs and branches against the background of snow or sky, to replace the green canopy of Summer verdure and the brilliant one of Autumn colors. And as a cemetery is not one of Nature's "measureless domains," but a place that is under the care and control of man, (a care and control that should be patent but not obtrusive), the style of fret work may legitimately be—what you will. As, for instance here, the picturesque outlines produced by the fantastic branches and corky bark of the Sweet Gum, (Liquidamber) or the Sour Gum, also called Tupelo and Pepperidge tree; there, the clean cut silhouette of any of the Magnolia family, while somewhere else the stately Elm may stand unabashed, though shorn of its garment, in all the pride of a magnificently sculptured figure.

Again it may be a group of Conifers, or a single specimen of some choice variety as the Blue Mount Atlas Cedar (Cedrus Atlantica), or of that most charmingly graceful Conifer—the Hemlock.

Of hips, haws and other decorative fruits there are many to aid in the winter pictures. Excellent effects are gained by the use of shrubs with bright colored bark—bark of such exquisite texture that it deserves far more attention at close range than it often gets, and were it not so effective in masses, after the leaves have fallen, would be even more neglected.

By judicious planting, groups may in some cases be made to produce more than one especially good effect each year. Of course this is a simple matter with those sorts which show flowers in spring or summer followed by ornamental fruits in fall or winter; or those varieties that wear gay autumn colors after giving character to a copse by their form and foliage, as for instance, the common sumach. And the effect at both seasons is improved by using the comparatively low-growing cut leaved sumach in conjunction with the taller, better known kind. But it will sometimes be possible, (though probably not often,) to group shrubs together that, while harmonious in foliage, will give two seasons of bloom.

The only example of this desirable plan, promising good results, that comes to mind is the inter-

BLUE MOUNT ATLAS CEDAR.
Engraving used by courtesy of *Gardening*.

mingling of the African Tamarix, which flowers in May or June, with the late flowering variety of Tamarix (Sinensis,) which shows its pale rosy flowers in August. But probably there are other plants that, massed together, would be as homogeneous in foliage as these and yet flower at different seasons.

Rhododendrons and Auratum Lilies have come to be grown together wherever both are planted, but equally good effects may be obtained with lilies, as well as with some of the best herbaceous perennials, among shrubs that are reliably hardy, where Rhododendrons could not safely be used. As, for instance, Auratums or other Japan Lilies among hardy Hydrangeas. Other combinations might be named, but bulbs and herbaceous plants will receive further attention in a later paper of this series.

FANNY COPLEY SEAVEY.

Send your problems to the "Question Box."

Suggestions to Lot Owners.

MOUNDS OVER GRAVES.

In the best cemeteries in the country the surface above graves is now kept flat, as it is almost impossible to make grass live, or to mow it properly on high mounds; and a smooth, unbroken surface is far more beautiful. Mounds are not necessary to mark the place of interment, as an accurate record is now kept of every grave.

DESIGNS FOR MONUMENTS AND HEADSTONES.

Great care should be taken in selecting designs. A monument should be designed with reference to its surroundings, consideration being given to the number, size and character of other monuments standing near it. A good design need cost no more, and it may cost much less than a bad one. Where a monument is to be placed on a lot, headstones, if used at all, should be made very low—the lower the better for permanence, for the appearance of the lot, and for the effect of the monument. Lot owners are earnestly desired never to duplicate a monument already in the cemetery. Justice to owner forbids copying a design for which he has paid, and multiplying any one design only leads to a tiresome monotony.

LAKEWOOD CEMETERY, Minneapolis, Minn.

To Shakespeare.

The bronze statue of Shakespeare presented to the city of Chicago by a deceased citizen will be dedicated in Lincoln Park on Shakespeare's birthday in April. William Ordway Partridge, the sculptor, is also the author of these fitting lines:

Who models thee must be thine intimate,
Nor place thee on a grand uplifted base,
Where tired eyes can hardly reach thy face.
For others this might serve; thou art too great.
Who sculptures thee must grasp thy human state;
Until this sculptor comes the world must wait.
But when he comes, carving those deep-set eyes
'Neath brow o'erarching, like the heaven's great dome,
Then men will turn and look with glad surprise,
And say, slow wending from their toil toward home,
"I saw this Shakespeare in the street; he seemed
But man, like you and me, howe'er he dreamed."

Suggestions are in order for the Philadelphia convention.

RULES AND REGULATIONS.

Every cemetery should be governed by certain rules and regulations, which should be printed in pamphlet form for distribution among lot owners. While this has been done in most of the large cemeteries, where the rules are very much alike, we will, for the benefit of the smaller cemeteries, publish in this department such rules as commend themselves for general adoption. Contributions are solicited.

Rules for Stone Work in Graceland Cemetery, Chicago.

1. No stone work of any kind shall be admitted to the cemetery, or foundation built for the same, until a design for such work shall have been submitted to the superintendent and approved by him.

For headstones or footstones, a sketch on the back of the foundation order will be deemed sufficient; for monuments, designs drawn to a scale must be furnished, accompanied by a certificate signed by the lot-owner and contractor stating that so far as they know the design submitted is not a duplicate of any now in the cemetery.

The above rule is made to save stonecutters the loss which they sometimes suffer from executing a design not in accordance with the rules of the cemetery.

2. Mausoleums can be built only when the designs and locations for them have been approved by the board of managers.

3. All foundations shall be built by the Cemetery Company. They must be ordered fifteen days before needed, and must be paid for in advance.

The charge for foundations containing eighteen cubic feet or less will be 35 cents per cubic foot; between eighteen and twenty-one cubic feet, $6.30; more than twenty-one cubic feet, 30 cents per cubic foot. An extra charge of 5 cents per cubic foot will be made for foundations laid when the ground is frozen.

No coping, or any kind of lot or grave enclosure, or steps to lots, will be admitted to the cemetery.

Corner posts for lots are furnished and set by the Cemetery Company.

4. In * certain portions of the cemetery, no monuments will be permitted.

On certain lots in Bellevue section, monuments must not exceed eight feet in height.

In other portions of the cemetery not here named, one monument will be permitted on one burial plot.

6. Headstones and footstones, or any structures used to mark graves, must not exceed eight inches in height above the surface of the ground, must not be less than six nor more than fifteen inches thick, and must not exceed thirty inches in width. Where headstones are used, footstones will not be allowed.†

On certain lots in Fairlawn section, they must not exceed four inches in height.

In Maplewood section, and on certain lots in Bellevue section, they must not project above the surface of the ground.

At single graves, stones must not exceed the width of the grave, 18 inches for children's and 30 inches for adults' graves.

7. In certain sections, headstones or footstones must not exceed thirty inches in height and must not be less than four inches thick.

8. No monument or grave marker shall be constructed of other material than cut stone or real bronze.

No monument or grave marker will be admitted which is cut in imitation of a log or stump, or of any other object which would itself not be allowed to remain in the cemetery.

9. Persons engaged in erecting monuments or other structures are not permitted to attach ropes to other monuments, or to trees, except by permission of the superintendent; or to scatter material over adjacent lots or to leave the same on the ground longer than is absolutely necessary. They are required to set their work as soon as possible after it enters the cemetery, and will be held responsible for any damage done to the grass, trees, or any object whatsoever in the cemetery, and must be subject to the control and direction of the superintendent. On Saturdays and on the day before Decoration day, no material of any kind will be admitted to the cemetery after twelve o'clock at noon.

10. The managers reserve the right to make exceptions to the foregoing rules in favor of designs which they consider exceptionally artistic and ornamental, and such exceptions shall not be construed as a repeal of any rules.

The superintendent is directed to enforce the foregoing regulations, and to exclude from the cemetery any person wilfully violating the same.

11. Special rules for certain sections may be made at any time hereafter by the board of managers, and enforced without previous notice to stonecutters.

FORM OF CERTIFICATE.

So far as we know the monument shown by the accompanying design is not a duplicate of any monument now in Graceland cemetery

.... Lot-owner.

..... Contractor.

---

* The portions are indicated in the circular.

† This rule applies to certain parts of the grounds.

Thoughts on Transplanting.

Many people ask, when is the proper time to plant trees, in the fall or in the spring?

This is a question which has been asked thousands of times, and been answered both ways by people who have had special success, in the spring or fall, as the case may be.

Now, according to the studies of those who have used their eyes and experiences on the subject, one time is as good as the other. Trees in full health transplanted in the spring go on pushing their leaves and making young fibres on the roots as if nothing had been done to affect their usual habits. In trees as in a human being, health is a great factor in success. A good sound, healthy person who loses a finger or even a hand, feels or exhibits no signs of the trouble he has gone through. The blood is good and sound and goes on healing the wounded parts.

So with a tree: the spring is the healthy time of all nature; all plants are in their best health, and they naturally feel less the damage done to them than at any other time.

Planting in the fall also has its benefits, even perhaps more so than in the spring. In early fall transplanting, the leaves are picked off, and the tree is again planted. The advantage the fall planter has is this: the tree, we may say, has gone to sleep for the winter, the leaves being off, they do not need the life giving strength of the roots, which possibly may have been injured in the digging, and need all their strength for themselves. What does it matter if we *take* the leaves off, instead of waiting until they fall off? Does not winter weather sometimes come early, and again it comes late in the year? Two or three weeks make no difference, the trees are always prepared, and, "have gone to sleep." To return to the planting, we see the tree suffers very little or none by the leaves using the strength of the tree. Another point is that when spring does come, the plant has been made solid in its place, by the winter months.

In the first part of the article we say that it makes no difference whether trees are planted in the fall or spring. There is one exception in favor of fall planting, and that is in the larch family. Larches planted in the fall are invariably successful, while those planted at other seasons only pull through after a hard struggle.

Evergreens can be transplanted during the summer.—*Meehans' Monthly for March.*

I congratulate you upon the MODERN CEMETERY, which, in my judgment, is doing an excellent work.—*Burton Mansfield, Pres. Evergreen Cemetery.* New Haven, Conn.

◁ CEMETERY REPORTS. ▷

We have received from Mr. Burton Mansfield, president of the Evergreen Cemetery Association of New Haven, Conn., a copy of the director's annual report from which we extract the following:

"After a careful consideration of the subject, your directors became convinced that they should no longer neglect the establishment of a permanent fund for the care of the cemetery grounds. This should have been done years ago, for few if any of the affairs of the Association are of such great concern. Late in the year the directors voted to set aside ten per cent. of the receipts from the sale lots for this purpose and allow the same to accumulate until the income from other sources shall be sufficient to meet the expenses which the care and maintenance of the grounds involve.

The necessity of a permanent fund forces itself upon us the more we consider it. This is, as you know, distinct from the perpetual care fund, to which lot owners contribute for the care of their individual lots. The object of this fund is to make provision for the support and maintenance of the cemetery in years to come, long after many of the present owners shall have passed away and the Association shall have ceased, to a considerable degree at least, to have a source of income other than this, which can be devoted to these purposes. * * * As to the affairs of cemeteries in general, we reiterate what we said last year in regard to Sunday funerals. We believe that they should be abolished, as far as possible, and it is with pleasure that we notice that at the last convention of the cemetery superintendents, a resolution expressing this same thought met with hearty approval. There is certainly a growing public opinion in favor of this position. In the same connection we may speak of a matter of a very kindred nature, viz: burial reform, as it is commonly called. Less expense and less display in connection with the ordinary burial, than what we so often see now would be more in harmony with the quietness and solemnity due to the occasion and be at the same time an evidence of good taste, a desirable quality to cultivate.

Your directors think that it would be a very good thing for our superintendent to visit other cemeteries in the country, and to associate with others similarly engaged, see how they care for their several charges and exchange ideas with them. In this way he can learn how others solving some of the problems which bother him and impart from his own experience that which will help others. This is true in regard to the annual conventions of the superintendents, of which the next one is to be held at Philadelphia. Our superintendent should be allowed to attend at our expense.

* * *

Extracts from the annual report of Lakewood cemetery, Minneapolis, Minn. Receipts from lot sales, $30,606.98. Total receipts from all sources, $55,516.55. Expenditures, $30,363.14. 203 lots and 157 single graves were sold. The permanent improvement fund, which is accumulated by setting aside 20 per cent of all lot sales, now amounts to $59,593.08. Number of burials during the year, 636; total number to date, 7,103. To remove the possibility of marble yards, or other objectionable features being established near the main entrance, the association has bought considerable adjacent property at an expense of several thousand dollars.

Mr. Barker's report on Lakewood has been reproduced for the edification of the lot owners and the superintendent's convention is referred to as follows:

In September last we were favored by the meeting in this city of the annual convention of Cemetery Superintendents, your board took some pains to entertain the convention, and in our intercourse we found its members to be men of ability, full of the energy of a progressive spirit, and genial gentlemen whom it was a pleasure to meet. The discussions at the meetings were full of interesting and profitable suggestions and your board has come to believe that this body of representative cemetery enthusiasts can and does result in great good to all, in any way interested in the cemeteries of the country.

* * *

An interesting account of the work of exterminating the gypsy moth from the trees in Harmony Grove cemetery, Salem, Mass., was read at the recent annual meeting. The report which we take from a local paper states that in May, 1893, many of the trees were found to be infested. From 17 trees and adjoining fences, 1,018 new egg-clusters and 30 old egg-clusters were taken. At the same time 58 new and 1 old were taken from estates and street trees near by. To facilitate further care in inspection, the rough bark was hewed from the large trees and the dead branches were removed, and the rubbish was burned. Fourteen trees were banded with Raupenleim to prevent the larvæ from ascending the trees; 343 trees in the cemetery and 283 on adjoining estates were also banded with burlap during the spring. From these burlapped trees, in the cemetery, 3,031 larvæ were taken, also 8 pupæ; on adjoining estates and street trees, 283 larvæ, 9 pupæ and 4 moths were found. As a result of this work, only one new nest was found on the cemetery grounds during the fall. The first larvæ was found May 29, 1893. The number killed during the week ended June 3, was 1,198; in August, only seven nests were found, which attests the good work performed and effective methods employed.

* * *

Extracts from a summary report of the treasurer and superintendent of Fairmount cemetery, Newark, N. J., for the past year. Receipts from single grave and lot sales, $33,972. Total receipts, $43,157.84. Total expenditures, $41,872.35, of which amount $17,589 was for salaries and labor. Number of lots sold, 115, entire number sold to date, 2,909. Lots under perpetual care, 1,486. Total number of lots cared for, 2,013. Single graves sold, 677. Sodded, 1,654. Monuments erected, 49; headstones, 173. Hedges removed, 52.

Interments, 1,278. Total to January 1st, 1894, 27,921. Mr. Nichols writes that a number of improvements were made in and around the cemetery.

≳|Correspondence.|≲

State or Local Associations of Cemetery Superintendents.
Editor Modern Cemetery:

I desire to call attention to a matter which I think has not had a fair consideration.

On page 72 of the convention proceedings for 1893 we read that Mr. McCarthy, Chairman of the committee on Local Associations, stated that "the committee was not ready to report. A vote was taken which showed it was the sense of the meeting that State Associations were not advisable."

What was it that prompted the President at the Baltimore convention to call the attention of the members to this subject? On p. 5, proceedings of the sixth convention, we read, "I have been impressed lately that we are not extending our influence to the extent that it is our privilege to do, we do not reach all the superintendents that we ought. The proportion is far too small. The United States is a big place, and it needs no argument to convince you that any of the places where we have met, have been too far off for many at a remote distance from the place of meeting to come. In a recent number of MODERN CEMETERY a writer advocated the forming of state associations. This might do for larger states, but the smaller ones I am doubtful about. I think New England at least should have an organization, and I feel confident that we may reach many that we can not through this organization, and perhaps the other States may be divided in some such way, I think greater benefits may be derived through the local societies. I trust a committee may be appointed to carefully consider this subject and report at this meeting (Sep. 1892.)" The committee was appointed but did not report at that meeting and at the next meeting, Aug. 1893 were not ready then, and without any sort of consideration the whole matter was peremptorily squelched. The writer regrets that at that particular moment when action was taken he was called out, and so had no chance to speak upon the subject but having been requested to speak through the columns of the MODERN CEMETERY I gladly do so and will try to confine myself to facts in support of my position.

Out of a membership of 124 only about one-third, (41), were present. Massachusetts 4, Ohio 9, Illinois 3, Minnesota 6, Missouri 1, Michigan 2, Nebraska 3, New York 3, Indiana 1, Iowa 2,

Rhode Island 1, New Jersey 2, Pennsylvania 3, Wisconsin 1. I think the figures speak quite loud. Out of the six N. E. States only two were represented. Now I think there is room for a New England Association, and its meeting should not be at a time that would conflict with a National Association, as it would be purely instructive, and to help those who cannot go so far away. March or April could be selected, with expenses reduced to a minimum, and give our friends who have charge of the smaller places a chance to share with us who are able to attend the National Association meetings, the benefits we derive. I believe there are many such who would gladly go to Philadelphia this year but their salaries are not sufficient to allow them that privilege, and in many cases the managers have not the means to send them. Now I think we should be willing to spread out, we all have a thorough good time every year, while others equally faithful, are obliged to be at home year in and out, hardly ever knowing what a vacation is. I think that that vote came very near the border of selfishness, and is wholly unworthy of the broad minded intelligent body that passed it. It could not possibly have been in the least injurious to us, to have the matter fairly investigated, the superintendents of New England may not want an organization of their own, and that would end it, but, wherein could such an organization be a hindrance to the National Association? I think it would be a help. I have spoken, let the opposers give their reasons. Very much more might be added on this subject, but enough has been said to satisfy the reader I trust, of the honest purpose I had in suggesting local, or if you please, auxiliary associations.

JOHN G. BARKER.

QUESTION BOX.

ANSWERS.

Editor Modern Cemetery.

Regarding the extermination of ants I am unable to give any information, as we are not troubled with them. Moles, with us, are a constant and disagreeable nuisance and we have tried every known method, from poison to the most elaborate traps to get rid of them. Each year they seem more numerous than before and we have come to the conclusion that it will be money saved to offer a premium for every mole caught and destroyed. While it may appear expensive to pay, say ten cents for each mole caught and destroyed we think it will pay, as men who will be detailed to that work at certain hours of the day (early in the morning, at noon and again before sundown), become experts in catching these pests at work, so that the value of the benefit derived will be far in excess of the expense. One mole often destroys sod over an area which to repair or relay will involve more outlay than the premium on a dozen moles, including time spent, amounts to. We do not propose to discard traps altogether, and will always have several varieties in use but where moles appear too numerous we will try the premium plan.

Lining Graves.

As to the question of "Novice," I will say that in our estimation nothing is prettier and more economical than the lining of a grave from the box up with fresh twigs of evergreens, pinned to the sides and ends by means of stout crimped hairpins. We generally use Hemlock, Spruce or Balsam Fir and find that the latter has a deeper and denser green than the others. Hemlock having a more delicate foliage is used principally for children's graves. Nothing larger than the outer twigs are used, being fastened, one piece over laping the lower a trifle, so that the whole appears solid from above. The earth on one side of the grave is also covered with branches of larger size, or if desired it is moved entirely from the grave, which of course involves double expense. The charge for lining an adult's grave is $3 and a child's $2, which is ample to pay all expenses and leave a fair profit for the cemetery. I venture to assert that it will pay to raise stock for that specific purpose. Often, during the cooler months of the year the greens are used several times by keeping them in a moist shady place, thus reducing expense somewhat. This method of lining graves is much more pleasing to the eye than any artificial material, can be done at very short notice by experienced help and is practical, economical and profitable.—FRANK EURICH, Toledo, Ohio.

MONEYWORT:—The planting of Moneywort is not permitted in Springdale cemetery. It was introduced here some years ago and soon became a nuisance. I have tried in vain for something that will effectually remove it.

ANTS:—Chloride of lime or coal oil will destroy them.

MOLES:—We use Olmstead's trap and find it the cheapest and best method for killing moles.

JOHN F. BOERCKEL, Peoria, Ill.

A tombstone in the quaint old cemetery at Eddyville, Ky., bears the inscription:

> W. J. Bigwood, murdered in cold blood by Hylan Skinner, on the—day of—1887.

Skinner was tried last year for the crime, found guilty and sentenced to seven years' imprisonment.

Association of American Cemetery Superintendents.

WM. SALWAY, "Spring Grove" Cincinnati, O., President.
T. McCARTHY, "Swan Point" Providence, R. I., Vice-President.
F. EURICH, Woodlawn, Toledo, O., Secretary and Treasurer.

The Eighth Annual Convention of the Association will be held at Philadelphia in September, 1894.

Resolutions Adopted at the Seventh Annual Convention of the Association of American Cemetery Superintendents.

Resolved: That it is the sense of this convention that all Sunday funerals be discouraged as much as possible.

Resolved: That it is the sense of this meeting that all headstones or markers should be limited to the height of the sod or the level of the surface of the ground.

Resolved: That it is the sense of this meeting that vaults and catacombs be discouraged and if possible prevented in cemeteries.

TOLEDO, O., March 8th, 1894

To the Members of the Association of American Cemetery Superintendents.

FRIENDS:—As the time glides rapidly by we are reminded that our Eighth Annual Convention is not far distant and sufficiently near to consider what each one of us can contribute toward making the meeting a success. You all know how difficult it is to formulate a program of proceedings, and being satisfied that you all are interested in the success of our meetings I appeal to each and every one of you to aid the Executive Committee by suggesting subjects for papers and discussion or by volunteering to prepare such and to help in making the meeting both profitable and pleasant. As all the members are readers of this, our official organ, much money and time can be saved by communicating ideas and plans through its columns which Mr. Haight will be glad to devote for that purpose, or if you prefer, address your communications direct to the Executive Committee, the members of which you will find in our last proceedings.

Friends, this appeal is to each one of you personally the same as if I had written a letter to each of you individually and I trust that you will give the request proper thought and reflection and send in your ideas and suggestions without delay.

Respectfully, FRANK EURICH, Sec. and Treas.

Epitaph from the tombstone of a photographer:
"Here I lie taken from life."

The trustees of the Cedar Grove Cemetery, Dorchester, have resolved not to sell single graves for the interment of persons dying from smallpox.

Twenty-two iron fences were removed from Harmony Grove Cemetery, Salem, Mass., in the past twelve months.

The catacombs of Rome contain the remains of about 6,000,000 people.

Publisher's Department.

The receipt of Cemetery Literature and Trade Catalogues will be acknowledged in this column.

TO ADVERTISERS. THE MODERN CEMETERY is the only publication of its class and will be found a valuable medium for reaching cemetery officials in all parts of the United States.

TO SUBSCRIBERS. Cemetery officials desiring to subscribe for a number of copies regularly to circulate among their lot owners, should send for our special terms. Several well known cemeteries have already adopted this plan with good results.

Contributions on matters pertaining to cemeteries are solicited. Address all communications to
R. J. HAIGHT, 334 Dearborn St., CHICAGO.

Cemetery Literature received, Charter, Rules and Regulations etc., Highwood Cemetery, Pittsburgh, Pa.

Catalogues received: The Wm. H. Moon Co., Glenwood Nurseries Morrisville, Pa., Ellwanger & Barry, Rochester, N. Y. Trees, shrubs, plants, etc., McDonald Brothers, Columbus, O.

Sidney Heminsley Jr., succeeds his father as superintendent of Cedar Lawn, Paterson, N. J. A. D. Smith has been appointed superintendent of Mountain View, Oakland, Cal., in place of D. Edward Collins resigned. Charles Fitz George succeeds the late J. Harry Wolff at Greenwood, Trenton, N. J.

Situation Wanted.
Young man, experienced in cemetery management, steady and trustworthy, desires position to take charge, or as assistant superintendent. Apply, L. B., MODERN CEMETERY.

Situation Wanted.
By a person qualified to fill position of superintendent and secretary. Several years experience. W. F. L., care MODERN CEMETERY, Chicago.

Modern Cemetery: Enclosed please find check for which send us the MODERN CEMETERY for one year. Just the help we have been looking for, several years past. The typography of the paper is attractive and entertaining in all its parts.
C. E. PERRY, Superintendent Oakwood Cemetery. Beaver Dam, Wis.

J. S. ARMSTRONG, PRAIRIE DU CHIEN, WIS. If I was to ask the question, what do cemetery officials, and lot owners in particular, most desire, or rather stand in need of, the answer would be, more light as to cemetery improvement, and for that light, I would say see the MODERN CEMETERY.

THE NEW HANDY BINDER

Will be found a most valuable invention for keeping the numbers of the MONUMENTAL NEWS in good condition. The method of binding allows the pages to lie perfectly flat, whether one or a dozen numbers are in the binder. Any number can be taken out and replaced without disturbing the other numbers. The binders are strong and durable and have the title of MODERN CEMETERY on the side in gilt, an ornament to any desk or reading table. We will supply them to subscribers in embossed cloth covers, 90 cents. Heavy flexible paper covers for 35 cents. By mail post-paid.

MODERN CEMETERY, 334 Dearborn St., Chicago.

THE MODERN CEMETERY.

THE MODERN CEMETERY.
AN ILLUSTRATED MONTHLY JOURNAL DEVOTED TO THE INTEREST OF CEMETERIES

R. J. HAIGHT, Publisher,

344 Dearborn Street, CHICAGO

Subscription $1.00 a Year in Advance.   Foreign Subscription $1.25.
Special Rates on Six or More Copies.

VOL. IV.   CHICAGO, APRIL, 1894.   NO. 2.

CONTENTS.

BURIAL REFORM	13
CEMETERY PLANTING, III	15
ELECTRIC FUNERAL CARS	16
INJURY TO TREES	17
*THE SHAW MAUSOLEUM, ST. LOUIS, MO	18
THE LILY POND	19
CEMETERY NOTES	20
*ENTRANCE TO THE MONTEFIORE BURIAL ASSOCIATION GROUNDS, MINNEAPOLIS	21
RULES AND REGULATIONS—CEMETERY REPORTS	22
CREMATION	23
ASSOCIATION OF AMERICAN CEMETERY SUPERINTENDENTS	24
PUBLISHER'S DEPARTMENT	24
*Illustrated.	

Burial Reform.

The Rev. Jenkin Lloyd Jones, of Chicago, recently preached a sermon on "The Selfishness of Grief," in which he discussed the several features of mourning and prevailing funeral customs in a manner we believe at once instructive to his hearers and worthy of pointed consideration, and we give the following extended extracts:

"Pain always breaks or makes the will. Grief will sweeten or sour the life. Sorrow makes one life somber and sullen, selfish and sordid; it makes another gentle and tender, helpful and holy. All depends upon the spirit in which we accept the bitter fruit. Our griefs may fertilize our lives and cause them to bear more abundantly the holy fruit of the spirit, or they may blight whatever they touch, depressing whomsoever we approach. The pleasures of life are accepted by most people as a trust; their administration is a matter of thought, and a misuse of the same brings prompt reproach, merited rebuke, wise counsel. We must not be selfish in our pleasures. But grief also is a responsibility. Why should we abandon ourselves to its sway without thought and without conscience? It is not easy to speak plain words of advice or rebuke when the heart is torn, but surely they are unworthy tears that blind the eyes to duty.

It is not a gracious task to speak of the faults born out of the tenderest and profoundest experiences of the soul, but there is need of plain speech here. Let me with love and all tender consideration try to speak plainly of these matters. This life is sad enough at best. Pain, weakness, separation and death are our inevitable attendants, ever near and ever ready to visit us with fresh surprises. Shall we maximize or minimize them? Shall we convert them into inward peace, moral earnestness and spiritual trust, or shall we allow them to overlay us, cripple our powers, limit our influence and pervert our natures until we become a burden to the society which we ought to serve? Let us then frankly confess that selfishness is unseemly by the coffin as it is by the festal board. Self-control is as necessary and admirable by the one as by the other. There is need of consideration in the sick room as on the play-ground. Death, mysterious visitant with a shrouded face and chilling hand, is ever an unwelcome friend, at best, a sorrow bringer; but we, the living, are not on that account released from the exactions of prudence, economy, cheerfulness and service. Death may leave us sad, but it should not make us mean. Death will make us sorrowful, but let it not make us selfish.

There is nothing more archaic in modern life than our attitude toward death and the customs that cluster about it. We are all slaves in that respect, of customs and fashions rooted in past error and false premises. There is nothing more barbaric surviving in our life to-day than a conventional funeral. The more proper it is, the more offensive it is to delicate sensibilities and common sense. Let me particularize.

Why should we, when the inevitable comes, yield to such wild rebellious grief as is so often witnessed? Let us in life prepare not only for our own death but for the death of those near and dear to us. Who is to go first we know not, but let all arm themselves beforehand with that holy fortitude that will enable the survivors to accept unhesitatingly the unfinished task and to bend willingly the shoulder to the added burden. Why should the last memories of the forms of our dear ones be so clouded with artificial gloom, with the grim crape at the door, the lowered curtains, the darkened house? Let the calm be illuminated with all the sunlight available. Let the quiet be sanctified by pleasant memories and high resolves. Oh, let the thoughts of the living be of life and not of death, or so far as possible let the thought of death be as that of an incident in life which does not change the relations and responsibilities of life. The hungry must be fed, the naked clothed, though your dear one is gone and his form lies silent in its chamber.

The minister has poorly filled his place if his ministrations have not been performed before the crape is on the door. The funeral sermon is preached long before the funeral if it is to be of real helpfulness. O soul, do not add to your bereavement bitterness; do not sulk because the Infinite God has touched you with the divine wand which leads the generations forward. Do not rebel against the benignant inevitable. You are richer by one more hope, richer in one more angel, richer in one more priceless gem that cannot be taken away from you. You have looked beyond the seen and the tangible and have felt the awe-inspiring mystery of eternity. If your soul sorrows as it must, let the grief reach your mind and your conscience, that they be quickened. Do not dwell amid the tombs; "let the dead bury the dead!" You should live while it is your privilege, that you may have a better right to the life and the reunion that await you when the discharge comes. I would not mock your tears, but let them be benignant showers falling upon the garden of your heart that it may bear more abundantly the lily-graces, the rose-loves and the apples of character. Sorrow, like love, obscures itself. True grief has no use for hired mourners, whether it be professional wailers hired to cry aloud over the dead, according to oriental customs, or the inanimate advertisers of grief employed by modern fashion. Alas for the widow whose sorrow for her husband must be estimated by the yard; pitiable is the servitude that uses money needed for children's clothes in buying crape in order to assure the world that the children's mother loved their father and realized his loss. Fashion is often tyrannical, frequently senseless, but never more so than in these mourning customs, which require that black should be worn for twelve months, and that black and white, not unbecoming to many women, should graduate the sorrow off into colors and gaiety. A reform in this direction is demanded for four reasons.

1. Black is a false symbol. Death is not an enemy, but a friend. Its symbol should be light and not darkness; it should suggest hope and not despair.

2. Practically it is a menace to the spiritual buoyancy of the community, particularly of the home, and most especially of the children in the home. What right have you to convert the memories of a strong father or a loyal mother into a twelve-months' gloom? Why should you fetter yourself with this grim reminder to others of a sorrow all your own, obscure joyous memories and blur your rising purposes with this swarthy mantle, which is not true either to night or day? It is not natures color. She uses it sparingly in her landscape.

3. These mourning customs are an abomination because they introduce the conventional and the artificial into the realm which ought to be preserved to the sanctities of sincerity. Of all ghastly pretensions a pretended sorrow is the most ghastly. Think of the young widow counting the time when she may lay off her weeds and it will be proper for her again to wear color; of the widower brushing the silken crape upon his hat as he is about to start out for his second or third wooing. There is a grim sarcasm (which ought to be reiterated from the pulpit) in the phrase, "mourning by the yard." It is a bit of modern Phariseeism against which religion, natural, wholesome, sincere religion, cries out. How extremely artificial and elaborate are the ramifications of this fashion which reaches to the coachman's dress and the horses' harness, only the dry-goods man and his expert customers know. As a measure of one's grief, how very expressive is the width of the black band on the mourning envelope. I ridicule the pretense because I bow in silent sympathy in the presence of the reality.

4. Lastly, I protest against the mourning custom for economic reasons. How grievous is the task even upon the favored, the well-to-do! how intolerable the burden upon those who walk the narrow plank that brings daily bread by daily earnings! I am not an adept at figures, but here is a case where figures should count. Take a family of mother and four or five children who, for fear of apparent disrespect to the memory of the father gone, must wear mourning, else "people will talk."

"Dear friends, I beg of you to do everything you can to further a social revolution in this direction: be sensible; be strong; carry the sweet sorrow in your heart; do not lose its benediction by parading it; do not make it vulgar by trying to wear it on your backs."

NOTE: The remainder of the Rev. Mr. Jones' sermon deals with funeral customs, and as it comprises so much of valuable suggestion, we propose to conclude it in our next issue.

Among other new rules recently adopted by Crown Hill cemetery, Indianapolis, Ind., is one that will rid the grounds of glass cases, boxes, toys and numerous other articles at the little graves. This rule should be enforced in all cemeteries.

LAWN AT DOSORIS.

Cemetery Planting. III.

To return to ligneous plants, there could be no more delightful or fitting cemetery ornament than a bank of Kalmia Latifolia, or native Mountain Laurel, in full bloom as it is seen in the mountains of East Tennessee, Virginia and elsewhere. Kalmias blossomed on the Wooded Island at the Fair about the last of May.

It would seem that a hardy small flowered Clematis, (C. flammula would probably be the best,) might be planted among Kalmias to supply a second crop of flowers. If C. flammula was used the second season of bloom would last all summer and be followed by an ornamental feathery, red starred envelope that would outlast many bleak wintry storms despite its fragile appearance. It grows so openly that it would not seem likely to be injurious to the small shrubs, especially if the old wood is kept cut out, but if they would not bear it there are larger ones that would.

It seems to me that wherever Lilacs, Syringas and Snowballs are used, (and no one wants to do without them,) it would be well to plant something to serve as summer drapery to make up for their lack of beauty after the flowering season.

A hardy herbaceous vine would be the right thing, and nothing could be better than Clematis Jackmanii, and for variety C. paniculata, where its white flowers in the fall would make a pleasing note in the general arrangement or composition.

Vines are excellent material and can be utilized in various ways. Hall's Honeysuckle, (Lonicera Halleana) would be delightful in some locations if left to assume any shape it liked. In this connection the new hardy creeping Japanese rose (R. Wichuariana) deserves special mention. Its foliage is so very pretty that it is worth growing for that alone, but it also bears lovely little roses—miniature wild roses in shape, but pure white. In leaf, flower and habit it resembles the Cherokee rose, of the South, and is very like it but on a daintier scale. This Japanese rose, as grown in the rose garden at the World's Fair, spread its vines out flat on the ground in all directions like a true creeper, but I was told by Mr. Thorpe, Chief of Floriculture, that it could easily be made to assume the cushion or mound shape into which the Cherokee rose builds itself when isolated on the grass.

These dark mounds are so numerous and have so much character that they are a marked feature of the scenery of the lower Mississippi River. They grow in perfection near the water in open sunny situations far from trees and shrubs, which suggests letting their little Japanese relation, (the Cherokee rose is a native of China,) have a chance to become an American mound builder in the north on the grassy border of lakes or streams. R. Wichuariana is very hardy.

Under the shade of trees, even where grass does not thrive, an authority (Mr. Falconer) says that the Japanese climbing honeysuckle (Lonicera brachy podia) will make a thick carpet of vines—a fascinating suggestion that makes one long to see such a rug forming for some fine tree to stand on.

Bitter-sweet is a good vine, especially if the fertile, seed bearing (female) plant is used, for its fruit is decorative and lasts well into the winter. While vines are legitimate material for working out various details of the scheme, they seem especially adapted to those parts that are to approach the nearest in effect to nature's pattern. So in a picturesque dell, or on the border of a glade near the edge of a naturalistic grove would be a home-like place for a tree, overgrown and literally draped by the wild grape. There is no vine that knows so well how to drape a tree, or that does it so successfully. It is a perfect vine for such places and schemes. It has the grace of a wood nymph, and the odor of its inconspicuous blossoms is like a breath of spring from some fairer world than ours. It comes into leaf early, and remains green and fresh from the ground up until the entire procession of summer growths has passed. It does not seem conscious of taking any part in the pageant, but it is there, in becoming dress, as a spectator who means to see all there is to be seen. It is too much absorbed in what is going on to grow old itself, and before it wakes to consciousness of self the end has come and it dies unruffled and happy, with its simple beauty intact.

An excellent example for its friends to follow.

FANNY COPLEY SEAVEY.

Electric Funeral Cars.

A system of funeral transportation service is coming to the front in many of our large cities and is rapidly gaining public favor, and with very good reason. The carriage service of the ordinary funeral has grown to be a severe tax both on the financial resources and the disposition of the community, for while generally expensive it is also quite unsatisfactory, and from what we learn, a department in the undertaking business which would cause very little uneasiness were it to be discontinued.

We refer to the funeral car on our street railways, which is being used in several of our large cities most noticeably on the "electric" routes.

On many of our steam roads the regular funeral train is now an institution and some of the companies have deemed it good policy to construct special cars fitted up expensively and tastefully to meet the circumstances.

This new progressive, but withal philosophical and economic feature of our "funerals" is now rapidly extending to our street railways, and we see no reason why such a system cannot be made a permanent feature, notwithstanding the frequent local inconvenience of distance from the residence to the car route. But we think that this is a matter of detail of the new order of things which the undertaking fraternity will quickly overcome.

The manifold advantages of economy, order and a minimum of discomfort are so pressing, in face of the obstacles, that once the community so signifies the car companies will rapidly frame themselves to the demand.

Atchison, Kansas, has a regular funeral street car, which was perhaps the first practice of the idea.

The City of Mexico has some thirty funeral street cars, equipped to suit the conditions of patrons, and the street railway system permits of these cars reaching almost any part of the city. Some of the more expensive cars are so arranged as to wheels that they can be drawn from the track and driven to the grave without infringing the rules of the cemetery.

In Seattle, Wash., the funeral car will be a permanent feature of street railway service and in Portland, Oregon, the system is about to be introduced.

In San Francisco the funeral car is an established fact on the electric road which is nine miles long and passes four cemeteries.

At Pittsburgh there is a switch upon which the funeral cars stand near the entrance of one of the principal cemeteries.

The tendency of the age is to modernize the funeral, in other words to remove from the occasion the outward paraphernalia of ancient times which have so obstinately clung to it and to perform the sad ceremonies in the spirit which our civilization has spread about us.

We have received from Mr. J. Mc Near, proprietor of the Cypress Hill Cemetery, Petaluma, Cal., a photograph of the entrance and one of his own lot. This cemetery was started in 1866 with 25 acres which has since been increased to 50. The entrance is some 2000 feet from the main traveled road and is reached by a private road 60 feet wide. The main avenues inside the gates are 50 and 60 feet wide and lead into others of lesser width, running on an up grade through the valleys. The main avenues are lined with palms, dracenas, magnolias and flowers. Mr. Mc Near's lot is a knoll 90 feet in diameter, the posts, steps and coping of which is cut from a solid piece of granite. Mr. Mc Near writes that this cemetery will compare favorably with the best cemeteries in the State.

Injury to Trees.

In the minds of many, a tree seems to have no rights they are bound to respect. It stands with them in the same category among useful things as stones, anvils, stumps, old barrels, snubbing-posts, and like insensible objects, to be kicked, pounded on, hacked, hitched to, stood on, cracked, bumped against, or set fire to, as the moment's need or a thoughtless fancy demands. But the careful guardian of a park regards the tree as exceedingly sensitive and liable to injury, and he holds himself as much in hand while dealing with one of his towering pets as when handling a tulip bulb. Trees go down to their death from seemingly insignificant hurts. A mere lad climbed up and stood in the fork of our fine thirty-foot Balm of Gilead while trying to recover his kite string. The bark was bruised where he stood, decay set in, limbs began to come down the next season, and the entire tree lay on the ground inside of three years.

I found in a neighboring thicket a neatly poised sumach and removed it to my yard, where for three years its symmetry and neat canopy of leaves made it an object of frequent admiring remark. A three year old child was playfully lifted up to stand among the branches of the "umbrella tree." The abraded bark where the little shoe had rested soon showed decay beneath it. The proper bacillus for the purpose made for it a case of "quick consumption," and my favorite was gone.

A black ash five inches through which stands near the street fence, carries a long, unsightly scar caused by a lad's beating a tattoo on the pretty bark with his stick while he sat on the fence idly humming in the sunshine. On a boulevard down the street a half-dozen young ash-leaved maples are trying hard to grow. A curious appearance of their having been girdled about three inches from the ground attracted my attention as I frequently passed. It was not a blazing by an axe, but a rumpled appearance of the bark. I speculated on ice damage, or hurts by mice or moles, or this and that, all to no purpose until I happened to come along when the young man was running his lawn mower and saw him vigorously bumping it against the trees to reach the grass about their trunks. It was all plain then. Bare patches of weather beaten, worm eaten wood now nearly encircle their trunks, and within a few months his fine trees will, more than likely, get antic some breezy evening and waltz away with the wanton winds.

Damage by fire is a ruthless and serious hurt to a tree. In "years agone" fire generally managed in our cemetery to do about all the raking of leaves that was undertaken. Indolence was uniformly sorry that the fire got the start of him, but "after all, it did a heap of good in clearing off the dead leaves." The falling and drifting leaves are apt to pocket deeply about the tree roots, making the burning especially hot just there, and it is no wonder that there is not now in all the cemetery a native forest tree that is not harboring a decay caused by fire singing,—away high in their tops amidst the green of summer there come dead branches,—look for an old scorch at the base of the trunk as the most probable cause of it.

But nature herself occasionally takes a hand in with unthinking men in wounding trees. You notice a young maple or basswood after a time of prolonged drought, with its leaves drooping and curling. You may save the tree's life by promptly and thoroughly saturating the earth about it with scores of pails of water; yet for all that, you will soon be grieved to see that a strip of its thin bark, from two to four inches wide, running up and down the trunk and on the side towards the 2 to 3 o'clock sun, is beginning to wrinkle. The sun has "scalded" it,—overdried it,—and you may as well, if you care to have nice trees, begin at once to look for one to replace it.

And I query if the sun does not sometimes get too attentive even in the winter. When a tree is frozen through, the expanding ice crystals cause a strain throughout the trunk. If now after severe cold the bright sun rapidly thaws a side of the trunk, it creates an area or line, up and down, of less resistance, and where there would occur a scald in the summer time there comes a crack in the winter. But the crack often runs high up among the branches, whereas the scald stops when it reaches the shadow of the leaves. Other forces may cause trees thus to burst open, but in my observation of such injury I have as yet found no crack not on the southerly side of the tree, and mostly they are toward the south-west. The suggestion is to provide trees with parasols of whatever sort. In nature, steep northern slopes are thus effective.

Yet of all the methods of inflicting injury upon a tree most imbued with the pure essence of wickedness, if you value the good will of the board of trustees you will not, in the cemetery, even presume to think of hitching your horse to a tree. This calls for the rarest exhibition of self-restraint, as the board well knows, and yet they hope it.

Red Wing, Minn. D. D.

Burglars tried their hand on the safe of Mt. Hope Cemetery, Rochester, N. Y., recently, and played havoc with the large office safe but failed on the money chest within. The records and books were uninjured. As the superintendent remarked this is a new departure in cemetery work.

The Shaw Mausoleum, St. Louis, Mo.

Probably the first impression of most visitors to the Memorial and tomb of Henry Shaw is one of surprise, and it is not unlikely that strangers visit the famous Garden where it stands without realizing that it contains a tomb.

It is so unlike all preconceived ideas of a tomb that from a distance it might easily be mistaken for a summerhouse. And instead of looking funereal it is a cheerful object. But on closer inspection its purpose can hardly be mistaken, although its details are sometimes misunderstood.

Taken as it stands it is by no means a gloomy adjunct to the garden, notwithstanding the remarks of a visitor, (overheard by the writer,) who tried to harrow up her soul by discovering the dew of death on the literally marble brow of the recumbent statue within.

The unusual shape of the building is accounted for when one learns that Mr. Shaw got his idea of its form from a structure described and illustrated in one of the Encyclopædias of Loudon, the noted Scotch Horticulturalist and Landscape Gardener. This pictured building was, however, roofless, being intended to enclose some sort of a tree which was to emerge from the top in its own good time.

The present building is the second of the same shape that has been built in the garden. The first,

THE SHAW MANSOLEUM.

which still stands at only a short distance from the newer one, was erected some forty years ago of rock-faced limestone. I was told by Mr. Barnett, (the architect who built both structures, and one of the few men who knew Mr. Shaw intimately, not only in a business way but socially,) that the first building originally, had neither roof nor windows, and in his opinion was not intended for a tomb by its eccentric proprietor. Later, it was roofed, the open arches glazed and a marble statue by the German Sculptor Von Muller placed in it.

There seems to be some difference of opinion as to whether the limestone structure was ever intended by Mr. Shaw for his tomb. Some think it was and that he merely became dissatisfied with the material of which it was built, while others hold that using such a building for the purpose was an afterthought. But, be that as it may, some four or five years before his death he gave Mr. Barnett instructions to reproduce the original building in substantial materials, on a slightly larger scale and on a far more solid foundation.

The Mausoleum stands in a grove of mixed trees, oaks, sassafras and sugar maples representing the deciduous class, and pines and hemlocks the evergreen class, in the garden proper, and about two hundred feet from the fence which separates the garden from the lawns surrounding Mr. Shaw's country residence, and in plain view from many of the windows. Every detail of its construction was carried out under the interested supervision of its owner. It is a well proportioned octagonal, red granite building, in what may be called the Italian style, since at least its details are Italian. It is twelve feet in diameter and about thirty-five feet high including the gilded bronze cross which surmounts the semi-oriental roof of copper. It is this roof which gives the structure its misleading summer-house appearance. It has tall windows on seven sides and a door on the eighth all protected for half their height by gratings of vertical iron bars finished at the top with gilded spear heads. The door is distinguished from the windows only by a padlock. The door and windows are of clear glass surrounded by a narrow border of indifferently good stained glass. The castings are all of bronze. The entire building is made as nearly indestructible as possible and its most unusual feature is the massive masonry which underlies the visible structure. This foundation is of stone and concrete to a depth of seven feet and projects beyond the building six feet on all sides. The projecting part supports a stone pavement of the same width. In the middle of this mass, which is also the middle of the diameter of the Mausoleum, is a solid block of limestone in which a space just large enough to admit the casket was cut. The question of the size of this opening troubled Mr. Shaw a great deal. After it was made he thought it too small and spoke to Mr. Barnett about it. The architect, whom Mr. Shaw jokingly alluded to as "his undertaker," made inquiries from a true undertaker and found that it really was too small.

Some three years before Henry Shaw's death there arrived from Germany the recumbent portrait statue of himself made by Von Muller of Munich, from photographs as the sculptor never saw his subject. With the statue were drawings of the marble sarcophagus on which it was to rest, together with the sculptured poppy leaves and seed pods and laurel wreaths in gold bronze which were to adorn the sarcophagus itself. The sarcophagus was made from these drawings in St. Louis under the direction of Architect Barnett and was put in place over the opening in the block of stone beneath the building. The plinth of the sarcophagus, rests on the top of the rock which now contains the casket and mortal remains of Henry Shaw.

The portrait statue was inspected many times by Mr. Shaw and pleased him thoroughly, but was not taken from its case until after his death. It was then placed in its permanent position on the sarcophagus facing the west, presumably because the walk connecting the Shaw mansion grounds with the Garden Conservatories runs by the west side of the Mausoleum and visitors pass that way.

The statue is of the purest white Carrara marble of finest grade, and is a full length, life size reclining figure, with the head and shoulders lifted well above the horizontal by cushions or pillows over which a simple drapery is thrown. The lower part of the figure also is concealed by well handled drapery, but the upper part is shown clad in a frock coat. The left arm falls naturally along the couch outside of the drapery, the fingers curved in an easy life like way, and the right rests on the figure, the hand holding a carefully and artistically chiseled rose. The face is calm, eyes closed, and the expression of it as well as the pose of the entire figure indicates sleep with no suggestion of "death dews" nor, I am sure, did the sculptor intend to represent or suggest anything of the kind.

The flower in the hand does at first glance suggest that it is the sleep of death, but on second thought one realizes its appropriateness as typical of the tastes and favorite pursuits of the founder of Shaw's Garden, now known as the Missouri Botanical Garden. And while the formal coat, collar, and old fashioned stock may seem a little out of place for a sleeping figure, they are quite in keeping with the dignified formality of the Englishman represented. The inscriptions are few and simple. On one side of the marble sarcophagus in sunk, gilded letters is seen:

Henry Shaw,
Born at Sheffield, Eng.
1800.

on the other:

Henry Shaw,
Died at St. Louis
1889.

and on a block of polished blue granite above the door, in larger sunk, gilded letters:

Henry Shaw.

There is no epitaph save the sculptured rose which at least, in some degree, indicates what manner of man bore the name, and lived the long life recorded by the graven letters.

The face of the marble figure leaves a pleasant recollection. It is as though a benevolent, flower loving old man had fallen asleep after a walk in his garden, a lovingly gathered rose still in his hand. The features are full of character, but a benign peacefulness overlies them which seems to indicate a mind at rest. Withal the marble is a work of art, and while one that would be inappropriate in many situations, is fittingly placed in this substantial building, under the shade of noble trees, in the quiet seclusion of a garden that will continue to be a garden as long as the present civilization endures. For the Missouri Botanical Garden is the only legal heir of Henry Shaw, and by his will, its support is provided for while time lasts.

FANNY COPLEY SEAVEY.

The Lily Pond.

I do not know of anything in the shape of floriculture that is so interesting to so many people as the lily pond and the interest increases every year. In the center of a circular bed fifty feet in diameter I made a pond fifteen feet in diameter and two feet six inches in depth, and made it tight with portland cement. I then put in about eighteen inches of loam and well decayed cow manure in equal quantity, and about 8 inches of water. I set in the center a Nelumbium Speciosum but was disappointed in its not blooming. But the lilies were gorgeous. Nymphae Devoniensis, N. Marliacea Chromotella, N. Albida Candissima and N. Cerulea, N. Zansibarensis azure and rosea. Red, yellow, white, and blue. Devoniensis is a night bloomer and it keeps open far into the day, and nearly all day if cloudy. They all bloomed constantly from about July 1st until stopped by cold weather. Around this pond separated by a path three feet wide I had four basins three feet in width. In these I grew Pontedercia Crassipes, (Water Hyacinths,) Papyrus (Egyptian Paper Plant,) Juncus Zebrinus, Sagittarias, double and single, Limnochavis Humboldti, (Water Poppy,) Lobelia Cardinalis, Typha Latifolia, (Cat Tail,) Thalia Devaricata. Sarracenias, several kinds, and wild Rice. Around all this I set out a promiscuous bed, with the different grasses both large and small. Pennisetum Longistylum is a beautiful grass and blooms readily from the seed the first year.

A few plants of Scotch Kale were very pretty and the question was often asked, "what is this?" Antirrhinums and Scabiosas of various colors, and Salvia Splendens, contributed their beautiful colors to make it interesting; Dativia Cornicopia and Wrightii were there, and received their share of attention. Nicotaina Affinis and Collossus, with a few Cannas and Ricinus gave a tropical aspect. Fern leaf Parsley and the low growing Sedums were around the edge of the pond and helped to make it interesting. Other perennials and annuals were there, and vied with each other to prolong the stay of the visitor. I started on Aquatics but found it necessary to deviate somewhat to fully describe my whole bed. This year I shall add Nymphea Laydekeri to my collection. For the bog garden Sagittaria Japeonica fl. pl. is very fine, constantly in bloom, and resembles a carnation pink. Water Hyacinths and water Poppies cannot be flattered. Enough cannot be said in praise of the above Lilies. They can be as easily grown in tubs, but the flowers may be smaller. Try a lily pond. There are two or three parties who make this business a specialty, not far from New York, who, I have no doubt will give any person any information they may desire. Their advertisements can be found in any of the leading papers on floriculture. If you cannot have a pond, grow one in a tub, in a sunny place near your door. And if you do not say the summer has been happier your tastes are different from the writer's.

WILLIAM STONE.

CEMETERY NOTES.

The permanent care fund of Greenwood cemetery, Brooklyn, N. Y., now amounts to $1,608,743.62.

* * *

By a special enactment of the legislature liquor cannot be sold within a half mile of Westview cemetery, Atlanta, Ga.

* * *

Undertakers in New York and Brooklyn, following the example of their brethren in Philadelphia, have started a movement against Sunday funerals.

* * *

Woodlawn Cemetery, New York, was fairly buried in flowers and potted plants on Easter Sunday, notwithstanding the rain. Mrs. Whitney's grave, the plots of Silas Lord, Austin Corbin, Lawrence Turnure, and the Singer family were conspicuous for the attentions bestowed upon them.

* * *

We take the following from a Pennsylvania exchange: "Joseph Pearl, who was refused admission to bury his child in a Hebrew Cemetery, at Bethlehem, because he was unable to purchase a lot, buried the child recently on Sunday night and was arrested for the theft of a grave on Monday."

* * *

The council ordinance committee of New Haven, Conn., on condition that the Grove Street Burial Association would accept an ordinance specifying proper side walk repairs and care of the same in winter, voted to abate the assessments for sewers. The Burial Association claimed that sewers and other street improvements outside bounds of cemetery were of no benefit to it.

* * *

The law of the state of Ohio provides that "burial lots shall be for the sole purpose of interments, subject to the rules prescribed by the management of the cemetery in which they are located, and shall be exempt from taxation, execution, attachment or any other claim, lien or process whatever, if used for burial purposes, and in no wise with a view to profit."

ENTRANCE TO MONTEFIORE BURIAL ASSOCIATION GROUNDS, MINNEAPOLIS, MINN.

A satisfactory settlement has been effected between the lot owners and stockholders of the Woodlawn Cemetery Association of Boston. The cemetery appears to have originated in a speculative investment, in 1853, of the late Henry W. Fuller, and has been so managed that finally the stock is practically owned by his three daughters. The original act of the legislature virtually gave the entire control into the hands of the stockholders and the situation has culminated in a determined effort of the lot owners to acquire rights. All is now peace and it has been agreed to pay the Fuller sisters 6 percent per annum on the $100,000 of stock held by them.

* * *

Catskill, N. Y., is laying out a modern cemetery on the lawn plan with larger sections than are usually found, and broad, well made, roads. There will be no paths or walks aside from the carriage roads to avoid injury to lots which it is necessary to cross in the erection of monuments. The Association will furnish plank for a perfect roadway to any interior lot. There will be five small lakes, one or more fountains, with a collection of rare trees and shrubs so arranged as to produce the best of landscape effect. The grounds are rolling with a gradual slope which have been drained to the depth of six and one-half feet; the soil is sandy loam which will not cave. The Association is incorporated under the general Act of the State as the Catskill Rural Cemetery Association. There is a board of nine directors composed of the representative men of the town and is to be conducted as a public benefit and not as a moneyed investment.

Entrance to the Montefiore Burial Association Grounds, Minneapolis.

We give herewith a front view of the Entrance to the Montefiore Burial Association Grounds, at Minneapolis, Minn. The building will be faced with brown sandstone and red pressed brick, and the roof covered with slate, tile and copper. The size of the chapel, which will be coved, is 22 ft. by 22 ft., and Georgia pine will be used for floor and finish. The gates will be of wrought iron. Mr. S. J. Bowler, the architect, informs us that the improvements, including some 1500 feet of wrought iron fencing and grading, will cost $7,000.

* * *

The necessity of providing the medical schools with subjects for dissection and study, is being recognized as a matter for legislative action in the interests of the profession and the public good, and the enactment of laws enabling public officers to furnish unclaimed bodies to medical societies without public scandal is always a step in the right direction. We note that the people of Milwaukee have recently taken renewed interest in the matter in view of the prospects of another medical school there, and the revised statutes of the state regarding the question have received pointed attention and amendments are suggested.

* * *

The managers of the Elmwood Cemetery, Memphis, Tenn., are moving to lower the mounds over the graves in the "single interment" portion of the grounds, but will not do so without permission. Such an improvement would greatly benefit the appearance of Elmwood.

RULES AND REGULATIONS.

Every cemetery should be governed by certain rules and regulations, which should be printed in pamphlet form for distribution among lot owners. While this has been done in most of the large cemeteries, where the rules are very much alike, we will, for the benefit of the smaller cemeteries, publish in this department such rules as commend themselves for general adoption. Contributions are solicited.

It is very gratifying to note that the management of the principal Catholic cemeteries of the leading cities is in harmony with the progressive ideas now prevailing in cemetery work. The following extracts from the Rules and Regulations governing Calvary Cemetery, Cleveland, O., recently received from the Rev. G. F. Houck, manager, will testify to this:

No fence coping or enclosure of any kind will be permitted on burial lots. Boxes, shells, stone, toys and similar articles scattered upon the graves and lawn are inconsistent with proper keeping of the grounds and will not be permitted.

Hedges, wooden or metal head boards, wooden trellises, chairs or settees, wholly or in part of wood, and large vases or urns, other than of stone, marble or durable metal, are prohibited.

Tablets or crosses of wood, being considered detrimental to the general appearance of the cemetery, are strictly prohibited.

Only one monument of proper design, material and workmanship may be erected upon a lot. Monuments shall not be erected at *single graves*, nor upon lots of a less area than 128 square feet.

No marble or granite *tablet* set in a socket will be allowed in the grounds, and no head-stones or grave mark must be set above grade. Grave marks may be of any form or thickness, but must be set horizontally. Graves will not be mounded to exceed three inches above grade after the ground is settled.

No monument shall be placed on a lot containing less than 128 square feet.

Inscriptions for monuments and head-stones, *stating more than names and dates*, must be submitted to the manager for approval.

The bottom of the lower base of every monument must be squared sufficiently to allow it to rest firmly on the foundation as no wedging will be allowed.

The soliciting of contracts or orders for monuments, head-stones, memorials or any other work will not be allowed in the Cemetery. Signs, notices or advertisements of contractors, stone-cutters, undertakers or any other persons will not be permitted on the cemetery grounds.

Graves will not be mounded to exceed three inches above grade after the ground is settled. *The sodding on graves must not be removed*.

SUGGESTIONS REGARDING FUNERALS.

1. Christian hope and tender resignation ought to prevail at the burial of the dead. Christian thought on such an occasion should instinctively dwell on the immortal soul, not on the corruptible body. Hence the simpler the burial of the dead, the more Christian, the more Catholic it will be.

2. The pomp and display so common at funerals spring from mistaken respect for the dead, and are intended as signs of honor and affection; hence the long line of carriages and the pagan display of flowers. True sorrow avoids ostentation. Simplicity in funeral arrangements is therefore to be recommended. Let the casket be modest, the carriages few and let flowers be omitted, except in the burial of children.

3. The friends of the deceased can best pay their respects to the memory of the dead by accompanying the remains to the church. The family and near relatives should be allowed to inter their beloved dead in private.

4. Another abuse, only too common, is the Sunday funeral. Unless imperative necessity obliges, as in contagious diseases and in times of epidemics, funerals should not be on Sundays. Public sentiment, founded on the best of reasons, is opposed to them, and in many cities they are prohibited, in Catholic as well as in public cemeteries.

☞ In Calvary Cemetery no interments will be allowed in the *forenoon* on Sundays, and it is desired *that as far as possible no interments take place on that day*.

We ought to add that Mr. F. Eurich, of Woodlawn Cemetery, Toledo, O., was entrusted with the laying out of Calvary Cemetery.

◁ CEMETERY REPORTS. ▷

We have received the report of the Board of Trustees of the Greenwood cemetery of Brooklyn, N. Y., for 1893. Much work in the way of improvement was carried on, and some adjacent lots purchased to prevent unsightly surroundings. The damage caused by the storm of last summer required an outlay of some $5,000 for repairs. The trustees completed the work of removing unsightly hedges enclosing burial lots, and it is the intention the present year to remove all dilapidated structures enclosing burial lots unless the owners give proof that they themselves will attend to it.

A close privet hedge was set out some 500 feet long to serve as a screen to the plant of the cemetery.

The General Fund for the Improvement and Permanent Care of the cemetery now amounts to $1,608,703.62, the year's addition being $106,794.36. The Trust Fund for the Special and Permanent Care of Lots amounts to $375,658.91, $19,065 being added the past year. 5,263 interments were made, making a total of 276,577. The receipts for cemetery lots and graves were $194,952.05; disbursements for labor and openings of graves and care of same, $118,201.55. The average number of men employed was 224, and of horses 32, 22 of which were owned by the cemetery.

* * *

The report of the Board of Trustees of Forest Hills cemetery, Jamaica Plain, Mass., for 1893, states that the past year has been as financially prosperous as any previous one. There were 108 lots sold and 927 interments made, making a total to Dec. 31, 1893, of 27,120. Special attention has been given to the improvement of the grounds. 62 monuments have been erected, and 314 headstones, tablets and markers. 3 iron fences and 2 curbings were removed. An average of 77 men were employed during the year.

The system of grass paths has proved a complete success both in economy and appearance, and the flowering shrubs which have been liberally planted are becoming noticeable features of the cemetery. The number of lots under perpetual care is 2,718, and annually 688. Four new greenhouses, costing $10,724.47 have been completed.

The Permanent Fund now amounts to $16,863.93, an increase of $5,798.94. The Perpetual Care Fund has been increased $34,595.03, and is now $543,825.96. Receipts for lots and graves amounted to $44,886.50; for use of chapel and receiving tomb and chapel, $3,725; for annual care of lots, $9,344.40. In the expenditures there is a sum of $180 for labor cleaning headstones.

✢ CREMATION. ✢

In a circular recently received from the Cincinnati Cremation Company, the following advantages are set forth, which commend themselves:

There is none of the dangerous exposure of mourners to the weather, which attends open air services in cold and wet seasons; none of the jar upon the sensibilities of the friends which accompanies the throwing of earth upon the coffin. The health of the living, which is often seriously assailed by the nearness of decaying bodies to habitations, is scrupulously protected by reducing the bodies at once to harmless ashes; an end which is accomplished by burial only after a very long period of corruption; while in times of pestilence, or in contagious diseases, the spread of infection is wholly prevented by cremation. And on the score of economy, the great and burdensome cost of the funeral is diminished, as the active energies of all friends of the system are being directed toward encouraging simpler coffins and an inexpensive last disposal of the ashes in urns.

The price charged by this company for incineration is $25, which includes the use of chapel, when desired, and a plain receptacle for the ashes.

* * *

A correspondent of the Manchester, N. H., *American* has gathered the opinions of four of the leading clergymen of that city on the subject of cremation. It is interesting to note in this connection that the clergy in many localities are falling into line in favorable discussion of the question.

Rev. W. C. McAllester, pastor, First Baptist Church: "I am in favor of this mode of disposing of dead bodies, and I believe that it is only a question of time before cremation will be adopted as the best and most practical way of solving a difficult problem. It shocks the sensibilities of the people, I know, to have the bodies of their friends burned, but it is like other great innovations, the people will overcome their prejudices in time."

Rev. W. H. Morrison, pastor, First Universalist Church: "I am a firm believer in cremation and always have been. I believe in it for sanitary reasons and I can see no possible objections to this method of disposing of the bodies of our dead from a religious point of view."

Rev. Francis S. Bacon, People's Tabernacle: "I can see no objections to cremation, and I am in favor of it for many reasons. From a religious standpoint I believe it makes no difference as far as the soul is concerned what becomes of the body."

Rev. W. H. Ramsay, Unitarian Church: "I believe cremation is the only rational and scientific method of the disposal of dead bodies, and I believe that in time the civilized people of the world will come to view the matter in this light. It has always been my wish that my body should be disposed of in this manner after my death, and as I said, my opinion is that this is the only rational and scientific method of disposing of the body after the soul has departed from it."

* * *

Miss Frances E. Willard places herself on record as follows:

"I have the purpose to help forward progressive movements even in my latest hours and hence hereby decree that the earthly mantle which I shall drop ere long when my real self passes onward into the world unseen, shall be swiftly unfolded in flames and rendered powerless harmfully to affect the health of the living. Let no friend of mine say aught to prevent the cremation of my cast-off body. The fact that the popular mind has not come to this decision renders it all the more my duty who have seen the light to stand for it in death, as I have sincerely meant in life to stand by the great cause of the poor, oppressed humanity. There must be explorers along pathways, scouts in all armies. This has been my 'call' from the beginning both by nature and by nurture; let me be true to its inspiring and cheery mandate even unto the last."

* * *

The New York legislature has just been asked to amend the law passed in 1888, whereby the seller of a monument placed in any cemetery of the state has a lien on such monument for any purchase money remaining unpaid, by permitting large monuments to be sold for debt by public auction in the cemetery itself. While there were many considerations in regard to the old law which entitled it to approval we object decidedly to the proposed amendment. A serious conflict of ideas would immediately result.

Association of American Cemetery Superintendents.

WM. SALWAY, "Spring Grove" Cincinnati, O., President.
T. McCARTHY, "Swan Point" Providence, R. I., Vice-President.
F. EURICH, Woodlawn, Toledo, O., Secretary and Treasurer.

The Eighth Annual Convention of the Association will be held at Philadelphia, September 11, 12, and 13, 1894.

Resolutions Adopted at the Seventh Annual Convention of the Association of American Cemetery Superintendents.

Resolved: That it is the sense of this convention that all Sunday funerals be discouraged as much as possible.

Resolved: That it is the sense of this meeting that all headstones or markers should be limited to the height of the sod or the level of the surface of the ground.

Resolved: That it is the sense of this meeting that vaults and catacombs be discouraged and if possible prevented in cemeteries.

Notice!

To the Members of the Association of American Cemetery Superintendents:

The Executive Committee has decided upon the 11th, 12th and 13th of September as the dates for holding the Eighth Annual Convention of the association in the city of Philadelphia.

FRANK EURICH, Sec'y and Treas.

Strangers in China have the greatest difficulty when meeting a funeral or wedding procession on the street to distinguish one from the other. The same red cloth coolies, carrying roasted pig and other dainties, appear in the procession, the same smaller coolies carrying cheap paper ornaments, and the same noisy turnout. And all this when some old person is being carried to his last resting place, as when the youngest and most beautiful of celestial maidens is being carried to the new home prepared by her husband. The crowd at the funeral is as noisy as at a wedding and the guests eat just as much. The only difference, indeed, between the two is that in the center of one the bride is carried in an inclosed sedan chair, borne on the shoulders of some men, and followed by her bridesmaids. In that of the other the coffin is carried and the mourners follow. Indeed, an English writer says that no event in the life of a Chinaman is half so important as his funeral.

The MODERN CEMETERY is becoming very valuable to superintendents. * * * I hope you will continue in your good work making it still more interesting and valuable.   L. J. WELLS.

CHAS. N. SNYDER, Sec'y, WEST LAUREL HILL CEMETERY, PHILADELPHIA. No association can afford to manage a cemetery in our day upon the narrow conception of a single individual, be he engineer, landscape gardener and veteran grave digger combined—the MODERN CEMEERY shows him the true work.

H. H. PARK, PRES'T CYPRESS LAWN, SAN FRANCISCO. ** The MODERN CEMETERY is doing a great work by educating the public to the appreciation of burying their dead in a beautiful park instead of a stoneyard.

Publisher's Department.

The receipt of Cemetery Literature and Trade Catalogues will be acknowledged in this column.

TO ADVERTISERS. THE MODERN CEMETERY is the only publication of its class and will be found a valuable medium for reaching cemetery officials in all parts of the United States.

TO SUBSCRIBERS. Cemetery officials desiring to subscribe for a number of copies regularly to circulate among their lot owners, should send for our special terms. Several well known cemeteries have already adopted this plan with good results.

Contributions on matters pertaining to cemeteries are solicited. Address all communications to
R. J. HAIGHT, 331 Dearborn St., CHICAGO.

Cemetery Literature received: Rules and regulations, Cypress Hills cemetery, Petaluma, Sonoma county, Cal. Descriptive circular, with rules and regulations, of the crematory of the Cincinnati Cremation Company.

Annual Report, Forest Hills Cemetery, Boston, Mass., 1894; Report of the Board of Trustees of the Greenwood Cemetery, Brooklyn, N. Y., for 1893; Charter, By-Laws, Rules and Regulations, Lowell, Mass., Cemetery, 1894.

A New Flower Vase.

The accompanying illustration represents a new flower vase for graves made by M. D. Jones & Co., Boston, Mass, which displays some novel and useful points. The design is attractive, and it is finished in enamel white, which gives it the appearance of marble. It is equally serviceable for bouquets or for sprays of flowers, while its shape admits of more than the ordinary supply of water. It is furnished with an iron stem and stands 10 inches high out of the ground.

Its durability and reasonable cost should lead to the displacement of many of the fragile and less substantial ornaments now so largely used.

It will be remembered by members of the Association of American Cemetery Superintendents that the matter of the necessity of a fender on lawn mowers was discussed at some length at the last convention and left in the hands of a committee. One of the lawn-mower manufacturers who gave the question prompt consideration was the Philadelphia Lawn Mower Co., of Philadelphia. In this company's advertisement which appears on another page is an illustration of a lawn mower with the improved fender which has been adopted for its simplicity and durability. This improvement, consisting of a steel rod, rubber covered, would seem to meet every requirement suggested in the aforementioned discussion.

THE MODERN CEMETERY.

THE MODERN CEMETERY.
AN ILLUSTRATED MONTHLY JOURNAL DEVOTED TO THE INTEREST OF CEMETERIES

R. J. HAIGHT, Publisher,
334 Dearborn Street, CHICAGO.

Subscription $1.00 a Year in Advance.   Foreign Subscription $1.15.
Special Rates on Six or More Copies.

VOL. IV.   CHICAGO, MAY, 1894.   NO. 3.

CONTENTS.

BURIAL REFORM (Concluded)............................. 25
SANITARY SEPULTURE....................................... 27
*CALVARY CEMETERY, ST. LOUIS, MO..................... 27
*THE HUMBOLDT MONUMENT, BERLIN..................... 30
THE VIRGINIA LAW LICENSING EMBALMERS............ 30
*CEMETERY PLANTING IV................................... 31
CEMETERY NOTES... 33
RULES AND REGULATIONS................................... 35
CORRESPONDENCE.. 35
EDUCATING ANTI-MONUMENT IDEAS...................... 36
QUESTION BOX... 36
PUBLISHER'S DEPARTMENT.................................. 36
LANDSCAPE ARCHITECTURE................................. IV
ROADS... V

*Illustrated.

Burial Reform.*

I wish I might next say the wise word concerning our funeral customs. They are happily much modified. The long argumentative sermon is happily gone from most communities, I trust. But there still remains the too public invasion of private homes, the long delays, the exposure and expense of the carriage procession to the cemetery, and the sad desecration of nature "called floral decorations." The torture to the artistic sense as well as the waste of the delicate product of nature involved in the so-called "set pieces" of our city funerals, is so great, that happily the abuse seems to be in a fair way of correcting itself. Let me outline my idea of a funeral, hoping that you will take it as a suggestion which may recur to you in some Gethsemane moment of your lives. If the deceased was an inconspicuous member of society, let the sacred privacy of life be not disturbed in death; let there be a quiet tender memorial half hour at home, where the family and their nearest friends will gather to listen to a few chosen selections from deathless writings, a breathing of sympathy and aspiration, a word of commemoration for the dead and of companionship with the living. Flowers? Yes,

*Continued from April issue.

indeed, a few if brought by loving hands and arranged in the simple wholesome way of the home. Singing? yes, if the dear familiar things are sung by loving and familiar voices. No, if it means the professional quartet hired for the occasion. After this memorial half hour let the friends take loving leave and go to their homes leaving the bereaved with their dead. At another hour, sufficiently removed to effectually break up the temptation to stay and see, let the undertaker and the necessary friends come and take the body away. Why should the family in their overstrained condition expose themselves to the profitless ride to the cemetery, and prolong the added strain of the unsatisfactory leave taking? If the deceased is a public character, one, who in his life made himself a part of the community, let him serve once more, and let the memorial service be held either before or after burial in the church of his choice or the hall where the community are wont to congregate, but let the vulgarity of a public funeral be reduced to a minimum.

Instead of the expensive interference with nature's law of decomposition in the way of hard wood or metalic coffin in outer box, let the body be encased in an osier or pine casket, that which will readily relinquish to mother earth her earthly treasure.

The next extravagance I would correct is the monumental burden. It is estimated that there is an investment of two million dollars in monuments in Graceland cemetery alone. Monuments are among the most perishable of stone structures. An authority says but few monuments survive even a century, but even then they survive the memory of the lives they commemorate. And their fulsome compliments are read as flippantly as the amusing epitaphs that form the staple of the funny column of the newspapers.

Oliver Wendell Holmes, remembering that three of the graveyards of conservative Boston have been tumbled over during this century says: "The stones have been shuffled about like chestnuts. Nothing short of the day of Judgment will tell whose dust lies beneath."

But all this only crowds us to the ultimate logic of our reform. The graveyards themselves are only a menace alike to the physical and spiritual well-being of the community. They are a relic of barbaric and superstitious ages, and they will have to vanish eventually before the mandates of reason, science and poetry. To-day we are complacent over our burying ground simply because we are ignorant of what is the clear testimony of science in the matter. Already Chicago has overrun several sets of cemeteries. The one redeeming feature of a city cemetery is that the dead are made to serve the living by holding ground for awhile, which eventually will be wrenched from them and given back to the living in the way of parks.

What is the remedy for all this danger and expense, this idle land, these plague-breeding homes of the dead? Happily for us there is a solution of this perplexity, a solution that is at once economic, effective, simple, beautiful. A solution that meets at once the requirements of sentiment and of science. I mean the prompt restoration of the body to its primal elements by the quick and pure element of fire,—the modern crematory. Scientifically speaking, inhumation and incineration accomplish exactly the same results. Decomposition is but slow combustion. Combustion is but prompt decomposition. In an hour's time there is left but a few pounds of ashes, which are gathered in an urn, preserved in the crematory, given to the friends for burial, or, more fitting and beautiful as it seems to me, scattered upon the grass,—and nature has accomplished in one hour by fire what it would take from twelve to sixty years to accomplish by inhumation; for with mawkish sentimentality we stupidly contest with nature and retard her processes as much as possible by our embalmings and metalic cases. I hope the reform will progress, until by law every cemetery shall be required to offer this alternative to its patrons. I hope the reform in our funeral customs will go on; that our street car companies all over the country will follow the example of the Atchison street railway by putting at the service of the public a funeral car, which may be chartered at a less cost than a hearse and which will carry forty attendants at the price which must now be paid for the carrying of four. I hope these funeral reforms will go on until white and not black will be the symbol of the great mystic nuptial occasion where death woos and wins its groom or bride. Let the funeral reforms go on until the consolation of the bereaved will be found in services of love.

But these reforms will not come any faster than does the growth of reason in religion. They cannot come as long as men in the toils of a mediæval theology tremble in the presence of death as in the presence of an arch-fiend, and go about this world with an ever open ear listening for the crack of doom, when in response to Gabriel's trumpet the ghastly graves are to open and the wasted bodies come forth crawling from under the crushing tons of granite which their successors and kindred ostentatiously piled upon them. These funeral reforms will never come so long as men regard this world accursed and deem the only glory over there. So long as they think that it is one thing to prepare to die and another to prepare to live.

Dr. Charles W. Purdy, before the Chicago Medical Society some years ago, offered the following as a careful estimate: "One and one-fourth times more money is expended annually for funerals in the United States than the government expends for public school purposes. Funerals cost this country in 1880 enough to pay all commercial liabilities in the United States during the year and to give each bankrupt a capital of $8,630 with which to resume business. Funerals cost annually more money than the value of the combined gold and silver yield of the United States in 1880." Now this is not a case of bad financiering nor of bad morals; primarily it is a case of bad theology. It is fetichism. It is superstition. It is the slavishness of dogma. What we want is to emancipate souls. Out of a petition of 23,365 Germans to the Reichstag for a law permitting cremation, there were only ten names of Protestant ministers appended, and three of rabbis. We must give to the world the sweeter thought of nature, of diviner trust in God, a holier calm in the presence of the inevitable, more restfulness in the eternal arms. We want a new emphasis on character, not on show or creed. We want to realize the truth which dear old Sir Thomas Browne stated over two hundred years ago in his "Urn Burial." In this he says: "There is no antidote against the opium of time. Our fathers find their graves in our short memories. Gravestones tell truth scarcely forty years. To be nameless in worthy deeds exceeds an infamous history. The greater part must be content to be found in the register of God, not in the record of man. Egyptian ingenuity was vanity, feeding the wind and folly. Mummy has become merchandise. Mizraim cures wounds and Pharaoh is sold for balsam. Five languages secured not the epitaph of Giordanus."

"The noblest monument in Graceland," said the superintendent, "is the great elm that was moved fifteen miles to mark the resting place of the man that loved it." It will outlast your granite shaft.

O let us have done with the miserable graveyard business; let us not think of death but of life. Let the dead bury the dead. Selfishness in tears is no more noble than selfishness in smiles. Let the tears of the sorrowing be illumined with love and they become crystaline lenses showing forth in magnified and clearer outline the present duty, the near opportunity, the deathless life, the endless love, the life in God, with man, for truth, the life that is free from the terrors of the grave, the life that is now eternal, triumphant and ever blessed.

Sanitary Sepulture.

The science of chemistry has given us a knowledge of the dangers to which our ancestors exposed themselves when interring their dead beneath their churches or in the grounds immediately surrounding them says a writer in the *Independent*:

"When land grew scarce in London the graves were opened and used over and over again, till in some of them the surface was raised to a level with the church windows. With the progress of science men began to discern that the dead could exercise a most deleterious influence over the living. Early in this century the subject attracted the attention of thoughtful men, among them Sir Edwin Chadwick, and in 1843 he made a report to Parliament on the enormous number of burials taking place in London annually; and he never remitted his efforts, till in the burial act of 1855, intramural interments were finally forbidden. While it is an easy matter to discover and point out evils, it is quite another affair to devise and supply remedies. After the passage of the act, the next step was to provide some other place which should be equally desirable in the eyes of surviving relatives. It took many years to win the victory that forbade further interments within the city limits; and when one sees a funeral group committing a body to the earth in Trinity church-yard in New York city, one wishes that the English law could, for the nonce, stretch across the Atlantic, for certainly there are already sources enough of pollution in that crowded vicinity.

The burial act led to the establishment of cemeteries in England, and the agitation of the subject there led to early and vigorous action here. Scientific and sanitary considerations caused trees and shrubbery to be planted. The scientific theory on which the planting proceeded was that the vegetation would necessarily absorb the carbonic acid and other gases generated by bodily decay.

In London it had been proved that shallow wells in the vicinity of grave-yards were polluted by the drainage from them, and the general awakening to the matter of pure water supply caused them to be closed, and then the question was asked: Cannot these old, disused burial places be made of use to the living? and now they have been converted into pleasant parks and playgrounds, till there are no less than 173 of these breathing places within the city, and of course these places have long ago become perfectly harmless to the living. Seymour Haden, an experienced medical man, as well as a charming artist, in a paper read before the Liverpool medical institution defines what he and the other burial-reform champions consider perfectly sanitary sepulture—that is to say, burial in an easily perishable envelope. He says a body buried in such a way that the earth may have access to it, does not remain in the earth, but returns to the atmosphere. Suppose a body buried three or four feet below the surface, the earth as earth affects it in no way whatever. The part played by the earth in its resolution is that of a mere porous medium between it and the air that is above it. Through this medium the air with its dews and its rain filters, and when it reaches the body oxidizes it—that is to say, resolves it into new and harmless products; and then these new products passing upward again, through the same sieve-like medium, re-enter the atmosphere and become the elements of its renewal, and of the nourishment and growth of plants. The body, in fact, literally, as well as figuratively, ascends from the dead, and fulfils the cycle of its pilgrimage by becoming again the source and renewal of life.

Calvary Cemetery, St. Louis, Mo.

On my way to Calvary, the large and widely known Catholic Cemetery of St. Louis, I tried to recall the impressions of a previous visit, made some twelve or fifteen years before, and found them to be: outside; a high, shaky and dishevelled picket fence: inside; dense shade, deep ravines, and an impenetrable wilderness of stones.

Returning after so long an interval striking alterations are observable, but enough remains of the former conditions to make the old impressions partly those of to-day, especially in one direction—the stones are still there. Indeed in some parts of the grounds they have increased and multiplied marvelously.

Head stones, foot-stones, corner-stones, coping-stones, stones as gate posts where there are no gates, at the head of flights of stone steps, often where no steps are needed.

Other changes are all in the line of improvements, most of which are marked, and of a character that places the cemetery in the front rank of those leading the modern movement that will result in the universal establishment of tasteful homes for the dead—an evidence of civilization as essential as tasteful homes for the living, and as sure in time to be the rule rather than the exception.

If interior decoration followed in the wake of the Centennial, surely exterior decoration may be expected as part of the outcome of the World's Fair.

The present superintendent of Calvary, Mr. Matthew P. Brazill, who has been in charge of the cemetery about ten years, is a progressive man. He has had the taste and perception to catch the modern idea in cemetery matters, and is not only in touch with the good work that is being done here and there in the United States, but as far as possi-

FLORISSANT AVENUE ENTRANCE, CALVARY CEMETERY, ST. LOUIS, MO.

ble is putting the best features of such work into practice at Calvary. But he finds it difficult to apply some of his good ideas, and were it not that he is so fortunate as to have the vigorous backing of the Vice-President of his board (who is acting President,) Mr. J. B. C. Lucas, a man of taste as well as of great influence, his position would be more trying. But intelligent appreciation of one's work is a great factor in its successful conduct.

Since Mr. Brazill's appointment many improvements have been made, and the cemetery has been enlarged by the purchase of an adjoining farm of 240 acres. It now contains about five hundred acres and is the third in size in the country; Greenwood, Brooklyn, and Spring Grove, Cincinnati leading it. Its situation is the same as that of Bellefontaine, being on the bluffs that face the Mississippi River north of St. Louis.

The two cemeteries are separated by a street which runs east and west connecting old Bellefontaine road, (formerly the Post "trail" and now Broadway,) with Florissant road, which street forms the western boundary of both cemeteries. The entire grounds are now enclosed by a neat and durable wire fence seven feet high, with suitable iron railings and gates at the two entrances. The "lower" and older of these gives old Broadway, which is the eastern boundary of the cemetery, for its entire length, and is down on the level of the low land lying between the bluffs and the river. Just inside this gate is the old lodge, (for many years this was the only entrance to the grounds.) The entering roadway at once divides and curves away up the natural ravines, around the face of the bluffs and out of sight.

Mr. Brazill says that he finds the landscapes ready made and only has to lay out roads. Which, however is not the whole truth, for he has also cut out a forest of trees, all told, to open up the vistas which make the beauties of the landscapes visible. This cutting has been judiciously done, and there are fine views with charming play of light and shade in the picturesque ravines, down the gently declining roadways, and out over the almost naturally terraced hillsides to the sunny valley and great sweeping river, pouring in these early spring days a wonderful flood of turbulent yellow water towards the Gulf.

The "lower" entrance is to my mind more artistic than the more pretentious new "upper" entrance, which is at the west side of the grounds and is now much more used, because more accessible than the old one. At the new one there are duplicate gateways for carriages and pedestrians, and the entrance is flanked by two semi-gothic buildings, the office and lodge, built of rock-faced limestone with rubbed sandstone trimmings. Their rather high pitched roofs are of six sided red slates with geometric designs in green slate. In general appearance this entrance is rather picturesque, an effect that will be increased when the good planting already done has time to show its character more fully.

Ampelopsis Veitchii is appropriately used as a climber for the buildings and its delicate tracery is distinctly outlined against the light stone although at this time (March) quite leafless. When it surrounds the square gothic windows and gets up to the eaves the entrance will be a pretty picture. There are also Clematises and well selected shrubs so placed that they cannot fail to greatly increase the beauty of the ensemble, and which do much already to take from the bare newness of this part of the cemetery.

Calvary is conducted on good business principles, and everything is kept in good shape. The barns are one hundred feet long and there are tool houses, repair shops, a neatly kept brick and stone yard, and all appliances for the proper conduct of the work.

There is a large Nursery filled with thousands of

young deciduous and evergreen trees, and much good shrubbery, all of which will come in nicely in reclaiming the old farm recently purchased, and which is now being fitted for cemetery purposes by plowing, grading, sowing to grass, planting and road making.

A good many summer flowers are supplied by the inexpensive method of starting annuals such as Phlox Drummondi, Pansies, Verbenas, Salvias, etc., in hot beds; a long line of them testify to the numbers grown. Cannas, Hollyhocks and Gladioli

"Wooded Island," and in certain beautiful plantings on the terraces, at the World's Fair, will be glad to see their use become more general.

At all available points in the old grounds, bits of tasteful planting are seen which give promise of even better things on the new ground where control can be exercised from the outset.

No new copings, fences, or hedges are allowed in Calvary and lot owners are encouraged to remove old ones, as well as vigorously discouraged in the matter of setting up any useless and meaningless stones. Good monuments, those that mean something, and teach mankind lessons worth remembering are heartily welcomed.

Calvary abounds in old historic names, as Knapp, Lucas, Chouteau, Benoist, VonPuhl, etc., but no monument in it receives the attention that is given the

ENTRANCE AT BROADWAY.

are also used, and some good hardy herbaceous plants, as Japanese Irises, Clematises and Pæonies are well established in some parts of the grounds. In a small valley from which the ground rises rather abruptly on all but one side is a lakelet. The steep slope directly behind it, as seen from the drive, is thickly set with evergreens which, when larger, will carry out the desired effect of a tiny mountain lake. At present this plantation is at a stage that draws from Mr. Brazill glances of mingled pride and despair such as one fancies that Mrs. Robbins is still bestowing on the piney sand hill she describes so graphically in her "Rescue of an old Place." At a good point on the lower, more cultivated side of this little body of water, it is pleasant to note that ornamental grasses have been given a place, and even in winter they have a charm. Eulalia Japonica, Zebrina and E. Gracillima, as well as Erianthus Ravenna look at home in this location. Those who saw the delightful effects produced by these hardy grasses, last fall, on the shores of the

VIEW OF TERRACE NEAR BROADWAY ENTRANCE.

unpretending one that marks the resting place of Gen. Wm. T. Sherman. It was designed by the General himself and is a simple head stone on which are carved crossed flags that droop in heavy folds on either side of the inscription which merely records the name and facts of birth and death. Above the flags appears the cartridge box inscribed with the famous "Forty Rounds"—the well-known motto on the badge of Sherman's Army Corps.

This is a departure from the stereotyped monumental style prevalent at Calvary, (as indeed, in every large cemetery,) and so is the monument recently completed in memory of Mrs. Winifred Patterson, a notably charitable woman who died in 1891. It is called the "Widow's Mite" and is an adaptation of Dore's Bible illustration of the same name. It is beautiful in itself and it typifies a living virtue that every passer-by is the better for having been reminded of. It belongs to the order of memorial designs that it is hoped will become more general, designs that mean something, that are fitly chosen, and that have artistic merit.

The beauty spot of Calvary is the Lucas Plot—one which any cemetery might be proud of. It occupies a naturally lovely site on the rounded point of a hill top. The grass slopes up in a gentle swell from the drive that outlines two sides and the blunt point of a triangle. The planting is admirable. At the back, the highest part of the plot, on either side are groups of tall evergreens, White Pines being prominent, in front of them and near the border of the turf as it slopes to the roadway are handsome plantations of well grown dwarf evergreens, Mugho Pines and Prostrate Juniper; while still lower and nearer together, as the blunt point of the triangle is approached, two large groups, (really small plantations), of fine hardy deciduous shrubs flank the entering graveled walk, and complete the outline of the plot against the driveway. As it should be the shaft is the only stone on the lot, (unless, indeed, inconspicuous markers,) and it is a pity it is not in better keeping with its surroundings. It is badly proportioned and clumsy, so noble a setting deserves a perfect monument. But, barring the shaft, the Lucas plot is the most satisfactory I have seen.

Calvary being the only prominent Catholic Cemetery in this Catholic city it is naturally a busy place. It takes always as much as one-fourth, (and sometimes the proportion rises to one-third,) of the mortality of St. Louis. This means a vast amount of attendant work as well, removals, of course, being very numerous. Some forty men and ten teams are employed.

The work is conducted in the most methodical way. A system of bells, something after the manner of the plan of fire-bells, is in use and works well, tending to save time and prevent confusion. One tap announces to the Supt., wherever he may be that he is wanted at the office; two, calls the sexton, Anthony Dwyer, who has spent 33 consecutive years in the service of Calvary; and other taps and combinations direct the movements of the various squads of men. The calls are announced to the man in the bell tower near the middle of the grounds, by telephone from either the upper or lower entrance.

As in all cemeteries where modern ideas are sought to be put in practice the public look upon them as useless, if not improper innovations, and it is difficult to overcome the feeling that dreary, iron bound customs that have become honored solely through the dignity of repeated observance, are right and should be continued. Here a vast number of the owners of single graves and small lots belong to the class that gets its ideas of the fitness of things from those who sell the "things." In this case they take the very material form of stones, and the vendors are of the opinion that the more there are of them the better. And among the prejudiced foreigners, of whom there are so many represented here, there is the feeling that if one buys a stone all the rest must do likewise. The pity of it is seen to be the greater when it is remembered that in nine cases out of ten the buyer needs bread rather than a stone.

But where every thing good and fitting is so heartily welcomed, and every evidence of taste encouraged, progress is bound to be made. And the entering wedge is already in place. As is to be expected the changes are evident on the plots of enlightened owners, and as soon as enough of these accept the better class of improvements the others will follow suit, and the new part of Calvary will undoubtedly be a far less stony way to travel.

FANNY COPLEY SEAVEY.

The Humboldt Monument, Berlin.

In the new park, in the northerly part of the City of Berlin, the Humboldt-hain, a park in many respects fuller of promise than the older ones, the great naturalist Humboldt is at last commemorated in a most fitting manner, and as if for emphasis in this same park by a most unique monument. It is described by Mr. C. Bolle, of Berlin, in *Garden and Forest*.

"The Marsh of Brandenburg is situated in a vast plain, far from any mountains. No minerals exist there except scattered boulders—those 'foundlings' which were transported to us by the disturbances of the glacial epoch. Nowhere do the foundation-rocks pierce the soil to recall, amid these sands and meadows, the hills and ridges of other lands. Even the great isolated stones are becoming rare, having been used in the construction of buildings and highways. But where they still exist they attract attention all the more strongly on this account.

It was by the use of these accumulations of boulders that the tumuli of very ancient times were built—monumental sepulchres of forgotten generations. The idea was quickly conceived that the memory of Humboldt should be honored with a prodigious cairn. Unchiseled stone was appropri-

THE MEGALITHIC HUMBOLDT MONUMENT, BERLIN.

ate for him, since he began his career as a miner and geologist. The Archæological studies of Herr Friedel pointed toward the same end, and I had the happiness to assist these slowly ripening projects with my most ardent sympathy. At the outset the intention was to construct the cairn with stones picked up on all the sites, in every part of the globe, which Humboldt had visited, or, at least which were connected with his studies. This plan was not without its attractions, it was finally abandoned, and, perhaps, not to the disadvantage of the monument; for, from an æsthetic point of view, it would have been a mixture of very heterogeneous elements that would have violated the geological conscience of Humboldt. Certainly it was better to confine the material to the products of this land itself. In the severe grandeur of its accomplishment the fundamental idea now appears dignified and appropriate, and speaks to the heart with a truly antique simplicity.

On a gently sloping elevation rises the primitive structure of rough stones, vaguely recalling the cyclopean walls of Greece or Italy. No trace of the hand of man is visible upon it. Two enormous longitudinal blocks seem to have been set, one upon the other, by the arms of giants. A third, equally colossal, but round in shape, lies beside them, while a multitude of large and small stones advance unsymmetrically to the right and the left, in an irregularity which is at once harmonious and picturesque, the whole being a faithful copy of primitive Nature as revealed upon this very soil.

The upper of the two great monoliths was found near Charlottenburg. It is of a pure deep rose-color and strangely traversed by irregular blackish veins, which mingle upon its surface as in a mystic design. With the other, placed at a lower level, it forms a little grotto, which is sealed with a slab of marble —the only trace of human art—bearing, in German, this inscription:

TO THE MEMORY OF A. VON HUMBOLDT,
THE CITY OF BERLIN.
1869.   1887.

A Lotus-blossom is sculptured beside it. The date 1887 marks the completion of the monument, which, contrary to custom, was never inaugurated by any official solemnity, but only by a modest ceremony organized by the Historical Society of Berlin, with Herr Friedel, as president, at its head.

A living spring of water trickles from the concavity of the rock, to disappear in the neighboring grounds as a little rivulet From the platform in front of the cairn there opens a charming view across the vast lawn, separated into two parts by a bosquet of foliage. Farther away the eye wanders amid the verdure of the park, rich in rare plants, beyond which, are groups of houses which, according to the character of the district, have nothing remarkable about them. Above all rest the golden vapors of the city.

Happily, trees existed here before building was begun. The middle distance behind the megalithic monument is, therefore, verdurous with a little grove of Locusts already fully grown. A new plantation would have contrasted too forcibly with the archaic aspect of the structure. Citizens of the great Republic so beloved by Humboldt, may well consider it an homage to their country that trees of an American species throw their shade upon this sacred soil. Certain Spruces from Norway, sickly and smothered by the urban atmosphere, count for little. The plants which adorn the cenotaph itself are few and provisional. Lost among these blocks of stone, they will always play a subordinate role. In the near vicinity, however, a richer development of vegetation will probably be secured later on. At present some Heaths and Saxifrages suffice to give an appearance of verdure to these solid masses which nourish nothing else except some dwarf Yews and a little Ivy."

To Virginia belongs the honor of being the first state to pass a law for the licensing of embalmers. Its action is limited to cities of five thousand or more of population. It creates a state board of embalming consisting of five members, appointed by the governor, one of whom shall also be a member of the State Board of Health. From the passage of the act, every person engaged, or desiring to engage in embalming within the State of Virginia, shall apply to the state board of embalming for a license, accompanying the same with the license fee of five dollars, whereupon the applicant, shall present himself or herself on a fixed date before said board for examination, when if the applicant is of good moral character, with skill and knowledge of the science of embalming and the care and disposition of the dead, and has a reasonable knowledge of sanitation and the disinfection of bodies of deceased persons, and the apartment, clothing and bedding in case of death from infectious or contagious diseases, the board shall issue to said applicant a license to practice said science of embalming and the care and disposition of the dead, and shall register such applicant as a duly licensed embalmer. Such license shall be signed by a majority of the board and attested by its seal.

Cemetery Planting.—IV.

So, let us not neglect to use vines. No planting can be picturesque without them, and they can and often do, transform the commonplace into something irresistibly charming.

One who has seen the City of Vicksburg in April or in May, when smothered in her creamy odorous honeysuckle draperies, or New Orleans hidden away under climbing roses, Confederate Jessamine, Bignonia, both yellow and pale lilac, climbing masses of Ficus repens, Chinese Wisterias, which they say down there is satisfied with nothing less than a four story house to climb over; honeysuckles in variety, English Ivy and many others, is not likely to underestimate the glorifying effect of vines.

But there are plenty of other good things to be remembered. Something for sun and shade, for every variety of surface and for every situation.

Among the shrubs that promise good results in cemetery work are the various Spiræas but best of them all, it seems to me, S. Van Houttei which appears able to withstand heat and cold, drouth and overplus of moisture wonderfully well, besides being pleasing in foliage and surpassingly lovely when in flower.

And the hardy Japanese single roses, Rosa rugosa and R. rugosa alba, are excellent—barring their sometimes annoying habit of suckering. They flowered all summer at the World's Fair and were green, vigorous and full of buds when frost came. Another thing that did remarkably well during the hot, dry and really trying summer of '93 was the Weeping Mulberry. Despite all drawbacks it trailed its slender branches far out over the grass on all sides and was beautifully green to the end of the season, and it bears a feast of fruit for the birds that find in cemeteries more satisfactory conditions for a happy life than any where else, which I take to be an unfavorable, but deserved comment on the manners and customs that obtain around the home of the living.

Hardy Hydrangeas are desirable not only for their fine flowers but because they show them at a season when flowers are comparatively scarce.

Many agreeable effects may be produced by using hardy herbaceous perennials among shrubs. Some of the most pleasing features of the landscape border of the Wooded Island at the Fair were secured by this method.

The shrubberies contained enough perennials to furnish a running accompaniment of flowers quite through the season. There were campanulas in variety, C. platycodon and C. turbinata, being the best because of their continuous flowering. There were Delphiniums, Columbines, and Oriental poppies of which one blossom makes as great a show as half a dozen ordinary flowers; big mats of the pretty, rather low-growing, Saponaria Ocymoides, Rose Campion, English Daisies, bright scarlet Geum Coccineum, and clumps of the tall rich blue Polemonium coeruleum, all of these were placed at or near the border line where the shrubberies met the closely shorn lawns. To these many others could be added. Phlox Subulata or moss pink, and the white form, P. Sub. Alba, being especially good either as mats for covering the bare ground under larger plants or as border plants where lawns merge into shrubberies.

Farther out among the shrub plantations rose spikes of crimson vervain (there should also have been the splendid color of our native cardinal flower, Lobelia Cardinalis,) all growing in scattered colonies; and here and there the beautiful red Bee Balm, (Monardia Dydima) brightened the border for weeks.

These showy colors were, however, introduced sparingly after nature's woodland fashion. The border was intended to represent natural growths, and did so to perfection. There are copses and thickets, certain corners and spaces, where such treatment would be a charming addition to cemetery planting. And where they occur the style and coloring can be carried through to the end of the season with the many varieties of Golden Rod and Asters. In just such situations I should like to see the season open with carpets of violets and racemes of dainty "squirrel corn" swaying gently above their rosettes of filmy foliage. They would both be lovely crowding around the feet of Berberry and Witch Hazel bushes. Indeed I would bring in the whole troop of wild flowers, everything that would thrive, from ferns up, should have its appropriate place and setting. If there is any better promise of an awakening from the wintry sleep of death, than that furnished by the fragile wild flowers of spring lifting their delicate forms at the first breath that comes from the erstwhile frozen lips of winter—I dont know what it is, unless, indeed, it is the crocuses crowding each other to see out the moment the door is unlocked.

If some one wants a unique and lovely decoration for a cemetery plot let them have a smooth carpet of sward and throughout the space let snowdrops, crocuses, and Poets Narcissus star the spring grass.

Lilacs are so charming when in flower and so lacking in charm at all other times that their inattractiveness should be disguised, or mitigated, by careful treatment. I have already suggested the use of hardy herbaceous vines as a summer drapery for them, and in the interval between their own flowering and the growth of their summer garments attention might be diverted by banking Pæonies about them for an intermediate season of bloom, and, for variety, Day Lilies (Funkias) might be put to the same purpose.

FANNY COPLEY SEAVEY.

CEMETERY NOTES.

The Evergreen Cemetery Association of New Haven, Conn., is creating a chapel fund by yearly contributions from the receipts from lot sales, etc.

* * *

The enforcement of the new rules of the Laurel Grove Cemetery, Paterson, N. J., relating to the sodding of graves and restriction of flower beds has called forth a vigorous protest from the lot owners.

* * *

The tomb of Lady Anne Grimston, at Tewin, in Hertfordshire, has been for years an object of interest for tourists. Long limbs of ash and sycamore trees have shot up from the vault below and pierced through the stone and twined around the iron work. The current tale is that Lady Anne was an unbeliever, and asserted before her death that if the scriptures were true then seven ash trees would spring from her vault.

* * *

It is a good sign when local papers show an interest in cemetery affairs. The subject is one in which every family should be interested, yet it is too frequently neglected by the press. Cemetery officials who are alive to the growing interest in cemeteries, should in every way possible cultivate the good will of their local press. It is the surest and readiest means of creating and fostering an active sentiment in the community, by which progress can alone be sustained.

* * *

During the past few years tombstones in the Schuyler, Nebraska, Cemetery have become much discolored during the summer. At one time it was charged that a local dealer was using some acid to cause the discolorations to discourage patronage of foreign dealers. Later developments disclosed that the injury arose from water used in sprinkling that passed through iron pipes. The Association has been laying galvanized pipe in place of the ordinary pipe with a view to remedy the evil.

* * *

The new rules of the Crown Hill Cemetery Board, Indianapolis, Ind., include the following, which is in keeping with the order of things now being rapidly instituted and enforced in the leading cemeteries of the country. The rule goes into effect the coming fall: "All persons are prohibited from planting trees, shrubs or plants on lots or graves, and on and after November 1., 1894, will be prohibited from planting any flowers in the cemetery grounds. Flowers are permitted in vases or urns, and cut flowers may be placed upon the graves, but will be removed as soon as they become faded and unsightly in appearance."

* * *

The cemetery receiving vault is beginning to attract the attention of Board of Health inspectors, and we note that an investigation of the vault of the New York Bay cemetery has been made, discovering a condition of things warranting immediate action;—bodies having been found which had been in the vault for years. Meeting the wishes of lot owners, prospective or actual, is a wise business practice, but it should undoubtedly be limited and brought within the bounds of common sense, which implies with due force, decency, notwithstanding that the dollar-bill may be a factor in the matter. In the questions of design, construction, ventilation, and even care, the receiving vault has been largely neglected, so that any action that will lead to proper attention to this important adjunct of the cemetery should be welcome.

* * *

Elsinore, or Helsingor as the Danes call it, is only a two hours train journey, or three hours sail from Copenhagen, and one would think should be a Mecca for travelers, for there is the tomb of Hamlet. At present it is however, seldom visited by American or English pilgrims, although otherwise an attractive spot. Within a mile of Kronborg castle, on the hills, which rise a little from the sea, in the verdant public grounds behind the pretty bathing place called Marienlyst, is found the shrine. A narrow path ascends the hill until a gate is reached, where a trifling toll must be paid. Passing on to the summit, in a forlorn, waste corner, sheltered by great elms there is found a mound or cairn of rough hewn brick, stone and earth, topped by a tiny monolith. Upon this monolith are two words, "Hamlet's Grave." It is a fitting spot for such a tomb. The everlasting murmur of the sea is heard afar. The breezes make strange music overhead, among the branches of the elms. A mossy wall forbids all access from behind and only rarely is the peace of Hamlet's melancholy resting place disturbed by the invading stranger.

* * *

An unfortunate circumstance of cemetery management has been brought to light in a prominent eastern cemetery, implying curious business relations existing between the cemetery and the undertaker. It is unfortunately true that such questionable business practices are by no means scarce, but nevertheless it is a serious reflection on cemetery management. The case in point was where a lawyer in settling an estate required to remove certain bodies in the cemetery, but permission was refused until the receipt for the grave was forthcoming which the undertaker had in his possession. Upon application he refused to deliver the receipt until interest on his bill was paid notwithstanding that the applicant held his bills fully receipted. The pecuniary advantages of such a condition of things to any cemetery association, will and should be fully negatived by the odium which publicity always casts upon the corporations so involving themselves.

* * *

A pertinent and practical suggestion is being materialized by a Ladies Cemetery Association of Ithaca, Mich., and that is that ladies committees can be most effective agencies for the care and improvement of our rural cemeteries, and that enlarged opportunities should be accorded to them for the exercise of the functions for which they are eminently fitted. The following from the pen of an Ithaca lady appeared in the *Journal* of that town. "Shall the walks between the lots be filled? My answer is emphatically 'yes' for several reasons. A few I will give. The walks as they are, act as surface drains, making it too dry to grow plants which do not root deep enough to reach down to the moisture on a level with the walks. It is almost impossible to trim those terraces in nice shape save with shears, and this process is too slow, for time means money to the association. A few will trim their own lots and the rest are left for us to hire trimmed. Until this is changed there will never be funds enough to beautify and improve the grounds, as it will be all one man can do to keep them clean. If the walks are filled on a common level with the lots and seeded, a lawn mower can be used on all the grass and leave time to cultivate and water plants and shrubs. This assured care will encourage individuals to procure and contribute many plants, which without care will survive but a short time. These are only a few reasons, but enough to stir up your thoughts on the subject. This is a work which principally falls on the ladies. We spend hours in arranging something dainty and beautiful to keep on our dressers where our jewelry is kept, only for a show, while the spot which contains all that was mortal of our God-given jewels—and which is viewed by the majority usually as often as once a week—lies neglected. This, to my mind, should be the most sacred and well cared for place in a community. Some learned person once said. 'Show me the cemetery and I will tell you what kind of people live in that community.' What judgment would he pass on the people of Ithaca? I am sure he would say we lacked system and regularity."

Action in harmony with the spirit of the above would transform the majority of our country cemeteries and add to the credit of the community.

RULES AND REGULATIONS.

Every cemetery should be governed by certain rules and regulations, which should be printed in pamphlet form for distribution among lot owners. While this has been done in most of the large cemeteries, where the rules are very much alike, we will, for the benefit of the smaller cemeteries, publish in this department such rules as commend themselves for general adoption. Contributions are solicited.

After an existence of fifty-three years, 1841—1894, the corporation of proprietors of Lowell Cemetery, Lowell, Mass., which is operated on the mutual plan, adopted new By-Laws and Rules and Regulations on April 1st, 1894. The officers of the corporation are President, twelve Trustees and Treasurer, acting as Clerk of the Board. The Board of Trustees make all ordinances and regulations governing the cemetery. Standing Committees on Finance, Cemetery and Personal property are appointed, with power to recommend only.—The committee on Finance has direct and general oversight of the finances of the corporation, audits accounts, supervises Trust Fund, Insurance, and recommends rules governing perpetual care of lots. The committee on Cemetery exercises general oversight over greenhouses, shrubbery, ornamentation of grounds, paths and avenues, lots and spaces. The committee on Personal Property has direct and general oversight over personal property and buildings of corporation, and repairs to same; drains, walls, fences, and of the help employed. All committees report to the Board.

The Superintendent has absolute control and direction of the cemetery under the direction of the President, selecting all help. Among the rules and regulations, which it will be observed are in harmony with the progressive spirit now largely prevailing are the following:

Funerals on reaching the Cemetery will be under the charge of the Superintendent or his assistants. Drivers must remain on carriages during funeral services.

All monumental foundation work shall be built by the Corporation under the direction of the Superintendent.

No lot shall be decorated by its owner, or other parties interested in it, with any tree, shrub, or flower without first obtaining the consent of the Superintendent. This does not however, exclude the placing of cut flowers on the graves.

No lot shall contain any auxiliary vase or seat, or any rock work or other architectural objects for which special permit has not been granted by the Superintendent.

The owner of a lot may have erected proper monuments, mausoleums, vaults, or sepulchral memorials, subject, however, in all cases, to the approval of the Superintendent or a competent committee of the Trustees.

The Superintendent may, under the direction of the Trustees, notify proprietors of neglected lots of their condition; and in case of continual neglect, so as, in the opinion of the Trustees, to impair the general appearance of the cemetery, such lots may be put in order by the Trustees at the expense of the owners thereof.

No double burials, that is one body resting on another, will be permitted in the Lowell Cemetery, except in the case of a mother and infant or two children buried in one coffin.

Single graves will be sodded level with the surrounding ground.

No lot or parcel of ground shall be inclosed or defined by any so-called fence, railing, coping or hedge.

The following are added to the Rules and Regulations governing Cambridge Cemetery, Cambridge, Mass.

"All Stone or Marble Work of any kind on Lots or Graves in this Cemetery shall be under the direction and subject to the approval of the Superintendent, who shall see that the same is performed in a workmanlike manner; also that in all cases, a sketch or plan of such proposed work shall be furnished the Superintendent before the work is commenced."

"No Burials, Care, or Work of any kind will be permitted in any lot or grave, in Cambridge Cemetery, on which a bill remains unpaid."

Correspondence.

Editor Modern Cemetery.

In consequence of an unusual amount of orders for spring work, my time has been so constantly occupied that correspondence of any nature aside from cemetery work, has, of necessity, been abandoned. But this evening finds me writing to our May issue of the MODERN CEMETERY to say a few words to our brother superintendents relative to the coming convention of the A. A. C. Superintendents, to be held at Philadelphia, Penn., this year.

We hope that our members will keep it in mind, and at this early day prepare themselves for the said meeting, as the time for holding our Eighth Annual Convention will be upon us before we are aware of it. Where our Ninth Annual Convention will be held is not to be considered at present, but the writer would like, even at this early day to suggest Cincinnati, Ohio, for that occasion as the West should have the preference.

Our Association was formed at Cincinnati, and to her belongs the honor of giving birth to the A. A. Cemetery Superintendents. Is not this then a strong argument for holding the Ninth Annual convention there; besides our members would again have the pleasure of visiting beautiful Spring Grove Cemetery, and the privilege of meeting the genial and efficient Superintendent, now the respected president of our Association. It would afford us much pleasure to hear from some of our brother superintendents their views with regard to holding the above named meeting at Cincinnati in 1895. In keeping with our annual custom we have commenced writing to our members to learn whether they will be at the Philadelphia Convention, this will be followed up from time to time. An answer received from one of our members aroused my sympathy; he states that it would afford him great pleasure to meet with us at Philadelphia, but owing to his meager salary he could not spare the money requisite to pay the expenses of the trip. This is a sad commentary on cemetery officials who only care to carry out their own purposes without any regard to the hard worked men having in charge their cemeteries. Most assuredly they could afford to give the managers of their cemetery at least one week's vacation during the year as well as defray their expenses to our convention.

Newark, N. J.   CHAS. NICHOLS.

Educating Anti-Monument Ideas.

In a circular recently issued by the managers of Graceland Cemetery, Chicago, the lots in the Maplewood section are offered for sale under the following rules: 1.—No stone-work or artificial material of any kind will be allowed to project above the sod. 2.—The graves may be distinguished by trees, shrubs, vines, or hardy perennial herbaceous plants of various kinds planted under the direction of the superintendent, but no greenhouse or tender plants can be planted. 3—No mounds will be allowed over graves.

This radical departure is taken in the belief that a sentiment is rapidly growing in favor of a burial ground without stone work. Mr. Eurich, one of the leading cemetery superintendents in America, and a landscape gardener of ability says: "In an ideal cemetery the lot owners should not only be encouraged, but they should be required by strict rules to discontinue the erection of monuments and grave memorials above the sod." Chateaubriand said: "I have seen the memorable monuments to Croesus and Cæsar, but I prefer the airy tombs of the Indians, those mausoleums of verdure, refreshed by the morning dew, embalmed and fanned by the breezes, and over which waves the same branch where the black-bird builds his nest and utters his plaintive melody."

It is expected that Maplewood is destined to become one of the most admired sections in Graceland.

QUESTION BOX.

What assurance can a cemetery give a lot owner that his last resting place will remain undisturbed by heirs after his decease? It is suggested that the best way to guard against such disturbance is for lot owners to deed their lots in trust to the cemetery, which would seem to afford the needed protection, but, the question arises, will this hold in every case? Where such provision has not been made, is a cemetery justified in defending deceased lot owners from removal to single grave sections to gratify the mercenary desires of heirs?

These are problems that cemetery officials frequently have to meet and we would like to hear from readers who have had any experience in deciding such cases. A correspondent suggests the question might be discussed at the next convention of the A. A. C. S.

Association of American Cemetery Superintendents.

WM. SALWAY, "Spring Grove" Cincinnati, O., President.
T. McCARTHY, "Swan Point" Providence, R. I., Vice-President.
F. EURICH, Woodlawn, Toledo, O., Secretary and Treasurer.

The Eighth Annual Convention of the Association will be held at Philadelphia, September 11, 12, and 13, 1894.

Resolutions Adopted at the Seventh Annual Convention of the Association of American Cemetery Superintendents.

Resolved: That it is the sense of this convention that all Sunday funerals be discouraged as much as possible.

Resolved: That it is the sense of this meeting that all headstones or markers should be limited to the height of the sod or the level of the surface of the ground.

Resolved: That it is the sense of this meeting that vaults and catacombs be discouraged and if possible prevented in cemeteries.

Publisher's Department.

The receipt of Cemetery Literature and Trade Catalogues will be acknowledged in this column.

TO ADVERTISERS. THE MODERN CEMETERY is the only publication of its class and will be found a valuable medium for reaching cemetery officials in all parts of the United States.

TO SUBSCRIBERS. Cemetery officials desiring to subscribe for a number of copies regularly to circulate among their lot owners, should send for our special terms. Several well known cemeteries have already adopted this plan with good results.

Contributions on matters pertaining to cemeteries are solicited. Address all communications to
R. J. HAIGHT, 331 Dearborn St., CHICAGO.

We have received from R. F. Robertson, Secretary of Los Gatos Cemetery, Los Gatos, Cal., photographs of the Entrance and birds eye view of the grounds of that cemetery.

We have received from C. McArthur, Superintendent of Pittsfield Cemetery, Pittsfield, Mass., a photograph of the McKay Mausoleum, a beautiful structure recently completed in that cemetery.

The Dille & McGuire Mfg. Co., of Richmond, Ind., has issued a handsome "Souvenir" illustrating their lawn mowers at the World's Fair, and also showing practical work in high grass. Their mower is already well known to Cemetery officials, but the recent improvements in manufacture, and material used in the wearing parts, greatly increases durability and efficiency in the machines now being turned out.

Readers of the MODERN CEMETERY who are interested in the Scherer Automatic Burial Device will be glad to know that a new company has been organized in New York City, and is now manufacturing the apparatus, which by the use of aluminium has been reduced in weight very materially. A show room has been established at 30 Bible House, where the invention may be seen in practical working order.

Mr. Geo. W. Williams, President of the Magnolia Cemetery, Charleston, S. C., took occasion on the 50th anniversary of the firm of Geo. W. Williams & Co., and the 20th of the Carolina Savings

Bank, which occurred in 1892, to revise and republish an address delivered by him to young men on the 32nd anniversary of the firm. It is full of good things gathered in the experience of a successful business man.

The Annual Report and Catalogue of Swan Point Cemetery, Providence, R. I., one of the handsomest cemetery publications issued has been received. It describes itself in its introduction as follows: "In this issue of the catalogue will be found eight half-tone views of interesting points in the cemetery, * * to awaken the interest of those proprietors who have allowed their lots to remain uncared for, trusting that they will * * do their share toward making the cemetery still more beautiful. The best way is to place all lots under perpetual care. We would call special attention to the view showing the river road, and the wooded banks of the river, and to that of the boulder wall, * this wall when completed, and covered with growing shrubs and vines, will, without doubt, be one of the finest pieces of clothed rock-work of the kind in the country. The Cemetery possesses great natural beauties, which, under the care of the Superintendent, have been emphasized and developed."

HITCHINGS & CO., Established 1844.
..Horticultural Architectural and Building,
GREENHOUSE HEATING AND VENTILATING.

IRON FRAME CONSTRUCTION.

Palm Houses, Conservatories, Greenhouses, etc., Erected Complete
Plans and estimates of cost furnished on application.
Send 4 cents postage for Illustrated Catalogue.

HITCHINGS & CO., 233 Mercer Street, New York.

O. S. KELLY CO., Springfield, O.
Steam Road Rollers

REFERENCES—Spring Grove Cemetery, Cincinnati, O.
Allegheny Cemetery, Pittsburgh, Pa. ☎ Send for Catalogue.

THOS. W. WEATHERED'S SONS,
INCORPORATED.
HORTICULTURAL ARCHITECTS AND HOT WATER ENGINEERS
Send for Catalogue, enclosing 4 cents in stamps.
No. 244 Canal St., NEW YORK CITY.

PLEASE MENTION THE MODERN CEMETERY.

Conservatories, Greenhouses, Vineries,
SHIPPED TO ANY PART OF THE COUNTRY AND ERECTED COMPLETE, READY FOR USE.

Plans Embrace the Latest Improvements.
Unequaled Facilities for Manufacturing.
Thirty-five Years Experience.

ADDRESS, STATING REQUIREMENTS,

Lord & Burnham Co...
IRVINGTON-ON-HUDSON, N. Y.

Conservatory in Newton Cemetery, Newtonville, Mass., designed and erected by Lord & Burnham Co. Catalogue sent on application.

Landscape Architecture.

Landscape architecture is attracting more attention to-day than at any previous time in our history. The wild, natural beauty of the country and the devotion to hard work, have combined to hold back attention from æsthetic matters, but it is coming to be admitted that we must feast the eyes as well as feed the body to maintain proper conditions. Messrs. Gray & Blaisdell, limited, landscape architects and engineers of 53 State St., Boston, have just issued a very attractive little pamphlet on "Gardens and the Landscape Architect," in which they draw particular attention to the gardens and parks of several parts of Europe, describing the styles and objects and pointing out the various tastes displayed. They suggest many directions in which we could add to the attractiveness of both our public and private property, and point out the particular features which should be retained and accentuated.

"Churchyards, with their surrounding cemeteries, formerly consisted of large tracts admitting of extended ornamentation, but the demands of sanitarians have led to their separation, thus taking from the church land necessary for its proper setting and embellishment. Excellent results can be obtained by leaving suitable grounds around churches and making a harmonious treatment;

and ideal cemetery grounds should be selected in spots having great natural charms and quiet situations."

CEMETERY ADORNMENTS
—ARTISTIC—
Iron Vases
WITH RESERVOIRS,
which are the best for Plants
BOUQUET HOLDERS
for Graves, 20, 25, 30 and 40c. each.
Our New Bouquet Vase
For Cemetery is just out.
Metallic Wreaths, Crosses, etc., 50c to $5 each.

SETTEES AND CHAIRS.
Both all IRON or IRON with WOOD SLATS.
Path, Avenue, and Keep off the Grass signs.
Ornamental Fountains and Drinking Fountains.
FLOWER SEEDS—2 packages, 5 cts. Grass seed, bulbs, etc.
LAWN MOWERS—Our new one, "THE HERCULES," far superior and different from all others.
GARDEN HOSE—We only sell the best grades, Nozzles, hoses, reels, etc.
JONES PATENT HOSE MENDER—No tools or hands required. We send four menders, postage paid, by mail, for 25 cts. Send inside diameter of hose.
LAWN SPRINKLERS—3, 4, 6 and 8 arms. Hub, Globe and Combination. All our own make. Prices to suit.
Wire Rose Bush Trellises, Garden Borders, etc.
Greatest Variety of Above Goods at our NEW Store.
Illustrated Price List on application.
M. D. JONES & CO.
368 Washington St.   BOSTON, MASS.

CAST IRON
ROAD BOXES
—AND—
Gratings.

TOM MOORE,
852-860 Monroe St.,
BROOKLYN, N. Y.

REFERENCES:
HENRY MORRISON, County Road Engineer, Richmond County, N. Y.
CHAS. G. BENNETT, President Evergreen Cemetery, Brooklyn, N. Y.

PATENT VAULT HEARSE.

Especially Designed For Removing Bodies from Vault to Grave.

NEEDED IN EVERY CEMETERY HAVING A VAULT.

CARRIES the heaviest body with perfect safety, and may be drawn easily by two men. Platform, 2' 6" x 7' 6", with silver plated rollers, pins, etc., similar to ordinary hearse. Substantially built. Highly finished.

Extra. from Testimonial: The Vault Hearse perfectly supplies a long felt want. * * We consider it indispensable where a vault is in use.—*Trustees, Marion, O., Cemetery.*

Send for PRICE LIST. **McMurray & Fisher Sulky Co.**, MARION, OHIO.

WATER and TRUCK CART COMBINATION

Any number of adjustable, swinging and dumping barrels can be used with our truck.
Send for circulars of our different Hand Cans & Barrel Trucks.
BELLE CITY MFG CO., Racine, Wis.

LAWN SWEEPERS
FOR sweeping lawns after mowing, for gathering leaves, sticks, stones and litter.
USED In Parks, Cemeteries, Tennis Courts and all public and private grounds.
Combines lawn roller, keeps lawns smooth and compact. Used when frost is leaving ground and after rain for re-sodding and laying out yards and flower arrangements.
THOMPSON MFG. CO., Elkhart, Ind.

FENCES (Wire, Iron & Steel) CRESTINGS **VASES** (Reservoir & Centre Drainage)

Do You Want

**LAWN ORNAMENTS — CHAIRS, SETTEES &c. &c.
STABLE FIXTURES, WIRE WORK, NETTINGS &c.**
Send For No. 31 Address **BARBEE WIRE & IRON WORKS,**
Catalogue 44 & 46 DEARBORN ST. CHICAGO, or LaFayette, Ind.

Roads.

It is remarkable, that of the thousands of intelligent people using the terms Macadam and Telford roads, rarely one can be found who understands what these roads are so says *Mechans Monthly* for May. Usually a broken stone road is called a Macadam road; but the principle of the Macadam road is to have the stone broken and arranged, that when the road is finally finished under this system, not a stone will move out of place. Whoever saw a modern "Macadam" road in which the stone would not move into ruts or be in some other way misplaced, or ground to mud in a short time? So in regard to Telford roads. It has come to be understood that a road with large blocks of stone at the bottom, and small ones at the top is a Telford road; but a true Telford road is made by having the lower blocks of stone somewhat of the form of wedges with the narrow points upward, the broken stone then fills in between the narrow points and makes a sheet of stone, which is almost self-supporting; but a simple large block of stone without the precaution required by Telford, of having the narow points

Slate Burial Vaults

are imperishable, impervious to dampness, proof against rodents and reptiles. Stronger than marble and as cheap as brick. Can be put in place by ordinary workmen.

Slate Headstones and Markers are recommended for **Durability** and **Economy**, do not weather stain or hold moss. Are known to have stood in cemeteries 100 years and retain their inscriptions.
Apply to manufacturer

JESSE R. KIMES,
1822 Filbert St.   Philadelphia, Pa.

TERRA COTTA
Grave and Lot Marks

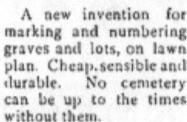

A new invention for marking and numbering graves and lots, on lawn plan. Cheap, sensible and durable. No cemetery can be up to the times without them.

MISHLER BROS.,
RAVENNA O.

GRAVE MARKS
J. F. WILLIAMS & CO.
Manufacturers of Cast Iron Grave and Lot Marks.
No. 237 Hamilton Ave.,   Cincinnati, Ohio.

It will pay you to examine our Marks before placing your order elsewhere, they are superior to all others.

upwards, simply sinks deeper into the ground with the first thaw, after the winter is over, and the whole roadway rapidly disintegrates. This is especially the case where the land is not under-drained. These principles in road making should never be forgotten—that a heavy body in the ground will sink in soft slush, and ground when thawed in the spring is in the condition of slush. The property of the writer of this paragraph occupies a portion of one of the heaviest battle fields of the revolution. Not unfrequently in digging deeply, leaden bullets are turned up. These are never found except at the depth of eighteen inches or two feet from the surface, yet it is evident that they were not driven this depth in the ground when the battle was going on; but they have gradually sunk. In the spring of the year, when the thaw comes, and the ground is soft, the heavy bullets go gradually down, so that at the present time they are found to the greatest depth that a frost has ever penetrated. So with the stone roads. Heavy blocks of stone, without something to keep them near the surface, must evidently sink.

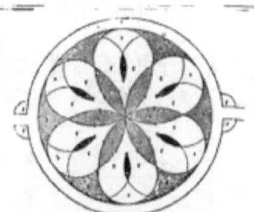

Ornamental Gardening.

SOLLY'S BOOK OF PLANS
Contains over 100 Designs of
Carpet and Ornamental Flower Beds.

Each design is drawn on a scale and is accompanied by a key, showing what plants should be used. A valuable book for cemetery superintendents and landscape architects. Mr Solly, the author, is a landscape gardener, with 36 years' experience. The book is 8x10 inches, substantially bound. Retail price, $3.00; with THE MODERN CEMETERY for one year, $3.50.

R. J. HAIGHT, Publisher,
334 Dearborn St., Chicago.

BOOKS FOR CEMETERY OFFICIALS

Landscape Gardening, by Samuel Parsons, Jr., 300 pages, 200 illustrations. Beautifully printed and bound, $3.50.

Ornamental Gardening for Americans, by Elias A. Long. Illustrated. Cloth, $2.00. The Nursery Book, by L. H. Bailey. Complete hand-book of propagation. Paper 50 cents, cloth $1.00. Sent postpaid on receipt of price.

The Nursery Book, by L. H. Bailey, assisted by several of the most skillful propagators in the world. In fact, it is a careful compendium of the best practices in all countries. It contains 107 illustrations, showing methods, processes and appliances. How to Propagate over 2,000 varieties of shrubs, trees and herbaceous or soft-stemmed plants. The process for each being fully described. All this and much more is fully told in the Nursery Book. Over 300 pages, 16mo Price, cloth, $1. Pocket style, paper, narrow margins, 50 cents. Address, **R. J. HAIGHT,** 334 Dearborn St., Chicago.

Interment Record and Lot Book.

This system is thought to embrace the best features of the most popular forms of burial records now in use and may be adapted to large or small cemeteries. The Interment Record gives all of the necessary information in regard to the deceased, and the Lot Book locates every grave, so that it can be readily found at any time. The books are printed on heavy paper, substantially bound and furnished in different sizes, depending upon the requirements of the cemetery.   **R. J. HAIGHT, Pub.,**   334 Dearborn St., Chicago.

EARNSHAW & PUNSHON

LANDSCAPE
ENGINEERS

Southwest Cor. Fifth and Race Streets,
Cincinnati,
Ohio.

30 YEARS experience in the profession, enables us to guarantee that our Modern Designs for laying out Cemeteries, Parks, and the Subdivision of Estates, will insure the best artistic effects and financial results, and at the same time involve the least expense in development and maintenance.

WE RESPECTFULLY REFER TO THE OFFICIALS OF THE FOLLOWING INSTITUTIONS:

Spring Grove Cemetery, Cincinnati, O.	Highland Lawn Cemetery, Terre Haute, Ind.
Lake View Cemetery, Cleveland, O.	Forest Lawn Cemetery, Buffalo, N. Y.
Linwood Cemetery, Dubuque, Ia.	Riverview Cemetery, East Liverpool, O.
Woodlawn Cemetery, Canandaigua, N. Y.	Forest Lawn Cemetery, Omaha, Neb.
Mount Pleasant Cemetery, Toronto, Canada.	St. Joseph's Cemetery, Evansville, Ind.
Lorraine Cemetery, Baltimore, Md.	Woodside Cemetery, Middletown, O.
Woodlawn Cemetery, Birmingham, Ala.	Mother of God Cemetery, Covington, Ky.
Forest Lawn Cemetery, East Saginaw, Mich.	Logan Park Cemetery, Sioux City, Ia.
Prospect Cemetery, Toronto, Canada.	South Indiana Hospital, Evansville, Ind.
Mount Olivet Cemetery, Detroit, Michigan.	Goodale Park, Columbus, O.
Hoyt Park, East Saginaw, Mich.	Park and Zoological Gardens, Cincinnati, O.

South San Francisco Land and Imp. Co., San Francisco, Cal.,
and to all our patrons.

PERSONAL INSPECTION AND ADVICE AS TO THE IMPROVEMENT OF LARGE PROPERTIES WILL BE PROMPTLY GIVEN, FREE OF CHARGE.

THE MODERN CEMETERY.

THE MODERN CEMETERY.
AN ILLUSTRATED MONTHLY JOURNAL DEVOTED TO THE INTEREST OF CEMETERIES

R. J. HAIGHT, Publisher.
334 Dearborn Street, CHICAGO

Subscription $1.00 a Year in Advance.   Foreign Subscription $1.25.
Special Rates on Six or More Copies.

VOL. IV.   CHICAGO, JUNE, 1894.   NO. 4.

CONTENTS.

*DEATH AS A FRIEND... 37
*THE McKAY MAUSOLEUM, PITTSFIELD, MASS.—ROCK-
LAND CEMETERY, NEW YORK 40
*DICKSON MEMORIAL CHAPEL AND CONSERVATORY,
GREENLAWN CEMETERY, SALEM, MASS.—MEMORIAL
TREES.. 41
CEMETERY PLANTING.—V.—ORNAMENTAL CEMETERY
MONUMENTS CONSIDERED AS TRADE FIXTURES..... 42
*THE MONUMENTAL CROSS 43
THE LAW WITH REGARD TO REMOVAL OF BODIES..... 44
ANNUAL CONVENTION OF AMERICAN CEMETERY SUP-
ERINTENDENTS—DECORATION DAY.................... 45
CEMETERY NOTES—TREASURED TEARS , ... 46
RULES AND REGULATIONS—CEMETERY REPORTS..... 47
CREMATION—QUESTION BOX—PUBLISHER'S DEPART-
MENT.. 48
*Illustrated.

Death as a Friend.

Daniel French's beautiful plaster cast "The Angel of Death Staying the Hand of the Artist" in the Sculptors gallery at the World's Fair, drew from the Rev. Jenkin Lloyd Jones an eloquent discourse on "Death as a friend," in which he discussed art and its effect on religion, referring to the above piece of work as his inspiration. From this discourse we extract the following:

"'The Angel of Death Staying the Hand of the Artist.' You all remember it. You must often have noticed how it held in thoughtful reverence its ever-present cluster of students and admirers. Its story is an interesting one: Designed as a monument for the grave of the lamented young sculptor, Milmore, who died in Boston some years ago, it was intended to be put in granite and placed in Forest Hills; a destiny scarcely to be wished for it. It deserves to be put in rarest marble; it is fitting that it should commemorate a devotee of the sculptor's art, but let it be kept mid the haunts of the living, rather than relegated to the abode of the dead. * * * Let us in imagination go again into the Art Palace at Jackson Park and look intently at this masterpiece, that we may catch its Easter message. Note the young sculptor quivering with inspiration, intense, eager, impetuous. He must not be interfered with. He cannot stop. The half-formed lines under his chisel are peremptory; he must proceed. But lo! there interposes a deeply hooded figure, strange but gracious, gentle but imperious. Her outstretched hand arouses impatience on the part of the artist; but the arrest is commanding. It stays his mallet in mid-air. The mighty wings suggest a visitant from beyond the ken of mortal. The poppy in her hand speaks of Lethean rest. There is a great change pending. A mystery strange and wonderful surrounds her. The sphinx growing so strangely beautiful under his chisel, every line in its contour a matter of such absorbing interest to him, seems to be unnoticed by her. She comes from beyond the vale which the syhinx symbolizes. She has come to solve the riddle which the sphinx propounds. He is life, living; and the sphinx is the problem of life, the mission of life, the something to do, to perfect, the goal to gain, a task to be accomplished. She is the Angel of Death. She seems apathetic to all this; to the strong young life in his veins, to the work he is striving to accomplish. Yet there is that gentleness and sympathy in her whole bearing that proves

"Contrariwise she loves both old and young,
Able and weak—affects the very brutes
And birds—how say I?—flowers of the field—
As a wise workman recognizes tools
In a master's workshop, loving what they make."

"And still she is inexorable. Whatever her message may be, one thing is sure: it cannot be a message of hate. Whatever her mission may be, it cannot be a fell one. Death is here, but it is a friend not a foe. Here is power inevitable, unflinching; it is not, however, malevolent, but benevolent. Here is a benign figure.

"We have come to the first great and obvious lesson which this art prophet gives us. This group would have been impossible at any other period of the Christian era. It shows a conception of death quite foreign to that which has inspired what is known as Christian art as well as so-called Christian theology. The masters of brush and chisel in Christendom have heretofore reveled in the grotesque, the hideous and the hateful, whenever they have undertaken to portray death. * * * It has remained for this age of humane instincts, * * * to restore to us the diviner conceptions of pagan Greece, which made of death twin angel of sleep, and to enlarge upon that conception making death an inviting spirit, a welcoming angel.

"And is not art justified by science? This

"THE ANGEL OF DEATH STAYING THE HAND OF THE ARTIST."—BY DANIEL E. FRENCH.

beautiful relief represents sense as well as sensibility. The common sense of the world is beginning to assert itself and organize itself into the systematized thought of science, which affirms that no matter how mysterious life may be, it cannot be meaningless. Whatever death may be it is not lawlessness. There is no fiend in all the universe, because law is everywhere. * * * There is method, meaning, order, development all the way from the gold in the mountain crevice to the truth in the mind of Socrates and Emerson. * * * In all the fields of space there is law, rhythmic, benignant, divine law. And the man with a microscope says, 'I have peered into the realms of littleness, penetrated the chambers of the most attenuated beings, and there I find beauty; the rose and the rainbow written small.' Life is there, pulsing upward; and the student of human history goes back to lowest savage or climbs up Parnassus, and finds, all the way from cave-dweller to the maker of libraries, a common brotherhood of hope and suffering, of joy and pain, of life and death. * * * The artist is justified, then, by science, history and philosophy, in shaping death as a friend. It is a kindly hand that stays the restless, struggling children of men, and not the hand of an enemy.

"The artist is justified in this picture by the profoundest voices in literature. The poet as well as the sculptor in his highest moments regards death as a friend. It comes as an angel. * * * Daniel French has but put into plaster our own experience, interpreting for us what we could not interpret for ourselves. This hooded figure has been indeed an angel to us. How it has quickened our energies! The thought that 'I must do the work of Him that sent me, for the night cometh wherein no man can work,' has been the inspiration of the lordly souls of the race. The thought that our time is

limited is a holy spur that puts us to work. *
* * Death is a noble task-master and keeps us busy. It is the inspiration of progress; musters out of service the disabled veterans, making room in the files for new life and fresh courage, and thus the banner of progress is borne forward. And then, how death consecrates life! What were this world without its memories! This winged figure, the mother of grief, carries poppies in her hand, but she opens more eyes than she closes. It is only the tear-washed eyes that read the common-place text with inspiring accents. How hallowed is the place where the brave man once walked; sacred the chair where the patient one sat and talked; holy the book upon which are left the mind marks of a gentle spirit vanished! With every death there comes into our life a new cabinet of sanctities. The old volume, the cane or cup, the picture, the empty chair, the favorite word, the happy haunt, these are the real shrines of humanity. * * * fundamental altars of the race. Worship begins here, aye, worship ends here also. For these sanctities lead us on and up. From the baby shoes, sacred mementoes of holy mother's grief, up to the shrines consecrated by pilgrim feet, the martyr places, the Bethlehem spots, up and up until the whole earth becomes a sacred mausoleum, consecrated by the blood of the martyrs, the lives of the heroes, the unnamed, but not on that account the unrecorded or unrecounted, triumphs of the humble workers for God. All the way from the earth-worm that makes the soil up through the pioneer who through pestilence and danger subdues it, the patient hand that tills it in cheerful obscurity that the world may be fed, to the loyal legion who laid down their lives in the trenches that their country might be free, until at last we arrive at the ultimate shrine, the permanent beneath all this transient, the ever-lasting love, the undying principle, the all-pervading and all-adorable spirit. * * * Thus it is that death widens our horizon, gives us sympathies that are noble and hopes more inspiring than knowledge.

Let us back again to our sculpture. For the artist has groped his way along beauty lines into thought too subtle for words. How silent, shy and elusive is this figure. The youth scarce can see the angel face. She speaks not; does not explain; does not justify; makes no promises; gives no assurances. And the figure is true to the fact. Death does not explain the riddle of being, but by her and through her we are willing to trust. Once we recognize the benignity of her form, we prefer her benevolent silence, the divine obscurity of her presence, to the garrulous assurances of assumed knowledge. * *
* A God that is understood, an immortality that is already anticipated, described and outlined, is not the God of the devoutest soul, nor is it the immortality that touches life with the divinest awe and profoundest peace.

"Yes, this thought of death as a friend, this revelation through art, does charm every wave of being, and we find ourselves in league with the stars and in the confidences of the lilies.

"There is something exquisitely comforting in this thought of death as a friend. It is the new thought.

"One other interpreter of the new Easter thought, I want to mention. * * * —a collection from the masters of English verse, the bards of the soul, -Wordsworth, Browning, Emerson, Lowell, Tennyson, Whittier and others,—a rare collection of choice spirits summoned unwittingly to help interpret this relief of Mr. French, to lead us into the higher trust of Easter, a clear confiding in the methods of God, a trustful shelter under the mantling of his law. Confidence, not curiosity, most becomes Easter. Patience, not petulance, is the becoming attitude of an immortal spirit. Let us then be worthy this great confidence. We will not fear nor run away. We will

"Counsel not with flesh and blood;
Loiter not for cloak or food;
Right thou feelest, rush to do."

"Welcome, then, this thought of death as a friend. Surely science and reason are to-day conspiring with art and religion to put down the last enemy, robbing death of its sting and the grave of its victory. Dear mother of Grief! Holy Angel of awe and trust! we will not dread thee; we will not flee thee, neither will we court thee nor fret thee with our idle impatience or imbecile curiosity, but will, nothing daunted, work out our tasks, chisel away, like the youth in French's group, at the sphinx upon which it is given us to work, and then, when thou dost come, we will not ungratefully remonstrate but remember that thou will not separate us from the love of God, that 'no evil can happen to a good man in life or in death,' and that—"

"All hope, all memory,
Have their deep springs in thee,
And Love, that else might fade,
By thee immortal made,
Spurns at the grave, leaps to the welcoming skies,
And burns a steadfast star to steadfast eyes."

The epidemic of "vandalism" in our cemeteries seems to be raging again, according to reports from different parts of the country, in some instances causing serious loss. Most drastic measures should be adopted in these cases; it is inexcusable, betokens morbid conditions, and the individuals displaying the disease cannot be dealt with too rigorously to ensure beneficial results.

The McKay Mausoleum, Pittsfield, Mass.

The fine mausoleum, of which we give an illustration, has recently been completed for the McKay family, in the Pittsfield Cemetery, Pittsfield, Mass., at a cost of over $20,000. It stands on slightly rising ground in the western portion of the cemetery and is built of white Lee marble. It is hexagon in shape with each corner ornamented with a round pilaster or column surmounted by a delicately carved capital. It is 22 feet 6 inches in diameter and 20 feet 6 inches high from the base to the marble ball from which a small white cross rises at the summit of its stone-arched roof. Its walls

THE McKAY MAUSOLEUM, PITTSFIELD, MASS.

are 15 inches thick and it is supplied with modern fixtures for ventilation. Over its bronze doors above the portal is a marble tablet with inscription.

The inner door posts, door arch and catacombs are of Numidian marble. The floor has a center circular block of marble 18 inches in diameter, which is surrounded by a mosaic setting of half-inch colored tile of handsome design.

Rockland Cemetery, New York.

A new cemetery association has been formed in New York City, with Andros B. Stone president, and a purchase has been made of a large tract of historic land on the Hudson, involving it is said $1,000,000. The purchase includes the old Rockland Cemetery, near Sparkill, Rockland County, overlooking the river.

Besides the 200 acres included in the original purchase, it is expected that within a short time adjoining plots will be bought, making Rockland Cemetery one of the largest and most beautiful in the world. The entrances to the burying-ground are near the little villages of Sparkill and Piermont, on the west side of the Hudson, about twenty miles from New York. Four broad plateaus rise by gentle slopes to the summit, 700 feet above the Hudson. Each plateau has its hills and dales and its woodlands. The cemetery, as a whole, was a camping ground in the Revolutionary War, and as a battle-ground it is historic. Several miles of it front, and in fact, touch the Hudson River. From the third plateau can be seen the Tappan Zee, and across the water on the eastern bank lies Tarrytown, the summer home of wealthy and well-known New-Yorkers, with the Sleepy Hollow Church and the old home of Washington Irving in plain sight.

From the summit of the highest plateau can be plainly seen the land of seven states, New York, New Jersey, Pennsylvania, Massachusetts, Connecticut, Vermont and New Hampshire. Miles of the winding Hudson can be seen northward, ending in the hazy outlines of the Catskills and Highlands. From another portion of the cemetery can be plainly seen, only a short distance away, the little old-fashioned Dutch Church where Major Andre was tried and condemned, and a short distance away the clump of trees which mark the place where he was executed.

In the old Rockland Cemetery, which was founded many years ago by Eleazer Lord, the former president of the Erie Railroad, much money has been expended in improvements. The new syndicate, however, will immediately begin improvements on a larger scale, in landscape gardening, and the cost of these changes will probably exceed the purchase price of the tract of land. Three thousand burials have already been made in the old cemetery. In the receiving vault lies the body of General John C. Fremont. A handsome mausoleum will be built to his memory as soon as sufficient funds can be raised. Among the other prominent persons buried there are Commander Gorringe, H. C. Seymour, Henry Shipman, Thomas Lippincott and Jerome B. Stillson. In case the cemeteries now within the limits of New York are ordered removed, it is probable the bodies will be removed to Rockland Cemetery, where the old cemeteries will be reproduced in detail.

Andros B. Stone, is well known both as a philanthropist, and as president of the Cleveland Rolling Mill when it turned out the first Bessemer steel rails. It is believed that this cemetery has been evolved from his charitable instincts, and it is stated that the charges will be very much less than the other prominent New York Cemeteries,—being de-

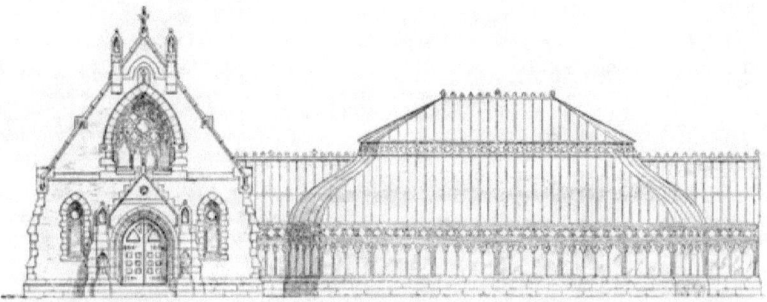

DICKSON MEMORIAL CHAPEL AND CONSERVATORY, GREENLAWN CEMETERY, SALEM, MASS.

signed to cover expenses for support and improvements. It is an established idea that some of the grave yards in New York City will have to be moved and the present project offers a solution.

Rockland Cemetery is within an hour over the Erie and the West Shore railroads, while from Forty-second Street it is a drive of only nineteen miles over a good roadbed. Within a short time desirable locations will probably be given to certain deserving charitable organizations.

Dickson Memorial Chapel and Conservatory, Greenlawn Cemetery, Salem, Mass.

The accompanying sketch represents a Chapel and Conservatory recently dedicated in Greenlawn Cemetery, Salem, Mass., erected in memory of Mrs. Georgia L. Dickson, by her husband Mr. Walter S. Dickson, and by him presented to the city.

The chapel is of sap-face granite with brown stone trimmings. It is 20 x 40 feet, and about 35 feet high. The interior is walled with bevelled terra cotta bricks and Cleveland sandstone trimmings. There are six stained glass windows in the body of the chapel, and six dormer windows. The ceiling is sheathed with hard wood and the hammer beams are carved by hand.

Five marble panels adorn the back of the pulpit which is of oak and is raised above the floor, with a settee at the back. Behind the settee there is a gothic screen, containing five tablets of polished Knoxville marble, set in oak frames. On the centre one, the following inscription has been cut:

> "Erected to the memory
> of Georgia L. Dickson
> by her husband.
> 1894."

On the right, as one faces the altar, are three arches of Cleveland sandstone, which lead into a small corridor. These arches are supported by large pillars of sandstone.

The conservatory 35 x 50 feet and 20 feet high, is connected with the corridor by similar arches of iron and glass. The corridor and vestibule are tiled.

The conservatory is of iron construction and wood trimmings.

The work and materials throughout are of the best and the whole forms a handsome and useful gift to the city as well as an endearing tribute to the departed.

Mr. George F. Meachem of Newton, was the architect.

Messrs. Thos. W. Weathered's Sons, of New York City, built the conservatory and heated both the chapel and conservatory. The chapel is warmed by the indirect hot water system, and the conservatory with 10 lines of 4 in. outside diameter cast iron pipes on each side of the house.

Memorial Trees.

On Arbor Day, in the state of Pennsylvania says *Garden and Forest*, a number of prominent Philadelphians connected with the Pennsylvania Forestry Association planted, with appropriate ceremonies, at the south end of the Centennial Concourse, in Fairmount Park, nine saplings; a sugar-maple in memory of Rev. J. P. Lundy, D. D., the first President of the American Forestry Association; an American Elm in memory of Dr. D. Hayes Agnew; an Oak in memory of General Meade; an Ash in memory of George W. Childs; another Ash in memory of Furman Sheppard; a Sugar-maple in memory of Governor Hartranft; a Linden in memory of Dr. Joseph Leidy; another Linden in memory of John Welsh, and a Sweet-gum in honor of Thomas Meehan, who will live, let us hope, to watch its growth for many years. Memorial plantings of this sort are certainly a very appropriate way of observing this holiday, and the trees, if properly cared for, will be invested with an affectionate interest which will increase with coming years.

Cemetery Planting.—V.

EULALIA GRACILLIMA UNIVITATTA.

Among the choicest of the hardy perennials are the Irises, German Siberian, and finest of all, Japanese. Classic blossoms these, more beautiful to the majority of flower lovers than Orchids and *certainly* more human notwithstanding the so-called "laughing" orchid and others. For orchid faces are only masks— Pansies have the real faces. The Japanese Irises like lots of moisture and would be at home fringing a little stream or lake.

The Lemon Lily, (Hemerocallis Flava) is a flower that should abound in cemeteries; it thrives best when left long undisturbed. Then there are the hardy tall Phloxes; masses of the pure white ones, or the clear red ones, that have come to take the place of the old time disagreeable magenta shades, would be well placed in the vicinity of shrubs that flower early, or interspersed among Pæonies.

Pyrethrum Uliginosum, and, for yellow Coreopsis lanceolata and C. tinctora are among the best of the late flowering perennials, and last of all, as well as best, are the Japanese Anemones—the pink ones are pretty but the white ones when well grown are as lovely as flowers can be.

Of the decorative plants that are particularly good for cemeteries are the big reed, Arundo Donax; Giant Parsnip (Heracleum Giganteum.) Yucca filamentosa and better still, that chaste plant, Yucca Augustifolia which builds itself into picturesque groups that present the same appearance the year around except while in flower. And in connection with hardy perennials the ornamental grasses should not be forgotten.

Eulalia Japonica and E. Jap. Zebrina are perhaps the best known and are both good, but the graceful fountain-like form of E. Gracillima Univitatta is even better and is especially effective for blending a shrubbery plantation with a lawn, or for softening the line where lawn and water meet.

And this brings us to Aquatics; than which there is nothing more satisfactory nor charming in the vegetable kingdom. Those that are hardy should certainly be seen in cemetery ponds and lakes, and the slight trouble and expense of starting water poppies and water hyacinths each spring is recompensed by such a wealth of beauty that those who try them once will have them always.

There is in planting a place for everything as well as something good for every location, and the best way to study artistic planting is to note Nature's arrangements under various conditions. Not to the end of reproducing exactly what is seen, or even using the same materials, for neither may be suited to the conditions at hand. But the seeing, comprehending eye will find suggestions in every combination of tree, vine and shrub; in every charming tangle, along each country lane; beside the wayside spring, the woodland walk, the winding stream, and in the quiet meadow.

And those to whom:
> "A primrose by a river's brim
> A yellow primrose was to him.
> And it was nothing more"—

have no part or parcel in what we have had to say in these papers, and happily of that sort there are none among our readers.

FANNY COPLEY SEAVEY.

Ornamental Cemetery Monuments Considered as Trade Fixtures.

"Fixtures" have been defined as "those things, which personal in their nature, become realty by reason of their annexation to the soil, such annexation being made by some one having an interest in the soil." Trade fixtures were the first which the law permitted to be removed to the injury of the owner of the soil. In the case of the Oakland Cemetery Company v. Bancroft, recently before the Supreme Court of Pennsylvania, (28 Atlantic Reporter 1021,) the principal question for adjudication was whether a certain ornamental monument was a trade fixture, so as to determine the ownership of certain copings, base, and marble statue levied on as the property of the Mt. Auburn Cemetery Company, under execution issued on a judgment against it in favor of the defendant Bancroft, and claimed by the Oakland Cemetery Company under a sheriff's deed executed pursuant to a foreclosure sale of the land on which such monument was erected, and constituting the grounds of the Mt. Auburn Cemetery Company. While this last mentioned company was the owner of the cemetery referred to, a burial lot was inclosed by a stone curbing, and a monument was erected on the ground, consisting of a stone foundation extending down below the frost line, and upon this foundation a marble base was placed, surmounted by a marble shaft, and upon the shaft the statue in question was erected. The whole of the structure was cemented together, and constituted a solid mass. The entire work, including the curbing, was built by the cemetery company for the ornamentation of the grounds, and manifestly was intended to be a permanent part of the cemetery property. Under these circumstances, the court holds it too plain for argument that the articles levied upon in execution in this case as personal property were a part of the realty, and could in no sense be regarded as personal property, and consequently could not be removed as a trade fixture.

THE MODERN CEMETERY. 43

THE MATHER MONUMENT, LAKEVIEW CEMETERY, CLEVELAND, O.

The Monumental Cross.

Of very early origin is the Cross, and for a very barbarous purpose does it appear to have been first devised. Traces of its use for execution by crucifixion dates back to very remote times, and for other purposes a cross device has been discovered among the researches into the histories of some of the early Asiatic nations.

But the triumph of Christianity brought the cross into honor and dignity, and it was soon made to assume an endless variety of proportions and form, and even to become an object of great effort in decorative art.

No position was too exalted for its use as a distinctive ornament, from the insignia of rank, to the hilt of the warrior's sword.

Mediæval ecclesiastical architecture fines the cross in most profuse use in the design of ornament, and the cathedrals were built on the ground plan of a cross.

It is easy to see how naturally the cross would find a place on the early grave from its venerated associations, apart from its use as a simple device for recording the departed:

The fundamental forms were the well known Latin cross; the Greek cross with the four arms of equal length; the St. Andrew's cross, like the letter **X**; and the cross of St. Anthony, like the letter **T**. Of these, the Latin cross has lent itself more directly to monumental service in the cemetery; and in Europe, crosses of innumerable varieties as to size and decorations may be found marking the resting places of the dead, in every cemetery and churchyard one visits.

The design of the cross is simple, but it admits of much latitude in decoration, and many elaborate cross monuments may be found. What are called the Runic and Celtic crosses, where a circle connects the arms, have been the origin of several handsomely decorated monuments.

The example we illustrate, that of the Mather monument in Lakeview Cemetery, Cleveland, O., cut from Westerly granite, is quite a striking piece of work, though comparatively simple in ornament. Another fine example, and perhaps the best known, is the Sidney Dillon monument in New York city. It is cut from an unusually large and finely carved stone. The cross stands upon a rustic base, overgrown with ivy.

The Law with Regard to Removal of Bodies.

Of all things, it would seem as if the expressed or implied wish of a person as to his last resting place would be treated as the most sacred. Still there are persons, inhuman and improbable as it must sound, who will even go to the length of removing ancestral remains from valuable burial lots so as to sell the latter. Besides, there are many more removals for less censurable reasons which ought never to be permitted, if on no other ground than that they violate the will of the dead.

The policy of the law is entirely against any removals alter interment, except for good cause. "A proper respect for the dead," said Mr. Justice Pratt, in Secor's case "a regard for the tender sensibilities of the living and the due preservation of the public health require that a corpse should not be disinterred, or transported from place to place, except under extreme circumstances of exigency." "There is a vast difference," the Philadelphia Court of Common Pleas declares, "between the question who is originally entitled to bury a human body and the question of the removal of that body subsequently to some other place of sepulture after it has been committed to the earth with the rites of religion in the presence of sorrowing relatives and friends. Questions which relate to the custody and disposal of the remains of the dead do not depend upon the principles which regulate the possession and ownership of property, but upon considerations arising partly out of the domestic relations, the duties and obligations which spring from family relationship and the ties of blood; partly out of the sentiment so universal among all civilized nations, ancient and modern, that the dead should repose in some spot where they will be secure from profanation; partly out of what is demanded by society for the preservation of the public health, morality and decency, and partly often out of what is required by a proper respect for and observance of the wishes of the departed themselves."

The Supreme Court of Rhode Island states, in the leading case of Pierce v. Proprietors of Swan Point Cemetery, that the right of a person to direct his place of sepulture is generally recognized. Strictly speaking, a dead man cannot be said to have rights. Yet it is common so to speak, and there is a qualified sense in which it is allowable to speak of the rights of the dead there being what may be termed "rights" which ought to be protected. There is a duty imposed by the universal feelings of mankind to be discharged by some one towards the dead; a duty, and we may also say a right, to protect from violation; and a duty on the part of others to abstain from violation. The person having charge of a body cannot be considered as the owner of it in any sense whatever; he holds it only as a sacred trust for the benefit of all who may from family or friendship have an interest in it, and a court of equity may well regulate it as such, and change the custody if improperly managed. In the case of Stephen Girard, the court said that if it had been applied to in time it would have prevented the removal of his body, when it did not consider that, under the circumstances of the case, it should interfere after the removal had been made. In this Rhode Island case, the court required the widow to restore the remains of her husband to a lot provided by him where she first had his body buried and from which she afterwards had it removed.

Another famous case is that of Reg v. Sharpe, decided by the Court of Criminal Appeal of England in the year 1857. In this case it is held an indictable misdemeanor at common law to remove a corpse without lawful authority, although the motive of the person so acting may be pious and laudable. This was a case, where it is so held, in which a son, from motives of filial affection and religious duty, removed the corpse of his mother from a dissenter's burial ground, for the purpose of its interment together with that of his father, in a consecrated churchyard. The accused, in person, argued that the grave was the private property of his family; and there had been no indecorum or improper motive in his proceedings. He alluded to the circumstance that the bodies of many illustrious persons had, at various times, been removed from one place of interment to another. The court says, among other things, that there is no authority for saying that relationship can justify the taking of a corpse from the grave where it had been laid. Furthermore, statutes have been passed in several of the states forbidding the removal of bodies, except under certain circumstances.

Besides all this, whoever has the freehold of the soil, may bring an action of trespass against such as dig and disturb it.

The law would, therefore, appear to be ample to secure the protection of graves and prevent improper removals. But to accomplish this it is necessary for some one to set the law in motion. If the heirs and friends of the deceased are indifferent, or connive at the removal of his remains there is not likely to be any one else who will care to interfere. There is, however, another pertinent suggestion in the Rhode Island case to be noticed in this connection. The court says that the cemetery corporation holding the lands for certain purposes had no doubt a certain control over same, but that control was to be exercised in such manner as to carry out, at least not to interfere with, the legal rights of those holding burial lots under them; that they were in fact trustees for certain purposes, and when the trust was not properly executed, the court would have the same jurisdiction to compel its execution as in case of any other trust.

Greater certainty might also be attained by having the title to lots conveyed in trust, providing so clearly for and limiting their use that no one would ever care to divert them in any way therefrom.

Annual Convention of American Cemetery Superintendents.

Preparations are actively on the way for the Eighth Annual Convention of the Association of American Cemetery Superintendents to be held in Philadelphia, September 11, 12, and 13, 1894.

The meetings will be held at the Hotel Lafayette, Broad and Chestnut streets, Philadelphia, one of the best hotels in the city of "Brotherly Love," where accommodations may be had either on the American or European plans, which will afford some freedom of action, in this regard, to visiting members.

The progressive advantages which the Association is assuring its membership, both from social and educational standpoints, warrants the belief that the coming convention will eclipse in beneficial results, all that have gone before, and it is urged upon all members to use every effort to be present. One grand result of the Association's meetings, and which is quite apparent, is the harmonious march of improvement now in progress all over the country. A fund of information is gathered, new ideas promoted and materialized, and a certain concert of intentions reduced to a formula for active work when returning to regular duties again. So, after all, the pleasure is really a duty, and this view can be carried right to the doors of the Cemetery Corporations themselves, who in their own interests should see to it that their superintendents have every facility at their command to attend the convention.

The following partial program has been so far prepared:

9 A. M. Tuesday, Sept. 11th.
Meeting called to order and Roll call.
Receiving new members.
Announcement of Executive Committee.
President's Address.
Secretary and Treasurer's Report.
Communications.
1st. Paper. How to Manage a Modern Cemetery.—A. W. Hobert.
2d. Paper. What are the Advantages to the Management, also to the Lot Owners of the Modern, or the Lawn Plan Cemetery?—Robert Scrivener.
Discussion of papers.
Afternoon and Evening—Arrangements not yet completed.

9 A. M. Wednesday, Sept. 12th.
Roll call.

3d. Paper. Civil Engineering in Cemeteries.—D. Z. Morris. Discussion.
4th. Paper. How to Make and Maintain a Cemetery with the Restrictions of Mounds and Memorials of any kind above the General Surface of the Lawns, and to Substitute a satisfactory Method of Marking Graves.—Timothy McCarthy. Discussion.

Questions from members for general discussion, with use of black board.
Afternoon—Arrangements not yet completed.

Evening, 8 P. M.
5th. Paper. What qualifications are Necessary to Become an all around Successful Cemetery Superintendent?—W. D. Primrose. General discussion.

9 A. M. Thursday, Sept. 13th.
6th. Paper. What is generally the Best and Most Approved System of Blending New Territory with an Old Cemetery?—Joseph Jewson.
7th Paper. The Theoretical System for the Perfect Management of Cemetery Employees, Teams, etc.—H. J. Diering.
Report of Committees.
Election of Officers, and Unfinished business.
New business.
Adjournment.
Afternoon—Arrangements not yet completed.

Decoration Day.

Decoration Day has come and gone once more, and the fact that it has received more public attention than before points to the conclusion that it is rapidly becoming one of the great festal days of the American people.

It is true that being a public holiday, the real intention of the day is in many directions overlooked in the interests of current human pleasures, yet there still remains the potency for good of the day, and the custom of decorating the graves of the fallen brave, while largely at present maintained in its integrity by those whose memories are still green, will more and more be merged into a public duty, and the day will, perhaps, become indeed a Memorial Day of a happy solution of a national crisis.

As long as the government maintains the national cemeteries, we shall still have, year by year, the reports from those cemeteries. While there remain communities who have not honored their fallen soldiery, we shall still have monuments to be unveiled; and as long as there are any G. A. R. men left, we shall still have interesting ceremonies at the graveside.

But apart from all this there has been springing up in the community a custom of using Decoration Day as a limit for completing monumental memorials to the departed in individual and private cases in our cemeteries, which all tends to concentrate about Decoration Day a truly national interest,—an interest hallowed by the conditions which created it and fostered by the further interest which mutual sympathy will always attach to it.

CEMETERY NOTES.

The Supreme Court has just affirmed the unconstitutionality of the Act of June 8, 1891, which prohibits the establishment of cemeteries within one mile from any city of the first class. This decision was rendered in affirming the judgment of Common Pleas Court No. 4, in the case of the City of Philadelphia against the Westminster Cemetery Company. The City of Philadelphia had asked for an injunction to restrain the Cemetery company from using their land for burial purposes, such land being within the act. The Westminster Company demurred to the bill, not in respect to the facts as to its location, etc., but as to the unconstitutionality of the Act, it being local and not general. The judge of the lower court sustained the demurrer, and the City of Philadelphia took an appeal with the above result. Among the points made by Judge Williams of the Supreme Court are:

"If, however, we look into the provisions of the Act, we shall find that they do not relate to cities of the first class or any other class. They relate distinctly and clearly to a strip of territory lying on the outside of the city of Philadelphia, having a breadth of one mile and a drainage into any stream from which the water supply of the city is obtained.

"It lays its hand on cemeteries and forbids their establishment within this narrow strip of territory. Now cemeteries may be more numerous and more necessary in the neighborhood of cities than in the country, but it will hardly be asserted that they are part of the municipal machinery of a city, even when located within its limits. This Act does not undertake, however, to deal with cemeteries within cities of the first class, but with those that are wholly outside of them.

"It does not attempt to deal with all cemeteries that are outside, but only those that are within one mile from the city lines. Even this limited territory is subdivided so that in the neighborhood of Philadelphia the law is applicable to those cemeteries lying in the valley of the Schuylkill, but it is not applicable to those in the valley of the Delaware. It would be difficult to imagine a better example of a law both local and special than this. We have held that the classification of cities rests on population, and may be sustained for the purposes of municipal government.

"When an effort has been made to extend legislation for classified cities to other subjects not municipal in their character, we have in every case refused to sustain such legislation."

The judge quoted a number of cases and closed by saying: "These cases are absolutely conclusive upon the question now raised, and the learned judge of the court below could not have done otherwise than to hold the Act of 1891 relied on to be local, and therefore unconstitutional. The judgment is affirmed."

* * *

Marcus A. Farwell, President of the Oakwoods Cemetery Association, Chicago, died June 12, at Waukesha, Wis., of typhoid pneumonia. Mr. Farwell was born July 8, 1827, in Coshocton County, O., where he grew up and was educated. He came to Chicago in 1851 and from 1855 to 1884, when he retired, was actively engaged in the wholesale grocery business. At the time of the Chicago fire when the house was entirely destroyed, Mr. Farwell was the first man to telegraph to New York that his firm would pay 100 cents on the dollar. Of later years he engaged a little in politics. For twelve years past his time has been devoted chiefly to Oakwoods Cemetery. He leaves a widow and four children. Mr. Farwell was an honorary member of the Association of American Cemetery Superintendents, and took great interest in the welfare of the association; he became personally known to many of its members by his frequent attendance at the meetings.

Treasured Tears.

In some districts of the Tyrol a quaint custom prevails which is singularly like the ancient Oriental custom of collecting the tears of mourners in bottles and preserving them. A traveler who has spent some months among the peasantry in that lovely district between Austria and Italy says that when a Tyrolean girl is about to be married and before she leaves her home to go to church, her mother hands her a handkerchief which is called a tear-kerchief.

It is always made of newly-spun linen, and has never been used. It is with this kerchief that she dries her tears when she leaves her father's house, and while she stands at the altar. After the marriage is over, and the bride has gone with her husband to their new home, she folds up the kerchief and places it unwashed in her linen-closet, where it remains untouched. The tear-kerchief has only performed half its mission. Children are born, grow up, marry and move away from the old home. Each daughter receives from the mother a new tear-kerchief.

Her own kerchief still remains where it was placed in the linen-closet on the day of the marriage. Generations come and go. The young rosy bride has become a wrinkled old lady. She may have survived her husband and all her children. All her friends may have died off, and still that last present which she received from her mother has not fulfilled its object. But it comes at last. At last the weary eyes close for a long, long sleep, and the tired wrinkled hands are folded over the pulseless heart. Then the tear-kerchief is put to the use for which it has been saved all those years. It is taken from its place and spread over the placid features of the dead before being laid away in the tomb.—*The Christian Herald.*

RULES AND REGULATIONS.

Every cemetery should be governed by certain rules and regulations, which should be printed in pamphlet form for distribution among lot owners. While this has been done in most of the large cemeteries, where the rules are very much alike, we will, for the benefit of the smaller cemeteries, publish in this department such rules as commend themselves for general adoption. Contributions are solicited.

Greenlawn Cemetery Association, Columbus, O., was organized in 1848. The cemetery is situated about two and one half miles from the Court house, in a southwesterly direction, and contains about 160 acres of land admirably adapted for the purpose. Most of the grounds are covered with native forest trees. Among the rules and regulations of this cemetery are the following:

No orders for Sunday interments will be taken by the Secretary after 10 a. m. on Saturday, unless for some exceptional reason the order could not have been more promptly given.

The preference shown for Sunday as a day for funerals is deprecated by the Board, and in justice to the employes of the Association, the selection of other days than Sunday for funerals, so far as practicable, is recommended.

No fences, hedges or stone coping will *hereafter* be allowed. Corner stones now set above the level of the lawn will be reset by the Superintendent at the expense of the Association.

All stone work more than two feet in height and more than eighteen inches square, will be classed as a monument, and should be set in the center of the lot.

Only one monument may be erected in one platted lot. Only one marker may be placed at a grave, and no marker should be less than six inches thick, nor more than twelve inches above the level of the lawn.

With regard to a change of improvements heretofore made, the wishes of lot owners will be consulted; but it is desired, at the expense of the Association, to effect the removal of all fences, hedges, copings and other like improvements, and to substitute for the same corner stones set level with the lawn.

Double head-stones embracing two or more graves will not be allowed.

No marker or other stone should be set in a socket or with a dowel.

No marble or granite tablets, cradles or horizontal marks, such as are made to cover the grave all over the top, will be allowed.

The use of spawls between base-stone and foundation or the removal of any part of the foundation to accommodate irregularities or other defective workmanship in the base-stone, will not be allowed. The Superintendent or his assistants are authorized to inspect every base before it enters the grounds, and if it be not up to the standard, it will not be allowed to enter the grounds until made satisfactory and according to the rules.

All foundations for monuments and head-stones will be put in by the Association at 30 cents per cubic foot.

No material for monuments or stone work will be received at the cemetery unless all that is necessary for its completion is ready for delivery at the time. The material for monuments can in no case be on the ground longer than is actually necessary for the purpose of erection.

No stone steps will be allowed in any part of the cemetery.

No gravel walks will be allowed in any part of the cemetery.

Only one flower bed will be allowed on lots that contain less than three hundred square feet of ground.

All vases that are not filled with flowers by the 1st of July each year, will be removed from the lot and taken to the tool house.

Small toy houses, wire arches, wooden trellis, glass globes, tripods, shells, toys, and like objects, are considered injurious to the beauty, dignity and repose of the cemetery, and the Trustees recommend the removal by lot owners of such objects now there.

◁ CEMETERY REPORTS. ▷

From the Annual Report of Woodlawn Cemetery, New York, we gather that 203 monuments were erected in 1893, at an estimated cost of $121,675, besides eight mausoleums and five side-hill vaults, costing $141,000. Arbor vitæ hedges were removed from around three lots, making a total removed of 517, leaving only 34 lots thus enclosed. The report notes a steady improvement in monumental work. Attention is called to the practice of erecting a "half" tent upon the lot and laying matting around the grave on lots, when interments are made.

A new Receiving tomb has been erected, adjoining the old one, containing 157 catacombs, built of stone quarried from the grounds. The interior walls are covered with hygienic cement. Cost, $12,880.96.

The cemetery contains 157 acres of graded ground; 10.8 miles of drains, and 9.4 miles of gravel and macadam roads.

The total receipts for the year amounted to $174,629.33, of which $152,878.51 was for lots, graves and receiving tomb fees. The expenditures were $160,232.09, which includes $28,050.00 paid for salaries.

* * *

Magnolia Cemetery, Charleston, S. C., has recently rendered its report for the year ending May 31st, 1894. This cemetery suffered very severe damage by the cyclone of last August, necessitating an outlay of five thousand dollars for repairs, which are being rapidly carried out. Since the cemetery was opened in 1850, twenty-one hundred lots have been sold, and eight thousand, two hundred and seventy-five interments made, with total receipts of $165,000. The Permanent fund now amounted to $32,000. The Perpetual Care fund now amounts to $20,000, and is constantly increasing, showing it to be a growing idea in the community.

Beyond the outlay for repairs, the cemetery is in a prosperous condition.

CREMATION.

In the annual report just issued of the Cremation Society of England, of which Sir Henry Thompson, F. R. C. S., is president, the council offer to the supporters of cremation their congratulations on the success of the Society's efforts during the past year. During the year one hundred and one bodies were cremated at the Society's crematorium, St. John's, Woking, Surrey, as compared with one hundred and four during 1892. The decrease, however, is only apparent, because it has to be borne in mind that a crematorium now exists near Manchester, where thirty bodies were burnt during the past year, as against three during 1892. Altogether during 1893, one hundred and thirty-one bodies were cremated in England, as against one hundred and seven in 1892. The accounts of the Society show a loss of nearly £200 on the year's working; but the council point out that it must be borne in mind that the fees for cremation are now reduced, and that it has also been found necessary to submit to a heavy outlay in repairs to the furnace, which is rapidly injured by the extreme alternations of great heat and cold to which it is exposed, the number of cremations at present being insufficient to maintain a more even temperature. The council are able to point to the increased facilities that now exist at Woking for carrying out a cremation. Since 1885, when the crematorium was started at Woking, four hundred and fifty-eight bodies have been disposed of there. The number of cremations in the successive years are as follows:—1885, three; 1886, ten; 1887, thirteen; 1888, twenty-eight; 1889, forty-six; 1890, fifty-four; 1891, ninety-nine; 1892, one hundred and four; 1893, one hundred and one. When the crematorium was first started at Woking, many of the local residents were highly indignant, and the villagers used to climb the trees in the vicinity with the object of witnessing a process which they regarded with undisguised disgust and horror. They could, however, see nothing, and now a cremation arouses not the least excitement or interest.—*Funeral Directors' Journal.*

QUESTION BOX.

"We recently made a large number of paths in our cemetery,—first carefully removing all turf and vegetation, and then covering carefully with coarse crushed bluestone. We have been bothered a great deal by grass growing up in spite of the stones. Can you give us any advice that will be useful in destroying vegetation in the paths? By so doing you will oblige," W. H. F., Peterborough, Ont.

ANS. Gasoline, properly applied, will satisfactorily destroy growing weeds in paths and gutters. It should be applied by means of a fine sprinkler, in such a way that the whole surface of the path or gutter is covered. One application is generally sufficient, provided enough of the gasoline is used.

A question is asked the Box as to what charge is made for watering grass in private lots per superficial foot for the season, and whether it is practicable to water grass in cemeteries on account of monuments.

ANS. It is difficult to make a price for such service, conditions varying so greatly, and then watering is included in the care of the lots, together with cutting grass and top dressing. For this work the price per annum appears to vary between three and four dollars for lots of from 200 to 400 superficial feet. No harm can befall the monuments of a cemetery for watering,—from observation, we should say, a goodly number would be improved by a more plentiful application.

Association of American Cemetery Superintendents.

WM. SALWAY, "Spring Grove" Cincinnati, O., President.
T. McCARTHY, "Swan Point" Providence, R. I., Vice-President.
F. EURICH, Woodlawn, Toledo, O., Secretary and Treasurer.

The Eighth Annual Convention of the Association will be held at Philadelphia, September 11, 12, and 13, 1894.

Resolutions Adopted at the Seventh Annual Convention of the Association of American Cemetery Superintendents.

Resolved: That it is the sense of this convention that all Sunday funerals be discouraged as much as possible.

Resolved: That it is the sense of this meeting that all headstones or markers should be limited to the height of the sod or the level of the surface of the ground.

Resolved: That it is the sense of this meeting that vaults and catacombs be discouraged and if possible prevented in cemeteries.

Publisher's Department.

The receipt of Cemetery Literature and Trade Catalogues will be acknowledged in this column.

TO ADVERTISERS, THE MODERN CEMETERY is the only publication of its class and will be found a valuable medium for reaching cemetery officials in all parts of the United States.

TO SUBSCRIBERS, Cemetery officials desiring to subscribe for a number of copies regularly to circulate among their lot owners, should send for our special terms. Several well-known cemeteries have already adopted this plan with good results.

Contributions on matters pertaining to cemeteries are solicited. Address all communications to
R. J. HAIGHT, 334 Dearborn St., Chicago.

Cemetery Literature Received:—Tenth Annual report of the Trustees of cemeteries of the city of Malden, Mass. Articles of association, by-laws and rules and regulations of Greenlawn Cemetery Association, Columbus, Ohio. Accompanying this was a card of rules for employes. Annual report of Woodlawn Cemetery, New York, for the year 1893. This report is illustrated with several fine half tone engravings.

Situation Wanted.

By a person qualified to fill position of superintendent and secretary. Several years' experience. F. L. R. Box 577, Eaton, Preble Co., Ohio.

THE MODERN CEMETERY.

THE MODERN CEMETERY.
AN ILLUSTRATED MONTHLY JOURNAL DEVOTED TO THE INTEREST OF CEMETERIES

R. J. HAIGHT, Publisher,
334 Dearborn Street, CHICAGO.

Subscription $1.00 a Year in Advance. Foreign Subscription $1.25.
Special Rates on Six or More Copies.

VOL. IV.   CHICAGO, JULY, 1894.   NO. 5.

CONTENTS.

CEMETERY MEMORIALS OTHER THAN GRAVE MONUMENTS... 49
CEMETERIES FROM THE SANITARY VIEW POINT—FUNGICIDES 50
*ANCIENT MONUMENTS—ARTEMISIA AND THE MAUSOLEUM 51
*OAKWOODS CEMETERY, CHICAGO 52
*OBELISKS 55
THE PATTERSON MONUMENT, CALVARY CEMETERY, ST. LOUIS, MO 56
CEMETERY NOTES.. 57
CEMETERY REPORTS.—CREMATION............................ 58
REFLECTIONS IN GREENWOOD CEMETERY.—THE CEMETERY SUPERINTENDENTS' CONVENTION 60
PUBLISHER'S DEPARTMENT 111
*Illustrated.

Cemetery Memorials other than Grave Monuments.

"Old things shall pass away; all things shall become new," said the old apostle, and while the prophetic warning has been working wonders in the spiritual life of man for which it was uttered, it has been equally potent, during the centuries which have passed, in the development of man's condition and surroundings, though there still remain much to be renewed both in his material and moral constitution.

No more radical change has been progressing in the past few years than in the ideas connected with our cemeteries and the disposal of our dead. An era of common sense, enlightened study, and a keener regard for the rights of our fellow man—though this feature will yet admit of considerable extension—is upon us, and a higher discernment and understanding of nature and her laws, are bringing us to endeavor to imitate her more closely in her methods and results,—and these results are harmony and beauty.

In the matter of our cemeteries this is especially apparent; the degree of favor with which the "lawn plan" is being received, and the rapidity of its development is an emphatic endorsement of the conclusion that an educated sense is taking the helm in cemetery management. That our cemeteries should be parks, decidedly not for recreation, but assuredly for contemplation, is the answer to the hitherto silent yearning of our better nature. This is a period of evolution in the cemetery, and yet not evolution, for the original cemetery was nature's landscape, which as the centuries moved along, lost its charm in the eager desire of man for improvement, display, and the vain effort to perpetuate himself. This resulted in the overloading of the cemetery with stone and metal work wherever room could be made for it, and the display of individual taste which created an incongruous variety of spurious adornment and a lack of harmony which invited disrespect and neglect. The decided turn in the tide of public taste, or lack of taste, is approaching the point where frequent discussion of the individual monument question, is rapidly leading the thoughtful and far-seeing mind, to consider in what more useful way can one perpetuate the memory of himself or those dear to him, than by expending large sums in monuments which after all only testify to selfish considerations.

Fortunately to show that there are other, more beneficial and praiseworthy means of keeping the "memory," not only green, but revered, many examples exist, principally in the way of cemetery chapels, to commemorate departed individuals.

Such a method of "memorial" has this great, unqualified advantage, it records for once something of benefit done for one's fellowbeing, while often times the costly monument in the owner's lot is the record of what has not been done.

This idea of erecting useful and necessary adjuncts to the cemetery is worthy of prompt and careful consideration. It carries with it the assurance of comparative perpetuity to a more comprehensive extent than the lot monument. No family complications as to heirship and other possible legal difficulties present themselves to mar the inviting prospect; on the contrary the fact that, beyond the enlarged prospective satisfaction of meeting and meriting the approval of the community, there will always be that indefinable solace which the intuitive faculties invariably prescribe for a good deed done.

Then the idea need not rest with the Memorial Chapel, or the Memorial Window and the Receiving Vault. There are other adjuncts of a cemetery which in the new order of things will become necessaries. For instance, Fountains and Shelter Houses.

What more graceful and albeit useful adornment

of a cemetery could there be than a chastely designed Fountain? Capable of infinite variety of design, and, moreover, wherein memorial statuary could be incorporated. It offers a scheme embodying the useful, ornamental, and "Memorial" ideas away ahead of the lot monument.

Something that is, and will be more needed in our improved cemetery, is what might be termed, "Shelter Houses." Here again architecture in its most refined form might be called upon to provide a fitting, enduring and most appropriate "memorial." Shelter Houses in properly selected spots to harmonize and give life to the surroundings, would add to the beauty of the scene and provide that comfort and means of rest which are generally deficient in such places.

Going to larger things there are many opportunities for carrying out these views in Cemetery Entrances. Memorial gateways afford an excellent field for perpetuating the memory of the departed, and much or comparatively little might be expended in such embellishments to our grounds.

Another field, presenting plenty of scope is the Conservatory. Memorial Conservatories offer an interesting and quite appropriate opening for the consummation of these views. While the planting of annual and tender flowers in profusion is discouraged, there is no more delightful recreation, no purer and brighter leading string to our higher sensibilities than a simple stroll through a well ordered conservatory—a pleasure that never tires, a refreshment always exhilarating.

We are not forgetting in our few suggestions in the direction of useful memorials—the Trees. Those noble, speaking examples of nature's most wondrous handiwork. Objects of admiration and affection through all the ages, and moreover, of certain species, well nigh imperishable. As memorial objects they have spoken for themselves through all the past and continue to speak with no uncertain voice.

Cemeteries from the Sanitary View-Point.

Investigations of the Paris cemeteries, says the *Journal of the American Medical Association*, strengthen the arguments against intramural interments and in favor of cremation for the disposal of the dead in the interests of the quick. Although M. Rochard asserts that the belief that bad smells emanate from cemeteries is unfounded and that there is an absence of noxious gases in well-kept cemeteries, there are other evils more insidious and more dangerous. Water filtered through the soil of cemeteries becomes polluted, and wells more than 100 meters from the graveyards of Mont Parnasse and Pere Lachaise were found to be contaminated from this source. With regard to the theory of germs being stored up in graveyards and later spread about, resulting in epidemics, M. Rochard believes that it is not impossible that when graves are dug microbes rise to the surface and mix with the surrounding atmosphere; but no fact has yet been demonstrated that this possibility has been recognized. It might be added that the well-known longevity of grave-diggers and their general immunity from the zymotic diseases is a disproof of the theory.

Fungicides.

One of the most valuable discoveries in modern gardening is the fact that there are appliances that will destroy fungus vegetation without any injury to vegetation of higher organization. Until comparatively recent times, sulphurous acid was the only dependence of the cultivator; but this had only a local and limited application. The farmer then discovered that when grain was steeped in copperas water, there was no injury to the seed, and the wheat which followed was wholly free from smut. It was easy to travel from this point to the Bordeaux mixture, and other solutions of copper, and the general application of spraying which has followed. At present the line of thought is in the discovery of cheapening and rendering less laborious the application of these solutions. A good step in advance is in the employment of ammoniacal solutions in connection with the copper. In about 45 gallons of water, three pints of concentrated ammonia and five ounces of copper carbonate are dissolved. The cost is less than one dollar a gallon.—*Meehan's Monthly for July*.

Several correspondents have written to *Meehan's Monthly* recently, as to how to destroy noxious weeds. Poison Ivy, Dock, Canada Thistle, and Dandelions are the subjects of these varied inquiries. In reply the editor states that intelligent gardeners know that no plant can live long without leaves. If, therefore, a plant is cut off to the ground soon after making leaves in spring, it is generally destroyed at once, but sometimes another or second growth will appear, of a more or less weak character, and if this is again cut, the plant will surely die. Nothing is easier than to destroy these weeds when this principle is kept in mind. The writer of this paragraph has known a whole half acre of Canada thistles entirely eradicated by having a boy cut them beneath the ground with a knife early in the spring. Very few shot up leaves the second time, but these were again cut as soon as perceived, and the result was to eventually destroy every plant. It did not cost $10. to do it.

Ancient Monuments.—Artemisia and the Mausoleum.

WIFE OF MAUSOLUS.

The illustrations we give of the ancient statue of Artemisia and of the Mausoleum she erected to the memory of her husband, Mausolus, make an interesting combination.

Considerable mythological history attaches itself to Artemisia, but like many of the women whose fame has been recorded in classic lore, or by the aid of Art, she seems to have won renown both in war and peace. Her husband, Mausolus, was king of Caria, who, in carrying through a warlike reign, changed his capital from Mylasa, the ancient seat of his kingdom to the city of Halicarnassus, the birth place of Herodotus, where he died in 353 B. C. He was succeeded by his widow, Artemisia, by the way, she was also his sister, who immortalized both herself and husband by the construction of a magnificent tomb, one of the seven wonders of the world, to honor and perpetuate his memory.

The illustration of the statue shows a queenly woman, with the marked characteristics of form and feature generally credited to the ruling woman of classic times, and with that repose and grace in the modeling of the statue, for which the great sculptors of Greece are so justly celebrated.

The picture of the Mausoleum gives the presumptive restoration, and from the ruins sufficient has been recovered by the excavations made by Mr. C. E. Newton in 1867 to enable a fairly complete understanding of the grand structure to be attained. The building appears to have consisted of five parts, a basement or podium, an enclosure of columns, a pyramid and pedestal, and the chariot group, or quadriga. An estimate of the basement gives 51 feet of height and an area of 114 by 92 feet. This was constructed of blocks of greenstone cased with marble, the monotony of the plain course being possibly broken by belts of frieze, suggest the investigators. The columnar enclosure, 37½ feet high, Pliny says consisted of 36 Ionic columns, enclosing a square space, the walls of which were relieved by friezes. Some portions of the principal freize of this enclosure represent combats of Greeks and Amazons. Mr. Newton, in describing these, says there is a "skillful opposition of nude and draped male and female forms, but the groups and figures are much less intermixed than in the Parthenon and Phigalian friezes. The whole surface was colored, the ground of the relief being ultramarine, and the flesh a dim red, while the drapery and armor were picked out with various hues." Some other fragments of friezes have also been found, but their position on the monument has not been exactly determined. One represents a chariot race and another a centaur fight.

A pyramid rose above this columnar enclosure, which has been estimated to be 108 feet long by 86 feet wide at the base; 24 steps carried one up to an apex or pedestal of, perhaps 15 feet 6 inches long by 20 feet broad. Upon this pedestal stood the quadriga, or chariot containing a statue of Mausolus himself, with an attendant charioteer,—some deity. According to all accounts the Mausoleum deservedly ranks as one of the seven wonders of the world. The statue of Mausolus is now in the British Museum.

TOMB OF MAUSOLUS.

ENTRANCE TO OAKWOODS CEMETERY, CHICAGO.

Oakwoods Cemetery, Chicago.

In appearance Oakwoods is materially improved by the new steel picket fence, six feet high, that now encloses it; and the entrance has gained dignity and impressiveness by the new fence being set out to the north line of the cemetery property, taking in the strip of land left vacant by the recent removal of the Illinois Central R. R's. branch track that formerly ran across the entire north front of the grounds.

The curved part of the fence on either side of the entrance, and the gates, are of handsomely hammered iron; and the pointed columns that support this part of the unusually elaborate and expensive boundary, are of polished Wisconsin granite, the lower ones being eight feet and the three taller ones, at the gates, twenty feet in height.

The effect of the light tracery of iron and steel, and of the brilliantly polished, richly colored columns seen against the light gray St. Lawrence marble of the office, and against the background of foliage is extremely good. The unfortunately placed pole of the electric railway that detracts from the appearance of the accompanying illustration is less noticeable in the real scene, and the entrance is now of a character calculated to create that first good impression that is credited with being a potent factor in later opinions.

But there are important improvements going forward in the interior of the Cemetery that, while more subtle and less likely to catch the eye of the ordinary observer, (at least in detail), are quite as satisfactory, and even more necessary than the new fence.

Oakwoods has always been pretty in spots, but only of late has one noted evidences of a coherent plan to make of the grounds a harmonious whole—a complete picture. The superintendent, (whom we take for granted deserves the credit of trying to bring about this happy condition), should have less difficulty in accomplishing so desirable an end there than in any cemetery of the same size and age with which we are acquainted. If he has the backing of the Association and the intelligent co-operation of the many enlightened lot owners, he will doubtless make Oakwoods lovely. And in these days when the best cemeteries are good examples of landscape art, and many of the cemetery superintendents are artists, it is likely that he will have the requisite co-operation and backing—especially as this is progressive Chicago where the legitimate ambition to set a good example is rife.

It should be easy because there is less bad work to be undone, as well as because much very good work stands as a foundation to which still better can be added.

For instance, some excellent planting is already well established; and the place is free from examples of objectionable old customs that have crept into newer cemeteries. Here there are no fences around lots—as though they were likely to run away; no cumbersome copings to help cut up the simple expanse, and, barring the misguided efforts at decoration seen in some unsightly borders of summer bedding plants, there are no symptoms of an intention to turn the grounds into a checker board.

It should be an expanse of closely cut, well watered sward—a great sweep of lawn where flickering leaf shadows weave delicate tracery, or long fingers of light and shade lie like a benediction.

It is a pity that in our day when Art has come to be more than a name, that bad taste in planting should be tolerated for any reason; it is doubly a pity that it should be publicly encouraged in high places by the ones to whom so many look for guidance. If *all* lot owners would but expend a fair

THE MODERN CEMETERY.

"A WELL SET GEM," OAKWOODS CEMETERY.

sum annually for the care of the grass, and of such hardy shrubs and perennials as would really enhance the beauty of Oakwoods as a sylvan picture —what a delightful picture it could be made.

Since spring, Mr. Lawson has accomplished some good and much needed work in thinning out the trees that have for years been crowding each other to the point of suffocation. Few shrubs find room for proper development when set at a distance of only five feet apart, and to set trees so close is simply to grow lumber—not pleasing plantations, and still less characteristic specimens.

The acre owned by the U. S. Government and used as burial ground for Confederate soldiers has alone furnished six hundred trunks to the axe. Heretofore this space was nothing but a solid and clumsy block of foliage—merely a wall of leaves. It now looks vastly better, the grass is already improved by the admission of air and sunlight, and with the contemplative figure on the monument that now marks the spot, the south end of the grounds is made far more interesting and attractive. But the weeding out of superfluous and inferior trees is being carried through the enclosure, and while in many instances it plainly should have been done long ago, their removal will still be of marked benefit to individual trees, and to the general effect.

Many of those taken out are soft maples, of which there was a superabundance; Box Elders, too, are also being taken up in numbers, (in every case where there is a better tree in close proximity), because they are shabby trees of shabby habits. They lose so many leaves during summer that their neighborhood is kept constantly untidy, and the grass sometimes permanently injured, all of which is a fruitful source of that *bete noir* of cemetery superintendents—unnecessary work.

The deciduous trees grown at Oakwoods that do especially well are the English and German Linden, their American relative the Basswood, Elm (American) White Ash which is extra good, and above all, the hard or sugar Maple, which seems to be about everything a tree should be for cemetery purposes in this latitude. Among others that thrive nicely and are not commonly seen are the southern Tulip, and Salisburia Adiantifolia, or Maiden Hair tree. There are two or three fairly good little specimens of the last named, but they are too shaded to do their best. I saw no Tupelo, or Sour Gum trees, although they are very desirable for cemetery planting, and grow well around Chicago. Conifers are faring badly at Oakwoods. Nearly all of the older trees are dead or dying, Spruces, White Pines, Arbor Vitæs and Junipers having suffered

LAKE SHORE PLANTING, OAKWOODS CEMETERY.

most. Their failure is attributed by Mr. Lawson to the smoke and foul gases from manufactories that sometimes envelope the entire neighborhood at night. The deleterious effect of these poisonous vapors on the evergreens is frequently so marked as to be seen at once, and their constant recurrence has wrought sad havoc. So far, Scotch Pines seem to withstand their influence, and handsome young specimens of Colorado Blue Spruce are doing remarkably well and promise pleasing variety in foliage effects.

I saw no Hemlock Spruces and wonder that they are not given a trial. The introduction of several Willows not yet used here, as the Royal and Laurel leaved Willows, would increase the beauty of the scheme, particularly if handled with an eye for color effects, and the charm brought about by judicious massing, and the varied results of light, shade and passing breezes. Probably all of these and many more will come into use as the planning and planting of the new section goes on.

The charm of the illustration "A well set Gem" will be seen to result in no small degree from the way the willows on the tiny island catch the light on their upper branches. I believe the effect would have been even better had the trees been Royal willows, because of their silvery foliage—the yellow tinge of common willows showing up darker in a photograph than in nature.

The lakes in the older parts of the grounds, with their surroundings, are the present beauty spots of the grounds. The illustration referred to shows a lovely bit, and "Lake Shore Planting" gives another glimpse of water view that is charming as a whole and that also shows several good points in detail. Two aspects of water side planting are fairly illustrated by it, the grouping on the farther side being seen to better advantage than that on the nearer shore—and more honestly too. The latter is so near the eye that only a part of a fringe-like plantation is shown, and the group seen in this incomplete way looks rather stiff and formal, an effect that will be overcome when the growing shrubs sweep the grass on one side and droop to the waters edge on the other. The spacing and arrangement of the group on the other side can be more correctly gauged as a wider stretch is visible, and one can estimate the relative distances. But the near planting plainly shows the pretty effect of shrubbery seen against a background of water. The introduction of small isolated groups of graceful hardy grasses, (like Eulalia Gracillima Univitatta,) near the water at some points, instead of shrubs, softens and improves such scenes wonderfully.

This illustration also shows the picture making results of well placed, boldly contrasted masses of light and shade, as well as the quick changes wrought by a passing breeze—one-half of the water being placed with the masses of dark foliage lying deep in undisturbed reflection; the other half broken into a thousand running ripples, each one with its bit of light and corresponding shadow.

The same breeze stirred all the trees it touched into gentle whispering atoms that put a new aspect on nature. Small things, small changes, small differences count for so much in these living landscape pictures, as they do in the sum of human existence —they make or mar a life. So also they make and unmake thousands of landscape scenes as the endless round of sunlight and gray mist, moonlight and frost rime, snowflakes and cloud shadows are shifted across numberless combinations of sea and sky, mountain and meadow, dim forest and glimmering stream, picturesque dell and awe inspiring canon.

Like all cemeteries Oakwoods contains a mixed showing of stone work, good, bad and indifferent— principally indifferent. Nevertheless it has some very expensive and elaborate monuments, as well as some that have decided artistic merit. But in all fine cemeteries the style of the memorial stones of all sizes should be required to meet an established artistic standard. The number of conspicuous ones would then be few, while every one, (whether costing much or little,) would be in good taste. Each lot could then be considered in relation to those around it, and the grounds would be beautiful and symmetrical as a whole instead of being spotted, (as is too often the case,) with all sorts of incongruous, inharmonious, meaningless and even grotesque designs and objects. Small wonder that so many persons are averse to visiting cemeteries, when they are so filled with cheerless stones that they strike a chill to the heart of the sensitive.

Every cemetery should be a park; a quiet, peaceful landscape; a place of velvet sward, clear waters, beautiful foliage and singing birds. Markers for recording names and dates should be so low and inconspicuous as not to count at all in the general view; and all monuments should be subordinated to the large general effect—each being designed especially to suit the location where it is to stand, thus gaining the proper setting and at the same time adding a harmonious feature to the picture.

Then cemeteries will be places where Nature's soothing balm will envelope the troubled spirits of the living, assisting poor sorrowing humanity to take up the broken strands of life and go its way comforted.

Stones are but cold comfort at the best. They would better take on forms of beauty, or breathe a wholesome meaning before being set up where sadness culminates, and bruised hearts congregate.

Better to see the stately swan sailing majestically on the water, or the helpless baby robins meandering in safety across the fresh grass, and better far a pure white rose blooming but for a day or two to make the world more fair, than pretentious stones that have no gentle meaning, no noble quality to lift the heart towards higher, holier things. FANNY COPLEY SEAVEY.

Obelisks.

The obelisk which is so frequently used as a form of cemetery monument, is of very ancient origin, and seems to have been originally intended to mark important events in old Egypt. The stock of the ancient forms of these monuments now to be found in Europe, principally at Rome, were all brought from Egypt by the Romans, and there is record that at one time Rome possessed six great obelisks and forty-two small ones, ranging in height between 108 feet and 8½ feet.

The ancient Egyptian expended an immense amount of labor and care on this form of "memorial" shaft, and it appears to have been used in contrast with the long lines of the peculiar arrangement of their temples, and from the fact that the despoiler's hand has so ruthlessly been displayed in the transportation of these relics from their original sites, it has not been possible to arrive at really just conclusions as to their value in Egyptian architectural schemes.

The largest monolith at Karnak is estimated to weigh 297 tons, and the one standing close to the church of St. John Lateran, at Rome, which is a little over 108 feet high and 8 feet square at the base weighs in the neighborhood of 450 tons.

The obelisk in Central Park, New York city which was brought over by Commander Gorringe some years ago, is one of the finest left of the ancient shafts, and a similar one now stands in London. Unfortunately the severity of our climate has rendered it necessary to resort to measures to preserve the hieroglyphic carvings on the faces.

These monoliths were generally cut from red granite or syenite.

The accompanying illustration is a good example of the obelisk monument, with modern ideas as to details. It is of Barre granite, 53 ft. high, shaft 36 ft.; bottom base 16 ft. square. The monument is fine hammered, with richly carved bottom molding.

THE SPRY MONUMENT, ROSEHILL CEMETERY, CHICAGO.

The Patterson Monument, Calvary Cemetery, St. Louis, Mo.

THE PATTERSON MONUMENT.

The memorial statue recently erected at Calvary in memory of Mrs. Winifred Patterson is a decided and refreshing departure from the prevalent distressingly stereotyped monumental styles. The design is an adaptation of Dore's Bible illustration of the widow's mite. I have not seen the illustration, so do not know in what details it differs from the original, but it is safe to say that it differs widely from it in pose and expression. An able critic has said that "Dore makes love, pity, charity and faith absurd," that "under his influence one feels that honest emotions or any trait of common humanity, much less piety, are evidence of weakness or nonsense." There is certainly nothing in the calm face and quiet, self-forgetful bearing of this beautiful figure to suggest anything of that kind.

The monument was designed by Mr. McNamara, a St Louis architect, and executed in Carrara marble by an Italian.

The statue is seven feet high, and stands on a draped altar table five feet square, which in turn rests on a granite plinth six feet square. On the face of the plinth is the name Patterson, and on the face of the altar, the drapery drawn up in heavy folds, discloses this inscription:

MARK XII.

"For they all did cast in of their abundance. But she of her want, did cast in all she had, even her whole living."

On the opposite side of the altar the inscription reads:

In Memory
of
WINIFRED PATTERSON
Born March 13th 1805
Died October 2nd 1891.
May she rest in peace.

On each end of the altar are reversed torches. And on both sides and ends the well carved drapery is drawn up in heavy folds as on the front.

The design is beautiful in its idea and its simplicity.

The well poised figure is appropriately clothed in a long flowing garment that falls in graceful, easy folds from the knotted scarf which girdles it at the waist. Deep drooping sleeves carry out the long lines and excellent drapery effects of the entire work. The head is closely coifed in a charmingly folded kerchief. The right hand is extended in the act of dropping a coin for the poor. The pose and expression of the entire figure is that of modest charity. The statue really means something.

The lesson of applied virtue is so clearly shown, and the work in its entirety so distinctive, that it can hardly fail to be remarked. And it seems impossible that any one should fail to recognize the fact that the expression of an idea gives that meaning to marble which is the only reason for its prominence in cemeteries.

The statue is a fitting tribute to a charitable woman, and it is an object lesson in monumental designs.

Fitness should be the first point considered. If it were, there would be fewer pretentious blocks of stone remarkable for nothing save their size, and fewer tall shafts that often serve only to call attention to the difference between their height and the small deeds they commemorate.

The Patterson monument is joyfully hailed by the Calvary authorities as a move in the right direction. They are proud of it and with good reason.

Cemeteries will become something more than places to be melancholy in when landscape beauty is freely introduced, when low, unobtrusive markers are used when only names are to be recorded, and, (where money is to be expended,) when monuments, statues and monoliths are only set up in remembrance of great names, of great deeds, or fittingly record in tangible form striking examples of human virtue.

FANNY COPLEY SEAVEY.

The Directors of Spring Grove Cemetery, Cincinnati, have suggested the following form of conveyance with a view to correct the practice of lot owners disinterring and removing bodies and disposing of their lots: "I give and devise to the proprietors of Spring Grove Cemetery my lot in the said cemetery, located in Hamilton County, Ohio, designated as Lot No.—, Section—, to be held by them and their successors forever in trust for the permanent interment of myself and (here insert names of persons whose interment therein is to be permanent, wholly free from control of my heirs at law or any other person whatever," etc.

CEMETERY NOTES.

It is proposed to create a city park out of Greenlawn Cemetery, Indianapolis, Ind., if the legal obstacles can be removed.

* * *

Mr. Frederick M. Farwell, son of the late Marcus A. Farwell, has been elected President of the Oakwoods Cemetery, Chicago.

* * *

Toledo Av., Detroit, Mich., is to be opened through Woodmere Cemetery, legislation of 1893, for that purpose having been declared constitutional.

* * *

A Sunday-School convention at Springtown, Bucks Co., Pa., decided that it was improper and sinful to strew flowers on the graves of departed friends on Sunday.

* * *

The Odd Fellows held their annual memorial meeting at Spring Grove Cemetery, Cincinnati, on June 17, some 500 members participating. The decorations were very elaborate.

* * *

A project is on foot to establish a new cemetery in Hamburg, a suburb of Buffalo. It is the idea of the projectors to make it the burial place of the dead of Buffalo after Forest Lawn shall have been filled.

* * *

At the 4th anniversary dinner of the Essex, Union Co., Funeral Directors Association held at Newark, N. J., last month, among the toasts responded to was, "Our local Cemeteries," by Mr. Charles Nichols, Supt. of Fairmount.

* * *

The ladies of the Cemetery Association of Parker, S. D., have raised the money and placed a windmill in their cemetery for irrigation purposes. All our small towns have just such ladies and there must be cemetery work to do.

* * *

Proposed reduction of pay and fines for trivial causes led to a meeting of the employees of Calvary Cemetery, Brooklyn, N. Y., at which it was resolved to submit the matter to Archbishop Corrigan, Chairman of the Board of Trustees.

* * *

The Board of Health of Philadelphia, has instructed the City Solicitor to proceed with the bill in equity filed by him to stop interments in Westminster Cemetery. The grounds for action are the possible contamination of the City Water supply from the Schuylkill River.

* * *

A new cemetery, Riverside Cemetery, is in preparation at Norristown, Pa. Mr. Acker of Phoenixville, prepared the plans for the residence and offices, and the receiving vault. Mr. Bellett Lawson, Jr., of Chicago, has been chosen superintendent and he is now busy pushing forward landscape work.

* * *

From the fact that the Queen's County boundary line passes through most of the large cemeteries on the outskirts of Brooklyn, N. Y., these cemeteries are assessed one dollar for every interment made over the boundary line in that county. In 1891 an income of $20,000 accrued to Queen's county from this source.

* * *

The Mount Auburn cemetery corporation of Lewiston, Me., is expending about $3000 this year in beautifying that place. A complete system of water works has been put in, the receiving vault is to be enlarged, and other improvements made. A tower for the purpose of distributing water has been built. It is pumped to the top by a windmill.

* * *

An Ohio State law provides for the erection of fences around all cemeteries at the expense of the county in which the cemetery is located. Fence companies at least seem to have taken advantage of the suggested possibilities in this law and have caught the attention of the "press" which is asking where all the fencing which the county pays for is going.

* * *

The selectmen of Canaan, Conn., have been remiss in their care of the lower cemetery of that town and are being editorially censured. Numbers of rural cemeteries suffer from similar official indifference and the remedy would appear to be a local association of lot owners whose personal as well as mutual interests would tend to devise ways and means to properly meet the question.

* * *

There is trouble for the Health officers of Toronto, Canada. It appears that a reported outbreak of diphtheria is claimed to be due to the exhumation of some children's bodies in Mount Pleasant Cemetery. These children had been the victims of the fell disease and had been exhumed by permits of the Health officers. The superintendent took active steps to prevent further trouble.

* * *

An association has been formed at St. Louis, the Undertakers and Liveryman's Association, for the purpose of regulating the prices of coffins and caskets as well as hire of hearses, carriages, etc. It is also proposed to keep a "dead beat" book to black-list such families as do not pay their funeral bills. It is possible that proceedings will be taken against the association under the anti-trust law of Missouri.

* * *

The old observatory tower on Highland Way, Cypress Hills, Cemetery, Long Island, has been taken down owing to decay. It had been frequently used by the U. S. Government for signal and geodetic purposes. It is the intention of the cemetery authorities to replace the observatory with a shelter or pavilion, one story in height, which will answer the purpose of accommodations for visitors as well as that of an observatory, it being located on very high ground.

* * *

There is a graveyard at Siegfried's Bridge., Pa., that was established in 1720—174 years ago. The ground on which it is located was deeded by one David Chambers to Joseph Showalter, Henry Funk, Peter Fried and Jacob Bear in trust for the Mennonites for burial purposes only. It originally consisted of one acre, but by an act of Assembly the trustees were granted the right to sell a part of the ground in order to secure means for erecting a yard wall around the remaining portion. The plot enclosed is about 75 by 100 feet in dimensions.

* * *

A little girl sat upon a grave in Mt. Hope Cemetery last Decoration Day, crying bitterly. A benevolent lady noticing her grief approached and laid her hand kindly on the child's head and inquired softly: "Poor child! Why are you crying dear? Is some soldier friend of yours buried here?" "Oh! no ma'am," said the child between her sobs. "I'm crying because I havn't any grave to decorate. Almost all the girls I know have got 'em. There's Lucy and Mary and Jennie, all have got graves, but there wa'nt none o' my folks killed in the war." And her grief broke forth afresh.

* * *

A correspondent of the Boston *Transcript* sends the following anecdote concerning the inutility of cemetery fences. An eccentric person known on the turf as "Billy Nicholl" of the Nottingham Town Council, in a warm discussion about rebuilding a wall around a disused churchyard was asked by a gentleman sitting next to him: "Well, Councelor Nicholls, what is your opinion on this question?" "Well," said Billy, "them poor devils what's inside, there's no fear of them getting out, and them blokes what's outside don't want to get in; so I don't see what you want a blooming wall at all for."

At a meeting of the Juneau (N Y.) Cemetery Association, the question was raised of assessing the lot owners one dollar each, the amount collected to be used for keeping the entire grounds in good order. This is a move in the right direction and should be carried out. The plan is in operation at a number of small cemeteries and ought to be more generally adopted. Nor should it be considered an unjust one by lot owners. It would surprise the lot owners of most of our small cemeteries what increased interest the community would take in them were they only to be kept trim and neat as they should be.

◁ CEMETERY REPORTS. ▷

The fiftieth annual meeting of the incorporators of the Allegheny, Pa., Cemetery was held June 30. The following are features of the report of the president :

During this fifty years there has been paid on the purchase of ground the sum of $299,861, and the amount expended in improvements, including labor, repairs, salaries to employees and expenses of all kinds, was $977,817, or an average per annum of $19,557.

There has been expended in these fifty years for permanent improvement, viz: for two handsome gateways, greenhouses, stables, fencing, etc., a total of $203,877.

The receipts for the sale of lots for each decade respectively were $139,809, $154,801, $417,004, $243,216, and $290,760, making a total of $1,245,590. The total receipts from interments were $277,982, and from interest on mortgages and invested capital, $396,857, a total of $674,839. The receipts from the sale of plants was nothing for the first ten years, and for the following forty years was $43,081.

During the past year 55 lots were sold for a total of $29,564, or an average of $537. There has been erected by lot holders three vaults, 65 tombs, 17 monuments and 335 headstones at an estimated value of $106,000.

There has been put down 1,720 yards of asphalt roadway from the entrance to the exit gate on Butler street, and 1,357 yards of new roads constructed.

36,817 persons have been buried in Allegheny cemetery.

At a low estimate, $2,000,000 have been expended by lot owners for monuments and other forms of memorials.

One hundred and twenty notices have been sent out requesting lot owners to either repair or remove the enclosures around their lots, and quite a number have already acceded to the request.

* * *

Mr. Geo. H. Olney, president of Pine Grove Cemetery, Hope Valley, R. I., in his recent report stated that a petition to the General Assembly for amendments to the charter included "giving the corporation power and authority to receive and hold funds in perpetual trust for the care and improvement of lots." Another important matter he touched upon was:

The necessity of lot owners providing in some way for the proper care of their lots from year to year. After the lots have been graded and put in first class order, more or less labor will be required on them each and every year, or the result will be that they will soon deteriorate and become over-run with bushes, briars and with grasses, and thus present a slovenly and most unattractive appearance, and in addition to this defect, the seeds from such wild vegetation will be scattered and sown upon other lots and the cultivated portions of the cemetery grounds, and thereby necessarily increase the labors and expense of the lot owners and superintendent in keeping the lots and grounds in good order.

A marked improvement was reported in the condition and appearance of the grounds, and an earnest appeal was made to lot owners to induce them to make arrangements with the board for the care of their lots.

✢ CREMATION. ✢

The Siamese employ cremation as a means of disposing of the dead, but they connect the burning with heathen rites. A missionary in Siam describes the cremation of the King's brother, the King being present.

On either side of the hall in which the dead man lay, stood long rows of idols, and near by groups of priests praying for the dead. All about the hall were theatrical performers, a shadow pantomine, a "Punch and Judy" show, music of Siamese bands and Chinese gongs, men dressed in skins of animals dancing through the crowd, huge animals made of paper stretched over bamboo frames and illuminated, darting in every shade in all parts of the grounds. Suddenly all noise was hushed, when the King kindled the fire, which, in a very short time, consumed the body to ashes. At a signal from the King the fireworks were lit, and the festivities recommenced with vigor and great noise. Such a funeral, conducted by the highest class of Japanese, costs a considerable sum, which the friends blindly believe will somehow purchase prosperity for the departed soul, and favor for the living.

Forest Home Cemetery, Milwaukee, Wis., is considering the question of a crematory. Milwaukee has a large German population, many of whom are anxious for such an addition to this cemetery. Mr. J. A. Pirie, the secretary, has been investigating the subject in view of future developments.

At the recent congress of the church of England, in the course of a paper on "Cremation" Professor A. Bostock Hill said: The time was coming in Great Britain when all available land would be required for the purpose of food supply, and the conversion, therefore, of thousands of acres into burial grounds which it was not intended to utilise for agricultural purposes, must be looked upon as a serious limitation to the food-growing of the country. After condemning the earth-to-earth system and burials in the sea, he said the object of cremation was to destroy the organic constituents of the body as soon as possible, and thus prevent the evil effects of the gases of putrefaction on the health of the living. That it was possible to carry out cremation efficiently, reverently, and without nuisance, had been proved by the establishment in this and other countries of crematoria, where many bodies had been burnt. One of the advantages of cremation was, that the body after death could, in the course of a couple of hours, without nuisance to anyone, be converted into three or four pounds of white ashes which were absolutely innocuous. The most serious objection that could be urged against cremation was, however, that which pointed out the danger of the destruction of evidence which might, at some future time, be utilised for the discovery of crime. As a matter of fact, there was practically no danger in the loss of traces of possible crime by the practice of cremation, because it had always been a rule, both adopted by the Cremation Society of England and in foreign countries, that no body should be cremated unless the most clear and satisfactory evidence could be adduced that nothing in the nature of foul play had occurred. It was most important that efficient means should be taken to prevent the spread of the disease to the living, and this could only be done by the process of disinfection. He knew of no disinfection which could be relied upon to satisfactorily perform that function except great heat. All thinking men deplored the great waste of money taking place in connection with funerals, and he believed that if cremation became popular there would be a saving of expenditure, amounting annually to a very large sum.

For those who have witnessed the ghastly spectacle of a modern funeral, no description of that barbarous rite is necessary. Who has not seen it all—the darkened room, stifling with its mingled odors of flowers and disinfectants; the somber, hideous casket; the awful ceremony of screwing down the lid over the beloved face; the black army of pall-bearers; the long, slow, mournful journey to the desolate, disease-breeding cemetery; the damp, dark, yawning pit, the lowered coffin, the sickening thud of the earth as dust returns to dust. Oh! could the most savage race invest death with more terrors than this frightful custom of the civilized world? Then follows the long process of decay, the darkness, the gloom, the weight of the earth upon that dear breast, the grave-worm slowing eating his slimy way into the flesh which has thrilled under our warm kisses?—God! are we not cruel to our dead?

Compare with this the beautiful ceremony of cremation. A snowy cloth envelopes the dead. A door swings open noiselessly, and the iron cradle, with its burden clothed as for the nuptial bed, rolls through the aperture and disappears in a glory of crimson light, as a dove sails into the summer sunset skies and is lost to view. There is no smoke, no flame, no odor of any kind. Nothing comes in contact with the precious form we have loved, but the purity of intense heat, and the splendor of great light. In a few hours, swiftly, noiselessly with no repulsive or ghastly features in the process, the earthly part of our dear one is reduced to a small heap of snowy ashes. All hail the dawn of a newer and higher civilization, which shall substitute the cleanliness and simplicity of cremation for the complicated and dreadful horrors of burial!—*Ella Wheeler Wilcox.*

There has been considerable difficulty with regard to the disposal of the remains of Mr. Kerr, who accompanied his brother-in-law, Lord Dunraven, at the yacht race last year. He was cremated and it was the wish of his widow that his ashes should be placed in an urn and deposited in a niche in the wall of St. Saviour's church, Belgravia, where her husband had been in the habit of attending divine service during his lifetime. This request, however, met with many obstacles; among others, the statute based on sanitary grounds which prohibits intramural interment of remains. Of course, no sanitary objections could be raised to a handful of ashes in a small urn, but, nevertheless, the statute was in the way and the matter was finally taken into court, where a decision has been given to the effect that the urn containing the ashes may be deposited under the floor of the church, but not in the wall.

Those who visit the boulder-marked grave of the poet John Boyle O'Reilly in Holyhood Cemetery, Boston, will find in position the stone from the wall of the Dowth (Drogheda) Church, on which thirty-four years ago he scratched his initials with a nail. It was once the poet's wish to be buried in the church-yard at Dowth, where he was born, but, as this could not be, his wife secured the stone indented with the letters of his name, and it has been let into the great rock above his grave. The initials "J. B. O'R." can be plainly read, but the date '60 has been almost effaced. The medallion executed by John Donohue, his sculptor friend, has also been placed in position. The medallion is thirty-six inches in diameter and shows the poet's head and shoulders. The representation is more than life size. The face is shown in profile. The poet could not have been buried in a spot more after his own heart. The lot is shaded by shrubbery transplanted from his native land, including golden cedars from Newton Ards, County Down, and purple beeches, yews, junipers, and rhododendrons from the same neighborhood. The boulder in whose shadow he lies is twelve feet in height and weighs seventy-five tons. Around its base 100 ivies from Dowth castle were recently planted. The scenery about the grave is rugged and picturesque.

Reflections in Greenwood Cemetery.

These polished urns may glint and gleam,
   With gaudy show their transient day,
But still the gnawing tooth of time,
   Shall wear their chiseled form away.

But generous deeds their records keep,
   In glowing fame shall live on high,
When marble shafts shall crumbling fall,
   And mouldering fanes in ruins lie.

Then bend, oh man, thy God-like mind
   To aid thy struggling fellow's needs,
And angel hands shall rear thy tower
   In deathless form with generous deeds.

Each act thy life hath ever wrought,
   Fraught with pure love for human kind,
In that fair structure angel built,
   Aglow with beauty thou shalt find.

Nor, as the ages come and go
   Shall storms e'er mar or time decay,
But it shall gleam with added charms
   In that elysian endless day.

Hence when few generations pass,
   Thou shalt not be forgotten there,
But thy life's record thus inscribed
   Shall glow with brightest beauty rare.

Then shall thy children call thee blest;
   Thy neighbor too with outstretched hand
Shall greet thee with o'erflowing joy,
   And life's great object understand.

—DR. W. H. HAMBLETON, in Atchison *Champion*.

The fee system, coming up from remote days in "Merrie England," has always been very liberal to ministers of the established church in connection with consecrated burial grounds, but trouble is brewing. Several Burial Boards have petitioned the Home Secretary, asking for legislation to curtail these privileges which have covered fees for the erection of tombs, headstones, iron work, etc., in fact pretty well everything in a cemetery. In the petition of the Worcester Burial Board appears the following:

"That your memorialists would not have been surprised to find that the excessive regard for vested interests which prompted the provisions of the Burial Acts dealing with the fees of the clergy, has led to the introduction of a clause securing such fees to every incumbent or minister who had possession of a benefice at the date of the passing of those Acts; but your memorialists submit that no justification can be found for continuing the right to receive the fees to which objection is taken in perpetuity by incumbents and ministers who have never received or been entitled to receive any fees in respect of burials in the churchyards of their parishes.

"Your memorialists therefore pray that you will be pleased to initiate legislation having for its object the repeal of those portions of the Burial Acts which confer upon incumbents and ministers the right to receive fees in respect of the sale of the exclusive right of burial, either in perpetuity, or for a limited period, in a cemetery provided by a Burial Board, or of the grant of the right of constructing any vault or place of burial with the exclusive right of burial therein, in perpetuity, or for a limited period, or of erecting and placing any monument, gravestone, tablet, or monumental inscription in such cemetery."

The Cemetery Superintendent's Convention.

The Eighth Annual Convention of the Association of American Cemetery Superintendents, to be held in Philadelphia in September, should attract a large attendance from Delaware, New Jersey and Eastern Pennsylvania cemetery officials. The object of the association is the dissemination of helpful information pertaining to cemetery management, and the practice of holding the annual meetings in different localities affords opportunities to all centering about such localities to avail themselves of the benefits to be had from participating in the discussions. The committee of arrangements have prepared an interesting program; the arrangements for the afternoons, which are not yet completed, will include visits to the best of the many local cemeteries, parks and other resorts, and as on other occasions, will form a most enjoyable feature of the meeting. It is hoped that all of the principal eastern cemeteries will be represented.

9 A. M. Tuesday, Sept. 11th.
Meeting called to order and Roll call.
Receiving new members.
Announcement of Executive Committee.
President's Address.
Secretary and Treasurer's Report.
Communications.

1st. Paper. How to Manage a Modern Cemetery.—A. W. Hobert.

2d. Paper. What are the Advantages to the Management, also to the Lot Owners of the Modern, or the Lawn Plan Cemetery?—Robert Scrivener.

Discussion of papers.

Afternoon and Evening—Arrangements not yet completed.

9 A. M. Wednesday, Sept. 12th.
Roll call.

3d. Paper. Civil Engineering in Cemeteries.—D. Z. Morris. Discussion.

4th. Paper. How to Make and Maintain a Cemetery with the Restrictions of Mounds and Memorials of any kind above the General Surface of the Lawns, and to Substitute a satisfactory Method of Marking Graves.—Timothy McCarthy. Discussion.

Questions from members for general discussion, with use of black board.

Afternoon—Arrangements not yet completed.

Evening, 8 P. M.

5th. Paper. What qualifications are Necessary to Become an all around Successful Cemetery Superintendent?—W. D. Primrose. General discussion.

9 A. M. Thursday, Sept. 13th.

6th. Paper. What is generally the Best and Most Approved System of Blending New Territory with an Old Cemetery?—Joseph Jewson.

7th Paper. The Theoretical System for the Perfect Management of Cemetery Employees, Teams, etc.—H. J. Diering.
Report of Committees.
Election of Officers, and Unfinished business.
New business.
Adjournment.

Afternoon—Arrangements not yet completed.

Association of American Cemetery Superintendents.

WM. SALWAY, "Spring Grove" Cincinnati, O., President.
T. McCARTHY, "Swan Point" Providence, R. I., Vice-President.
F. EURICH, Woodlawn, Toledo, O., Secretary and Treasurer.

The Eighth Annual Convention of the Association will be held at Philadelphia, September 11, 12, and 13, 1894.

Resolutions Adopted at the Seventh Annual Convention of the Association of American Cemetery Superintendents.

Resolved: That it is the sense of this convention that all Sunday funerals be discouraged as much as possible.

Resolved: That it is the sense of this meeting that all headstones or markers should be limited to the height of the sod or the level of the surface of the ground.

Resolved: That it is the sense of this meeting that vaults and catacombs be discouraged and if possible prevented in cemeteries.

Publisher's Department.

The receipt of Cemetery Literature and Trade Catalogues will be acknowledged in this column.

TO ADVERTISERS. THE MODERN CEMETERY is the only publication of its class and will be found a valuable medium for reaching cemetery officials in all parts of the United States.

TO SUBSCRIBERS. Cemetery officials desiring to subscribe for a number of copies regularly to circulate among their lot owners, should send for our special terms. Several well known cemeteries have already adopted this plan with good results.

Contributions on matters pertaining to cemeteries are solicited. Address all communications to
R. J. HAIGHT, 334 Dearborn St., Chicago.

For the purpose of stimulating an interest among lot owners in a class of cemetery memorials that will be useful both to the present and future generations, we desire from time to time to illustrate memorial chapels, receiving vaults, etc. Will our readers kindly furnish us with photographs or sketches of such memorials accompanied by brief description of the work?

"What shall we do with our dead?" is the title of a handsomely gotten up book issued by the Cremation Cemetery Co., of Baltimore, Md. It is intended that a perusal of the book shall answer the question, which its entertaining contents serves to confirm. There has been much scattering literature on the subject of Cremation, the best of which is herein epitomized.

THE NEW HANDY BINDER

Will be found a most valuable invention for keeping the numbers of the MODERN CEMETERY in good condition. The method of binding allows the pages to lie perfectly flat, whether one or a dozen numbers are in the binder. Any number can be taken out and replaced without disturbing the other numbers. The binders are strong and durable and have the title of MODERN CEMETERY on the side in gilt, an ornament to any desk or reading table. We will supply them to subscribers in embossed cloth covers, 50 cents. Heavy flexible paper covers for 35 cents. By mail post-paid.

MODERN CEMETERY, 334 Dearborn St., Chicago.

PATENT AUTOMATIC BURIAL APPARATUS
MANUFACTURED BY

This machine is a valuable, indispensable and useful invention. It is a necessity for the modern undertaker, cemeteries and the public. It is made of the best material, with best workmanship, and combines both lightness and durability. It is simple in its operation, cannot get out of order, dispenses with all extra labor and works without any noise or disturbance. A child could operate it with ease. Accidents are impossible.

We furnish two sizes:
Size A, inside opening 7 ft. 3 inch. long; weight, 150 lbs; Price $200.

Size B, inside opening, 5 ft. long; weight, 125 lbs; Price, $175.

HOW IT IS USED.

The frame is set level around the grave and the pall bearers place the casket on the straps. With a little pressure of the foot upon a small treadle on the side of the frame, the casket will descend slowly and silently into the grave. Then the operator draws up on two small cords, so as to unbuckle or disconnect the straps under the coffin, when by turning the crank the straps are rewound on their respective drums.

With each apparatus we furnish a complete set of Wrenches, one Crank Lever and a Water Proof Cover.

SCHERER MANUFACTURING COMPANY,
OFFICE AND SHOW ROOM— Bible House, Corner 4th Avenue and 9th Street, NEW YORK City.

THE MODERN CEMETERY.

Caloric Pumping Engines.

Nearly fifty years ago Ericsson first built a small caloric engine for pumping purposes, and it has been used for railroad, domestic and other purposes ever since. In the matter of economy, it is difficult to make any estimate because the cost is so small. When the water supply for twenty families can be lifted from 50 to 75 feet, with the expenditure of perhaps 1½ or 2 scuttles of coal and half a dozen drops of oil, the figures are too low to be of interest.

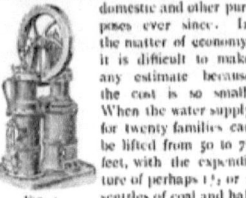

Fig. 1. DE LAMATER - RIDER PUMPING ENGINE.

The hot-air engine has passed through many modifications and improvements, and the two forms which we illustrate now practically hold the market in the United States. The De Lamater-Rider shown in Fig. 1, is generally used for the larger and heavier work. The DeLamater-Ericsson shown in Fig. 2 is of an entirely different type from the engine first built, and is adapted to both light and heavy work. The history of this latter engine is exceedingly interesting.

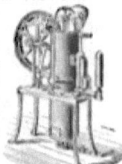

Fig. 2. DE LAMATER-ERICSSON PUMPING ENGINES.

During the last ten years this pump has worked under all sorts of conditions, and in the hands of all sorts of men, from the most experienced to the very poorest. It rarely needs repairs, and has been practically always ready to go to work when the fire was lighted. It is used with gas, coal, wood and kerosene burners. The larger engine, the De Lamater-Rider, is usually fitted to burn coal. Recent expedients for taking up wear, etc., have greatly increased the durability of both machines, and, taken altogether, they are probably the most satisfactory pieces of machinery in general use that can be found.

These engines are being largely used by florists, nurserymen, etc., and we would suggest that anyone desiring further information should write the DeLamater Iron Works, 87 South Fifth Avenue, New York.

.......BOOKS........

LANDSCAPE GARDENING ...

By SAMUEL PARSONS, JR., Supt. of Parks, New York City. Notes and suggestions on Lawns and Lawn Planting, Laying out and arrangement of Parks, etc. Deciduous and Evergreen trees, shrubs, flowers and foliage. Ornamentation of Ponds and Lakes. 300 pages, nearly 200 Illustrations. Beautifully printed and bound. A charming book for landscape gardeners. Price $3.50. With the Modern Cemetery one year, $4.25.

Local exchanges continue to report more or less reprehensible acts of vandalism in our cemeteries. It would seem that of all places in the world the cemetery should be safe from the depredations of the heedless and dishonest, but unfortunately it is not so. Owing to the conditions involved in cemetery management, a thorough police service is out of the question, yet to offset this apparent need, the penalties for such offenses against the public as well as the cemetery associations should be so severe as to afford a complete protection. Especially should this be the case in such criminal acts as the defacing of monuments and other structures; and for the petty, but none the less aggravating, though far more frequent, thefts of flowers from the grounds and graves, while the punishment must of necessity be modified, it should be of such a nature as to prove an effective deterrent. It is surprising that this latter offense is so general and not even confined to the lowly classes, for recently in a leading Chicago cemetery the occupant of a fine equipage was seen to go from lot to lot and take flowers until she discovered that she had been detected, when her coachman was told to make a hasty exit and she escaped. The local press should take up this matter and by creating a strong sentiment in the community against such acts lead to the enforcement of laws, the application of which would soon make the offense very rare.

* * *

It is gratifying to note the increasing interest taken by the local press in the welfare of the cemetery. We have all along, and time and time again urged lot owners to make every necessary effort to induce their local press to become interested. The discussion of improvements, policy of management, needs and requirements, through the columns of the local paper draw more attention to the general subject than perhaps any other course, and a public interest is fostered which can be depended upon to aid and encourage any efforts toward clearing up, improving and beautifying neglected spots, or of adding to the attractive features of such cemeteries as have been fortunate enough to have been well cared for.

J. B. Turner of Peabody, Mass., refused to allow the G. A. R., to decorate a grave which occupied a plot he had purchased, because the stipulation made at the time of purchase that the body should be removed had not been carried out. A Mrs. Spangler, at Myerstown, Pa., the wife of a dead soldier, forcibly opposed the decoration of his grave by the G. A. R. Post, because said Post had opposed her application for a pension.

* * *

Greenwood Cemetery, Brooklyn, N. Y., formed part of the battlefield of Long Island.

CEMETERY ADORNMENTS
......ARTISTIC......
Iron Vases
WITH RESERVOIRS, which are the best for Plants

BOUQUET HOLDERS
for Graves, 20, 25, 30 and 40c. each.

Our New Bouquet Vase For Cemetery is just out. Metallic Wreaths, Crosses, etc., 50c to $5 each.

SETTEES AND CHAIRS.
Both all IRON or IRON with WOOD SLATS.
Path, Avenue, and Keep off the Grass Signs.
Ornamental Fountains and Drinking Fountains.

FLOWER SEEDS—2 packages, 5 cts. Grass seed, bulbs, etc.
LAWN MOWERS—Our new one, "THE HERCULES," far superior and different from all others.
GARDEN HOSE—We only sell the best grades. Nozzles, hose, reels, etc.
JONES PATENT HOSE MENDERS—No tools or bands required. We send four menders, postage paid, by mail, for 15 cts. Send inside diameter of hose.
LAWN SPRINKLERS—3, 4, 6 and 8 arms. Hub, Globe and Combination. All our own make. Prices to suit.
Wire Rose Bush Trellises, Garden Borders, etc.

Greatest Variety of Above Goods at our NEW Store.
Illustrated Price List on application.

M. D. JONES & CO.
368 Washington St., BOSTON, MASS.

PATENT VAULT HEARSE.

Especially Designed For Removing Bodies from Vault to Grave.

NEEDED IN EVERY CEMETERY HAVING A VAULT.

CARRIES the heaviest body with perfect safety, and may be drawn easily by two men. Platform, 2' 6" x 7' 6", with silver plated rollers, pins, etc., similar to ordinary hearse. Substantially built. Highly finished.

Extract from Testimonial: The Vault Hearse perfectly supplies a long felt want. * *
We consider it indispensable where a vault is in use.—*Trustees, Marion, O., Cemetery.*

Send for PRICE LIST. **McMurray & Fisher Sulky Co.**, MARION, OHIO.

THE MODERN CEMETERY.

THE MODERN CEMETERY.
AN ILLUSTRATED MONTHLY JOURNAL DEVOTED TO THE INTEREST OF CEMETERIES

R. J. HAIGHT, Publisher,
334 Dearborn Street, CHICAGO.

Subscription $1.00 a Year in Advance.   Foreign Subscription $1.25.
Special Rates on Six or More Copies.

VOL. IV.   CHICAGO, AUGUST, 1894.   No. 6.

CONTENTS.

THE APPROACHING CONVENTION OF CEMETERY SU-
 PERINTENDENTS—CEMETERY ENTRANCES 61
THE FRIENDS' BURIAL GROUND, PROSPECT PARK,
 BROOKLYN, N. Y. 62
THE MODERN CEMETERY A SOCIAL FORCE............... 63
*METAIRIE CEMETERY, NEW ORLEANS, LA............... 64
THE CEMETERY SUPERINTENDENTS' CONVENTION 66
*HARDY HERBACEOUS PLANTS FOR CEMETERIES....... 67
THE SOIL OF GRAVEYARDS....................................... 68
CEMETERY NOTES 69
POWER TO TAKE LAND IN IOWA—POLICE POWER OF
 STATES OVER BURIAL GROUNDS—REMOVALS FROM
 UNPAID FOR LOTS 70
CORRESPONDENCE—ATTEND THE CONVENTION—LAWN
 GRASS—PUBLISHER'S DEPARTMENT..................... 71
*Illustrated.

The Approaching Convention of Cemetery Superintendents.

Before the next issue of of the MODERN CEMETERY the Eighth Annual Convention of the Association of American Cemetery Superintendents will have been held at Philadelphia. On another page will be found a communication from the President of the Association, Mr. Salway, supt. of Spring Grove Cemetery, Cincinnati, strongly urging the importance of this meeting and the work of the Association to cemetery officials.

The program, which will be found in part elsewhere in this issue, includes the discussion of important current features of cemetery work, and visits to adjacent parks and cemeteries.

It would seem hardly necessary to further emphasize the importance of this meeting to cemetery officials. The objects sought by the Association are of such obvious value to all cemeteries that it is the unquestionable duty of cemetery corporations to unite in furthering work, the benefits of which so largely accrue to themselves.

Cemetery Entrances.

The importance of appropriateness in our cemetery entrances very properly presents itself with the modern ideas of design and management. How often do we experience positive disappointment in the entrances of the majority of what are regarded as leading cemeteries, and the necessity of improvement in this direction is already recognized. It is not so much the character of the gateways that creates this disappointment, as the view usually presented after passing the gates.

In many cemeteries, and especially the older ones, the only object sought seems to have been the sale of lots, regardless of the advantages to be derived from attractive surroundings. Instead of the impressions that might be created by pleasing landscape effects, stonework of all classes and in all stages of dilapidation, oftentimes confronts the visitor.

The effect of such an entrance on the average mind must, naturally, be anything but conducive to the development of that spirit of restfulness and contemplation which should prevail.

Professor Weidenmann has well said that: "A cemetery without ornamental grounds is a mere graveyard."

The cemetery entrance would appear to be the most fitting place for the display of the highest skill of the landscape artist, and although the reservation of sufficient land for the purpose may be at first sight regarded as a sacrifice, the permanent results from such an improvement will more and more assert themselves as the years go by.

We have in mind a cemetery entrance that for years presented just such a spectacle as to stone work as has been suggested. But it has been changed, and the good work of beautifying what has for years been an eyesore, is still going on. It has taken time to work this out, but one by one the lot owners have been induced to exchange their holdings for others, perhaps larger, in newer and more attractive parts of the grounds. This plan has enabled the cemetery to gradually recover the ground around its entrance. The trees, with the green turf comparatively free from its burden of stones of all sizes, and doubtful perpendicularity, present an impressive picture. Here is a suggestion for cemeteries to adopt where it is not possible to change the entrance or add a new one.

We might enlarge upon the value of this suggestion to a greater extent. First impressions are forcibly said to be the best, at least from a business standpoint this should be true, and the first impressions of a cemetery will be those induced by its entrance, and hence a sound business policy dictates such improvements.

The Friends' Burial Ground, Prospect Park, Brooklyn, New York.

The gentle nature of the Quaker as we call him, Friend as he desires to be called, is reflected from everything pertaining to his sect, and the same serene, peaceful quiet of the Meeting House naturally finds more expression in the Burial Ground. Who that has read it once has not read it over and over again—that gem of our language, Charles Lamb's, "A Quaker's Meeting." Note his opening paragraph, and we shall better appreciate the following on a Friend's Burial Ground:

"Reader, wouldst thou know what true peace and quiet mean; wouldst thou find a refuge from the noises and clamors of the multitude; wouldst thou enjoy at once solitude and society; wouldst thou possess the depth of thine own spirit in stillness, without being shut out from the consolatory faces of thy species; wouldst thou be alone, and yet accompanied; solitary, yet not desolate; singular, yet not without some to keep thee in countenance; a unit in aggregate; a simple in composite: come with me into a Quaker's meeting."

Comparatively few of Brooklyn's residents know that within their beautiful Prospect Park limits, a Friend's burying ground has been in active operation for many years, and that it occupies one of the many choice sites. It lies hidden away in a dense and almost impenetrable mass of foliage, near the south-western corner of the park. The cemetery is finely situated upon the summit and gently sloping sides of a large knoll of ground, which commands an unimpaired and excellent view of New York bay with the Jersey shores as a rich background, and large sections of the cities of Brooklyn and New York. The cemetery covers a space of about fourteen acres of ground in its irregular and picturesque boundaries. An old board fence, built many years ago and now gray with age, half covered with clinging mosses and vines, hedges in the consecrated ground, which is pierced all over with little headstones that uniformly mark the repose of some faithful, God fearing Friend. The knoll is divided irregularly by a miniature ravine. Its borders are thickly wooded and within noble trees, studding the soft, velvety turf at frequent intervals, lift their towering trunks high into the air and throw out their broad leafy branches until they all but overlap overhead, and form a dense canopy of green, to shade the silent sleepers in the graves beneath.

Amid these peaceful surroundings and undisturbed by intrusions, some fifteen hundred of the faithful sleep in quiet. That same simplicity which has ever characterized Friends is carried in undiminished strength and intensity into the grave itself. Uniformity among all the brethren is the rule of life and seems to be that of death also and the life that is to come. Each of the fifteen hundred graves, with but very few exceptions, is marked with stones of like size and design. The headstones stand about ten inches to a foot in height and are as a rule, of white marble, with the names and the dates of birth and death carved thereon in the stone. With but few exceptions these are the only carvings upon the stone. The graves themselves, apart from the stones, are of the simplest character, small mounds thickly covered with smooth, well cared for turf. Running irregularly across the cemetery from east to west and dividing it into two unequal parts is an old roadway originally used as an entrance driveway when the cemetery was opened in 1826.

Next year came the great schism in the church which divided it and has kept it divided ever since, and the burial plot was also divided, the southern portion being assigned to the Hicksites, while the orthodox section took the northern. There are about 1,000 graves in the southern part, and 500 in the northern. The present cemetery may be called a continuation of the first Quaker cemetery, which was situated in New York. There is a stone in the present cemetery marked "Edward Hazard, died 1820," which is the earliest one that can be deciphered now. "Anna Rodman, 1762-1845," and "Thomas Hazard was born 11th month, 15th, 1758, died 7th month, 24th, 1828" also mark early interments in this cemetery. Notwithstanding the fact that the ground was purchased several years before, the first new burial in the present cemetery took place as late as 1848.

The cemetery is the absolute property of the monthly meeting of the Society of Friends of New York and Brooklyn, which holds all property for the society. The lots are assigned to each family, but are not bought or sold. It is impossible to purchase a grave in the cemetery. When Prospect park was originally planned in 1861, the Friend's cemetery had been established for a number of years, and the society refused to sell the property. The park was laid out in 1865 by Olmsted & Vaux, and by agreement between the city authorities and the Friends, their cemetery was embraced in the park limits. They owned a much larger tract of land at that time than they do now, and sold it to the park commissioners, preserving, however, a perpetual right of way through the park for all intercourse. The official entrance is the Tenth avenue and Fifteenth street. The burials in the cemetery average from thirty to thirty-five a year, rarely ever amounting to a larger number. The superintendent is James C. Stringham. There are no walks through the grounds, only a fine turf in every direction, broken at intervals by the trees and shrubbery, which are allowed to grow in luxuriant profusion. The Friends' funerals are devoid of all formal ceremonial. There is heartfelt grief visible, veiled with a calm dignity that surmounts misfortune and turns tears of bitterness into thanksgiving to the great God above for his innumerable mercies. A Quaker funeral is as sad and impressive as is a Quaker meeting house. There is always present with them that reserve and dignity which has come to make them respected and admired wherever they have lived and been known.

The Modern Cemetery a Social Force.*
(Copyrighted 1891 by the Memorial Art League.)

In rejecting the English law of primogeniture and entail we have denied ourselves much that is good in order to avoid more that is evil. The entailed estate is the balance wheel of English Society. It is to that more than to any other one cause that England owes that persistency of laws and of institutions which has placed her in the forefront of civilization. To it the Englishman owes that pride of ancestry which acting through many generations, has made him the straightforward, intolerant, sturdy and adorable bigot who is instantly recognized as an Englishman. His family name is his fetich, but his worship of it is in many ways a public benefaction.

But this pride of birth can flourish only when its roots are struck deep into the soil, and it bears transplantation no better than an English Oak. In the "turbulence of transition" that threatens to become the normal condition of the American's life, the homestead that has sheltered three successive generations is becoming more and more a curiosity and the flood of forgery, defalcation and embezzlement advances commensurably, yet we do not question the wisdom of our fathers in safe guarding us against the dangers of the "cumulative estate."

Are we then hopelessly adrift upon a shifting sea of dispersion? Have we nothing that can serve as a stable nucleus around which our family traditions may gather—about which a saving family pride may crystallize?

Our modern cemetery, we believe, may be made to answer exactly these conditions. "There are few occupations more wholesome to the soul than the care of a tree that one's grandfather planted"—and, we may add, this is never more true than when that tree shades its planter's grave. The unconscious recognition of this truth is the underlying cause of the vast popularity that greeted the establishment of our first Rural Cemeteries.

Opened less than fifty years ago; in many ways unskillfully managed as was to be expected where

*This article is the first of a series of articles by the Memorial Art League of Philadelphia, Pa.

there were no guiding precedents; encumbered and disfigured by useless and barbarous stone-work, whose producers, wholly mercenary and generally ignorant, were quick to see and to seize their opportunity, and whose monstrosities quickly antagonized the most exquisite effects of the landscape gardener; notwithstanding all these adverse influences—some of which have persisted to this day in spite of the present admirable management,—The Modern Cemetery has developed with a constantly accelerating rapidity.

That the family lot may become to us very much what the entailed Homestead is to the Englishman, we are certain; that it will quickly become so we firmly believe when our cemetery companies fully open the way for it.

1st. By encouraging and facilitating the purchase of ample plots.

2nd. By inducing interest on the part of lot-owners, in the *personal* care of their lots.

3rd. By discouraging ostentation and teaching that stone-work is an adjunct of the lot—not the reverse—as so many seem to consider.

4th. By a constant insistence that nature, under judicious guidance, is not excelled (except in costliness) in her products, even by some stone-cutter.

Let the members of the A. A. C. S., at their pending convention take up this aspect of the subject in earnest; let them find a way to formulate the idea definitely and clearly to their intending lot-owners; let them adopt a system by means of which the wishes (as they certainly find them to be) of our most cultured classes can be fully realized, and our modern cemeteries will very quickly assume their rightful position—that of a veritable saving force upon our character as a people.

It would be a gross impertinence in us to attempt to suggest ways and means to such a body of men as will make up this convention; and besides, we have no coal to send to that Newcastle; but there is much preparatory work to be done in freeing the minds of prospective lot-owners from false and pernicious notions regarding lot "improvements." In clearing away this rubbish, we do feel a moderate confidence in our ability, and shall enter upon the task *con amore* in our next paper; in the meantime will the convention adopt as a subject of discussion, this:

"How shall the Modern Cemetery be enabled to realize its grandest Potentiality?"

The Supreme Court of Vermont will not allow any extension of the Barre Cemetery, which makes the purchase of a new cemetery imperative. Barre is one of the most important towns of the state on account of the granite industry, and the decision is probably a wise one as the town is growing very rapidly.

Metairie Cemetery, New Orleans, La.

The cemeteries of New Orleans are among its most novel and interesting features and are in strong contrast to those seen elsewhere in the United States.

They are literally "cities of the dead," with avenues of spacious and stately tombs; streets of less pretentious ones, and by-ways walled by solid blocks of tenement houses. The latter are the oven tombs, and represent the single grave sections of localities where dust can be returned to dust as Nature intended and Hygiene demands.

Here, burial above ground is necessitated by the swampy nature of the site of the city, and its environs. Water stands within two or three feet of the surface at all times, and there is not only a possibility, but a strong probability of an annual overflow in many localities.

Metairie contains about one hundred acres, and is the most important and attractive of the numerous cemeteries, most of which are of small area, and none of which approach the size of the principal ones in northern cities corresponding in importance and population to New Orleans. It is one of a group of comparatively modern origin that cluster along the canal at a point about midway between the heart of the city and the West End—a resort on Lake Ponchartrain that is in great favor during summer. Metairie is accessible by the "shell road," famous in former days among the drives of America, but which now wears a shabby and neglected air, although not without attractions. These are principally due to the proximity of the distinctly picturesque canal with its channel crowded in places by floating islands of water hyacinths, its overhanging trees, trailing dewberry vines red and black with fruit, and tangles of pretty things growing with the free grace of all unhampered wildlings.

The cemeteries are also easily and quickly reached by steam dummy trains that run at frequent intervals from a point on Canal street, within a few blocks of the Clay statue,—the hub of the big, rambling town.

The triple-arched entrance to Metairie is distinctive by reason of the clinging cover of Ficus-repens which clothes it in every part with a close fitting garment. This vine is popularly used in New Orleans for covering plain surfaces, just as Japan Ivy (Ampelopsis Veitchii) is used in the north. It clings as the Ivy does, but resembles it in no other respect. In the north the Ficus is a greenhouse climber, here it is used extensively as an out of door evergreen. Besides the three arches of the entrance and part of the enclosing wall being covered with it, it is also used on the gate keeper's lodge, a concrete building just inside the entrance, and on the big receiving vault, (through which runs an open arch way with oven-like receptacles on either side from floor to ceiling), the exterior walls of which are hidden from ground to gable by its green covering.

Metairie has an open, spacious air unlike the crowded effect in the older cemeteries. Each tomb stands on its own plat of grass, a little apart from those on either side, and there are vines, shrubbery and flowers about them, while these wider avenues are lined with fine

AN AVENUE OF TOMBS, METAIRIE CEMETERY.

shade trees including Live Oaks, bitter Oranges, (which are much used as street trees throughout the city), Magnolias, etc. A gray stone wall tomb almost smothered in Confederate creeper, (Rinkesporum), whitened by loose drifts of snowy star-like flowers is not unusual, and altogether, with its Fig and Oleander trees, vines bright with yellow Bignonia blossoms, Pomegranates heavy with a burden of scarlet bloom, and many other plants and flowers unusual to northern eyes, the cemetery seems a Garden city of the Dead—its small white palaces set in unexpected greenery and bloom.

Gardening in Metairie goes on the year round. About the middle of November the winter planting is done, the varieties then set out, or started from seed corresponding with the Spring gardening work of the north. Phlox Drummondi and similar plants spring up from self sown seed of the preceding winter and spring; and Pansies started in cold frames in August, as well as Calendulas, Asters, etc., started in boxes in fall (to protect them from heavy rains) are set out for winter bloomers. Other similar work furnishes forth the decorative beds that are kept up in certain parts of the grounds throughout the twelve months by the cemetery authorities. Then in the spring, April or May, according to the season, these fading plants are replaced by those used for summer decorations, such as Hibiscus and Abutilons in variety, (these are wintered indoors), Geraniums, Coleus, Plumbago, etc. The Plumbago is wintered where it stands as it dies down like any herbaceous plant during the colder months, and starts up in the spring. It is very handsome too. Most of the annuals used in northern gardens are in their prime in New Orleans in April or May. Beds of roses are left undisturbed year after year, the Tea's being mostly used. They bloom well in spring, more or less throughout the summer, and again abundantly in the fall. The gardener at Metairie told me that Duchesse de Brabant (pink) was their best summer bloomer. Certain roses, notably Gen. Jacqueminot do not thrive in New Orleans, because the weather is never cold enough to induce the season of complete rest required. John Hopper, however, does well, as do Mrs. Laing, Baronesse Rothschild and Mabel Morrison; the latter being a pink rose in the far south instead of a white one as in the north. Their best white rose is a pillar climber, Celia Praedell; its flowers deepen to cream at the centre, and during the fall months are said to be as double as Camellias.

There is a plant house in connection with the cemetery where stock is propagated and tender plants are given the winter protection they need. Cannas remain outside the year round, and bloom all the time except in January and February. Gladioli are also left undisturbed, and form clumps that astonish a northerner by their size, and also by the number of their big flower-laden spikes. The splendid Gardenia grandiflora (Cape Jasmine) are woody shrubs that are neither disturbed nor protected in any way; they begin to bloom about the middle of May, and continue to flower during summer. They are preceded by Gardenia Florida, which bears smaller flowers that open some two weeks earlier. Verbenas continue alive, growing and blooming throughout the year. Zinnias are counted among the summer bloomers, but Dahlias and Chrysanthemums flower in the fall. The latter are left in the ground the year through, and are merely divided for increase.

Enough has been said to demonstrate that the difference between northern and southern vegetation and gardening is as marked as between the burial customs. In both directions the duties of cemetery superintendents would seem to be easier there than here. Mr. Scholz, the former superintendent of Metairie, who is highly spoken of by those who knew him, committed suicide in the fall of '93, and has been succeeded by Mr. Frank Ponjos. An important and interesting feature of the cemetery is seen just inside the entrance—the Albert Sidney Johnston equestrian statue of bronze, which surmounts a grassy mound built over the catacombs of the Louisiana division of the Army of the Tennessee, (Confederate.) It is a handsome bronze, and is one of the most prominent among southern martial memorial statues. A lengthy epitaph seen inside the tomb is of great literary merit, and has a history. It was written on the battle field by a soldier just after he heard of the General's death, and was found fastened to a board set up on the battle ground, by an officer who recognized its fine character; and when suggestions for a suitable epitaph were called for, this effort was offered and accepted.

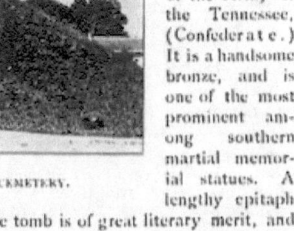

ALBERT SIDNEY JOHNSTON STATUE, METAIRIE CEMETERY.

In the back part of the cemetery stands a curious historic feature that might be called "the restored tree." It is an enormous Live Oak, the trunk of which was partly burned out during the war, but although so much of the life giving bark was destroyed the tree continued to live and thrive, and being so tenacious of life, such a fine specimen and so historically interesting, the hollow trunk was filled with concrete, (some brick being used too, I believe), until the original size and contour were

RESTORED LIVE OAK.

nearly reproduced. The bark and the general exterior were imitated while the material was plastic, and, at first glance at least, the tree now stands forth complete. Whether so-called "rustic sculpture" is the outgrowth of this attempt at restoration, or this work was the result of a knowledge of that style of handiwork, at all events the progress of decay has been retarded, and the noble old tree bids fair to outlive the generation that had actual knowledge of the desecrations of war. This dignified southerner wearing not only the green symbol of perpetual summer, but draped in a misty mantle of Spanish moss of the tint held dear by the South, seems to typify the proud southern spirit standing silent and stately guard over days, deeds and friends that have passed.

In this dreamy land one easily fancies that everything, even bitter regrets are soon overgrown with the moss of forgetfulness, even as the "sun and the dew," and the soft moist air weaves over their old tombs a dainty burden of moss, ferns and delicate plant life that soon softens their hard outlines and takes away their grim meaning.

And it is good to think that this may be true. This lovely, dreamy land should hold place not alone for its own warm-hearted, generous people, but furnish a refuge for those who live amid sterner surroundings—peaceful nooks where such may come and for a season possess their souls, while they fancy that they, too, dwell in the fair land where it is "always afternoon."

FANNY COPLEY SEAVEY.

A valuable prehistoric discovery is reported to have been made in in a mound at Egan, S. D. A tomb was uncovered lined with cement. In its compartments were twenty-two male skeletons of unusual size. A rude altar and many bronze utensils were exposed.

The Cemetery Superintendents' Convention.

The time for holding the convention of the American Cemetery Superintendents is drawing near, and I am especially anxious that it shall be a success in every respect, and the only way to make it such is for every member of the association, and as many others who are interested in cemetery work to be in attendance, and come laden with knowledge to impart, and ready to ask for all the information they desire to obtain.

The gathering has always been a kind of a family reunion, where good feeling is beaming through every eye, and the fraternal tie makes freedom of word and action which must be experienced to be appreciated. If we desire to be well developed, and properly informed in the things pertaining to our business, we should put ourselves in the position to become such, where can we go? Or what can we do better than meet with a gathering of men whose daily experience and life interest is directly in harmony with what is most interesting to us? I am aware that many superintendents are not able to stand the expense of going so far, and for such I ask the managers of the cemetery they represent to pay all their expenses and see that they attend, and I know it will be the best investment that can be made. It will yield the fruit of knowledge, and at the same time change the old one idea into new channels. I have had no other vacation since the organization of the association, although I have borne my own expenses it has yielded to Spring Grove Cemetery many thousand dollars; I never go to one of the meetings that I do not learn something that I can apply to advantage in Spring Grove. I therefore entreat the managers of cemeteries to show interest enough in their superintendent and the work he is doing, to see that his expenses are borne, on his attendance to the convention of the Association of American Cemetery Superintendents to be held in Philadelphia at Hotel Lafayette, on September 11, 12 and 13, 1894. I will here suggest that every member bring his note book, that he may retain, for future use, what he may see and hear, and I am sure that his store house of information will have additional stock well worth the gathering.

The committee have made arrangements which will ensure a profitable and enjoyable time, and at the season of the meeting, the cemeteries and parks in and around Philadelphia will be in a favorable condition for inspection, all of which affords object lessons not to be forgotten.

WM. SALWAY, President,
American Cemetery Supt. Assn.

* * *

The meeting will convene at the Hotel Lafayette, Broad and Chestnut streets, Philadelphia, at 9 a. m., Tuesday, September 11th, and will continue three days. Tuesday will be occupied in the morning by the preliminaries and discussions of:

"How to Manage a Modern Cemetery," by A. W. Hobert, supt. Lakewood Cemetery, Minneapolis; and

"What are the Advantages to the Management, also to the Lot-owners, of the Modern or the Lawn Plan of Cemeteries?" by Robert Scrivener, supt. Cedar Hill Cemetery, Hartford, Conn.

In the afternoon a visit will be made to Harleigh Cemetery, Camden, N. J.

On Wednesday morning discussions will be resumed, as follows:

"Civil Engineering in Cemeteries," by D. Z. Morris, supt. Mount Hope Cemetery, Rochester, N. Y.; and

"How to Make and Maintain a Cemetery with the Restrictions of Mounds and Memorials of any kind above the General Surface of the Lawns, and to Substitute a satisfactory Method of Marking Graves," by Timothy McCarthy, supt. Swan Point Cemetery, Providence, R. I.

A drive in Fairmount Park will be the feature of the afternoon, and the evening will be devoted to a paper by W. D. Primrose, secretary Loudon Park, Baltimore, Md., on:

"What Qualifications are Necessary to Become an all around Successful Cemetery Superintendent?"

On Thursday morning papers will be read by Wm F. Jewson, supt. Glenwood Cemetery, Mankato, Minn., on:

"What is generally the Best and Most Approved System of Blending New Territory with an Old Cemetery?" and

"The Theoretical System for the Perfect Management of Cemetery Employes, Teams, etc.," by H. J. Diering, supt. Woodlawn Cemetery, New York.

Thursday afternoon will be in charge of the Executive Committee.

* * *

Mr. Geo. E. Rhedemeyer, supt. Harleigh Cemetery, Camden, N. J., or Mr. Geo. M. Painter, supt. West Laurel Hill, Philadelphia, members of the Executive Committee, offer their services in securing accommodations for such of the members as desire to make arrangements in advance The Hotel Lafayette is conducted on both the European and American plans.

* * *

Visiting members who intend going to New York will be glad to know that in reply to a solicitation by the editor of the MODERN CEMETERY, Mr. C. A. Dana, of the New York *Sun*, has responded that; "he would be very glad to have the superintendents visit the grounds at Dosoris," and has instructed Mr. Wm. Falconer, his well known gardener, to be prepared to receive them. Dosoris is one of the most famous of American country seats, and is a "Mecca" to all interested in landscape gardening.

Hardy Herbaceous Plants for Cemeteries.

Among the hardy herbaceous plants suitable for cemeteries those that bear heat and drouth, as well as cold, must be accounted the most useful, and cemetery superintendents must needs keep themselves informed regarding the desirability of the species and varieties adapted to their various needs and to different localities.

Having been familiar with all of the out of door planting at Jackson Park that was included in the preparation for the World's Fair, as well as with the exhibits during the Exposition, and also with the treatment of the plants retained by the South Park Commissioners after its close, I have seen some things thoroughly tried and tested. And the reliability of the varieties named herein cannot be questioned for they have done well under trying conditions, having lived through two hot, dry summers during neither of which did they receive a supply of water equal to their needs, (if the best results were to be attained,) and have wintered as best they could without care or protection.

For carpet plants Veronica cupestris and Cerastrum tomentosum can be recommended. By carpet plants are meant dwarf plants that make close growth, quite hiding from sight the ground occupied. Such plants are a necessity if one would garden well, for bare earth with here and there a straggling plant is not good gardening. We do not find examples of this sort in Nature's garden. *There* things are finished off, not left half done. The ground around and beneath hazel bushes, wild blackberries, or sumachs is occupied by colonies of tall or medium sized plants that rise from beds of violets or wild strawberries, and the interstices between these are filled with delicate trailing plants, ferns, grasses or mosses. Everywhere some such charming plan will be found carried out with fine breadth of effect, great beauty of detail, and, withal, infinite variety of form and color. In all favored climates vegetation literally *clothes* the earth.

To return to our pretty, unassuming little friends the carpet plants: Veronica cupestris is a neat, compact, low-growing plant that spreads a layer of sprays nearly parallel with the ground, (but a little above its surface,) each closely filled with small dark green leaves that look fresh and living after weeks of heat and insufficient watering; it also gives itself a nice finish by carelessly lifting a loose spray of the same pretty leaves here and there to take from the formality of its appearance, and in early summer it is decorated with many small spikes of pretty blue flowers—good while they last, yet not greatly missed when they are gone because the foliage retains its admirable qualities throughout the season.

Cerastrum tomentosum attains an average height of about six inches, being a little less dwarf in effect than the Veronica, and in direct contrast to it in color, as it is silvery green or greenish white in tone. It has small pointed leaves set closely along the nearly upright stems, bears a good crop of starry white flowers in spring, and endures drouth remarkably well. These plants are useful for covering the ground around taller ones in hardy borders. In moist partly shaded situations For-get-me-nots are a good selection for the same purpose. And in all situations the Moss Pinks (Phlox subulata and P. subulata alba) are excellent low plants for edging beds of hardy perennials or for smothering the ground around their feet.

FANNY COPLEY SEAVEY.
(To be continued.)

The Soil of Graveyards.

At a special meeting of the Royal Society of Edinburgh, on May 28, a paper was read on the "Chemical and Bacteriological Examination of Soil," by Dr. James Buchanan Young. The question was whether the present method of the disposal of the dead was inimical to the public health. He had approached the subject from the point of view of examining virgin soil and soil which had been used for inhumation, and he had done so chemically and bacteriologically. He had tested the soil for organic carbon and organic nitrogen, and also for nitrates. Such work was not easy to carry on in England on account of restrictions imposed on investigators in graveyards, but great facilities were given for it on the Continent. The result of an examination of virgin soil in the Grange Cemetery which had never been used for inhumation, was this: Organic carbon, .265; organic nitrogen, .0257; and ammonia, .0005 per cent. The Arboretum soil which had been used for cultivation gave organic carbon, .842; nitrogen, .0936; ammonia, .0096; while in soil that had been used for inhumation the figures were—carbon, .87; nitrogen, .1073; and ammonia, .0115. It was apparent from these figures that the soil used for burial purposes was not rendered materially impure, and when the graves were opened the soil was in such a state of purification as not to differ greatly from other soil which had never been used for burial. Schutzenberger had made investigations into soils in Paris with this result, that whereas in virgin soils the figures were—carbon, .835, nitrogen, .01—in the soil of the *fosse commune*, in the Mont Parnasse Cemetery, they were .14 carbon and .15 nitrogen. The soil of Mont Parnasse was thus richer in organic carbon than the cemeteries of Edinburgh, but it was not a bit worse than the soil which was often found in sites of houses, for the reason that in such cities as Edinburgh, the ground naturally had been polluted by the want of sanitary arrangements in the past. The result, therefore, of the investigations was this, that, from a chemical point of view, there was no reason to consider that inhumation as at present practised was inimical to public health. This question had been dealt with in Germany by testing the ground air for carbonic acid, both at and below the levels at which interments were made. Statements had been made that there was a large amount of carburetted hydrogen, carbonic oxide, and sulphuretted hydrogen in graveyards, and when one read the evidence of the witnesses given before a Commission many years ago as to the state of the London graveyards, one could only wonder at their vivid imaginations. Some of them actually spoke of fires bursting forth from the graves. Well, Hesse of Saxony had worked this out, and had found that after ten years in fairly good porous soil the carbonic acid in the gases aspirated from the soil had almost come down to the normal of ordinary soil, and that in twenty years the soil had purified itself. It had been said that graveyards polluted the air by the gases which rose from them. Tests had been made of the air in the Rue de Rivoli and in Pere la Chaise Cemetery, and there was no difference at all; and as regards carbonic acid, it had been found that the air in St. Cuthbert's Churchyard was rather purer than the air in Princes Street. In testing for micro-organisms, it was found that these diminished in the ground from above downwards, the soil acting as a filter—an important result, as bearing on the pollution by organisms of water courses passing under graveyards. Figures were given to show the relative number of micro organisms at different depths in graves, and above and below the coffin. The largest number seemed to be found about four feet six inches down, in one case there being 7,222,000 per gramme. These results were calculated to reassure them, and to keep inhumation from falling into disrepute. At the close of the paper, Professor Geikie said he had only one remark to make, and that was from a sentimental point of view. He was afraid it completely extinguished the corpse candles which country folks supposed they saw in churchyards.

CEMETERY NOTES.

Jasper, Mo., now has a handsome cemetery, and the Jasper *Bee* calls on the citizens to give it their "hearty support."

* * *

A City Improvement Society has taken in hand the improvement of the local cemeteries of Newburyport, Mass. It is a timely project and pursued with intelligence and with proper support will create renewed interest to the permanent pleasure and profit of the community.

* * *

It is interesting to note that all people are not inclined to favor giving over the parks to public monuments. This is evidenced by the opposition manifested in Syracuse, N. Y., of the residents about Fayette Park to the proposition to place the soldier's monument there.

* * *

A cemetery near Providence, R. I., is offering special inducements to people to die early. A large sign board proclaims that lots will be sold at the lowest possible prices, and that they can be paid for in monthly installments. This is reported to be the sequel to proposed auction sales at the same place which did not materialize for lack of audience.

* * *

The long continued drought has had a disastrous effect on the appearance of many of our cemeteries, and such a general diffusion of dry weather has seldom been known in the United States. Even with ample water facilities it has been difficult to take sufficient care of large tracts to keep up appearances, while in a majority of cases such attempts have been futile.

* * *

At a recent meeting of Pine Grove Cemetery Association, Deering, Me., a new code of by-laws was adopted. Every lot-holder is now a member of the Association and the officers form a board of directors ex-officio. Lot-holders have a vote for every 200 square feet in area of their lots. A plan for perpetual care of lots is to be prepared and submitted. The invested fund of the Association now amounts to $2,100.

* * *

We are very busy, says Mr. William Salway, superintendent of Spring Grove Cemetery, Cincinnati, O., excavating for two new lakes, and raising low land with the earth taken out. We shall use the part so raised for single graves, which will be worth when completed between $50,000 and $60,000, and at the same time much improve the locality by the change. We have recently built a new shelter house at a cost of $1100, with modern conveniences.

* * *

I see in your notes a statement concerning an old cemetery at Seigfrieds Bridge, Pa., writes the secretary of Cedar Grove Cemetery, Long Island, N. Y., "and it might be of interest to note that in one part of our cemetery, now at the end of its initial year, there is a burying ground with some well preserved stones with clear cut inscriptions and queer epitaphs, dating from 1706 to 1720 and later. It has been trimmed up and new trees and shrubs planted, and with the exception of well worn marks of time, is the same burying ground of colonial Long Island."

* * *

Lot owners in Brooklyn cemeteries seem to have good cause for complaint against the annoyances imposed upon them by the numerous florists and gardeners who have established themselves in close proximity to the entrances, the better to push trade. This of course could be obviated in large measure by the cemetery corporations operating their own greenhouses, and it is quite open for discussion whether it would not be better to do so and take what revenue might result, than negatively to encourage conditions which involve unpleasant consequences and sometimes imposition on their patrons.

* * *

The mausoleum in course of construction by Chauncey M. Depew, in memory of his wife, in the Hillside Cemetery, Peekskill, N. Y., is of granite, classical in design and almost devoid of ornamentation. It will be twenty feet long, sixteen feet wide and seventeen feet high. The roof will consist of two huge slabs of granite, with a granite cap. The entrance will face the west, and will have bronze doors. A wreath carved in the stone over these doors and the scroll work on cornices under the corners of the roof will be the sole ornamentation. Openings cut in the granite in the shape of a Greek cross in the north and south walls will admit air and light. The mausoleum will cost about $20,000.

* * *

In the District Court of Douglas county, Neb., in the case of Barber vs. Baldwin and Callahan, president and sexton of Prospect Hill Cemetery, suit was brought for $125 damages on account of the cemetery employes entering on the said Barber's lot, trimming some trees and shrubs, and removing two small markers. After two full days' trial, the court decided that inasmuch as the said cemetery had no rules or regulations at the time of the purchase of this lot, nor for twenty years after, the said cemetery association had no right to enter this lot without first obtaining the consent of the lot owner to make this or any other improvement. Court decided in favor of the plaintiff. $35 damages and costs.

* * *

A monument erected in the Church of St. Saviour, London, preserves the memory of Dr. Taylor, a famous pill maker. This monument represents the doctor in a reclining attitude. In one hand he holds a scroll, bearing a most enthusiastic eulogy of "Taylor's pills." It stands near the pulpit, where the congregation could not help seeing it. In the church at Godalming, there is, against the south wall of the south transept, a mural monument bearing the following inscription: "Sacred to the memory of Nathaniel Godbold, Esq., inventor and proprietor of that excellent medicine, the Vegetable Balsam, for the cure of Consumptions and Asthmas. He departed this life the 17th day of December, 1799, aged 69." At the Pere la Chaise Cemetery, Paris, there stands, or stood, in a conspicuous position, a monument to Pierre Cabochard, grocer, with a pathetic inscription, which, after relating the many virtues of the defunct, closes thus: "His inconsolable widow dedicates this monument to his memory, and continues the same business at the "old stand, 187 Rue Mouffetard."

To the foregoing, which we take from the *Funeral Directors' Journal*, might be added the inscription on the tombstone erected at the grave of a marble dealer's wife in a southern state, which informs the reader of the cost of the monument and where it was made.

Power to Take Land in Iowa.

The township trustees are empowered, in Iowa, to condemn or purchase, pay for, and enter upon and take, lands, for cemetery purposes, in same manner as is provided for incorporated cities and towns. The Code also provided that, "When it shall be deemed necessary by any such corporation to enter upon or take private property for any of the above uses, an application in writing shall be made to the district court. After such notice has been given the court shall proceed to determine the compensation to be paid for the taking of the property, and for that purpose shall empanel a jury, and the mode of precedure therein shall be the same, so far as applicable, as in an action by ordinary proceedings." Construing these enactments, the Supreme Court of that state holds, in the case of Barrett v. Kemp, recently decided, that it is contemplated that only the question of compensation shall be submitted to the jury. It is also clear, it holds, that the necessity for the taking of the property is a matter which the trustees alone can determine. But their determination must be made before the court has jurisdiction to act in the matter of ascertaining the compensation to be awarded, and whether they have so acted is a matter for the determination of the court alone.

Police Power of States over Burial Grounds.

The Court of Errors and appeals of New Jersey has rendered an important decision in the case of the Mayor and Common Council of Newark v. George Watson and the Trustees of the Second Presbyterian Church of that city. It says that all rights are held subject to the power of the state over the public health and morals. The power of the legislature to restrain or prohibit the use even of private property in a way detrimental to the public health or safety is beyond dispute. It being competent for the legislature not only to change and modify political districts, but also to dissolve them at pleasure, its power to control and extinguish the uses to which property may be held by such political districts, must be wider than that which pertains to the property of private persons. The rights of the legislature to forbid a municipal corporation to appropriate or use its lands within corporate limits for burial purposes is incontrovertible. Such enactments are not unconstitutional, either as impairing the obligation of contracts, or taking private property for public use without compensation. They are unassailable as an exercise of the police power. Whether there is any limitation upon this rule as applicable to private cemetery companies may present a different question. Moreover the Court holds that the title to lands held by the municipal corporation above named as plaintiffs in this case, under a grant from the proprietors of East New Jersey for burial purposes, to be appropriated for no other use or uses whatsoever, reverted to the proprietors when an ordinance of the municipality and an act of the legislature prohibited the use of such lands for burial purposes.

Removals from Unpaid For Lots.

The question has been asked by an Iowa correspondent if, when a body is buried in a lot that has never been paid for, nor a deed given, but the title to which is still in him, whether he can legally remove the body to some other lot in the same cemetery, if he so desires. This is a common practice in most incorporated cemeteries, and is made a part of their agreement in the transfer of lots. But in the latter case there is introduced a condition not specified in the above question, namely, the existence of an agreement, either made with the deceased in his lifetime, or with the person having the burial of his body in charge, that it may be removed to some other location if the lot be not paid for. This is, on principle, somewhat like giving the body a temporary resting place in a vault awaiting preparations or determinations for its final interment. The question as propounded cannot safely be answered, as must already begin to be apparent, by a direct affirmative or negative declaration. In a few of the states there are statutes which might prevent such removals. But the subject is controlled for the most part, by what may be called considerations of sentiment and public policy. Of decisions throwing light on the matter there are few; of decisions right in point, there are none.

By the civil law of ancient Rome, a body once buried could not be removed except by the permission, in Rome, of the pontifical college, and in the provinces, of the governor. In England, by the ecclesiastical law, the whole matter of burial was under the direction of the ordinary, and was of ecclesiastical cognizance. And once buried, the body could not be removed without license from the ordinary. The courts of common law were left to confine themselves to the protection of the monument and other external emblems of grief erected by the living, and these they guarded with singular solicitude. Here is the explanation of Blackstone's statement that, though the heir has a property in the monuments and escutcheons of his ancestors, yet he has none in their ashes; nor can he bring any civil action against such as indecently, at least not impiously, violate and disturb their remains, when dead and buried. But there is quite an old decision to the effect that though a dead body by law belongs to no one, it is therefore under the protection of the public. If it lies in consecrated ground the ecclesiastical law, it is said, will interpose for its protection; but, whether in ground consecrated or unconsecrated, indignities offered to human remains in improperly and indecently disinterring them are the ground of an indictment. Since then the current of judicial opinion has been gradually changing, so that the courts, if applied to in time, would now doubtlessly interfere to prevent the removal of bodies under many circumstances where they could afford no relief after the removal. Thus in the Stephen Girard case it was said that where a person was buried in a common burying ground, where the title did not pass, the law did not furnish a remedy in reference to a removal; but a chancellor of a court of equity would intervene to prevent the desecration of the grave.

This much seems to be clearly settled, according to a high authority, that when a body has once been buried, no one has the right to remove it without the consent of the owner of the grave, or leave of the proper ecclesiastical, municipal or judicial authority. A purchaser of land upon which is a burial ground has no right to remove the bodies against the wishes of those interested. Every one of the interments, it is said, is to be regarded as an assertion by the one party, and an admission by the other, of the existence of the privelege of burial, with all that implies, as belonging to those who exercised it, the legal effect of which concession the purchaser cannot repudiate. In a North Carolina case which turned largely upon practically this same principle, it was suggested, on the argument, that the owner of the land on which there was a burying ground had the legal right to remove the monuments, however indecent, improper, and censurable it might be in a moral point of view, to do so. This view, the supreme court of that state pronounces wholly untenable. Granting that he was the owner of the land, it says that it was decent, orderly and proper to bury the dead, they were buried, and he, or those under whom he claimed title to the land must be presumed to have assented to and sanctioned the use of it for burial purposes, and having done so, he had not the right to remove the bodies interred there, or the memorial stones erected by the hand of affection and respect, and much less had he the right to desecrate the place, by felling the trees, ploughing the ground, and throwing down and scattering the grave stones. The law does not tolerate, but on the contrary, forbids such acts, as criminal offences of serious moment. Causes might arise that would require and justify the removal of dead bodies from one place of interment to another, but such removal should be made, with the sanction of kindred, in a proper way, or by legislative sanction.

Returning now to the original question, it would seem plain that, where anything like an unconditional license to bury, either express or implied, has been granted, no matter if it is not accompanied by any transfer of title, the owner of the land has no right to remove the body so buried without at least the consent of the next of kin, or the proper legislative or judicial authority. Where the burial is made under a conditional license or permission, as that the lot must be paid for or the body will be removed to another location, it might well be that the removal, if done carefully, and not objectionable on any sanitary grounds, would be regarded by the courts as justified. And, as before stated, the courts would be more apt to prevent, on application, a removal of this kind, than to afterwards punish it. The Indiana case of Hamilton vs. The City of New Albany is a strong one in some respects, and a good illustration of this last statement to close with. Proof was made on the trial, that the city had, by mistake, resold a lot in which years before the first purchaser thereof had buried the body of his deceased child, and that when about to inter a corpse in the lot at the request of the second purchaser, the sexton discovered the box containing the remains of the child, which he carefully removed and placed in a place set apart for single graves. The first purchaser of the lot had removed from the city and had no knowledge of this until he sent to have the body of his child removed to another city. There were no special damages shown or expenses incurred The first purchaser instituted this action to recover damages. The finding of the jury was for him, with one cent damages, and this the supreme court says that it does not feel at liberty to disturb, but affirms, with costs.

* * *

The foregoing article has been prepared for THE MODERN CEMETERY by a member of the Chicago bar and is therefore a legal view of the question.

It will interest our enquirer to know what action has been taken under similar circumstances in one of the adjoining states. Mr. D. Densmore, Pres. Oakwoods Cemetery, Red Wing, Minn., says: The Board of Trustees, after taking charge of the city's cemetery, gave six months' notice to all delinquent lot holders, which was extended a further six months to pay up, or in default the bodies would be removed to the Potter's field and the lots placed on sale at a higher valuation. This was carried out. The ordinance contained no special clause as to right to make such removals, but the ground was taken that parties burying their dead in lots which after due time had not been paid for were trespassers and had no rights.

In Pennsylvania in a sale of a burial lot no title passes, except by deed, and Mr. R. D. Fletcher, Superintendent Woodlawn Cemetery, Titusville, Pa., says: We make a removal to single burial ground in case of nonpayment, having a legal right to remove as no title is passed.

Correspondence.

Attend the Convention.

The next convention of the Association of Cemetery Superintendents is near at hand. Every superintendent should be present, and do what he can to make this convention better than the last.

It is not merely an outing, we should look at it from a business standpoint. Whatever business a man is engaged in, he should meet with others similarly engaged. It must be beneficial, it cannot be otherwise. I care not how well a man thinks he is posted, there is always something that he can learn. Our work must be kept up, and we must keep our eyes about us, if we do not, we will open them some day, and find ourselves falling behind, and will also find it pretty hard to catch up. Rather, let the times catch up with us. The world will continue to move, and we must move with it. Let us then all strive to be present at Philadelphia, and attend to the important business before us. The papers that are read, the points that are discussed and the general conversation, in, and out of the meetings, will give us plenty to think of, and will prevent us from becoming narrow minded. We have many minds to cater to. Our works are open to praise or criticism, we are human and are much better pleased to hear words of praise, and we will not get them unless they are merited, and only by diligent work can we hope to merit them. Let us all endeavor to be present and put our shoulders to the wheel and keep our eyes on that word *Excel*, which is generally at the top of the ladder.

WILLIAM STONE, Lynn, Mass.

Lawn Grass.

Questions are often asked as to the proper amount of seed to sow per acre in order to get the best results in lawn grass; the usual quantity is about 75 pounds to the acre. This depends, however, a good deal on the kind of grass used, some being lighter per bushel than others; but when what is generally known as mixed lawn grass seed is employed, this is about the quantity to use. It may be remarked in this connection, that very much of the beauty of a lawn depends on its being properly weeded. The first season, in spite of every precaution, weeds will appear. It is not that the seeds of the weeds are mixed with the seeds of the grass as a general thing; but the weeds come from the seeds which will lie in the earth sometimes for several years before germinating. These coarse weeds should be dug out with a pointed trowel or sharp knife, and if comparatively large holes are made, these should be filled with earth. Towards the dry weather of summer the whole should be thoroughly rolled. Of course many weeds can be pulled by hand. After the grass gets started and has thorough possession of the ground, it will itself keep down the most undesirable weeds.—*Mechans' Monthly for June.*

Several costly memorials have recently been completed in Elmwood Cemetery, Detroit, Mich., for prominent citizens. Among them is the Gen. R. A. Alger mausoleum, the Luther Beecher mausoleum and an imposing canopy monument for James F. Joy. The aggregate cost approximates $50,000.

Association of American Cemetery Superintendents.

WM. SALWAY, " Spring Grove " Cincinnati, O., President.
T. McCARTHY, "Swan Point" Providence, R. I., Vice-President.
F. EURICH, Woodlawn, Toledo, O., Secretary and Treasurer.

The Eighth Annual Convention of the Association will be held at Philadelphia, September 11, 12, and 13, 1894.

Resolutions Adopted at the Seventh Annual Convention of the Association of American Cemetery Superintendents.

Resolved: That it is the sense of this convention that all Sunday funerals be discouraged as much as possible.

Resolved: That it is the sense of this meeting that all headstones or markers should be limited to the height of the sod or the level of the surface of the ground.

Resolved: That it is the sense of this meeting that vaults and catacombs be discouraged and if possible prevented in cemeteries.

Publisher's Department.

The receipt of Cemetery Literature and Trade Catalogues will be acknowledged in this column.

TO ADVERTISERS. THE MODERN CEMETERY is the only publication of its class and will be found a valuable medium for reaching cemetery officials in all parts of the United States.

TO SUBSCRIBERS. Cemetery officials desiring to subscribe for a number of copies regularly to circulate among their lot owners, should send for our special terms. Several well known cemeteries have already adopted this plan with good results.

Contributions on matters pertaining to cemeteries are solicited. Address all communications to
R. J. HAIGHT, 331 Dearborn St., CHICAGO.

Trade Circulars Received. Catalogue of Holland bulbs, Hardy plants, etc. Ellwanger & Barry, Mount Hope Nurseries, Rochester, N. Y.

The Scherer Manufacturing Co. extend an invitation to superintendents who may be in New York City, to visit their offices in the Bible House, corner of 4th Avenue and 9th street, to inspect the operation of their improved Automatic Burial Apparatus. Those who inspected the apparatus at the Minneapolis convention will be gratified to see the many improvements introduced since that time. Its weight has been reduced from 400 to 150 pounds, and it can now be carried easily by one man.

To Superintendents

Desiring to secure one member of our League in each principal city of the U. S. and Canada, we beg you will send us the name of a marble dealer in your city whom you would recommend to us for honor, intelligence and energy. Your communication will be held strictly confidential if you so wish.

THE MEMORIAL ART LEAGUE,
1341 Arch Street, Philadelphia, Pa.

The Country Graveyard.

There's a graveyard in a city
  Rich in marble, vault and shrine,
Where the deeds of men are blazoned
  In many a fulsome line.
There the stately, costly granite
  Lifts its head above the sod,
And amid its cold magnificence
  You are pretty far from God.

There's a rustic little graveyard
  In the shadow of the trees,
And a bird is gently swinging
  On the lazy summer breeze;
You can walk among the daisies,
  As they peep above the sod,
And the flowers seem to whisper
  That you're very close to God.

Traffic does not roar around you,
  And no stately columns rise,
But stones half-hidden in the grass
  Elude your wary eyes;
And the bees are in clover
  Where the gentle blossoms nod,
In the little country graveyard
  You are pretty close to God.

O! the silence and the beauty
  Where the rural folk repose,
In the shadow of the cedar
  And beneath the modest rose;
O! the peace that steals upon you
  O'er the violet sprinkled sod,
In the little country graveyard,
  That seems so close to God.
— *T. C. Harbaugh, in Middletown Register.*

HITCHINGS & CO.
Established 50 Years.

...Horticultural Architects and Builders,
AND LARGEST MANUFACTURERS OF
Greenhouse Heating and Ventilating Apparatus.

Conservatories, Greenhouses, Palm Houses, etc., Erected complete with our Patent Iron Frame Construction. Plans and Estimates of cost and illustrated catalogues sent on application.

233 Mercer St., NEW YORK.

THOS. W. WEATHERED'S SONS,
INCORPORATED.
HORTICULTURAL ARCHITECTS AND HOT WATER ENGINEERS
Send for Catalogue, enclosing 4 cents in stamps.

No. 244 Canal St.,   NEW YORK CITY.

☞ PLEASE MENTION THE MODERN CEMETERY.

Interment Record and Lot Book.

This system is thought to embrace the best features of the most popular forms of burial records now in use and may be adapted to large or small cemeteries. The Interment Record gives all of the necessary information in regard to the deceased, and the Lot Book locates every grave, so that it can be readily found at any time. The books are printed on heavy paper, substantially bound and furnished in different sizes, depending upon the requirements of the cemetery.   **R. J. HAIGHT, Pub.,** 334 Dearborn St., Chicago.

Conservatory in Newton Cemetery, Newtonville, Mass., designed and erected by Lord & Burnham Co.

Conservatories, Greenhouses, Vineries,
SHIPPED TO ANY PART OF THE COUNTRY AND ERECTED COMPLETE, READY FOR USE.

Plans Embrace the Latest Improvements.
Unequaled Facilities for Manufacturing
Thirty-five Years Experience.

ADDRESS, STATING
REQUIREMENTS,

Lord & Burnham Co...
IRVINGTON-ON-HUDSON, N. Y.

Catalogue sent on application.

Cemetery Interment Record AND Lot Book.

A perfected system for recording the essential particulars regarding each interment and for accurately locating the position of every grave. The most thorough and satisfactory system of Cemetery Records ever published. It embraces the best features of the records used in the leading American Cemeteries. Printed on heavy paper, and substantially bound in different sizes.

R. J. HAIGHT, 334 Dearborn St., Chicago.

BOOKS FOR CEMETERY OFFICIALS

Landscape Gardening, by Samuel Parsons, Jr., 300 pages, 200 illustrations. Beautifully printed and bound, $3.50.

Ornamental Gardening for Americans, by Elias A. Long. Illustrated. Cloth, $2.00. The Nursery Book, by L. H. Bailey. Complete hand-book of propagation. Paper 50 cents, cloth $1.00. Sent postpaid on receipt of price.

The Nursery Book, by L. H. Bailey, assisted by several of the most skillful propagators in the world. In fact, it is a careful compendium of the best practices in all countries. It contains 167 illustrations, showing methods, processes and appliances. How to Propagate over 2,000 varieties of shrubs, trees and herbaceous or soft-stemmed plants; the process for each being fully described. All this and much more is fully told in the Nursery Book. Over 300 pages, 8vo. Price, cloth, $1. Pocket style, paper, narrow margin, 50 cents. Address,

R. J. HAIGHT,
334 Dearborn St., Chicago.

CEMETERY ADORNMENTS
—ARTISTIC—
Iron Vases
WITH RESERVOIRS,
which are the best for Plants

BOUQUET HOLDERS
for Graves, 20, 25, 30 and 40c. each.

Our New Bouquet Vase
For Cemetery is just out.
Metallic Wreaths, Crosses, etc., 50c to $5 each.

SETTEES AND CHAIRS.
Both all IRON or IRON with WOOD SLATS.
Path, Avenue, and Keep off the Grass Signs.
Ornamental Fountains and Drinking Fountains.

FLOWER SEEDS—2 packages, 5 cts. Grass seed, bulbs, etc.
LAWN MOWERS—Our new one, "THE HERCULES," far superior and different from all others.
GARDEN HOSE. We only sell the best grades. Nozzles, hoses, reels, etc.
JOVE'S PATENT HOSE MENDERS. No tools or bands required. We send four menders, postage paid, by mail, for 25 cts. Send inside diameter of hose.
LAWN SPRINKLERS—3, 4, 6 and 8 arms. Hub, Globe and Combination. All our own make. Prices to suit.
Wire Rose Bush Trellises, Garden Borders, etc.

Greatest Variety of Above Goods at our NEW Store.
Illustrated Price List on application

M. D. JONES & CO.
368 Washington St., BOSTON, MASS.

PATENT VAULT HEARSE.

Especially Designed For Removing Bodies from Vault to Grave.

NEEDED IN EVERY CEMETERY HAVING A VAULT.

CARRIES the heaviest body with perfect safety, and may be drawn easily by two men. Platform, 2' 6" x 7' 6", with silver plated rollers, pins, etc., similar to ordinary hearse. Substantially built. Highly finished.

Extra. From Testimonial: "The Vault Hearse perfectly supplies a long felt want. * * We consider it indispensable where a vault is in use."—*Trustees, Marion, O., Cemetery.*

Send for PRICE LIST. **McMurray & Fisher Sulky Co., MARION, OHIO.**

Patent Fence Cresting
Especially designed for Cemeteries and Orchards. This fence surrounds Calvary and the fountain in Cemeteries in St. Louis.

F. I. GRAYDON,
Sole Agent,
7201 N. B'dway, ST. LOUIS, MO.

PATENT AUTOMATIC BURIAL APPARATUS
MANUFACTURED BY

This machine is a valuable, indispensable and useful invention. It is a necessity for the modern undertaker, cemetery and the public. It is made of the best material, with best workmanship, and combines both lightness and durability. It is simple in its operation, cannot get out of order, dispenses with all extra labor and works without any noise or disturbance. A child could operate it with ease. Accidents are impossible.

We furnish two sizes:
Size A, inside opening 7 ft. 3 inch. long, weight, 150 lbs; Price $200.
Size B, inside opening, 5 ft. long; weight, 125 lbs; Price, $175.

HOW IT IS USED.
The frame is set level around the grave and the pall bearers place the casket on the straps. With a little pressure of the foot upon a small treadle on the side of the frame, the casket will descend slowly and silently into the grave. Then the operator draws up on two small cords, so as to unbuckle or disconnect the straps under the coffin, when by turning the crank the straps are rewound on their respective drums.

With each apparatus we furnish a complete set of Wrenches, one Crank Lever and a Water Proof Cover.

SCHERER MANUFACTURING COMPANY,
OFFICE AND SHOW ROOM— Bible House, Corner 4th Avenue and 9th Street, NEW YORK City.

THE MODERN CEMETERY.

THE MODERN CEMETERY.
AN ILLUSTRATED MONTHLY JOURNAL DEVOTED TO THE INTEREST OF CEMETERIES

R. J. HAIGHT, Publisher.
384 Dearborn Street, CHICAGO.

Subscription $1.00 a Year In Advance.   Foreign Subscription $1.25.
Special Rates on Six or More Copies.

VOL. IV.   CHICAGO, SEPT. 1894.   NO. 7.

CONTENTS.

*ANNUAL CONVENTION OF THE ASSOCIATION OF AMERICAN CEMETERY SUPERINTENDENTS	73
CONVENTION NOTES	78
ARE WE GOING FROM ONE EXTREME TO ANOTHER?...	79
*HARDY HERBACEOUS PLANTS FOR CEMETERIES.....	79
SOME PARASITIC GROWTHS AND RECIPES FOR THEIR REMOVAL	80
CEMETERY NOTES	82
FOUNDATIONS—SUGGESTIONS TO LOT OWNERS.......	83
RULES AND REGULATIONS — PUBLISHER'S DEPARTMENT	84

*Illustrated.

Annual Convention of the Association of American Cemetery Superintendents.

The Eighth Annual Convention of the Association of American Cemetery Superintendents was held at the Hotel Lafayette, Philadelphia, September 11, 12 and 13th. The occasion was one of unusual interest, and will form an important part in the annals of the Association. No former meeting has witnessed so many additions to the membership of the association, nor has any meeting been more largely attended than this. The diversity of topics discussed and the character of the entertainment provided by the local cemeteries made the occasion one of rare interest and enjoyment.

President Salway called the meeting to order and introduced Mayor Stuart who welcomed the superintendents to the city of Brotherly Love in a happy speech, in which he alluded to the many historical associations which cluster about the homes, the cemeteries and various institutions of the city.

President Salway made a fitting reply and the business of the convention was proceeded with.

PRESIDENT'S ADDRESS.

Gentlemen: It gives me pleasure to welcome you to the eighth annual meeting of our association. The preceding meetings have been pleasant and profitable to all of our members who have been in attendance, and I trust this will prove equally so and that its benefits may go out to many who are not with us, that it will tend to advance largely the interests of the economic management of cemeteries. The few words I have to say must not be styled an address, my time has of late been so constantly taken up by my official duties that little was left to permit me to look over the field of progress in the line of cemetery work. The association and its objects are too well known to need an introduction. Our chief aim is the improvement of the management of cemeteries by meeting annually to exchange ideas and renew our interest in each other and the work we are doing. I believe that my own busy life is no more so than most of you experience. I know from the nature of your duties that you are all intensely interested in what you are doing, and few of us would ever have an opportunity of meeting others similarly engaged, and exchanging ideas, were it not for this yearly gathering. As the pebbles in the ocean have by constant contact with each other worn off their angular roughness and become polished and refined, so man's contact with man, is helpful in the development of his better qualities and in the ever moving tide of life our aim should be to become like polished gems reflecting the light of our experience to those around us. Our conventions of the past lead one to expect much in the future. We all know that this association has done much good, but it is impossible to say how much. It reminds one of a young healthy plant full of energy within, causing it to unfold and stretch out in every direction.

The papers produced, and discussions which have formed part of the program of previous meetings have been read by hundreds of interested persons, so the topics to be considered at this meeting are worthy of our best attention, they are calculated to furnish valuable suggestions, and practical application will alone prove their success. It is not to be expected that all that is said or recommended at this time will be of the same benefit to every cemetery, but I doubt if there is anyone here who cannot put into profitable use some idea or suggestion which is advanced to the better management and success of the institution he is interested in.

The landscape and lawn plan seems to be fully established as the favorite system on which to make and operate cemeteries. The idea seems to have originated in J. C. Loudon, who wrote a series of letters a short time before his death in 1843 to the *Gardeners' Magazine*, on the "Principles of Landscape Gardening and Landscape Architecture as applied to Cemeteries, and the Improvement of Church Yards." The letters are well worth reading, for he advanced many valuable ideas, and yet some that at the present stage of progress would be considered absurd. The main principles are in harmony with what is generally considered as the best method of making and maintaining cemeteries. He gave a brief description of the London cemeteries, also those of this city at that time, and mentioned the fact that "he was received with the greatest civility and attention from the superintendents, and at the respective offices every information was given." Few men ever did more or stood higher in his profession than J. C. Loudon. His writings are studied and considered an authority for the best ideas on Landscape Architecture. With such a preceptor, and his own experience, the cemetery superintendent can justly take courage. Fifteen years ago you could count on your two hands all the cemeteries in this country working on the lawn plan. To-day all new cemeteries are laid out in that way, and nearly all new additions to old cemeteries are being formed on those principles. The evidence we have assures us that all efforts are approved; let us then take courage.

THE MODERN CEMETERY.

THE SUPERINTENDENTS AND THEIR FRIENDS AT HARLEIGH CEMETERY, CAMDEN, N. J.

and with renewed energy go forward to our duties with true and firm determination to do our part, and to help others who need our assistance.

In his annual report, Secretary Eurich said: "I would be untrue to my convictions did I not express my increasing pride in the name, achievements and progress of our Association. Cemetery managers have realized that they are directly interested in our association, and gain as much, if not more from our annual meetings than their representatives can. In many instances they have given substantial testimony of their appreciation by paying the expenses of their superintendents to our conventions." The report showed that eleven new members had been enrolled during the year, which, with the additions at this meeting, viz: 23, made the present membership 147. The expenses of stenographers and printing and circulating the reports of the seventh annual convention aggregated $300. Notwithstanding this generous contribution towards disseminating valuable cemetery literature, the treasurer's report showed a substantial balance on hand. The first paper of the meeting was read by A. W. Hobert, superintendent of Lakewood Cemetery, Minneapolis, Minn., on: *"How to Manage a Modern Cemetery." Mr. Hobert outlined in a very interesting manner the methods that had been adopted in managing the affairs of Lakewood, a cemetery that is conducted exclusively on the most approved lawn plan.

Owing to the absence of Mr. Robert Scrivener, who was detained on account of ill health, the time allotted to the paper to have been read by him was devoted to an impromptu address by O. C. Simonds of Chicago, in which he told of London and Paris cemeteries which he visited last year. He said that the statistics as to area, interments, etc., were interesting, but he found but little that would be regarded as instructive in cemetery management by a modern cemetery superintendent. The afternoon was devoted to a visit to Harleigh Cemetery, Camden, N. J., across the Delaware river. The party went by train from Camden to Harleigh, where they were the guests of President Cooper and Superintendent Rhedemeyer. A pretty cottage at the entrance answers as superintendent's office and residence, from the porch of which a pleasing view is had of well kept lawns and drives, with a background of natural woods. Two lakes add a charm to the grounds in which graceful swans disport themselves among handsome specimens of the Egyptian lotus in bloom. The lover of nature finds much of interest in the wild, unimproved sections of Harleigh. In a secluded spot, rich in rustic beauty, is the rock-faced granite vault, shown in our illustration, in which are entombed the remains of Walt Whitman. After reviewing the grounds the party

---

*All the papers will be published in full in pamphlet form, with the entire proceedings of the Convention, and furnished by Mr. F. Eurich, Secretary, A. A. C. S., Toledo, O.

THE MODERN CEMETERY

WALT WHITMAN VAULT, HARLEIGH CEMETERY, CAMDEN, N. J.

was grouped for the photographer, and the regular order of exercises taken up. Addresses of welcome were made by Mr. Howard M. Cooper, president of Harleigh, Mayor J. L. Westcott of Camden, and the Hon. J. G. Engard.

Mayor Westcott, in extending the welcome to Camden, said: "Whenever good work has been done it has been done through organization. The individual may succeed in making some improvement, but will not get beyond his own province. The results end with him. But when he imbues others with his ideas, these consult together, and by considering different plans and means accomplish what was needed. It is only a little time since burial grounds were looked upon only as such, and the keepers were nothing more than grave diggers. To-day we have the evidence of something different, and this organization is evidence of different ideas. There are still a good many graveyards wherein nothing in the line of improvement has been tried for, and again, there are beautiful spots that show the superintendent has come to an idea beyond the grave. He is an artist; must be, or he could not accomplish the results he has."

A paper on: "Suitable Trees and Shrubs for a Modern Cemetery," was read by Thomas Mechan, Jr., of Philadelphia, and addresses by President Salway and Messrs. J. G. Barker, T. McCarthy and O. C. Simonds. This enjoyable feature of the entertainment was followed by a banquet of most tempting menu. Tastefully decorated tables were spread under a large tent on the lawn, where more than one hundred guests did ample justice to the repast. A vote of thanks was extended to Mr. Rhodemeyer and the officials of Harleigh for their hospitality, and soon after dusk the party departed for Philadelphia.

SECOND DAY.

Fifty-eight members answered roll call on convening for the second day's session.

"Civil Engineering in Cemetery Work," a paper written by D. Z. Morris, superintendent of Mt. Hope Cemetery, Rochester, N. Y., was read by Secretary Eurich. "No more judicious investment can be made in organizing a new cemetery than the employment of a competent engineer with a knowledge of its peculiar requirements from a landscape point of view. Drainage, road making, waterworks, grading, the economic handling of earth and stone, and other features of a cemetery engineer's work were dwelt upon, and the value of a knowledge of engineering to cemetery superintendents clearly demonstrated. An interesting discussion followed on the subject of engineering instruments required in cemetery work, foundation building, etc.

The second paper: "How to Make and Maintain a Cemetery with the Restrictions of Mounds and Memorials of any kind above the General Surface of the Lawn, and to Substitute a Satisfactory Method of Marking Graves," was read by Timothy McCarthy of Swan Point, Providence, R. I. He said in part: "This subject is worthy the best thought and attention not only of superintendents of cemeteries, but by every intelligent citizen or association who feel and understand that the great object of our association is to educate the public how to properly embellish their burial lots in a more simple and less costly manner than prevails at present. Our association has accomplished very much by inducing the public to dispense with the costly curbing, iron fences, hedges, etc., and the

BELL TOWER, WEST LAUREL HILL CEMETERY, PHILADELPHIA.

enormous outlay for such things has been saved to the public, while the natural beauty and attractiveness of the cemetery is often acknowledged and appreciated." Quotations were read from the writings of many superintendents who favored restrictions in the character of stone work erected in cemeteries, and from Hawthorne, who said: "The marble keeps merely a cold and sad memory of a man who would else be forgotten. The man who needs a monument never ought to have one." While there are no restrictions at Swan Point, Mr. McCarthy said his people were taking kindly to low corner posts, grass walks, etc., and he was hopeful of having a law adopted by his trustees restricting head stones to two or three inches above the grass. Let our object be to make the cemetery beautiful by bringing it nearer to nature and to God, and further removed from the stone yard.

In conducting a cemetery on the lawn plan, Mr. Eurich said: "Whatever unnecessarily breaks the continuity of the lawn or obstructs the view should be prohibited. Markers and corner posts flush with the ground will answer their purpose, and reservation grounds in every section for planting trees and shrubs will form an artistic background." The advisability of cemeteries retaining absolute control of their grounds in regard to the erection of monumental work, and the planting of trees, shrubs, etc., and the importance of educating lot owners to consult with cemetery officials before placing orders for stone work was strongly advocated.

Mr. Hamill, of Baltimore, said that since the convention met in his city two years ago he had met with much encouragement in the introduction of reforms. On two hundred lots, mounds and corner posts had been levelled even with the ground, while many other things evidenced a desire on the part of the lot owners for something better than the old plan.

In the afternoon the entire party, occupying seven large stages, were driven through a number of the city cemeteries, including Mount Peace, Mt. Vernon, Laurel Hill, North, South, Central and West Laurel Hill, Westminster and Fairmount Park. Many of the older cemeteries are beautifully located, overlooking the picturesque Schuylkill. The possibilities of artistic landscape effects, however, have not been taken advantage of, and the result is only acres of stone and iron. Many handsome monuments and costly mausoleums are to be seen, but not always to advantage, owing to their crowded situation. The Pencoyd entrance to West Laurel Hill Cemetery, with its winding drive making an ascent of two hundred feet; the broad lawns, sloping hill sides, and beautiful trees and shrubs that meet the eyes on every side bring us nearer to nature. The cemetery contains about 150 acres of rolling land, with much natural beauty. In many of the sections, lot coping is prohibited and markers are restricted to eight inches in height. Corner posts are allowed to rise above the surface, which mars the otherwise pleasing continuity of the lawn.

Standing on the highest point in the grounds is a massive stone bell and clock tower with chimes, partially covered with ampelopsis. Near it is the superintendent's office and waiting rooms, complete in their appointments. After inspecting Superintendent Painter's system of records, the party was photographed on the lawn, and after a stroll over the grounds the stages were again resumed and the hotel reached after another pleasant ride.

EVENING SESSION.

At the evening session, M. E. Hibbs read a practical paper on "Roads, and How to Maintain them." The "Sanitary Relations of Cemeteries," was treated in a scientific manner by Dr. Henry Leffmann, a local sanitarian of some renown. He said in part: "Of all methods, other than cremation, of disposing of the dead body, especially when dead of contagious disease, earth burial is the best, and it is a strictly natural method, for it is by means of the action of soil microbes that the organic mass is converted into harmless materials. The principal objection to intra-mural cemeteries is that they interfere with proper use of land and offend the aesthetic taste of the inhabitants. These are indeed the main reasons that lead to their abandonment. The charge that they are prejudicial to the health is often a mere pretense. Of course there must be a limit to the use of such places. Earth is a natural disinfectant, but it is not an inexhaustible one. A limit must be fixed for depth of covering, but with a few feet of earth over a body there is no reason to suppose that any dangerous emanation could arise. As regards the possibility of disease germs passing downwards, we have proof that even coarse particles of soil will act as a complete filter. Soil is almost sterile a few yards below the surface, notwithstanding the large numbers of microbes present in the upper layers, and the constant downward movement of the water falling on the surface. If microbes lived forever, they could not work their way through any ordinary soil, not even through considerable layers of sand; but in reality they soon perish. There is every reason to believe that a few months after the burial of the corpse the disease producing microbes are dead; that even if a body containing them were buried uncovered in the soil, it would be unlikely that it would contaminate the sub-soil water."

"How to Make and Care for a Lawn," was the

subject of an instructive paper by J. Otto Thilow, of the Henry A. Dreer Co. A representative of the Memorial Art League of Philadelphia, read an interesting paper on "Memorial Art," during the reading of which examples of sculpture were exhibited, showing the beauty of a truly artistic creation in comparison with a production that closely resembled a model of a prevailing type of cemetery statuary at the present. The speaker appealed to cemetery officials to exert their influence in favor of better class of memorials. Addresses were made by R. R. Bringhurst, of Philadelphia, and J. S. Pierce, of Ardmore, Pa., prominent funeral directors who proffered some good advice on the subject of cemetery employees who had to do with the burying of the dead.

THIRD DAY.

"What Qualifications are Necessary to Become an All-around Successful Superintendent?" was the subject assigned W. D. Primrose, of Baltimore, Md., for the opening paper, but as he was not present the President substituted Mr. Barker, of Boston, who made an excellent impromptu address, in which he gave his hearers some good advice as to how they might become "good all-around superintendents." Among other qualifications he thought necessary was that of being sympathetic with those who had been bereaved. He considered the purchaser of the cheapest single grave as worthy of kind and considerate treatment as the person who bought the highest priced lot.

In the absence of W. F. Jewson, of Mankato, Minn., his paper on "How best to Blend New Ter-

VIEW FROM BELL TOWER IN WEST LAUREL HILL CEMETERY, PHILADELPHIA.

A SIDE HILL VAULT IN WEST LAUREL HILL CEMETERY, PHILADELPHIA.

ritory with an Old Cemetery," was read by the Secretary.

The final paper, and one of the best of the convention was read by H. J. Diering, of Woodlawn Cemetery, New York, on the "Theoretical Management of Cemetery Employees, Teams, etc." Mr. Diering outlined the practical workings of his large force of men at Woodlawn, and gave some valuable suggestions as to the careful system observed there. He stated that his grave men are all uniformed. The suit consists of coat and trousers of black cheviot. In rainy weather the men wear waterproof coats and leggings.

Mr. J. R. Hooper, of Richmond, Va., extended an invitation to the association to hold its Ninth Annual Convention in that city, and the invitation was unanimously accepted.

Appropriate resolutions were adopted on the death of the late Marcus A. Farwell of Chicago, who was an honorary member of the association.

The committee on nominations for officers for the ensuing year named Timothy McCarthy, of Providence, R. I., for president, and although urged to accept the office by a unanimous vote, he positively declined, on the plea that he could not give so important an office the attention it required. His refusal was accepted with regret, and the following named officers were elected: President, O. C. Simonds, Graceland, Chicago; Vice President, G. W. Creesy, Harmony Grove, Salem, Mass.; Secretary and Treasurer, Frank Eurich, Woodlawn, Toledo, O. Executive Committee—J. R. Hooper, Hollywood, Richmond; C. W. Hamill, Mt. Olivet,

Baltimore; William Salway, Spring Grove, Cincinnati, O.

A committee was appointed to select extracts from essays that had been read before the association, and have them printed and circulated among cemetery officials throughout the United States at the expense of the association.

The convention adjourned to meet in Richmond, Va., at a time to be fixed by the Executive Committee.

* * *

AFTERNOON MEETING.

Although the business of the convention had been attended to, there still remained an unfinished portion on the program of entertainment, which proved to be a most enjoyable treat. From 2 o'clock in the afternoon until 10 in the evening the party was entertained on the excursion steamer Elizabeth, which had been chartered expressly for the occasion. Cramps' shipyard was visited where more than three thousand men are at work. The massive hulls of the steel steamers St. Louis and St. Paul, sister vessels to the City of Paris and City of New York, engaged attention for some time, as did an inspection of the recently tested war vessel Minneapolis, whose time of 23.073 knots broke all former records. League Island, where the navy yard is situated, eight miles down the river was the next objective point, and here the visitors were permitted to go on board several of the old war ships and monitors. This unique feature of the entertainment was especially enjoyable to the visitors from the interior. The balance of the evening was passed in steaming up and down the beautiful waters of the Delaware. The Camden band of eight pieces discoursed sweet music, and singing and dancing were indulged in. A luncheon was served that would have done justice to a Delmonico, after which, ex-president Salway and his wife were invited into the cabin, where they were given a most pleasant surprise. In a few well chosen remarks, Mayor Westcott, of Camden, expressed the appreciation in which the ex-president was held by the members of the association, and as a token of their esteem, presented him with a handsome diamond ring. The surprise was a complete one, and for the moment Mr. Salway's vocabulary failed him, but he soon responded in a very happy speech.

President Simonds then presented Mrs. Salway with a handsome cut glass olive dish from the ladies of the party. This delightful excursion and the ride through the cemeteries on the previous day was provided by the proprietors of West Laurel Hill, Laurel Hill, Cathedral, Greenmount, Fernwood, Knights of Pythias, Mt. Peace, Mt. Vernon, Hill Side, Westminster and Cedar Hills Cemeteries.

Convention Notes.

Richmond in '95, Cincinnati in '96.

* * *

Messrs. Rhedemeyer and Painter are to be congratulated on the successful outcome of their arrangements. The entire program was a complete success.

* * *

Father Nichols was an active participant. Long may he live.

* * *

Enrolling twenty-three new members surpasses all previous meetings.

* * *

A successful exhibit was made of the Scherer automatic burial apparatus at West Laurel Hill.

* * *

Philadelphia has sixty cemeteries, and the best of them were represented at the convention.

* * *

One who believes that the Schuylkill river is contaminated with seepage from the cemeteries, says that Philadelphians are "drinking their ancestors."

* * *

G. L. Transue, of Easton, Pa., extended an invitation to visit his cemetery, which was accepted by quite a number of the superintendents.

* * *

The visit to Dosoris had to be abandoned.

* * *

The association entered its ninth year with a larger membership and a larger fund in the treasury than ever before. This means progress.

* * *

"Cemeteries should be considered as features for the living rather than for the dead. We select the most beautiful spots we can find, not because the dead can admire their beauty, but to charm the eye of the living; to make us feel our dead are resting where we find a pleasure in being, and not that they are in the solitude and gruesomeness of the graveyard."—*O. C. Simonds.*

* * *

"A good, all-around cemetery superintendent is a many sided individual who should possess many requirements, not the least of which is a sympathetic nature.—*J. G. Barker.*

* * *

Among those present at the convention were: *John G. Barker, Forest Hills, Boston; G. W. Bechel, Riverside, Defiance, O.; J. F. Boerekel, Springdale, Peoria, Ill.; J. M. Boxell, Oakland, St. Paul, Minn.; *R. B. Campbell, Holy Cross, Fernwood; J. Y. Craig, Forest Lawn, Omaha; G. W. Creesy, Harmony Grove, Salem, Mass.; *H. J. Diering, Woodlawn, N.Y.; *John C. Dix, Riverside, Cleveland; W. H. Druckemiller, Pomfret Manor, Sunbury, Pa.; Mr. English, New Haven, Conn.; *Frank M. Floyd, Evergreen, Portland, Me.; Geo. Gilmore, Maple Grove, Uhrichsville, O.; C. W. Hamill, Mt. Olivet, Baltimore; *Mr. Haskell, Portland, Me.; A. W. Hobert, Lakewood, Minneapolis; J. R. Hooper, Hollywood, Richmond, Va.; Philo King, Maple Grove, Ravenna, O.; *Bellett Lawson, Oakwoods, Chicago; W. J. Lockwood, Sleepy Hollow, Tarrytown, N. Y.; T. McCarthy, Swan Point, Providence; A. McKerrichar, Glenwood, Washington; C. Nichols, Fairmount, Newark; *G. M. Painter and W. J. Phillips, West Laurel Hill, Philadelphia; C. D. Phipps, Franklin, Franklin, Pa.; George Renshaw, Elm Lawn, Bay City, Mich.; *G. E. Rhedemeyer, Harleigh, Camden; J. Reid, Mt. Elliot, Detroit; T. B. Robinson, Woodlawn, Des Moines; Henry Ross, Newton, Newtonville, Mass.; *W. Salway, Spring Grove, Cincinnati, O.; *Henry Schroder, Mystic, Conn.; G. Scherzinger, Calvary, Fond du Lac, Wis.; *O. C. Simonds, Graceland, Chicago; W. Stone, Pine Grove, Lynn, Mass.; *J. J. Stephens; *G. L. Transue, Easton, Easton; H. F. Torrey, Arlington, Jersey City, N. J.; †J. Gunn, Pine Grove, Whitingsville, Mass.; †W. Harris, Uniondale, Allegheny, Pa.; †John Dunn, South Laurel Hill, Philadelphia; †H. Wilson Ross, Newton, Mass.; †A. B. Forest, Oakwood, Raleigh, Va.; †Theodore Elsasser, Westminster, Philadelphia; †Dr. J. B. Mayer, Hillside, Philadelphia; †Charles Fitz George, Greenwood, Trenton, N. J.; †J. M. Holden, Mt. Peace, Philadelphia; †J. C. Hepler, Charles Evans Cemetery, Reading; †John F. Shapleigh, Cedar Grove, Dorchester, Mass.; †*W. H. D. Cochrane, Edgewood, Nashua, N. H.; †Bellett Lawson Jr., Riverside, Norristown; †E. P. Frich, Green Mount, Philadelphia; †G. C. Naylor, Riverview, Wilmington, Del.; †J. K. Bettson, Lafayette, Philadelphia; †George Redford, Mt. Vernon, Philadelphia; †D. S. Grissinger, Odd Fellows, Philadelphia; †D. C. Penrose, Wilmington and Brandywine, Wilmington, Del.; †Frank A. Sherman, Evergreen, New Haven, Conn.; †J. C. Knox, Cedar Hill, Frankford; †A. L. Smith, West Laurel Hill, Philadelphia; *R. J. Haight, Chicago.

*Accompanied by Lady. †New members.

Are We Going from One Extreme to Another?

During recent years we have heard much concerning the adoption of the "Lawn Plan" in cemeteries. It is almost universally conceded that it is an improvement over the old plan, and we are shown bare lawns dotted here and there with monuments and headstones as an example of what is best. Let us test our theories and practice occasionally by going to the fountain head. Mr. Strauch abolished the fences, hedges, railings, chains, etc., formerly used so extensively as boundaries of cemetery lots, and replaced the gravel walks with grass. He then planted trees or shrubs arranged singly or in groups so as to make a background for monuments, suitably frame in the best views and make a varied outline for the sky and the continuous lawn. This he called the "landscape lawn plan." Some of those who design cemeteries seem to forget the first part and regard the lawn as the only essential feature. A carefully graded piece of ground covered with a growth of grass abundantly watered and closely mown pleases the eye with its color and the foot with its softness, but it has no more artistic merit than a piece of clear sky. Introduce a few fleecy clouds in the latter, let them be partly in shadow and partly lighted up and colored by the setting sun, and we have an effect which painters—the best judges of beauty—would be glad to imitate on canvas. In the same way, by the introduction of varied masses of foliage about a lawn in an artistic manner, we get light, shade, color, a pleasing outline—in a word, beauty. A work of art, whether a poem, a painting, a song, a statue or a landscape, does not tell all the facts. It leaves something to the imagination. Just so an attractive section of a cemetery has some portion hidden from every point of view. There is a chance for the exercise of one's imagination, and curiosity leads a visitor from place to place to observe all the views. The monuments are not seen all at once as in an open lawn, but each receives attention as it comes in sight. There is unity with variety. Nothing produces the desired result so quickly and satisfactorily as the judicious use of shrubs. Trees should be planted to give shade and to vary the sky line, but it takes them much longer to give character to a landscape than it does shrubs. We need both to make cemeteries beautiful, to clothe the lawn, and to take away the stone-yard effect seen in many sections where no planting has been done.

O. C. SIMONDS.

Hardy Herbaceous Plants for Cemeteries.
Continued from page 68.

Among the numerous good taller plants the long spurred hardy Columbines are exceedingly useful for early flowering. Aquilegia Canadensis being one of the best, and a later flowering extra long spurred yellow one is the most airly graceful of them all. Monarda Didyma is desirable because it is able to care for itself, its long flowering season and the rich red shade of its blossoms; but in most situations its growth is likely to be so rampant as to require thinning out every two years to keep it within bounds, and it looks best when grown in naturalistic plantations for it has an air of the highways and byways.

PYRETHRUM ULIGINOSUM.—Courtesy of *Gardening*.

Mimulus Cardinalis and Lobelia Cardinalis (the first sometime called Monkey flower and the latter well known as Cardinal flower,) are good in rather damp partly shaded situations; they are hardy and beautiful in color. The Mimulus does quite well in any location even when rather dry, but the Cardinal flower must have moisture.

Polemonium is another good one for the wild, or naturalistic border as it seems like a wild flower. It sends its flower stalks up some two feet above a full rosette of handsome foliage that is fresh, green and luxuriant in summer even when furnished but little water—it does better; however, when it gets more.

The soft gray tone of Rose Campion is good at all times, but the color of its flowers tends so strongly towards magenta that it requires nice handling to prevent a war of colors. The safest plan is to keep it well away from other flowers unless white ones—they are the floral peacemakers.

Eringenum Purpureum and E. Americana are handsome plants in a style quite unlike all other perennials. Their flowers do not amount to very much, but in form and color the plants are effective when grown in large groups. The stems and leaves of the terminal shoots are of an odd metallic blue tone that is unusual if not unknown elsewhere in vegetation.

Coreopsis lanceolata is invaluable as a summer bloomer, and so are the hardy perennial Gailliardias—G. grandiflora being especially good.

Anthemis tinctoria is another desirable yellow flower for midsummer, while Veronica Spicata is a good blue one, and Platycodons both blue and white should not be missing for they are at their best when no other blossoms of their size are found. Two of the best tall hardy Phloxes are Queen, which is white, and the beautiful clear red Lothair. They are finest when massed in large numbers and so used are extremely satisfactory. And there is nothing better than Acolia ptomica to furnish snow drifts of bloom in midsummer.

For late flowering nothing excels Pyrethrum Uliginosum and white Japan Anemones, (the pink variety of the latter is also good,) they are both white, and of white flowers there can never be too many in cemeteries, nor in gardens either.

Elimus glaucus is a hardy ornamental grass of merit. It is in its prime before the fall grasses are in plume, and it is graceful in form and good in color at all times.

The three Eulalias are now so well known and appreciated by all who are interested in decorative planting that their good qualities need not be described, it is sufficient to say that those who have not tried them should get them forthwith

FANNY COPLEY SEAVEY.

Some Parasitic Growths and Recipes for their Removal.*

"That we find out the cause of this effect:
Or rather say the cause of this defect,
For this effect defective comes by cause,
* * *
Perpend." —*Hamlet, Act II, Scene 2.*

PREFATORY NOTE.—An amputation cannot be made a pleasant operation though the life of the patient may depend upon it. Before applying the knife we beg that the sufferer will freely voice his agony through these columns, and the surgeon pledges himself to apply soothing lotions after the operation is over.
* * *
Was it Prof. Tyndal who said, "Too exuberant life develops the conditions of death"? So a phenomenal success generates the causes of failure.

In a previous paper we noted the marvellously rapid evolution, from the primitive graveyard, of the modern cemetery. We wish now to call attention to some parasitic growths that have struck root in that success, and which, we fully believe, have become a serious menace to the parent body.

Minor among these is the Florist whose wire frames still hold together the faded and tattered remnants of his "Gates Ajar." Of himself he is not intolerable; it is when he joins forces with the Taxidermist, and leaves the ghastly remains of the symbol of the Holy Spirit to moult its feathers in pitiful decay that he becomes intolerable and means should be found to suppress him.

More mischievous than he is the undert——, we mean—the Funeral Director whose chief function in the order of things seems to be to devise and encourage new means of that very ostentation which we should most carefully eschew.

It is true that the cemetery management is in no degree responsible for him; but it is also true that in the public thought he gets himself involved with it—that he is helping to create the atmosphere through which the cemetery is already beginning to be viewed. Though he is rapidly working out his own *reductio ad absurdum*, a protest from our cemeteries against him and most of his works would be a valuable adjunct to the action of many of our churches on the same subject.

Thus far the evils considered are comparatively trivial and can bring but small, and chiefly indirect, reproach upon the cemetery. But there is an evil that is colossal in its proportions and especially fraught with danger to our present system of sepulture in that no one has seemed to recognize its extreme viciousness. That danger is the Monument-man.

"Ridicule is more deadly than argument," and the monumental work that is being done in our ceme-

*Copyrighted, 1894, by the Memorial Art League.

teries is making them ridiculous. Culture follows close after wealth and our reproach, as a people ignorant of art, is being taken from us. Upon every other department of architecture and sculpture, our Chandlers, Hunts, Furnesses and Richardsons of the one, our Bailys, Bitters and Boyles of the others, have left their indellible impress; in the cemetery, alone, where, equally without churches, it would seem the services of the artist are especially needed, we have accepted the tradesman as our architect and the granite cutter as our sculptor; there, only, we permit mass to usurp the place of meaning—mere mechanical feats of stone cutting to pass for art.

Look about your grounds and tell us if there be a single section, the original beauty of which has not rapidly deteriorated or been converted in positive ugliness in process of "improvement" at the hands of the marble-man.

Examine closely the "Art Monuments" and "Artistic Memorials" that fairly cumber the ground and see how many of them bear the impress of the noble names that are making us respectable in art circles! Look again and note, of the few pieces that are not absurd in themselves, how many are not rendered tedious by repetition at the hands of the "Mortuary Architect," "Cemetery Decorator" or (not to be outdone) "Designer and Constructor of Artistic Memorials."

There are a few firms and individuals, alas, how few! who have done much conscientious work; but but even of these it may be said in Weggian quotation,—

"They know the right and they approve it, too;
Abhor the wrong and yet the wrong pursue."

(Sometimes and because there is big money in doing so, Mr. Boffin.) But for the rest—it verily seems as though they had said, "Evil be thou my good," and are sticking to it manfully.

That our progress in art should halt at the cemetery gates seems too great an anomaly to be true, and yet the reason is simple. The modern cemetery was established at just the time when art-culture was at its lowest among us—when the meaning of the word "monument" was, as Dr. Holmes has put it, *polarized* in our minds, and stood for certain blocks of stone placed one upon another and engraved with names. A large trade-interest was involved in keeping the lot owner away from the artist; the cemetery officials were too much occupied in conquering the new and perplexing difficulties in their front to give any thought to what the monument-man was doing (so to speak) in their rear; the lot-owner was solicited at a time when recent bereavement so obscured his vision that he was easily induced to accept the package as being what the label called for, and once accepted its associations were too sacred to permit of criticism.

But the time is near at hand when culture will supersede conventionality, and when that day arrives, are you not likely to be arraigned somewhat thus:

"You must have known that this structure which our father was induced to place here, was preposterous, and that the fellow who cajoled him into doing it was a quack and humbug. You have connived at the doing of a thing which will make this place repulsive to us forever."

Have we made clear the necessity for a remedy?

Turn on the light, as is your bounden duty not only to your lot-owners but to yourselves; the growths that flourish in darkness are mostly poisonous.

To do this effectually will cost no more than you expend annually in the destruction of moles and caterpillars, and whereas, in the latter case the warfare has to be continuous, in the former it needs but an original impulse.

RECIPES.

First. Prepare a pamphlet with contrasted views within your own grounds—the letter-press pointing out exactly wherein the one is good and the other the reverse.

Second. In this pamphlet group together a monument of original design and all the copies of it (large and small) showing distinctly the names of the owners, and in the letter-press "show up" the downright immorality of this form of theft and the monument men who encourage it.

Third. Rigorously prohibit this theft, within your grounds, by photographing, sketching or measurement of monumental work.

Fourth. Procure the authority of your lot-owners and, by prosecution for trespass, make an example of the operative partner in such theft.

Fifth. Restrict the size of central monument to a reasonable proportion (both as to ground plan and height) to the plot in which it is to be placed.

Sixth. Restrict the location of monument within the plot to the actual centre.

These restrictions will tend to minimize the evil effects of injudicious selection and, in many cases, make the placing of any monument impracticable.

Seventh. Encourage lot-owners to consult you before selecting a design; qualify yourself to criticise judiciously and do not spare your criticism. The hope of our established modern cemeteries is now in the artist; *you can do more than any other man towards securing him a hearing.*

In our next, we shall try to establish some definite canons of criticism—a subject that admits of being treated good-naturedly.

CEMETERY NOTES.

The commissioners of Highland Lawn Cemetery, Terre Haute, Ind., have decided to build an Entrance Gateway to cost some $3,000.

* * *

The Homewood Cemetery Co., Pittsburgh, Pa., is erecting a handsome lodge at the main entrance from designs of J. T. Steen, architect.

* * *

A movement is on foot among the various lodges of the Knights of Pythias of New Orleans to organize a Pythian Cemetery Association. Committees have been at work investigating as to sites and probable cost.

* * *

In the will of the late Silas Evans, of East Vincent township, Montgomery County, Pa., is a bequest of money to put the cemetery of Vincent Baptist Church in good order. For this purpose funds are provided for 200 headstones for unmarked graves, and they have been contracted for.

* * *

The tendency to discourage Sunday funerals is spreading. The Aulenbach Cemetery Company of Reading, Pa., has been seriously considering the matter, but it is a fact that, compared with years ago, the practice of Sunday funerals has largely abated without any prohibitory efforts.

* * *

The Arcade Rural Cemetery, Arcade, N. Y., has carried out a scheme of improvement this year, with the usual experience. The original amount intended to be expended was $600, but the bills have footed up $2,000. The authorities may safely conclude, however, that it will be a good investment.

* * *

The Utica, N. Y., *Herald* reports that the superintendent of Forest Hill Cemetery has been sued by the New Forest Cemetery Association for "slander and misrepresentation," and damages laid at $10,000. Cemetery officials more than all other people should be above this low order of competitive methods.

* * *

In Grand View Cemetery, Johnstown, Pa., the first interment took place April 30, 1887. Since that time until June 1, 1894, 2,556 burials are recorded. Of this number 430 were drowned in the terrible flood of 1889 besides 772 in the Unknown Plot. Including the unknown and deducting two bodies removed, the total number of interments have been 3,326, of which 1,201 were flood victims.

* * *

Mount Hope Cemetery, Rochester, N. Y., made its fifty-thousandth burial on June 1, 1894. The first purchase of land was made January 2, 1837, and the first burial took place in 1837. There appears to be no record as to how the cemetery came by its name, but it has always been called Mount Hope. Some of the deeds date back to 1841; at the present time each lot has a separate deed of which there are some 14,000.

* * *

Brookside Cemetery, the new cemetery at Carbondale, Pa., will soon be ready for dedication. The landscape work has been under the care of Mr. B. F. Hatheway, of Stamford, Conn., and is designed on modern plans and with a view to modern improvements. The natural beauty of the site, aided by a liberal management, will make this an attractive cemetery. The tract comprises 100 acres, only a small portion of which will be fully improved immediately.

* * *

In the 138 years since Fairview Cemetery, New Britain, Conn., was opened, hardly over a dozen people have been buried there who were over 90 years of age when they died. There are a great many five, and even three years less than that. The eldest noted is 94. Mr. Gladden's record was copied in part from the Rev. Dr. Skinner's record of nearly a century ago. In those days the town pastor kept whatever record of that kind there was kept. There are over 8,000 bodies interred in Fairview Cemetery.

* * *

Cemeteries in small towns are gradually seeing the necessity of limiting admissions to the grounds to lot owners, and then by tickets of admission. The flagrant violations of the rules of propriety by so many visitors, and the utter disregard, that in some minds prevails, of the conditions imposed by the acceptance of privileges, are compelling cemetery authorities to use what means may be at their disposal to protect their properties and lot owners, and preserve the conditions that should exist in cemetery grounds.

* * *

The snap shot and kodak man is having a hard experience nowadays in our prominent cemeteries, from many of which he is rigorously excluded. The bad practice of photographing monuments for copying purposes, a practice which is universally condemned, has had the effect of compelling restrictions in permits for picture-making purposes. One of the most strictly enforced rules of Mt. Auburn Cemetery, Boston, is that: no one shall be permitted to take photographs of any monument without the permission of the owner. Applications by marble workers and dealers are invariably refused.

* * *

The Hobart Mausoleum in course of construction in Cypress Lawn Cemetery, San Francisco, Cal., will be twenty feet high and is to be in the form of a Greek temple. The entire exterior, with the exception of the four fluted columns, is to be of granite from Raymond, Cal. The capitals of the four columns will be of granite, of the Ionic order, and the columns themselves will be fluted and made of Mexican onyx. Each of these columns will be a single stone, and will be imported from Mexico. The entire exterior of the building, from the ground up, will be line hammered. The interior will be highly polished, and the double doors will be of solid bronze. It is expected that the cost will reach between $65,000 and $70,000.

* * *

There are over 2,400 acres of cemetery property in Queens County, L. I., used principally for interments of dead from New York and Brooklyn, and to the end of prohibiting future growth of such property, the following proposed amendment has been offered in the Constitutional Convention at Albany: "It shall not be lawful for any person or for any cemetery or corporation hereinafter incorporated to use, set apart or take by deed, devise or otherwise any land for cemetery purposes in either of the counties of Westchester, Kings, Queens, Rockland or Richmond without first obtaining the consent of the Town Board and the Board of Supervisors in the town and county wherein said land is located. The legislature may provide for the manner and method by which said consent may be obtained."

* * *

On the summit of a high hill in Evergreen Cemetery, Brooklyn, N. Y., stands what is known as the sailors' monument. This monument has an interesting history, particularly so to "Jack" and his friends. The death of some unfortunate sailors in New York decided the Chamber of Commerce in 1852 to petition Congress to appropriate $5000 for the purchase of a suitable burial plot. This was granted, the Seamen's Cemetery Association formed and the three acre plot bought. It was formally opened January 31, 1853, and immediately transferred to the Government. Every nation has its own space set apart, which is marked by granite blocks placed thirty feet from each other. The name of the country is cut on the front of each block. The United States Government seems to be the only one in the world that has provided for the decent burial of sailors of all nations.

Foundations.*

Before becoming superintendent of a cemetery, an experience of some thirty-five years in the practical work of a brick and stone mason leads me to offer the following in relation to foundations as applied to cemetery work particularly:

It is a great mistake, in my opinion, to use pure lime for underground work, but there is lime that is one-half cement which persons used to working in lime and cement can detect at once when using it. Lime mixed with cement can be used, but the purer the lime the less fit it is for use underground; it should only be used above ground. Cement, or water lime, as some call it, is the proper material for foundations, or underground work. In my own practice, I use all cement. American cement, such as is made in Pennsylvania or New York states, is good enough for the majority of foundations. Of course, should an extra good job be desired, Portland cement should be employed.

In mixing all cements with sand, the materials, in proper proportions, should be thoroughly mixed *dry* at first, and when water is applied in the mortar box, care must be taken *not to drown the miller*, as they say. In mixing, a strong hoe should be employed and also plenty of "elbow grease" in a lively way, so as to ensure thorough mixing before use.

If the foundation is to be of brick, and the weather is warm, the brick should be not merely wet down but thoroughly soaked with water. A dry brick will absorb about one pound of water,—equal to a pint. So the advantage of soaking the brick is to prevent its drawing the water out of the cement mortar, which will prevent adhesion and there will be no bond. There is much more moisture in stone than in brick.

Cemetery foundations should go down to the full depth of the adjoining graves, no matter what depth that may be. This is still more a necessity in large foundations. This will absolutely ensure them from toppling over.

With good, hard, stone or good, hard, well burned brick laid in good cement mortar, and carried down to the depth of the graves, there will be no danger of losing the perpendicular or of falling over as is so often observed.

It is necessary to use good, clean, sharp sand to secure good mortar, and the cement or lime should be as fine as flour. It forms a paste and sticks the particles of sand together, so that when it drys out it all becomes like a stone. Good cement will harden under water better than when exposed to the sun and air.

*By R. B. Campbell, Superintendent of Holy Cross Cemetery, Fernwood, Pa.

A fair mortar may be made of a proportion of two barrels of sand to one of cement; if the cement is not considered extra good use one barrel of sand to one of cement.

A few years ago I built some six little dams in a brook, which I was told I would have to build every year. I said: I guess not. They are there yet and are the beauty of my cemetery entrance. A stone wall foundation one foot thick was put in one foot below the bottom of the brook, and upon this a nine inch brick wall was built, arched up stream to form the dams. The arch form holds the structure secure against spring freshets, which in the case of straight walls would carry them out.

Suggestions to Lot Owners.

The Lakewood Cemetery Association of Lake City, Minn., have displayed praiseworthy enterprise in the issue of an Annual for distribution which contains some good things. It is stated that one object of the Association is: "A labor of love, prompted by the tender recollections of the loved ones that are buried in our cemetery." Another is: "It is an organized effort to keep the grounds in a neat and tidy manner." It states plainly that: "It costs money to mow and rake, dig and cultivate, plant and water, mend and paint," and suggests to lot owners that they can extend help by contributing to the Permanent Care Fund, or at least, provide for annual care.

The following form is suggested for bequeathing money for Perpetual Care with Guaranty of Lot: "I hereby direct my executors to pay to the Lakewood Cemetery Association of Lake City, Minn., such sum of money as may be found necessary to obtain from said corporation a contract for the perpetual care of my lot .... in said cemetery.

For convenience in mowing and raking, lots should be kept as nearly level as possible; also gravel walks replaced by grass paths, and on a level with the lots.

"A good and well kept cemetery is one of the highest recommendations a people can have. With shabby churches, poor school houses and disarranged cemeteries, there is little to boast of in any community. They are an index to the moral standing and social pride of a city or people, and when they go uncared for it is useless to expect an influx of good people, for they will look elsewhere for homes."

"Familiarize yourself with the rules governing your cemetery, and do what you can to assist in their enforcement."

The unusually dry season has most forcibly suggested that an efficient water supply is one of the actual necessities of the modern cemetery.

RULES AND REGULATIONS.

Every cemetery should be governed by certain rules and regulations, which should be printed in pamphlet form for distribution among lot owners. While this has been done in most of the large cemeteries, where the rules are very much alike, we will, for the benefit of the smaller cemeteries, publish in this department such rules as commend themselves for general adoption. Contributions are solicited.

Among the Rules and Regulations of the Riverside Cemetery Company, of Norristown, Pa., incorporated this year, are the following. The cemetery has been laid out and will be conducted on the Lawn plan:

The purchasers of lots in this cemetery will receive a deed from this company, guaranteeing to them and their heirs a burial place forever, or for the burial of such members of their family as they may choose to admit; but owners can not sell or transfer their lots, or any part thereof, to any other person whatever, without the consent of the Managers first had and obtained in writing. Upon the surrender of the deed, a new deed will be issued to the assignee upon payment of one dollar.

The Cemetery Company will give perpetual care to all lots and graves without charge.

No enclosures of any kind will be allowed around lots, nor will cradles be allowed around graves. All lots are to be marked by corner posts set flush with the sod. In order to insure permanency no headstones will be allowed higher than one foot above the surface of the ground, or less than six inches thick, or more than twenty-four inches in width, and a headstone must be in one piece with stub sufficiently long to enable the Cemetery Company to build it in a foundation.

The Managers have no desire to interfere with the individual taste of the lot holders, but to protect the interest of each separate purchaser they reserve to themselves the right to prevent the erection of any construction which may be considered detrimental to the cemetery. Not more than one monument will be allowed to a lot. This does not include headstones, of which one will be allowed to each grave, but no headstone must mark more than one grave.

All foundations for stone work will be done by the Cemetery Company at the expense of the lot or grave holder. No work shall be done on Sunday, and no material for work shall be delivered on Saturday. All debris and obstructions must be removed before Sunday. Stone men are requested not to put their name on any work within the cemetery with a view to advertising, nor to duplicate any work except headstones already on the grounds.

Workmen must not scatter material over adjoining lots, or leave the same on the ground any longer than necessary, and to prevent injury to the lawns, planks must be laid when any heavy material is to be moved over them.

No money shall be paid to attendants at the gate or on the grounds. The beauty of the whole cemetery is considered, rather than the decoration of individual lots; trees, shrubs and plants may be cultivated, but no tree or shrub growing within or overhanging any lot shall be cut down, removed or trimmed without permission of the superintendent or acting officer. Neither shall trees or shrubs be planted without permission.

A safe rule to adopt in visiting the cemetery. "Touch nothing in the cemetery that does not belong to you."

The following is the By-law governing Perpetual Care: The Board of Directors shall annually set apart ten per cent. of the gross receipts from the sale of lots for a Principal Fund for the perpetual care of the cemetery, and shall pay over the same annually to "The Norristown Title, Trust and Safety Deposit Company," of Norristown, Pa., as Trustee thereof. The said Trustee shall invest and reinvest the said principal fund from time to time in safe securities, and annually pay the income arising therefrom to the said Cemetery Company, to be used in keeping the cemetery in good order and repair. If the Cemetery Company for any reason fails, neglects or refuses to keep the said cemetery in good order and repair, then the said Trustee or any successor in trust shall use and apply the said income for the said purposes.

Association of American Cemetery Superintendents.

O. C. SIMONDS, "Graceland," Chicago, President.
G. W. CREEVY, "Harmony Grove," Salem, Mass., Vice-President.
F. EURICH, Woodlawn, Toledo, O., Secretary and Treasurer.

Publisher's Department.

The receipt of Cemetery Literature and Trade Catalogues will be acknowledged in this column.

TO ADVERTISERS. THE MODERN CEMETERY is the only publication of its class and will be found a valuable medium for reaching cemetery officials in all parts of the United States.

TO SUBSCRIBERS, Cemetery officials desiring to subscribe for a number of copies regularly to circulate among their lot owners, should send for our special terms. Several well known cemeteries have already adopted this plan with good results.

Contributions on matters pertaining to cemeteries are solicited. Address all communications to
R. J. HAIGHT, 334 Dearborn St., CHICAGO.

We have received a photograph of a Shelter House, Cave Hill Cemetery, Louisville, Ky.; and photograph and blue prints of a Receiving Vault for the Canton Cemetery Association, Canton, O., which will be illustrated in an early issue.

Mr. Aaron Sonneborn, secretary, Pueblo Cemetery Association, Pueblo, Colo., will be pleased to receive from secretaries or superintendents, annual reports, maps of grounds, etc., for which he will feel under obligations and gladly reciprocate.

Earnshaw & Punshon, Civil and Landscape Engineers, Cincinnati, O., whose advertisement regularly appears in the MODERN CEMETERY, have just issued a very neat little pamphlet of references of over 50 pages. In it a wide, varied and reliable experience is practically detailed and corroborated.

A most comprehensive catalogue and price list of Stable Fittings is that of Tom Moore, of 1367 Broadway, Brooklyn, and New York City, which has just come to hand. It is replete with varieties of stable necessities, descriptions, prices and illustrations, and offers an abundance of information in this line of supplies.

Cemetery Literature received: Rules and Regulations, By-Laws, etc., of the Riverside Cemetery, Norristown, Pa., 1894. Rules and Regulations of the Evergreen Cemetery Company, El Paso, Texas, 1894. Origin, History, By-Laws, Regulations and Catalogue of Fair Haven Union Cemetery Association, New Haven, Conn., 1894; illustrated by several half tone engravings.

The contract for the new receiving tomb for the Island Cemetery, Newport, R. I., has been awarded to Mr. William Gosling, and it will add both to the conveniences and the attractiveness of the cemetery. It is designed by Mr. Edwin Wilbur, and will be built of granite, with Indiana limestone trimmings, and in the Grecian-Tuscan order of architecture, with a portico and handsome stone pillars. There will be little ornamentation. The granite will be quarry-faced, and the trimmings, which include the steps, tablets and columns, of Indiana limestone, will be fine-cut. The structure will be 31.8 by 42.10 feet in size, exclusive of the portico, and will be lined with white enameled brick. The catacombs, sixty-four in number, will be arranged in tiers on either side and at the end opposite the door. Each catacomb will be provided with a separate system of drainage and have a door of white marble. The building will be set on plateaus of steps, running on all sides. The tomb will be placed on the site of the Gilliat tomb, near the Perry monument, and the contract calls for its completion by December 1.

Editor Modern Cemetery: Herewith please find $2.00 renewal for myself and new subscription for our superintendent. Your journal is most valuable, and is accomplishing much good. The progressive ideas of cemetery improvement as enunciated in your columns are taking root, and will surely have a beneficial effect.—W. H. D. COCHRANE, Sec'y, Edgewood Cemetery, Nashua, N. H.

HITCHINGS & CO.
Established 50 Years.

...Horticultural Architects and Builders.
AND LARGEST MANUFACTURERS OF

Greenhouse Heating and Ventilating Apparatus.

The highest awards received at the World's Fair for Horticultural Architecture, Greenhouse Construction and Heating Apparatus. Conservatories, Greenhouses, Palmhouses, etc., erected complete with our Patent Iron Frame Construction. *Send Four Cents for Illustrated Catalogue.*

233 Mercer St., NEW YORK.

THOS. W. WEATHERED'S SONS,
INCORPORATED,

HORTICULTURAL ARCHITECTS AND HOT WATER ENGINEERS

Send for Catalogue, enclosing 4 cents in stamps.

No. 244 Canal St., NEW YORK CITY.

We Grow Three Quarters of a Million of Roses Annually

Many other things as largely. **Are headquarters for the choicest Fruit and Ornamental Trees, Shrubs, Vines, Roses, Plants,**

BULBS. No finer assortment of Large or Small Fruits, Shrubs or Roses in America. With more acres of Ornamentals than any other Nursery can show. Planters as well as Nurserymen, Florists and Dealers are cordially invited to call and inspect our stock. **FALL PRICE LIST AND BULB CATALOGUE FREE.**

41st YEAR. 1,000 ACRES. 29 GREENHOUSES.

STORRS & HARRISON CO., Box 10, Painesville, Ohio.

Conservatories, Greenhouses, Vineries,
SHIPPED TO ANY PART OF THE COUNTRY AND ERECTED COMPLETE, READY FOR USE.

✱ ✱ ✱

Plans Embrace the Latest Improvements,
Unequaled Facilities for Manufacturing
Thirty-five Years Experience.

ADDRESS, STATING REQUIREMENTS,

Lord & Burnham Co...
IRVINGTON-ON-HUDSON, N. Y.

Conservatory in Newton Cemetery, Newtonville, Mass., designed and erected by Lord & Burnham Co

Catalogue sent on application.

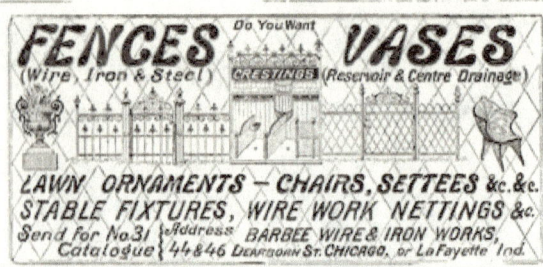

FENCES (Wire, Iron & Steel) Do You Want VASES (Reservoir & Centre Drainage) CRESTINGS

LAWN ORNAMENTS — CHAIRS, SETTEES &c. &c.
STABLE FIXTURES, WIRE WORK NETTINGS &c.
Send for No. 31 Address BARBEE WIRE & IRON WORKS,
Catalogue 44 & 46 Dearborn St. CHICAGO, or LaFayette Ind.

☞ PLEASE MENTION THE MODERN CEMETERY.

CEMETERY ADORNMENTS
---ARTISTIC---
Iron Vases WITH RESERVOIRS, which are the best for Plants
BOUQUET HOLDERS for Graves, 20, 25, 30 and 40c. each.
Our New Bouquet Vase for Cemetery is just out.
Metallic Wreaths, Crosses, etc., 50c to $5 each.
SETTEES AND CHAIRS, Both all IRON or IRON with WOOD SLATS.
Path, Avenue, and Keep off the Grass Signs.
Ornamental Fountains and Drinking Fountains.
Flower Seeds—2 packages, 5 cts. Grass seed bulbs, etc.
LAWN MOWERS—Our new one, "THE HERCULES," far superior and different from all others.
GARDEN HOSE—We only sell the best grades. Nozzles, hose, reels, etc.
JONES PATENT HOSE MENDER—No tools or tacks required. We send four menders, postage paid, by mail, for 25 cts. Send inside diameter of hose.
LAWN SPRINKLERS—3, 4, 6 and 8 arms. Hub, table and Combination. All our own make. Prices to suit.
Wire Rose Bush Trellises, Garden Borders, etc.
Greatest Variety of Above Goods at our NEW Store.
Illustrated Price List on application

M. D. JONES & CO.
368 Washington St.   BOSTON, MASS.

PATENT VAULT HEARSE.

Especially Designed
For Removing
Bodies from
Vault to Grave.

NEEDED IN EVERY CEMETERY HAVING A VAULT.

CARRIES the heaviest body with perfect safety, and may be drawn easily by two men. Platform, 2' 6" x 7' 6", with silver plated rollers, pins, etc., similar to ordinary hearse. Substantially built. Highly finished.

Extract from Testimonial: The Vault Hearse perfectly supplies a long felt want. We consider it indispensable where a vault is in use.—*Trustees, Marion, O., Cemetery.*

Send for PRICE LIST. **McMurray & Fisher Sulky Co.,** MARION, OHIO.

Patent Fence Cresting

Especially designed for Cemeteries and Orchards. This fence surrounds a library and Bellefountaine Cemeteries in St. Louis.

E. L. GRAYDON,
Sole Agent.
7201 N. B'dway,   ST. LOUIS, MO.

PATENT AUTOMATIC BURIAL APPARATUS
MANUFACTURED BY

This machine is a valuable, indispensable and useful invention. It is a necessity for the modern undertakers, cemeteries and the public. It is made of the best material, with best workmanship, and combines both lightness and durability. It is simple in its operation, cannot get out of order, dispenses with all extra labor and works without any noise or disturbance. A child could operate it with ease. Accidents are impossible.

We furnish two sizes:
Size A, inside opening 7 ft. 3 inch long; weight, 150 lbs; Price $200.

Size B, inside opening, 5 ft. long; weight, 125 lbs; Price, $175.

HOW IT IS USED

The frame is set level around the grave and the pall bearers place the casket on the straps. With a little pressure of the foot upon a small treadle on the side of the frame the casket will descend slowly and silently into the grave. Then the operator draws up on two small cords, so as to unbuckle or disconnect the straps under the coffin, when by turning the crank the straps are rewound on their respective drums.

With each apparatus we furnish a complete set of Wrenches, one Crank Lever and a Water Proof Cover.

SCHERER ⁂ MANUFACTURING ⁂ COMPANY,
OFFICE AND SHOW ROOM— Bible House, Corner 4th Avenue and 9th Street, NEW YORK City.

Epitaphs.

In a church in Lincolnshire, on the tombstone of a blacksmith, are these lines:

> My sledge and hammer are reclin'd,
> My bellows, too, have lost their wind;
> My fire's gone out, my forge decay'd,
> And in the dust my vice is laid;
> My work is done, my last nail's driven—
> So I now resign myself to heaven.

The Philadelphia *Times* is responsible for the following epitaph on a tired woman:

> Here lies a poor woman who always was tired,
> Who lived in a house where help was not hired,
> Her last words on earth were: "Dear friends I am going
> Where washing ain't done, nor sweeping nor sewing,
> But everything there is exact to my wishes,
> For where they don't eat, there's no washing of dishes
> I'll be where loud anthems will always be ringing,
> But having no voice I'll get clear of the singing,
> Don't mourn for me now, don't mourn for me never,
> I'm going to do nothing for ever and ever."

The tombstone of William Bell, Erroll, (1651-65), bears this inscription:

> "Here ceast and silent lies sweet sounding Bell,
> Who unto sleeping souls rung many a knell,
> Death crackt this Bell, yet doth his pleasant chiming
> Remain with those who are their lamps a-trimming.
> In spite of death, his word some praise still sounds,
> In Christ's church, and in heaven his joy abounds."

A huge boulder stone at the foot of one of Colorado's rocky cliffs is said to bear the following:

> An unknown man lies buried here,
>   Whose name was probably Davedge.
>   (From papers found about his clothes)
>   Slain by the lordly savage.
> We found him by his broken gun,
>   His hand gripped round the stock yet,
> A good big lead mine in his head,
>   But no gold in his pocket.
> Only a well-thumbed deck of cards,
>   All blackened on their faces;
> With kings and queens in duplicate,
>   And sixteen extra aces.

At the Dr. Edward Dean cemetery, at the Furnace village, (Mass.), on the tombstone of him who gave the land, and for whom it was named, is the following epitaph:

> The third physician Easton ever lost,
> Those Guild and Pratt not five months past.
> A short time since we lived as friends,
> Godfrey, Guild, Pratt, Bryant too,

> Physicians all our labor ends.
> We've bid the world adieu;
> To brighter worlds our spirits rise
> And view at distance there
> The vain results of busy man,
> And smile at human care.

Another in the same yard reads:

> Joyless sojourner was I,
> Only born to weep and die

On another stone:

> The lids he so seldom could close
> By sorrow forbidden to sleep,
> Sealed up in a lengthy repose,
> Have now forgotten to weep.

On another:

> Ten thousand talents I did owe,
> But Jesus Christ has paid the debt;
> Believe and sure you'll find
> To glory Death is but a step.

Thomas Blair of Coldstream, Scotland, (1686-1728), is thus commemorated:

> Here lies the Reverend Thomas Blair,
> A man of worth and merit,
> Who preached for fifty years and mair
> According to the Spirit.
> He preached off book to shun offense,
> And, what is still more rare,
> He never spoke a word of sense—
> So preached Tammy Blair."

VIEW IN CEDAR HILL CEMETERY, NEW YORK.

Half-Tone Engravings for Cemeteries
MADE DIRECT FROM PHOTOGRAPHS.
When writing for prices please state size of cut wanted.

R. J. HAIGHT, 334 Dearborn St., Chicago.

Interment Record and Lot Book.

This system is thought to embrace the best features of the most popular forms of burial records now in use and may be adapted to large or small cemeteries. The Interment Record gives all of the necessary information in regard to the deceased, and the Lot Book locates every grave, so that it can be readily found at any time. The books are printed on heavy paper, substantially bound and furnished in different sizes, depending upon the requirements of the cemetery.   **R. J. HAIGHT, Pub.,** 334 Dearborn St., Chicago.

EARNSHAW & PUNSHON
Landscape Engineers

Southwest Cor. Fifth and Race Streets,
Cincinnati,
Ohio.

30 YEARS experience in the profession, enables us to guarantee that our Modern Designs for laying out Cemeteries, Parks, and the Subdivision of Estates, will insure the best artistic effects and financial results, and at the same time involve the least expense in development and maintenance.

WE RESPECTFULLY REFER TO THE OFFICIALS OF THE FOLLOWING INSTITUTIONS:

Spring Grove Cemetery, Cincinnati, O.
Lake View Cemetery, Cleveland, O.
Linwood Cemetery, Dubuque, Ia.
Woodlawn Cemetery, Canandaigua, N. Y.
Mount Pleasant Cemetery, Toronto, Canada.
Lorraine Cemetery, Baltimore, Md.
Woodlawn Cemetery, Birmingham, Ala.
Forest Lawn Cemetery, East Saginaw, Mich.
Prospect Cemetery, Toronto, Canada.
Mount Olivet Cemetery, Detroit, Michigan.
Hoyt Park, East Saginaw, Mich

Highland Lawn Cemetery, Terre Haute, Ind.
Forest Lawn Cemetery, Buffalo, N. Y.
Riverview Cemetery, East Liverpool, O.
Forest Lawn Cemetery, Omaha, Neb.
St. Joseph's Cemetery, Evansville, Ind.
Woodside Cemetery, Middletown, O.
Mother of God Cemetery, Covington, Ky.
Logan Park Cemetery, Sioux City, Ia.
South Indiana Hospital, Evansville, Ind.
Goodale Park, Columbus, O.
Park and Zoological Gardens, Cincinnati, O.

South San Francisco Land and Imp. Co., San Francisco, Cal.,
and to all our patrons.

PERSONAL INSPECTION AND ADVICE AS TO THE IMPROVEMENT OF LARGE PROPERTIES
WILL BE PROMPTLY GIVEN, FREE OF CHARGE.

THE MODERN CEMETERY.

THE MODERN CEMETERY.
AN ILLUSTRATED MONTHLY JOURNAL DEVOTED TO THE INTEREST OF CEMETERIES

R. J. HAIGHT, Publisher,
334 Dearborn Street, CHICAGO.

Subscription $1.00 a Year in Advance.   Foreign Subscription $1.25.
Special Rates on Six or More Copies.

VOL. IV. CHICAGO, OCTOBER, 1894. NO. 8.

CONTENTS.

SUITABLE TREES AND SHRUBS FOR A MODERN CEMETERY	85
*AQUATIC GARDEN, PINE GROVE CEMETERY, LYNN, MASS.	88
*MT. AUBURN, AND SOME OF ITS FAMOUS DEAD	89
FUNERAL CUSTOMS OF ANCIENT NATIONS	90
SHRUBBY HERBACEOUS PERENNIALS	91
SOME CANONS OF CRITICISM	91
WESTLAWN RECEIVING VAULT, CANTON, O.	92
CEMETERY NOTES	94
CORRESPONDENCE	95
PUBLISHER'S DEPARTMENT	96

*Illustrated.

Suitable Trees and Shrubs for a Modern Cemetery.*

To obtain the best and most satisfactory result from trees and shrubs in connection with cemetery planting is one of more than usual importance. We have only to look around us in many cemetery grounds to recognize how desirable improvement, from a practical stand-point, and by a judicious selection and arrangement of cemetery trees and shrubs becomes. It is generally found as time rolls on, that a large proportion of the trees originally planted are where they should never have been, and, as a consequence, have to be cut away before they have really served any useful purpose. The great object of modern cemetery planting is not so much to afford shade, form screens or accomplish other objects of practical importance, as it is that the beautiful picture presented by a skilled display of trees, shrubs and flowers should rob death of the many terrors which the ignorance and superstitions of olden times surrounded it.

The modern idea of a cemetery is not so much that the grave is the end of all as it is that it is the beginning of a new career of happiness which we

---

*Paper read before the Eighth Annual Convention of the Association of American Cemetery Superintendents, Philadelphia, by Thomas B. Meehan.

are taught the new life is to be. The earliest idea of paradise was that of a beautiful garden, and it is impossible to rob the paradise of the future of the same surroundings. The modern cemetery is, therefore, the ideal garden of the future, so far as it is possible for the human intellect to accomplish, and it should be the aim to make pleasurable the visits of the living, by making beautiful the resting places of the dead, leading the mind from gloomy thoughts such as ancient cemeteries fostered; but this beautiful garden must necessarily be subservient to practical details. It is impossible to accomplish anything in this world, that is not a financial success, and there is no reason why financial success and the ideal cemetery garden cannot both go hand in hand. And, in fact, the financial aspects require close consideration in connection with the adornment of the grounds. In the planting of the cemetery, therefore, the possible desires of future lot-holders should be considered. I knew once of a cemetery which prided itself on the number of rare trees it contained, and which had among its arboreal treasures one of the finest specimens of the Cedar of Lebanon to be found in the United States. The majority of lot-holders would have been proud to have possessed such a rare gem. Not so, however, the one who owned it at the time in mind. The superintendent of the company was amazed when the lot-holder came one day to insist on cutting down the tree, because it shaded over the grave and moss grew on his marble monument. Determined to save his tree, the superintendent had to make arrangements to give the owner a large price for his lot and sell him another one, and have the interred removed rather than have his beloved tree taken away. Such occurrences as this cannot always be foreseen, but they may be sometimes, and thought should be given in the arrangement and planting of cemeteries to the possibility of such unpleasant occurrences. With this end in view, it would seem desirable, therefore, that portions of the grounds should be reserved expressly for planting in order to beautify and make as nearly as possible an ideal garden spot, while that portion devoted to the lot-holders should be as free from planting as would be consistent with the necessary landscape effect. By the judicious selection of these spots, a general landscape effect would be produced which is lacking in very many cemeteries, even in those of recent beginning.

I have frequently felt that sufficient importance has not been attached to the artistic arrangement and planting of the entrance to the cemetery. It was with great pleasure when visiting the Forest Hill Cemetery of Boston, I saw that this had evidently been taken into consideration when the plans of the cemetery were drawn. Who having driven along that broad, sweeping drive, planted on both sides with most beautiful specimens of Blue Spruce, Nordman Fir and other choice evergreens, supplemented with banks of Rhododendrons, Azaleas and handsome thickets of shrubs, and on up through the Ivy covered archway, has not felt that he was indeed entering a beautiful Paradise! I really believe that more attention should be given to the approach to, and the entrance of, the cemetery grounds proper, for it is there that visitors get their first impression,—and first impressions are always the most lasting.

Perhaps this was more impressed upon my mind when I visited Forest Hill, because it was only a few days before this that I saw another cemetery in western New York, where the entrance was directly from the street, through the conventional gate-way with its stern granite posts and iron railings. Not but what the grounds of this cemetery were very artistically arranged, but the entrance to it did not give me the same feeling of rest that I experienced when I visited Forest Hill. Yet, the entrance to the cemetery of which I speak could very easily have been arranged so as to give one the idea of entering a beautiful park, simply by placing the entrance proper a little distance from the street, and massing a number of choice evergreens, trees and shrubs on both sides of its sweeping driveway.

It is not my intention to go into the details of how to plant a cemetery, because that is the province of a landscape gardener; I merely wish to throw out a few hints or points which to me seem to be frequently overlooked, and this question of an artistically planted entrance is, I think, one that particularly needs attention. It seems to me that it is your duty, gentlemen, to let no opportunity escape to instruct your lot-holders how to keep in touch with the improved and more advanced aims of the modern cemetery. Every one is prone to do a certain thing because custom has made it popular, and this is as true in cemetery matters as in everything else. The huge marble or granite shaft, rarely an object of beauty and sometimes but a mere display of wealth, is usually erected with the best intentions, and its use is still a custom mainly because it is believed to be the most fitting thing to do, and lot-holders have not learned a more advanced idea. And this is just where the question arises— what is the most advanced idea by which we can satisfy that desire to do something to show how the dead are missed or loved? Would not the planting of rare trees and plants be more fitting and bear testimony to our love to a far greater extent than does the erection of monuments? Do not visitors at a cemetery show more real love for the trees and flowers than they do for a block of marble or granite, upon which more frequently they look with more curiosity than respect? There is no doubt that our dead soldiers are more honored and the living more inspired by the strewing of flowers annually on their graves, than they would be by mere monuments alone. We must get lot-holders to remember with us that beautiful trees and shrubs produce beautiful thoughts, and keep us, as it were, in closer communion with those we have lost, and that trees, shrubs and flowers are, therefore, more fitting than monuments. The most choice and beautiful evergreens that could be selected would cost but a small portion of the value of a monument, and would leave a handsome fund to be placed in the hands of the superintendent for the annual care necessary to keep the lot in a beautiful condition.

I understand that no marble monument or headstone marks the spot of the famous Nicholas Longworth, one of the pioneers in the industrial development of Cincinnati, and possibly the father of modern strawberry culture, but that he sleeps beneath the spreading branches of a noble elm tree.

I think that you all will agree with me that the time is here for some changes in this direction. Many of you have already passed rules forbidding the erection of marble copings, iron railings, and I think in some cases tall headstones. A few years ago this would not have been possible, but to-day the people have more advanced ideas, and through your teachings are becoming willing to discard these things. Even in the matter of headstones and monuments they are showing a desire to design them after ideas more natural than the marble shaft and square or rounded top headstone. This is shown by the imitations of tree trunks, and boulders now frequently seen in cemeteries. The monument in Harleigh Cemetery, near the main entrance, representing a column of stones, doubtless attracted the attention of many of you, and each of you perhaps have in the cemeteries which you superintend, monuments, the erection of which has been suggested by some seemingly appropriate object in nature. It is but a step from the imitation of nature to the real, and I firmly believe that the transition would not be so difficult of accomplishment as one might suppose. Let but a few of your lot-holders start the work, and others will quickly follow. It is probable that the idea may be too radical for its full accomplishment at an early date, but I have no doubt but what it will come in time just as other reforms have been adopted after persistent efforts have been made to bring them about.

It is always a source of regret that there is not more desire for more meritorious trees and shrubs in cemetery planting. Why should quantities o Arbor-Vitæ, Norway Spruce, Austrian or Scotch Pine be used, when the more rare and vastly more beautiful Nordman Fir, Oriental Spruce, Englemans Spruce, Douglas Spruce and the superb Colorado Blue Spruce, and Swiss Pine could be used to as great advantage. It certainly should not be because the first named are cheaper,—for first cost in planting should not be a consideration, as the work is to last one may say forever. To be sure, there are portions of the United States where some of these named may not be hardy, but there are many that will thrive almost anywhere. The Blue Spruce, Douglas Fir, Englemans Spruce and the Picea concolor are all natives of the mountains of Colorado, and should thrive in almost any portions of the United States, unless the soil of the particular spot be unfavorable. It is not commonly known that plants which are apparently not hardy in a more northern climate than where they are indigenous prove quite so if they are protected when they are small until they become established. The most northern limit of the Magnolia grandiflora is I think North Carolina, yet we in Philadelphia and vicinity have no difficulty in getting it to grow if we protect the tree for a few years until it can force roots below the frost line. There are several of these trees in Philadelphia that are not less than twenty-five feet high.

It is impossible for any one to say positively what might or might not thrive in a certain locality. This can only be learned by the individual efforts of yourselves. Select what you believe would thrive in your soil and climate, and test it for a year or two; the cost would be trifling, and every time you find something new or uncommon that will grow in your cemetery, you will have added a new subject of interest to your grounds.

Of late years the planting of evergreen beds has become quite popular; and in many of the more recently designed cemeteries and, in fact, in a number of the older ones, numerous beds are now planted. There is scarcely any form of Spruce, Fir, Arbor-Vitæ or Retinospora that cannot be used in this connection, as by frequent trimming, even the larger growing sorts can be kept within reasonable bounds, and at the same time a much finer color will develope from the constant pruning. The great labor and cost of planting large beds of greenhouse plants annually have had much to do with the advancement of the evergreen bed,—as in the latter case the first cost is the greatest one.

During the last few years there have been many introductions of plants from Japan which have been found to be extremely hardy, and also many from Europe and remote parts of our own country, and it may be desirable to mention a few of these that would doubtless be valuable for cemetery work. The Cercidiphyllum, a Japanese tree, has proven hardy in many sections of the country where it has been tried. It is a pyramidal tree, but rather more spreading than either the Lombardy Poplar or the Pyramidal Oak. It seems particularly adapted to heavy soils, and especially to low and damp situations, where it makes quite a strong and rapid growth. The Kolreuteria is a Chinese tree, making a low, spreading growth. In July it is densely covered with very large panicles of yellow flowers,— and is particularly attractive at that time. It is not a new tree, but rather uncommon. One of the prettiest trees adapted to cemetery planting which has recently been introduced is the Styrax Japonica,— few things can be more beautiful than the pearly white flowers, abundantly produced in the early part of July. The Pterostyrax hispidum is also a valuable addition,—a rather spreading tree, of moderately rapid growth, and covered in May with drooping racemes of white flowers entirely covering the tree. This I think will become extremely popular, when it is thoroughly well known.

Of improved varieties of our native trees, nothing seems to have become more popular than the forms of Cornus florida,—the red flowered and the weeping. These with the parent plant seem to be adapted to all soils, situations and climates, and consequently are found largely in all cemeteries. The red flowered form is particularly beautiful in spring when covered with bloom, though later, as with the other two, when it assumes its varying tints of autumn coloring, few plants exceed it in gorgeousness.

The recent introduction among shrubs are too numerous to mention, doubtless they have been brought to your notice many times. A class of plants which have sprung into great prominence in a short period is hardy perennials,—and they need more than a passing word,—indeed, a whole chapter could be written of the many useful positions they might occupy in our ornamental planting. A class of plants which after planting become more and more beautiful every year as the roots become stronger, and which, by judicious selection of varieties give a continuation of bloom from early spring to late fall,—and exist in form from those of low and dwarf habit to plants making a growth from five to six feet are what perennials comprise. It would be useless for me to attempt to name desirable varieties, as this would depend upon the soil and location where the particular bed is to be planted,—

AQUATIC GARDEN, PINE GROVE CEMETERY, LYNN, MASS.

but I can assure you that you would never regret the use of these plants in your work, and would find the study of varieties particularly adapted to your necessities of great interest to you.

Aquatic Garden, Pine Grove Cemetery, Lynn, Mass.

Mr. William Stone, superintendent of Pine Grove Cemetery, Lynn, Mass., writes us as follows on his Aquatic Garden. In plan it is of circular shape, with a walk extending around the centre pond, from which four paths at right angles cut the bog garden and promiscuous bedding into segments:

"As you look at the picture the Nelumbium Speciosum (Egyptian Lotus) is seen in the center. In front of this is Nymphaea Albida Candidissima, (white); at the right, Nymphaea Marliacea Chromatella (yellow), and to the left is Nymphaea Zanzibarensis (dark blue). On the back, not visible, is Nymphaea Devoniensis (red).

"Around the edge of the pond I planted dwarf morning glories, portulacca, and some fern parsley, while on the other side of the walk was my bog garden containing water hyacinths, water poppies, Sagittarias, double and single, Lobelia Cardinalis, wild rice, etc. In the tubs on the outside corners I placed lilies of different colors, and also the water snow flake (Limnanthemum Indicum).

"In the adjacent promiscuous planting I used castor beans, tobacco, the various tall grasses, Zea Japonica, and the low growing grass, Penissetum longystylum, a beautiful grass blooming from the seed the first year, Brazilian beets of various colors, which attracted much attention, hollyhocks, and other plants too numerous to mention. The whole scheme was a source of attraction all the summer, as the thousands of visitors will testify.

"Aquatics should be more generally grown and in fact, they are becoming more in favor every year, and every year we are more convinced that an all wise creator has furnished them for our pleasure."

The old negro burying ground, Mount Zion, in Washington, still presents the curious customs of the colored people in regard to their dead. The articles that were most used and enjoyed by the departed while living, and the bottles containing the residuum of the medicines last administered are placed upon the graves. The cemetery thus decorated forms a striking contrast to the beautiful cemetery close adjoining, but withal its rank growth of weeds and grass and generally unkempt appearance, there is a peculiar interest attached to the place, and its patrons are strong in the belief that the things used by the departed while alive will be needed on the other side.

Mt. Auburn, and Some of its Famous Dead.

There is perhaps no cemetery in the country that possesses more interest from the associations connected with its dead; or that displays more natural beauty within its confines; or that considering the noted names inscribed on its memorials is marked by greater simplicity in such memorials. The stones have a usefulness, it is true, in denoting the last resting place, but the pages of history, science, art, literature, are imperishable records of many of the occupants of Mount Auburn, Boston.

Mt. Auburn was consecrated over 60 years ago, and its area of about 140 acres contains about 30,000 persons. It is one of the pioneers of the rural cemetery idea, and is a hallowed park which invites contemplative communion with those who have passed away. Every lot is now disposed of under the "perpetual care" provision which enhances the beauty of the place and ensures the most intelligent attention to seasonable requirements.

Under the early system lot owners were permitted to take care of their own property, and it worked well in many instances, but when succession of ownership placed it in other hands a carelessness usually developed, a condition which neither bespoke affection for the living nor respect for the general appearance of the home of the dead. In other cases change of abode, and in still others the dead were too quickly forgotten, which all resulted in lack of care and general untidiness which seriously interfered with the best interests of the cemetery. The modern system does away with all this, and so rapidly is the change being made that only in a comparatively few cases does the old method obtrude itself.

One of the recent additions to memorial art in the cemetery is that in memory of Edwin Booth, of which an illustration is given. It is a marble slab, on one side of which is a bronze tablet, with the head of the great actor in bas-relief, and the inscription; and on the other side a quotation from the poet the interpretation of whose works made him famous.

A plain headstone of white marble, simple as the nature of the great preacher himself, marks the grave of Phillips Brooks, late bishop of Massachusetts, in the Brooks family lot. On the stone is carved: "Phillips Brooks, Dec. 13, 1835. Jan. 23, 1893. Rector of the Church of the Advent, Philadelphia, 1859-1862. Rector of the Church of the Holy Trinity, Philadelphia, 1862-1869. Rector of Trinity Church, Boston, 1869-1891. Bishop of the Diocese of Massachusetts, 1891-1893." On the base of the stone is the sentence: "Him that overcometh I will make a pillar in the temple of my God."

A very modest lot is that in which James Russell Lowell lies. A small slate headstone marks the spot, so unpretentious that one must be careful not to overlook it, and there are other stones in close proximity, equally unassuming, which direct the eye to the last resting places of a distinguished company. The inscription on the headstone of James Russell Lowell reads as follows: "Sacred to the memory of James Russell Lowell, born 1819, died 1891, and of his wife Maria White, born 1821, died 1853, and also of his second wife, Frances Dunlap, born 1825, died 1885."

A simple gravestone points to where the great humanitarian Dorothea L. Dix rests. The stone only carries her name, but the soldiers annually give plain notice that her work for them still holds their remembrance.

From the Edwin Booth lot some of the most noted graves in the cemetery can be seen. Just back of it is the memorial to the famous Margaret Fuller erected in the family lot. It will be remembered that Margaret Fuller and her husband, Count Ossoli, were lost at sea in 1850.

Near by is a large brown stone monument with an urn on top, the inscription on the front of which tells a story: "Sacred to the memory of Charles Bulfinch, born in Boston, A. D., 1763; Graduated at Harvard College, A. D., 1781; Chairman of the Selectmen of Boston from 1797 to 1817; Architect of the State House of Massachusetts from 1795 to 1798, and of the Capitol of the United States from 1817 to 1830. He closed a pure and honored life with Christian submission April 15, 1844. Mourned by a numerous family."

The boulder monument in a neighboring lot distinguishes the grave of that genial and celebrated scientist, Louis Agassiz. The boulder was brought from Switzerland, his native country.

A bit of the work of St. Gaudens, the sculptor, is to be found on the stone at the grave of Henry Coffin Nevins, the Methuen millionaire.

Not far from this is the monument to Charlotte Cushman, and higher up the hill the Harvard College lot. Here lie President Kirkland, Professors

Herman August Hagen, Evangelinus Apostolides Sophocles, and Count de Pourtales, the friend of Agassiz.

Among the few names mentioned there must not be omitted those famous sons of Massachusetts, Charles Sumner and the poet Longfellow, whose graves attract many a pilgrimage.

A red granite Runic Cross marks where Prof. Horsford, Leif Ericsson's champion lies. William Ellery Channing's grave draws many visitors, while such names as Fanny Fern and Rufus Choate lead numbers interested in their lives and works to visit their last resting places.

On the road to the chapel, which is situated on a commanding knoll, the monument to Nathaniel Bowditch is passed as well as the family lot of Bishop Lawrence. Nearly opposite the chapel is the grave of Col. Robert Gould Shaw, whose memory is held in grateful remembrance by the colored people. Not far off is the monument erected to the memory of Benjamin Franklin. The most recent addition to this galaxy of notables is the last of the New England coterie of literary giants, Oliver Wendell Holmes, who now lies buried beside his wife.

Funeral Customs of Ancient Nations.

The nations in their childhood had different ways of disposing of their dead.

In Egypt we find them embalming the remains of their departed and placing them in immense tombs—Pyramids—or we discover whole cities of the dead under the ground in the mountain sides. Monuments all through Asia, proof against the effect of time, bear evidence that a great many nations resorted to the burial of the bodies of their dead. The Persians placed their dead in the open air to be disposed of by the animals of the night. To them earth and fire were sacred, so that they could not use these two common elements for such purposes.

Of the Indo-European races a great many used the burning process with more or less funeral rites. The Celts and Latins had the funeral-pile, but not to a great extent, the burying of the body was a more common practice among them; but the Teutonic race loved the funeral-pile, it was part of their religion, it was sacred to them.

Slaves were left unburned, but the free man must go the right road from the funeral-pile to the land of souls. It was considered dishonorable to subject the body to the ravages of worms.

In "the Odyssey." Odysseus meets one of his friends in the other world, walking around unable to find Hades' house, and he complains bitterly to Odysseus that his body is left unburied, and implores him to burn it when he goes back. The old Greek view of the funeral-pile is furthermore seen in the story of how old king Priam, unable to get possession of the body of his beloved son Hector, burns Hector's clothes as a substitute for the body.

Charles Keary says in "The Mythology of Eddas:" "In the tenth century an Arab traveller, Ibn Haukel in his Kitab—el Meshalik na—i Memalik, (Book of Roads and Kingdoms), tells about how he visited the Russ or Varings in the centre of Russia, (near Kief) to which they have given their name. They were a Gothic race.

A Russ was speaking to his interpreter and Ibn Haukel asked what he said. "He says," was the answer, "that as for you Arabs, you are mad, for those who are the most dear to you and whom you honor most, you place in the ground, where they will become a prey to the worms; whereas with us they are burnt in an instant and go straight to Paradise."

The Teutonic race has composed a hymn of untold beauty in honor of the sacred funeral-pile in the myth "The Funeral of Balder," where we see Balder placed in his ship on the funeral-pile, his wife Nanna throwing herself at his body in a grief which burst her heart, and she is placed by his side. We see gods and elves and dwarfs, warriors and giants, all forces from heaven and earth gathered around this burning ship; costly trinkets are thrown in the fire, and the god Thor makes it holy with his hammer-sign.

It was as a whole very common to put the ship of the dead warrior on the funeral-pile and burn his body in it. He was then supposed to go in his ship to the land of Paradise after the burning.

In the old Teutonic poem "Brynhildskvide," Brynhild is placed in a car hung with costly weavings upon the funeral-pile, and after the burning she rides to the land of the souls in this car.

Still no nation seems to have clung to the burning of the dead as part of their creed more than did the old Greeks, the nation of the highest standing in art and literature among all nations in the ancient world, the nation never yet surpassed in love of all that is beautiful. NICO BECH-MEYER.

One of the most celebrated Roman sculptors has now almost completed the sepulchral monument for the Pope, ordered by himself. It is of Carrara marble. On the cover of the sarcophagus lies a lion, with one paw on the papal tiara. On the right is a statue of Faith, holding in one hand the Holy Scriptures and in the other a torch. On the left is a statue of Truth, holding the arms of the Pope. Under the lion, on the face of tomb, is a Latin inscription.

Shrubby Herbaceous Perennials.

Certain herbaceous plants are so shrub like in their appearance that they serve to merge the one class into the other. Some of them are well adapted for use in connection with plantations of true shrubs, others are more in keeping with the plants grown in herbaceous borders, and a few have enough character to be effectively used alone, either as isolated specimens or in clumps or beds apart from other species. Under this head we will speak of three species that are shrub-like in appearance, but are, in fact, herbaceous, the shrubby tops dying to the ground in the fall just as Pæonies do. The first, Cassia Marylandica, looks well only when used in connection with shrubs, and looks best when set at the edge of a planting, next to the grass. It is attractive in foliage retains its bright green color through the season despite heat and drought, and in late summer it bears yellow flowers that are similar in shape and manner of growth to those of the Locust tree.

The second, Clematis Davidiana, throws up a number of leafy stems as shrub-like as Hydrangeas, and in August begins to put forth axillary clusters of beautifully blue, hyacinth shaped flowers that are deliciously fragrant and that keep on coming for several weeks. It is hardy, and looks most at home in the neighborhood of other herbaceous plants, although it might fringe a small plantation of true shrubs. It is, however, not at all conspicuous, and would not be effective at a distance, unless, indeed, if used in a large mass. The third and most showy of the trio is itself a trinity. It belongs to the Mallow family, and the three varieties are white crimson eyed, cream crimson eyed, and rose colored Hibiscus. They are all remarkably handsome, with flowers like very large single hollyhocks, and the large bed of white ones shown in our illustration is one of the chief August attractions of the island flower garden in Jackson Park.

It is in ordinary garden soil, and the plants have been fairly well watered, but, like all Mallows, these are happiest near the water, and single plants or clumps of either variety make splendid ornaments on the margin of lakes or ponds, where they may be planted only a foot or two from the water. The white and the cream colored should not be used together, but the pink ones go very well with the white, though in placing them it must be borne in mind that the rose flowered makes a slightly taller growth than either of the others. The exquisite shade of this pink, or rose colored Hibiscus is, so far as I know, distinct from anything in the floral world, and captivates every colorist by its purity.

FANNY COPLEY SEAVEY.

Some Canons of Criticism.*

In our article on "The Modern Cemetery a Social Force," in the August number, we tried to show what the modern cemetery is capable of becoming; in "Parasitic Growths," in the September issue we pointed out the influence that, beyond all others,

CRIMSON EYED HIBISCUS.—BED OF PLANTS IN BLOOM.

threatens to defeat its ideal development; but all that we have said will be of little avail if we fail to establish criterions of taste in Memorial Art by which the false may be distinguished from the true.

Memorial Art, like literature, is, and should be, an admixture of prose and poetry—the sculptor being the poet and the architect the prose-writer, and thus memorial art seems to us capable of an analysis that shall be thoroughly qualitative.

The cardinal considerations in Memorial Art are three:

1. BEAUTY OF DESIGN. 2. DURABILITY, AND 3. COST.

Beauty of Design. This is so far above and beyond every other consideration that the other should not occupy a single thought until this is secured. This wanting, durability is no longer a

---

*Copyrighted, 1894, by the Memorial Art League.

merit, but rather a vice. A painting for the parlor, or a statue for the lawn, if, after familiar study it proves a disappointment (and how often is this the case!) may easily be gotten rid of; a monument that is not satisfactory, is of all things the most persistently unsatisfactory. Therefore urge upon your lot-owners to take time in its selection; this is not a matter requiring haste; on the contrary it is a matter requiring the most thoughtful and studious deliberation. Impress upon them that any one who seeks to hasten their decision, does so because his own schemes will not bear investigation. You have your lot-owners' confidence:—do not abuse it by refraining, through diffidence or timidity, from using your influence to prevent his making a mistake that not only himself, but his children to the remotest generation, are sure to regret.

Beauty of Design may be resolved into three elements, viz: Fitness, Harmony of Outline, and Repose.

Fitness. The adaptation of the structure to its purpose and to its environment. Thus the Colonial style of architecture, though ugly in itself, becomes beautiful by reason of its pre-eminent fitness in home-building; conversely, the Grecian orders which, abstractly, have been the world's ideal of beauty for twenty centuries, become ugly when applied to our modern commercial uses, so obvious is their unfitness. Thus the Washington monument has pre-eminent fitness; its mass is justified in the name it commemorates; its form is exactly suited to the level plain upon which it is located.

In our cemeteries, no regard whatever seems to have been had for Fitness; obelisks placed upon hill sides where the eye cannot fail to make them incline from the perpendicular; mausoleums of Grecian order squat upon level plains or even in valleys, where their lines become actually offensive; lofty shafts crowded together until the effect is that of factory chimneys; duplication and reduplication of forms in a "meaningless and damnable iteration."

When we see the Muse of History employing her stylus to engrave the name of a rich pork butcher, it is only a more startling exemplification of the less obvious violations of Fitness which abound in our grounds. Mausoleums and vaults—whatever structure tends to withold the products of decomposition from the clean, sweet earth (nature's universal disinfectant) are conspicuously unfit. Interment ("in-earthment") or cremation, civilization has a right to demand.

Fitness is readily determined by the exercise of an enlightened common-sense.

Harmony of Outline. This is what the eye first recognizes in a structure, and no excellence of detail on closer inspection can overcome the repugnance impressed upon the mind by a deficiency in it, and no fault in details can seriously mar the pleasure we find in the recognition of excellence in it. It is the most subtle and evasive of qualities—the achievement of it is a rapture, the recognition of it a delight. Consistency is never more a jewel than in the designing of a monument, and a good design was never produced when the designer had not a clearly defined idea in his mind of what he wished to accomplish. He must see the end from the very beginning.

Fitness demands that the work should be in keeping with its surroundings.—Harmony of Outline, that it should be consistent with itself—integral—not a patchwork.

Repose. It is the office of Memorial Art to soothe and tranquilize—not to startle or astonish.

Unlike other departments of art, wherein even violent action may be admissible, here every line should be quiet—restful.

Flamboyant details, tawdry decoration, feats of stone-cutting and engineering have no place in it. Repose excludes dynamics; and the moment our thought begins to wander from the contemplation of beauty to the admiration of mechanical or engineering skill, we know what we are looking upon is not an expression of true Memorial Art; its place is at the exhibition, not in the cemetery.

Finally. An artisan can execute a design, but the design itself, if artistic, is the work of an artist, and we say again: You can do more than any one else to open the way for him; it is your duty to your clients, to your profession and to posterity, to do it.

(*To be concluded.*)

Westlawn Receiving Vault, Canton, O.

The accompanying illustrations present the main features of the Westlawn Receiving Vault, built for the Canton Cemetery Association of Canton, Ohio, from plans by the architect, Mr. E. G. Essig, of Canton, Ohio.

The vestibule is 10 feet square with gothic arch

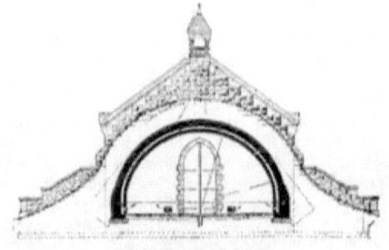

TRANSVERSE SECTION.

WESTLAWN RECEIVING VAULT, CANTON, O.

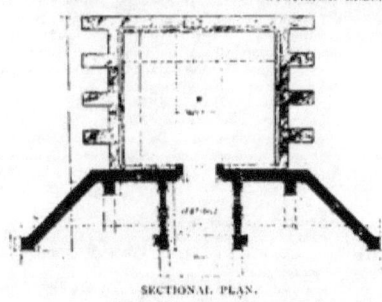

SECTIONAL PLAN.

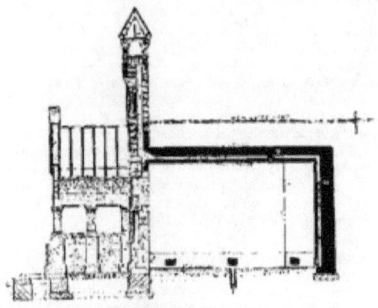

LONGITUDINAL SECTION.

front, constructed of a rockfaced and clean cut Ohio stone. The framework is of open timber work covered with green slate, finished with a neat terra-cotta cresting.

The main wall is of the Romanesque type with a wide flank wall on either side; the base of main and flank walls is of clean cut Ohio stone, the ballance of walls is constructed of rock-faced stone laid in uniform courses, finished with a wide coping of clean cut stone; the main wall is finished at top with stone cupola 4 feet square and about nine feet high. This cupola is connected with inside air chambers affording an excellent ventilating shaft.

At the end of each flank wall a square base carries a large vase.

The main entrance is a Gothic arched door-way with two heavy open iron day gates, above which is an enriched grill, and a pair of heavy solid steel burglar proof doors on the inside of the day gates.

Both vestibule and vault floors are of flagging; the vault floor has a fall from all the outer walls to the center whence the drainage is carried through a grating to a small gravel bottom cesspool.

The arch or crown is constructed of hard vitrified brick beginning with a 20 inch wall at base to a height of 4 feet above vault floor; then 12 inches is the thickness adopted. Inside of this wall is a 4 inch air chamber and inside that is another 4 inch brick wall, the air chamber is connected with the inside by a series of valve registers at bottom of wall and the air chambers are then connected with ventilating shaft. By this means the air on the inside can be kept fresh and sweet. The outer walls all have air chambers entirely around them which keeps them perfectly dry. Both the outside and inside of these walls are covered with a coat of cement plaster.

The structure is said to have given great satisfaction, and moreover, it is well located in the cemetery.

CEMETERY NOTES.

A Boston lady seeing a mile-stone marked 1 m. from Boston and taking it for a tombstone and taking the 1 m. for I'm, exclaimed, "how simple, yet how sufficient."

* * *

This is how the Fenton, Mich., *Independent* gives the public a cemetery note: "An Owosso family is erecting a house for their dead in the Owosso cemetery, at a cost of $7,000. Such things make very pretty spots in cemetery landscapes."

* * *

By the will of the late William V. Lippincott, of Philadelphia, who died in 1893, and which now becomes operative, $10,000 is left to the West Laurel Hill Cemetery Company, Philadelphia, to be applied to the keeping of his mausoleum in good repair. This structure is one of the finest of its kind in the East.

* * *

The trustees of Forest Hill Cemetery, Dunkirk, N. Y., are making preparations to expend about $6,000 on their grounds. One of the most needed improvements will be the erection of a chapel and a new residence for the sexton. A large new entrance arch will also be erected, fountains arranged, and the grounds generally improved.

* * *

Master in Chancery J. S. Biery, has filed his decision in favor of the defendants in the case of Aaron Jacobs, of South Bethlehem, Pa., against the Union Cemetery Association and Mayberry S. Weidner, of Allentown. Edward Denhard had owned a cemetery lot, which he sold to Mr. Jacobs, but the transfer was never recorded on the books of the association. When Mr. Denhard died his heirs sold the lot to Mr. Weidner. They did not know of its prior sale. The deed being missing, they had a duplicate issued to Mr. Weidner. This transfer was recorded on the books of the association. The lot now had two owners, and to decide the dispute Mr. Jacobs entered suit against the association and Mr. Weidner.

* * *

A special telegram to the Chicago *Inter-Ocean* from New York reports the following from an interview with John M. May, of Chicago: "I am interested with several others, in the establishment of graveyards for domestic pets in the large cities of this country. We are already well under way in Chicago, and expect the scheme to pay well on the investment. The idea is to start these burial places in all the cities and all under one management. It was our intention originally to have secured a plat of ground in a cemetery, but lot-holders made such a strong objection that we gave it up. We shall buy a piece of land of from two to five acres in extent, far enough on the outskirts to avoid offending the supersensitive. Then we will proceed to fence it in, lay it out in walks, and issue our prospectus.

We shall charge a moderate price for interment, and will stand ready to receive orders for monuments, mausoleums, or statues of dogs, horses, cats or birds."

* * *

A correspondent of a London paper thus writes of a dog cemetery: The idea of a dog cemetery is not by any means a new one in England, as such an enclosure is to be found in one or two garrison towns. There is such a place of sepulture in Edinburgh Castle, in particular, the small space behind the battlements, on the north side of that fortress, just in front of the battery on which stands that huge historic piece of ordnance, Mons Meg. The cemetery is filled with stones erected to the memory of regimental pets, with the names of the corps and dates, the last going well back to the beginning of the present century. The spot, which is not open to the general public, is very much neglected. The castle guides, as a rule, point out this curious dog cemetery to visitors.

* * *

In regard to Burial Reform, a New York correspondent of the Middletown, N. Y., *Press*, remarks that the objects of the New York Association will be impossible of accomplishment, notwithstanding the active co-operation of Bishop Potter, so long as the rich indulge their pride at funerals. The poor are as proud as those better off, and follow an example rather than advertise their poverty on so public an occasion. The floral mania still continues and is a heavy tax. The correspondent declares it is the rich who need to reform, and their poorer brethren will readily follow. Pride in funerals has always been a ruling feature in society, and so has been the equally improper display of mourning. A striking contrast to the usual well-to-do is that of James Lenox, a wealthy man, who was averse to all display, and ordered that his funeral should be private, and that even the day and hour should be kept secret. No notices were given out, and only the hearse gave sign of the funeral. No funeral sermon was preached and no stone marks the grave. This may be carrying privacy too far, but there is a wide gulf between this and the prevailing custom.

* * *

The following comes from London *Tit-Bits*: In the churchyards of Britain several tombstones exist with the accusations of murder deeply engraved upon them. A stone over the grave of three children in Merrington (Durham) churchyard bears the following inscription:

Sleeping we were slain,
And here we sleep till we must rise again.

In Sandridge churchyard, Surrey, on the tombstone of a custom house officer who was shot in an encounter with smugglers is the following:

Thou shalt do no murder, nor shalt thou steal
Are the commands Jehovah did reveal.
But thou, O wretch, without fear or dread
Of thy tremendous Maker, shot me dead.

On a stone in Cadoxton churchyard, Glamorganshire, is inscribed the most fearful accusation of murder to be found on any tomb in Great Britain:

"TO RECORD MURDER.

"This stone was erected over the body of Margaret Williams, age 26, living in service in this parish, who was found dead with marks of violence upon her in a ditch on a marsh below this churchyard on the morning of Sunday, the 14th July, 1822.

"Although the savage murderer escaped for a season the detection of man, yet God hath set his mark upon him either for time or eternity, and the cry of blood will assuredly pursue him to certain and terrible but righteous judgment."

A tombstone stood in Dulverton churchyard a few years ago on which was inscribed:

Poisoned by the doctor, neglected by the nurse,
The brother robbed the widow, which made the matter worse.

An accusation of murder appears on the tomb of Edwin, the Irish comedian, who was buried in St. Werburgh's churchyard, Dublin, and also on tombs to be found in Acton churchyard, Gloucestershire; Hoo, near Rochester; Little Stukeley, and Mytton, near Clitheroe, Lancashire.

* * *

The annual election of directors and officers of Spring Grove Cemetery, Cincinnati, O., resulted in re-election to office of those whose terms had expired. This included Capt. Robert Hosea, who is the oldest living member of the board, having served for nearly 50 years, and having watched the growth of the cemetery from 160 acres to its present 600 acres. The financial statement shows receipts for sale of lots $44,080.15; Interments, foundations, etc., $21,550.06; Care of lots and trust funds, $6,444.50. Total receipts including last years balance $89,065.32. Among the disbursements were: Labor, materials and watch, $37,460.94; Interments and foundations $8,972.12; Salaries and stationery, $9,475.37. The immediate resources of the corporation are: Cash on hand: $347.78; U. S. 4 per cent. registered bonds, $133,000; U. S. 6 per cent. currency bonds, $20,000; C., H. & D. R. R. 4 per cent. preferred stock $10,000; ground rents, $100,000; total $263,347.78; Trust fund investment for perpetual care of lots, U. S. 4 per cent. registered bonds; $27,000.

Number of lots sold during the year, 117; area, 61,965 square feet; number of vault permits issued, 62; number of burial permits issued, 1,461, of which 42 were for removals from other grounds; number of single graves occupied, 11,068; number of interments to date, 56,945; number of lot holders to date, 9,408. The endowment fund being a systematic accumulation of a certain sum from the sale of lots, etc., to be used for perpetual care now amounts to $290,000. It is well invested and produces a good income. The intention is to increase this fund to at least $1,000,000. The cemetery is not, however, anywhere near the occupancy of its whole tract of land. Of the six hundred acres within its boundaries only 375 are now improved so that in due course the directors may well expect to carry out their scheme of the $1,000,000 endowment long before the time comes when interments at Spring Grove will have to cease.

There is also the rule allowing a lot owner to make a permanent deposit of $400, the income of which is to be used forever in the particular care and ornamentation of the specified grave or lot.

≼|Correspondence.|≽

A Timely Suggestion.
To Cemetery Superintendents:

It is not too soon to begin thinking of the work of the next convention. It has occurred to me that if we could have in addition to papers on appropriate subjects, photographs from different cemeteries illustrating points of excellence or objectionable features, our meetings would be more interesting and instructive. Not only this but the instruction will begin when a cemetery superintendent is looking about his grounds to select a position from which a photograph should be taken. He will notice something which he does not wish the camera to record, and perhaps correct the weak spot by a little planting during the coming month. There are many features which photographs might illustrate; the arrangement of groups of trees and shrubs, the margins of drives, the borders of lakes, good and poor grades; cemetery boundaries, the landscape lawn plan in contrast with cemeteries all covered with stone work, railings, hedges, etc. It would not be a bad idea to photograph some natural groupings from the surrounding country. Take an old fence corner that has grown up with sassafras, sumach, etc., and see if the effect is not better than any found in the cemetery. A paper on cemetery entrances with a discussion of the subject and photographs illustrating the ideas advanced, might be a great help to a new cemetery.

A series of notes of the season giving under successive dates the plants in blossom, the appearance of foliage on trees and shrubs, good effects in fruit, the different colors assumed by different varieties of foliage from time to time, the most attractive winter effects, together with a general record of the weather would be interesting and valuable to the person making the notes and might furnish something of value for the members of the Association or for the "Modern Cemetery."
O. C. S.

* * *

The Colored Race in our Cemeteries.
Editor Modern Cemetery:

Please let us know if the officers of cemeteries in the United States allow the interment of "Negroes" within the cemeteries, and if the colored race is assigned a certain plot, for their burials, or are allowed to make their selection of a lot anywhere within the cemetery? Ours being a southern city, and there being an unfriendly feeling entertained for the negro, we thought little objection would be made if we assigned a remote portion of the cemetery for this race's dead. We received the first interment to-day, which has aroused quite an animated debate among the citizens here. We feel that we have acted in the right, and any information that you may be able to furnish us upon this subject will be appreciated, as we are anxious to convince ourselves as well as the public if there has been an error made.
MANAGER.

It is the practice in the south to have separate cemeteries for the white and black population, and where controlled by the cities, separate cemeteries are maintained. Correspondence from Louisville, Savannah, Richmond and Charleston establish the fact that the cemetery corporation rules are exclusive on the subject of the burial of the colored people. A correspondent in Atlanta states that a section is set apart in West View Cemetery which is called the "colored grounds" and to which all interments of the colored race are confined. There has never been any trouble here as the negroes "appear to be just as particular as the white people" in this matter.

It would appear that the correspondent making the enquiry has adopted a wise course and one that should satisfactorily settle the question in his neighborhood.

* * *

Editor Modern Cemetery:

If any member of our Association has paid for the picture taken at Harleigh, and has not received same, please address:
GEO. E. RHIEDEMEYER, Camden, N. J.

* * *

We have received a copy of the Easton, Pa., *Free Press*, containing a communication from Mr. Charles Nichols, Fairmount Cemetery, Newark, N. J., regarding the visit of members of the A. A. C. S. to the Easton Cemetery at the close of the Philadelphia convention. The visitors were escorted over the grounds by directors of the cemetery, and were agreeably entertained by superintendent Transue at his home. Mr. Nichols writes in most complimentary terms of the present condition of the cemetery, and the improvements contemplated and in course of completion.

* * *

Editor Modern Cemetery:

At the convention in Philadelphia, I was asked about a peculiar inscription in our cemetery, and for the interest of the readers generally I send you a copy for publication. It is altogether an unique affair, the monument is of marble, and below the inscription is, as perfectly carved as possible, a locomotive.

The deceased was an engineer, and was killed in a collision down south. Very truly,
JNO. R. HOOPER.

James E. Valentine,
Killed in a collision,
Dec. 20, 1874. Aged 32 years.

"In the crash and the fall he stood unmoved and sacrificed his life that he might fulfill his trust."

Until the brakes are turned on Time,
Life's throttle-valve shut down,
He wakes to pilot in the crew,
That wear the martyr's crown.

On schedule time, on upper grade,
Along the homeward section,
He lands his train at God's round-house
The morn of resurrection.

His time all full, no wages docked,
His name on God's pay-roll,
And transportation through to Heaven
A free-pass for his soul.

⁂ CREMATION. ⁂

The objection that has been recognized by the advocates of cremation as serious, is the one, that in the case of poisoning all traces of evidence would be destroyed by incineration, and the murderer might go free without even a trial. This objection has been greatly overestimated; it is not as serious by any means as has been urged by the enemies of cremation and has been granted by its friends. If a supposed murderer should occasionally get off scot free without a trial it might not be so serious a matter to the tax payers, or so serious a matter for society, as to have hundreds of murderers set free by juries who have been fairly convicted of murder by the evidence after a long and expensive trial. Again, there is perhaps not one death in 10,000 where there can by any possibility be even a suspicion of poisoning; and, again, every health office should have a medical officer at its disposal to verify the physician's certificate as to the cause of death in every case before a permit is given to dispose of the body. If an inquest be considered necessary, or if there be any suspicion of any such necessity, an examination should be made then. Mr. Danford Thomas made a very careful and systematic inquiry as to the number of exhumations which involved questions of poisonings for the past twenty years in England and Wales. He found that exhumations did not average one yearly, yet the number of deaths in England and Wales is about 800,000. Could anything be more absurd than to oppose cremation on the grounds that it deprives the officers of the law the chances of exhuming a body in cases of suspected poisoning, that it lessens the chances of convicting the murderer, —while in burying the dead they are but depositing poisonous masses beneath the surface of the earth, which experiment, reason and science teach, poisons thousands of living beings. The one who administers poison to his fellow is committing a crime.—*The Urn.*

Association of American Cemetery Superintendents.

O. C. SIMONDS, "Graceland," Chicago, President.
G. W. CREESY, "Harmony Grove," Salem, Mass., Vice-President.
F. EURICH, Woodlawn, Toledo, O., Secretary and Treasurer

Publisher's Department.

The receipt of Cemetery Literature and Trade Catalogues will be acknowledged in this column.

TO ADVERTISERS. THE MODERN CEMETERY is the only publication of its class and will be found a valuable medium for reaching cemetery officials in all parts of the United States.

TO SUBSCRIBERS. Cemetery officials desiring to subscribe for a number of copies regularly to circulate among their lot owners, should send for our special terms. Several well known cemeteries have already adopted this plan with good results.

Contributions on matters pertaining to cemeteries are solicited. Address all communications to
R. J. HAIGHT, 334 Dearborn St., CHICAGO.

A photograph of the entrance to LaFayette cemetery, Philadelphia, with description of the grounds, have been received from John K. Betson, Supt., and will be used in a future issue.

We are in receipt of a handsome brochure, published by Messrs. Burger & Eurich, containing 17 pages of most artistically arranged groups of views, about 100 in all, of Woodlawn Cemetery, Toledo. These views together with letter press form a most attractive souvenir of this beautiful burial park, and is dedicated to present and future lot owners in the cemetery. Copies of the work may be obtained of Mr. Frank Eurich, superintendent, for thirty cents post paid, the actual cost of production.

Cemetery Superintendent's Library.—Will every reader of the MODERN CEMETERY who has one or more books that have been helpful to him in the pursuit of his cemetery duties kindly furnish us with a list of the titles and names of publishers. It is our wish to publish a list of books suitable for a cemetery superintendent's library, and we shall arrange to furnish them at publishers' prices. At the Philadelphia convention, a number of books and pamphlets are referred to as being of value to superintendents, and doubtless there are many more. Please send in your list of names at once.

Wood ashes and their use by T. Greiner, is a practical treatise on the value and use of wood ashes for fertilizing purposes published in pamphlet form for distribution by Munroe, Lalor & Co., Oswego, N. Y. The fertilizing and regenerative properties of wood ashes are well known to the scientific investigator and are also of common practical knowledge to the farmers in wooded districts; and the beneficial results already made known are having the effect of inducing a more rapid use of this fertilizing material elsewhere. Wood ashes is already in use in many cemeteries and superintendents will be interested in perusing this pamphlet which may be obtained by addressing as above.

THE MODERN CEMETERY.

THE MODERN CEMETERY.
AN ILLUSTRATED MONTHLY JOURNAL DEVOTED TO THE INTEREST OF CEMETERIES

R. J. HAIGHT, Publisher,
584 Dearborn Street, CHICAGO.

Subscription $1.00 a Year in Advance.   Foreign Subscription $1.25.
Special Rates on Six or More Copies.

Vol. IV.   CHICAGO, NOV. 1894.   No. 9.

CONTENTS.

RECOMMENDATIONS.................................... 97
INDIVIDUAL RIGHTS AND STATE REMOVALS......... 98
*SHRUBS FOR CEMETERIES............................ 99
SOME CANONS OF CRITICISM......................... 100
REMOVAL OF BODIES FROM UNPAID LOTS.—ALL SAINTS
  DAY IN NEW ORLEANS............................. 101
*WOODLAWN CEMETERY, TOLEDO, O................. 102
*CEMETERY NOTES..................................... 104
CHINESE SANITARY BURIAL.—EXTREMES IN CEMETER-
  IES.—THE GARDEN.................................. 106
*A PLEA FOR THE OLD STYLE—CORRESPONDENCE.—A
  CANINE GRAVEYARD................................ 107
PUBLISHER'S DEPARTMENT............................ 108
  *Illustrated.

IN the papers which have been written and the discussions which have ensued in regard to improvements in our cemeteries, in relation to modern ideas on the subject, it must have been observed how strong the tendency is growing to promote the conclusion that the cemetery memorial, which has found expression in so much that is inappropriate, inartistic and disproportionate, should be subordinated to landscape effect. And it must be conceded that even an inspection of the many cemetery illustrations, photographic and otherwise, which this prolific age brings so frequently to one's notice, offers such an argument in favor of the landscape plan that anything but an indorsement of the modern idea would appear to be behind the times.

It is particularly observable that this sentiment is at least firmly engrafting itself on the minds of those most closely identified with cemetery management, where associations have naturally had that refining influence which most certainly leads up to the better appreciation of the beautiful, and whose mandate once understood admits of no disloyalty.

Yet few cemetery associations have, so far, taken any steps towards imparting these advanced ideas to their lot owners, with a view either to an improvement in the character of the memorials, or of educating them to work harmoniously with the management, in order to secure a more rapid advance along the lines of modern thought in cemetery development. It is, perhaps, forgotten that the constant education of the cemetery official in the ethics pertaining to his associations is in no wise parallelled by the irregular and intermittent attention to the same object by the lot owner.

Experience has clearly demonstrated that it is imperatively the duty of cemetery officials, who would advance their own best interests and promote an enlightened taste, to educate their lot owners to the result desired.

While it is true that there is considerable current literature treating of matters connected with the cemetery, it does not, as a rule, reach the lot holder; certainly not to the extent that can be construed as of having an educational value in the broader sense. It is mostly in the department of trade journalism. It seems to follow that the main source of information tending to create and elevate public opinion in the expanding ideas relating to the modern cemetery is the cemetery management. The work has become a broad one, needing careful thought, good judgment, and constant attention, for the uprooting of old prejudices takes time and patience.

The course to be pursued to attain this end may vary according to the community and prevailing conditions, but the methods of the business world are established facts, and can always be adopted beneficially. Here the value of printer's ink is appreciated, and is a constant medium of inter-communication. By this medium, brief extracts from articles which may have appeared in these columns, or from the printed proceedings of the meetings of the Cemetery Superintendent's Association, may be disseminated in the form of tracts, and these will yield returns in a constantly increasing interest in the cemetery, and a more or less active co-operation in the work of improvement.

The fiscal year of many cemeteries is now drawing to a close, and this prompts us to suggest that in the printed annual reports usually distributed such matter as has been alluded to should be incorporated therewith. But a new era is opening out in which the relations of the community to its cemeteries promises to be entirely modified, and the best results will the more speedily accrue in proportion to the enlightenment mutually enjoyed.

Individual Rights and State Removals.

The reported cases are not harmonious upon the question as to the character of the title which a lot owner has to a burial plot in a cemetery controlled and governed by a corporation. The courts have differed as to whether it is a right of use analogous to that of a pew owner in a church, or whether it is an ownership in the soil. The general term of the Supreme Court of New York holds, in a recent decision on the subject, that the question of title cannot be determined solely by the terms of the deed given to the lot owner. Reference must be had to the act of the legislature creating the corporation from which title is derived, and to the limitations upon its power, and to the manifest intent of the parties to the instrument. Every owner of a cemetery lot must be deemed to have purchased and to hold it for the sole purpose of using it as a place of burial, and he is bound to know at his peril that it may become offensive by the residence of many people in its vicinity, and that its use must yield to laws for the suppression of nuisances. Every cemetery within or near large cities must give way to the advance of population. Interments ultimately must cease, and the remains of the dead that are capable of removal must be reinterred in new grounds. Every lot owner holds his title subject to that contingency, and no conditions or covenants contained in deeds appropriating the lands to particular uses can prevent the legislature declaring such use unlawful, and compelling the removal of all bodies from the grounds. All individual rights of property whether they rest on absolute conveyances or mere license, are subject to laws of this character. The power of the legislature to prohibit interments in or to remove the dead from cemeteries which, in the advance of urban population, may be detrimental to the public health, or in danger of becoming so, is not at this day a debatable question. Assuming, therefore, as must be done, that the use of a cemetery as a burial place may be interdicted, and the bodies of the dead removed, it cannot, the court thinks, be seriously claimed that it was within the contemplation of parties to a deed for a burial plot that when that contingency should arise the individual owner should hold title to his lot for general uses, the same as he would hold other property. Individual ownership, under such circumstances, would only create confusion of title, and eventually leave a large tract of land without the care or supervision of a responsible owner. The lots would be small, and of no use for building purposes, inaccessible in many instances from the city streets, and where the original grantee had died, probably owned by many persons having widely separated residences, and in many instances unknown. A construction should not, therefore, be put upon deeds of this character that would produce such a result, unless the rules of law applicable to such instruments forbid any other conclusion. It is settled by a long line of authorities that a pew owner has no claim for compensation when the church is taken down from necessity arising from the condition of the building or other imperative exigency. It cannot be said in any sense that in such case his property is taken for a public use. For all of which reasons the court holds here not only that a deed to a cemetery lot from an incorporated association, even though absolute in form, conveys no title to the soil which subsists after a removal by legislative requirement, but that the rights of burial which the lot owner loses, in the old ground will be fully restored to him in the new, so that, in legal contemplation, he suffers no damages. Nor is another statute providing that a lot in which an interment has been made is forever thereafter inalienable, a limitation upon the power of the legislature to order a sale of the property by the association in such a case as this to defray so far as necessary, the expenses of the required removals.

The South Bend, Ind., *Sunday News* says: When so prominent a churchman as Bishop Lawrence openly advocates cremation, as he recently did before a Boston audience, it is an indication that the question has passed beyond the speculative stage and is confronting us as a vital issue. The opposition to the new method of disposing of the bodies of the dead has chiefly in this country come from those who believe in the literal bodily resurrection of the departed, and who have held that this was a part of the christian belief. Bishop Lawrence boldly assailed this opinion and affirmed that cremation is not out of harmony with christian principles, and that it should be regarded as a reverent and christian method of disposing of the remains of the departed. The existence of churchyards for the burial of the dead within the limits of large cities is now considered as hostile to the living on sanitary grounds, and Bishop Lawrence has taken a forward step in this matter, in which he he will have a large number of supporters.

* * *

A better idea, because of the higher conception suggested, has been bequeathed by the late Prof. Swing, the lamented Chicago divine, in that by his last testament he desired that the casket containing his remains should not be opened for public observation. It is due to the spirit of the departed who lived for good, that the public pay fitting and worthy tribute in the final ceremony of putting the earthly tabernacle away, but the taste of the times now loudly protests against the former practice.

Shrubs for Cemeteries.

As shrubs are indispensable in Cemetery work, consideration of the desirability of various species and varieties is always in order, and may be helpful, especially to those having few opportunities to see well grown collections. While it is possible to have too much of a good thing, no harm can result from repeatedly reminding people what the good things are. There is so much to distract attention that it is necessary to say a thing many times before making much impression. And if the shrubs mentioned here are already familiar to our readers, they know them to be worth talking about; while if they are not, our advice is to make their acquaintance forthwith.

Having personally a strong liking for the Cut leafed Sumach I have photographed a group of them growing on the wooded island at Jackson Park. They are on the lawn at a little distance from the boundary of the border proper, but still forming a part of it—a slightly detached annex.

It is a happy arrangement, taking from the formality of an unbroken border line, while the selection of this particular shrub for the purpose cannot be too highly commended. Its graceful fern-like foliage and habit of growth adapts it to the location when looked at broadly as a part of the general view, and it is handsome enough in itself to bear close inspection as a detail of the planting.

This illustration shows very well the good effect of an occasional accent in shrubbery borders. The irregularly placed group of three sumachs is in one sense an accent, although it serves to melt the border into the lawn at this point, and, farther along the graceful, but not too sinuous, line of planting is seen an accent of another kind in a shapely, double, white Althea standing boldly to the front and showing up well against the foil of mixed greenery behind it. This single large shrub is also set out in the grass beyond the line of the mass of the plantation, and it is a marked and admirable note that during several weeks in late summer, sings out clearly enough to dominate the scheme—just as a pianist makes a certain note sing quite through a passage above the many that are woven into a harmonious accompaniment or background.

Both the Sumach and hardy Althea (Syriacus Hibiscus) are well adapted to cemetery work, and usually the former is more effective than those shown in the illustration because it generally bears showy spikes of scarlet berries.

Common Elder is too well known to need description, and is always good, but there are four other varieties of the species, all of them hardy, that are handsomer in foliage, although not bearing more charming flowers nor, as I have seen them, are they so free flowering.

They are Sambucus Nigra, S. Nigra lacinata (excellent), S. variegata argentea, and S. var. aurea or Golden Elder. The last is the most effective, and is a very desirable golden leaved shrub.

By far the best purple leaved shrub shown in the World's Fair exhibits is the Purple Plum

CUT LEAF SUMACH.—RHUS LACINIATA.

(Prunus pissardi) a nice group of which still stands on the Island, has done well, and is decidedly handsome.

The delicate foliage and soft grayish green tone of the Rosemary leaved Willow is seen to much advantage in a number of round headed specimens grafted on common willows at about five feet above the ground. And there are a couple of beautiful little trees of the Russian Golden Willow, a variety that seems excellent.

FANNY COPLEY SEAVEY.

A stone in Copps Hill burying ground, Boston, bears this inscription:

> A Sister of Sarah Lucas lyeth here
> Whom I did Love most Dear;
> And now her Soul hath took its Flight
> And bid her Spiteful Foes good-night.

Some Canons of Criticism.*
(Concluded.)

"Monuments are the grappling-irons that bind together successive generations;" accordingly Beauty of Design having been secured:

Durability—Permanence, is the next essential. The monument is not so much for the present as for future generations—"*vos non vobis ædificatis.*"

In the search for a material that should combine a desirable color, susceptibility to art treatment and durability, we have seemed almost to witness the clash of the proverbial irresistible force with the immovable body. Slate, sandstone, limestone, marble, bronze, zinc:—each in turn has been tried for sepulchral monuments and has been (or is being) abandoned as defective in one or more of the above requirements. Granite, has seemed to approach the nearest to our requirements among the natural stones—and for what we may designate as the severest prose of Memorial Art, it is doubtful if it ever will be superseded. But to the sculptor granite is an absolute impossibility. (Please note that by "sculptor" we do not mean "stone-cutter" though even the latter term is not strictly applicable to the worker of granite, since granite has to be crushed into form by tools that do not *cut*, but *break*.) Even when (as very rarely happens, since really it is scarcely worth while to do so) a model from the studio of a real artist is procured, all the delicate touches that distinguish the artist's technique are lost in the coarseness and hardness of the stone, and most of even the broader treatment which distinguishes it as a work of art, is dissipated in the lower intelligence (we come near saying "lowest") that necessarily intervenes between the model and the finished statue.

No, while granite is adapted to the prose of Memorial Art, any attempt at the *poetry* of it can result only in doggerel.

Leaving, for a moment, this subject, let us consider our third requirement, which is intimately connected with this, viz:

Cost. Before the Ohio Marble and Granite Dealer's Association (see MONUMENTAL NEWS, for August '94) Mr. O. A. Coltman after recognizing the deplorable character of our sepulchral monument, says (in substance:)

"The monument man cannot be expected to be a teacher of the public taste. He is more concerned to learn, and cater to, his customers' ideas than to supply his own. If our cemetery memorials are bad, it is the fault of the purchaser; he gets what he wants and all that he is willing to pay for."

We believe, and, (since ignorance is less deplorable than dishonesty,) for the sake of the monu-

*Copyrighted, 1895, by the Memorial Art League.

ment man, hope that this is not true. That the buyers of monuments are penurious, is proven false by the too lavish expenditures made by them in our cemeteries. Instead of looking upon *cost* as we wish them to, as the last and least consideration, *many have evidently regarded it as no consideration at all.* That there has been fierce competition is true, but this is of the monument man's own making —he (whose name is Legion) has fairly thrust himself upon the customer and demanded a hearing; he has called himself (and probably believed himself) an authority upon the subject; each of him has urged a little greater ostentation than the other—generally (such, in this respect, being the fatal facility of granite) in the direction of a larger structure. When the doctors *agree*, is it to be wondered at that the patient has confidence in their prescriptions? *Cost* then, is, though the last, still a very serious consideration; but our purpose is rather to restrict than enlarge it—more especially when it is misdirected to the transportation of enormous blocks of stone that when set up, go to the disfiguration of our cemeteries; or to the attempt to sculpture a stone that is in its very nature unsuited to sculpture.

It will be apparent from what we have said, that Memorial Art demands an art-medium in which are combined, (1) Susceptibility to Art Treatment (2) Durability and (3) Delicacy of Color.

We have endeavored to show that the quarry and the foundry have failed to supply a material that satisfies these requirements. History tells us *the kiln does this*; the very earliest forms of art were produced from it, and the only wonder is that we should have sounded the entire gamut of other materials before having recourse, again, to it.

It is the material in which the Greek sculptors delighted to work; the material in which the Della Robbias executed their immortal, and now priceless, productions; the material that has transmitted to us the world's history from a period so remote as otherwise to have been beyond conjecture; the material that all authorities agree in pronouncing to be practically imperishable; the material that fully equals in fineness of texture and delicacy of color the most fragile marble; and the material that retains and exhibits unchanged, the most subtle touch of the sculptor and we look to its early recognition.

In concluding these papers, which have stretched themselves out to an extent the writer did not dream of at their beginning, we urge upon you to secure, by doing—and much more by leaving undone,— that which shall so consecrate our cemeteries to all that is pure and lovely, that even the casual visitor shall hear again the Voice that Moses heard saying:

"Cast off thy shoes from off thy feet; for the place whereon thou standest is holy ground."

Removal of Bodies from Unpaid Lots.

In connection with the recent discussion on the subject of the legality of the removal of bodies from unpaid lots, Mr. L. L. Mason, supt., Lake View Cemetery, Jamestown, N. Y., sends us the following opinion. In regard to the opinion he says that the Hon. R. P. Marvin, referred to, was long a judge in high standing on the bench of New York state:

JAMESTOWN, N. Y., Sept. 9, 1892.
L. L. MASON, Supt., Lake View Cemetery.

Dear Sir: Some time ago you submitted to me a statement of facts and an inquiry based thereon, substantially as follows:

Statement of Facts. Lake View Cemetery Association which is a corporation duly created under the acts authorizing the incorporation of Rural Cemetery Associations, owns certain lands known as Lake View Cemetery, in the village of Jamestown, which lands are devoted to cemetery purposes.

Upon certain lots in said cemetery are interments, such interments being made with the consent of the cemetery authorities and upon a verbal arrangement for a sale of the lots to the person obtaining the consent, but no money was ever paid and no deed given.

The persons who were to have purchased now refuse to pay for such lots, or remove the bodies therefrom or take any action whatever.

The Cemetery Association has a place provided for single interments and the lots where these interments were made are desired by persons wishing to purchase and unless the Association can remove these bodies it must suffer loss and inconvenience.

The Inquiry. Can the Association remove these remains to the place provided for single interments, without the consent of the persons who were to have purchased the lots and now refuse to do so? In my opinion it can. The Association has control over its property, the management and protection thereof, and the power to regulate burials therein and the consent that the interments could be made upon the lots in question was upon the condition that the promise to purchase should be fulfilled.

Upon a failure to purchase the Association could order the bodies removed or could remove them itself, I think. They should be properly reinterred and kept separate, preserving and removing with each, all identifying marks, head-stones or monuments.

I come to this conclusion after an examination of the law upon the subject. I confess I am not without doubt as to the correctness of my opinion. I have, however, presented the whole matter to the Hon. R. P. Marvin and he is of the opinion that my position is correct.

Respectfully yours,
(Signed)   E. GREEN, JR.

All Saints Day in New Orleans.

All Saints Day, which occurred November 1, in New Orleans, is a holiday which perhaps has a greater hold upon the hearts of the people of that city than any other festive occasion. All differences and grievances, creeds and dogmas are forgotten, and all spontaneously turn out to pay reverence to the dead without distinction of race or calling.

The New Orleans *Daily Picayune* of November 2, devotes several columns to an account of the doings of the day at the several cemeteries, from which we take the following: "The custom of decorating the graves of the dead on the 1st of November is an old and beautiful one in our Crescent city, and perhaps no other city of the union can present such a peculiar spectacle as that of an entire community laying aside absorbing duties and business cares, opportunities for speculation and moneymaking, pleasures and amusements, and devoting the livelong day to communion with silent friends in the cities of the voiceless throng.

"By 9 o'clock the streets were filled with a living, moving mass, which increased as the hours went on, and by evening the entire city seemed deserted, while the cemeteries teemed with life and animation. Many thousands wended their way towards nightfall to the beautiful Metairie cemetery, after visiting the spots where their own dead lay, merely to see the exquisite decorations in this beautiful city of the dead.

"A stroll from cemetery to cemetery was a study in itself, outside of the beautiful sentiment underlying the festival. Beginning with the old St. Louis cemeteries, from tomb to tomb adown the narrow aisles, were read the names of the old French and Spanish noblesse, the last remnant of the ancient regime, inseparably connected with the history of Louisiana. The quaint oven-shaped tombs, which once were so typical of the New Orleans cemetery, are only to be found in St. Louis No. 1, and St. Louis No. 2. Many of these have fallen into decay, and above the crumbling vaults one may decipher: "Ici Cigit Jean Jacques," and then follows an indistinct medley of letters, which show that the family name has passed out of the life of the people since that grave received its dead, in 1798. Others of the ancient tombs have been built upon and modernized, and are handsomely kept.

"In St. Louis No. 3, the graves of the colored remnant of the olden people of New Orleans showed that All Saints' was a day of hallowed memories. Gorgeous paper wreaths of black and white, with gold letters glistening, and the typical "A Mon Epaux," "A Ma Mere," were familiar decorations, while lights and flowers and crucifixes and statuary of saints formed striking features. Out in Esplanade street, near the bayou St. John, is the new St. Louis cemetery, where the Aldiges, Infantes and other prominent families have their tombs. These handsome mausoleums were beautifully decorated, the Infantes' especially, telling the recent and touching story of sorrow.

"Away out in the rear of the Third district is St. Roch's cemetery, that quaint, old world spot grown like an olden ivy in the earth of New Orleans. The cemetery is the last resting place of the children of the Fatherland, and the nationality of the dead spoke in every line of decorations from lighted tapers and pictures of the dead enshrined in lights and flowers to the ancient chapel, where the pilgrims kneel in prayer, and at the feet of whose altar repose the remains of the late Rev. Father Thevis, founder of St. Roch's cemetery and builder of the ancient and historical chapel. His grave beneath the dimly lighted altar was beautifully decorated. The new St. Roch's was also handsomely decorated from the new and beautiful tombs to the graves of the very poor lying in the eastern aisle. At the St. Vincent de Paul's cemetery, sometimes called the Louisa street, the decorations were on a scale of beauty seldom seen in the quiet spots. In the old St. Louis cathedral, a massive pillow of flowers rested on the marble slab at the base of the altars, which marks the grave of Don Andreas Almonaster, who donated the cathedral and Jackson square to New Orleans. The grave of the Chevalier Mandeville de Marigny and of the deceased bishops and archbishops of New Orleans who repose in the old cathedral were also decked with flowers.

"In beautiful Metairie cemetery, art is not needed, for nature has done much for this city of the dead. The trees are always green, the flowers constantly in bloom, the grass spreads out like a verdant carpet. Just at the entrance is the handsome monument of the Army of the Tennessee which was elaborately decorated in honor of the late General G. T. Beauregard. The effect of the ornamentation was unique and beautiful. The tomb, with the statue of General Albert Sidney Johnston, was a centre of attraction in the cemetery.

"Another grave attracted much notice, that of a man, who as a soldier fought gallantly and well, as a journalist rose to the highest rank, and who as a citizen received that respect due to his stainless character, Major William Robinson, late city editor of the *Picayune*. A simple tribute was placed upon his grave, a wreath of white immortelles, etc., and the sentiment of his confreres expressed on a streamer of satin ribbon, "Faithful Even After Death," "From the Picayune Staff."

"Metairie is rich in beautiful memories. Leaving Metairie, beautiful Greenwood comes in sight, where the confederate monument tells the story of heroes and saints, and just over the way is St. Patrick's, dear to every Irish heart. Here sleep the noble sons of the sturdy isle. Near by is the Hebrew's rest, where is gathered the dust of the sons of Israel. The Firemen's cemetery was beautifully decorated, and at the Odd Fellow's Rest, three links of flowers, with the letters, "F. L. T" within, illustrated the beautiful sentiment of the association."

"Up town, at Washington No. 1, there are many handsome mausoleums, conspicuous among which are the family tombs of the Toledanos and Rices. The Rice mausoleum was a spot toward which many wended their way.

"At Cypress Grove and the Masonic and Girod street cemeteries the most beautiful decorations were seen, and so, from cemetery to cemetery, one might go hearing their songs and stories, and listening to the silent teachings of poet and philosopher, patriot and soldier, Christian and philanthropist. And it seemed well to bring flowers on this sainted day to scatter on the graves of the dead. It seemed beautiful to let them mingle their fragrance with the prayers of the living. Together they form an offering worthy of human love; together they sing their flight like messenger angels to loved ones on the spirit shore."

The May Mausoleum.

A mausoleum for the late Frederick De Courcey May has been built in Bonnie Brae Cemetery, Baltimore. It cost $25,000, and is said by a correspondent of the St. Louis *Globe-Democrat* to be the finest tomb in the United States. The structure is modeled on pure classical lines. It is in the form of a doric temple. Standing on the slope of a hill this modern temple of white Beaver Dam marble is an imposing feature in the landscape surrounding it. The colums, roof and walls of the mausoleum are of marble. The only other material distinctly visible in the structure is a heavy bronze doorway, paneled and ornamented with a cross, which cost $1,000. Four immense marble slabs, each weighing ten tons, form the ceiling. Above the ceiling is a pitched roof, also of stone. The sarcophagus is chiseled out of a solid, cream colored stone, imported from France.

Woodlawn Cemetery, Toledo, O.

Fourteen years ago, Woodlawn Cemetery, Toledo, O., was a comparatively uncultivated, uncared for farm, and if the wilderness has not been made during the interval, to "blossom as the rose," it comes about as near to that consummation as time and conditions have permitted, and under the care

THE MODERN CEMETERY.

VIEW IN WOODLAWN CEMETERY, TOLEDO, OHIO.—From *Picturesque Woodlawn*.

of Mr. Frank Eurich, superintendent, improvement is still the watchword.

The rude ravine, by the landscape artists' skill, has been transformed into a gentle slope, dotted with shrubs and trees, and avenues and walks curve gracefully between undulating, well cared for, lawns. The sloping hill sides trend downwards to the lake, which is a transformation from the old time sluggish stream. Transplanted trees dispense their cooling shade and present a darker background for the better display of lighter objects in front. Nature and art have entered into partnership to provide a peaceful resting place for the dead, and a charmingly attractive spot for the contemplative living.

The cemetery is situated just outside the city limits, easy of access, but remote enough to make it secure from urban encroachments for a long time to come. Its area is 160 acres, subdivided into some 80 sections, containing about 10,000 lots, and ample space for single graves.

The ravine, which aided in the formation of the artificial lake, divides the grounds, but the whole area is of the gently undulating character, so well adapted for the best cemetery landscape effects, in that it does not present violent contrasts between adjoining lots.

A structure combining chapel, receiving vault, and conservatory is in course of erection, which has been planned in accordance with the latest principles of modern burial systems. Its design is conceived to moderate the feelings of sadness and sorrow prevailing on the occasions of its use. A receiving vault is situated beneath the chapel, into which the departed will be lowered by a noiseless elevator. This plan will avoid out of door services in inclement weather, with all the possible contingencies. On three sides of the chapel conservatories will be added, connecting with the audience room by sliding doors. Spacious verandas will form useful additions to the structure, and will afford charming views of the grounds.

The view presented above gives some idea of the development of this park-like cemetery, and exemplifies the possibilities in landscape effect where enlightened taste, combined with skill, is brought to bear on the results sought. Such a landscape view is elevating to the mind as well as refreshing, and must tend to excite the healthy living soul to brighter and loftier conceptions.

CEMETERY NOTES.

The Mount Albion Cemetery commissioners, of Albion, Orleans County N. Y., advertises the following on its letter-heads: "By the terms of all notes given for cemetery lots, the commissioners have the right to take possession of said lots upon the nonpayment of the note, and remove all bodies buried therein to the public ground at the expense of the purchaser, without notice." Such information is good to keep before some lot owners.

* * *

Mrs. Alice N. Lincoln, in New York *Times*, thus describes her feelings while watching a cremation: As we stood in silence watching the rosy glow which played over the white surface of the retort a feeling came to us of awe certainly, but also of peace and rest. There was something so spiritual, so elevating in the absolute purity of the intense heat that it seemed to all of us who stood there far less appalling than the blackness of an open grave.

* * *

Mr. J. A. Pirie, many years secretary of the Forest Home Cemetery Association, Milwaukee, Wis., died at his home Oct. 19, after an illness of several months. He was born in Irie Wells, Scotland, in 1832 and came to Milwaukee in 1849. After many years in the banking business he associated himself with the Forest Home Cemetery Association of which he has been secretary for over fifteen years. He was widely known and esteemed by all who knew him.

* * *

A curious source of wealth is reported by the French council at Mongtze, as belonging to Upper Tonquin, in its wood mines. The wood was originally a pine forest, which the earth swallowed in some cataclysm. Some of the trees are a yard in diameter, and lie in a slanting direction. As the top branches are well preserved, it is thought the geological convulsion which buried them cannot be of great antiquity. The wood, varnished, is imperishable and the Chinese gladly buy it for coffins.

* * *

An interesting case, says the New Bedford, Mass., *Mercury*, in which an undertaker, and the pastor of St. Lawrence church will be the principals, is likely to come up for trial soon in the local court. The undertaker objects to a custom which has been in vogue many years, of taxing undertakers an entrance fee of three dollars whenever they take a body inside the Catholic cemetery on Kempton Street. Last month while entering the cemetery the undertaker's hearse was stopped by the assistant in charge of the cemetery by order of the reverend father. Council has been retained.

* * *

Periodically the old crime of grave robbing develops in sufficient seriousness to make it of more than local interest from the fact that the bodies so procured are destined for points outside of the locality where the crime is committed. A grand jury of St. Joseph, Mo., has been investigating what is claimed may prove a wholesale business in this line with bodies taken from the various cemeteries of that city. Subjects for dissection are distinctly necessary in the medical colleges, and legitimate means should be possible for obtaining such subjects, but unquestionably to the seats of medical learning must be laid the onus of stimulating the gruesome business of body snatching periodically recorded.

* * *

Members of the A. A. C. S. who attended the Minneapolis convention will remember the address of Mr Charles Nichols, secretary and treasurer of the Oakland Cemetery Association at the Aberdeen, and will regret to hear of his death which occurred October 24. With the exception of an interval of one year he had served as an active trustee of the Oakland Cemetery since 1868 and a member of the executive committee. He first reached St. Paul in 1858 and after two years residence was appointed postmaster by President Lincoln, his term closing with the rebellion. He has been connected with many of St. Paul's business enterprises, and was a highly honored and respected citizen. At the time of his death he was serving in the capacity of assistant master in chancery of the Union Pacific system.

* * *

The Tyrone, Pa., *Herald*, recently published a petition which was being circulated for signatures, expressing unqualified disapproval of the employment of any person in Tyrone Cemetery "as has been the case sometimes heretofore, we believe, of any person who has or does allow to be kept on his premises in our midst a brothel, or house of ill fame, or of any self styled employe who, for the sake of gain, has been known to extort from bereaved friends in time of their distress, undue amounts for the work done, or of any persons known to have been guilty of theft or crime; to the employment of any such as sexton, assistant sexton, or employe, we earnestly remonstrate," etc. If this protest be well founded, the management of Tyrone Cemetery needs investigation and in the interest of the community an enforcement of the regard due to the established ethics of cemetery control.

* * *

A New York lawyer is said to have been retained by some twenty-five descendants of persons buried in St. John's Churchyard, which belongs to the Trinity corporation, and for which the city has offered the sum of $520,000 in order to turn it into a public park. The lawyer contends that the Trinity corporation has no right to sell it, that the lots occupied were originally paid for, so that their descendants still own them, as the receipts do not show that the land should ever revert to the cemetery authorities. He believes the dead have rights, and in any event it shall be insisted upon that the bodies be re-interred in Greenwood, Woodlawn or some other well known cemetery. It is said that the Trinity corporation does not fear any action, claiming not to have made a cent from any of its burying grounds. Many inquiries have been made by persons having dead in the churchyard as to what disposition was going to be made of the bodies.

* * *

A suit in mandamus has been brought against the German Roman Catholic cemetery association, Cincinnati, which controls the St. Mary's cemetery at St. Bernard to compel the issue of a permit to parents for the disinterment of the bodies of their two children who died in 1890. It is desired to remove the bodies to the German Evangelical cemetery and the directors of the Catholic cemetery refuse to allow the disinterment. A similar proceeding was begun by the same parties some time ago and the court refused to grant a writ, but since that time a law has been passed making it obligatory upon cemetery trustees to permit a disinterment upon application of the next of kin, provided that no such disinterment shall be made during the months of April, May, June, July, August and September, and in no event where the deceased has died of a contagious or infectious disease, and not until a permit has been issued by the local health department. In case the directors refuse a permit, the act makes it the duty of the Court of Common Pleas to issue a writ of mandamus.

* * *

Further excavations recently made on the site of the Anglo-Saxon Cemetery on the top of High Down Hill, near Worthing, England, have yielded some interesting results. The ground has been trenched under the direction of Mr. C. H. Read, of the British Museum, who regards it as the largest and most important Saxon cemetery yet found in Sussex. Many interments have been traced. The most notable discovery has been that of a collection of glass vessels, which vie with those of the same period now preserved in the British Museum. One of these is described as shaped like a tall wine glass without a stem, and ornamented with loops of thick white glass. Another is a vase of slender shape, with raised figures and some Greek characters upon it. In one grave some fifty or sixty small beads were found. In another grave, in which part of a child's skull was recovered, were found several glass beads and some thin discs of bronze, decorated with a pattern composed of dots and perforated, as well as a thick ring of bone or ivory, which, it is conjectured, might have been a plaything, or possibly a teething ring. Most of the bodies, but not all, are buried from west to east.—*Funeral Director's Journal.*

* * *

THE GATEWAY AT HIGHLAND LAWN CEMETERY.

The new gateway at Highland Lawn Cemetery, Terre Haute, Ind., illustrated below is now in course of erection according to the plans by Mr. Paul S. Lietz, the Chicago architect, by Heidenreich & Co.

Its cost is set at $6,500 and the stone work is in the hands of the Terre Haute Stone Company. It consists of a circular tower containing a lodge, a semi-circular arch for a gateway and a

NEW ENTRANCE, HIGHLAND LAWN CEMETERY.

waiting room, together with iron fences and stone fence posts for approaches. The foundation is of lime stone and the body of the entire structure is of Buff Bedford stone with trimmings of Blue Bedford stone. The fence leading to the gateway is of wrought iron with stone piers at given intervals. The letters "Highland Lawn" in one side of the main arch are to be made of wrought iron in rustic design. The gates leading to the main avenue will be 18 feet wide and the smaller gates at each side four feet wide. The waiting room in the large arch will have a concrete floor and can be used for a carriage entrance whenever desired. Handsome lamps will be placed beneath the arch. The roofs will be of slate and the towers capped with tiling. The gate is located 160 feet up the main avenue from the old fence, making it 200 feet from the center of the National road. The handsome iron fence will curve east and west until it reaches the present fence line and the approach will be laid out in a handsome manner. The frontage of the entire structure will be 72 feet. The main tower will be 60 feet in height. The clock shown will be omitted for the present and the lodge will not be completed for immediate use.

* * *

The people of Columbus, Ohio, are discussing Sunday funerals. Criticisms have been made that it is impossible to conduct a private funeral in Green Lawn cemetery on Sunday because of the presence of thousands of idle curiosity and pleasure seekers. This charge appears to be unfounded owing to the stringent rules observed in admissions,—only such as are entitled by ticket to enter being permitted to do so. This condition which is quite a prevailing one, emphasises the wisdom of those who are trying to do away with the Sunday funeral. Sunday must naturally be a day on which in fine weather the cemetery has peculiar attractions for those bereaved, as well as for those who can appreciate its restful atmosphere, and consequently a well kept cemetery will always be more or less occupied by the living on that day. Hence the desire for privacy and quiet can be far better satisfied on week days. The officials of all well regulated cemeteries are generally doing all in their power to discourage funerals on Sunday and the effect is becoming quite apparent. Already a diminution in number is recorded from many points. Ministerial conventions and unions are taking up the subject in good earnest, and undoubtedly the minister will appreciate the change. Mr. John J. Stephens, the superintendent of Green Lawn cemetery, who read a paper at the Minneapolis convention of cemetery superintendents, is a strong advocate of private funerals, and believes a great reformation is under way in funeral appointments. While of modern origin, the reform will undoubtedly become permanent.

* * *

The agitation on "Funeral Reform" is another of the many striking evidences of the activity in enlightened progress of the present day. On the subject of costly burial the London *Lancet* makes the following potent remarks: The majority of intelligent persons are more or less indifferent as to the disposal of their bodies after death, but it may be safely asserted that not one would be found to express a wish that his or her body should be preserved in a polished oak or elm brass mounted coffin and in a walled grave or vault. It is the result partly of tyrannical custom and partly of leaving all to the undertaker. The latter has been shorn of much of his former profits derived from the sale of scarves and hat bands and the hire of palls, plumes, feathers and other trappings of woe. The polished coffin and the brass furniture are the surviving relics of the "funerals completely furnished" of a past age and are clung to with affectionate tenacity by those whose interest it is to have them continued. But the undertaker is, after all, what the public make him. The courage and persistence of a few individuals swept away the costly and useless trappings of woe; only a very little more courage is required to substitute cheaper and perishable coffins for the pretentious upholstery exhibited in the coffin of the day. If the upper classes would set the example and make perishable coffins fashionable it would soon spread to the working classes, who are still tempted to spend upon a coffin and a burial money which would be much more wisely expended in providing additional comforts and even necessaries for the living.

* * *

A writer speaking of an Iowa cemetery some time since said that when creditable appearing lots were contrasted with neglected ones, there was lost not only a general attractiveness, but the moral bearing and influence; for properly considered there is an object moral lesson to be learned from a thoughtful familiarity with the cemetery. Beecher said these bodies, now lost to sight are but being transformed and fitted for the higher sphere of life; we shall see them again. Talmage speaks of the cemetery as a resurrection factory from which shall come the radiant and resplendent forms of our interred friends on the brightest morn the world will ever behold. Nor is this mere sentimentality, but according to our Christian faith and teaching, a divine, as well as sublime truth fittingly expressed.

Chinese "Sanitary" Burial.

The U. S. Consul at Hong Kong gives estimates by Dr. Grant, a missionary physician, of the ravages of smallpox in his part of the district of Ning Po: cases, 50 per 1,000 inhabitants; ratio of mortality, 70 per cent. Dr. Grant reckons by the number of coffins sold, added to the capacity of the five "baby towers" in which the uncoffined sucklings are deposited like garbage. Baby towers, the Consul explains, "are buildings about twenty-five feet high, built of stone and brick with tile roof, by various charitable organizations, for the reception of babies that have died before cutting all their teeth, as such are not considered worth boxing. There is a room with a platform raised about two feet from the floor. On this the baby is placed, the little body being wrapped only in a piece of straw matting. They are piled one above another like pieces of wood, until the room is full, when the bodies are put in boats and taken into the country and buried. Ordinarily these towers are cleaned out twice a year, once in winter and once in summer, but, as Dr. Grant says, it was necessary to clean them twice during the past winter.

"The people of this section do not in this case bury their dead, but place the coffin on the ground in a spot sometimes away on the hillsides, but in this city near their doors or along side the paths. The coffins are sometimes rolled in and covered, but thousands of coffins can be seen in a short walk protected from the elements only by a straw covering. Only a short distance away from this office are immense 'charnel' houses; one is filled with corpses of those who died of cholera, the bodies being covered with lime after being placed in the coffins."—*The Sanitary Era.*

Extremes in Cemeteries.

An article on page 79 of the MODERN CEMETERY for September, touches somewhat on a chord of my own thought as to cemetery work—only just touches it. I have never seriously given attention to cemetery design, because I have never been able to satisfy myself that a true gardener could ever expect to justify his art in a cemetery. I have noticed that the motive of those who visit either cairn or crypt, either vaulted Westminster, or picturesque Rock-creek, is centered upon the personalities of those who have gone before, and it is but rarely that any work of man can distract their attention for long, if at all. It is now and then possible to find a person intent *only* upon the sculpture, they are students perhaps, or even artists, but the great bulk of those interested in a burial place would rather lose the monument than the epitaph. Perhaps there are no burial places in the world of such great and commanding interest as the little country churchyards, known to be the resting places of those great thousand lights of our race who never needed any monument whatever, except to identity the spot. No monument can for one moment compare in interest with Stratford on Avon, or Stoke Pogis, whether it be to soldier or statesman. How immensely it would be a loss if those spots were unknown needs scarcely to be said.

Well then, if the living desire to mark the places of interment, will they not also desire to do so in their own way? And will not the cemetery giving the greatest freedom be best appreciated, other things being equal? I fancy it will.

But as everyone knows such freedom is destructive to a lawn, or park or garden idea. The two things—the show-yard of the gravestone maker, and the natural picture of the gardener are utterly discordant, and I frankly confess that I have come to the conclusion in a moment, whenever I would approach it, and think.

Can a modern cemetery be beautiful? And I answer, only in parts uninvaded by the marble slab. Beauty in a cemetery must be looked for, I think, in private rather than in public cemeteries; to such I would give the full power of creative conception, but I would never pretend that I could extract beauty out of a surface covered as I know a modern cemetery must be.

There is, I think, too much sameness in cemetery design—probably due to work by the same minds on similar conditions and with similar environment. I imagine a very great improvement would be observed if superintendents of known tastes were engaged by the cemetery associations from the first, and the work of design and construction entrusted to them. The same remark applies to public parks,—the country will never find the genius within it until it finds fields of action.

Trenton, N. J.   JAMES MACPHERSON.

The Garden.

Under the gloom of the shivering pines,
  That whisper when it blows,
Behind the creeper-covered wall,
  Is a garden that always grows.

In summer and in springtime,
  And when the winter snows
Bend the dark branches to the ground,
  The garden always grows.

The hand of man has made it,
  The white stones stand in rows,
The tears of the world have watered it,
  And the garden always grows.

There are many gardens like it,
  Their number no man knows.
Each day, till the world is ended,
  This garden always grows.

—*Lorimer Stoddard.*

A Plea for the Old Style.

Mr. John K. Betson, superintendent of LaFayette Cemetery, Philadelphia, thinks the MODERN CEMETERY is too pronounced on the question of the modern idea to the exclusion of the old fashion. Regarding LaFayette Cemetery, he says: I send you a picture of the main entrance, with a brief sketch of one of the latter. The "LaFayette" is situated in a thickly settled, and built up section, of our good City of "Brotherly Love." It occupies a full "block," or as it is called here a "square," and is

MAIN ENTRANCE, LA FAYETTE CEMETERY, PHILADELPHIA.

surrounded by prominent streets; on the north, which is the front, and main entrance, it is bounded by Federal St., on the south by Wharton, east by 9th, and west by 10th St., and it is enclosed with an iron railing seven feet high. On the Federal St. front it has a granite coping 18 in. high surmounted with iron railing five feet six inches above the coping.

The Cemetery Society was incorporated by act of the State Legislature of Pennsylvania in January 1839. It covers an area of about four acres; it is governed by a board of Directors, ten in number, who must be lot holders, elected annually by the lot holders. Each holder, being a member of the Society, is entitled to one vote for every eighty square feet, which is the contents of a lot, 8 x 10 ft. The ground is laid out in lots of this size. "Immediately after every election the Board shall from among themselves choose a President, Treasurer, and Secretary to the Corporation." The ground is laid out in sections of ninety-two lots each, which are known by letters from A to Q. There is a drive running north and south, through the centre of the ground, fourteen feet wide, which is patent paved with Portland cement. The sections are separated by a gravel walk four feet wide, giving every lot frontage on a walk. The ground is encumbered with numerous head and foot stones, iron railings and other ancient contrivances. But it also has many very pretty and costly monuments. A great many of the lot holders have their lots cared for by the Society and many others living in the vicinity of the ground, care personally for their lots. The drive and walks are kept clean, and borders kept trimmed. Altogether the Cemetery presents a very nice appearance, although the modern folks would class it a "Stone Yard."

Correspondence.

The Colored Race in our Cemeteries.

OMAHA, NEB., October 30, 1894.

Editor Modern Cemetery:

In answer to enquiries of Manager on page 95, October number of MODERN CEMETERY, in regard to burial of negroes, I found it necessary to set apart a section exclusively for that purpose for family lots. The white man will not purchase a lot alongside that occupied by a negro if he knows it; but for single graves we make no distinction,—white, negro or red Indian. We find no objections to this system.   J. V. C.

A Canine Graveyard.

Just behind the lodge at the Victoria entrance to fashionable Hyde Park, London, is a plot of ground, shaded on two sides by towering elms and chestnut trees, embellished with many carefully tended flowers and shrubs, and which the orderly rows of little graves and head stones declare to be a burial ground. A glance at the inscriptions quickly decides that this neat little graveyard is devoted to the care of the remains of pet dogs.

Nearly all the graves have white gravestones, upon which inscriptions dictated by the varied eccentricities of the sorrowing owners are cut, and they are further bordered with tiles, and decorated with flowering plants.

One inscription simply reads:
> To dear little "Smut."

Others, more elaborate, run as follows:
> Alas! poor "Zoe,"
> Born 1 October, 1889,
> Died 13 August, 1892.
> As Deeply Mourned as
> Ever Dog was Mourned
> For Friendship rare
> By her adorned.

> To faithful
> "Mimie,"
> Yorkshire Terrier
>   weight 3½ lbs.
> Died
> Also Beautiful "Pet"
> Died
> Ever Remembered Friends
> To "Bobby" over the way.

"They were lovely and pleasant in their lives, and in their deaths they were not divided."

My Dear Dog
"Sam"
June 3, 1894.
A. E. P.
After Life's fitful slumber
He sleeps well.

Love's Tribute to Love,
Dear Little "Tommy,"
Sweet Little Skye.
Sept. 1882.

Dear "Impy,"
Loving and Loved,
April 7, 1896.

Darling "Sammie,"
July 14, 1894.
Aged 12.

A police dog is recognized by this:
"Topper,"
Hyde Park Police Station.
Died 9, 6, '93.

One grave was reported to have a cross at its foot, bearing a wreath of immortelles and this inscription:

"Prince Charlie,"
May 29, 1894.
A Faithful Friend.

In Loving Memory of
Dearest "Chin Chin,"
A Perfect Dog.
May 26, 1894.

The following is an extract from Mr. O. C. Simonds remarks on foreign cemeteries at the Philadelphia Convention of the A. A. C. S. : "Among the cemeteries I visited while in Europe is the Metropolitan Cemetery in London, containing twenty thousand graves. It is nicely laid out and very well kept. As far as landscape gardening and the care of the cemetery is concerned, it is very beautiful. There are some things that might be of much interest to you; in the first place, there is a consecrated ground where they charge a little more for a lot or burial than in the unconsecrated portion. The association carries on the whole business of the cemetery; they attend to the funerals and sell flowers in connection with the care of the cemetery. * In one large cemetery in Paris where there are 300,000 bodies buried, the cemetery is built in form somewhat like our cemeteries here; but the graves are twenty, thirty and forty feet deep, the bodies being buried one above the other."

Association of American Cemetery Superintendents.

O. C. SIMONDS, "Graceland," Chicago, President.
G. W. CREESY, "Harmony Grove," Salem, Mass., Vice-President.
F. EURICH, Woodlawn, Toledo, O., Secretary and Treasurer

Publisher's Department.

The receipt of Cemetery Literature and Trade Catalogues will be acknowledged in this column.

TO ADVERTISERS, THE MODERN CEMETERY is the only publication of its class and will be found a valuable medium for reaching cemetery officials in all parts of the United States.

TO SUBSCRIBERS, Cemetery officials desiring to subscribe for a number of copies regularly to circulate among their lot owners, should send for our special terms. Several well known cemeteries have already adopted this plan with good results.

Contributions on matters pertaining to cemeteries are solicited. Address all communications to

R. J. HAIGHT, 334 Dearborn St., CHICAGO.

With the issue of October 27, *American Gardening* (New York City) completes its first twelve months under the new management. The occasion is celebrated by the adoption of a newly designed and appropriate cover, and also by the introduction of an interesting department devoted to woman.

The Cemetery Superintendents' Library.—Mr. C. W. Hamill of Baltimore, Md., recommends *Farm Drainage*, by Henry F. French, as a valuable book for superintendents interested in the drainage of land. The book contains over one hundred illustrations and costs $1.50. Orders may be sent to the publisher of MODERN CEMETERY. Will other readers kindly send in the names of books that should be in the Superintendents' Library.

We have received from Mr. John Gunn, Supt., Pine Grove Cemetery, Whitinsville, Mass., photographs of views of that cemetery which will be published in our next issue.—From W. T. Lockwood, Sec. and Supt., Sleepy Hollow Cemetery, Tarrytown, N. Y., photographs of two views of the Revolutionary Soldiers' Monument, recently dedicated in that cemetery.—From M. E. Dupre, Supt. of the Notre Dame des Nieges Cemetery, Montreal, views of the imposing entrance to the grounds, and a copy of the recently adopted by-laws.—Illustrated descriptive pamphlet of Cedar Grove Cemetery, between Newton and Flushing, L. I., containing also information on interments, rules and regulations, etc.

Interment Record and Lot Book.

This system is thought to embrace the best features of the most popular forms of burial records now in use and may be adapted to large or small cemeteries. The Interment Record gives all of the necessary information in regard to the deceased, and the Lot Book locates every grave, so that it can be readily found at any time. The books are printed on heavy paper, substantially bound and furnished in different sizes, depending upon the requirements of the cemetery.   **R. J. HAIGHT, Pub.,** 334 Dearborn St., Chicago.

SITUATIONS WANTED, Etc.

Advertisements, limited to five lines, will be inserted in this column at the rate of 50 cents each insertion, 7 words to a line. Cash must accompany order.

WANTED — position as manager or superintendent of cemetery by a thoroughly practical man, understands grading lawn and road making, draining, etc., is also a practical florist and landscape gardener; extensive experience in the erection of greenhouses and cultivation of choice plants and flowers. Full particulars by applying to P. H. S., care of MODERN CEMETERY, 334 Dearborn St., Chicago.

Patent Fence Cresting
Especially designed for Cemeteries and Orchards. This fence surrounds Calvary and Bellefontaine Cemeteries in St. Louis.
E. L. GRAYDON, Sole Agent,
7201 N. B'dway, ST. LOUIS, MO.

A Paris florist charged the Emperor of Russia $1,000 for a wreath ordered for the funeral of President Carnot. — *Meehan's Monthly.*

* * *

The first interments in King's Chapel burying ground, Boston, were made in June, 1630.

* * *

Please renew our subscription to the MODERN CEMETERY, as we get much help from its columns. — C. A. NOBLE, Catskill, N. Y.

* * *

I take much interest in the paper as do the trustees, as is shown by their paying for the paper. — C. C. BURDICK, Mason City, Ia.

HITCHINGS & CO.
Established 50 Years.

...Horticultural Architects and Builders,
AND LARGEST MANUFACTURERS OF
Greenhouse Heating and Ventilating Apparatus.

The highest awards received at the World's Fair for Horticultural Architecture, Greenhouse Construction and Heating Apparatus. Conservatories, Greenhouses, Palmhouses, etc., erected complete with our Patent Iron Frame Construction. *Send Four Cents for Illustrated Catalogue.*

233 Mercer St., NEW YORK.

THOS. W. WEATHERED'S SONS,
INCORPORATED.
Horticultural Architects and Hot Water Engineers
Send for Catalogue, enclosing 4 cents in stamps.
No. 244 Canal St., NEW YORK CITY.

Every copy of the MODERN CEMETERY is worth a dollar to a cemetery superintendent, writes Mr. David Grinton, Supt. and Sec'y., Oak Grove Cemetery, Delaware, O., when renewing his subscription.

The MODERN CEMETERY has been and is a great help * * it is pleasing to see it maintain a high standard. * * Cemetery superintendents should consider themselves favored to be represented by so excellent a publication. — N. C. WILDER, *Supt. Spring Grove, Hartford, Conn.*

Find enclosed one dollar for the MODERN CEMETERY. Cannot get along without it. — *Jno. F. Mabin, Supt. Oak Hill Cemetery, Owosso, Mich.*

BOOKS FOR CEMETERY OFFICIALS

Landscape Gardening, by Samuel Parsons, Jr. 300 pages, 200 illustrations. Beautifully printed and bound, $3.50.

Ornamental Gardening for Americans, by Elias A. Long. Illustrated. Cloth, $2.00. The Nursery Book, by L. H. Bailey. Complete hand book of propagation. Paper 50 cents, cloth $1.00. Sent postpaid on receipt of price.

The Nursery Book, by L. H. Bailey, assisted by several of the most skilful propagators in the world. In fact, it is a careful compendium of the best practice in all countries. It contains 107 illustrations, showing methods, processes and appliances. How to Propagate over 2000 varieties of shrubs, trees and herbaceous or soft-stemmed plants; the process for each being fully described. All this and much more is fully told in the Nursery Book. Over 300 pages, 8vo. Price, cloth, $1. Pocket style, paper, narrow margins, 50 cents. Address, **K. J. HAIGHT,** 331 Dearborn St., Chicago.

A GREAT IMPROVEMENT IN INTERMENT!
The Patent Automatic Burial Apparatus, Endorsed by Prominent American Cemetery Superintendents.

An Exhibition Given Before Their Association at Philadelphia With Gratifying Results.

At the convention of the cemetery superintendents from all parts of the Union, held last month in Philadelphia, an exhibit was made of an apparatus for lowering coffins into the grave, that evoked the warmest admiration. It is a disagreeable sight at best to see the casket lowered in the olden way, by straps or ropes, since accidents happen at times that involve the personal safety of the bystanders while the lowering of the body with straps or ropes is revolting to one's finer sensibilities, and surely these ought to be regarded, particularly at a moment when loved ones naturally feel that the form of their departed should be consigned to its home with the utmost tenderness.

The convention in question represented a body of men of superior intelligence, men who look upon their work as a profession rather than as a business, and it is not surprising that the satisfaction afforded by the exhibit of the Burial Apparatus in question found vent in the following communications:

EIGHTH ANNUAL CONVENTION ASS. OF AMERICAN CEMETERY SUPERINTENDENTS, PHILADELPHIA, Sept. 14, 1894.
Scherer Manufacturing Co., New York — We have witnessed the exhibition of the Scherer Automatic Burial Apparatus at West Laurel Hill Cemetery, Philadelphia, and are gratified at the improvements you have made in it since the apparatus was last exhibited at Minneapolis. As a means of obviating accidents in the lowering of caskets this apparatus should commend itself to the careful consideration of cemetery officials.

It is easily handled, is simple in construction and possesses merits that cannot fail of recognition. Yours respectfully,
WM. SALWAY, Supt. Spring Grove Cemetery, Cincinnati, O.
FRANK EURICH, Supt. Woodlawn Cemetery, Toledo, O.

The Patent Automatic Burial Apparatus can be seen on exhibition at the office of the Scherer Manufacturing Co., Room 22, Bible House, New York. It is safe, simple, moderate in price, substantially built, and can be operated by a child. The one exhibited in Philadelphia was operated by a boy of 15 years.

OFFICE OF THE SUPT., SALEM FIELDS CEMETERY,
EAST NEW YORK, Sept. 20, 1894.
The Scherer Manufacturing Co. — I have watched with much interest the development of the Automatic Burial Apparatus manufactured by you, and have studied its workings carefully. It is simply made and operates easily, and its general use in cemeteries is destined to mitigate the anguish of mourners at the final moment when the body is consigned reverently to the grave. I hope to see it introduced generally.
Respectfully yours, PETER J. HILTMAN, Supt.

MOUNT NEBOH CEMETERY,
EVERGREEN P.O., LONG ISLAND, Sept. 10, '94.
To the Scherer Manufacturing Co. — It affords me pleasure to testify to the excellence of the Automatic Patent Burial Apparatus manufactured by you. I find that it is in general demand, and the small additional charge that is made for its use brings in quite an income to the cemetery. The oftener it is used, the more it is appreciated by those participating in interments. Respectfully yours, HERMAN GRAUPNHOLZ, Supt.

PATENT AUTOMATIC BURIAL APPARATUS, Manufactured by the

SCHERER M'F'G CO., Office and Show Room: BIBLE HOUSE, Cor. Fourth Ave. and Ninth St., NEW YORK CITY.

☞ *For a more definite description of the Burial Apparatus and its use send for Catalogue, which will be mailed free.*

EARNSHAW & PUNSHON
LANDSCAPE
ENGINEERS

Southwest Cor. Fifth and Race Streets,
Cincinnati,
Ohio.

30 YEARS experience in the profession, enables us to guarantee that our Modern Designs for laying out Cemeteries, Parks, and the Subdivision of Estates, will insure the best artistic effects and financial results, and at the same time involve the least expense in development and maintenance.

WE RESPECTFULLY REFER TO THE OFFICIALS OF THE FOLLOWING INSTITUTIONS:

Spring Grove Cemetery, Cincinnati, O.	Highland Lawn Cemetery, Terre Haute, Ind.
Lake View Cemetery, Cleveland, O.	Forest Lawn Cemetery, Buffalo, N. Y.
Linwood Cemetery, Dubuque, Ia.	Riverview Cemetery, East Liverpool, O.
Woodlawn Cemetery, Canandaigua, N. Y.	Forest Lawn Cemetery, Omaha, Neb.
Mount Pleasant Cemetery, Toronto, Canada.	St. Joseph's Cemetery, Evansville, Ind.
Lorraine Cemetery, Baltimore, Md.	Woodside Cemetery, Middletown, O.
Woodlawn Cemetery, Birmingham, Ala.	Mother of God Cemetery, Covington, Ky.
Forest Lawn Cemetery, East Saginaw, Mich.	Logan Park Cemetery, Sioux City, Ia.
Prospect Cemetery, Toronto, Canada.	South Indiana Hospital, Evansville, Ind.
Mount Olivet Cemetery, Detroit, Michigan.	Goodale Park, Columbus, O.
Hoyt Park, East Saginaw, Mich.	Park and Zoological Gardens, Cincinnati, O.

South San Francisco Land and Imp. Co., San Francisco, Cal.,
and to all our patrons.

PERSONAL INSPECTION AND ADVICE AS TO THE IMPROVEMENT OF LARGE PROPERTIES WILL BE PROMPTLY GIVEN, FREE OF CHARGE.

THE MODERN CEMETERY.

THE MODERN CEMETERY.
AN ILLUSTRATED MONTHLY JOURNAL DEVOTED TO THE INTEREST OF CEMETERIES

R. J. HAIGHT, Publisher.
334 Dearborn Street, CHICAGO.

Subscription $1.00 a Year in Advance. Foreign Subscription $1.25.
Special Rates on Six or More Copies.

VOL. IV. CHICAGO, DEC. 1894. No. 10.

CONTENTS.

FUNERAL REFORM 109
FORETHOUGHT NECESSARY IN ACQUIRING LAND FOR
  CEMETERY PURPOSES... 110
*ST. ROCH'S CHAPEL, NEW ORLEANS...................... 111
RUBBLE AND CONCRETE FOUNDATIONS................... 113
*PINE GROVE CEMETERY, WHITINSVILLE, MASS...... 114
*CEDAR HILL CEMETERY, HARTFORD, CONN 116
WOMEN IN WESTMINSTER ABBEY............................ 117
CEMETERY NOTES.. 118
SUGGESTIONS TO LOT OWNERS—CORRESPONDENCE—
  ST. JOHN'S CHURCHYARD, NEW YORK 119
PUBLISHER'S DEPARTMENT..................................... 120
  *Illustrated.

Funeral Reform.

The movement toward reform in funerals appears to be in a state of rapid advancement, and much is being accomplished in educating the public in this important matter by the clergy. There is a ministerial association in north Chicago which has adapted the following rules:

First, no public invitations; second, no funeral on Sunday; third, casket closed upon conclusion of service; fourth, service concluded at house, without any addition at the grave; fifth, only those accompany deceased to grave who are personally requested to do so; sixth, no expense incurred for carriages, flowers or other matters; seventh, no heavy mourning. These are printed suggestions to all.

There is also in contemplation a Burial Reform Association, which will undertake the conduct of funerals at a minimum of expense. The association will be financed under a policy or certificate system, subscription or dues for which will be collected at regular intervals, and when a certain amount is subscribed, a certificate would be issued entitling the holder to the grade of funeral prescribed by the certificate.

Some of the religious organizations are being drawn into line on the subject, and the hitherto ostentatious display attending the funeral occasion, will be relegated to the past, whence in the darker times of human progress all the follies and exagerations emanated.

In connection with this matter it will be interesting to note what the Fall River Philanthropic Burial Society, of Fall River, Mass., has accomplished and is doing. Its object is to provide the funeral expenses on a sort of benefit plan. It started without capital, has always been officered by working men and shows what honest and careful management can do. It was established in 1878 and incorporated in 1879.

The receipts for the half-year ending July 31, 1894, amounted to $10,971.63, and the expenditures to $8,389.46, showing a gain of $2,582.17. During the year ending July 31, 1894, the receipts amounted to $21,175.42, while the expenditure was $19,054.32, showing a gain of $2,121.10 during the year. During the half-year ending January 31, 1894, there was expended about one thousand dollars in improving the property.

Eighty deaths occurred in the last six months costing $5,565.; during previous six months, 93 deaths, costing $6,895. Since the establishment of the society there has been 1,032 deaths and an expenditure of $60,950. The monthly subscriptions from members range between ten cents for a four months old child to twenty cents for adults up to fifty-five years. The benefits range between thirty and sixty dollars after four months membership to sixty and one hundred dollars after two years membership.

The following are among the rules: All regular subscriptions are due on and dated for the first day of each month. * * Extra collections to be due when ordered to be levied.—Any member who is three months' subscription in arrears shall be declared out of benefit, and if four months' subscription in arrears to be excluded from the society. Arrears owing by deceased members will be deducted from the funeral allowance.— Every member shall have been a member of the society at least four months, and have paid all subscriptions or collections due within the said four months, before being permitted to vote, to hold any office, or become entitled to any funeral allowance specified by the rules.—Any false statement as to age, state of health or bodily infirmity, at time of admission, subsequently proved, is met by expulsion from society and reversion of accrued benefits.

Forethought Necessary in Acquiring Land for Cemetery Purposes.

A very important question is decided by the supreme court of Vermont in the case of Camp vs. Town of Barre, which was a suit to enjoin the town authorities from laying out into lots, and disposing of the same, or from utilizing for burial purposes, that portion of the cemetery grounds in Barre village purchased November 5, 1885, which is within 20 rods of the dwelling houses of the complainants. These dwelling houses have all been erected since the date of the purchase. The situation at the time of the purchase was substantially as follows: There was a need for the enlargement of the cemetery grounds, and at the time none of the dwelling houses in question had been erected, but the cellar of one had been partly completed. The town had laid out the street on which these dwellings were subsequently located, (presumably to accommodate such dwellings as might be erected thereon; no other necessity for the street being suggested). The owner of the land now occupied by the dwelling houses was using it for a pasture, but had had it plotted into building lots, and, by an arrangement, the cellar on one had been partially completed. The town authorities did not know that the owner had had this land plotted into building lots, but they knew that the land would soon, if it were not then, be in demand for building lots. They did not think the digging of the cellar on one of the lots would prevent the use of the land purchased for burial purposes. Considerable of it could be used for that purpose if the injunction should be granted. The purchase by the town was apparently made at the time it was to anticipate the use of the land occupied by these dwelling houses for such purpose. It was not found on trial that the use of the addition adjoining the house lots of the complainants for burial purposes, if the burials were properly made, would create a nuisance to the dwelling houses, but it was found that such use would materially diminish the value of them. The suit was based principally upon a statutory provision prohibiting the town from burying any deceased person upon the purchased addition within 20 rods of their dwelling houses. That provision follows those sections of the Vermont statute which authorize towns to acquire land by purchase, or by condemnation under the right of eminent domain, for the enlargement or establishment of public burial grounds. It reads: "This chapter shall not authorize the acquiring of land for the purpose of the enlargement or establishment of a burial ground so as to bring the same within twelve rods of a dwelling house, and no remains shall be buried in such burial grounds so enlarged or established, within twenty rods of a dwelling house." It is apparent, the supreme court holds, that this relates to the enlarged or newly-established part of such burial grounds. The town authorities contended that this provision related only to such dwelling houses as were in existence at the time of the enlargement or establishment. Whether this section of the provision should be construed, as claimed by the complainants, as prohibiting the burial of any remains in the newly-enlarged or newly-established part of any burial grounds within 20 rods of any dwelling house, although erected after such enlargement, or, as claimed by the authorities, is applicable only to dwelling houses in existence at the time of the enlargement, was not considered very material to be determined in this case. In equity, it was said, the intention and spirit of the requirement is to be regarded more than the strict letter of the law. This is a police regulation passed to secure the health of the public and of individuals. Disease germs are propagated and distributed so insidiously and beyond common observation, both through the air and percolating water, that it is next to impossible to trace them, and determine by ordinary methods whether a public or private nuisance is created by the burial of the remains of a deceased person within given limits to a dwelling house. To prevent the communication of disease from such source the legislature thought it wise to prescribe a limit within which such grounds should not be brought to a dwelling house, and within which no remains should be buried. When the town authorities, at the time of acquiring the land to make this needed enlargement, acting solely for the public, knew that the land occupied by these dwelling houses would very soon be needed for such purpose, had laid out a street to make it available for that purpose, and knew that the owner had commenced to dig the cellar for one such dwelling house thereon, it was a clear breach of the spirit of the statute for them to make the purchase, and for the town to lay that portion of the purchase out into and sell lots to persons, giving them the right to bury thereon for all time. It was a breach of the spirit if not the letter of the statute, which equity would regard and restrain, both in the interest of the complainants and the public,—to enforce the law in essence and spirit, and to protect the health of the complainants and the public from the insidious propagation and distribution of disease. It was urged that the complainants had waived their right by allowing a few burials to be made on the inhibited tract. It might be so as regards such burials. But such interments are quite distinguishable from laying the inhibited tract into lots, and selling the lots for permanent use by the purchaser and his family and friends and assigns for all time. The decree in complainants' favor did not disturb them, and was affirmed on this appeal.

St. Rochs' Chapel, New Orleans.

The Chapel of St. Rochs, (pronounced St. Rox), is one of the sights of New Orleans. It was built in 1875 by Father Davis—whose tomb is beneath the floor in front of the altar—as a mortuary chapel, and stands in Campo Santo Cemetery. The cemetery is only two blocks in extent, and is divided by a street so that the ground is in two separate sections, each inclosed by a brick, cement covered, wall, with quaint, low towers or bastions at the corners. It fronts on Washington Avenue, away out on the edge of the swamps in the third district of the city. The surroundings are unprepossessing and apparently unwholesome. Stagnant water stands in the open drains that are cut through the

ST. ROCHS' CHAPEL, NEW ORLEANS.

waxy black soil on both sides of the streets, and the entire appearance of the vicinity suggests malaria, yet the streets are fairly built up with dwellings quite out to the cemetery walls.

The main entrance is overhung by a large weeping willow that droops about the iron gates, and partly shrouds a little lodge just inside, where an attendant is always at hand to sell at five cents each, candles, of which dozens are constantly burning before the chapel altars.

The chapel itself has been likened by some one, (Charles Dudley Warner, I think), to a kitchen clock, and when seen from the front, its tall, narrow outline does give it an odd resemblance to an old fashioned clock, the bell opening far up the front of the gable standing for the dial face. It is dressed in living green, its covering of Ficus repens clinging so closely that the walls of concrete are almost hidden and the roof will soon be smothered in foliage. Altogether it wears an old world aspect that sets it apart from the general run of American cemetery architecture.

The interior of the building is even more contracted than the exterior leads one to expect, because the slight projections on either side, like rudimentary wings, are tiers of tombs, the inner closed ends of which form the side walls of the narrow, high room. The blue domed ceiling is sprinkled with golden stars that show faintly in the dim light filtering through windows of stained glass. A small gallery above the entrance is used by a choir for the infrequent chapel services, of which the principal one is the annual celebration of the Feast of St. Rochs, held on August 16th, St. Rochs' Day.

Although built as a mortuary chapel, St Rochs' was turned into a votive shrine by the public during the Yellow fever scourge of '78, (St. Rochs being the patron saint of the sick and troubled), and has grown famous in its new role. Persons from the most distant parts of the city make Novena there when desiring relief from illness or sorrow. They come in person for nine successive weeks, (always on the same day of the week), to burn candles and say prayers before the altars. The interior of the chapel is decorated with paintings illustrating the principal events in the life of St. Rochs, who, according to tradition, or Church history, was born at Montpelier, France, in 1312, of noble parents, being the only child of a mother who had long prayed for a son. He was found at his birth to bear on his left breast a red cross, and was consecrated by his mother to a holy life. But his own heart seems to have turned from earliest childhood in love and pity to the sick, the poor, and the afflicted; to these he gave not only his time and strength, but his inheritance—himself wearing the garb and living the life of a member of the order of St. Francis. After suffering poverty, sickness and distress, he was mistaken for a spy on his return from a pious pilgrimage to Rome, and being thrown into prison, died in 1337, alone and uncared for in a dungeon. On the site of his prison, the original Chapel of St. Rochs was built.

The popularity and efficacy of the patron saint of illness and trouble find abundant proof in this new-world chapel of St. Rochs in the numerous canes and crutches abandoned there by persons restored to health; by occasional waxen feet and hands that are hung on the altars as thank offerings, representing the restoration of the use of those members; and especially by small marble tablets inscribed with "Thanks" or "Merci" that are so numerous as to face the fronts and sides of the altars, and the walls in their vicinity. Some of these marks of gratitude also bear the names of the donors. Most of the tablets are about six inches square, though some are larger, and occasionally there is one in heart shape. The last undoubtedly stand for the satisfied affection of some maid who has made Novena there, seeking relief for that illness of the heart called Love.

St. Rochs is in high favor with the young folks of the Crescent City as a mediator in lover's quarrels. I strongly suspect that an innocent faced young girl in a fresh, crisp muslin, whom I ventured to ask a few questions as she hastened towards the chapel, candle in hand, was begging the saint's intercession to untangle a difficulty between herself and some happy-go-lucky man, who knew full well that she would bring it out all right some way and save him the trouble. When the same little maid learned that I was making my first visit to St. Rochs, she lost no time in advising me to wish for something before leaving, as it was certain to come true; which in itself was convincing proof of a kindness of heart that would put the masculine half of the quarrel in the wrong in the mind of every reasonable man or woman.

Scattered through the enclosure are the twelve stations of the cross, and before their altars some one is ever stopping to breathe a prayer. Near one of the stations there is growing what is called there, sacred heart clover. The leaves are a tre-foil, about the size of white clover leaves, but *on each one there is a small heart, blood red in color*. I believe it to be the so-called Calvary clover, (Medicago echinus) said to be native to Palestine. The name of Calvary clover is due to several peculiarities. It is alleged that if the plant is to thrive the seed must be sown on Good Friday; then when the plants are young the leaves bear the heart-shaped spots, like freshly spilled blood, that are said to remain bright for a time and then gradually fade away. The three leaves composing the trefoil stand erect during the day in the form of a cross; but at sunset the arms of the cross are drawn together and the upper leaflet bows over them as if in prayer. In good time the plant bears small yellow flowers that are followed by little spiral pods bearing sharp prickles, and as the pods ripen these curl up and interlace with one another, forming a ball which when fully ripe, may be unwound, (the soft lining to the pods being first removed), and easily twisted about the fingers into a miniature crown of thorns.

So, by its blood-stained leaves, extended arms, bowed head, and by the day when the seed is placed in the ground to await resurrection, the plant has gained its name of Calvary clover.

Campo Santo Cemetery contains both tombs and graves. That the latter should be permitted seems unaccountable, for when graves are dug water stands in them before interment takes place, so that the boxes are put directly into the water unless temporarily baled out. This being the case, how any one can choose the vicinity as a place of habitation is incomprehensible. The crying need of New Orleans, of all places, seems to be Crematories, and the compulsory use of them.

In New Orleans, funerals are made occasions of much ceremony, especially by the colored people,

ST. ROCHS' CHAPEL, NEW ORLEANS.—FRONT VIEW.

and an imposing funeral cortege does much to assuage grief, and is also good ground for subsequent pride and satisfaction. In view of this fact, the story of a bright young woman resident of New Orleans is apropos. Having taken a northern friend to see St. Rochs, they chanced upon a colored funeral, and knowing the race fancy for a large company, she did not hesitate to join the procession for the purpose of further study of the cemetery practices. On reaching the open grave, the coffin was deposited at one side, (it would be strict truth to say shore), until the water was baled out, and the first part of the service read. Before many words were spoken there was a commotion on the outskirts of the company, which became a regular stampede when police officers were seen approaching. The colored people, minister, mourners and all, fled in every direction, taking refuge in and behind tombs, forsaking the coffin where it stood, and not reappearing until a man, who was inclined to make a good fight for freedom, was overpowered and taken away—but not before the frightened yet plucky southern girl had insisted on the officers telling why they invaded the sacred precincts at such a time and for such a purpose. She learned that the man had committed a crime, and thinking to escape detection, had assumed the guise of a mourner in the first funeral he came across; an opportunity he knew he would not have to go far to find.

But there are compensations for all things. Funeral notices in French and English are tacked to corner trees and posts throughout the city. On reading one of them one day, the writer commented to a resident on the high death rate. The characteristic answer was: "Yes, but the people here do enjoy funerals so much."

FANNY COPLEY SEAVEY.

Rubble and Concrete Foundations.

For any class of ordinary massive work in foundations composed of rubble stone, work laid in even courses and filled with concrete, making practically a solid concrete block foundation, is about the best that can be employed.

The excavation should be made to a depth one foot greater than any adjoining excavation, and of sufficient area to distribute the load, so that a pressure not exceeding 2,000 to 3,000 pounds per square foot shall be imposed. The nature of the soil and form of the superstructure will modify and govern the case. Care should be taken that the bottom of the excavation should be shaved to a level even grade with no loose material therein.

A light course of crushed stone should be evenly spread over the bottom and all the interstices thereof washed full of sharp sand and other fine material. On this footing, stone should be laid in even courses, making tight outer joints. In this class of work interior joints had better be open rather than too close. Into the space thus enclosed a good amount of stiff concrete mortar should be put and upon this a light course of broken stone may be thrown which should be well rammed into the mortar.

The spall filling for this purpose should be clean and in size should not exceed one-third the space they are to occupy. They should be drenched to saturation before being placed and incorporated with the mortar. A more solid job is secured by ramming the stone into the mortar than by mixing them first and then endeavoring to dispose of the mass among the interstices of the stone work. In no case should the stone be put in any work first and the mortar thrown upon them, for a thoroughly solid and compacted mass can never be thus obtained. Grouting, a practice sometimes employed to that end, is a practice that should very seldom be employed, for in grouting the sand and cement separate and setting does not properly take place; when it does, if ever, a frail stratum of sand will be found in each succeeding batch of grout which will destroy the strength of the whole. The object sought in concrete work is to obtain a compact cohesive mass, that can only be secured where the adhesive base, the cement and lime, are thoroughly incorporated with every part of the mass.

Where extreme solidity and a quick setting job is not essential, the work may be cheapened by well slacking good lime for working in double the amount of clean sand. Again, let the mass lay for several days, and when ready for use spread out so much as is required at a time for use, and quickly and evenly spread over it one-fourth to one-third part of cement, taking pains to promptly and thoroughly work and incorporate the materials for immediate use.

The work can be carried up one course at a time, taking pains of course to make any stone used overlap underlying joints so as to make a well bonded job.

The strength of masonry depends very much on the mortar and how it is applied. Adhesion in mortar is the object sought. This can be had only by selecting clean material and a thorough drenching of both the sand, spalls, and stone employed in the work. Whatever the material at hand is, nothing is so essential as a little thought and care directed by good judgment.

L. C. W.

The mausoleum for C. P. Huntington, president of the Southern Pacific R. R., in Woodlawn Cemetery, New York, which has been under construction for the past five years is nearing completion. With the possible exception of the Vanderbilt mausoleum on Staten Island, it is the most expensive piece of work of the kind in this country. The structure stands on the crest of Chapel Hill and occupies a commanding view of the surrounding country. The approach from the roadway up to the mausoleum is covered by a massive granite stairway, the main platform consisting of a single stone weighing 40 tons. The mausoleum has the appearance of a Roman temple; its principal dimensions are, length 42 feet, width 28 feet, height 24 feet. It contains 16 catacombs. The exterior is of Quincy granite, and the interior is finished in Italian marble. The cost is said to approximate $250,000.

Pine Grove Cemetery, Whitinsville, Mass.

The accompanying illustrations speak louder than words in describing Pine Grove Cemetery, Whitinsville, Mass.

However, there are conditions and features in

ENTRANCE TO PINE GROVE CEMETERY, WHITINSVILLE, MASS.

connection with its existence and maintenance, that offer such excellent lessons for other localities and cemetery organizations, that some facts in addition to its pictorial representation will be of value.

Pine Grove Cemetery Association was formed about twelve years ago, and it evidently comprised advanced men, of broad intelligence and views, for it is the only cemetery in Worcester county, Mass., laid out under modern ideas. The wisdom of its projectors has been justified by the fact that numbers of the lot owners come from the towns and villages along the Blackstone valley and surrounding country.

The cemetery contains thirty-five acres, all of which has not yet been improved; but the rule is to prepare a section every fall. At present about one-third of the area is laid out in improved lawns.

No wall, fence, coping, hedge or any boundary whatever is allowed about the lots, but the limits are marked at the corners by granite posts, sunk in the ground so that the tops do not appear above the surface, and the trustees reserve to themselves the right to remove any monument, structure or inscription that may be determined by a majority of the board to be offensive or improper; and no tomb can be constructed or allowed within the cemetery, unless by special permission of the trustees, and only in such places and manner as they may decree.

The sections are laid out in lawns averaging fifty-five feet, and the lots are not separated by paths of any kind. In the single grave section no monuments are allowed except headstones, not exceeding four feet high by sixteen inches wide.

The cemetery charges throughout are reasonable, practically a nominal charge is exacted for the use of the receiving vault.

The cemetery has the usual and necessary buildings, all carried out in harmony. There is a main green house, eighty-five by twenty feet, with two smaller attachments; and near by a pretty cottage for the superintendent, Mr. John Gunn. There is also a substantial and well finished barn on the grounds.

The by-laws, rules and regulations of this cemetery are so ordained that the trustees have the deciding voice in its control and management. The officers of the corporation are: President, Secretary, Treasurer and a Board of nine Trustees, and one Auditor, all of whom, except the president, are chosen by ballot at the annual meeting of the association.

The proceeds of all lots and burial places are applied to the necessary expenses and indebtedness of the association, and as much of the remainder as may be deemed necessary by the Board of Trustees is used for laying out, fixing and ornamenting the cemetery.

The association comprises the original members and all lot-owners owning lots of not less than one hundred and fifty square feet of land in the grounds.

The perpetual care of lots has not been overlooked in this beautiful cemetery and the trustees have continued to impress upon lot-owners the im-

VIEW IN MAIN PART OF CEMETERY.

portance and desirableness of providing for the perpetual care of their lots. It is manifest that the beauty of the whole cemetery depends largely upon the care bestowed upon individual lots, and that the care should be constant and as much as possible removed from the uncertainties of the future. To provide for this want so that all interested can guard against all contingencies, certain rules have been adopted by which lot-owners can by making a deposit with the treasurer, based upon the size of the lot, provide for the care and attention so necessary to make beautiful the home of the dead."

The charges are as follows, or such sums may be bequeathed by will:

For single grave $10.00; for a lot containing not exceeding 150 square feet, $50.00; for a lot containing over 150 and not over 300 square feet, $75.00; for a lot containing 300 square feet or more, $100.

This sum is invested with other like deposits under the name of "perpetual care fund," and the income therefrom is expended under the direction of the trustees in keeping the depositor's lot in order forever, in cutting grass, etc., but does not include care of monuments, headstones, etc., unless specially provided for.

For the annual care of lots charges are made as follows: For single graves, 50 cents; for lot not exceeding 150 square feet, $2.00; for lot over 150 and under 300 square feet, $3.00; for lot over 300 square feet, $4.00.

Modern ideas are seen to prevail throughout Pine Grove Cemetery, and even the regulations concerning visitors are made with due regard to the protection of the lot-owners and the respect demanded by the hallowed surroundings. It all results in a cemetery which is at once a pride to its owners, a place of rest and peace to those whose loved ones have found eternal repose, and a spot to which any and all can turn to feast their eyes on nature's quiet beauties, and their souls in contemplation and reflection.

Whitinsville is a town of only 4000 inhabitants, and this cemetery clearly demonstrates what can be done, when wide-awake, liberal men, of the necessary qualifications, and there are many such in every community, take hold of cemetery matters. If only two or three of the right kind of men in each community, could be induced to interest themselves in their local cemeteries, new conditions would rapidly grow and the rural cemetery,

VIEW FROM FOOT OF GROVE—IVY-COVERED TOMB, ETC.

VIEW FROM CENTRAL LAWN, SHOWING GROVE, ETC.

instead of being a reproach, would be the measure of the development of the community in which it exists.

Mention has been omitted of the fact, that all purchasers of lots from outside territory, are compelled to place such lots under "perpetual care." This is a wise precaution, preventing the inconvenience attaching to communication and other matters with non-resident owners.

In the last annual report, dated April, 1894, seven lots and fifteen graves had been sold for $340 and the total net receipts for 1893 were $3,813.59, and the total expenditures $3,246.23. The greenhouse sales amounted to $801.95 and the net income from investments $1,905.02.

On April 1, 1894, the "perpetual care" fund amounted to $41,695. There were thirty-eight interments during the year, and the number of lots under annual care was 132.

The development of Pine Grove Cemetery should be a positive encouragement to all small communities to go and do likewise.

Cedar Hill Cemetery, Hartford, Conn.

It is proposed in forthcoming issues to give more or less frequently, plans of some of our cemeteries, showing their designs and lay-out, and with these maps such notes of their main features as may lead to a clearer comprehension of their details which are most striking and useful for study.

The plan herewith is that of Cedar Hill Cemetery of Hartford, Conn., which was organized under a special charter by the state legislature, in 1864.

In area it is 268 acres—the original purchase being large in order to control land enough to secure a site in every way desirable. Of this area some 50 acres are improved and laid out in lots and sections, and 6 acres are in lakes and running water.

The nature of the ground is gravelly hardpan, and the landscape is markedly undulating. Its greatest elevation is 255 feet above mean low water at Saybrook, Conn., on Long Island Sound, and the highest point of the cemetery is 102 feet above its entrance. Its location is superb, commanding a view of over 40 miles up the Connecticut river, and from 13 to 20 miles east and south. A public road, it will be seen, bounds three sides of the cemetery. The general lay-out was made upon suggestions of the late Adolph Strauch, of Spring Grove, Cincinnati, and the development by the late Jacob Wiedenmann. The roads throughout are generally constructed on the Telford system.

The method of improvement is first to bring up a section to an established grade, and then to lay out the lots in reference to the section as a whole. The lots are generally square—from twenty feet to fifty feet square—and owing to the irregularity of outline of the sections, straight lines and rows are avoided; moreover, lots do not touch each other, a reasonable amount of space being left between. For these reasons monuments seldom line with each other for any distance.

Only about a quarter of an acre is laid out for

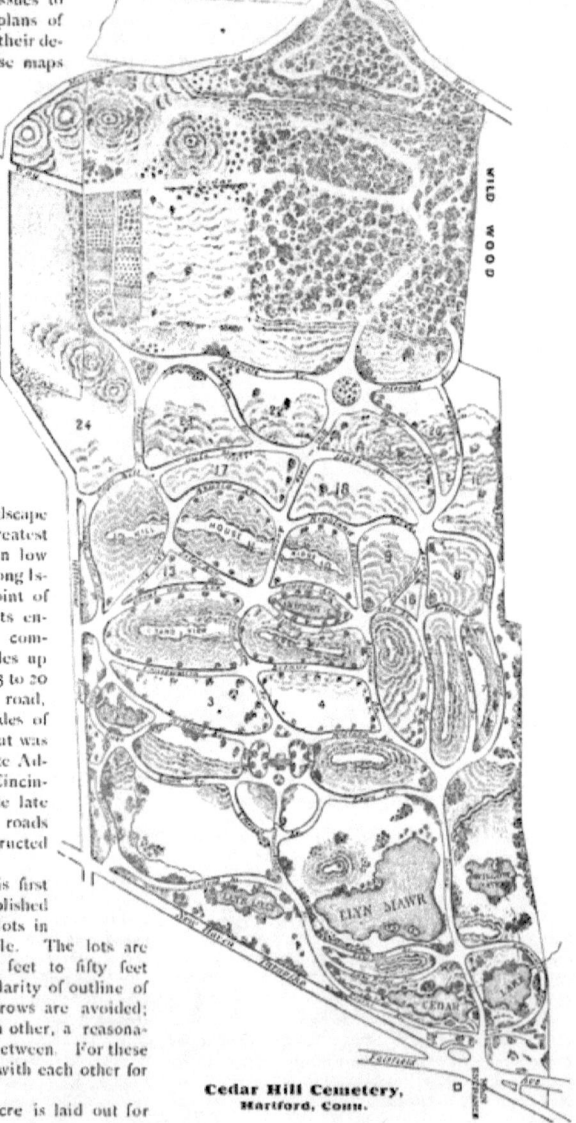

Cedar Hill Cemetery, Hartford, Conn.

single graves. Experience here has shown that such use is only temporary, the tendency being to buy lots and re-inter.

The cemetery has a Receiving vault of a capacity for 60 bodies. No greenhouses have been established on the grounds.

The cemetery has always been conducted strictly on the lawn plan. The graves are generally level, though some mounds have been allowed not more than five inches high. The lots are designated by stones set flush with the ground. No hedges, fences, or copings are allowed. Stone grave markers must be, if shallow, set on a stone foundation, if of granite, set not less than 3 feet in the ground. Headstones are permitted not higher than 2 feet, and foot stones not more than 8 inches. No metal markers or monuments are permitted. The cemetery has, generally speaking, a fine display of monumental work.

All work about the grounds, including the building of foundations for monuments is done by employees of the cemetery, and no workmen from the outside are admitted, except such as are required to erect monuments.

That important feature of modern cemetery management, Perpetual Care, has not yet received due attention, owing to the large capital that has been expended on improvements, but it is expected that a fund will soon be established. However, there are a number of special trusts in operation. The cemetery company at present cares for all lots equally, whether occupied, sold or unsold, and whether for resident or non-resident owners.

Women in Westminster Abbey.

The old gray Minster of Westminster, whose records date back over twelve hundred years, has found room for numbers of women in its long line of honored dead. Ethelgoda, wife of Sebert, King of Essex, who founded the Abbey on the site of a temple of Apollo, and his sister were the first women to be buried within its sacred precincts. Edward the Confessor commenced the building of the great edifice as it now stands, and Edith his wife was the next woman to repose in it. Since that time quite a large gathering of historic dames have found a final resting place in the old Abbey. Queen Maud, wife of Henry I., through whose marriage the Normans and Saxons were reunited, sleeps here. Then came Henry III., who from his own purse nearly rebuilt it in a splendid manner, and laid therein his little dumb daughter. Then we have Lady Aveline of Albemarle, wife of Earl of Lancaster, he of the Red Rose; Eleanor of Provence in whose honor on her last journey, Charing Cross, the twelfth cross, was erected; Philippa, mother of the Black Prince, founder of Queen's College, Oxford. A recumbent statue marks her tomb, to which it is said Tennyson bears a strong resemblance. The poet claimed descent from this line. The first protestant queen of England, Anne of Bohemia, followed, then came Catherine of Valois, wife of Henry V. The first to rest in Henry VIII's chapel was his wife Elizabeth of York, who was followed by her mother-in-law, Margaret Beaufort, countess of Richmond and Derby who founded two colleges at Cambridge and a chair of divinity at Oxford. "Bloody Mary" lies in an unmarked grave, Queen Elizabeth's coffin resting on top of Mary's; Mary, Queen of Scots lies near by and both these tombs have life size portrait recumbent statues, which distinctly display the historic characteristics of the two women. It was in Elizabeth's reign that men and women renowned in politics, arts and letters were first given entrance to the Abbey for final repose. The mother of Lady Jane Grey lies under a monument erected by her second husband. One of the women of the Russell family has a monument representing her sitting at ease in an osier chair, and her sister who was born in the abbey precincts, where her mother had taken refuge from the plague, lies near her. Catherine Knollys was granted privilege of interment in the abbey on account of faithful service to Queen Anne Boleyn, and the Norrises, deadly rivals, because Henry Norris alone of the family went with her to the scaffold. Lord Burleigh erected a high monument to his wife and daughter, whose loss overwhelmed him. He kneels in the monument in his robes of state, a picture of grief.

The monument of the beautiful Duchess of Richmond, is a curious one. It is her effigy in wax, dressed in her conventional robes, accompanied by a stuffed parrot, an old pet, the whole enclosed in a glass case.

Mary Beaumont, mother of George Villiers, Duke of Buckingham, lies in a splendid family tomb. Elizabeth Claypole, Cromwell's favorite daughter, found a place in the abbey, but her illustrious father was cast out. The great actress, Sarah Siddons, rests in this pantheon, as well as Anne Oldfield and Anne Bracegirdle. Perhaps the best known monument in Westminster is that of Lady Elizabeth Nightingale. That cruel figure of Death stealing up from the tomb beneath to cast his dart at the girl slipping from the arms of her husband above. The family vault of the Delavels of Northumberland brings to notice "Wild Lady Tyrconnell" who lies here. Lady Strathmore, she of the Strathmore secret, was buried in the Abbey in 1800.

History attaches some important incident to the large majority of silent sleepers here, and no short note can do justice to any feature of such history.

CEMETERY NOTES.

In Hillsboro Cemetery, Hillsboro, O., while some excavation was in progress, a spring of water was struck, of sufficient quantity to form a lake five to seven feet deep. There is no suspicion of surface water in the outflow.

* * *

Extensive improvements are contemplated for immediate prosecution in Mountain Grove Cemetery, Bridgeport, Conn. The proposed work will cost some $25,000 and will include the macadamizing of the principal drives and the erection of a handsome arch at Burr road entrance. This is to be one of the handsomest structures to be found anywhere.

* * *

The contract for the transfer of some 13,000 bodies from the old Machpelah Cemetery, Philadelphia, has been awarded to C. A. Quimby, and it is expected that the work will have been completed in two or three months. This old burying ground was closed in 1890 by the Health Board, when the number of interments became a menace to the living. The vast majority of bodies that lie in Machpelah are to be removed to a high plot of ground, ninety acres in extent, adjoining Mount Moriah.

* * *

Locust Hill Cemetery, Dover, N. J., is carrying out some extensive and commendable improvements since the organization of the new board. It is one of the small cemeteries, some six acres, well situated, which always repay to the community in a large sense any care and improvement expended upon them. A new vault has just been constructed bearing the name of Bickley, the president of the cemetery association, above the doorway and above the name is the date "1894." The style is after the Egyptian and adds much to the appearance of the adjacent grounds.

* * *

The Lakewood Cemetery Association, Minneapolis, Minn., held its 24th annual meeting recently, when the old staff of officers were reelected. A committee was appointed to secure amendments to the state law with reference to the cemetery management and it was decided that all mounds over graves in Lakewood be eliminated as much as practical. The treasurer's report showed the receipts of the association during the past year to have been $45,202.20, and the disbursements $70,450.63 of which amount about $40,000 was applied on the payment for new lands, leaving a net gain of $15,000.

* * *

One might well be at a loss to know to what natures an advertisement worded as the following appealed. Good taste, appropriateness and every essential element have been sacrificed:

What a solace and comfort it is to know that after the trials and cares of this life are o'er, and we have been laid away in the "silent city of the dead," that there are those who will remember and mourn us, and who will erect a suitable monument to commemorate our good qualities. These pleasant thoughts help to remove the fears of death. Monuments and tombstones from $2.00 to $10,000.00. Satisfaction is guaranteed; skillful and artistic work; save you 25 per cent. Inscription cut upon and erected at grave without extra charge.

* * *

At the annual meeting of the Oakland Cemetery Association, St. Paul, Minn., the matter of securing better roads in the grounds was discussed and it was decided to do so. The receipts from all sources were $21,757.28; the expenditures for all purposes were $16,720. The perpetual care fund increased during the year $5,133.92, and now amounts to $87,116.84. Of this amount $85,500 is invested in interest bearing securities. The sale of lots has been very small during the year. Sales of lots during the year, $8,473; sales of single graves, $1,343; greenhouse sales, $3,243.77. The assets of the association include: real estate unsold, 44 3-10 acres at $5,000, $221,500; securities, investments for perpetual care fund, $84,000; buildings, fences, water service, $71,147.24. Total, $383,643.76. Liabilities include, perpetual care principal, $76,225.82; perpetual care working fund, $10,891.02. Accumulations, $296,202.92. Grand total, $386,643.72;

* * *

Late last month a local speculator of Paterson, N. J., bought at sheriff's sale 7000 square feet of the Reformed Cemetery which the city authorities had confiscated in default of payment of a sewer assessment. The area had been subdivided into building lots and the lines actually cut through individual lots and in some cases divided graves, leaving headstones on one side and footstones on the other. The purchaser claimed all monuments, tombstones and everything on the ground. This unquestionably outrageous method of the Paterson city council aroused public indignation to a high pitch, and the bravado of certain of the city fathers has rightly given way to "chills." The lot owners have retained counsel and if the city does not have to pay heavily for the ill considered action of its rulers, it would seem to be due to good fortune rather than deserts. Common sense should suggest that no law in the civilized world countenances the spoliation of graves even to pay taxes.

* * *

The death of the late Dr. James McCosh, of Princeton, N. J., draws attention to one of the oldest and most unique burying grounds of the Union, Princeton Cemetery. Near its center it holds within one little iron-railed enclosure the graves of almost all the college presidents from the beginning of the institution, which had its birth even before the dawn of the nation. There is a single tomb, however, in this curious area of God's acre which to the average American will suggest a more impressive sense of the strange mystery, strength and sorrow of life than any of the rest, for under its sacred stone lie the ashes of Aaron Burr, who once occupied the next to highest seat in the nation, and who fell to the depths of disgrace and ignominy in the hearts of his countrymen. Burr lies at the foot of his father's grave, and not far from the tomb of his grandfather, Jonathan Dickinson; and today it is best to remember him sleeping the last, long, dreamless slumber in the cemetery of the school where he passed, probably, the happiest hours of his life as a phenomenal young student.

* * *

The noted clan, the "Giant Macnabs," at one time owned the territory on the south bank of the river Dochart, Scotland, and what is now known as Kinnel house was for many centuries the principal residence of the successive chiefs. Nearly seventy years ago, however, the late Marquis of Breadalbane purchased from Colon Macnab, the then chief, the house and lands, which were thus absorbed into the Breadalbane estates. All that now remains of the old clan and their ancient patrimony is, significantly enough, the romantic little island—Inchbhuid, "beautiful island," that was for centuries the burial place of the clan, and it is a strange and not inappropriate peculiarity that in shape it resembles a coffin. Access to this interesting old place of sepulture is obtained by a steep flight of steps from Dochart bridge, near which stands, in a good state of preservation, two massive gate pillars, which at one time were surmounted by a figure of a dragon. The wall and doorways guarding the entrance to this ancient God's acre are quaint looking enough, and quite in keeping with the character of the surroundings. The island is fully two hundred yards long, by about sixty yards broad, is protected by rocks, and crowned by splendid Scotch firs of great age—although here, too, last Winter's storm has wrought sad havoc, the damage done detracting in no small degree from the picturesque appearance of the romantic old place. At the head of the avenue is an enclosure, formed by a thick high wall, in which many chiefs of the Clan Macnab and their near relations lie buried; while outside and all around repose the remains of the common clansmen.—*Philadelphia Item.*

Suggestions to Lot Owners.

BY A LOT OWNER IN LOWELL CEMETERY, MASS.

If your circumstances will not admit of depositing as large a fund as you would like for "Perpetual Care," deposit $25 or $50 and allow the deposit to accumulate. In a few years it will reach an adequate sum, you meanwhile paying yearly charges as rendered by the superintendent.

If your lot does not grow a good sod, consult with the superintendent. Perhaps there is no soil to support the sod, perhaps it has "run out." New soil and new turf may be the easy remedy.

If you have rubbish to dispose of, throw it on the carriage way. Employees will then easily gather the same. Don't throw on spaces that do not belong to you, or behind trees or banks.

Consider if there is anything more beautiful than nature itself in cemetery adornment. Is there anything prettier than the green sward? Then why break its beauty with the hideous corner post protruding above the level of the lot? It is well enough to bound your lot with markers level with the surface, but you disfigure your own lot and that of your neighbor when you do more. There is but one benefited—the stone-cutter.

Thousands of dollars are spent in the effort to produce effective stone work in our own and other cemeteries. Beautiful work is shown, but far too often is defective material used. In a short time the defects appear. You cannot be too painstaking in the selection of stock to be used.

Study for simplicity in all inscription work. The greatest indignities to the dead are to be found in burial places throughout the land, in the way of inscriptions. Much is ludicrous, some horrible, and by far too much in very bad taste. No doubt much that we read on cemetery stone work is the ingenuity and suggestions of the stone-cutter. There is only one rule—study for brevity.

If you buy stone work and pay the cutter for it, there is no reason why he should forever after share with you the surfaces for advertising purposes. The mark is for the dead, and it is not erected for the purpose of displaying the name of the enterprising dealer.

It would be well if the custom followed at the grave should be to have the cemetery authorities do all concerned with the handling of the casket and lowering into the grave. Especially should this be the case when the bearers are of advanced years.

If you have a sloping front to your lot, don't cut it for flower beds. It breaks the symmetry of the avenue, and will not look presentable without constant care.

Don't turn your carriage in an avenue. If you do the chances are that you will cut the margin turf, and if you do, it means expense.

Don't give too much weight to the sayings of sidewalk orators who see so much that is bad in the management of your corporation's affairs. If your mind is uneasy on any point, go to the president or treasurer and ascertain if the evil actually exists. If the management is inefficient the remedy is at the annual meeting, but first, be correctly informed. —*Lowell Cemetery Report.*

Correspondence.

Removal of Bodies From Unpaid Lots.

GROVE HILL CEMETERY, SHELBYVILLE, KY., Nov. 23, 1894.
Editor Modern Cemetery:

On page 101 of the November issue, I find under the head of "Removals of Bodies From Unpaid Lots," a certain judge's decision in favor of such removal. He is certainly correct in his judgment. On first taking charge of Grove Hill Cemetery, as Secretary and Superintendent, I was informed that I would have all classes of people to deal with, and human nature is more or less the same in every age. In my sixteen years experience I have found people who, after burying their dead on a lot in a cemetery, and after most solemn promises, have deferred payment and become both callous and careless, from whom no satisfaction could be got. Your correspondent *asked what to do*. Give them a written notice that if all charges are not paid in thirty days, the remains will be removed and decently buried on the ground which a committee appointed for that purpose has set apart; then place the lot in good condition for resale. This is a plan adopted here for which a saving clause is inserted in our charter. I have furnished many superintendents copies of this for revision of their charters, and we furnish lot owners with an abstract for their guidance. Before I had charge of the cemetery five or six lots were taken back and resold after notification.

Yours truly, G. W. Ricly.

St. John's Churchyard, New York.

"Good friend for Jesu' sake forbear
To dig the dust enclosed here.
Blest be the man that spares these stones,
And curs't be he that moves my bones."

I imagine the Shakespearian sentiment inspires everyone who commits the remains of loved ones to the earth.

Then what can be said for a rich corporation such as the Trinity Corporation of New York, who for "$530,000" (p. 104), or any consideration whatever, would disturb the tombs of St. John's Churchyard? It is rare enough in this country to find an old churchyard guarded by twenty-five survivors, and it is monstrous that they should be compelled to employ a lawyer. The Trinity Corporation claim not to have made any money you say. Is it their province to make money out of property which would never have existed—except for the interments? There can be no objection to throwing the property open to the public and improving it, but no grave should be desecrated, nor should a bone be moved. If this shall be permitted the whole system of interment will be violated, the sentiment of a burial place mocked, perverted, and subordinated to the commercial instincts of a corporation no one of whom you may be sure have ancestors lying in the graveyard.

I cannot imagine a gardener who would willingly advise an improvement involving the disturbance proposed. Nor do I believe the people of New York would desire it—if the facts were properly presented.

The graveyard may be acquired by the city for improvement, as any graveyard might be acquired, but it should remain a graveyard, or it would be infinitely better to adopt cremation generally.

The headstones can be laid flat either on lawns or walks, and monuments can be moved with the consent of survivors, marking the place of interment with a suitable flat slab. Where they cannot be moved, they can *usually* be worked into the design of the landscape gardener. There are hundreds of old graveyards which might be acquired by cities and improved at slight cost, without injury to the feelings of any survivor; and the purposes of a breathing place not only secured, but heightened in interest.

It seems to me that common decency would impel a body of Trustees to consult the feelings of survivors, before proceeding to desecrate the graves of their ancestors, and I say again that cremation is a better plan in a country where such Trustees are possible.

Trenton, N. J.   JAMES MACPHERSON.

The funeral of Alexander III, of Russia, must have been an extraordinary sight, especially so to citizens of Western civilization. Both in the streets of St. Petersburg and in the Cathedral, which was packed with visiting royalty, nobility and native potentates, and with tributes of all kinds and sorts, the scene must have been remarkable. There were a thousand or more wreaths in the Cathedral, besides quantities left outside. There were enormous specimens of the goldsmith's work, ten feet across and five feet high, jostling with humbler offerings of inmortelles and violets.

Notice to Cemetery Officials.

Persons desiring copies of the Philadelphia Proceedings of the convention held in that city by the Association of American Cemetery Superintendents can have them at the following rates: 25 cents for single copies, $2.50 per dozen.

In order to save time and postage please remit with order.
FRANK EURICH, Secy. and Treasurer.
Auburndale, O., Dec. 10, 1894.

Association of American Cemetery Superintendents.

O. C. SIMONDS, "Graceland," Chicago, President.
U. W. CREESY, "Harmony Grove," Salem, Mass., Vice-President.
F. EURICH, Woodlawn, Toledo, O., Secretary and Treasurer.

To Members of A. A. C. S.:
Three copies of the Philadelphia Proceedings have been mailed to each member; those who will want additional copies will please send in their orders at once and remit at the rate of $2.50 per dozen or 25 cents for single copies; six or more sent at dozen rate.   FRANK EURICH, Sec. and Treasurer.
Auburndale, O., Dec. 10, 1894.

Publisher's Department.

The receipt of Cemetery Literature and Trade Catalogues will be acknowledged in this column.

TO ADVERTISERS. THE MODERN CEMETERY is the only publication of its class and will be found a valuable medium for reaching cemetery officials in all parts of the United States.

TO SUBSCRIBERS. Cemetery officials desiring to subscribe for a number of copies regularly to circulate among their lot owners, should send for our special terms. Several well known cemeteries have already adopted this plan with good results.

Contributions on matters pertaining to cemeteries are solicited. Address all communications to
R. J. HAIGHT, 334 Dearborn St., CHICAGO.

Our readers who may wish to place their subscriptions for horticultural books or periodicals, can be supplied through the MODERN CEMETERY office, and frequently at a saving. Clubbing rates on any publication will be sent on application.

Our many readers who have promised contributions to the MODERN CEMETERY should avail themselves of the long winter evenings that are now with us, to prepare them. Contributions on any subject of general interest to cemetery workers will be appreciated.

Cemetery officials should send for specimen pages of the new Record of Interment and Improved Lot Book before making changes in their system of keeping records. The method adopted in these books is recommended by leading cemetery officials. The publisher will mail specimen pages on receipt of request.

It is to be regretted that the photographer who took the group of cemetery superintendents at Harleigh Cemetery, has failed to fill his order. It has entailed upon Mr. Rhedemeyer considerable inconvenience and no little annoyance. As he is in no way responsible for the photographer, he is certainly entitled to due and proper consideration.

Received. From R. K. Wood, secretary, By-Laws and rules of the Los Angeles, Cal., Cemetery Association, proprietor of the "Evergreen Cemetery." The pamphlet contains the history of the cemetery.—By-Laws, Rules and Regulations, and Acts of Assembly of St. John, N. B., Rural Cemetery. Mr. Joshua P. Clayton, Supt., besides several of the forms used by the management, also sends us three winter scenes in the cemetery.—By-Laws, Rules and Regulations of Fair Lawn Cemetery, Prattsville, N. Y.

THE MODERN CEMETERY.

THE MODERN CEMETERY.
AN ILLUSTRATED MONTHLY JOURNAL DEVOTED TO THE INTEREST OF CEMETERIES

R. J. HAIGHT, Publisher,
334 Dearborn Street, CHICAGO.

Subscription $1.00 a Year in Advance.   Foreign Subscription $1.25.
Special Rates on Six or More Copies.

VOL. IV.   CHICAGO, JAN'Y 1895.   NO. 11.

CONTENTS.

THE USE AND ABUSE OF BOULDER MONUMENTS 121
EMBALMING AS A SANITARY MEASURE........................ 122
DRY RUBBLE FOUNDATIONS.. 123
"FALL AT GRACELAND, CHICAGO.................................. 123
CEMETERY GREENHOUSES.. 12
SOME RIGHTS OF OFFICIALS OF CEMETERY ASSOCIA-
  TIONS—"OAKWOOD CEMETERY, AUSTIN, MINN. 127
*THE G. P. MORISINI MAUSOLEUM, WOODLAWN 129
CEMETERY NOTES... 130
CEMETERY REPORTS.—TREES AND SHRUBS.—THE
  LAWN.. 131
CREMATION... 131
PUBLISHER'S DEPARTMENT... 132
*Illustrated.

The Use and Abuse of Boulder Monuments.

In many of our cemeteries, especially in the east, the use of natural boulders for memorial purposes is becoming quite common, and within certain limitations and with surroundings inviting the use of such natural monuments, many appropriate effects have resulted. The example so set in the use of such memorials, has, however, had the tendency to create a "fad," if we might term it so, and we find very many instances reported of persons making long and expensive journeys into favorite localities to discover boulders and rocks to meet their desires. One instance at hand is that of the transportation of a twenty ton boulder ten miles in Indiana for a cemetery memorial. Another where a citizen of Ohio traveled to Rhode Island to search for a satisfactory boulder on the beach at Quonochontaug, and went to the expense of getting it home.

The original idea clinging to the boulder for memorial purposes was that of ruggedness or stability, and such memorials have frequently been chosen to perpetuate the names of men whose local or public character created this general impression, and in such cases nothing more appropriate as memorials could be found. But this granted, even then comes in the important question as to whether the spot to be thus marked will detract from the monument, or the monument impair the natural characteristics of the ground, and the whole value of the project thus be ruined. So that under the most favorable circumstances the cemetery authorities should exercise their prerogatives in the admission of such a class of memorials.

But it has come to pass that the "fad" before suggested has grown so rapidly that there is eminent danger of the beautiful idea being overwhelmed in the demand for boulder monuments, and our cemeteries dotted with unmeaning stones, having no significance whatever but that of thoughtless "copyism."

But the evil has gone farther than this, for the impossibility of supplying natural boulders to meet the demand has resulted in the manufacturers supplying quantities of what is called rock face work, which, in the majority of cases, is the poorest possible substitute for mother natures handiwork. That rock face work can be produced in large masses to, in a certain measure, simulate natural cleavage and fracture, may be admitted, but it is actually practically impossible to do so in the smaller class of monuments, so that the general result will be, if not checked by common sense or cemetery management, a continued degradation to memorial art.

A cemetery either besprinkled with boulder stones or recklessly ornamented with so-called rock face work, will very shortly find itself loaded with the responsibility of reform, to meet the enlightened taste happily rapidly engrafting itself on our institutions, and which should be even now the governing principle of our cemetery management.

The use of the boulder for memorial purposes, after all, loses nearly all its value, divorced from the idea with which it has usually been associated. To the ordinary being there is no beauty in a boulder, and as we all know, in localities where they abound, they are usually an abomination to man. To a person of a searching, enquiring nature the boulder is enveloped with a wealth of information, and carries locked up in its ruggedness secrets only to be revealed to the seekers after natures facts and processes.

To commemorate man after he has passed away, the boulder, held to represent certain qualities and characteristics, if appropriate is unique, and fills a place no other memorial very well can; but used inappropriately and without due regard to all the conditions involved, both as to man and the cemetery, it is only a huge stone, and very likely to be a blot on the landscape.

Embalming as a Sanitary Measure.*

For years we have been embalming bodies with the one object in view of preserving them. To-day we add to this a more important object, and that is to destroy contagious and infectious diseases, and protect the living. All over the world scientists are much interested on the subject of sanitation, and they are devoting more time to the question of diseases and their germs, than to any other subject now before the people. It is a subject which we must study if we wish to understand what we are doing when we embalm the bodies of the dead. We are at the present time asking for legislation to protect in the science in which we are engaged, and in order to secure such legislation we must show that we are qualified to properly and intelligently do the work entrusted to our care. While it is important that a body should be preserved, it is still more important that the living, and especially those who come in contact with the dead, should be protected against the germs of infectious and contagious diseases.

In all infectious and contagious diseases we have to deal with some of the smallest forms of plant life, called bacteria. These are micro-organisms, which are present in the body, the air, and water. They are classified to some extent only, as they are not all thoroughly understood, but they have been classified enough to know that some live on live tissue, called parasitic germs, while others live on dead matter, and are called saprophytic germs.

Among the latter are those that the embalmer must destroy when decomposition takes place, while in infection and contagion he must understand how to reach and destroy the parasitic germs.

That we can destroy these parasitic germs by the chemicals which we use in embalming is a positive fact. With the aid of the microscope, we learn that we have two forms of development; one by simple division, and the other by what is called sporing, the mother cell containing a daughter cell, and these developments take place in the living subject at the normal temperature of the body generally. To prepare cultures for laboratory use, some of these germs are put into a propagating medium, usually an extract of beef-bouillon, with which we may mix gelatine or agar-agar, or on a sliced boiled potato, these media having the elements on which these micro-organisms live. To properly develop them in these, it is necessary that they be kept at the temperature of the living body. After death, when the temperature of the body falls to that of the surrounding air, these germs cease to develop, but they do not die, and are present either in themselves or in the spore. * * *

I call attention to this fact, because from it we can demonstrate that these germs, even though they have stopped developing, if brought into contact with a propagating medium with the necessary temperature, will again assume vitality. * * *

As acids will destroy some of these germs, we take advantage of that fact by making use of them in embalming fluids. Still, they cannot be depended on entirely, as experiments have proven that the spores of anthrax will withstand the action of a 5 per cent. solution, it is necessary to use something more effective. There are many chemical agencies which prevent the development of germs and destroy them, as well as the spores, but the principal one used all over the world, and always in the laboratory of the bacteriologist, is bi-chloride of mercury, which, in a solution of one in a thousand, is an absolute destroyer of all germs.

The next question is, as to how we can reach these germs, as in different diseases the germs are found in different portions and organs of the body. In septicæmia and anthrax they are found in the blood; in diphtheria, in the membrane of the throat, and in typhoid fever, in the spleen, lympathics, and intestines.

In scarlet fever they are supposed to be only on the surface of the skin. * * *

It is the duty of the embalmer to understand how to absolutely destroy these germs. We have two ways of doing this: By the direct application of our antiseptics on the parts infected, or by injecting them into the arterial system.

In the circulation of the blood through the system, we have everything to favor us in doing thorough work. While the blood can only flow in one direction through the veins, we have in the arteries a system in which circulation can be had in both ways, either to or from the heart. We have in these arteries and their capillaries a way of reaching every portion of the body, and should there be a blood clot, or any other cause to impede the flow of the fluid through any branch of this system, the circulation is still made complete by the anastomosis of the vessels in all parts of the body. We are on this account absolutely sure of reaching at least every portion of the body outside of the organs.

Should it so happen that an infected organ should not receive the injection of the antiseptic fluid, say, for instance, the spleen, in typhoid fever, we are still surrounded by other tissues that are in-

---

*Extracts from a paper read before the National Association of Funeral Directors, by W. P. Hohenschuh.

jected, that it would be impossible for the germs to pass out of the body in any way without being destroyed. * * * * *

Study and learn where to look for these dangerous germs. Know that to destroy them they must be brought in contact with the proper antiseptics. With this knowledge at your command, there can be no doubt but what the embalmer can do much toward the stamping out of infectious and contagious diseases.

Dry Rubble Foundations.

In a former article on foundations for monuments, attention was called to the fact that different characters of foundations might be required for different classes of superstructure, and that specifications for each should be adopted. Local conditions will suggest where to draw the line between these different classes of work. There is a certain small class of work which may be set upon what may be designated as dry rubble. Such, however, should never be used on a yielding soil under a load of more than one-fourth of a ton per square foot, or under a job standing more than four or five times its *narrowest width of base* in height.

Dry rubble should have a footing one-half greater than its upper bearing face, which face should be double the area of the surmounting superstructure. The bottom of the pit should be evenly graded to an even natural soil bed. No stone should be permitted in any part of the foundation exceeding in its greatest dimension one-fourth the least dimension of said foundation.

All stone larger than common course gravel must be broken so as to have an angular form that will interlock and hold position.

The largest stone should be placed in the bottom and otherwise evenly distributed in courses throughout the work. After the first course is placed in the bottom, fine sand and chips small enough to fill in all the interstices shall be lightly spread over and thoroughly washed in by a stream of water. When the course refuses to receive any more fine filling and an even surface is made, another course of larger stone may be laid and the same process of filling and washing in is repeated, and the whole procedure continued until a sufficient height has been attained to receive the bedding stone or concrete on which the base is to rest

The proper drenching in of fine clean stuff is the important part in securing a comparatively solid mass, and in the which each stone is so embedded as to prevent any change in its position, thus ensuring the rigidity of the entire mass. The whole foundation must be given time for the water to drain out carrying each particle that can be moved to its place, before work on the *superstructure* is carried on.

No coping, marker, or other stone should be set without some such foundation as described above.

J. C. U.

Fall at Graceland, Chicago.

It so happens that I have never seen Graceland in the Spring, but I can say with as much truth as enthusiasm that it is a right royal place in the fall.

How much better that name is than Autumn. What does Autumn mean? It is a word for those who strive after fine language! Fall, has a meaning—the season of the falling leaf, it is poetic and satisfying.

Even at Graceland there are too many stones, but in the parts of the grounds where control in this matter is exercised, they are neither numerous nor intrusive enough to spoil the landscape effects. And what fine effects they are! Beautiful in line and in boldness of mass, as well as in the combinations of foliage that are so telling. As, for instance, distant billowy masses of Royal Willows, blue in tone; in the middle distance, clumps of rich crimson, scarlet sumachs; and in the foreground, fantastic little Pepperidge trees all aflame in their lighter colored garments. Seen thus at a glance, the coloring almost takes ones breath.

Probably there is not a more effective bit of planting in the country than that around the larger pond. In October it is a gem set in a rim of shaded Carnelian. The border is not continuous, and it is artistically varied in height and breadth—but the general effect is of an enclosing rim of color, brought about by the extensive and admirable use of a common shrub—just plain Dogwood in two or three varieties. Other shrubs and small trees are used, but they are introduced in such a way as not to interfere with the October color effect. The illustration, "A waterside tomb," gives a good view of part of this planting. One feels that if there must be a tomb, this is the way it should be placed and treated—at least, one of the few satisfactory ways. It gains much from its happy situation, and the tasteful planting. Yet if I am not mistaken, some one interested in this very tomb has asked that some of the "brush" be cleared away. Brush! But there is unspeakable satisfaction in the thought that such sacrilege will never be permitted. It is the surroundings that make the place seem more like a temple than a tomb.

This illustration is a fair example of the art that prevails in the planting, not only around the pond, but throughout Graceland. The touch of a hand that has mastered the use of its chosen medium is recognizable. This complete, and apparently easy

A WATERSIDE TOMB.— GRACELAND CEMETERY, CHICAGO.

control of material is, in this case, partly due to the large use made of native shrubs that were bound to thrive from the outset, because they were acclimated and in their accustomed environment.

By using well chosen native shrubs for the basis of various plantations, good, inexpensive and quick results may be depended on in any given locality, if practical knowledge is available for the work of transplanting, and taste for the correct grouping. And with such a foundation it should not be difficult to add less common or even rare hardy shrubs year by year, providing always that provision is made in the original plan for such additions. But Mr. Simonds goes to the wilds not only for tangible raw material, but for inspiration. Every happy combination of tree, shrub, vine and herbaceous plant is an object lesson of which he makes mental note. Sometimes he even transports the object lesson bodily, and naturalizes it in some sylvan nook of Graceland, where it feels so much at home that it goes right along making itself beautiful in undisturbed serenity; as witness a small oak tree, its crimson foliage partly smothered by the fresh leaves of a vigorous Bitter-sweet vine that makes a green tent all about its trunk. This was seen in a woodland drive and brought home in triumph.

Of course one may not expect to often find portable object lessons ready at hand; but suggestions abound, and happy the man who can see, appreciate and grasp them.

Taste can transform a mud puddle into a lovely pool; a stone pile into a picturesque rockery, it can see and seize the possibilities in sandy, tree grown ridges alternating with damp, swamp like depressions such as lie both to the north and the south of Chicago, and, making the most of each natural advantage as well as of each seeming defect, produce a fine general effect. Just as the late Dion Boucicault had the art to make his defective eye an actual advantage.

In fact, taste can take *any* material at hand and evolve from it something else, that, without losing the spirit of the original scene, will be more beautiful. Could planting for cemetery purposes be more practical or more pleasing than that shown in our illustration, "A peaceful glade." The grouping of trees and shrubs is admirable. The planting beautifies every lot, and fortunately, the graves, mostly level with the surrounding lawns, are located by unobtrusive markers.

The glade is delightful as a picture and idyllic as a loitering place.

But the attractions here are manifold, and there is much to be learned from them. One learns, for instance, how much better and artistic in most locations irregular belts of shrubbery are than formal hedges. There is a screening belt of Japan Quinces that must be a glorious mass of color in the Spring; others of Barberry, now hung with heavy fringes of long, coral colored berries, so lovely! Again it is the graceful Indian currant, its slender, drooping sprays set closely in fall with round red berries that, while not as showy as some other ornamental fruits, are yet pleasing; and at all seasons this little shrub is good, because of its graceful habit, sweeping in wide curves quite to the ground on all sides. It is pretty either in hedges, belts, groups, or grown singly. In the south, this plant is known as Buck Bush, and a writer in a recent number of *Garden and Forest*, says that the name is said to be due to the fondness of wild deer for its fruit.

The fall color combinations at Graceland are endless. Dogwoods, (largely *Cornus stolonifera* and *C. paniculata*), show crimson against the brownish red of the Blue Beech, or Silver Poplar in their cool, gray-blue foliage; a Prickly Ash draped with a wild grape is charming; clumps of gorgeous little Pepperidge trees are seen to the best advantage against the rich feathery green of Cutleaf Alders—the latter being one of the most attractive trees I know, and appropriate in every way for use in small grounds.

But if there was nothing else to make fall interesting in these grounds, the ornamental fruits would be enough.

My favorite among the many fruiting trees and shrubs seen there this fall was a symmetrical English White Oak, *Quercus pedunculata*, its small well shaped leaves as green as in June, and bearing a full crop of medium sized, exquisitely shaped acorns, on flexible stems, two or three inches in length—quite unlike any other oak I know, and a perfect beauty.

The most showy among them was a fair sized Thorn Apple tree, heavily laden with fruit that is midway in size, shape, color and flavor between an ordinary Siberian Crab apple and a large hip of Rosa Rugosa—the fruit of which, if I am not mistaken, is much darker in color than that of R. rugosa alba. The fruit, though edible, is of inferior quality. Then there were Buckthorns that bear inconspicuous flowers, followed by smooth, round, and very black berries, thickly massed along the twigs; and one of the Dogwoods that bears cymes of white berries; and open groups of Sweet Briar starred all over with bright little hips after having blossomed, and shed refreshing perfume from every leaf since earliest spring. Sweet Briar is a surprising shrub, so frail and dainty, yet so hardy and trustworthy.

Also there were white banks of Snowberries—the whitest, I believe, of all ornamental fruits; and its modest and always pleasing relative, the Indian Currant, with dark crimson berries rather dull in shade, but pretty nevertheless; and Sweet Viburnum, *V. lentago*, its fruits growing singly, each half an inch long, first green, then scarlet, and finally blue-black and covered with a glaucus bloom. These, too, are edible. And there were Barberries,

A PEACEFUL GLADE.—GRACELAND CEMETERY, CHICAGO.

both the common and the purple leaved varieties, the first loaded every fall with slender oval fruits that depend from slim twigs like fringe; also the pretty Spirea Thunbergii, with shining red berries, as well as numerous sharp thorns; and Winterberry with brilliantly polished scarlet ones.

A bouquet of all these fruits is doubly attractive if interspersed with sprays of glossy, reddish bronze leaves of Mahonia; and the same shrub is a useful and beautiful addition to hardy borders.

FANNY COPLEY SEAVEY.

Cemetery Greenhouses.

The cultivation of flowering and ornamental plants is encouraged, or tolerated, as the case may be, in almost every cemetery in the land.

Some few there are who advocate their total exclusion from the modern cemetery, but this is hardly worth consideration at the present time.

The opinion has frequently been advanced, and stoutly maintained, that hardy plants alone are suitable for cemetery planting. How we prick up our ears at the word "hardy." What a seductive sound it has! What visions arise before us! We have to but exchange a few paltry dollars for some of the wondrous things advertised in the list of hardy plants, go forth with our spade, put them in the ground, and without further care or toil on our part, they will become things of beauty and joys forever. But alas and alas! The lily toils not, neither does it spin, but the gardener must toil mightily, would he have it bloom at its best, and all his toil in these days of the lily disease is more than likely to end in disappointment.

Of the published lists of hardy plants, more than one half of them are worthless for our purpose—valuable possibly for massing in broad landscape effects, but for close scrutiny—weeds. Of the remainder, many are not reliably hardy, except in the most favorable locations. Our list is at once reduced to quite modest dimensions. If we then strike off all those which are too tall, too rank in growth, too much inclined to spread and sucker, too slow in reaching maturity, too scant or uncertain of bloom, or whose period of bloom is too short, we have but a handful left, and of them all there is not one with so many sterling qualities as the much villified geranium, to say nothing of a dozen other tender plants.

The writer would not be understood as decrying the use of hardy plants. Many of them are indispensable, but they should not be used when better results can be obtained with those which are not hardy.

The great saving in expense is another argument strongly advanced in favor of hardy plants. Any one who has had the care of a large collection of hardy plants, who has fertilized them, cultivated them, tied, pruned and staked them, dressed them for cold weather and undressed them in spring, who has endeavored to guard them against those terrible instruments of destruction, the lawn mower and the steel rake; any one, we say, who has nursed the sick, replaced the dead ones and secured the best results for a number of years, will find it hard to see when any great saving is made. Recognizing, then, the fact that plants are used, and that they will continue to be used, the question of interest to all having the care of cemeteries, large or small, is how can the planting best be regulated; how can the evils with which we are all so familiar, in this connection, be abolished, and the proper use of plants be encouraged.

The adoption of proper and judicious rules and restrictions will do much, but the workings of the human mind are past comprehension, and the number of hideous schemes of planting and discordant color combinations which can be evolved to come within the letter of the best set of rules, is infinite. The most artistic plans may result in any but a desirable way, if the mechanical part of the work is improperly done, or the individual requirements of the plants used are not provided for, points very difficult to reach by rules.

Let the cemetery be equipped with proper greenhouses, supply the plants, do the planting and provide subsequent care, and the difficulty is at once greatly lessened. The lot owner is forced to consult the superintendent or gardener before the work is commenced, and before he has bargained for, or perhaps paid out his money for something undesirable. If, then, the superintendent is possessed of a reasonable amount of tact, (and he needs it, of all men), it becomes, in most cases, a simple matter to guide the lot owner's footsteps in the way they should go. The average man, or woman, relies largely on the advice of the one from whom the plants are bought, and it makes a great difference in the result whether the adviser is interested in the general good appearance of the cemetery, or only interested in disposing of surplus stock on the best terms possible. (If the plants do not do well, it is so easy to charge it to the lack of care on the part of the cemetery management).

The gain in quality of the work done and the bringing the management in closer touch with the lot owners would alone amply justify us in considering the greenhouse an essential part of the modern cemetery, but there are many other advantages besides.

A well managed greenhouse, no matter how small, adds greatly to the attractiveness of the cemetery in the eyes of the average man and woman, and we must not forget that it is the average man who owns most of the lots in our cemeteries.

The average man is oftener right than, perhaps, we think he is; at any rate, his wishes, as he foots the bills, are entitled at all times to careful consideration, and when there is doubt, we should always give him the benefit of it.

The greenhouse can be not only made a material source of revenue to the cemetery, but at the same time, in nearly all cases, the work can be cheapened to the lot owner.

The greater part of the work in the greenhouse comes at a time when there is little to do outside, and in growing bedding plants, the ordinary hands kept for outside work can put in their spare time to advantage. A moderate amount of planting, in a somewhat formal manner, at the entrance to the cemetery or in connection with the buildings, if judiciously done, adds much to the general effect. The greenhouse will supply the material at a trifling expense.

A small greenhouse or conservatory, from which perfectly satisfactory results may be had, can be built and equipped at the present time so cheaply that no cemetery need be without some form of glass house. While a competent gardener is a valuable man in any cemetery, and a necessity when extensive glass houses are operated, yet the lack of such a man or inability to meet the expense of employing him, need deter no one from putting up a small conservatory and cultivating a few of the commoner and easiest handled bedding and flowering plants. Any man of fair intelligence, and having a love for flowers, can by a little care and study get surprisingly good results, if the beginning is on a small scale. Of course he must creep before he can walk.

A final and not unimportant point in favor of the greenhouse as a part of the cemetery equipment, is that it enables the management to exclude from the grounds all outside workmen except the monument setter. When the millenium comes, perhaps we can abolish him also.

WILLIS N. RUDD.

Some Rights of Officials of Cemetery Associations.

In an action for libel, where the publication made the basis of the suit, falsely charged, in effect, that the secretary of a cemetery association had embezzled funds, it was recently held by the supreme court of Nebraska that the law presumed him to be innocent of the crime; that it presumed the publisher was actuated with a malicious intent; and that the party suffered some damages thereby, so that no proof of actual injury by reason of the publication was necessary to entitle him to recover damages, the amount of which would, however, have to be determined by the jury. The trial court charged in this case that a cemetery association, organized under the general laws of the state, was a private corporation, and that the corporation, its officers and servants, had the same and equal immunity and protection from criticism that a private individual possessed, and that the publisher of any newspaper, who published a criticism of and concerning the officers and servants of a private corporation, was responsible to the same extent for such criticism as though it had been published of and concerning a private individual. This is upheld by the supreme court, which further declares that the secretary of a cemetery association organized under the incorporation law of Nebraska is not a public officer, in such a sense as to enable the publisher of a newspaper to claim that an article published concerning him, and charging him with embezzling the funds of such cemetery association, is a privileged communication, and thus compel such secretary, in an action for libel, to prove express malice.

Oakwood Cemetery, Austin, Minn.

The Association owning Oakwood Cemetery, Austin, Minn., is the out-growth and successor of a rather peculiar combination, the old cemetery being partly the property of an association and partly that of a private individual.

The methods by which this reorganization was brought about, may be of interest in other locations where there is need of such action.

As it seemed difficult to interest the business men of the place in the matter, the ladies formed a club, having for its objects the beautifying of the cemetery, and the establishment of a library and reading room; it is sufficient to say that their efforts have been fully successful; as one of the present cemetery officials put it, "the men folks had to take hold of it to keep peace in the family."

The old cemeteries being well filled some new land adjoining on the north was purchased, and as it was decided that the time had come to abandon the old "checker board" system which prevailed in the old division for the modern lawn plan, the designing and preparing plans for the addition was entrusted to Messrs. Arthur W. Hobert, Superintendent of Lakewood Cemetery, and Frank H. Nutter, Landscape Architect, both of Minneapolis, Minn., and the results are seen on the accompanying map.

The tract shown comprises an area of about thirteen acres, situated about one mile north-west from the center of the city, and has a gently rolling surface, sloping gradually from the highway to the

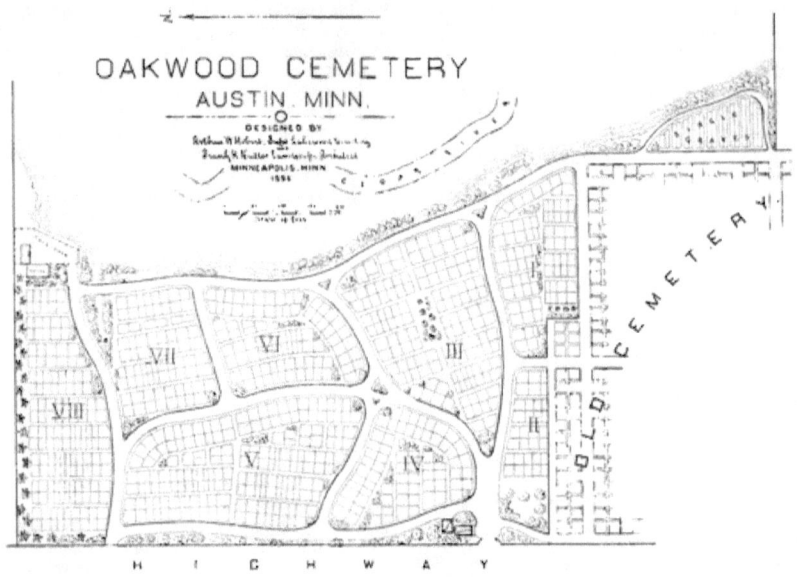

top of a steep bluff some fifteen feet in height, at the foot of which is a wooded swamp, through which winds a small stream, known as the Cedar River.

As economy of construction and maintenance was of prime importance and surface drainage for the present at least, the only reliance, the drives were laid in conformity with the surface of the ground, in such a manner that the deepest cut is only about two feet, and the greatest fill only about half that.

In subdividing the sections the lots are of a uniform depth of twenty feet, while the frontages are either nine, twelve, fifteen, eighteen or twenty feet, to meet the varying needs of purchasers. It will be observed that these different sizes are well mingled, by which two ends are accomplished; it obviates a too monotonous succession of monuments and markers, and prevents the establishment of a "cheap" section which results when all the small lots are grouped together.

Although the north half of the property is well wooded and fine specimen trees of the burr oak are scattered over a portion of the rest, the unplatted corners and other vacant spaces in the sections are proposed to be devoted to ornamental shrubberies, as are the sides of a ravine in section seven, with also an occasional group along the bluff; while on the north side an evergreen screen will shut off both the cold winds and a rather disagreeable outlook.

The portion of the plateau to the east of the old cemetery is devoted to single graves, and in view of future needs, locations are suggested for Gate Lodge, Receiving Tomb, and Tool Yard and Sheds.

Grades have been established over the whole tract that there may be no unconsidered problems arise in the matter of drainage, and in the spring it is proposed to complete a sufficient portion in the south part of the cemetery to meet the demands for several years to come.

The present officers of the Association are: J. S. Decker, President; T. F. Leonard, Secretary; C. A. Pooler, Actuary and Geo. Baird, Treasurer.

A bill to regulate the practice of embalming and undertaking has just passed both houses of the legislature in Alabama. California was the first state to pass such an act, but it was vetoed by the governor. The same fate attended the New York law, but that of Virginia became a law last year, and the MODERN CEMETERY at that time gave its chief provisions. The Alabama bill is very similar, in fact, almost identical with that of Virginia. The board of examiners is to be appointed on May 1st, whose duty it will be to examine all persons now in the business, and those intending to enter it, and after September 1st, it will be unlawful to practice embalming without a license in places of 1,500 inhabitants or over in that state.

The G. P. Morosini Mausoleum, Woodlawn Cemetery, New York.

The mausoleum stands on a lot about 75 feet in diameter. It is in the form of a Greek cross, 25 feet square, architecturally in the Byzantine style, and of a total height of 35 feet. The external material is Westerly, R. I., red granite of fine quality, finished in hammered effect. The sides of the structure are pierced by windows of green veined, white marble, the grille of the main window over the doors being of the same material, while the rear window is in stained glass with a grille of rich yellow bronze. The interior is adorned with some of the finest examples of Florentine mosaic work, the design of the floor and the ceiling is beautiful in colored marble. It is of cruciform shape, and a pendentive ceiling above the catacombs, supported by four columns, is composed of mosaic of Venetian marble made in Venice. The four columns composing this vaulted ceiling are carved from Cippolino marble, an Italian stone noted for its beautiful creamy tint and violet and green veins. The building contains ten catacombs, four being placed on either side of the central hall, and two beneath the rear window. The faces of these catacombs are of fine Venetian work. The caps of the four columns are of statuary marble, harmonizing with the general artistic tone of the interior, and formed after four different models, the floors and capitals being adapted from the motive of the design of St. Mark's, Venice. The bronze doors, cast by the Henry-Bonnard Co., of New York, are eighty-four inches high by thirty-six inches wide, of right and left design. The doors and framework are of heavy bronze, and the lintel bears the date MDCCCXCIV. Above this the polished granite lintel has the name G. P. Morosini. The underlying pattern of the doors is geometric in design, with smooth panels alternating with fruit and flowers. The dome is composed of four monolithic stones, the largest being thirteen feet six inches in diameter. Recesses are provided in the vestibule between the bronze doors and the cruciform centre for statuary. In the main doors there are small casement windows of heavy plate glass, with a grille of bronze to allow for the circulation of air, which is further enhanced by the rear window being hung on lateral pivots. There is also an aperture leading up through the interior of the dome, with vents under the foliated work of the finial. The architects are Messrs. Jardine, Kent & Jardine, New York. The cost of the building has been $50,000, and the work has been carried out under contract with the New England Monument Company.

MAUSOLEUM FOR G. P. MOROSINI, ESQ., AT WOODLAWN.—JARDINE, KENT & JARDINE, ARCHITECTS, NEW YORK.

CEMETERY NOTES.

The authorities of the Vale Cemetery of Schenectady, N.Y., have prohibited public funerals on Sunday.

* * *

Portland, Me., is to have a new cemetery, under a private association. The cemetery will be situated at Deering Centre, and will contain about 60 acres.

* * *

The city fathers of Flint, Mich., recently decided that they had no jurisdiction on the matter of the establishment of new burial grounds within the city limits.

* * *

At the funeral of a woman in Baltimore, Md., some time since, six women attired in black acted as pall-bearers. With the exception of a priest, not a man officiated at the ceremony. —*Sunnyside*.

* * *

Mr. Rufus Howe, the oldest native resident of Marlboro, Mass., died suddenly recently, aged ninety-two. He was a market gardener, and had been superintendent of Mount Auburn Cemetery for many years.

* * *

A bequest of money to put the cemetery of the Vincent Baptist Church in good order, and furnish headstones for those who have never had anything to mark their resting places, was made by the late Silas Evans, of East Vincent township, Pa. A contract for some 200 headstones has been let.

* * *

The directors of Mountain Grove Cemetery at Bridgeport, Conn., will probably begin an era of improvement in that cemetery early in the spring, which will possibly absorb some $25,000. These improvements will include the macadamising of the principal drives, which have been badly abused by a general traffic, and the erection of a handsome arch entrance. Other improvements will go on simultaneously.

* * *

Cold marble is too perishable and insignificant to longer serve for monumental purposes. The only fitting monument of the noble is something that will house an idea, foster souls, and develop love. The richest men can hardly preserve their names on earth with costly monuments and extensive estates. But the world will not permit the name of him who founds a library, causes a park to be made for man, or helping a church to thrive, to pass from the minds of men.—*Unity*.

* * *

A new cemetery, to be called Wildwood Cemetery, containing some 240 acres, will add to the list of Detroit, Mich., cemeteries. It is located about nine miles from the City Hall, and is picturesquely situated, the Rouge river running through it, and the landscape is rolling and drainage good. A. C. Varney, architect, has in charge a $10,000 chapel, and a vault will be built with a capacity of 50 bodies. The spot offers grand facilities for landscape work, and improvements are to begin in earnest in the spring. The company is capitalized at $200,000.

* * *

Among the many unmarked graves at Oak Hill Cemetery, Washington, so far as monumental art is concerned is that of James G. Blaine. A small foot stone with the initials J. G. B., marks the precise spot where the remains repose, but to the large number of pilgrims visiting the grave, a blasted hickory tree is the most telling sign post. At the death of his favorite son, Walker Blaine, Mr. Blaine purchased a lot in this cemetery, and when soon after he was called upon to bury his daughter, he bought the adjoining lot on which this fine old hickory stood. It was in a somewhat shabby condition, having been struck by lightning, but the statesman expressed a wish that it should be taken care of as he would like it to mark his resting place, and so it stands, care having restored its vitality which bids fair to sustain it as long as the other fine trees in the cemetery.

* * *

Dr. George Francis, who died last month in Alameda, Cal., was cremated a few days later without any religious services whatever. A codicil in his will relieved his friends of their surprise and shows that the deceased thought that the preparation by the undertakers for the grave was a disgusting proceeding, and he therefore forbade his body being washed, or that his clothes be changed, and directed that all unnecessary expense be avoided after his demise; that there be no religious ceremony whatever, and that his body be cremated as soon after death as possible.

* * *

To show what the women can do by organization, in the matter of improving rural cemeteries, the history of Glendale Cemetery, Akron, O., gives an excellent example. In 1837, the town council put the project on its feet, and some 8 acres were secured. It now contains 58 acres. For several years it remained unfenced, and the sexton was superintendent. In 1850, the city transferred rights and title to the Akron Rural Cemetery Association. In 1866, several prominent women organized an association to assist in beautifying the cemetery, of which Mrs. Evans, a woman devoted to the cause, was president until her death in 1869. Under her active work the entrance lodge was built, and much work of improvement accomplished. She bequeathed her energy to her associates who, since her death, have raised and expended over $20,000 in adding to the beauties of the cemetery. The ladies' association appears to be as active as ever, and is on the war path for funds for further improvements and renovations.

* * *

In Loudon Park Cemetery, Baltimore, an elaborate monument has just been completed for Mr. John F. Wiessner. The structure rests on a bed of Portland cement concrete two feet thick and twenty feet square. On this is built a foundation of hard brick laid in cement, in which are set heavy copper anchor bolts. The height of the monument is fifty feet and consists of four main divisions, viz: The base, the surbase, the pedestal and the pedestal proper, forming the top division and supporting a colossal figure of Hope. The base, of Beaver Dam marble is sixteen feet square, and consists of four monolithic plinths, from the diagonal angles of which spring four huge consoles, forty feet high, with steps between, each carrying pedestals supporting recumbent draped figures of Grief. The surbase is eight feet square and eleven feet high, boldly molded and reinforced by circular buttresses at the angles based upon the tops of the consoles. It is crowned by a rich cornice and frieze. On each side central between the molded bases of the buttresses, are sheafs of wheat cut in full relief. The pedestal is seven feet square and twelve feet high. It has four niches flanked by pilasters with molded bases and carved capitals, spandrils and keystones. At each of the exterior angles are detached circular columns supporting a heavily molded entablature, with cinerary urns over each column. At the base of the niches are elaborately carved corbels for the support of four life-size statues—that on the front or west side representing the Angel of the Resurrection, on the south side Faith, on the east side the Recording Angel, on the north side Resignation. All the statues were cut in Italy. The pedestal is four feet square at the base and fourteen feet high, the base and capital richly molded and carved. The die block, a stone three feet square and five feet high, is sculptured with festoons of drapery in graceful folds, and its capital is crowned by the figure of Hope nearly nine feet high. The monument was designed by Hugh Sisson & Sons, Geo. A. Frederick, architect.

Cemetery Reports.

The annual report of the Mount Royal Cemetery, Montreal, Canada, for the year ending Nov. 30th, 1894, shows that considerable improvement was done during the year, and that the perpetual care system received much encouragement from proprietors of lots under old tenure deeds. The general receipts for the year, with balance from 1893, were $31,622.86, and disbursements $28,718.92. Number of interments 1376. The invested funds of the cemetery amount to $35,206.09.

* * *

The annual meeting of the Riverside Cemetery Association, Cleveland, Ohio, has been held and the report published. A bonded indebtedness of $70,000 has been discharged, and the Association has now also cash and book account assetts of over $20,000. The total receipts for the year ending Nov. 30th, 1894 of $23,138.64 include $17,858.74 for lot accounts and $2,712.40 for interments and receiving tomb fees. The total disbursements, including $41,000 for redemption of balance of outstanding bonds amounted to $31,463.36. The old officers were re-elected and in his report the president strongly urged the formation of a fund looking to the perpetual care of the cemetery.

* * *

The annual report of the Oakland Cemetery Association, St. Paul, Minn., gives receipts from all sources $21,757.28 and total expenditures $16,720. The increase in the perpetual care fund for the year ending October 31st, 1894, was $5,133.92 and the aggregate of these funds $87,116.84. The amount received by sale of lots for the year was $8,473.00 and for single graves $1,343.00. Interment and tomb fees amounted to $2,686.00. Greenhouse sales were $3,243.77. The expenditure for labor for the year was $8,384.46. The work of improvement was restricted by reason of the comparatively small sales of lots and an unusually expensive season.

Reconveyance of Lots in Trust.—An important subject that should be carefully considered by every lot owner, is that of securing the undisturbed interment of himself and family by rendering it impossible for his heirs at law, induced by poverty or cupidity, to remove their bodies and dispose of the lot, which has been done in several instances. This can be accomplished by reconveying the same to the Corporation, to be held by it in perpetual trust for the permanent interment of himself and such others as may be designated by him. This reconveyance does not deprive the owner of any privileges he enjoys as lot owner; does not prevent him from making any improvements on his lot, erecting monuments or headstones, or enjoying a sense of ownership. In fact, the ownership is secured to himself and those dear to him, beyond all danger of alienation or desecration forever.—*Uniondale Cemetery, Allegheny, Pa.*

Trees and Shrubs.--The Lawn.

Go around among your trees and shrubs and mark all that you wish to cut down or root out, says Mr. Falconer, in *Gardening*. You can do this rooting out better now than later on, because so far there is very little frost in the ground, hence you can do the work more expeditiously than you can in mid-winter, don't leave anything of this sort till the spring for then between planting, grading, and fixing up things generally, we are apt to be very busy. Use a little discretion in thinning out, however. In the case of evergreen trees that you wish to get rid of, but which serves a good shelter for other plants in winter, if practical, leave them stand till the winter is over and get the good of their shelter. At Dosoris, as we use a good many evergreen branches for covering somewhat tender or little plants in winter, and also for temporary wind breaks, we strain a point in thinning the belts of pines, spruces and firs. Instead of clearing away every unnecessary tree in one season, we keep thinning out these supernumeraries, a few every fall, to use them for protecting purposes. In this way, those that are left are always pretty specimens.

* * *

From the same periodical we take the following on the Lawn: Having raked off the roughest of the tree leaves, we are now prepared to apply a little top dressing. This is a light coating of loose manure, either fresh horse manure from the city stables, or rotted, well broken up farm yard manure preserved on the place. This dressing may be put on any time after the middle of November, but as there is so much lawn to go over here, we wait till a frosty spell of weather, when we can drive the loaded wagons on the grass, without cutting the turf. This saves labor and we do better and cleaner work. But where there is only a small lawn, or it isn't necessary to drive the wagons on the grass, don't wait for a frosty time, but spread the top dressing at once. It is nice to get it on before snow comes. Put it on about half or third as heavy as you would on to cultivated garden lands.

A young man, struck down at the age of 19, left this warning to his companions:

> In health and strength put not thy trust,
> The strongest man is made of dust;
> Repent in haste, make no delay
> For I in youth was called away.

✢ CREMATION. ✢

The Other Side of the Question.

In cremation *versus* earth burial, leading scientists are to be found arrayed against each other on the two sides of the question. It has been pretty positively proved, according to the testimony of some prominent professional experts, that earth burial does not menace public health as set forth in the main arguments of those testifying on the side of cremation. Take this argument out and the battle must be fought on the lines suggested by the many other arguments used in favor of the latter method of disposing of the dead. But a new argument has been most forcibly brought to bear on the subject by Sir Francis Seymour Haden in an address before the British Institute of Public Health, in which he took issue with the cremationists, and on which the *New York Tribune* gives the following: He declared in the strongest language that earth burial, if properly conducted, can never endanger the health of the living, and carried the war into Africa by asserting that cremation is itself insanitary, and therefore so serious a menace to the public health that it ought to be prohibited by law. The earth, he maintained, is the one great purifier and renovator. There resides in the soil the chemical power of forming new and innocuous combinations out of the poisonous and miasmatic substances buried in it. Not only that, but the earth needs to be enriched by the restoration to it of dead matter, whose substance was drawn from it by the protoplasmic energy of life. So that, if all the effete residuum of the world were to be burned, the earth would soon be deprived, according to Sir Francis, of the chemical elements that support life, and all life would cease. * * * It is pertinent to observe, however, that it is not the purely speculative question that it may seem to be at first. It has a practical application as well. If the contention of Sir Seymour Haden is true, then the system of burning garbage, so frequently advocated and in many cities adopted, is unwise, for it is destroying valuable nutrient elements that ought to be returned to the soil.

There is, says the Detroit *Free Press*, a misapprehension in the public mind as to one of the objections made to the practice of cremation. It has often been said, not only by those who favor but by those who approve the practice, that the chief objections are based upon the doctrines of the church and have their foundations in religious beliefs or scruples. While pronounced opposition may be based upon this idea, Reverend Hogan claims that the objection of the Catholic church, at least, instead of being, as so many have assumed, doctrinal or even religious, is substantially sentimental; and, what is more important, that the church holds itself ready to sacrifice the sentiment whenever it is shown to be necessary for the general good.

Association of American Cemetery Superintendents.

O. C. SIMONDS, "Graceland," Chicago, President.
G. W. CREENY, "Harmony Grove," Salem, Mass., Vice-President.
F. EURICH, Woodlawn, Toledo, O., Secretary and Treasurer.

To Members of A. A. C. S.:

Three copies of the Philadelphia Proceedings have been mailed to each member; those who will want additional copies will please send in their orders at once and remit at the rate of $2.50 per dozen or 25 cents for single copies, six or more sent at dozen rate.
FRANK EURICH, Sec. and Treasurer, Auburndale, O., Dec. 10, 1894.

Publisher's Department.

The receipt of Cemetery Literature and Trade Catalogues will be acknowledged in this column.

TO ADVERTISERS. THE MODERN CEMETERY is the only publication of its class and will be found a valuable medium for reaching cemetery officials in all parts of the United States.

TO SUBSCRIBERS. Cemetery officials desiring to subscribe for a number of copies regularly to circulate among their lot owners, should send for our special terms. Several well known cemeteries have already adopted this plan with good results.

Contributions on matters pertaining to cemeteries are solicited. Address all communications to
R. J. HAIGHT, 358 Dearborn St., CHICAGO.

Our readers who may wish to place their subscriptions for horticultural books or periodicals, can be supplied through the MODERN CEMETERY office, and frequently at a saving. Clubbing rates on any publication will be sent on application.

Our many readers who have promised contributions to the MODERN CEMETERY should avail themselves of the long winter evenings that are now with us, to prepare them. Contributions on any subject of general interest to cemetery workers will be appreciated.

Cemetery officials should send for specimen pages of the new Record of Interment and Improved Lot Book before making changes in their system of keeping records. The method adopted in these books is recommended by leading cemetery officials. The publisher will mail specimen pages on receipt of request.

Received.—Mr. W. S. Loomis, superintendent of Forestdale Cemetery, Holyoke, Mass., sends a photogravure of a view in that cemetery showing Mt. Tom in the distance.—Maps of the cemetery grounds of the Oneida Cemetery Association, Oneida, New York, from Mr. T. F. Hand, secretary.—The descriptive catalogue of the Syracuse Nurseries, Smiths & Powell Co., Syracuse, New York, whose advertisement appears in another column, contains lists and prices of Fruit and Ornamental trees, Vines, Shrubs, Roses, etc., with many illustrations, and hints and suggestions in this line of work. Attention is also drawn to their thorough bred stock farms, of which a separate catalogue is published. The nurseries were established in 1825, and have been practically under one management for 50 years. Between 400 and 500 acres are under cultivation, and stock is grown in large quantities.

SITUATIONS WANTED, Etc.

Advertisements, limited to five lines, will be inserted in this column at the rate of 50 cents each insertion, 7 words to a line. Cash must accompany order.

SITUATION WANTED—By experienced superintendent, now in charge of a prominent cemetery. Practical and thoroughly competent in every respect. Preparation of new grounds a specialty. First class testimonials and best of references, correspondence invited. SUPERINTENDENT, care MODERN CEMETERY, Chicago.

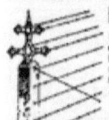

Patent Fence Cresting

Especially designed for Cemeteries and Orchards. This fence surrounds Calvary and Bellefontaine Cemeteries in St. Louis.

E. L. GRAYDON,
Sole Agent,
7201 N. B'dway, ST. LOUIS, MO.

HITCHINGS & CO.
Established 50 Years.

...Horticultural Architects and Builders,

AND LARGEST MANUFACTURERS OF

Greenhouse Heating and Ventilating Apparatus.

The highest awards received at the World's Fair for Horticultural Architecture, Greenhouse Construction and Heating Apparatus. Conservatories, Greenhouses, Palmhouses, etc., erected complete with our Patent Iron Frame Construction. *Send Four Cents for Illustrated Catalogue.*

233 Mercer St., NEW YORK.

THOS. W. WEATHERED'S SONS,
INCORPORATED.

Horticultural Architects and Hot Water Engineers

Send for Catalogue, enclosing 4 cents in stamps.

No. 244 Canal St., NEW YORK CITY.

PLEASE MENTION
THE MODERN CEMETERY.

Mr. E. L. Remsburg, Fayetteville, N. C., sends the following epitaph copied from a tombstone in an old cemetery in his state. The lines were composed by the old sailor at whose grave the tombstone stands:

> I crossed the seas till I was tired,
> To gain some port I long desired,
> From Rocks and Shoals this place seemed clear,
> So I in peace have anchored here.

LAWN MOWER SHARPENER.

WE invite the attention of the public to our **Lawn Mower Sharpener** as one of the most useful and indispensable inventions of the age. It fills a long felt want for the cemeteries and the public. It is simple in its operation, trues the cylinder knives and thoroughly sharpens the mower in a few minutes; it dispenses with all bother of sending your mower to a machine shop, also all trouble of trying to sharpen the mower by hand filing or with oil and emery which process never proves satisfactory. We furnish two sizes, one for hand and one for horse mower. Send for circulars and price list to

ADAMS & DOSWELL, Ft. Wayne, Ind.

Conservatories, Greenhouses, Vineries,

SHIPPED TO ANY PART OF THE COUNTRY AND
ERECTED COMPLETE, READY FOR USE.

Plans Embrace the Latest Improvements.
Unequaled Facilities for Manufacturing.
Thirty-five Years Experience.

ADDRESS, STATING
REQUIREMENTS,

Lord & Burnham Co...

ARCHITECTURAL OFFICE:
160 Fifth Ave., cor. 21st Street,
New York City

FACTORY:
Irvington-on-Hudson, N. Y.

Catalogue sent on application.

Conservatory in Newton Cemetery, Newtonville, Mass., designed and erected by Lord & Burnham Co.

Cemetery Interment Record AND Lot Book.

A perfected system for recording the essential particulars regarding each interment and for accurately locating the position of every grave. The most thorough and satisfactory system of Cemetery Records ever published. It embraces the best features of the records used in the leading American Cemeteries. Printed on heavy paper, and substantially bound in different sizes.

R. J. HAIGHT, 334 Dearborn St., Chicago.

BOOKS FOR CEMETERY OFFICIALS

LANDSCAPE GARDENING...

By SAMUEL PARSONS, JR., Supt. of Parks, New York City. Notes and suggestions on Lawns and Lawn Planting, Laying out and arrangement of Parks, etc. Deciduous and Evergreen trees, shrubs, flowers and foliage. Ornamentation of Ponds and Lakes. 300 pages, nearly 200 illustrations. Beautifully printed and bound. A charming book for landscape gardeners. Price $3.50. With the Modern Cemetery one year, $4.25.

Ornamental Gardening for Americans, by Elias A. Long. Illustrated. Cloth, $2.00. The Nursery Book, by L. H. Bailey. Complete hand book of propagation. Paper 50 cents, cloth $1.00. Sent postpaid on receipt of price.

The Nursery Book, by L. H. Bailey, assisted by several of the most skillful propagators in the world. In fact, it is a careful compendium of the best practice in all countries. It contains 167 illustrations, showing methods, processes and appliances. How to Propagate over 2,000 varieties of shrubs, trees and herbaceous or soft-stemmed plants; the process for each being fully described. All this and much more is fully told in the Nursery Book. Over 300 pages, 16mo. Price, cloth, $1. Pocket style, paper, narrow margins, 50 cents.

Greenhouse Construction, by Prof. L. R. Taft. A complete treatise on Greenhouse structures and arrangements of the various forms and styles of Plant Houses for professional florists as well as amateurs. All the best and most approved structures are so fully and clearly described that anyone who desires to build a Greenhouse will have no difficulty in determining the kind best suited to his purpose. The modern and most successful methods of heating and ventilating are fully treated upon. Special chapters are devoted to houses used for the growing of one kind of plants exclusively. The construction of hotbeds and frames receives appropriate attention. Over one hundred excellent illustrations specially engraved for this work, make every point clear to the reader and add considerably to the artistic appearance of the book. Cloth, 12mo., $1.50.

Bulbs and Tuberous Rooted Plants, by C. L. Allen. A complete treatise on the History, Description, Methods of Propagation and full directions for the successful culture of Bulbs in the Garden, Dwelling and Greenhouse. As generally treated bulbs are an expensive luxury, while, when properly managed, they afford the greatest amount of pleasure at the least cost. The author of this book has for many years made bulb growing a specialty and is recognized authority in their cultivation and management. The illustrations which embellish this work have been drawn from nature and have been engraved especially for this book. The cultural directions are plainly stated, practical, and to the point. Cloth, 8vo., $2.00.

Address, **R. J. HAIGHT,** 334 Dearborn St., Chicago.

Hardy Ornamental Trees, Shrubs, Vines, Evergreens and Hardy Herbaceous Perennials.

The finest general assortment of Hardy Ornamental Plants in America. 200 page Illustrated, Descriptive Catalogue on application.

Send your list of needs for special rates.

Jacob Manning, Prop.,
The Reading Nursery, - Reading, Mass.

New, Rare, and Beautiful Plants!

[illegible descriptive listing]

JOHN SAUL, Washington, D. C.

GARDEN AND FOREST
A JOURNAL OF HORTICULTURE, LANDSCAPE ART AND FORESTRY

Garden and Forest ably discusses the principles of landscape gardening as applied to the improvements and care of public grounds, and contains practical suggestions regarding the management of American Cemeteries, together with beautiful and useful illustrations.

"Should be in the hands of every progressive superintendent."—*A. H. Sargent.*

"I have gained much useful and practical knowledge from the numbers of *Garden and Forest.*"—*F. Enrich.*

"*Garden and Forest* ought to be worth to any cemetery many times the cost of a year's subscription."—*O. C. Simonds.*

Published Weekly, - **$4.00 a Year.**

Specimen copy free on application.

Garden and Forest Publishing Co.,
Tribune Building, New York.

SYRACUSE NURSERIES!

ORNAMENTAL TREES AND SHRUBS!

Suitable for Cemetery Grounds, Lawns and Avenues.

Write and let us know your wants and we will make you low prices on a high grade of stock. We also are large growers of FRUIT TREES of all kinds.

SMITHS & POWELL CO., - Syracuse, N. Y.

A GREAT IMPROVEMENT IN INTERMENT!

The Patent Automatic Burial Apparatus, Endorsed by Prominent American Cemetery Superintendents.

An Exhibition Given Before Their Association at Philadelphia With Gratifying Results.

At the convention of the cemetery superintendents from all parts of the Union, held last month in Philadelphia, an exhibit was made of an apparatus for lowering coffins into the grave, that evoked the warmest admiration. It is a disagreeable sight at best to see the casket lowered in the olden way, by straps or ropes, since accidents happen at times that involve the personal safety of the bystanders while the lowering of the body with straps or ropes is revolving to one's finer sensibilities, and surely these ought to be regarded, particularly at a moment when loved ones naturally feel that the form of their departed should be consigned to its home with the utmost tenderness.

The convention in question represented a body of men of superior intelligence, men who look upon their work as a profession rather than as a business, and it is not surprising that the satisfaction afforded by the exhibit of the Burial Apparatus in question found vent in the following communications:

EIGHTH ANNUAL CONVENTION ASS. OF AMERICAN CEMETERY SUPERINTENDENTS, PHILADELPHIA, Sept. 12, 1894.

To the Scherer Manufacturing Co., New York—We have witnessed the exhibition of the Scherer Automatic Burial Apparatus at West Laurel Hill Cemetery, Philadelphia, and are gratified at the improvements and have made in it since the apparatus was last exhibited at Minneapolis. As a means of obviating accidents in the lowering of caskets this apparatus should commend itself to the careful consideration of cemetery officials. It is easily handled, is simple in construction and possesses merits that cannot fail of recognition. Yours respectfully,

WM. SALWAY, Supt. Spring Grove Cemetery, Cincinnati, O.
FRANK EURICH, Supt. Woodlawn Cemetery, Toledo, O.

The Patent Automatic Burial Apparatus can be seen on exhibition at the office of the Scherer Manufacturing Co., Room 42, Bible House, New York. It is safe, simple, moderate in price, substantially built, and can be operated by a child. The one exhibited in Philadelphia was operated by a boy of 15 years.

OFFICE OF THE SUPT., SALEM FIELDS CEMETERY,
EAST NEW YORK, Sept. 20, 1894.

The Scherer Manufacturing Co.—I have watched with much interest the development of the Automatic Burial Apparatus manufactured by you, and have studied its workings carefully. It is simply made and operates easily, and its general use in cemeteries is destined to mitigate the anguish of mourners at the final moment when the body is consigned reverently to the grave. I hope to see it introduced generally.

Respectfully yours, PETER J. HILTMAN, Supt.

MOUNT NEBOH CEMETERY,
EVERGREEN P. O., LONG ISLAND, Sept. 19, '94.

To the Scherer Manufacturing Co.—It affords me pleasure to testify to the excellence of the Automatic Patent Burial Apparatus manufactured by you. I find that it is in general demand, and the small additional charge that is made for its use brings in quite an income to the cemetery. The oftener it is used, the more it is appreciated by those participating in interments. Respectfully yours, HERMAN GRAUSHOLZ, Supt.

PATENT AUTOMATIC BURIAL APPARATUS, Manufactured by the

SCHERER M'F'G CO., Office and Show Room: BIBLE HOUSE, Cor. Fourth Ave. and Ninth St., NEW YORK CITY.

☞ For a more definite description of the Burial Apparatus and its use send for Catalogue, which will be mailed free.

THE MODERN CEMETERY.

THE MODERN CEMETERY.
AN ILLUSTRATED MONTHLY JOURNAL DEVOTED TO THE INTEREST OF CEMETERIES

R. J. HAIGHT, Publisher.
334 Dearborn Street, CHICAGO.

Subscription $1.00 a Year in Advance.   Foreign Subscription $1.25.
Special Rates on Six or More Copies.

VOL. IV.   CHICAGO, FEB'Y 1895.   NO. 12.

CONTENTS.

FUNERAL REFORM	131
VALIDITY OF ORDINANCE RELATING TO PLACES OF BURIAL	134
*SLEEPY HOLLOW CEMETERY, CONCORD, MASS.	134
CEMETERY GREENHOUSES—WHAT TO BUILD. II	137
SHRUBS FOR CEMETERIES	138
*NEW GREENHOUSES, ALLEGHENY CEMETERY, ALLEGHENY, PA.	138
CEMETERY NOTES	140
CORRESPONDENCE	141
*THE HOUGHTON MONUMENT	141
CEMETERY REPORTS	142
PLANTING AND GOOD PLANTING	143
EPITAPHS	144
PUBLISHER'S DEPARTMENT	144

*Illustrated.

With this issue the MODERN CEMETERY closes its fourth year. It is, as many of our oldest subscribers know, the outgrowth of the cemetery department of the *Monumental News*, the field appearing to present an opportunity for a paper devoted exclusively to Cemetery interests. Four years experience has justified the assumption, and numerous expressions of opinion from subscribers have testified to the value of the work which has been accomplished.

The course of this experience has developed this, however: that in the quest for information for MODERN CEMETERY purposes the greater part of the material obtained, and the sources of that material, have been such as would be equally instructive and necessary to that other public feature of our civilization,—the Park. The prevailing ideas governing the cemetery of to-day so far as the physical conditions obtain, outside the grave and mortuary monument, are practically those necessary for the care and improvement of our parks.

A due consideration of these facts has resulted in the decision to amalgamate these interests, and the next issue of the MODERN CEMETERY which commences Vol. V., will be under the title PARK AND CEMETERY.

In thanking our subscribers generally for their support and interest in the past, we cordially solicit and hope for its continuance in the future.

Funeral Reform.

The matter of Funeral Reform is assuming wide spread proportions, and is establishing itself in a very positive way in the centers of population. Two years ago a committee of Episcopalian church dignitaries was appointed in New York to consider the question, and it has recently made a most exhaustive report commending the Burial Reform Association, and especially approving certain of the recommendations of that body. The following is taken from the report:

Your committee has examined with a great deal of care, the constitution of the Burial Reform association. They are convinced that the more closely the recommendations of said association are adhered to, and the more closely and intelligently the archdeaconry co-operates with said association in the dissemination of its principles, the larger and more beneficial will be the results. The recommendations of the Burial Reform Association are as follows:

"1. The exercise of economy and simplicity in everything appertaining to the funeral.

"2. The use of plain hearses.

"3. The disuse of crape, scarfs, feathers, velvet trappings and the like.

"4. The avoiding of all unchristian and heathen emblems and the use of any floral decorations beyond a few cut flowers.

"5. The discouraging of all eating and drinking in connection with funerals.

"6. The discouraging of any but immediate members of the family from accompanying the body to the grave; but nothing in these rules and methods shall be considered as discouraging the attendance of persons at the grave in connection with the holding of religious services.

"7. The dispelling of the idea that all club money or society money must be spent on the funeral.

"8. The use of such materials for the coffin as rapidly decay after burial, and the disuse of the box in which it is commonly inclosed.

"9. The early interment of the body in soil sufficient and suitable for its resolution to its ultimate elements.

"10. The substitution of burial plots for family vaults.

"11. The encouragement, on sanitary grounds, of the removal, in crowded districts, of the body to a mortuary, instead of retaining it in rooms occupied by the living.

"12. The impressing upon the officers of public charity and correction the claims of the poorest to proper and reverent burial.

The report adds the following further recommendations for New York evolved form the committees investigation:

"1. The substitution of a simple garb of muslin or linen for dressing the dead, in place of clothing that might be of use to the living.

"2. The use of a very light, soft wood coffin, for the reason that it will decay quickly; or else of the wicker coffins, which have found favor in England and are now manufactured in this country.

"3. Abandonment of the custom, once prevalent and even now not infrequent, of building brick and stone inclosures for coffins with in graves.

"4. That the rectors and vestries of churches should loan the use of some suitable places for mortuaries in connection with said churches, to which remains could be removed as quickly as possible after death.

"5. That so far as possible the clergy should make known the fact that the churches and not the homes are the proper places for the conduct of burial services and that they offer the entirely free use of said churches for funerals."

The report closes with the following statement of the methods which may be used to reduce materially the cost of burials as pertaining to New York:

"For a coffin, with plate, hearse, one coach, Newtown permit and ferriage for hearse and coach from house the sum of $25, extra, from church $1.50. A shroud if necessary, $2, a box, $4, or a top cover for coffin, $1, the cost of preserving the remains on ice, $8. These prices would be for Long Island cemeteries, near by, and for funerals below 100th street, and for more northern localities, up to Harlem bridge, say, $1 extra for the vehicles. For $15 a plain coffin will be furnished and remains be conveyed to St. Michael's cemetery from points south of 100th street."

The clergy seem to be quite alive to the necessity of a change from the practices of by gone days in the light of our present civilization, and their active co-operation will most assuredly hasten the consummation of this much needed reform.

Validity of Ordinance Relating to places of Burial.

Several questions of interest to cemetery associations are discussed and decided by the supreme court of Texas in the recent case of the city of Austin v. Austin City Cemetery Association.

It holds that a city ordinance providing, under penalty, that it shall be unlawful for any person to bury, or cause to be buried, or to in any manner aid or assist in the burial of a dead body, of any human being, within the corporate limits of the city, except in three specified cemeteries, if void, and though the city is not immediately seeking to enforce it, and there might exist a legal remedy against its enforcement, an injunction will lie on the petition of a cemetery association to restrain its execution, and to declare the ordinance void, especially when it is shown that the right and privilege of using its property for cemetery purposes is destroyed or impaired by virtue of the existence of the ordinance, as no one in the control of dead bodies is willing that they should be buried or interred there for fear of violating the ordinance in question.

On the other hand, the court holds that a provision in its charter, empowering a city "to regulate the burial of the dead and to prohibit public funerals in cases of death from contagious or infectious disease; to purchase, establish, and regulate one or more cemeteries within or without the city limits" authorizes the passage by the city council of such an ordinance as the above.

Moreover, such a charter provision as this one, the court does not think can be construed to be intended by the legislature to confer power upon the city council either to prohibit the burial of the dead within the limits of the city, or to unreasonably restrict the right of its citizens to provide places for the purpose within such limits. In a case like this, whether the ordinance be reasonable or not, it says, must depend upon the circumstances of the particular restriction as affecting the people who are to be subjected to its control.

An ordinance of this nature, it is further held, is presumably valid, and cannot be declared void upon the mere fact that it designates only three cemeteries in which the dead bodies of people can be buried, within a portion of the city which embraces 4,500 acres, part of which is thickly, and part thinly settled, in the absence of a showing that there are no other localities outside such limits accessible and suitable for such purposes.

Finally it is held that when an ordinance like the one in question is attacked upon the ground that it is unreasonable, and therefore void, it is incumbent upon the party who alleges its invalidity to aver and prove the facts which make it so. If the facts be controverted, they must be determined by the jury; but whether the facts relied upon show the ordinance to be unreasonable or not is a question for the court.

Sleepy Hollow Cemetery, Concord, Mass.

In no place of equal size in the country is there a cemetery so universally admired for its natural beauties and situation, as Sleepy Hollow, in the historic town of Concord, Mass.

Visited each year by thousands of tourists, it has become noted the world over, from the fact that so many famous men and women are buried there.

The new portion which has the greatest interest, was purchased by the town in 1855 and covers about twenty-five acres. In the same year a receiving vault was built, and the cemetery opened with suitable ceremonies. Up to the present time about one thousand interments have been made, and in the old portion twelve hundred and fifty.

At the main entrance on Bedford Road are the iron gates presented to the town by one of its well known men, Wm. M. Pritchard. These gates which were erected in 1891 at a cost of three thousand dol-

THE MODERN CEMETERY.

ENTRANCE TO SLEEPY HOLLOW CEMETERY, CONCORD, MASS.

lars, are of wrought iron, the masonry being of buff brick with sandstone trimmings. An excellent idea may be had of them from the accompanying photograph by the writer.

Passing through the gates and following the winding driveway to the left, we come to Ridge Path which ascends a steep knoll; on this well trodden path and on the crest of the incline to the right is the Thoreau lot. The original tablet marking the grave of Henry D. Thoreau, who died May 6th, 1862, was of brown stone, but within a few years this has been replaced by a more durable monument of granite.

In the next lot, on the same side, lie the remains of A. Bronson Alcott and his daughter, Louisa M. Alcott, that great favorite and friend of the young people the world over, whose books have attained a circulation unparalleled in the history of juvenile literature. The stones marking these graves are perfectly plain, except for the initials of each. Bronson Alcott died March 4, 1888 and his daughter two days later.

Directly across from this lot is that of the Hawthornes. The grave of this great novelist is marked with a very simple marble stone bearing the words "Hawthorne, Died May 19, 1864." The mound is covered with shining myrtle. The lot is enclosed by an Arbor Vitæ hedge and since the accompanying photograph was made it has been necessary to erect a wire fence outside of the hedge, as visitors entering destroyed the myrtle upon the grave, and when this was gone, broke the hedge down nearly level with the ground merely for the sake of a memento from the burial place of the noted author, whose fame is also world-wide.

THE GRAVE OF NATHANIEL HAWTHORNE.

THE GRAVE OF RALPH WALDO EMERSON.

Walking a short distance along Ridge path we come to the grave of Ralph Waldo Emerson. Here on this wooded hill, guarded by the gaunt massive pines, singing their never ending songs, rests the great philosopher, beloved by all the world which sends hundreds of persons every year to pay his resting place their homage.

At the head of the grave is a huge rough boulder of rose quartz, weighing three tons. His son, Dr. Edward W. Emerson, experienced great difficulty in finding such a stone, and only after several months search did he finally succeed. It came from South Acworth, N. H. The tablet was put in position only this last August. It is of bronze, twelve by eighteen inches, and was designed by Newton McIntosh of New York.

The design consists of a border four inches wide representing a species of pine cone of which the dead author was very fond. The inscription reads:

"THE PASSIVE MASTER LENT HIS HAND
TO THE VAST SOUL THAT O'ER
HIM PLANNED."
Ralph Waldo Emerson
Born in Boston, May 25th, 1803.
Died in Concord, April, 27th, 1882.

The fine lettering upon the tablet made it necessary to place the camera near the stone, therefore the stone is made to appear wider and not as high as it actually is.

THE MINUTE MAN.—BY D. C. FRENCH.

The famous minute man, while not connected in any way with Sleepy Hollow Cemetery will be of interest to the many readers of this paper. It stands on the battle ground and marks the spot where the first forcible resistance was offered to the British on the morning of the 19th of April, 1775. The statue was designed by Daniel Chester French, when a man yet in the twenties. It was cast from cannon furnished by the state, and for many years was considered the finest bronze casting in the country. On the face of the granite base is Emerson's well known and oft repeated verse.

Here by the rude bridge that arched the flood,
Their flags to April's breeze unfurled,
Here once the embattled farmer stood
And fired the shot heard round the world.

The statue was unveiled April 19th, 1875, at the Centennial Celebration.

Henry F. Walcott, Jr.

Cemetery Greenhouses—What to Build.—II.

Having decided upon adding greenhouses to the cemetery equipment, the first question that arises is, what, of the many forms of glass houses now in use, is best adapted to our needs.

There are three general classes of greenhouses which we may call plant houses, forcing houses and show houses.

The plant house is one especially adapted for propagating and growing the ordinary assortment of moderate sized plants used for bedding and similar purposes. The sunny months of late winter and spring being the time when this class of plants makes the greatest growth, and an extraordinary amount of light is not needed. Glass of moderate size and fair quality can be used, and all glass is dispensed with in the sides, being used in the roof and one gable only, in most cases. The plants are not tall, hence a low house can be used. (It may be said in this connection that, with but few exceptions, the closer plants can be kept to the glass without touching it, the better the growth). Finally, as these plants generally do not require a high temperature, the cost of heating apparatus is not excessive. For these reasons the plant house is the cheapest of the three in construction and in operation.

Houses for the successful forcing of plants for winter flowers, especially roses, must be built very differently. Light and heat are essential for strong growth and good flowers. As the flowers are in great demand during the period of shortest days and cloudiest weather, the house, in order to secure best results, must be so built as to admit the greatest possible amount of light, and the heating apparatus must be sufficiently powerful to maintain an even temperature, at all times, and considerably higher than is needed in the plant houses. We must then have large glass of extra quality; the bars on which the glass is laid must be as thin as possible, requiring additional supports, preferably of iron; the front must be partly of glass, the house must be higher and most complete provision must be made for ventilation. In this way a first class forcing house may cost double that of a good plant house of the same capacity.

The show house is used for the growing and exhibition of specimen plants. The varieties generally used are tropical plants, which remain in the house winter and summer and attain large size. A very high roof is needed, with glass, also, on at least two sides, and we must be able to maintain a high temperature. The very best of glass will be none too good, any imperfections being likely to act as lenses and cause burned spots on the foliage. All parts must be made very carefully so as to avoid cold drafts, or the dripping of water upon the foliage, leaves or flowers.

The show house is, therefore, when properly built, the most expensive of the three classes.

The plant house may be regarded as a necessity, and can easily be made to pay its expenses if not more. The show house will be an expensive luxury, and will bring in little or no returns. It will be found a source of interest to visitors, however, and should be provided for, if we can afford it. The forcing of roses, carnations, etc., for winter flowers will not be advisable, except in the larger cemeteries, or when the surplus product, not required for use in the cemetery, can be disposed of elsewhere to good advantage. We have already seen that the houses designed for this purpose are expensive, and, in order to secure best results, a separate house must be provided for nearly every variety grown. This necessitates a large investment at first. Great skill and very close attention is required for this work, and a thoroughly competent gardener is absolutely necessary. The thoroughly competent gardener is a rare bird, and many otherwise competent are absolutely unreliable through too great a fondness for the cup that cheers and also inebriates, or through an inability to refrain from considering and using their employer's dollars as their own individual perquisites.

To summarize, then: the plant house should be built, by all means, the show house, if it can be afforded, the forcing house only after careful study of the situation with reference to all the points above mentioned.

By the use of flowering bulbs and the easier handled flowering plants, a moderate amount of flowers for cutting may be had at all times, even in the planthouses, while extraordinary demands for flowers can be met by express shipments from the wholesale markets in the larger cities, at a much less expense than they can be grown for on a small scale.

It being settled what to build, the next question is how to go about it. In building any other structure the wise man, unless he has an exceptional knowledge of such matters, will at once intrust the preparation of plans to an architect. When the plans are ready, the next move is generally to advertise for bids and contract with the lowest bidder for the erection of the structure complete (that is, we offer every inducement for the use of poor material, poorer workmanship, and general bad results). In greenhouse building, the good architect unless he is one of the very few who have had long and successful experience in this class of work, will be as detrimental to the best and cheapest results as he is essential in other building operations. He seems unable to comprehend how light and seemingly frail such structures may be, and still answer their purposes admirably, and he will cheerfully sacrifice all the requirements of the plants to his ideas of architectural beauty.

It is claimed, with seeming truth, that greenhouses constructed entirely of iron and glass, are sufficiently durable to render them the most economical notwithstanding their excessive first cost. We have hardly, as yet, in this country, had sufficient experience with them to decide the matter positively. It will probably be found that when architectural beauty and also adaptability to the wants of the plants is desired, the iron frame construction, with some wood, of our best horticultural builders is the best, if the question of first cost can be made a secondary one. These firms, having in their employ experts who are thoroughly posted in all the branches of horticultural building, and who have a thorough knowledge of the requirements of plants, can be relied upon to develope the plans from the beginning, after an examination of the ground, and to erect the buildings complete. This is by all means the easiest and most satisfactory way of building, but it is expensive.

By omitting the iron frame work, excepting a few gas pipes for supports, and building entirely of wood, houses can be erected that for all practical purposes will answer as well as the more expensive and ornate structures. If this method is adopted, it will be necessary to work out the general features of the plan, and make a rough sketch or description of what is wanted. This can be forwarded to any of the mill men advertising greenhouse material in this paper, who will furnish all mill work complete, much of it cut to length, mitred and ready to put up. They will also, without charge, furnish full and complete working plans. From these plans and with this material, any good carpenter or in fact, anyone "handy with tools" can put up a building which, while not being particularly ornate, will possess that element of beauty which is inherent in all things that are perfectly adapted to the purposes for which they were created.

There must be no contract work about the erection of it. The durability of the house will depend largely upon the pains taken in doing the work, upon the quality of the paint, oil and putty used and the faithfulness with which every detail is attended to. The points which are always slighted by the building contractor, are the very ones of most importance to the life of greenhouse structures.

In the succeeding articles we shall discuss that part of the work to be done on the ground, omitting largely the detail which is so completely described and illustrated in the circulars of the mills, which make a specialty of greenhouse wood work, and is so fully shown in the plans they are always ready to furnish.

Willis N. Rudd.

Shrubs for Cemeteries.

The few varieties of "Shrubs for Cemeteries" mentioned in an article under that heading in the MODERN CEMETERY for November are unquestionably well adapted for certain kinds of planting where natural effects are desired, and abundant space for shrubs of spreading habit. In many of the finer cemeteries, however, where space is valuable and but very little room left for planting adornment, smaller growing shrubs than the Altheas and Elders are requisite, and are also much more effective.

From the large number of perfectly hardy ornamental varieties there is no difficulty in selecting shrubs that will be much more effective in flower and foliage.

The purple Plum (Prunus Pissardii) is unquestionably a very effective hardy plant for color effects, especially when grown on plum stock, closely pruned, and kept in compact form either as a specimen or in groups. The Purple Filbert (Corylus atropurpurea) is also very effective as a red or crimson-leaved shrub, and the foliage being very much larger than any of the other hardy shrubs of this color, is very effective in contrast. The Purple Berberry (Berberis atropurpurea) can be grown more compact, hence may be preferable for many locations.

Of the smaller growing Shrubs especially desirable for fine ornamental planting Andromeda floribunda, the hardy Azaleas, Berberry Thunbergii, Mountain Laurel (Kalmia latifolia,) Mahonia aquifolia and the new variegated Yucca are especially good and can be advantageously included in any plantings where quality is the first consideration rather than size. All of these are usually more effective planted in masses or groups by themselves, or in beds or borders of other shrubs.

The fine hardy Rhododendrons are always most effective and appropriate, and with proper treatment there is no difficulty in growing them in most places with perfect success.

Viburnum Plicatum, the beautiful Japanese Snowball, can also be advantageously included in every list of fine shrubs; as also Hydrangea paniculata grandiflora, both as dwarfs (bush form) and standards. These standards are quite new but can be grown as successfully as the ordinary bush Hydrangeas, and will undoubtedly take the place of standard Roses to quite an extent for certain kinds of planting. Besides the advantage of being a decided novelty, they are perfectly hardy, bloom freely and transplant readily.

The well-known California Privet, grafted on 4 to 5 feet stocks and grown as standards are also effective. The hardy Japanese Maples should not be overlooked. There is no more beautiful hardy tree or plant known than a good specimen or bed of the finer varieties of these beautiful shrubs. Fortunately the most effective of these Japanese Maples are the hardiest, and such varieties as Atropurpureum, Sanguineum, Scolopendifolium, Ornatum, etc., will succeed well with ordinary treatment in many, if not most, situations in this climate.

Those who have not given this subject special consideration can hardly appreciate the opportunities for improvement of cemeteries by the proper use of all this finer planting material now available at reasonable prices, and the MODERN CEMETERY will accomplish a great amount of good in bringing out from time to time the best thoughts and experiences of various subscribers and correspondents on this important question.

Fred. W. Kelsey.

There are a couple of bills in the legislature of Minnesota relating to cemetery matters, and in which the cemetery officials of St. Paul and Minneapolis are interesting themselves. One is to expedite the settlement and make certain the ownership of cemetery lots after the death of the first holder. Superintendent Hobart, of Lakewood, Minneapolis, is of opinion that the lots should descend by statute to the direct heir to be him held in trust for the other heirs. The other bill is to enlarge the land holding power of cemetery associations in the large cities. Under the present statute, as it now exists, 180 acres is the limit, which frequently imposes inconvenient restrictions on the larger cemeteries.

There is an activity now apparent in many parts of the country, looking to the remedying of defective legislation in relation to our cemeteries. There is much to be done in this direction.

NEW GREENHOUSES, ALLEGHENY CEMETERY, ALLEGHENY CITY, PA.

New Greenhouses, Allegheny Cemetery.

The accompanying illustrations give a plan and perspective view of a range of glass recently erected for Allegheny Cemetery, at Allegheny City, Pa. The houses which formerly stood on the site of the present structure were found inadequate for the requirements of the cemetery, and the present range was accordingly built, using as far as possible the old foundations.

The plan will show the arrangement of the various houses. The Palm House is one hundred and thirty feet long by thirty feet wide with a vestibule 9 ft. by 17 ft. on the front. The height from top of cement walk to base of lantern is twenty-five feet. The lantern is seven feet from base to ridge, while

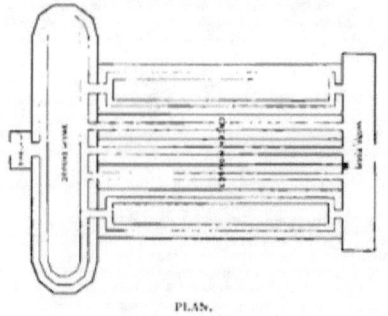

PLAN.

the central tower rises ten feet above this point. The total height is forty-two feet from top of cement walk to top of tower. The Palm house is executed throughout in the Gothic style of architecture, and presents pleasing exterior and interior views. Extending from the Palm House is a group of five Green Houses with straight roofs.

The framework of all the houses is iron, bent to shape of the various sections, and properly proportioned to sustain the various weights and strains which it will be called upon to sustain. Wide iron gutters capping the brick walls are placed between the green houses, to which the iron rafters of the roofs are secured. Wood is used in the construction of the houses, to a very limited extent and only where it is found to be indispensable to form a secure setting for the glass.

Iron framed tables with slate tops are placed in all the houses except in center of Palm House which is utilized as a natural bed; the walks are concrete with Portland cement finish. The houses are heated throughout with steam. Sufficient ventilating sash to secure the proper amount of ventilation is placed in each house, operated by special machinery.

In designing the range the practical use for which the various houses were intended has in no case been sacrificed for appearance sake alone. An inspection of the houses and the plants which are there unmistakeably thriving will attest to the fact that when glass houses are built in a thorough manner, and skilled services employed to superintend them, the result must be great benefit to a cemetery, both as regards its own necessities and as a source of income.

These houses represent the latest improvements in horticultural architecture and building, and cemetery officials contemplating such improvements would be well repaid by a visit to this range at Allegheny.

The range was designed and erected by Lord & Burnham Co., Horticultural Architects and Builders of 160 Fifth Ave., New York City, and Irvington, N. Y. The same firm also designed and erected the Schenberg Park conservatories at Pittsburg, which is the largest range of glass in America.

Apropos of the "ghoul" who is again busy, if exchanges can be relied upon, we read of one who has bequeathed his body to a hospital on condition that his skeleton, properly mounted and inscribed, be placed in the museum.

CEMETERY NOTES.

The deed used by the Catskill Rural Cemetery Association, N. Y., embodies features worthy of notice. In the body of the deed which is notably brief occurs the following paragraph relating to perpetual care: "And the said party of the first part in consideration of the said payment hereby agrees to and with the said party of the second part...... heirs and assigns forever to cause the grass which shall grow on said lot or plot to be cut and to cause said lot to be resodded and forever kept in order by top-dressing at such times and in such manner as the trustees of said Association shall deem most expedient for the proper care of said lot and of said cemetery." Besides the form of witnessing, the deed also included a ruled section for the record of burials, grave numbers, date of interment and names of such bodies as may be buried in the lot covered by the instrument, and space for a diagram of the lot itself. These records are made by the superintendent on the deed as occasion necessitates.

* * *

The Court of Appeals has affirmed a judgment in favor of Martha E. Seymour against the Spring Forest Cemetery Association and others of Binghamton, N. Y. The action was brought to recover a percentage of receipts from the sales of lots. When the cemetery was organized in 1853, it issued bonds to pay its way which pledged a certain portion of the receipts, but were no lien on the fund, and never affected the cemetery itself, or any lot owners. Some ten years ago the trustees refused to pay over the usual percentage, and in 1889 Mrs Seymour brought suit and recovered a judgment for $14,000. This case was appealed to the supreme court, and the judgment was affirmed. The Court of Appeals has again affirmed the judgment, which is that Mrs. Seymour is entitled to the percentage of the moneys which have been received.

* * *

The Cedar Hill Cemetery Association, Hartford, Conn., is an example of business enterprise. It was started with a working capital of $100,000 which was secured by the issue of stock on the agreement that if the operation proved profitable this money with interest would be repaid to the stockholders. The growth of the cemetery, the rise in value of its lots, and its prosperity as a business enterprise has resulted most favorably. Within a short time stockholders have received checks for 50 per cent. of their stock, leaving interest and the other 50 per cent. to come along later. A report is current that the management has suggested to various stockholders the idea of waiving the right to interest and that the invitation has been declined with thanks.

* * *

The Jewish Cemetery of Troy, N. Y., is to be the recipient of a memorial entrance, erected to commemorate their parents by the children of M. Goldstone. It will consist of two arches, the main one to be a gateway for driving and a smaller one on the left for pedestrians. The main arch will be eleven feet wide by twelve feet high and the other four feet six inches and nine feet high. The pillars will rise to a height of nineteen feet. Over the main arch is to be the inscription, from Psalm XXXVII, 37, "Mark the perfect man, and behold the upright: for the end of that man is peace." On either side of the main gateway will be inscribed panels. The memorials will be constructed of Barre Granite. For the large arch there will be double gates and for the smaller one a single gate of wrought iron. The contract for the stone cutting and erection has been let to W. H. Young. The design, which is in the Moorish style of architecture, is from Architect C. Edward Loth.

* * *

The Dempster claim against the Rosehill Cemetery Corporation of Chicago, which has been in the courts for 12 years, contested by leading legal lights, has just been decided by the Illionis Supreme Court in favor of the plaintiff. The claim was based on some certificates of conditional scrip of the Rosehill Cemetery Company, issued to Rev. John Dempster by Francis H. Benson, founder of Rosehill Cemetery, in 1859, in consideration of $40,000 lost by Dempster in the failure of Benson's bank. The scrip was to be exchanged for cemetery stock of equal face value, when the indebtedness on Benson's stock, then pledged with Henry W. Blodgett, should be discharged. The value of the claim is now said to amount to $1,000,000 which probably accounts for the persistent litigation. It is said that the claim could have been settled in 1880 by the erection of a monument to Dr. Dempster.

* * *

A mausoleum has just been completed in Forest Hills Cemetery, Boston, Mass., as a tribute to Lillian Durell, the gifted singer. It is a simple but substantial structure of the renaissance order of architecture, the outside dimensions being 11 ft. 4 in. by 9 ft. 8 in. by 10 ft. 10 in. high. It is built of blue Westerly granite, the base and sides rock face finish with cut quoins at corners. The pilasters and cap at the doorway are of cut granite, and carries in the cap polished letters the name Atkinson. Light is admitted through a stained glass window in the rear end, having as its chief feature the lily of the valley, this being the favorite flower of Lillian Durell. The roof is composed of five stones. Entrance to the interior is through polished granite doors, protected on the outside by bronze gates.

It contains four catacombs on each side, the supports and frames being built of contrasting colors of Tennessee marble highly polished, in a sharp contrast with the marble tiled floor. The catacomb for the reception of the casket containing the remains of Lillian Durell is sealed with a bevelled edge plate glass screen, affording a view of the interior, and yet protecting its contents completely.

* * *

Hitherto the state of Vermont has had no provisions for the care of funds bequeathed or donated by those desirous of "perpetual care" of their burial lots, although instances are numerous of such funds being left for such purposes with churches. In the state laws just published for 1894, there is printed: "An act authorizing towns to receive money in trust for the benefit of cemeteries and burial lots." The working of the law is about the same as the course pursued by towns in the use of the United States Trust Fund, now applied to the support of schools. In places where there are cemetery associations, the trustees can easily secure the care of lots through the proper officers. The survivors of families, living at a distance, can delegate the Town Trustee to keep the lots in proper order and for all time.

* * *

A Frenchman who recently spent some time in the United States, has recorded an impression created by the American method of filling teeth with gold, in a French newspaper. It is to the effect that the amount of gold annually consumed for this purpose amounts to $500,000, all of which is buried in our cemeteries in due course. He figures that at the end of 30 years these cemeteries will be veritable gold mines containing some $150,000,000 of the precious metal. He fears that this will prove too tempting for the practical mind of the future American, and we shall see the day when companies will be organized to mine the cemeteries and recover the gold secreted in the jaws of dead ancestors.

* * *

The contest over the annual election of trustees of Green Lawn Cemetery, Columbus, O., passed off with less commotion than new paper reports previously anticipated, although great interest was manifested. The old trustees were reelected by large majorities. The cause of the opposition was attributed to the new rules put in force last year, which were said to be too arbitrary, especially in regard to prohibiting the use of limestone and sandstone bases and monuments, which has been argued, was a rule detrimental to the interests of the power lot owners. The officials of Green Lawn Cemetery have been alive to the advantages of modern ideas in cemetery management, and the new rules were adopted in order to conduct their affairs in accordance therewith.

* * *

The Parsees will not burn or bury their dead, because they consider a dead body impure, and they will not suffer themselves to defile any of the elements, says *The Nineteenth Century* speaking of the Tower of Silence. They therefore expose their corpses to vultures, a method, revolting, perhaps, to the imagination, but one which commends itself to all those who are acquainted therewith. And, after all, one sees nothing but the quiet, white-robed procession (white is mourning among the Parsees) following the bier to the Tower of Silence. At the entrance they look their last on the dead and the corpse bearers—a caste of such—carry it within the precincts and lay it down, to be finally disposed of by the vultures which crowd the tower. And why should the swoop of a flock of white birds be more revolting than what happens in the grave. Meanwhile, and for three days after, the priests say constant prayers for the departed, for his soul is supposed not to leave the world till the fourth day after death. On the fourth day there is the Uthanna ceremony, when large sums of money are given away in memory of the departed. The liturgy in use is a series of funeral sermons by Zoroaster. In superstitions, the Parsees have had more than they retain. Connected with burial is the popular conception as to the efficacy of a dog's gaze after death. Dogs are sacred, and supposed to guide the souls of the dead to heaven, and to ward off evil spirits; hence it is customary to lead a dog into the chamber of death, that he may look at the corpse before it is carried to the Tower.

⇒|Correspondence.|⇐

NEW HAVEN, CONN., January 19, 1895.
Editor Modern Cemetery:

In looking over the Proceedings of the Association of American Cemetery Superintendents, I saw two discussions on how to open graves through frozen ground, but I did not notice that anything was said about using salt. Here in New Haven we look upon salt as a great help. We cut a channel around the grave about three inches deep, and about the same in width, into which we put about one inch of rock salt and then pour upon it water enough to fill the channel. We then cover this with boards, canvas or snow, to keep it as warm as possible, so that the salt will melt. If this is done the night before the grave is to be opened, it frequently cuts a channel through 18 inches to 2 feet of frost all around the grave. We then take the frost pick or any other tools for cutting frozen ground, and pick out a hole at one end or side of grave. With the use of wedges the rest is easily done. Of course, the salt does not take all the frost out of the entire grave, but it gives the frozen earth a chance to give away from the wedge.

Our soil is a sandy loam, with loam and subsoil about 18 inches in depth, the rest is clear sand. The weather has a great deal to do with the operation of the salt. If the weather is near the freezing point the effect is much greater; if near zero the effect is much less. I do not know how many have tried salt, but to those who have not, try it, and I think the result will be satisfactory.

F. A. SHERMAN, Supt. Evergreen Cemetery.

* * *

Editor Modern Cemetery:

In lining graves we use white muslin, and nearly all our graves are so treated. We have a frame of boards around the top to which we tack the muslin, and let it drop down to the box. This and a few evergreens make a very pretty effect, is very cheap, and we charge only the cost of the material

We do not have as many Sunday funerals as we had a few years ago. There is quite a change in sentiment here on this subject. Several times the people have been themselves disgusted with the crowds that gather merely to look on. I think my people are in sympathy with me and our association on this subject.

A few years ago, private funerals were almost unknown, and now, more than half of ours are private, and the custom is steadily gaining. Our wealthy families were the first to start upon this reform. I have talked with all our lot owners in regard to all these current reforms, and they seem to think it best. I have them read the MODERN CEMETERY and our Convention reports and quite frequently, drop a few hints in our local papers. Our undertakers also, have a good influence, and if one can get their co-operation, much can be done on the new lines. I think we should do all we can in economy as well as appearance in these matters.
C. D. PHIPPS, Supt. Franklin Cemetery,
Franklin, Pa.

RULES AND REGULATIONS.

Every cemetery should be governed by certain rules and regulations, which should be printed in pamphlet form for distribution among lot owners. While this has been done in most of the large cemeteries, where the rules are very much alike, we will, for the benefit of the smaller cemeteries, publish in this department such rules as commend themselves for general adoption. Contributions are solicited.

The Rules and Regulations of the Prospect Cemetery association, Vergennes, Vt., which was first organized in 1892, have been amended in accordance with modern ideas of cemetery management to apply to their extension. Included are the following:

"No railing of wood or iron, or coping of any material will be permitted around lots.

"Posts of stone or marble at the corner of lots are all that will be allowed as boundaries (without special permission.) They must not be less than one foot in length, and placed not to project above the surface of the ground. Foot markers for graves will also be subject to the same rule.

"Lot owners are requested to consult with the superintendent in regard to designs for monuments and head stones, also before planting any trees, shrubs, or flowers on their lots."

Perpetual care is also considered, and earnest pleas made for more serious attention to this most important consideration.

The Houghton Monument.

The monument illustrated herewith is among the finest of the memorials recently erected in Forest Hills Cemetery, Boston. At a time when quantity seems to be more fashionable than quality, the design of this monument is well worthy of attention, from the fact that it combines both in such a manner as to create a very pleasing effect. The proportions are harmonious, and the details are so worked out in the design that no one part more than another obtrudes itself. It is executed in Westerly granite, a material admirably adapted to bring out the details. The monument is the work of the Smith Granite Co.

CEMETERY REPORTS.

The sixty-third annual report of the Trustees of the Cemetery of Mount Auburn, Boston, for 1894, shows a successful financial year notwithstanding the general business depression. The receipts from sales of lots and receiving tomb deposits show an increase of $10,500 over the previous year, while the expenses, due to cautious management by reason of the uncertainties of the times have been smaller.

The Repair Fund amounts to $812,216.82, an increase for the year of $40,532.44. This is, in fact the fund, the income from which is devoted to the perpetual care of lots, etc. The Permanent Fund to provide for the expenses of the cemetery after all the lots are sold, and which accumulates under provisions of the by-laws is $344,009.27, an increase of $13,218.51.

The general fund to provide for all large improvements, amounts to $119,456.63, a gain of $19,074.63.

The total receipts for sales of lots and deposits in receiving tombs were: $26,984.25; for work and material on lots, $54,823.67. In the total expenditures that for labor amounts to $37,153.68, and for materials and repairs of buildings and fences $11,425.04.

* * *

The annual report of the Mountian View Cemetery Association, Oakland, Cal., shows that a large amount of improvement was done, and many handsome monuments erected. The receipts for the year include lots sold, $17,278; single graves,

$3,604; interments, $3,754. Total receipts were $62,498.38. Total expenditures, $55,660.06. There was deposited on account of Perpetual Care Fund, $2,161.75. The new sections opened are laid out on the lawn plan, and the perpetual care and guarantee funds show a steady and healthy growth.

* * *

The annual report of the Rural Cemetery, Worcester, Mass., states that the fund for the perpetual care of lots and grounds amounts to $69,844.17; the general fund to $5,433.96. During the past year 62 lots have been graded, 13 inside curbs taken out, 8 iron fences removed; 42 lots have been curbed with an avenue curb of stone. The number of burials was 104. A sum of $2025 was received in gifts for the perpetual care of 24 individual lots in response to the appeal of the trustees, that all individual lots be placed under the perpetual care of the corporation.

* * *

The annual report of the Little Lake Cemetery Co., of Peterborough, Ontario, shows that our cousins over the line are adopting modern American ideas in cemetery management. The financial statement showed a cash surplus of $761, the largest for many years, although many improvements were carried out. There was also received a sum of $400 for the perpetual care of a lot. Several of the lot owners gave permission for the removal of cedar hedges and iron railings, affording great improvement. A report of a committee on legislation made an urgent plea in the direction of perpetual care, and recommended amendments to existing laws which were decidedly in the direction of modern views regarding cemetery affairs.

* * *

The annual report of Superintendent Fred C. Emde of the city cemeteries of Cleveland, O., for 1894 has been submitted. While the receipts were $5,868.85 less than in 1893, a balance of $7,709.34 is shown in the fund. In 1893 the sale of lots netted $22,911.56 and for 1894 only $1,645.27. The receipts from interments and extra work done on the lots sold amounted to $13,770.76 in 1893 and $14,268.20 for the past year. The difference in these receipts was due to the greater number of burials during 1894, there being 2,805 in 1894 and 2,665 in 1893. Notwithstanding the greater expenditures in improvement and labor the expenses were $2,256.68 less during 1894 than 1893.

Considerable loss in receipts was due to the fact that in the receipts of the first nine months of 1893, lots sold brought an average of $4 more per lot than for the corresponding months in 1894. Choice lots are also becoming less each year and it is only a question of a short time until the receipts from the cemeteries will not be enough to pay the cost of maintenance. The cemetery fund has been increased $18,730.85 and no necessary improvements or repairs were neglected. The interments during the year were: Woodlawn cemetery, 1,755; Erie street cemetery, 156; Monroe street cemetery, 677; Harvard Grove cemetery, 217.

The cash receipts and disbursements at the various cemeteries were as follows: Woodland avenue, total cash receipts, $19,222.27; total disbursements, $15,207.67.

Erie street; total receipts, $2070.95; disbursements, $2,263.92.

Monroe street: total receipts $7,269; disbursements, $3,500.43.

Harvard Grove: total receipts, $2,151.25; disbursements, $2,033.01.

The total number of persons buried in the various cemeteries from the time of their construction to Jan. 1 last, is: Woodland, 32,601; Erie street, 17,250; Monroe street, 17,557, Harvard Grove, 5,403; total in cemeteries owned by the city of Cleveland, 72,811.

Planting and Good Planting.

Tree planting claims prominent attention in spring work. Whether a tree should be pruned or not when transplanted, depends, in a measure, on the health and vigor of the tree to be planted. A weak tree, or a tree with mossy bark, or one which in any way seems to have been somewhat neglected, requires more pruning than a tree showing a lusty and healthy growth. In fact, a tree which shows excellent vigor and appears to have been well cared for before transplanting, seldom needs much help from the pruning knife.

Then the question of good planting comes in. What many people imagine to be good planting is frequently very bad planting. If a tree leans over after a rain or wind storm, it is a proof that it was badly planted. If the soil had been packed in properly about the roots, it could not lean,—a tree only leans under these circumstances, from there being vacancies which the settling of the earth finds out. It is almost impossible to pack the earth in too firmly about the roots, at transplanting, and it should be done as the hole is being filled.—*Meehan's Monthly for February.*

Chicago clergymen are quietly discussing the very delicate subject of whether the clergyman should accompany the remains and the mourners to the cemetery after the services in the home or the church. No decided opinion has yet been expressed.

EPITAPHS

Hang her an epitaph upon
her tomb.
—*Shakespeare.*

Mr. J. R. Guindon, of Lynn, Mass., writes: "I wish to add to your list of Epitaphs—as I take pleasure in reading them, and doubtless many others do the same":

A quaint one, which may be found on an old monument in a prominent cemetery in eastern Mass., reading after the names—Jane wife of James ———, and dates, etc:

> James sat holding in his hand
> The likeness of his wife,
> Fresh as if touched by fairy wand
> With beauty, grace and life.
> He almost tho't it spoke, he gazed
> Upon the treasure still,
> Absorbed, delighted and amazed
> To view the artist's skill.
>
> This picture is yourself, dear Jane
> 'Tis drawn to nature true,
> I've kissed it o'er and o'er again
> It is so much like you,
> And has it kissed you back, my dear?
> Why no, my love—said he,
> Then James it is very clear
> 'Tis not at all like me.

In Marblehead, Mass., a stone of 1787 says:

> "I charge you, O, ye
> Memento to take care of my dust."

The very next one to it, of date but a year later, 1788, enjoins:

> "Don't view my relicks with concern,
> O, cease to drop the pitying tear,
> I'm got beyond pain and fear."

In a French churchyard is a monument having an epitaph, of which the following is a translation:

> "Here lies Jean Pinto, the Spanish vocalist. When he reached Heaven he united his voice with the voices of the archangels. As soon as he heard him the Deity cried: 'keep quiet, all you fellows, and let us hear alone the illustrious singer, Jean Pinto!'"

In an old cemetery at Niantic, Conn., is a large family plot of five small graves in a row. At the foot is a full-sized grave, and in the middle of the latter is a marble slab bearing this epitaph on the side facing the smaller graves:

> "Children!"
> "Ma'am?"
> "Mother's come!"

A young man, struck down at the age of 19, left this warning to his companions:

> In health and strength put not thy trust,
> The strongest man is made of dust;
> Repent in haste, make no delay
> For I in youth was called away.

The following is on a tomb at Bath, England:

> Sacred to the memory of Miss Ann Man,
> She lived an old maid and died an old man.

From Peter Church, England, from *Funeral Director:*

> Sickness was my portion,
> Physic was my food,
> Groans was my devotion,
> Drugs did me no good.
> The Lord took pity on me,
> Because He thought it best—
> He took me to his bosom,
> And here I lies at rest.

On a man who was killed in a drunken brawl in California:

> This yere is sakrid to the memory of John Skaraken, who came to his death by being shot through the head with a colt's revolver one of the old kind brass mounted and of such is the kingdom of heaven.

The following is evidently on a shrew:

> Beneath this stone, and not above it,
> Lie the remains of Anna Lovett,
> Be pleased, good readers, not to shove it
> Last she should come again above it:
> For, 'twist you and I, no one does covet
> To see again this Anna Lovett.

Association of American Cemetery Superintendents.

O. C. SIMONDS, "Graceland," Chicago, President.
G. W. CREESY, "Harmony Grove," Salem, Mass., Vice-President.
F. EURICH, Woodlawn, Toledo, O., Secretary and Treasurer.

To Members of A. A. C. S.:

Three copies of the Philadelphia Proceedings have been mailed to each member; those who will want additional copies will please send in their orders at once and remit at the rate of $2.50 per dozen or 25 cents for single copies; six or more sent at dozen rate. FRANK EURICH, Sec. and Treasurer, Auburndale, O., Dec. 10, 1894.

Publisher's Department.

The receipt of Cemetery Literature and Trade Catalogues will be acknowledged in this column.

TO ADVERTISERS. THE MODERN CEMETERY is the only publication of its class and will be found a valuable medium for reaching cemetery officials in all parts of the United States.

TO SUBSCRIBERS. Cemetery officials desiring to subscribe for a number of copies regularly to circulate among their lot owners, should send for our special terms. Several well known cemeteries have already adopted this plan with good results.

Contributions on matters pertaining to cemeteries are solicited. Address all communications to
R. J. HAIGHT, 331 Dearborn St., CHICAGO.

Received: Form of Deed used by the Catskill Rural Cemetery Association, N. Y.—Treasurer's Report, 1893-94. Prospect Cemetery Association, Vergennes, Vt.—Charter, Rules and Regulations, Grove Cemetery, New Brighton, Beaver Co., Pa.—Sixty-third Annual Report, January 1, 1895, Mount Auburn Cemetery, Boston, Mass.—Constitution, By-laws, etc., Odd Fellows Cemetery Association, New Haven, Indiana.—Articles of Association, By-laws, and Rules and Regulations of Greenlawn Cemetery Association, Columbus, O.

A question among all gardeners at this season of the year is, what seeds shall I plant? We are in receipt of a 100 page catalogue from J. J. Bell, of Binghamton, N. Y., telling all about what to get and where to get it. Flowers as well as vegetables. The book is mailed free to all who send for it.

www.ingramcontent.com/pod-product-compliance
Lightning Source LLC
Chambersburg PA
CBHW021954220426
43663CB00007B/806